WILDERNESS COOKERY

Books by Bradford Angier

WE LIKE IT WILD

WILDERNESS COOKERY

HOW TO GO LIVE IN THE WOODS ON $10 A WEEK

ON YOUR OWN IN THE WILDERNESS
  (with Colonel Townsend Whelen)

LIVING OFF THE COUNTRY

HOW TO BUILD YOUR HOME IN THE WOODS

AT HOME IN THE WOODS

HOME IN YOUR PACK

FREE FOR THE EATING

SKILLS FOR TAMING THE WILDS

WILDERNESS COOKERY

BRADFORD ANGIER

Foreword by
Colonel Townsend Whelen

STACKPOLE BOOKS

Harrisburg, Pennsylvania

Printed in the United States of America

By THE TELEGRAPH PRESS

Harrisburg, Pennsylvania

DEDICATION

To my friend and partner

COLONEL TOWNSEND WHELEN

For years the Commanding Officer at Frankford Arsenal—from where in 1804 his great-great-grandfather, Commissary General of the Army Israel Whelen, equipped the Lewis and Clark Expedition—and later the Director of Research and Development at Springfield Armory, Colonel Townsend Whelen, U.S.A. (Ret.), is remembered as Dean of American Outdoor Writers, Dean of American Riflemen, and as the twentieth recipient of the Medal of Honor of the venerable Camp Fire Club of America. This book and its author owe more to him than can be expressed.

BRADFORD ANGIER
Hudson Hope, British Columbia

ACKNOWLEDGMENTS

The author is indebted for some of the illustrations to: David T. Abercrombie Company, Cooperative Extension Service of the University of Alaska, Brion Company, Lodge Manufacturing Company, Randall Made Knives, Sims Stoves, The Ski Hut, The Smilie Company, and the Williams Gun Sight Company.

Contents

There is no place where cooking and meals mean so much as in the wilderness or on a camping trip away from professional cooks and stoves. There the appetite is tremendous, and there the energy and warmth that come from food is in big demand. When, as a youngster, now over sixty years ago, I began to wander in the wilderness and to camp out, I knew absolutely nothing about cooking, much less about cooking over a campfire.

In my way of bringing up at home, neither a lady nor her children were supposed ever to enter a kitchen. Spending my boyhood summers in the Adirondack Mountains, I never saw any outdoor cooking save the frying of bacon and flapjacks. When I first started into the Wilderness, into British Columbia in 1901, I made a terrible mess of cooking until I ran into Bones Andrews, one of the old mountain men of the West, and we became partners to "hunt and prospect." He taught me how to cook over a wood fire; plain, delicious, wholesome meals after the methods of the old western trappers and hunters, and the Indians.

Then about 1906 Horace Kephart published his classic *Camping and Woodcraft*. In it he had several chapters on "Camp Cookery." I don't know where Kephart learned to cook, but his methods and his recipes were exactly the same as those of old Bones, practical and simple, and those days most anyone could become a good cook by following Kephart.

Then gradually there followed a whole deluge of books on the subject. Again I don't know where these later writers learned, but I think it must have been from their wives' cookbooks. So far as my experience goes, their methods and recipes were entirely impractical—foods that could never be carried into the wilderness with its limited transportation and lack of refrigeration, seasonings straight from Paris to disguise the taste of plain wholesome food, and methods that could be used only over a kitchen range. Not one of them, for example, told how to bake bread, cook oatmeal and cornmeal, how to fry or roast meat, how to

9

bake dry beans, or to stew prunes. Nothing was said about how to fry trout, or cook grouse, or broil venison. In the wilderness, my experience has been that often the only "store grub" that you can well take along is 2¼ pounds per day of plain, fairly waterfree food. You can live well on this, plus perhaps some wild game procured as you go along. With this basis you can live like a king, enjoy hearty meals, and do prodigious work.

Brad Angier, an old partner of mine, and his wife Vena have lived deep in the northern wilderness for some fifteen years, living largely off the country plus what store grub they could tote on foot, by pack horse, or boat miles and miles from the settlements. All their meals have been cooked over an outdoor wood campfire or on a little sheet iron stove in a log cabin. Those who happened by their board can attest to their plain, delicious, and wholesome meals. So when Brad asked me if I thought there was a need for a modern, up-to-date, real, practical, simple wilderness cookbook that anyone with no experience could use and live by today, I said, "Gosh, yes!" So here it is. I know you can use it; can succeed with its aid. By all means study it and take it into the woods with you.

TOWNSEND WHELEN

CHAPTER 1

SUSTENANCE IN THE SILENT SPACES

When your appetite is sharpened by the healthy sort of outdoor living for which mankind was made, the mealtimes can include some of the best moments of any vacation—if you outfit yourself with foods that keep well, cook readily, and are easy to handle.

Now is not too soon to get started on your provisioning for that next trip back of beyond, for done right it's going to take some time. You'll do best to take foods you personally like and know how to prepare. Experimenting at home and on weekend journeys is the soundest way to find out how much of each item you'll need to round out the sort of satisfying meals you're going to need to keep going under full power.

And they should be satisfying as well as sustaining. As the Hudson's Bay Company says after nearly three centuries in the farthest and most primitive reaches of this continent, "There is usually little object in traveling tough just for the sake of being tough."

Rough it, sure, if you want to prove to yourself the actually very important fact that you can rough it. One day, it's true, anyone at all may be thrown entirely upon his own resources and forced to get along the best he can with a minimum of comforts.

But as far as the preference goes, roughing it is a development stage. Once we've successfully tested our ability to take it, a whole lot of doubts and inhibitions disappear. We find ourself realizing that the real challenge lies in smoothing it. We come to appreciate that making it easy on ourselves takes a lot more experience and ingenuity than bulling it through the tough way.

"Nothing is more important on a camping trip than the

grub." As Colonel Townsend Whelen has pointed out, "Most of us go camping to have a good time. If the food is poor, unwholesome, or not what we crave, we have a continual grouch. If it is excellent and there is plenty of it, everything is rosy. Good food even makes up for rain and hard beds. Good fellowship is at its best around good meals.

"Unless you are lucky enough to have a professional cook booked for your party, it will pay you to study the commissary problem in advance. Exercise in the open air doubles the appetite and adds sauce to plain food. In quantity, quality, selection, and in preparation, this food should be good, wholesome, the kind you like, and attractively served."

Far from the humdrum concerns of man-made civilization, it is possible as nowhere else to appreciate the simple pleasures of life—browning frypan bread, steaming coffee, and bacon sputtering over apple-red coals. The crackle of your campfire takes on unexpected coziness, and even the smallest tent all at once seems as snug and satisfying as a mansion.

CHARCOAL GRILLS. Odd thing, wilderness! The instinct for it reaches far into the soul of man, mighty close to the steamy start of things. On this young continent even city dwellers live near their wilderness background, and the campfire remains an integral part of our pioneer heritage, even though it may often find expression today in the charcoal grill. The recipes in this book are adapted for use in the fireplace, backyard, patio, picnic ground, and National Park, as well as in more remote regions.

BASIC GRUBSTAKES. The standard foods taken by experienced outdoorsmen on trips into the farther places of this continent, and which in general form the basis of most grubstakes, include: all-purpose flour, triple-action baking powder, baking soda and a packet of dry yeast if sourdough breadstuffs are to be used, sugar, compact cereals such as quickly cooking rice and oatmeal, corn meal, side bacon which has nearly triple the calories of back bacon, salt pork, oleomargarine, salt, spaghetti and such, powdered milk and eggs, and dehydrated fruits and vegetables. All these are practically free of water.

Some of the more nutritious spreads such as honey, jam, and peanut butter work in well. So does cheese. Practical beverages are concentrated tea powder or tea itself, one of the instant coffees, malted milk, and chocolate. Bouillon solids and dry soup mixes, although short on nourishment, are often welcome because of the easy variety they afford, especially with small game that hasn't had time to age. Seasonings such as powdered celery and onion, pepper, a favorite spice or two, as well as an unseasoned meat tenderizer, may be desirable.

The old Three B days are gone; not that steady diets of beans, bacon, and bannock ever had much glamor in real life after the first couple of days.

THE LIMITING FACTOR. Available transportation will, of course, be the limiting factor in provisioning. A pack horse can balance 120 pounds or so day after day over mountain trails, while a full-size burro can double that. A canoe should not be loaded so deeply that it will have less than five inches of freeboard, depending on the water. This should be increased to at least six inches for windy lakes.

A husky man fresh out of the cement jungles can, without particular difficulty, shoulder about 75 pounds at a stretch over short portages, and he can take his time in making several such trips. He should not usually pack more than 35 pounds, of which 20 pounds may reasonably be food, when hiking day after day for pleasure over high country.

HOW MUCH OF EACH. No one can give you more than an idea of the quantities to take of various items. The tables near the end of the book provide specific and definite information, however, by which you personally can arrive at a reasonable and practical estimate. Detailed grub lists as such are ordinarily of little value, for they seldom suit anyone but the compiler. It all depends on the number of meals you expect to make of each food, how many are to be in the party, and how much of each particular nutriment it will take to make a satisfying portion for each individual concerned.

To determine quantities, you can experiment at home. If you want oatmeal every morning, for example, find out just how much rolled oats are needed to make the breakfast you will likely eat in the woods. Just as a suggestion, take at least double the amount of sugar and sweets you would use at home, for your desire for them in camp will be out of all proportion to what you want in the city.

Here's a yardstick that you may find valuable. Generally speaking, the total weight of reasonably water-free foods you will want to eat should not be less than 2¼ pounds per adult per day. This does not include fresh vegetables and fruits. For purposes of figuring, consult the previously mentioned tables to ascertain the weight relationship of these to their dehydrated equivalents.

All this takes time. But it will pay off in satisfaction, and it's fun.

THE LEAST WITH THE MOST. Fat is, in calories, the most concentrated food. It is also the hardest to come by when living off the wilderness. Butter, oleomargarine, lard, and cooking oils have double and triple the amount of calories that even such a quick energy food as honey contains. If you plan to augment your meals with fish and game, the staples you carry should include a large proportion of edible fats.

Other concentrated foods that have figured conspicuously in rations where space and weight have been stringently restricted include dried shelled nuts, peanut butter, chocolate, dried whole eggs, dried whole milk, and malted milk tablets. If you want a bulky starch, rice is one that cooks up appetizingly with nearly everything.

You can, if weight and space are at extreme premium, use a calorie chart as a basis for figuring how to go about packing the most nourishment with the least trouble. Briefly, you're burning up a certain amount of energy every second. Energy not supplied directly by a sufficiency of food is taken from the body's carbohydrates, fats, and proteins.

Even when you're sleeping relaxed in the most comfortable of eiderdowns, your system is consuming heat units (or calories) at the rate of approximately ten calories a day per pound of body weight. In other words, if you weigh 160 pounds, the least number of calories you'll use each day is 1,600. These basic requirements diminish but slightly, as a matter of fact, even when an individual is starving.

The more you move around and the more energy you expend in keeping warm, the more calories you use. Even lying in your sleeping bag and reading will increase your basic caloric needs about 25%. The city man who gets very little exercise consumes on the average 50% above his minimum requirements. To maintain his weight, therefore, such a 160-pound individual requires about 2,400 calories daily.

It is reasonable, both from these scientific facts and from personal experience, to generalize that a healthy and fit man enjoying a robust outdoor life can require 20 calories of food a day per pound of body weight—and perhaps more, depending on his activity and on the climate. Cold weather, for example, compels the system to put out more and more heat to keep itself warm. The same 160-pound city man hunting in the north woods can very easily take in 3,200 or 4,000 calories a day, and more, and still trim down lean and hard.

HOW TO PACK. Dry foods such as flour, cereal, beans, salt, and sugar may be packed in small waterproof sacks which are available in a variety of types and sizes from most camp outfitters. You can make them, too. Each should be plainly labeled. Repackage prepared dry foods whenever this can be done advantageously, cutting out and enclosing any special directions. Unless you've plenty of room, foods such as corn flakes should be compressed into as small a space as possible.

Dried meats may be wrapped in wax paper or aluminum foil. Lard, butter, and the like travel well in tightly closed tins such as half-pound and pound tobacco cans. Plastic flasks and bottles made for carrying most liquids are safer and lighter than glass for syrup, oil, and such; but not for most extracts. Powdered eggs and milk will keep better in

FOOD SACKS.

snugly closed receptacles. Beverages in powder form should also be kept tightly covered. See, also, Chapter 2.

FRESH PERISHABLES. Fabric sacks can be used for carrying oranges, potatoes, onions, and apples when you have room for these. Choose oranges heavy for their size. Thinner, smoother skins usually indicate more juice. If possible, try a few potatoes before outfitting to make sure they're what you want. Pass up any with wastefully deep eyes. Size and color do not affect either onions' flavor or quality. Any with wet necks should be avoided. The very hard, long-keeping varieties are stronger than the Bermuda and Spanish types. With apples, good color usually signifies full flavor.

Cabbage and head lettuce will keep fresh for several weeks if wrapped in waxed paper and then in several layers of ordinary brown paper. Select heads that are heavy for their size. Avoid cabbage with worm holes and lettuce with discoloration or soft rot.

KEEPING COOL. Foods can be kept cool by placing them in a pail that is partly submerged in a shady portion of a brook, lake, or spring. Small amounts of fresh meat will keep for several days this way in hot weather if air is allowed to reach it. Cooked meat, broth, mulligan, greens, and the like will keep better if covered individually. Several yards of inexpensive cheesecloth tucked in the outfit will protect such food when flies become pestiferous.

You can also knock a couple of bottom strips out of a wooden box so that water will circulate through it. Weigh down the bottom of the box with large flat stones and on them place a few perishables. If there is danger from slightly rising water, put these in containers that will safely float. It is usually a good idea to have a partially screened top, which can be held in place by another stone. See the next chapter, too, on this subject.

ABOUT FREEZING. Some of the foods will spoil if allowed to freeze. Days these can be wrapped in bedding. Nights they can be stowed near enough to the reflected warmth of a fire. When traveling with a small outfit and sleeping out in temperatures 60° and more below freezing, I've kept a few canned goods, that otherwise would be burst by the cold, stowed safely out of the way at the foot of my sleeping bag.

When food does freeze, it preferably should not be thawed until it is to be used. Fresh meat and fish keep well frozen. So do cheese and eggs, although their flavors are impaired. The taste and texture of such fruits as oranges are best preserved by letting them defrost in cold water. Frozen potatoes, which take on the aspect of marble, should be dipped in boiling water and their skins scraped off. Then drop them singly into boiling water that is kept bubbling. Cold weather increases a potato's sugar content, so you may find the resulting flavor especially appealing.

CANNED FOODS. Canned goods are usually ruled out except on trips when transportation is of little worry. Otherwise, their weight and bulk can quickly add up to prohibitive proportions. If you cannot expect to procure fresh game or fish, however, you may care to pack along a few of the canned meats. Canned tomatoes always go particularly well in the woods if you can manage them.

Canned butter, although expensive, remains sweet and fresh, but now there is nutritious oleomargarine whose taste for all practical purposes soon becomes practically indistinguishable from butter and which stays good for months at ordinary temperatures.

The most economical way to heat canned vegetables is to puncture the top of the can slightly, as with a small nail, and then to place the container in a deep pan of water. This should not cover the tin, which should be left in the hot water only the brief time necessary to heat the contents thoroughly. It will then give no trouble in opening. Incidentally, if a tenderfoot ever tries to heat that unopened can of soup or beans by dropping it in the campfire, either rake it out in a hurry or stand a long way back.

Nutriment that you may as well capitalize on to the fullest, especially after packing it for miles, is wasted by emptying commercially canned vegetables into a pan for heating. But if you do this, simply warm them before using. Boiling destroys much of their food value.

Don't throw away any of the juice in the can. Containing both vitamins and minerals, it can be profitably used in sauces, gravies, and soups. Seasoned if you want, it also makes a tasty beverage, especially in the bush.

If there are any cans without distinguishing markings except for paper labels and if there is a reasonable chance that your outfit may become wet, scratch the identity of the contents on an end of each tin. I neglected to take this precaution on a month-long river trip in Eastern Canada. We had ample room, no portages, and plenty of hunting and fishing to do in preference to cooking. Therefore, we had an abundance of canned goods, packed loosely in burlap bags so we could trim the canoe more easily. After paddling mostly in rain the first day, and shipping some water in rapids besides, we had to try from then on to pick what we wanted from a perfectly blank array of tins.

The cleanest and safest place to keep the contents of an open can, incidentally, is in that can. Cover this, perhaps with one of several elastic-rimmed little plastic fabrics brought for the purpose, and store away from squirrels and their like in as cool a place as possible. With acid foods such as tomatoes, however, a metallic though harmless taste may insinuate itself because of the acids' eating into the iron of the opened can, so these may as well be shifted to a non-metallic container. Unopened canned goods should preferably be kept at moderate temperatures.

Inspect all cans before buying them for a camping trip. Do this again before opening them. Such commonplaces of wilderness travel as denting, rusting, and freezing all can cause trouble. One test is to press each end of the can. Neither should bulge, nor should it snap back unless the can has been sprung or unless the contents have been frozen sufficiently to exert pressure against the ends although not enough to break the seal. Ordinarily, both ends should either be flat or should curve slightly inward. Seams should be tight and clean with no evidence of any leakage.

When you open a can, watch out for spurting liquid and for any off colors or odors. All are danger signals. Cans should be clean and smooth inside with very little corrosion. If the metal of a meat product can has merely turned dark inside, though, this is only a harmless reaction with the sulphur in the meat.

Whenever there are any signs of spoilage, the wise thing to do is to discard all contents without tasting, burying or burning them to protect wildlife. It's important enough to repeat; do not even touch your tongue to the product. Although you may expel any spoiled food at once, then thoroughly rinse your mouth, that one taste may be sufficient to cause an extremely severe digestive upset if not worse.

Tops should always be well cleaned before any canned foods are opened. For one thing, the metal often picks up poisonous insecticides sprayed in stores. The small roller type of can opener is the easiest to pack and to use. Just stow it, for example, inside the nested cups. The usual attempt to open a can with an ax or hatchet is wasteful at best, while performing the chore with a hunting knife makes cut hands a distinct possibility during and afterward, to say nothing of the damage done a good blade. To avoid metal slivers, begin opening the can beyond the side seam and, unless you need the top all the way off, stop before reaching this seam.

Instead of puncturing the evaporated milk can on top and plugging, taping, or sealing the holes with congealed milk, try making these small openings on opposite sides just below the rim. Then you can close them with a wide elastic band.

SALT. Add cornstarch or a few grains of rice to salt in shakers to keep it dry for easy pouring. A few grains of salt

SALT AND PEPPER SHAKER.

added to cooked foods such as stewed apricots will enhance the sweetening of the sugar content. On the other hand, it is sometimes possible in cooking emergencies to hide the taste of excess salt by adding a small amount of vinegar or sugar. Away from the table, salt is often invaluable as a preservative. The salt draws water from the game or other food to be preserved by the process of osmosis, forming a brine that prevents or retards the growth of microorganisms.

SWEETENING. You can buy one of several so-called sugar substitutes, one tiny pellet of which will sweeten a cup of coffee to the same degree as would a teaspoon of white sugar. Don't do it under ordinary circumstances unless for dietetic reasons. The minute pills furnish the taste, certainly, but they add no fuel to the body.

The various natural sweets such as sugar are among our most readily assimilated energy foods. Granulated white sugar provides roundly 1,750 calories per pound. An equal weight of brown sugar contains 1,670 calories. The same amount of pure maple sugar has 1,580 calories. A pound of honey has 1,400 calories. Good jams average some 1,260 calories per pound, jellies slightly less. For comparison, one pound of fresh lean venison runs about 630 calories. In other words, this isn't the department in which mistakenly to try to save weight.

WILD FOODS. These days you can dine about as easily and well in the wilderness as in the city. Matter of fact, you're likely to find yourself eating considerably better. There may be the drawback of not being able to pick up the numerous frozen specialties featured in modern markets. This disadvantage is more than offset by all the fresh foods that are at hand, free for the taking. Whenever you learn how to recognize and use a reasonable number of these, you're sort of like the old prospector who kneels on a lode of silver while he pans gold and platinum from a creek. Whatever your epicurean whim of the moment may be, you can satisfy it. See Chapter 10 about eating for free.

FATS. Oleomargarine, largely because it keeps so well, is recommended for general camp use. To cut hard margarine or butter cleanly, use a knife that has been heated in hot water.

To protect yourself from popping hot fat, stop the spattering by sprinkling a bit of flour in the frypan. If the grease catches fire, throw a handful of flour on it; either that, or extinguish the flames by covering the burning fat and shutting out the air.

The camp shortening pail can be replenished by pouring in your surplus bacon grease. Excellent lard can also be secured from game fat not eaten along with the lean. Cut this into small bits and melt them down in a pan over low heat. Pour the liquid grease into some handy container, such as a friction-top can, where ordinarily it will harden and become easy to pack. Save the cracklings to eat with lean meat or to munch for lunch some cold noon.

If you are in the fall woods and have bagged a black bear, the pure white grease rendered from the fat of such a trophy is unexcelled for such shortening. If you've collected a grizzly instead, the thick oil rendered from this fat is also excellent. Use it like any other liquid shortening.

THE BEAN FAMILY. Dry beans, peas, and lentils are old-time dehydrated foods that remain favorites in many a vacation camp. See Chapter 8.

JAMS. An outdoor trip is where you really appreciate jams and marmalades. Some campers are bothered by the white crystals that often form in these foods. Looking like mold, such crystals tend to spread through the mixture once the first of them have appeared. Actually, they're the result of sugar combining with the water in the preparation. Although they do nothing for texture and appearance, they are not at all harmful.

YEAST. It is a good idea when using sourdough bread-stuffs to carry a recently dated package of dry yeast in case something happens to the sourdough starter. It's true enough that a fresh starter can be made on the spot by mixing a cup apiece of flour and water in a scalded jar, covering it loosely, and stowing it in a warm place to sour. If the first results are not satisfactory, you can always try again with a new mixture. But the addition of yeast to these sourings will eliminate the guesswork. See details in Chapter 7.

VINEGAR. Here's a pioneer stratagem to stretch supplies of sometimes hard-to-pack vinegar. When half of the vinegar is used, dilute the remainder with an equal amount of water. Then restore its authority by adding a cup of sugar; brown sugar if you have it. The sugar will ferment and supplant the missing acid.

CHEESE. Cheese is one of the most versatile and delectable of camp foods. It may be relished in its natural state or added to everything from soups and salads to sauces to make all sorts of delicious combinations. More than one day I've enjoyed it at breakfast with scrambled eggs, at lunch in a sandwich melted over the noonday tea fire, and at night in a baked macaroni and tomato casserole. Preferences vary. A sharp, aged Cheddar keeps well, as does Edam and Gouda. Provolone is probably the best choice in high temperatures.

If heat makes the cheese rubbery, a solution is to wrap it well and to revive it in a cool stream. If you're going to spend a month or more away from civilization, sew one-week portions snugly in cheesecloth and immerse them in melted wax. You can harmlessly keep mold off cheese to a large extent by wiping the cheese with a clean cloth soaked either in baking soda solution or in vinegar.

MILK. Whether or not you use powdered milk and eggs will depend to a large extent on your preferences and upon where you are. As far as nutrition goes, both compare favorably with the fresh products. Which taste you prefer is mostly a matter of what you're accustomed to; in other words, nothing is the matter with either one, and you can become satisfied with each. A friend of mine, who wrangles dudes up by the brawling Liard River in Northwestern Canada, flew to California the other winter to visit a wealthy sportsman on the latter's dairy ranch. Only thing he couldn't stand was the fresh milk. For years he'd been mixing his with powder and water. Order a glass of milk in many a bustling Far Northern town today, and this is exactly what they set before you.

Powdered milk is especially handy in cold weather if only because the quality of evaporated milk is impaired by freezing, which, as far as that goes, may cause it to spoil entirely by bursting the can. Besides, evaporated milk is still ¾ water. Condensed milk is ¼ water and nearly ½ sugar. Depending on the product, one pound of whole milk powder makes one gallon of liquid whole milk.

Whole milk powder is sometimes a little difficult to mix with water, but there are several ways to get around this. When you open the container, stir the powder and lightly take up the amount you want without packing it down in any way. Even measures are best obtained by leveling off the top of the cup or spoon with the straight edge of a knife. Place the powder on top of the water with which it is to mix. Then stir with a spoon until smooth. The mixing can be speeded somewhat by having the water slightly warm. You can also shake the water and powder together in a tightly closed jar which will subsequently serve as a pitcher.

Better spray dryers have also improved the quality of dehydrated milk. The quick hydrating quality of the newer skim milk powders, however, is the result of a second drying step which gives the particles a porous, spongelike fluffiness that 30 years of research were required to achieve.

Dried skim milk has all the nourishment of fresh skim milk. It has the calcium, phosphorous, iron and other minerals, the B vitamins, natural sugar, and the protein that make liquid skim milk such an important food. Powdered whole milk has all these, plus the fat and Vitamin A found in the cream of whole milk. Adding two teaspoons of butter or margarine to a cup of reconstituted skim milk will make this equal in food value to a cup of whole milk. And it's often a lot easier to mix.

You can even use dried skim milk to make a whipped topping for desserts. Mix ½ cup of the milk powder with ½ cup of preferably ice water. Beat for 3 or 4 minutes until soft peaks form. Then add 2 tablespoons lemon juice, fresh or reconstituted, and beat about the same length of time until it is stiff. Fold in ¼ cup sugar. About 3 cups of topping will result. Serve while you're still ahead.

Containers holding any of the dry milk products should be kept tightly closed, as the powder attracts moisture and becomes lumpy if long exposed to the air. It also picks up odors unless care is taken.

Powdered milk, mixed dry with the flour, makes a valuable addition to biscuits and other breadstuffs. Mornings when you're in a hurry to get away hunting or fishing, milk powder can be mixed directly with cereals such as oatmeal and the breakfast food then cooked as indicated on the package.

Evaporated milk, which is what you may settle for, is homogenized whole milk concentrated to double strength by evaporating part of the water. If you use equal parts of evaporated milk and water, you can utilize evaporated milk as you would any other fluid whole milk. The lumps in evaporated milk are formed by solids settling during storage and are harmless. Cans of evaporated milk can be turned or shaken at frequent intervals during a vacation trip to prevent such lumping.

POWDERED EGGS. An egg is eleven percent waste unless you are going to bake the shells and then pulverize them, as many do to increase the calcium content of their dogs' feed. Seventy-four percent of the remaining yolk and white is water.

Yet dried whole egg has virtually the same food value, includes no waste whatsoever, and is only five percent water. More efficient processing equipment and methods have improved the quality of dried eggs. Varying somewhat with brands, a pound of dessicated eggs is the equivalent of some five dozen fresh eggs. One level tablespoon of the yellow powder, beaten until smoothly blended with two tablespoons of water, again depending on the individual product, equals one hen's egg. And you don't have to bother cushioning those perishable ovals with crumpled newspaper in the more stable types of their own cartons, nor arranging them with the large ends up while camping so as to keep the yolks centered.

The flavor of egg powder cooked by itself is not like that of fresh eggs. Most of us in the United States are accustomed to the latter. Our natural taste reaction, therefore, is that the former is inferior. With different eating habits, as many have witnessed in Europe and elsewhere, this taste prejudice also works the other way around.

In any event, scrambled eggs prepared from the powder come to taste mighty good in the farther places. If you haven't prepared these before, dissolve powdered eggs and milk in lukewarm water to make the proportions of these fresh products you might ordinarily use. Add salt, pepper, and any other seasoning, together with a chunk of butter or oleomargarine. A little flour may be stirred in for thickening. Scrambling all this with ham or bacon gives the dish added flavor.

Never wash whole eggs until you're ready to use them.

However, eggs with clean shells do keep better, so any soiled spots should be wiped off with a damp cloth. Regular washing, though, will remove the natural protective film which aids in keeping out bacteria and odors. Matter of fact, oiling the shells will help the eggs to retain carbon dioxide which, in turn, will serve to retard chemical and physical changes in the albumin and yolk. Such oiling also cuts down moisture losses.

DESSERTS. The dehydrated fruits such as raisins, apricots, apples, prunes, peaches, pears, dates, and figs give everyone plenty of choice. Numerous prepared dessert mixes of one sort or another also afford a wide selection, but find out by experimentation which ones you like before you take to the woods. Especially delicious and nutritious in the wilderness? That dense, heavy fruitcake that ordinarily seems a little too rich for city consumption.

MEAT TENDERIZER. Aging or ripening of meat permits its natural enzymes to become active and to induce tenderness. A number of commercial preparations containing an enzyme are available. The enzyme often used in such tenderizers is papain, obtained from the papaya. You sprinkle the preferably unseasoned variety of enzyme powder over the meat, piercing the meat with a fork to help get the preparation inside. For better results with game, I like to use more than the individual instructions suggest and to let the meat stand a shorter time.

SPICES AND FLAVORINGS. Everybody has his own ideas on these, which is as it should be. Nearly everyone wants a little pepper. Small containers of powdered (not salt) celery, onions, and garlic pack a lot of possibilities. Paprika and powdered parsley combine taste and eye appeal. Then there are nutmeg, cinnamon, and their ilk. Small containers of thyme and rosemary afford occasional taste variations with fowl and red meats respectively. Like the rest, they only cost a few cents and occupy little room. Among the flavorings that seem to taste particularly good in the woods are vanilla, banana, and the peppermint which really touches up chocolate. Then there are lemon and other pure fruit juice powders, crystals, etc. Suit yourself.

CAMP COFFEE. The way I like to make camp coffee is to put a rather coarse grind into fresh cold water, using 2 level tablespoons for every cup of water. Amounts can be varied, of course, for a stronger or weaker brew. Hang or set this over the fire. Watch it carefully. As soon as it boils up once, lift it to a warm sanctuary to take on body for five minutes. Then settle the grounds if you want with a couple of tablespoons of cold water and start pouring.

Unless you have decided preferences to the contrary, though, powdered instant coffee is far preferable to the ground article for general camp use except, perhaps, for those first cups in the morning. It is more economical in weight and bulk, cheaper, better lasting, and both quicker and easier to prepare. It can be made to individual order and without waste.

If you'd like to pocket several pleasant pickups before going on a hike or for a day's fishing, you can ready a number of these in a jiffy beforehand. For each, mix one teaspoon of your favorite instant coffee with an equal amount of sugar. Roll securely in foil. Dissolved pleasantly in the mouth, each will provide the same amount of stimulation and energy as would a similarly based cup of black coffee.

B'ILING THE KITTLE. The northern woodsman, particularly the Canadian, must sip his steaming cup of tea at noon, and contemplate its swiftly seething surface colors, even if he has nothing to eat. This is almost a religion up under the aurora borealis, and it's called "b'iling the kittle." Only a temporary fire is needed, a mere handful of dry wood that will flare up briefly and as quickly fall to ashes, a few feathers of which invariably seem to swirl up to float unheeded in the dark brew. Get the water bubbling. Drop in a roughly measured teaspoon of tea for every cup of water and set immediately from the heat in a safe place. Five minutes of steeping is sufficient.

Tea is something I've long preferred to carry in the usual form, if only for the pleasant rite of tossing a handful of palm-measured leaves into the bubbling kettle. There is powdered tea on the market, however, that mixes immediately with warm water and which tastes a lot closer to regular tea than any of the powdered coffees taste like regularly brewed coffee. This tea can't reasonably be spoiled by improper making, although I suppose some camp cook by trying to make enough for everyone at once can still somehow manage to boil it.

OTHER BEVERAGES. Fruit juices are particular treats in the bush. Lemon, for example, is also sometimes welcome with fresh rainbow trout. A number of consolidated fruit juices are now available, both dried and in concentrated liquid.

Bouillon cubes and powders make hot drinks that taste good around a campfire. A lot of times you'll appreciate them a lot more than you would either tea or coffee. They are also useful for flavoring broths, soups, gravies, and stews. Other worthwhile beverage concentrates include cocoa, malted milk, and chocolate.

CHOCOLATE. Hot chocolate and cocoa in particular have a way of easing those last few steps between fire and bed. As for chocolate bars, these are one of the best known and liked energy foods. It's a common thing on extended camping trips to find a whitish appearance in such chocolate. This does not indicate spoilage, however, but is due to cocoa butter that has separated out. At a temperature no more than 85°, the cocoa butter in ordinary chocolate melts and comes to the surface. It whitens upon hardening. Only the appearance of the chocolate is affected.

INSTANT EVERYTHING. Try the individual dehydrated product first. Do this before you leave home. Then suit yourself. Tastes differ. So do needs. A major error is to load up with dehydrated meals for the entire trip without everyone's doing considerable sampling beforehand. This is especially true when you've little to save but time.

Dehydrated grub is fine in its place. Many of the standards, such as the fruits, are welcome on any table. You can get to like most of the rest, but this often takes weeks and months, far more time than you'll spend on the usual vacation. The vitamins and minerals are there, too, but this is also a secondary factor as far as the average brief fishing, hunting, or camping jaunt is concerned.

Ordinarily, you'll be heading out for fun and relaxation, and the enjoyment of the meals is going to be a determining factor. Unless weight, space, and perhaps temperatures are basic considerations—as in mountain climbing, on extended back-packing hikes away from supply points, and during forced trips into remote regions—dehydrated foods despite their continuing improvements are still most satisfactorily used to supplement, rather than replace, regular victuals.

TRIP TIP. What you take on your camping, hiking, or family fishing trip is pretty much a personal matter. The main thing is not to drive off and leave some wanted item behind. Here are two ways to avoid that disaster.

Unless you live where there's plenty of room, make a check list with a separate column for each group of essentials. One column will be for dry foods, a second for perishables, another for eating materials such as dishes and tableware, and so on.

Tape or glue this list, if that is what you have to settle for, on a heavy piece of cardboard. Use it during preparations, of course, but also have it at hand when you pack for the start. At that decisive moment, recheck items one by one as a preventive measure against going off and forgetting some indispensable.

Those who have ample space can take advantage of the visual technique of building little piles. Place cooking utensils in one group, dining paraphernalia in a second, foods in another, etc. When a certain article is in use at the moment, or needs to be picked up at the store or removed from the refrigerator, a note to that effect weighed down in the proper pile will serve as a handy reminder.

Keep a record for future reference. Note, finally, what is left over at the end of the journey. Such intelligence can guide your efforts when you provision for that next sojourn in the silent spaces.

CHAPTER 2

HEATING AND EATING EQUIPMENT

What remain most fondly in our minds after a wilderness trip are the campfires. The handful of crackling twigs that boils the kettle at noon. The cooking coals at the end of the day's fun, when odors build up in such a way that you can hardly wait for that fresh liver or flaky rainbow. The cheerful flames behind whose sanctuary you sit, while the darkening forest comes to life, and watch moonlit magnificences reserved for those who venture into distant and deserted places.

Then there is that unforgettable first fire at dawn. Because of the air currents set into motion by the blending of day and night, it's colder now than it was during total darkness. The cook maybe deposits an old pine stump, saved for the purpose, in the center of the fading overnight embers. This gives him a blaze like the light of a pressure lantern, and it also helps him to get some warmth into his extended fingers. Pretty soon he's thawed out enough to shove the coffee pot grumpily into the heat. He then begins banging pans around, a little more expressively than necessary. Further sleep soon becomes impossible. The coffee smells too good, anyway, particularly when joined by the aromas of flapjacks and bacon.

Much of the success of a camping trip, as well as a considerable deal of the pleasure, is going to depend on your having the right kinds of cooking fires. This does not mean that campfires, if those are what you use, should be built in just one way. It all depends upon where you are, what you have, and whether your most pressing needs at the moment are for tea, steak, or mouth-tingling barbecue.

THE OPEN FIRE. When conditions are favorable, vacation meals never taste better than when they are prepared

over the red gleaming warmth of wild wood. It is so easy
to regulate the open cooking fire so as to take advantage of
quickly roaring heat, or to provide a ruddy bed of coals
that will break ardently apart for broiling, or to conjure up
such fringe benefits that a dumpling-festooned mulligan will
either simmer or just keep temptingly warm.

When you want to start those food smells tantalizing
your sensibilities in a hurry, the various dry softwoods,
especially when split, will chortle into a quickly flaring blaze.
For steadier and more conservative heat, the hardwoods
are more satisfactory. For an enduring expanse of glowing
coals, you will probably choose when possible such fuels as
oak, hickory, and ash. Or perhaps you'll split up one of the
sweetly black-smoking birches with its inherently hot enthusiasm even when green.

Although campfires can be made in numerous ways, the
principles remain the same. An understanding of these
renders fire making under every practical circumstance a
lot more easy. Firewood, for one thing, does not itself actually
burn. A gas driven from the wood by heat is what flames.
To be capable of this, the gas must first combine with the
oxygen in the air.

What we need for a campfire, therefore, is fuel that is
sufficiently flammable to give off combustible gas in sufficient quantity to be lit by the heat we are able to concentrate
on it. This initial fire, in turn, must be hot and lasting
enough to release and ignite more and more gas from
progressively larger fuel.

STARTING THE FIRE. If birch grows in your locality,
the very best kindling is birch bark. Enough small shreds
of this can be pulled off by hand so that seldom will there
be any need, even deep in the woods, to disfigure the tree.

In evergreen country you needn't ever have difficulty in
starting a blaze in any kind of weather. A fairly tight handful of the dead resinous twigs that abound in the lower parts
of all conifers will burst readily into flame at the touch of a
match. The only exception occurs in damp cold weather.
Then freezing moisture sometimes sheathes the forest with
ice. When this happens, the solution still remains simple.

You only have to expose the dry oily interiors of the dead branches.

Shavings from pitch pine light very easily. So do shavings from any dead wood you find adhering to standing evergreens. If no softwood is about, look for dead wood on other trees. If you do have to use fallen litter for kindling, be sure that what you choose is firm and dry.

Fuzzsticks, when you need to bother with them, start a fire quickly. They are made by shaving a piece of wood again and again, not detaching the accumulating curls. These fuzzsticks are commonly employed instead of paper, by the way, to start stove fires in the backwoods. Light fuzzsticks and all other kindling so that the flames will be able to eat upward into the fresh fuel.

Ordinarily, you will use dry materials to get the fire going. The job can also be done with live birch and live white ash, however, by splitting out kindling and making fuzzsticks.

One way to start a campfire, then, is to bunch a few wisps of birch bark on the bare ground. Pile a handful of small, dry evergreen twigs above this. Over this nucleus lean a few larger seasoned conifer stubs. Also in wigwam fashion, so that ample oxygen will reach all parts of the heap, lay up some dead hardwood. Then ignite the birch bark so that the flames will eat into the heart of the pile. Once the fire gets going well, you can shape it anyway you want.

The lighting should almost always be accomplished with a single match. Even on those occasions when plenty of matches are at hand, the thus slowly acquired skill may on some later day mean the difference between a warmly comfortable camp and a chilly and miserably damp one.

The ordinary wooden matches are best. These should be held so that any draft reaching them will feed the fire down the stem where it will be able to keep burning. This you will accomplish in whatever way seems best at the moment. You may face the wind with both hands cupped in front of the flaming match. You may stretch out between the breeze and the carefully heaped flammables so that your body will act as a shield. You may use your jacket or any other handy article, such as a large sheet of bark, to protect the first feeble flames.

There is no time in any wooded area when a campfire cannot thus be built from materials at hand. You can always either find or make a sheltered nook. Even when a cold rain is freezing as it falls, shavings and kindling can be provided with a knife. If you don't have a knife, you can still shatter and splinter enough dead wood with which to kindle a blaze. If, preferably, birch bark is available, one sheet will form a dry base on which to arrange campfire makings, while other sheets angled about and above will keep off moisture until the fire is crackling.

VARIOUS COOKING FIRES. When an experienced camper merely wants to get water boiling in his tea pail and to toast a sandwich or two, he builds a small fire in the easiest way he can, depending on what fuel is nearby. Then he cuts a green pole several feet long. This tea stick he shoves into the ground so that one end extends over the heat. He may adjust its height by propping it up with a rock, chunk of wood, or forked stick. If the ground is hard, he may weigh down the lower end with a billet or stone.

The pail he hangs by its bail at the end of the tea stick. The surface of this stick is generally rough enough so that this handle won't slide; also, branches are usually so trimmed from it that a few projections remain. If necessary, of course, a notch can very easily be cut. Incidentally, a practical tea pail is often only a large tin can with two opposite holes punched near its rim to accommodate a makeshift wire handle.

A larger meal is often prepared with the help of additional angled green poles. However, the round fire is generally not too convenient for cooking purposes. One answer is to arrange a number of such small fires of varying intensities, just as you use different burners on a city range.

But the problem becomes one of most easily supporting the various cooking utensils. As usual, solutions are numerous. One handy method that will do away with a lot of teetering and tipping is to scoop, scrape, or stamp a trench.

This may be about six inches wide and deep and perhaps two feet long. Running this trench in the same direction as the wind will assure a better draft. Get a good fire going in this trench, perhaps by raking it there after it gets blazing well. Then kettle, frypan, and pots can be steadied across it. Such a fire, however, probably won't be successful if either the day is quiet or the fuel is none too ardent.

The answer then may be the more usual above-ground fire but one that's some eight inches wide and four or five feet long. This fire may be contained by two fairly dry logs some four to six inches in diameter, laid either parallel or at a slight angle with the open end toward the wind. If these logs are raised an inch or two by stones or billets, air will be able to circulate advantageously beneath them. Fuel this fire with preferably long split hardwood, and if possible let it burn down either to a hot bed of coals or to a steady blaze which does not flame up more than a foot.

Meanwhile, cut two substantial forked green poles. Drive these upright into the ground at each end of the fire, so that a green crosspiece laid between the crotches will extend the length of the center of the fire. Make pothooks for each kettle by cutting handle-holding notches in forked sticks that can be inverted over this crosspiece. Or carry several pothooks made by bending short lengths of coat-hanger wire into "S" shapes.

A convenient variation of this technique is to use two green poles on either side of the fire instead of the somewhat seasoned logs. Take pains to raise these evenly above the ground, perhaps notching the supporting billets if that's what you're using. Such green poles will take a long time to burn through. Just set your cooking utensils across them.

GRATES AND IRONS. A substantial wire grid, available from dealers in camp equipment, will provide a convenient base on which to set pots and pans above a wood fire and over which to broil meat. Some of these have folding legs which, stuck into the forest floor, will hold kettles and frying pan above the heat.

My own experience, however, has been that these sharp extremities can be somewhat of a menace when one is on the move. I have removed them, also partly to save weight. The grids can as handily be laid across rocks or billets. In a stony and often in a treacherously soft spot, this has to be done anyway.

A similar arrangement, less bulky to pack, is two iron rods about one-half inch in diameter and four feet long, or flat or angle irons of similar stiffness. Support them above

CAMPFIRE GRILL.

your fire with rocks or logs at each end, and have them just far enough apart so the smallest kettle will not slip down between. If transportation is no problem, a sheet of metal to lay across these will give you much of the convenience of a stove.

SMOKE. Ever notice how smoke seems to follow you around a campfire? Matter of fact, it actually does follow you. Reason for this is that smoke is pulled into the partial vacuum made by any nearby object. The antidote? Create a larger attraction than that of your person. One way to go about this is by building the fire against a boulder or sandy bank. Or locate some other bulk or surface nearby, always a safe distance from the heat.

SAFETY. It does not pay to take chances with a fire. Never kindle one on surfaces made up largely of decomposed and living vegetation. Fire will sometimes eat deep into such footing. An individual may think he has put it out. Unseen and unsuspected, it may smolder for days and weeks. It may lie nearly dormant during an entire winter. With the warmth and increasing dryness of spring, it may regain new vigor until one hot day a strong wind may cause it to erupt into a growling, exploding, devastating forest fire.

When you leave a camp or bivouac in a potentially dangerous area for more than a few minutes, put out that fire. Saturate it with water. Stir up the ground beneath and around it, working and soaking ashes and dust into mud. Dig around it until you are certain no root or humus will lead the blaze away like a fuse. Feel with your hands to make sure that all heat has been safely diminished. Examine the vicinity for any activity resulting from sparks and flying embers.

Particular precaution must be taken in some country when a dutch oven is used underground. In a few areas, especially during the dry seasons, this shallow kettle with its rimmed cover should not be so used at all except when you remain on the spot. Make sure in any event wherever fire can be a menace that the oven is buried in mineral soil and that no combustible material of any sort, be it roots or decaying forest litter, is near enough to be started smoldering.

CAMP STOVES. In spite of all that can be said for an open fire, there are times when a stove either is necessary or is at least indicated by common sense.

The most popular camp stove today is one that uses gasoline for fuel under its one, two, or three burners. In many cases the gasoline stove solves the cooking problem admirably, especially when it comes to boiling and frying. A separate oven can be used for baking.

This type of stove is ideal and often a must for many public camping grounds. It is good for the places where firewood is no longer to be had and where space may be limited. It is excellent for those automobile tourists who like to cook their own meals beside the road, both for the

GASOLINE CAMP STOVE.

pleasure of eating outdoors and because of the very real economies thus afforded.

Such a cooking fire can be lighted immediately. The even and easily regulated heat will allow the refugee from the city range to put out good meals with a minimum of effort and guesswork. Such a stove is fine, too, for travelers in those areas where nonresidents are prohibited from lighting an open fire except when accompanied by a resident or a licensed guide.

Gasoline stoves are inexpensive, easily and compactly packed, and durable. They can be used if desired atop a handy metal stand that supports them at normal stove height and, when not in use, folds into a small bundle that is easily stowed in the car or boat.

TINIEST STOVES. The one-burner primus stove is often the answer for winter sports enthusiasts, fishermen and mountaineers who climb beyond the tree line, and even motorists who like to heat water or cook very small meals inside their cars. These light, efficient little heaters may be obtained in units burning alcohol, kerosene, gasoline, canned gas, and similar compact fuels. For example, there is a 2½-pound combination selling for about $15 which includes: one 3½-pint casserole, one 2½-pint casserole, one

PORTABLE PROPANE GAS COOK STOVE.

lid pan, one upper and lower wind guard, a pot holder, a strap, and a gasoline stove, all nesting into a space 8¼ inches in diameter and 4¾ inches high. Lightweight, leak-proof aluminum fuel bottles are also inexpensively available. The big, catalog-issuing camp equipment dealers stock a functional variety of these units and combinations.

WOOD-BURNING STOVES. Whenever a stove is to be

used where firewood is available, a sheet-metal model burning this fuel has decided advantages. You'll seldom see one today in city stores, and they're unfamiliar to campers with little experience. But along the receding frontiers in whose forests you still encounter old-timers, these wood-burning models usually are the only portable stoves ever considered.

PRIMUS COOKING COMBINATION.

Such a stove usually weighs a little more than the gasoline stove. Although available in folding types, it is generally bulkier. But there is no fuel to transport, and the sheet-metal stove is not difficult to carry even over a portage or on a pack horse.

You can cook on it in the rain. With a little care, it will safely warm closed tents. Many sourdoughs, as a matter of fact, have no other stove, not even in their home cabins. It is easy to dry clothing around it. Broiling and toasting over an open pot hole can be a comparative pleasure.

It is particularly handy for river trips in the large outboard motor boats that travel the broad and often sluggish streams at the roof of this continent. There, odds and ends

SIMS FOLDING STOVE WITH SHELF, OVEN, AND TANK.

of driftwood quickly afford concentrated heat, protected from the ravenous winds often howling along such shores. By providing a shallow box filled with sand, you can even cook afloat.

If the stove you select has an oven, baking and roasting will be possible. If it is without an oven, a folding reflector baker or a separate collapsible oven can be used.

COLLAPSIBLE OVEN.

CARBON MONOXIDE. Be sure there is plenty of ventilation when you have any sort of a stove going in any enclosed area including a tent. Carbon monoxide is more of a threat to outdoorsmen than is generally realized. It is a colorless gas. It has no odor. Being cumulative, it often so weakens a victim that by the time he is aware that something is wrong, he no longer has the strength to do anything about it. There is not even any prior difficulty with breathing to warn him. Carbon monoxide is a potential danger in any closed area where cooking or heating is going on. The best precaution? Good ventilation. You'd think that a tent, certainly, would therefore be a safe place. But when, for example, tent fabrics have been closed by waterproofing in some instances and by frost or rain in others, small stoves going overnight have sometimes killed all occupants.

DUTCH OVEN. Here is the one and only. It's not that this old-fashioned oven of cast iron doesn't have its disadvantages. It's awkward and heavy to carry unless you're traveling by pack train, boat, or car. Furthermore, although it holds the heat, it will rust if not kept well greased. Other varieties, such as those made of aluminum, are both lighter and easier to keep clean. But they're for city stoves if anywhere. They wouldn't even come close to getting the job done over outdoor fires.

What you want for food in the farther places is a heavy, thick, cast-iron pot with a similarly rugged top, lipped to hold a ruddy bed of coals. If your dealer doesn't have one, write the Lodge Manufacturing Company in South Pittsburg, Tennessee. The model I find most satisfactory for my own use with small parties is 12 inches in diameter, 4 inches deep, and 17 pounds in weight. Models are also available 8, 10, 14, and 16 inches in diameter.

The dutch oven you get should have squat legs both to keep the bottom safely above the otherwise scorching ardor of hot embers and to anchor the contraption levelly. It will also need a convenient handle by which the hot top can be lifted and a likewise easily manipulated bail by which the entire contrivance can be moved. Both of these jobs can be performed with the help of a forked stick cut on the spot. When I'm shifting the coal-heaped lid, though, I help balance it with a second stick held in the other hand. You'll also need a shovel. One of the husky, folding models available at surplus stores is convenient to carry. Dutch ovens are used both above and below ground, as detailed in the chapter on breads.

Old-timers season their dutch ovens, when they first buy them, by boiling grease in them. Otherwise, they'll tell you, the cast iron which is porous will give trouble in making food stick. This is a sound precaution when you buy those heavy iron frypans, too.

REFLECTOR BAKER. The way to add a really luxurious touch to meals cooked over open fires is to bring along a

REFLECTOR BAKER.

reflector baker. Described at length in Chapter 7, one of
these holdovers from pioneer years can also be effectively
utilized with ovenless stoves and with the most modern
charcoal grills. Dealers sell reflector bakers in sizes to fit
your needs.

Some hints? Because these contrivances roast and bake
with reflected as well as direct heat, you'll get better campfire results if the warmth from your open blaze is directed
toward the opening by some reflecting surface such as a

rock or a high back log. Two ways to keep this oven from cooking too fast on the bottom are to place the oven several inches lower than the fire or to base the blaze on a slow-burning green wood so that its concentration of heat will be a bit higher than the lower part of the oven. You need flames for this sort of cooking; not coals. The reflector baker may be set as close as 8 inches to the leaping blaze.

GRIDDLE. A griddle will clear the way for the quick serving of bacon, eggs, and flapjacks in quantity. One of

GRIDDLE.

these plates can be laid across a couple of logs between which a cooking fire has largely burned to coals. Matter of fact, such a griddle can also be used as a substitute stove top to keep cooking utensils steady and free of soot. Magnesium griddles are the lightest available. Unless you plan to wrap them in papers, it's a good idea to make or buy a protective traveling cover so as to keep the rest of the outfit clean.

FOIL. Aluminum foil cookery is the modern version of enclosing food for cooking by bundling it in moist leaves, clay, or dripping green seaweed. This modern method also encourages food to retain its juices and to warm evenly. Therein, as a matter of fact, lie the shortcomings. Meat wrapped in foil, for example, is steamed rather than roasted or broiled. The deliciously crisp brownness is missing. There are ways around, of course. But these largely erase the virtues of simplicity.

A fish can be roasted directly on the coals if it is first wrapped in oiled foil, and in the case of small catches you can impart a certain charred touch by toasting it unwrapped beforehand on a forked stick. With large fish, you can help along the taste by cooking sliced tomatoes, diced onions, bacon, chopped peppers, and the like in the foil along with the fish.

Then there are the vegetables and such whose taste this variety of cooking does not seriously impair. The major drawback to any large amount of foil cookery, from the vacationist's viewpoint, is that its nature is more that of an occasional novelty. It does not really lend itself to serious cookery. Once in a while it's fun. But in the long run you save no time or energy. Most importantly for go-light campers on extended trips, you also save no weight. This is not to say that aluminum foil does not have innumerable admirable outdoor uses. Many of these are considered elsewhere.

NESTED COOKING UTENSILS. You'll need cooking and eating paraphernalia. Pots, pans, dishes, and tableware from home will often do.

For the lone camper, the practical minimum is two small kettles with covers and with bails by which they can be hung over a fire, a frypan with preferably a folding handle, a table spoon and usually a light fork, and a cool cup. The frypan will serve as a plate; the cup as a bowl. One's pocket or sheath knife can be used whenever necessary.

Two nesting aluminum kettles, the larger holding about 1½ quarts, together with an 8-inch frypan with conveniently folding handle, are available from dealers in camping goods. Weighing less than two pounds, they add no appreciable bulk to a pack, inasmuch as food and other essentials can be packed within them. Even when there are two or three people in the party, this same outfit can suffice; along with a plate, cup, spoon, and fork for each individual.

Best of all for camping is a small nested cooking and eating kit made of a light, tough aluminum compound. Anyone who has ever burned himself on aluminum, however, will agree that the nested cups, and preferably the plates as well,

NESTED COOKING OUTFIT.

ONE-MAN NESTED OUTFIT.

may well be of stainless steel. The frypan, too, should be stainless steel. I bought an outfit of this sort when I first started going into the real wilderness, and I've used it without replacement or changes ever since. Matter of fact, many of the components are so handy that even when I'm in the city one or another of them is still used almost daily. How-

FOUR-MAN OUTFIT.

ever, some flimsy and highly impractical sets are on the market. Buy your nested outfit, if you get one, from the best established and most reliable sporting goods dealer you can get in touch with. Cost is surprisingly low.

Light fabric holders available for the pots and frypan permit their being cleanly packed, when camp is moved frequently, without a whole lot of work scouring off the black every time. Actually, a certain amount of this exterior blackness makes for faster and more even cooking. You can also secure fabric knife, fork, and spoon rolls that, when you set up camp, can be handily hung to a tree or tent.

KNIFE, FORK, AND SPOON HOLDER.

When you get home, spots and discolorations on aluminum ware can be removed by using a solution made by dissolving a tablespoon of cream of tartar in a pint of water.

A durable set of nested aluminum measuring spoons takes up very little space and can be handy in both the kitchen and eating areas. If you don't take a regular measuring cup, mark accurate proportions plainly on one of your drinking cups.

MIXING SURFACE. Simplest and handiest thing to take along for mixing and working purposes is a thin sheet of plastic. This can be easily washed, quickly refolded, and conveniently carried from one vacation spot to another with a minimum of bother.

Matter of fact, one of the most convenient things for each individual to carry when picnicking, camping, hiking, skiing, fishing, hunting, or otherwise vacationing outdoors is a thin sheet of lightweight plastic, perhaps five feet by seven feet. This will quickly fold into bandanna handkerchief size, small enough for the pocket of a sport shirt. It can be drawn over the head and shoulders as a protection against wind and rain, laid atop the lower boughs of a tree as a shelter from a storm, spread on the ground as a picnic cloth, and used as a clean waterproof wrapping for a deer liver or a string of sleek bright trout.

AXES. The ax is an almost indispensable tool for the woodsman, many of whom rate it even above matches as the most valuable item to have along in the bush. The full sized ax is not really needed in the average warm weather camp, however. That with a 2½- or perhaps a 3-pound head is big enough for most vacationists.

The handiest ax for packing outside an automobile, although not for any great amount of work, is the Hudson Bay model with a narrow butt and a face of normal width. This model, because of the narrow poll through which the handle is attached, does not hold up too well for heavy work. But for ordinary camping requirements, where weight is a consideration and you still want an ax, a Hudson Bay with a 1½-pound head and a 24-inch handle will do a lot of jobs. A metal-riveted leather sheath should ordinarily be added. The Hudson Bay ax, incidentally, is a convenient one to tie to your saddle.

If you are going to be using a vacation ax very much, you will probably be most satisfied with an ordinary single-bit model with about a 2½-pound head. A handle or helve about 26 to 28 inches long is generally enough, though some may find they can swing the longer 36-inch handle more naturally and therefore more safely. In any event, if you adopt one length handle and use it exclusively, you will come to do better and safer work.

AXMANSHIP. The main thing is to be careful. You can ruin a hunting or fishing trip mighty easily with just one stroke that lands a fraction of an inch from where you want it to go. The best general precaution is to anticipate the worst and to be so placed that even if it does occur no one will be hurt. A sharp ax is safer than a dull one in that it is not so prone to bounce off the wood.

Be prepared to have the ax glance off a knot and have

your feet and legs where they will not be hit. Take the time to clear away any shrubs or branches that might catch the blade. Don't take the risk of steadying a billet with hand or foot.

Avoid, too, the common practice of leaning a stick against a log and half-chopping and half-breaking it in two. A lot of head injuries from flying wood have resulted from that all too prevalent habit. When you're felling a dead tree for firewood, watch out that another tree doesn't break off the top and send it crashing back toward you. In other words, there are a great many possible misadventures. The more of these you can foresee and guard against, the less will be the possibility of an injury.

When you stop to think of it, axes are far less dangerous than such a common substance as glass. Shortcomings do not lie in the ax, but rather in the individual. Use the ax with a nice easy swing. Don't hurry your back stroke. Then let the gravity fall of the ax do most of the work, and you'll be able to cut for extended periods without pressing. Bring your eye to the exact spot where you want the edge to strike, and practice until it does always strike there. Give a slight twist to the blade at the very end of the stroke.

SAWS. It is usually much easier and faster for campers to saw wood than to chop it. If you are using a wood-

CAMP SAW.

burning stove, such a tool will be invaluable for working available fuel into the right lengths to fit the firebox. Even when you're bivouacking in weather nippy enough to argue the companionship of an overnight blaze, a saw will make the task of accumulating enough fodder for that campfire a comparatively easy one.

The long slender blade of the Swede is a favorite. It is so thin that it speeds through logs with a minimum of effort. It is so light that it can be handled easily in any position. The long narrow blade is so flexible that, except during extreme cold, it can be coiled to the circumference of a saucer, held together by a cord wound and tied among its teeth, and wrapped with a piece of canvas for carrying. The two-piece, light, tubular handle is easily slid apart and packed.

HATCHET. The light hand ax with about a 12-inch

HATCHET.

handle will do all the work necessary in many summer or auto camps and on backpacking trails. The average camper will use it with more effectiveness and greater safety than he will a long-handled ax. Such a hand ax can be useful when you're butchering, although you'll have to touch up the blade afterward. A neat way for even a novice to go through a heavy bone is to hold the hatchet in place, rather than trying to swing it, and to drive it by hammering on the back. This tool also works well enough in procuring wood for a small cooking fire. Secure a substantial sheath for it, but don't ordinarily carry it on your belt. Most of the time this is both inconvenient and uncomfortable. Stow it instead in a rucksack or in a game or saddle pocket.

MEAT SAW. A lot of hunters carry only hatchets or,

FOLDING SAW WITH BOTH MEAT AND
WOOD BLADES.

if they're traveling by canoe or cayuse, axes. I also like a meat saw, small enough to stow in my packsack. Besides other uses, such a saw is the only conservative way to cut up frozen portions.

COOK'S KNIFE. You need a knife constantly afield, and for many purposes. For example, the camp cook will require one for slicing bread and meat, paring vegetables, and for a dozen other chores. Any fair-sized knife will do for such duties. Unless you're traveling particularly light, however, it is better to have a special one for kitchen work. This blade is almost sure to get such rough treatment that it would take a lot of work to keep it sharp enough for other jobs. Aside from that, a kitchen knife both performs better and holds up more satisfactorily if not given the fine edge desirable for pocket and sporting knives.

COOK'S KNIFE.

One reason for this is that meat is carved and bread sliced more easily with what is actually a sawing action. A coarse edge made by sweeping the blade forward a few times against a carborundum diagonally from heel to tip, first on one side and then on the other, actually resembles saw teeth. This most functional edge can be quickly renewed by the same process.

A small butcher knife, particularly one of those stocked by specialists in outdoor equipment, goes well with most outfits. Have a sheath for it, and keep it in the bundle with the knives, forks, and spoons. Do not oil and thus soften this leather. Not only does the knife then become difficult to encase, but the point has a tendency to catch and puncture the flexible and often curling leather. Saddle soap the sheath instead, or use ordinary shoe polish on it.

CLEANING CARBORUNDUM. Carborundums are used so often in camp that it's little wonder that these abrasive stones become more and more clotted with grime, thus progressively losing their effectiveness. To restore the cutting ability of your dirt-clogged carborundum, just put the stone in a good bed of coals until it is red hot. Then it will be all right again.

COOLER. For fixed camps where refrigeration is a problem, capillary attraction may be harnessed to help solve food-keeping difficulties. Start by building a wooden frame in the general size and shape of an orange crate. Make one side a hinged door. Put in several shelves of slats or poultry wire, making them as open as possible so as to encourage circulation. Then screen the box to assure its being fly proof.

Tack burlap over the contraption, lapping this generously at the door and leaving the top and bottom folds both long and loose. Place a large pan of water on the top of this food container. Immerse the top burlap ends in the water. Capillarity will keep the burlap saturated. If the box is set or suspended in a breezy spot, evaporation will do the cooling.

PAILS. Plenty of water is wanted at most campsites, and sources of supply are often some distance away. Collapsible and folding canvas or rubberized buckets are procurable and are handy for certain kinds of camping. For other types of vacationing, such as automobile camping, two galvanized pails will be cleaner and more convenient. Breakables can be packed in them during traveling.

PACKING FOOD. Available inexpensively from a number of outdoor outfitters, small plastic bags are excellent for packaging all dry home mixes suggested in this book. These bags can be readily sealed by a hot iron. If you want to reuse them, close them instead with one of the adhesive cellulose tapes.

Lightweight unbreakable plastic bottles and flasks of a wide variety of styles and shapes are on the market. You can get these to carry cooking oil and other inert liquids. The storing of whisky and liquors in polyethylene is safe for periods of up to two and three months.

Both regular and high density polyethylene containers arc suitable for use with vanilla extracts. However, they have not proved satisfactory with other extracts because aldehydes and esters in these cause a softening of the polyethylene. Such extracts, therefore, are better left in their original glass containers which may be wrapped in tape for safety.

Although high density polyethylenes have been found suitable for use with spices, the essential oils present in significant quantities in black pepper, nutmeg, mace, etc. attack regular density containers of this sort.

In the case of motor campers in particular, regular packages and bottles can be carried without much difficulty if some semblance of order is maintained. A couple of minor hints? If the glass-top jar you take from home sticks, instead of risking injury by prying, just pull the jar rubber far enough out of position to release the seal. If you have to make a cork smaller, cut a small wedge out of the center so that the edges will fit closely.

Paraffined fabric food bags are light, sanitary, moisture-proof, and inexpensive. They impart no odor to the food, and they pack compactly. A good way to label them is with tags or wax crayons. When you transfer a packaged food such as a dessert mix to one of these bags, it's a sound idea to cut out and include the printed instructions. You can also get substantial cotton bags and stow a number of these in a large waterproof sack for protection. Strong, durable plastic bags with tie cords at the top leave contents visible from the outside, but during really rough going they must be protected from abrasion and puncturing.

CHAPTER 3

PREPARING GAME AND FISH

GAME ANIMALS

How good would the choicest corn-fed beef taste if the steer were shot four times through the paunch and chased several miles? Suppose the rancher hacked into the entrails while butchering it, letting additional juices and waste matter mingle with hair in the meat. He might then leave the unskinned carcass lying a couple of days, with the sun working on one side, the damp ground on the other, and flies all over. Eventually, suppose he hauled the beef over the sweltering hood of his car and jolted it through dust, heat, and fumes for a few hundred miles before flopping it down for the locker man to skin, section, and refrigerate. That's the way more than one deer is mishandled, and if the prime steers got the same treatment there'd be as much conversation about "gamy" beef as there is about "gamy" venison. When people honestly and open-mindedly react this way to wild meat, the odds are that the animal was not dressed out properly and that, in addition, the meat wasn't cared for afterwards as it should have been. There is no good reason for any of this.

IS THROAT CUTTING NECESSARY? When you shoot a large animal, it serves no useful purpose whatsoever to run in and cut its throat with the motive of bleeding it. A modern bullet so disrupts the chest or abdominal cavities that they fill with blood almost immediately. No more than a few spoonfuls of blood will be released by this kind of sticking.

But the animal should be gutted as soon as possible. Then turn the body belly down and drain out all the blood. If you're going to use the skin, try not to spill

56

blood on it, as this is difficult to remove. When the animal has been cleaned out, take fistfuls of grass, moss, or leaves and wipe the chest and abdominal walls clean and free of moisture. The blood itself acts as a good solvent in doing this. Get the inside walls as clean and dry as you can. Never use water.

BUTCHERING. When you come to your kill, don't try to hang up the animal unless this can be quickly and easily accomplished. Ordinarily, the job is apt to be difficult and unreasonably time consuming. If this is the case, it will be sufficient to have the carcass with the head uphill and the rest of the body slanting downwards. If even that is not possible, try to get the animal's chest up on a rock or log.

Turn the animal belly up, propping it in that position with rocks, logs, stakes, or whatever else may be handy. Or a line between a hind leg and a tree will hold it. Then make a very short center cut at the lower end of the breastbone just below the lowest ribs. As soon as the knife slits through skin, fat, and meat into the body cavity, insert the first two fingers of whichever is your master hand into the opening.

KNIFE.

Hold the entrails down and away so that the knife will not penetrate them. Then extend the incision down to the rectum, circumventing the active external milk glands if any and then returning to lift and cut away these easily disengaged tissues. Cut around each side of the major sexual organ and around the rectum, taking care not to puncture either. The contents can quickly taint the best meat unless any areas of contact are trimmed away. Carefully free the ducts leading to each. Preferably, tie them off with a piece of string or lace so that nothing will escape from them.

Then with your sleeves rolled up and wrist watch removed, reach up into the upper end of the abdominal cavity and cut the diaphragm loose all around. This is the membrane that separates the organs of the chest from those in the abdomen. Now reach with your secondary hand into the top part of the chest. Find and pull down on the windpipe, gullet, and large arteries. Cut them off as close to the neck as you can. This is one operation where, because of the close and obscure quarters, you have to take particular care not to slash yourself.

Now the entire contents of the chest and abdomen are free except for occasional adhesions along the backbone. These can be quickly torn loose by hand. You can now turn the animal on its side and dump out the viscera. As you work down towards the stern, take care to poke the two tied ends free so they will fall out with the remainder. It is then that you wipe the inside of the animal as dry as possible, after dragging it away from the discards.

DELICACIES. Save the heart, cutting this free from the little pouch of membrane in which it is lodged. Be sure to lay the liver beside it on some clean area such as a piece of bark, a rock, or a patch of snow. Secure the two kidneys as well. All are delicious. You may also care to save the white sheets of abdominal fat which will render into excellent lard for cooking. Unless you are going to have the head mounted, slit the underneath of the jaw deeply enough so that you can pull the tongue down through this opening and sever it near the base. A blood-proof bag is handy for carrying these back to camp.

COOLING. What you do next will depend to a large extent on circumstances such as weather, weight, and terrain. You may be able to hang the game by the head. You will at least be able to turn it so that the body opening can be propped open with sticks in order that the meat will cool as soon as possible.

Covering the carcass with a mass of well-leaved boughs will protect the flesh to a large extent from the shifting sun, as well as from birds which may be already waiting for a chance to whittle away at the fat.

If blowflies are bad, you should either have enough cheesecloth to cover the cavity or a cheesecloth bag in which the entire animal can be placed. Bluebottles and other winged pests will still probably get at it to some extent. When these have been particularly thick, I've found it effective to douse the underneath few of a mass of evergreen boughs with one of the effective and unobjectionable personal fly dopes such as Pellent, taking care of course to keep this off the meat. You can examine all openings and exposed spots when you pack the animal out, in any event, and wipe or cut away any eggs and larvae.

If rain is threatening, a better procedure is to turn the animal so that it is draped, back uppermost, over a rock or log. The body cavity must be freely ventilated in any event. Turning a freshly butchered deer on its belly in the snow, for example, will cause the meat to start to putrify noticeably even overnight in temperatures well below zero.

PACKING. The easiest way to get the venison out of the woods is usually with a horse. This is a common practice in the West. In the East, some hunting camps keep a horse for this purpose. If the animal is spooky, stroke and pet it some and during the process rub a little of the blood on its nose.

Ordinarily, you can tie a deer across or in front of the riding saddle. With something such as a moose, you'll perhaps cut it up and divide the sections between two animals. If snow is on the ground, you may drag a large unskinned quarry by its head after cutting off the legs.

Dragging is most easily accomplished with a harness. However, you can take a half hitch high around the tail, bend back the hair, and then take a second half hitch around the now doubled tail. The usual saddle horse will then skid out even a good sized moose or elk without any lasting discomfort if conditions are halfway favorable. If the experience is a new one, the horse will probably settle down better if you remain in the saddle as much as possible.

Snugging the rope around the saddle horn is not such a good idea.

MANPOWER. Deer can be dragged headfirst by a couple of husky hunters. They are often carried on a stout pole, back hanging down and feet tied up over the timber. The head should also be lashed up so that it won't dangle and continue to throw the load off balance. As a matter of fact, a deer lugged more than a short distance in this fashion will swing so much that you will very probably soon be weighing the advisability of cutting a second pole and using the two of them as a stretcher. This, once the animal has been tied on solidly, can be borne at any height.

One ordinarily rugged man can carry a fairly good size deer by himself. There are two handy ways of accomplishing this. I prefer to drape the animal over my shoulders like a scarf and to hold onto the legs. This way, if you start to slip or stumble, you can get rid of the load in a hurry.

If you've tied it into a pack by lashing the legs together, you may fall and find an uncomfortable amount of weight pressing you down. A common way of carrying deer, nevertheless, is by tying all four legs together and then running your head between body and legs, with the shank ends held down in front of your chest with one hand. The flats on the sides of one fore and one hind leg then rest on your shoulders and do not cut in. It is almost impossible to carry a heavy deer any distance piggyback because of the way the sharp bones bite into the shoulders.

If under any circumstances whatsoever you carry a deer through a forest frequented by other hunters, tie a brightly colored cloth or other red or orange material conspicuously around it. It isn't a bad idea, either, to whistle loudly.

SKINNING. If you are an old-time hunter, you'll very possibly prefer to complete the skinning on the spot. You may pretty well have to do this if your trophy is big. (To make rawhide, see Colonel Townsend Whelen's and my Stackpole book, *On Your Own in the Wilderness.*) There are exceptions, of course, depending generally on the available methods of transportation and to some degree on the weather.

You'll want to get the hide off as soon as reasonably practical. The meat should be allowed to cool thoroughly with the least possible delay. Unless the animal is a small one and is opened wide, it won't cool quickly in temperate weather with the skin on. And if you're in a cold climate, you'll want to be sure to complete the skinning before the hide freezes on, or what would have been a few minutes' work may very easily develop into a cold and disagreeable all-day chore. Besides, bacterial growth is prevented on the surface of the meat when the air can get to it.

To skin a deer, first remove the lower legs or shanks. The novice is likely to begin too high at what most of us think of as the knees. Cut deeply through skin, flesh, and muscle about an inch below these joints. Then brace your knee against what are actually the ankles. Pull forward briskly in the case of a front leg, backward with the hind leg, and the shank will snap off.

Your taxidermist can make very attractive gun and clothes racks, lamps, and other nostalgic items from the shanks with attached hoofs. Skin these all the way down. Cut all meat off the bones but leave the latter attached. Then salt thoroughly and send to the taxidermist, either with instructions or with a request for his suggestions.

Now we come to the actual skinning. Slit the hide along the inside of each leg to meet the belly cut. Extend this latter incision on up to the neck just short of the jaw. Then cut completely around the neck, close behind the jaws, ears, and antlers. If you may want to have the head mounted, however, you proceed a bit differently at this stage, as noted in a moment.

Slit the underside of the tail, also. Then start at each of these cuts in turn to peel the skin from the flesh. If you are working on the ground, use the hide throughout as a clean rug on which to keep the meat unsullied. Generally, the skin will come away neatly, particularly if the animal has just been shot. In places where it adheres rather firmly, such as along the neck, use your knife carefully to cut it loose.

Avoid as much as possible making any nicks in the hide. You will notice between skin and flesh a thin, white film resembling parchment which, as a matter of fact, it is in a sense. Touch this film with a sharp blade, and the skin will continue to peel off. If anyone is helping you, have that individual keep the hide pulled taut while you free it with the long easy sweeps of a keen knife.

Despite all your care, there will be a few places where thin layers of meat and fat will adhere to the skin. When you have the latter off and can find some time to work on it, perhaps leisurely beside the campfire at night, neatly flesh it. One way to make this task easier is to stretch the section on which you are working tightly and comfortably across a knee. Fleshing consists of cutting, scraping, or peeling off all pieces of meat and fat that adhere to the hide.

If a rug is what you want, lace the skin to a frame. Or stretch it, with the hair against a building or a big tree, with nails around the edge. Or, leaving the fleshed side up, stake it out on clean and dry ground by pegs driven around the perimeter through little slits made six inches apart. Let it dry away from moisture and sunshine. If there are blow-flies and bugs around, rub the inside of it with salt to discourage them. A day or so later, wipe the wet salt off and let the skin dry as before.

You may be on the go, however, and unable to stretch the skin. It can still be kept in fine shape for a rug by salting it thoroughly all over the fleshed side, turning the ends and edges in, and rolling the whole thing into a limp bundle that may be stowed in a loose burlap bag if one is handy and hung in a cool dry place. The hide does not have to be fleshed too closely when handled this way.

HEADS FOR MOUNTING. In case your game has excellent antlers and you want to have the head mounted as a trophy, instead of skinning as previously indicated, proceed in this manner. Starting at a point atop the shoulders, slit the hide down over each shoulder until the two incisions meet at the point of the chest between the forelegs. Commencing again at the top of the shoulders, cut forward along the top of the neck to a point just between the two antlers.

From these cuts, peel and skin off the shoulders and neck right up to the skull. Run the point of your knife deeply into the cartilages between the skull and the first vertebra, cutting this junction as free as you can. Then push the head hard one way and then the other, and the skull will break free of the backbone. Now you have the head with the cape attached.

Proceed to turn the skin inside out over the head, first cutting very closely around each antler. Then slice away down in the orifice of each ear, leaving these members on the skin, of course. Skin around the eyes, placing a finger in each to make sure you do not cut the lashes. Then cut to the junction of the upper gums close to the teeth, and in front of the front teeth or gums, leaving the nose on the skin.

Salt the ears, eyeholes, nose, and gums very thoroughly. Roll up the scalp, flesh side to flesh side, and leave it for two days while the salt works in. Then wipe as much wet salt off as possible. Hang up the scalp by the nose to dry in the shade, using a bent stick like a coat hanger. Do not stretch the scalp.

In the meantime, remove all flesh from the skull and the lower jaw. Incidentally, this meat is adjudged by many to be the tastiest on the animal. Using a small stick shaped like a small spoon, remove the brains through the hole where the skull was separated from the backbone. Brains, too, are a fine delicacy, scrambled for instance with eggs as suggested later. Send the dry or nearly dry scalp, the skull with antlers attached, and the lower jaw to your taxidermist.

QUARTERING. Once the carcass is free of the skin, which you have been shifting about so as to keep the meat as clean as possible, quartering will be in order. Unless you intend to save the head, ease the point of your blade deeply into the cartilages between the skull and the first vertebra, severing them as well as you can. Then twist

12-OUNCE PORTABLE SAW WITH 20-INCH BLADE.

the head abruptly in one direction and then in the other, and it will snap free.

With a hatchet, ax, or meat saw, split the bone from the belly cut to the neck. Open the neck on the same line and remove the windpipe and gullet. Then split the backbone from neck to tail. The animal will now be in two halves. Quarter it by dividing each of these halves along the line of the lowest ribs.

You may now wrap these quarters, perhaps rubbed with flour, separately in cheesecloth to discourage pests. Sprinkling black pepper on the flesh will, if necessary, also help to keep blue-bottles and such annoyers off while the meat gets a protective casing over its outside. You will also prob-

HATCHET.

ably want to examine the meat every day or so to make sure it remains unbothered, giving particular attention to bullet wounds and to folds and nicks in the flesh. Any eggs or larvae so detected can be quickly and harmlessly scraped, wiped, or cut away.

In any event, the quarters can now cool quickly, especially if you hang them high in a tree to hasten the chilling the first night. Some of the pack trains in the mountains, hunting early so as to be back down in the lowlands before snow drifts in too deeply, keep fresh game sweet by trimming the branches out of a tree and pulling the meat high up into the clear 20 feet or more from the ground where blowflies do not operate. Days, the quarters can be wrapped in canvas or bedding to keep them cool.

A meat tent is a handy thing to pack along in hot weather if you have a large enough outfit to warrant its inclusion. A handy model, often seen in work camps in the wilderness, consists of canopied netting with a zipper opening. This shelter is customarily tied in a dark, well ventilated spot by a single rope that runs from its top center.

REFRIGERATION. Keep these quarters as cool and as dry as possible. If you are heading outside, get them into refrigeration as soon as you can. If a long and warm auto trip lies ahead, try at the earliest opportunity both to pack each quarter in a carton of dry ice and to protect those containers in larger ones with crumpled newspapers between for insulation. Circumstances may be such, too, that you'll prefer to travel in the comparative coolness of the night.

If the weather is hot and the distance far, you will probably do well to lay over a day in some locality where you can have the meat frozen solid. This may be a desirable time to cut and wrap it in plainly labeled packages that can be retrieved from the freezer and used one by one. Odd portions can be ground into hamburger, along with a desirable proportion of beef fat unless you object.

It should then be an easy job, with the help of dry ice which these days is obtainable along most routes, to bring these packages frozen to your cold storage cabinet, drawer,

locker, or butcher's cold room. You'll have some really
fine meat.

FISH

TO CLEAN A FISH. Slit the abdomen from the vent
to the neck as soon as possible after catching. Take out
the entrails. Scrape the kidney tissue from along the backbone with the knife tip or thumbnail. Some of the sweetest
meat is in the head and tail, but if you'd prefer to have
them off, sever them with a sharp knife. If you're by a
stream, you'll probably rinse the cavity in cold running
water. Otherwise, it is preferable to wipe it out well with
a clean damp cloth. Keep the fish dry and cool.

TO REMOVE THE FINS. Cut into the flesh on either
side of the fin. Then grasp the fin and yank it abruptly
toward the head so as to pull out the bones. If you ever
trim fins with shears or knife, leave these bones in sight
so that they can be dislodged easily after being loosened
by cooking.

TO SCALE. Hold the fish firmly on a flat surface. Scrape
off the scales with a blunt knife, working swiftly from tail
to head. Scales are most easily removed if you can give a
few moments to the job while the fish is still wet from the
water.

TO SKIN. Slice off a thin ribbon of skin along the
entire length of the backbone once the back fins have
been removed. Then loosen the skin around the gills. Grasp
the skin, finally, and peel it from head to tail. With tough
hides like that of the ling, pliers are handy. Turn the fish
over and do the same thing on the other side.

TO FILLET. Cut down from the head to the tail, along
the backbone, with a sharp pointed knife. Turn the knife
flat and cut the flesh along the spine to the tail, letting the
knife slide over the ribs. Lift off the side of the fish in
one piece. Turn the fish over and remove the other fillet
the same way. Fillets are those slices, boneless or nearly
so, cut lengthwise along the ribs parallel to the backbone.
Steaks, on the other hand, are slabs cut at right angles to
the backbone.

TO BONE. Lay the fish on its side and with a sharp pointed knife cut from the head to the tail close to the spine. Turn the fish on its other side and make a similar cut. Sever the head if this hasn't already been done. Then carefully lift out the entire backbone. Pick out as many remaining small bones as possible.

TO KEEP FISH IN CAMP. Clean immediately after catching, wipe dry, and then put in a dry nest of grass or other green vegetation within a creel or similar container. Completely surround each fish with the grass or such, so that no fish touches another. The top layer of vegetation may be moistened slightly, inasmuch as evaporation will make for added coolness. But no more dampness should touch the fish. Keep them cool, dry, and clean.

KEEPING FISH. One way to keep such fish several days without refrigeration is to swathe the fish and vegetation in a lot of newspapers, early in the morning after they have been chilled by the night air. Then pick a spot that will remain shaded all day and bury the package underground. Or the package can be rolled during the day in dampened burlap or such, then laid out each night to air and cool.

Another method is to wrap each fish, sprinkled with salt or corn meal if you want, in wax paper after it has been cleaned and dried. Then roll in dry fabric or newspaper and wrap a second time. Sacking or other material may then be soaked, wrung out, and then lashed over the dry bundle with each end roped tight. Keep in as cool a place as possible, preferably away from open air. Do not open until the fish are to be used. This bundle can be successfully shipped in a box with ice, providing that the ice does not touch the fish.

Green grass or similar vegetation can also be used to insulate fish that are to be shipped with ice. Pad the bottom of a wooden box thickly with grass or similar green vegetation. Wrap each fish separately in more greens or in paper and nest them in the box, covering them with additional vegetation. Lay a quantity of large sheets of paper over the box, flatten their centers down across the fish, cover with some four to six inches of ice, then fold up and over the ice. Place more paper on top, nail on the cover, and plainly mark, "This Side Up, Perishable Fish."

Fish can also be tastily smoked, dried, or preserved by methods detailed in my Stackpole Company book, *How To Go Live in the Woods on $10 a Week*.

GAME BIRDS

For best results, unless you have preferences to the contrary, remove the crop and entrails as soon as possible. This may often be successfully delayed for a few hours, but if the bird is badly shot up, the flavor of the meat is apt to be affected. Also, such dressing, in the opinion of many of us, desirably hastens the cooling process.

The crop is situated loosely beneath the skin at the base of the throat. Slit open the skin, take it out, and pull out the windpipe.

Then make a crosswise slit below the breastbone. With small birds that are not going to be stuffed, you can often just hold the legs in one hand, the breast in the other, and pull the bird open. Reach into the abdominal cavity and carefully draw out the insides. Cut out the vent. Then wipe the bird dry. Do not leave any blood clots on the interior.

Save the liver, gizzard, and heart. Very gently cut out the little gall bladder intact and discard it. Its contents are so bitter that any dark portions where they may have spilled on the liver may well be cut from this delicacy as well. Clean the gizzard by easing the knife through to the hard center, then pulling the flesh away from this central sac.

Before using you may remove the oil sac at the base of the tail, disjoint the legs below the thighs, and cut off the head.

Birds should be cooled as quickly as possible. Separating them rather than piling them into a hot game pocket will speed this. If allowed to hang in a cool place soon after they have been shot and drawn, a protective glaze will be formed from contact with the air. They should be kept cool until used. Flavor will be better if they are hung for at least several days before being used.

To save yourself work and to avoid tearing the skin, dry pluck the fowl while it is still warm. Remaining pinfeathers may be removed with the fingernails or with tweezers. Singe the down off quickly, being careful not to burn the skin. Do not pass the bird through the flames of a lighted newspaper, however, as the ink has a blackening effect.

Birds may be plucked later, of course. Scalding is then recommended for grouse, pheasant, quail, and similar fowl. Hold the bird by the feet and quickly plunge it several times into hot, not boiling water, until the feathers loosen readily. Scalding waterfowl, however, usually makes the plucking even more difficult and results in loss of flavor.

Small duck, coot, and such may as well be skinned. Just slit open the back. Pulling in opposite directions with both hands if you want, peel off the skin like a glove. Cut off head, wings, and feet.

Despite a loss in flavor, many hunters skin other birds rather than bother plucking them. As a matter of fact, how you handle your game birds is decided by your own palate. Each of us is a gourmet in his own right.

SMALL GAME

Clean, skin, and cool as soon as possible. Remove any scent or musk glands if they do not come off with the hide. These small, waxy or reddish kernels or glands, located under the forelegs and along the spine or under the lower part of the abdomen, often pull away with the skin. Cut out all imbedded glands, removing them intact if possible so as not to give a musky flavor to the meat.

If you can handle big game, you'll have no trouble with small meat animals. Matter of fact, if you're not going to save the skin, just ring it with your knife around the middle part of the body. Pull half toward the head and the other half toward the tail. Cut off the head, feet, and tail, and that's that. Fur animals deserve more pains. Complete, detailed directions for handling these are to be found in the Stackpole book, *On Your Own in the Wilderness*.

Rabbit and certain other small game are susceptible to infections that can be passed on to man. These are less likely to exist after the first heavy frost and during cold weather. One precaution is to pass up all but lively game. The prudent hunter will also take particular pains to avoid cutting himself while handling any small game and will don rubber or plastic gloves whenever he has any cuts or wounds on his hands. Thorough washing of the hands with a strong soap, followed by the use of a disinfectant after dressing the game, will vastly reduce the danger of any infection.

The liver of each animal, the rabbit especially, should be examined for possible infection. The liver of a healthy animal is clear, dark red in color, firm, and unspotted. Small white cystlike spots, the size of peas or smaller, may indicate the presence of tularemia. Germs of this, incidentally, are destroyed by thorough cooking. But the thing to do when you are aware of its presence, of course, is to burn or deeply bury the infected carcass. Painstaking cleansing of the hands is essential after an infected carcass has been handled.

Thoroughly cooked meat, it may be repeated, is completely safe. By observing the above few simple rules for handling freshly killed small game animals, and by cooking the meat until well done, danger of contracting tularemia from infected animals is removed; one reason why more wild rabbits continue to be happily taken by hunters each year on this continent than any other game, large or small.

CHAPTER 4

FAME WITH BIG GAME

What too many well-meaning cooks do to big game meat shouldn't happen in a nightmare. The result? The hunter is crestfallen. The cook feels unappreciated. A lot of topnotch grub is wasted.

More game meat is ruined by overcooking than by any other misadventure. The major reasons for this are two. The cook has the mistaken opinion that an abundance of heat is the way to assure tenderness. There is also the erroneous notion that high temperatures will burn away the wild flavor.

If your deer or moose tastes best to you rare, that's fine. If not, there's still a way around. Overcooking is ordinarily fatal to most big game, with the exception of bear, because of its general lack of the layers of fat common to comparable domestic meats. Such wild meat dries out under heat, and the fibers quickly tend to harden and toughen. An antidote? A non-seasoned meat tenderizer. For best results with game, use more than the instructions suggest and let it stand a shorter time.

Whether or not some people like a particular game meat largely depends on their taste prejudices. In other words, individuals sit down for the first time to deer that's kept sassy on willow shoots, and they expect it to taste like corn-fattened beef. It doesn't. The instinctive reaction, no matter how delicious the venison may be in its own right? Unfavorable.

Such taste prejudices can work themselves out in a while, when repeated servings begin to assume a familiar taste. There are better ways around, however. One of these shortcuts is to present the meat in as favorable an aspect as possible, surrounded with familiar and favorite side dishes, especially the impressionable first time.

Most of the other methods have to do with actually reducing any objectionable wild game flavors. These latter efforts start in the field with immediate cleaning and rapid cooling, as already considered. They continue with proper handling and storage. When the meat reaches the cooking area, there is an even wider range of choices. Among them are the following general methods, often used both with modifications and in combination.

Cut and pull off all loose fat, inasmuch as this carries most of the game's flavor. Replace this, if at all possible, with beef fat. Your meat man, or any cattle raiser who's been butchering, will sell you a large bag full for a quarter, and it can make all the difference. While you're in the woods, other fat will do, of course. The whiteness or yellowness of fat, incidentally, is no indication of quality or age. Yellow fat merely indicates that the carotin, the yellow substance found in all vegetation, has not yet been converted to Vitamin A.

Trim the meat well before using it, removing all discolored and dehydrated portions and especially any hard or dry outer husk.

You can use spices, herbs, sauces, and the like if you want to alter or modify flavor. The trouble is that you're apt to get too far from the natural deliciousness of game meat. A more natural method? Plain, ordinary bouillon cubes, beef extracts, and similar preparations.

There's this, too. Roasts and stews will have far fewer unfamiliar flavors than steaks. As for such delicacies as heart and liver, these can seldom be distinguished from those bought at the butcher shop.

Finally, if you want, you may soak the meat overnight in a solution of vinegar, water, and spices. Some cooks employ wines, combinations of oil and weak acids such as lemon and tomato juice, barbecue sauces, and the like.

Most of us who love the woods prefer fine game meat quickly cooked, on the rare side, with only salt, pepper, and melting butter or margarine to bring out the delectable natural flavors. However, for one reason or another usually having to do either with age or mating, some meat is below average in savor. Also, everyone is a gourmet in his own right. If an individual prefers to marinate either a prime slab of beef or an equally choice moose sirloin, who is to say that he is wrong?

For those who may be interested, here is a better than usual marinade that will flavor and tenderize some 7 or 8 pounds of steak cut no less than 1½ inches thick. This marinade can be prepared at home by blending the following: 2 tablespoons olive oil, ½ cup wine vinegar, 1 rounded teaspoon oregano, and a sparsely measured ⅛ teaspoon apiece of salt, black pepper, Italian red pepper, and cayenne pepper. When ready to use, pour this into a flat dish where it will lie about ½ inch deep. Immerse the meat about suppertime, topping it with a thinly sliced medium-size onion and covering the dish. Turn the meat once the last thing at night. The steaks will be ready the next day.

This will give a general idea. Actually, if you taste occasionally, use a certain degree of restraint, and have the inclination, you can usually concoct an adequate marinade from the materials at hand. A virtually foolproof wild game marinade can be made, for example, by diluting a cheap red wine such as a claret with half its volume of water, then returning its authority by adding small amounts of pepper, bay leaf, rosemary, tarragon, thyme, mustard seed—anything that gives a pleasing taste.

WHAT TO EAT FIRST

The first parts of the big game animal to eat, while the body of the meat is taking on flavor and tenderness with age, include the liver, heart, kidneys, brains, and tongue. If you don't utilize at least most of these, you're passing up some mighty fine feasting.

LIVER. Slice about ½ inch thick. Brown in a heavy frypan in bacon drippings or other fat until done to taste. Include onions and bacon by all means if you want. Liver is best when it is kept on the rare side. Overcooking gives you a tough, dry, tasteless, and far less nutritious product.

Grilled liver beats the frypan product four ways from go. This is one reason why, if you're hungry by the time you've collected that deer, bear, or sheep, you may choose to emulate the Indian hunter. If so, build a small fire and drape the liver, or slices of it, over a rack made of green wood. Or just shove a pointed stick into the ground and impale the liver on it, turning it occasionally in any event. It will not take long to cook. Fresh liver is delicious without seasoning, although if you want you can do like many sportsmen and always carry a small container of salt.

Liver sliced an inch or so thick and briefly grilled over an open fire until crisp outside and pinkly juicy within is delectable. Cutting into the meat will show you when it is ready. Butter liberally just before serving.

HEART. Brown the heart in natural fat or shortening in a dutch oven. Season with salt and pepper. Then set the heart on a rack. Pour in a cup of boiling water. Cover and pot roast slowly in an oven or atop the heat for about 20 minutes per pound; only until the meat cuts easily. It should be rare to be tender. If you prefer yours well done, it is well to help it along with one of the tenderizers. Too much heat will otherwise give you a dry chunk of leather. Add more boiling water if necessary. Peeled onions, carrots, potatoes, and such may be put in toward the end. Basting the heart every half hour seems to improve the flavor. It certainly stimulates the appetite.

Big game hearts are also excellent broiled over cooking coals. Cut into thin slices, season, baste with butter or margarine, and cook about 3 minutes to a side. Eat while still sizzling. A tart jam or marmalade served on the side makes these taste even better. So does a kettle of hot black tea steeping within arm's reach.

KIDNEYS. "If I could eat just once more, I'd sure pick bear kidneys," King Gething told me up on the headwaters of the Peace River. "I'd want them simmered awhile with butter, salt, cloves, celery if I had any, and a mite of onion. Matter of fact, let's get 'em on the fire before somebody else shows up."

Cut or divide the kidneys into segments about the size of chicken hearts. All you have to do with bear kidneys to achieve this is strip away the connective membrane. Let the kidneys and other ingredients simmer in low heat until tender. Best way to establish proportions is by taste. These kidneys are especially tasty atop either steaming mountains of mashed potato or hot crusty bannock, streaming with butter or margarine.

BRAINS. This one is worth the trouble. It's also a practical way of reminding yourself how small and precisely positioned a target the brain of a big game animal actually is. Best way in is with a meat saw, although a battered woodpile bludgeon will get the job done. If you have a dog along, wire the head loosely to a tree, so he won't bury and forget it, and he'll worry away happily at it for as long as you're in camp.

Remove the outer membrane of the brains. Dip them in beaten egg, roll in cracker or bannock crumbs seasoned with salt and pepper, and saute uncovered in butter or margarine. These have a delicate flavor and go well with scrambled eggs.

If you haven't any fresh eggs in camp, however, immerse the brains in melted butter or margarine and then crumbs. Pan broil slowly until crisp outside and hot throughout. Serve with buttered toast, hot biscuits, or boiled potatoes.

MARROW BONES. "They can keep them filly-minions and sech," an old prospector told me once over coffee in Seattle. "Me, I'm heading back to where I can knock over a caribou. I'd roast me the tongue first, except the liver is durned near as good and won't keep so long. I ain't forgetting the leg bones, either. Ever heat them in your campfire, then bust them open with rocks to get at the marrow? Then you savvy what I'm palavering about."

Marrow bones from any of the large game animals are an epicurean's delight.

TONGUE. Tongue is another delicacy you shouldn't let get by you. Those from the larger animals are special tidbits, that from a moose being as big as a beef tongue.

Caribou tongue is also excellent. So is elk tongue. The only drawback to that from the usual deer is its small size.

In case you've heretofore passed up this choice bit, there's a trick to securing it. Feel for the bones under the lower jaw. Make a deep slit between them up into the mouth. Press the tongue down through this opening. Grasp and cut off as close to the base as possible.

Cover with cold, salted water. Bring to a boil. Spoon off any scum that has come to the surface. Then simmer until the tongue is tender. When it has cooled sufficiently in the stock to permit its being handled easily, skin it. A sharp knife will help, although much of the skin can be peeled off with the fingers alone. Remove any small bones at the base.

This meat is especially good thinly sliced, either hot or cold. If you want something special, smoke the cooked and peeled tongue over a smudge of ground birch, alder, willow, or similar hardwood for several hours.

MOOSE MUFFLE. The moose is far and away the heftiest game animal in this hemisphere that is widely hunted for its meat. Polar bear and grizzly grow bigger, it's true, but neither is famous for steaks. Moose meat is something else again. To put it briefly, it has been my main sustenance for a double handful of winters in the Far North, and by choice.

All that Horace Kephart said about this particular part (moose muffle), though, was: "Boil like a pig's head. Add an onion."

More bafflingly, as far as my schoolboy knowledge was concerned when I first read these brief instructions, he called it moose muffle. That made me think of the woolen muffler I wound around my neck in snowy New England weather, which in turn brought my conjectures to the moose's bell. It was some Crees, years later, who straightened me out. I'm happy they did, for if you, too, ever get a chance to eat any, moose muzzle is something you shouldn't miss.

I've roasted this delicacy before an open birch fire, picked out with my knife point what I could devour of the meat,

and given the remainder to my 180-pound Irish wolfhound
who was along as a packdog.

A more conservative method, after you've cut off the
upper jaw just below the eyes, is to drop it into a large
kettle of scalding water and parboil it an hour. Remove
and cool in cold water. Pluck out the loosened hairs and
wash.

Then put the moose muzzle in fresh water along with
some onions, salt, and pepper. Simmer until tender. Then
set away from the heat. After the muffle has cooled in its
juice, extract bone and cartilage.

You'll end up with the white meat from the bulb of the
muzzle and dark strips from along bone and jowls. Cut
these into slices. What you don't eat on the spot, pack into
a handy container and cover with the juice. This will jell.
When chilled, the jellied moose muzzle can be profitably
sliced for eating cold.

BROILING. Townsend Whelen and I were reminiscing
just the other day about different wild American meats we
have eaten—south through Mexico to Panama, all the way
across the original 48 States, northeast to New Brunswick
and Nova Scotia and Hudson Bay, and northwest into
British Columbia and the Yukon to Alaska.

That involves considerable feasting. But I went all the
way with the Colonel when he summed it up like this: "I do
think that there is no better way to cook the meat of large
animals than to broil it over the coals of an outdoor wood
fire.

"When I was a boy there was a very excellent artist named
Tappan Adney whose specialty was depicting the Indians
of our Northwest. I so well remember one painting of his
of a group of Siwash Indians cooking meat before a fire.
Chunks of meat, alternating large and small, were impaled
on a stick that was leaned over and towards the blaze. Way
back in 1901 in British Columbia I spent several days in
camp with an old mountain man and his klutch (squaw).
They had just killed a ewe, and that night she cooked it in
just the same way.

"She impaled large chunks of lean meat about the size

of baseballs, alternating with chunks of fat about as large as a golf ball, on a thin green stick about two feet long, and sticking one end of this stick in the ground alongside the fire, she leaned the stick over towards the blaze exactly as Tappan Adney had depicted it. Then she turned the stick every couple of minutes until the chunks were pretty well charred on the outside, but still almost raw in the center. I have never since tasted such delicious meat in my whole life. Since then I have always cooked my venison in that way when I had the opportunity."

As long as I can remember, I've used a modified version of this at noon when I have stopped to boil the kettle; threading inch-square chunks of already salted game meat onto a sharpened green stick, thrusting them briefly into the blaze to form a juice-restraining glaze, and then broiling them a few minutes in the fringes of the heat. These I bite off one by one to punctuate alternating mouthfuls of hot toasted sandwich. Choice cut for these kabobs among the really big game? The filet mignon; that is, the small end of the tenderloin. When you get through these and the rest of the tenderloins, move to the back steaks.

BROILED SPARERIBS. Indian hunters improvise racks in the reflected heat of campfires by sticking a few roughly trimmed green limbs in the ground and laying smaller sticks between the crotches. Over these they drape hastily hacked rib sections to sputter and sizzle while they're finishing dressing out the animal. Or sometimes they just shove a spread of ribs onto a single slanted stake. Charred a bit, all these taste fine without seasoning.

A more conservative way to come by the same delicacy in camp is to saw chunks of the rib area into serving pieces. Place on a greased, preheated rack over the coals. Turning occasionally, cook for about 20 minutes or until the ribs are crisp and brown. Then you'll probably want to salt and pepper, or to spice up some catsup if you're a barbecue fancier and season with that. In any event, big game ribs may well be used a few days before steaks and roasts, as they're susceptible to drying out and, when fat, to picking up off flavors.

SWEET AND SOUR SPARERIBS. Saw some 2 pounds of ribs into serving portions. Brown in a frypan over moderate heat about 5 minutes on each side. Add ½ cup water, ¼ cup raisins, and ½ teaspoon salt. Cover pan tightly and cook over very low heat 20 minutes. Add two sliced green peppers if you have them; a similar bulk of some other green such as celery, wild mustard leaves, watercress, peas, etc. if you don't.

Blend 1½ tablespoons of cornstarch with 1¼ cup sugar, 1¼ cup vinegar, and 1 cup of water. Mix this with the other ingredients in the pan. Re-cover and continue cooking over low heat for another 1½ hours. Stir occasionally and if necessary add more water to prevent drying. Before serving, perhaps with rice, sprinkle on soy sauce if possible. I most always keep some of this latter in my outfit. If you've never tried it, you'll better appreciate why when you discover the elusively different flavor a few drops give such wilderness dishes as cold venison and boiled wild greens.

BAKED VENISON CHOPS. Arrange four thick chops in an open baking pan. Measure out a cup of canned tomato, using the solid portions. Spoon this over the chops. Then distribute a sliced onion atop the meat. Salt and pepper.

Pour in a cup of water and bake in a moderately hot oven for 45 minutes. Turn the chops once. Another 30 minutes should see them tender and ready to serve, perhaps along with mashed potatoes into each serving of which a spoonful of the juice is depressed. If they've had this before, you'll only have to call them once for dinner.

STEAKS. These are always best over an open fire. Even when I'm surrounded on four sides by log walls, as admitted in *How To Go Live in the Woods On $10 a Week,* during reasonably warm weather we still take to the outdoors to broil steaks over hot wood coals. Cooler days we often open the cabin windows, remove a lid from the wood stove, and cook in a similar fashion. How about when temperatures get a snapping 60° below? The only difference is that the windows stay closed.

The rest of the time I mostly pan broil all top grade steaks, cutting them 2½ inches thick, quickly searing both sides in a hot and preferably heavy frypan, and then cooking with slightly less heat until done to taste. Salt the metal well before putting the meat in and have it really hot. No grease at all is used, and that sputtering from the meat is tipped out. Salt and pepper if you want, and daub with butter or margarine after cooking. Serve on preheated plates.

Cooking over open embers is still unbeatable, however. A good trick at the start is to get a glowing bed of coals, then to sprinkle on a few chips and shavings. These will flare up enough both to help seal in the juices and to give that flavorsome char relished by so many. As you're already aware, the grill should be greased beforehand to prevent sticking. A handy one for wilderness use? One of those lightweight campfire grates available from most large outfitters. Removing the folding wire legs will make for easier packing if that's any problem. It's a simple matter to lay such a grid between logs or rocks.

Individual steaks can also be very pleasingly grilled merely by holding them over the heat by means of sturdy, forked green sticks.

Lean meat cooks more quickly than fat meat. Aging also progressively shortens the cooking time. Then there are such factors as size, shape, and the amount of bone. Outdoor fires add another variable. A practical way to test is to prick the steak with a sharpened stick. If red juice wells out, the meat is rare; pink, medium rare; colorless, overdone unless that is the way you want it.

SWISS GAME STEAK. This is good both for a change and for those days when you're confronted with the tougher cuts. Flank handled this way will work into a tasty steak of sorts. Slitting such game meat every few inches along the trimmed edges will keep it from curling unduly.

For about a 3-pound slab, mix 2 teaspoons salt with ½ teaspoon black pepper. Season one side of the steak with half of this. Then with the back of your camping knife pound all the flour you can into the meat. Turn the steak and repeat both processes.

Melt 5 tablespoons of bacon drippings, bear grease, lard,

margarine, or the like in a dutch oven or in a large skillet which has a cover. Quickly brown the meat all over.

Then spread a large onion and an equal bulk of carrot, diced together, over the steak. Add a can of tomatoes. Cover and simmer over low heat 1½ hours. Then bank the meat with enough small, peeled potatoes for the ensuing meal. Cook for an additional half hour or until the potatoes are tender.

ROASTS. Tender big game roasts are best cooked rare so as to take fullest advantage of the natural savor of the meat. If the meat isn't tender, treat first with one of the unseasoned commercial tenderizers.

Moderately slow oven temperatures give the best results with the large roasts. About 12 minutes per pound should do it, to give you an idea. Searing, inasmuch as it keeps in no juices, is unnecessary. If one side of the meat is fattest, placing this uppermost will give you the energy-conserving advantage of some natural basting. Laying strips of beef fat over venison or similar roasts, or pinning on chunks of such fat with small whittled skewers, will vastly improve the final results. Meat should be left uncovered, salted beforehand if you want but not floured, and cooked without any addition of water.

The reflector baker does a particularly wonderful job in this department. Turn the roast occasionally to encourage uniform cooking. While you're at it, scrub enough potatoes for the meal. Slice off the ends to allow steam to escape. Rub with shortening or cooking oil. Place in the oven to cook along with the roast.

BUFFALO POT ROAST. Buffalo are occasionally legal game in Alaska and in the vicinity of Great Slave Lake in Canada. Tougher portions of the meat, which tastes like a heavy beef, cook up well as pot roasts. This same recipe for sort of a super-speed sauerbraten will also give you a change with other big game. For a 7- or 8-pound chunk, preferably in the case of a buffalo chunk shot through with orangish lines of fat, you'll need:

     3 tablespoons shortening
    1½ tablespoons vinegar

    1 tablespoon cinnamon
    1 tablespoon ginger
    1 teaspoon nutmeg
    1 tablespoon salt
    ¼ teaspoon pepper
  1½ cups water
    3 cups apple juice
    1 can condensed tomato soup
    1 cup chopped onion
    1 teaspoon chopped garlic (optional)
      flour

Melt the shortening in the bottom of a dutch oven and brown the meat atop the stove. Blend the vinegar, cinnamon, ginger, nutmeg, salt, and pepper. Add the water and apple juice, that from cooked dried apples being excellent. Pour over the meat. Spoon the concentrated tomato soup, the onion, and if you want some garlic atop the roast.

Cover and cook in enough heat to keep the pot simmering for 4 hours or until the roast is tender. Thicken the gravy with flour and clear a way to the table.

"BOILED" MEAT. Cut the meat into about 2-inch cubes. Drop these individually into just enough bubbling water to cover. Do not boil. Don't salt until almost ready to serve. Meat so cooked can best be relished after it has been simmering covered only 5 minutes or so. However, many get the habit of letting it cook an hour or more.

Often rice and other vegetables, particularly onions, are cooked along with the meat to make what is often called mulligan. The addition of any such components, except when included for flavor only, should be so staggered that everything will be done at the same time. Any extra fluid should be heated before it is added.

If you are going to use the meat cold, let it cool in the broth. For a taste treat with moose and caribou eaten this way, try sprinkling a little soy sauce over it and serving wild berry jam on the side.

The dutch oven will conveniently so "boil" a big solid chunk of game meat. Place the meat in the bottom of the oven along with onions if you have any, perhaps a sliced carrot or two, and 1½ teaspoons of salt per pound. Half cover the meat with simmering water. Cook about an hour for every pound, at the end of which time the meat should be tender but not stringy or mushy. If you want to use it in cold sandwiches, let it cool in the broth. Then move to a flat utensil that will also hold a little of the broth. Press it into shape with a weighted cover or plate so that it can later be more handily sliced.

MULLIGAN. The preceding is the basis of the stew called mulligan. What the end result of this staple will be depends more or less on ingenuity, imagination, and the materials at hand. Available vegetables go well in such a stew. So do odds and ends of steaks and roasts.

When a lot of us are off by ourselves, the tendency is to go in for one-dish meals. This we can easily accomplish with such mulligans, even to the extent of making bread unnecessary by adding a starch such as rice, potatoes, noodles, macaroni, one of the cooked cereals, or perhaps a steaming soft dome of dumplings.

PACK TRAIN MULLIGAN. This trail mulligan is a favorite of some of the cooks on big game hunting parties when their pack trains make camp late after a long ride. Cut 3 pounds of caribou or other game meat into inch squares. Brown with 2 tablespoons of margarine or lard in the bottom of a stew pail. Then put in 2 quarts of water and 1 tablespoon of salt. Cover and boil until the meat is done.

Add hot water as necessary to bring the water back to its original level. Add 1½ cups macaroni, spaghetti, noodles, or the like. When this is nearly soft enough to eat, put in two large (15 oz.) cans of chili con carne or anything of the sort that may be handy in an accessible pannier. Salt and pepper to taste. Cook only a few minutes, just long enough for the mulligan to thicken. Serve with piping hot bannock. And if you want seconds yourself, you'd better get your refill in a hurry.

STEWING. Stew meat, which can be the toughest in the critter, is best browned at the onset with fat, chopped onion, and seasonings in the bottom of the kettle. You can then if you want stir in enough flour to make a thick smooth gravy.

For liquid, use any fluid in which vegetables have been cooked or canned, broth from boiled meat, or water. Season to taste, bring to a bubble, and then place tightly covered where it will simmer all morning or all afternoon.

A dutch oven is a handy receptacle for stew inasmuch as you can dig a hole, always in a safe place where fire can not spread, and leave it buried there among hot coals while you spend the day hiking, fishing, or hunting.

BEAR. When I was writing *Living off the Country* for the Stackpole Company, I tasted every kind of wild meat that I could come by handily—wolf, lynx, cougar, muskrat, beaver, and so on, together with moose, caribou, antelope, and the like. I also sampled opinions. Those who dine on bear meat fairly often, I found, are almost unanimously agreed that the North American wilderness affords no more delicious game with the single exception of mountain sheep, and the last is only the best meat, wild or tame, I've ever eaten anywhere.

Many hunters, most of whom have never tasted bear meat nor smelled it cooking, are prejudiced against the carnivore as food for one reason or another. One reason often heard concerns the animal's eating habits. Yet the most ravenous bear is a finicky diner when compared to such delicacies as lobster and chicken.

It's true enough that not even a plump young yearling furnishes really good steaks, which is where many culinary attempts end. But even an oldster big enough to carpet a cabin will cook up into roasts and stews so moist and savory that you have to eat them to believe them. The meat then so resembles top grade beef that you can serve it as such to individuals who've vowed they'd never touch bear meat and actually have them coming back for second and third helpings. I've seen more than one convert made that way.

And the mulligans? Well, if bear weren't such good eating, I'd have given up hunting them after collecting my first two or three.

Any excess fat should be trimmed off before the meat is

cooked. This fat may then be heated in open pans to extract the grease. Strained into jars, that of the black bear hardens into a clear white solid that makes the best shortening that any user I've talked to has ever come across. That procured from a grizzly is also excellent and, when similarly rendered, remains a more easily measured oil. Both are prized in the farther places for everything from medicine to mixing with molasses for Yankee butter.

BROTH. When trophy hunting in pack horse country, you sometimes find yourself back of beyond with more good game meat than you can ever hope to bring out. Maybe you'll delay in camp a few days longer. Still, you can scarcely begin to eat it.

On occasions like this, why not really splurge on broth and enjoy all you possibly can? What I've done such times is get the kettle simmering, hang a ladle nearby, and let everyone help himself until the pot is exhausted. Then begin another. Thing to remember is that the liquid will boil down, so don't get it too salty at the start.

Just cut the meat into small pieces so that you'll get the most good out of it. Shot portions are fine. So are all lesser cuts that you haven't time or room to handle otherwise. Marrow bones, split or sawed, are unequalled. Those necks and backs of game birds can be used this way, too. Add about 1 cup of cold water for every ½ pound of meat and bone. Cover and simmer (not boil) upwards of 4 hours.

Incidentally, if you get hungry between meals, the meat itself is wonderful hot and swimming in melting butter or margarine.

SOUP. Start like the above. In fact, you can ladle out what broth you need for the liquid part of the soup. If the broth you want to use for the soup has somehow become too salty, let it simmer along with some raw potatoes. Then remove the potatoes. Gently saute in the bottom of the kettle whatever vegetables you're going to use. Figure out your times so that these will not be overcooked. (See the chapter on vegetables.) Then add the broth and cover. Do not boil or you'll spoil the flavor. Do not season until 5 minutes before you're ready to serve.

CAMP HASH. When you have cold vegetables left over and maybe not enough cooked meat to go around, here is a solution. Cut the venison or other meat up fine. If you're a bit short on meat, help the flavor along with a bouillon cube. Add enough chopped vegetables, usually potatoes mostly, to go around. Season to taste.

Be melting several tablespoons of fat in a frypan. If rawish onions bother anyone in the party, cook these first until thoroughly soft. Otherwise, chop up whatever amount you want and mix them with the other ingredients.

Press the hash down into the pan. Cook over slow heat until a crust has formed on the bottom. Fold over and serve while hot.

OTHER METHODS. There are other ways to cook big game meat: baking in a pit, steaming in a hole, baking in clay, baking in the hide, cooking with the help of hot stones in a hollow made by pressing the hide into a small depression scooped in the ground, suspending by a variety of methods over the open fire, roasting in ashes, boiling in bark dishes, etc. Unless you happened to be in the wilderness without cooking utensils, though, you wouldn't ordinarily use most of them once in a decade. Those who are interested in learning more about such primitive and elementary cooking methods, however, will find many of them discussed in my survival book, *Living off the Country*.

SUPPOSE SOME'S LEFT OVER?

PRESERVING MEAT. If you're camping in one place and have a quantity of fresh meat you'd like to preserve with a minimum of trouble, cut it into forearm-size strips, following the membranous divisions among the muscles as much as possible. Pull off as much of this parchment as you reasonably can.

Roll the pieces in a mixture made proportionately of 3 pounds of table salt, 4 tablespoons of allspice, and 5 tablespoons of black pepper. Rubbing this well into the meat, then shaking off any excess, will give the best results.

You can either drape the strips over a wire or similar

support, well away from any animals, or you suspend them there after first piercing an end of each with a knife and looping in a string or wire. The treated meat must be kept dry. If you have to travel, rehang it after reaching your destination. About one month is needed for it to shrink and absorb the seasoning properly; less in dry country and more in damp regions. Sliced thin, it's then really something to chew on raw. Scraped and trimmed some, and soaked overnight if you want, it also goes well in mulligan. Game meat so cured is still delicious after several decades, as I can personally testify.

JERKY. The simplest way to preserve meat is by drying it. When this is done most advantageously, it's also one of the most delicious methods. Try some of the beef jerky available in many markets if you have any doubts. And note the price. The amount charged for two or three slim, blackened strips of this dehydrated meat will often buy a good steak.

There's nothing complicated about making jerky. You cut lean deer, moose, elk, caribou, buffalo, and similar red meat into long straps about ½ inch thick. These you hang apart from one another in the sun, in the attic, or some other place where, kept dry, they will gradually lose most of their water content. At the same time, they'll become hard, dry, black and, incidentally, both nourishing and tasty.

The strips may be first soaked, it you want, either in brine or sea water. If you are along the sea coast, you may care to try the ancient method of boiling down ocean water until it becomes extremely salty. While it is still bubbling, immerse a few straps at a time for 3 minutes apiece. If there is no convenient place to hang this meat, it can be laid across sun-warmed rocks and turned every hour or so. You can also make your own brine by dissolving all the salt possible in boiling water.

After the meat has been allowed to drain, some makers sprinkle it with pepper. In many cases they also add favorite spices such as oregano, marjoram, basil, and thyme for increased flavor. Good? Friends of ours in New Mexico and California, with plenty of empty space in their freezers, jerk a deer or so a year in this fashion just for their own personal eating.

A common bush technique for jerking game meat involves draping the strips, or hanging them by string or wire loops, on a wood framework about 4 to 6 feet off the ground. A small, slow, smoky fire of any nonresinous wood is built beneath this rack. The meat is allowed to dry for several days in the sun and wind. It is covered at night and during any rain. The chief use of the fire is to discourage flies and other insects. It should not be hot enough to cook the meat at all.

When jerked, the meat will be hard and more or less black outside. It will keep almost indefinitely away from damp and flies. This covered wagon staple is best eaten as is. Just bite off a chunk and chew. It may also be cooked in stews. It is very concentrated and nourishing, and a little goes a long way as an emergency ration. Alone, it is not a good food for long continued consumption, as it lacks the necessary fat.

The fat, which would turn rancid, should be trimmed off before the drying operation is commenced. It may then be rendered for future use in cooking or in the manufacture of pemmican.

REAL PEMMICAN. Some frightful conglomerations appear on the market from time to time under the name of "pemmican." One which I recently sampled looked and tasted like spoiled fruit cake, this despite a price in excess of 20¢ per ounce.

To make real pemmican, one of the best concentrated foods ever, you begin by pounding up a quantity of jerky. Then take raw animal fat and cut it into walnut-size hunks. Try these out in a pan in the oven or over a slow fire, never letting the grease boil up. Pour the resulting hot fat over the shredded jerky, mixing the two together until you have about the consistency of ordinary sausage. Then pack the pemmican in commercial casings or waterproof bags. Despite some practices, no salt at all should be included. Dried berries? Suit yourself. Their function is as a flavor only.

The ideal proportions of lean and fat in pemmican is, by

weight, approximately equal amounts of well-dried lean meat and rendered fat. It takes approximately 5 pounds of fresh lean meat to make 1 pound of jerky suitable for pemmican.

Such genuine pemmican will afford practically every necessary food element with the exception of Vitamin C. The average individual can get along without this vitamin for at least two months if in good health to begin with. Furthermore, supplementing the pemmican with some fresh food (for example, just several fresh rose hips daily) will supply all the Vitamin C necessary to prevent any trouble with scurvy over even an extended period.

MAKING IT LAST. There are other standard ways of preserving game meat. For instance, I've salt-cured some flat slabs of grizzly, then smoked them. Served up with sourdough hotcakes and scrambled eggs, mornings while the northern lights still fired the sky, the crisp slices never lasted long.

Also, if you find yourself at all interested in canning game animals and birds to help spread the supply deliciously throughout the year—or in making your own sausage, or in smoking or corning meat—these subjects are covered in minute detail in my book, *How To Go Live in the Woods on $10 a Week*. You can almost hear creaking wheels of covered wagon trains when you eat grub like this.

CHAPTER 5

BIRDS AND SMALL GAME

Meat is the one complete food. To put it another way, plump fresh meat is the single food known to mankind that contains every one of the nutritional ingredients necessary for good health. It is entirely possible for man to live on meat alone. No particular parts need be eaten. Fat juicy sirloins, if that is what you prefer, will supply you with all the food necessary for top robustness even if you eat nothing else whatsoever for a week, a month, or a decade.

Each animal in the far and near places of this continent, every fish that swims in our lakes and rivers and streams, and each bird that inhabits the air is good to eat. Not only that, but nearly every part of North American animals is edible, even to the somewhat bland antlers that are not half bad roasted when in velvet and to the bitterish gall that has an occasional use as seasoning. The only exception is the liver of the polar bear, and of the ringed and bearded seal, which becomes so rich in Vitamin A at certain times that it is usually as well avoided.

Juicy fricassees, succulent stews, and sizzling roasts are fine fare. If anything, most of us would be happy eating more of this ideal grub which contains all the vitamins, minerals, and other nutriments necessary for full vigor. One way to accomplish this? By not passing up the birds and small game which are freely available to many of us throughout the entire year and which if not eaten will only be wasted.

GROUSE. Smoky fall days when you collect several young grouse or such from a covey, a worthy way to prepare them is by frying. Birds so cooked should be tender enough so that there will be no excuse to parboil them first.

Neither should they be encased in a thick shell of batter, nor kept soggy beneath a lid.

Disjoint the birds. Dip the sections in milk. Roll very sparingly in flour, salt, and pepper. If you've any thyme, try adding ⅛ teaspoon of that.

Get about 4 tablespoons of bacon drippings, bear fat, margarine, or the like sputtering in a heavy frypan large enough to hold all the pieces. Put the chunks in with the skin toward the bottom. Move to a cooler part of the stove and cook slowly, uncovered, until the uppermost meat is golden brown.

Turn the pieces just once. Cook another 15 or 20 minutes or however long it takes to make the skin tan and crisp. Then lay the chunks on a paper that will absorb the excess grease. Keep them warm while you ready the gravy.

For the gravy, leave only enough grease in the frypan to cover the bottom. Stir in 2 tablespoons of flour until thoroughly blended. Then very gradually add 2 cups of milk, along with ½ teaspoon salt, ⅛ teaspoon pepper, and ⅛ teaspoon paprika. Cook slowly, short of boiling, for 15 minutes, adding milk if thinning becomes necessary.

UPLAND FOWL. The trouble many cooks have in cooking some of the upland game birds stems from the fact that woodcock, quail, pheasant, and the like tend to run on the lean side. For half a dozen woodcock or quail, or an equivalent bulk of quartered pheasant, try:

¼ cup margarine
¼ teaspoon thyme (optional)
¼ cup chopped onion
 1 teaspoon dried parsley
 1 cup apple juice
 1 teaspoon salt
⅛ teaspoon paprika (optional)
    flour

Spread open the small birds, cutting along the backbone and removing the nearly meatless bony parts. Quarter the pheasant. Roll sparingly in flour.

Melt the margarine or other fat in a heavy frypan. When

it is hot, brown the fowl. Sprinkle on the thyme. Cover and cook over low heat for 10 minutes.

Mix the chopped onion, dried parsley, and cup of juice which may be from cooked dried apples. Cover and keep simmering an hour or until done. About 10 minutes before the cooking is finished, sprinkle on the salt and paprika. A good accompaniment is rice—wild rice, by all means, if you can gather this expensive seed in your neck of the woods.

CREAMED GAME BIRD. Cut into strips or cubes the cooked meat of any leftover partridge or similar game bird. For every cup of meat, you'll want 2 tablespoons margarine, 2 tablespoons flour, ⅛ teaspoon salt, and 1 cup milk. A little powdered or plain dried celery will further enhance the flavor, as will a small amount of dried parsley.

Melt the fat in a heavy frypan. Stir in the seasoned flour until it is smoothly blended. Continuing to stir, gradually pour in the milk. Cook over low heat until creamy. Season to taste. Then put in the fowl and slowly cook until warm. Sprinkle lightly with dried parsley and serve.

TWO GAME BIRD SAUCES. In some regions, even when your major objective is big game, you can dine on ptarmigan, partridge, and other game birds about as often as you want. Here's a sauce that will afford a change of taste.

> 2 tablespoons margarine
> 1 medium-size chopped onion
> 1 tablespoon flour
> 1 can evaporated milk
> 1 tablespoon vinegar
>   salt and pepper to taste

Melt the fat and fry the onions at low heat, turning them constantly and not allowing them to brown. When the onions are tender, gradually stir in the flour. Then add milk and vinegar. Bring to a boil and allow to simmer 15 minutes, stirring frequently. Season. This sauce goes well with all upland fowl.

When gunning is so good that you have a quantity of breasts to cook separately, mix:

½ cup cooking oil
1 cup vinegar
2½ tablespoons salt
1½ teaspoons poultry seasoning
¼ teaspoon pepper
1 minced clove of garlic

Bring these to a simmer. Then set off the stove and permit to cool. Soak the breasts in this sauce for an hour. Then broil or roast them until tender, basting with the remaining sauce. See if this one doesn't prove to all doubters that grub can be a pleasure as well as a necessity.

ROASTED WILD DUCK. Early season duck that are still in the pinfeather stage, duck that are to be stored frozen, badly shot birds, and those with fishy and other strong odors in the fatty tissue just beneath the skin will be considerably choicer eating if skinned.

Wild duck ordinarily are not stuffed. However, chopped or sliced onions, stalks or leaves of celery, soaked prunes or dried apples, or a few juniper berries are frequently placed in the cavity.

Set the well wiped duck in an open roasting pan with the breasts uppermost. Roast up to 25 minutes or so, depending on the size, in a very hot oven. Baste about every 5 minutes by spooning the hot juices over the birds. Duck will be tastier, juicier, and tenderer if kept very definitely to the rare side. Season to taste with salt and pepper after cooking.

This recipe is good, too, for sand hill crane.

WILD GEESE SPUTTERING. Roast wild geese in a slow oven until well done, allowing 18 to 20 minutes per pound. If you'd care to try a dried apricot stuffing, I can recommend this one:

¼ cup chopped onion
½ cup margarine
3 cups cooked rice
1 tablespoon celery seed or powder
1 teaspoon dried parsley
2 cups chopped dried apricots
1 diced carrot

1 teaspoon allspice
½ teaspoon salt
⅛ teaspoon pepper

Saute the onion lightly and politely in the margarine, only until tender. Remove from the heat. Add the other ingredients. Mix them together with just a few stirs. Stuff the goose. Truss. Roast in a moderate oven.

Wild geese, unlike their less active domestic brethren, tend to be dry and need frequent basting. The bird will be ready for the table when legs are loose and skin is appetizingly bronzed. Gravy may be concocted with drippings and giblets.

GEESE, SENIOR VERSIONS. Sometimes it is the older and less agile members of the flock that are bagged, whereupon the dutch oven may be called for.

Stuff the honker with equal amounts of well-soaked prunes and apple along with an onion to lend authority. Crisscross it with strips of bacon or salt pork. Set it in the heavy pot on a nest of carrots, potatoes, onions, parsnips, and any similar vegetables. Add hot water, with a chicken bouillon cube dissolved in each cup of fluid, until the fowl is about ⅓ covered. Put on the lid and cook very slowly atop the heat, or in a slow oven, until tender.

MALLARD. "My method of preparing this supreme wild fare is fairly simple," says Duncan Hines. "After washing and drying the duck, put a whole onion, a tablespoon vinegar, and a stalk of celery cut into long pieces inside it. Then set in a covered pan in a cold place overnight. This is for the purpose of eliminating all fishy flavor. These contents should be removed and discarded the next day.

"A sliced apple and a cut stalk of celery go inside the mallard next, but these, too, are discarded after the roasting. Lay 2 slices of salt pork diagonally across the breast of the duck. Put ½ cup olive oil and 3 tablespoons butter into a small roaster, and be certain it is very hot before putting in the duck. Roast in a hot oven for 15 to 20 minutes, basting every 4 to 5 minutes. My favorite accompaniment is wild rice and cranberry sauce."

QUAIL. Here is another savory and mouthwatering

delicacy passed along to me by Duncan Hines. Dredge 6 quail lightly in 1 tablespoon of flour, salted and peppered to taste. Now heat ½ cup butter and a tablespoon lard as much as possible without scorching. Add the birds and, turning them, brown fast to seal in the juices.

Then lower the temperature, add a cup of boiling water to the birds, cover the pan, and cook until tender. Add water as needed until you are ready to brown the breasts. After the water is gone, place the quail breasts down in the butter and brown over low heat.

For the gravy, remove the birds and stir a tablespoon of flour into the butter and juices. Add 1 to 1¼ cups of water to the flour mixture and scrape all the brown coating off the roaster into the gravy. Stir and cook until quite thick.

GIBLETS. These are just about the best part of any fowl, for my money. Clean the gizzards by carefully cutting to the hard center, then pulling this sac away from the meat with the fingers. Gently separate the bitter gall bladder from the liver, cutting out any part of the liver that is left with a greenish tinge.

Here's a good dish for sometime when you have a lot of these giblets; enough, say, for a couple of hearty eaters. Place the hearts and sliced gizzards into enough cold water, with ½ teaspoon of salt, so that you'll end up with 2 cups of broth. Adding feet and necks will give you a richer broth. Simmer for about 2 hours or until the hearts and gizzards are tender. Put in the livers the last 5 minutes of cooking.

Now get 2 tablespoons margarine or other fat melting in a frypan. Gradually add 2 tablespoons flour, stirring until it is smooth and thick. Saute ½ cup onion and ½ cup celery over low heat until tender. Then add the 2 cups of broth and get everything hot.

The hearts, gizzards, and liver go in next. Stir everything together over the low heat. If you want the gravy a little thinner or a little whiter, add evaporated milk. Salt and pepper to taste. Top with paprika and powdered parsley if you happen to have any.

All giblets taste pretty much the same. So, during off

seasons back in town, you may like to buy frozen chicken hearts so that you can repeat this repast often.

MUD HEN, ETC. Are men the best cooks? The Hudson's Bay Company says so. In its cooking course, prepared for the bachelor managers among its some 200 far-flung fur trading posts, the *Governor and Company of Adventurers of England trading into Hudson's Bay* state unequivocally, "The best cooks in the world are men."

My wife Vena suspects that this statement may be inserted largely as a morale builder, because a few sentences further along the potential "world's finest chef" is cautioned not to use his dishcloth to wipe off the stove. Yet the majority of good cooks in the North, certainly, are male. Some visiting sportsmen never do recover completely from the spectacle of hairy-armed sourdoughs lounging about a fur press and swapping recipes.

These old-timers go in mostly for plain cooking, although occasionally you'll meet a bannock puncher with a flair for the exceptional. One of these was rotund Ted Boynton, famous for more than a quarter century as one of the best trail cooks in the continental Northwest.

Whenever I see someone discarding some less favored waterfowl because they're "too fishy" or "too gamy," I remember how Ted Boynton used to handle birds of this sort. It's too bad, for several reasons, that more hunters don't know about it. Anyway, I guess one party figured they had Ted stopped the day they lugged in a brace of mud hen. One sportsman allowed as how he'd tried mud hen before. He said that if the part he got went over the fence last, somebody must have given it a boost.

Maybe it was the odors sifting into the atmosphere from the direction of Ted Boynton's fire. Maybe it was just curiosity, for a mud hen, although kind to its family and all, is generally about as tender and tasty as a discarded moccasin. At any rate, there was no second call that evening to the pan-banging accompanied, "Come and get it." There these fowl were, browned and bulging, looking as handsome as canvasback and smelling no less tempting than fat ptarmigan. Someone stuck his fork gingerly into a drumstick.

Moist steaming meat fell invitingly away from the bone.
Everyone dug in hungrily.

"Even a loon don't cook up too bad," Ted told us, and
later proved it, "if a yahoo don't try to gentle it aitch-for-
leather. So don't throw mud hens or other such critters
away, particularly in times like these. Cram them with
onions. B'il real easy for three hours. Then start brand new
with a crumb stuffing. Tuck a mess of sow belly or bacon
strips where they'll do the most good. And roast nice and
quiet like until a hungry man can't wait no longer."

PIGEON AND DOVE. The meat is dark of color and
fine of flavor, that of pigeon having a tendency to be tough.
Both are best cooked, tightly covered, in a small amount of
water or tomato juice at low temperatures, either atop the
heat or in the oven or reflector baker. Brown the birds first
in a bit of cooking oil. Season with salt, pepper, celery or
parsley flakes, and a small amount of chopped onion. Simmer
usually from 30 to 45 minutes or until just tender.

CROW. Just as muskrat is more successfully merchan-
dised as musquash and swamp rabbit, crow finds more takers
when sold as rook. However, the dark meat is well worth
cooking under any name. Tasting like chicken with appetizing
overtones of duck, young crow is excellent either broiled
or sauteed. Older varieties respond better to fricasseeing.
If you've too many for friends and deep-freeze, then concentrate on the breasts.

H.B.C. PASTIES. Some of the best eating you'll find
in northern Canada is at the Hudson's Bay Company trading posts. The following flexible recipe, geared in this instance to 4 partridge, is one of the reasons.

You'll also need 1 cup of raw potato and 2 tablespoons
onion. Chop and mix these and the meat thoroughly. Salt
and pepper to taste.

Now roll and cut some pastry dough into rectangles,
about 1/4 inch thick. Moisten the edges. Put generous portions of the meat mixture on one half. Then fold over the
other half and seal the edges of the pastry well. Prick with
a fork to make an escape vent for steam. Place on a pan
and bake in moderate oven or reflector baker 3/4 hour or

until done. If any last that long, these are also memorable cold.

WILD TURKEY. It's hard to realize that back during early colonial years wild turkey was far more familiar to handhewn American tables than was domestic poultry. Remove the craw at once, or you are in for a disappointment. Matter of fact, the bird should be drawn as soon as you shoot it to make sure that it won't become too strong. This feast is worth all the personal attention you can give it. Cook by your favorite domestic turkey recipe.

BLUE GROUSE. The subtly flavored white meat of one of these big, plump fellows is just about the best you're going to sit down to in the game bird realm. Way I like them is cut into serving pieces, well rubbed with cooking oil, liberally salted, dusted with a few flakes of pepper, and then slowly broiled over hot coals. Start with the bony side toward the heat. Turn after about 10 minutes, again basting and seasoning. When a fork slips in easily and there's no gushing of red juices, the grouse is done.

You sometimes get a coat full of blue grouse, though, in high windy country where there's no satisfactory hardwood for coals. One way around is to use just the legs and breasts, saving the giblets and the rest for soup. Dredge the legs and breasts in salted and peppered flour. Now bring 6 slices of bacon slowly to a sputter in a heavy frypan. Remove the bacon to a hot dish when it is crisp. Quickly brown the grouse on both sides in the hot fat. Salt and pepper it, then remove to more moderate heat. Cover and cook 15 minutes, turning at about the halfway point.

Put the grouse on the hot dish with the bacon. Stir 2 tablespoons of flour into the fat and juice. Still stirring, slowly add 1½ cups of rich milk. When this has thickened the way you like it, season it to taste. Let each banqueter spoon his share over grouse, bacon, and any vegetables. With one ridge after another lifting in front of the late northern sun as you eat, and a breeze starting to trumpet a cool blue note, this is grub you're never going to forget.

LYNX. Lynx meat, served up to hearty appetites alongside a campfire, is except for fiber almost indistinguishable from the white meat of chicken. Because the larger lynx in particular are apt to be somewhat stringy, we like to cut the meat into very small pieces and fricassee these.

This you can do in a dutch oven if you want, preparing the meal before you leave camp in the morning and leaving it to reach a state of perfection by the time you get back ravenous at night. Or if someone is going to be in camp during the morning or afternoon, the meat can be trusted to cook slowly in a big kettle suspended over the fringes of the fire.

Start the meat as you would a stew in the bottom of a large receptacle. Allow it to simmer gently until tender. Such vegetables as onions, carrots, chopped celery, and in fact any you'd include with chicken go equally well with this dish.

You can make a gravy on the side if you want by blending 6 tablespoons of flour with a small amount of cold water, then adding 3 cups of the liquor from the pot and stirring until a thick sauce is the result. This may be poured over the lynx and vegetables. The fricassee goes well atop mashed potatoes, hot steaming bannock, or fresh fluffy rice. A little paprika will give it character. The flavor is surprisingly delicate. Unless so informed, no one would realize he was eating game.

BEAVER. One way to collect a heavily furred grizzly robe in the continental northwest is to accompany a trapper when he goes out in the spring for beaver. The great bear are so fond of fresh beaver meat that it's not unusual for them to raid a camp. When you've sat down to a feed of *amisk* after a day of making your way past steaming snow-drifts and seething streams, you'll better appreciate why.

Beaver meat is particularly rich. It's best, when possible, to stick to the tender youngsters. If you ever do cook up one of the big fellows weighing 40 to 50 pounds, a good thing to remember is that the meat will become more and more fibrous and stringy the longer it is cooked.

The ordinarily moist dark flesh is reminiscent, both in odor and flavor, of plump turkey. It is particularly excellent roasted, and when so cooked it has the advantage of not requiring any basting. For best results, trim off any excessive fat first, and keep grease from accumulating in the pan. Cook in moderate heat. Cold, such meat is still moist and tasty in sandwiches.

"Noble creature," Dudley Shaw, Peace River neighbor, decreed once at lunch at my cabin, anchoring a slab of roast beaver between two slices of bread. "Glutted himself joyously with poplar."

"How can you tell?"

"*Amisks* who bog themselves down on willow," the old trapper explained, "are permeated with a bitterish flavor. And if they're crowded back into spruce, as happens on some congested ponds, the result is notoriously ghastly. Then the only thing you can do is parboil it copiously. Indians still scrape fat for a quick snack from even those hides, though. They roast the blinking stuff on green sticks propped by the fire while finishing skinning out the plunder. Cheers them up nobly."

BEAVER TAIL. Beaver tail was always something I very much wanted to try since reading, when a boy, Horace Kephart's regretful observation: "This tidbit of old-time trappers will be tasted by few of our generation, more's the pity." Because of wise conservation practices, the species has been making considerable of a comeback recent years, and, like you probably, I've had the pleasure of eating this delicacy on a number of different occasions.

Strung on a cord, as they're often carried, beaver tails look like nothing quite so much as scaly black fish whose heads have been removed. Heat causes the rough dark skin to puff and lift away, exposing a white and gelatinous meat. Somewhat resembling pork when boiled, this goes particularly well with such dishes as baked beans and thick pea soup.

PORCUPINE. "Many campers would pass up a porcupine, and yet he is one of the purest of all vegetarians. Again my memory goes back to when Bones Andrews, one of the last of the old mountain men of the breed of Jim Bridger, and I were compelled to spend several weeks in a region where there was no game. At the end of that time we had about the worst case of meat fever you can imagine. So we saddled up our little pack train and made tracks for higher altitudes and game country. On the way up I shot a porcupine. I skinned it, starting at the smooth underneath, and tied it to the back of my saddle.

"That night we made it into a stew. First, we cut it into small pieces and boiled these an hour. Then we added a handful of rice and salt, a dozen small dumplings of biscuit dough, and covered all that to boil 20 minutes longer. This was tall country. With air pressure lessening with the altitude, the higher you climb the longer you have to boil. We finally finished by adding a little flour to thicken the gravy and by stirring in a teaspoon of curry powder.

"Then the two of us sat down and finished the whole pot in one sitting. That pot held 9 quarts and was full. The quill pig, incidentally, should be a young one." (Colonel Townsend Whelen)

'POSSUM. The opossum's light colored and fine grained meat, all the tenderer because of mild flavored fat that's well distributed among the bands of lean, make it one of the most prized game animals in the southern states particularly. I prefer to skin them, at the same time removing the glands in the small of the back and inside the forelegs. The meat is better after it has aged a few days. If the 'possum is particularly plump, the answer as with bear is to cut off most of the outside fat and to keep grease from accumulating in the cooking pan. Salt and pepper. Roast in an oven or reflector baker.

'Possum is also exceptionally good when broiled over the open coals of the campfire. Cut it in half for this purpose. Or divide it into serving pieces. A small 'possum can then be individually cooked on forked sticks. If you want, baste it with your favorite barbecue sauce, although a lot of us would rather keep this latter for some less delicately flavored meat.

You can also brown 'possum in its own fat in the bottom of a dutch oven, season it with salt and pepper and perhaps ⅛ teaspoon of sage, add enough vegetables including sweet potatoes to go around, pour in 2 cups of hot water, and cook slowly until the meat is tender.

COON. The raccoon, one of the very cleanest of the game animals both in its eating and living habits, has dark, somewhat coarse, long fibered flesh whose flavor surpasses a lot of the veal and other meat for sale at the nearest market. Remove the kernel-like scent glands that are similar to the 'possum's. Trim off most of the exterior fat, and cook the same as 'possum. Roast coon, which takes 3 to 4 hours in a moderate oven, is famous. Coon is also excellent braised or broiled.

SQUIRREL. Squirrel, too, has little if any gaminess. The firm, lean meat needs added fat, but it can be advantageously cooked about every way. Lard it with bacon, season, and roast 1½ hours in a moderate oven. Or broil about a half hour or until tender, basting frequently. Or fry uncovered in a small amount of fat for from ½ to 1 hour, turning occasionally.

Or, particularly if the squirrel are the elders of their tribe, cut them up and roll each piece in flour. Brown slowly in a small amount of bacon drippings in a heavy frypan or dutch oven. Season with salt and pepper. Then add enough tomato juice or water to cover the bottom of the receptacle. Cover tightly and simmer in low heat from 1 to 1½ hours or until the meat is tender, turning it occasionally and if necessary adding enough liquid to maintain steam. Remove the cover the last 15 minutes for a crisper crust. Serve hot with gravy made by adding a small amount of water to the pan drippings, stirring it diligently over the heat, and seasoning to taste.

SQUIRREL STEW. If you only have a couple or so squirrel and some robust appetites to satisfy, the following stew may be the solution. Cut up the squirrel. Brown the pieces in the bottom of a pan in 3 tablespoons of margarine. Then cover with 3 cups water. Season only with 1 teaspoon salt and ⅛ teaspoon pepper so as to maintain the distinctive natural flavor. Simmer 1 hour.

Add ¼ cup chopped onion, ½ cup diced celery, and ½ cup sliced carrot. Thicken with a smooth paste made by blending 3 tablespoons flour with ¼ cup water. Cook an additional 15 minutes. If you want really to top this one off, roof it with dumplings made by one of the recipes suggested elsewhere.

ROAST MUSKRAT. Moist dark roast muskrat tastes like turkey, only better. The thing to remember is to remove the little glands under the hind and forelegs. Rub inside and out with an onion, and season all over with salt and pepper, using more pepper than you usually do.

If you want, fill loosely with a stuffing made in the proportions of 2 parts of soaked dehydrated apples and 1 part pitted and chopped cooked prunes. If you've any horseradish, include a teaspoonful of that.

Place the meat on a greased rack in a shallow pan. Brush generously with melted margarine or other fat. Lay several strips of bacon over the top. Roast in a moderate oven or reflector baker until tender, basting frequently.

Muskrat is also excellent both fricasseed and fried. For the former, make a well-seasoned brown gravy and simmer onions and pieces of muskrat in this until tender. Serve with rice. For the latter, disjoint the muskrat, parboil for 20 minutes if not young and tender, dip in flour, and fry in deep fat until golden brown.

WOODCHUCK. These are very much worth saving, particularly if after skinning you carefully remove the small glands from under the forelegs. Unless too grizzled and tough, they're generally best roasted. But if you run into a patriarch, brown the pieces in a small amount of fat. Then cover with water, season, and simmer 2 hours or so until tender. For a stew, add vegetables when the meat is nearly done. If any 'chuck is left over for serving cold, it'll be juicy and more flavorful if allowed to cool in the stock.

WILD GAME SOUP. This recipe is another from the Hudson's Bay Company. It calls for cutting up a rabbit or ptarmigan, although any similar game is also satisfactory. Put in a pot and simmer slowly for 2 hours with some left over vegetables, either 1 onion or 1½ tablespoons onion flakes, ¼ cup rice, 4 cups cold water, and salt and pepper to taste.

BRUNSWICK STEW. This huntsman's stew has been famous for centuries, so the recipes vary. The following is a good one, particularly when a day outdoors has whetted everyone's appetite. For four servings, disjoint a large rabbit or several squirrel or partridge so as to come by about 2 pounds of meat. Brown this in 2 tablespoons of fat in a heavy pot or frypan, along with ¼ cup of diced onions.

Add 1 cup tomatoes, 1 cup boiling water, and ⅛ teaspoon pepper. Cover and simmer until the meat is tender. Then put in 1½ cups lima or other green beans and 1½ cups of corn. Simmer 10 minutes or, if the vegetables were raw, until everything is ready. Season to taste with salt.

PICKLED RABBIT STEW. "Would you like a Midwestern recipe for the foremost American game animal, some 50 million of which are brought to the pot annually? If you would enjoy hasenpfeffer, 'First catch your hare,' goes the old saying. Some say it should be, 'First case (dress) your hare.' Anyway, you start with a 3-to-5 pound rabbit. Here is a good recipe:

"Cut the rabbit into pieces. Place in a marinade of: 2 cups vinegar, 1 cup claret, 1 cup water, 1 sliced large onion, ½ teaspoon salt, ⅛ teaspoon pepper, 1 teaspoon mustard seed, 1 teaspoon crushed juniper berries, 8 whole cloves, and 6 bay leaves. Marinate 1 or 2 days, turning at least every 12 hours.

"Then dry the meat carefully and sprinkle with flour. Saute in ⅓ cup of either butter or salt pork until well browned on all sides. Drain, then place in a pot. Strain the marinade through a sieve, add ½ cup water, and pour over the pieces of rabbit. Bring to a boil, cover, and simmer over low heat for about 45 minutes. Additional salt and pepper may be added if desired. Serve on a platter with the gravy—thickened somewhat with flour if you want—poured over it. Traditionally, hasenpfeffer is served with dumplings." (Duncan Hines)

RABBIT. The mildly flavored, finely grained meat of the rabbit and hare can be cooked like chicken, which it resembles. First, remove the glands from under the forelegs. Rabbit is so lean that even if you had all of it you could eat, you'd still starve to death on it alone. Add fat, though, and it's both nutritious and delicious. Cook like fowl and like other small game.

Smothered rabbit is a way out when you run into some of the older animals. With 2 rabbit, you'll need:

    1   teaspoon salt
    ⅛   teaspoon pepper
    ½   cup flour
    ¼   cup fat
    ½   cup diced onion
    1   cup milk

Mix the flour, pepper, and salt. Roll the serving pieces in this and brown them with the fat in a frypan or dutch oven. Add the onion and milk. Cover and simmer slowly for about an hour or until tender. Then remove the meat. Stir enough flour into the remaining juices to make gravy. Pour this over the meat. Sprinkle on paprika if you have it. Garnish if possible with parsley, either fresh or powdered, or with watercress. Serve over potatoes, rice, or hot bannock.

RABBIT FRICASSEE. One hungry wet night up by Sherwood Lake in New Brunswick, when our tent was leaking so much that we pitched it under an old brush leanto, Old Bill MacDonald took a couple of small rabbit I'd managed to bag, clattered around some in the grub box of our canoe, and came up with a fricassee that pushed back the rain and the shadows. By the next morning the rain had turned to tracking snow, and we were soon paddling back toward his Seven Mile Lake camp with a heavy buck.

Old Bill cut those rabbit into serving pieces and rolled them awhile in flour, salt, and pepper. Then he got ½ cup of butter sizzling in the bottom of a big iron frypan and slowly browned the chunks, forking them around all the time. He then poured in 2 cups of hot water from the boiling kettle, covered the frypan, and shoved it to one end of the grate where enough birch coals were falling apart to keep it simmering merrily.

After about an hour, he tested a meaty slab with a fork, nodded, and then stirred in a large chopped onion and a small can of peas. It couldn't have taken any more than 15 minutes to whip together a steaming batch of baking powder biscuits. Our stainless steel plates were so hot by then that I remember we had to put on a glove apiece to handle them. Old Bill eased a couple of biscuits on each plate, saturated them with butter, and then spooned rabbit over them until I begged quits. There was still enough for the seconds, at that.

CHAPTER 6

BY HOOK AND BY COOK
FISH

The way you cook your fish may be determined to some extent by their fatness. Plumper varieties such as lake trout, salmon, and whitefish are best for baking, as in a reflector baker or dutch oven, and for broiling over the cherry-red coals of a campfire. Their fat content helps keep them from becoming too dry.

Leaner catches such as pike, bass, perch, and Arctic grayling are preferable for poaching and for steaming because they remain firmer. They can also be satisfactorily baked and grilled if frequently basted or if topped with a sauce.

All fish are eminently suitable for frying. As far as that goes, any fish may be satisfyingly cooked by any of the basic methods if allowances are made for the fat content.

The main thing is not to overcook the catch. To keep fish moist and tender, and to bring out its delicate flavor, cook only until the flesh is no longer translucent. Once the fish is easily flaked, it is done. The taste will be further enhanced if the fish is salted, inside and out, as much as an hour in advance of cooking.

Second thing to avoid? Never soak any fish before or after it is cleaned.

SPITTED FISH. Some time when you have a mess of small brook trout or such, let everyone roughly trim and peel his own green hardwood wand. Thread a slice of bacon on the wand and broil it over ruddy coals until translucent. Then place the opened and cleaned fish lengthwise over the bacon, fastening the fish by skewering it with sharpened twigs. Cook slowly over glowing embers. Repeat as long as fish and appetites hold out.

Large fish may also be spitted and roasted over hot coals.

They have a tendency to roll on the stick, however, and usually must be lashed to it with twine or old fishline. Unless the fish is fat, it will be the better for basting.

KITED FISH. Naturally fat salmon, being self-basting, really lend themselves to this way of cooking which was a favorite among the Indians of the Northwest. I have also found this method effective with the Atlantic salmon of such famous Eastern rivers as the Southwest Miramichi and the Grand Cascapedia.

Open a salmon along the belly and remove entrails, fins, head, tail, and finally the backbone. Take care not to sever the back skin. Select a long, sturdy hardwood sapling and with your knife carefully make a split in it about twice the length of the fish. Open the fish like a book and ease it into the split, so that the sapling will loan the fish a solid spine and will extend well beyond it on both ends. Wrap some twine or wire securely around the split end of the stick.

You now need to spread the fish open. This you can accomplish by working a half dozen or so wooden crosspieces through the split stick and against both sides of the fish. Tie the ends of each pair of these together to hold the fish flat. You'll end up with something resembling a crude kite.

Sharpen the solid end of the sapling and stick it in the ground, so that the fish angles over a campfire that has burned to glowering coals. If a little smoke is wisping from the hardwood embers, the flavor will be all the better. Turn the fish after it has cooked to umber crispiness on the skin side. And be prepared to go fishing again tomorrow, and the day following, and the day after that.

SAUTEED FISH. This is hard to beat when it comes to fillets and small fish. Open and clean these latter as soon as possible after catching, saving the livers, hearts, and any roe. Unless you object to them too strenuously, leave on the head and certainly the tail where, in that order, lies the sweetest meat. Keep dry, cool, and well ventilated.

Get the frypan just hot enough that the butter or margarine in it barely begins to brown. You can roll the fish in flour, crumbs, or corn meal if you want, although I much prefer the rich crispy skin when it is unadorned. Brown on both sides only until the flesh flakes easily. The heart, liver, and any roe will then also be well done and tender. Transfer to a hot plate, unless you're eating alone maybe, and add any desired salt. If near civilization where such supplements are available, you may also like to squeeze on a few drops of lemon juice.

FRIED FISH. Dip the fillets, steaks, or the cleaned but otherwise whole pan fish into evaporated milk. For a richer crust, immerse next in beaten eggs. Roll finally in cracker, bannock, or bread crumbs. This will seal the flavor in and the cooking fat out.

Get this latter ½ inch deep and thoroughly hot, just short of smoking, in a heavy frypan, so that a protective coating will be quickly formed on the fish. Do not let the fat get any warmer, as this will cause both dryness and loss of flavor. Turn each piece of fish once. Although the cooking time will depend on the thickness of the catch, keep it on the under side if anything. When the fish flakes easily with a fork, it's ready for eating.

Fish so prepared can also be cooked in a hot reflector baker. Once they have been rolled in crumbs, place them in a warm greased pan and either dot with butter or margarine or pour a small amount of oil over them. This cooking method will give you more time for other chores. In about a dozen minutes, depending on the fish and the fire, the flesh will flake easily and be ready for the table.

BAKED FISH. A reflector baker and a large fish make a winning combination. Cover the fish well with butter, margarine, or cooking oil. Place in the greased pan with the skin down. Bake in front of a rousing fire as you would bannock. Baste occasionally. Turn the pan end-for-end about halfway through. About the only thing to beware of is overcooking. Test for flakiness as usual with a fork or twig. Too, baked fish must be fresh, or it will fall to pieces.

The larger fish can also be stuffed and baked if you want. A bread filling is a favorite. For a 5-pound fish, come as close as you can to:

¼   cup chopped onion
¼   cup margarine
5   cups bread crumbs
1   teaspoon salt
⅛   teaspoon pepper
1½   teaspoons thyme or poultry seasoning
¼   cup water

Cook the onion in the margarine until tender. Mix with crumbs, salt, pepper, and seasoning. Then add the water. Fill the fish loosely so that it won't burst and close it with whittled skewers. Bake in a hot oven or reflector baker, basting frequently. This will take about 10 minutes a pound. The usual flaking test will indicate when done.

With leaner fish in particular, this bread stuffing may seem somewhat dry. If you want and have the raw materials, substitute sliced tomatoes for the crumbs and omit the thyme and poultry seasoning.

FISH H.B.C. Hudson's Bay Company fur trading personnel have a recipe for whitefish that's good with other varieties as well. Fillet a large whitefish and divide it into 6 portions. Put 2 cups milk in a large frypan. Add a thinly sliced, medium-sized onion. Heat to the bubbling point and add the fish. Simmer until flaky, which will take about 20 minutes.

Now mix 1 tablespoon cornstarch in ½ cup milk. Remove the fish from pan and add the cornstarch mixture to the remaining liquid. Stir until it thickens. Then remove from heat and add a small piece of butter. Pour the sauce over the fish and serve with dry toast.

GRILLED FISH. The smaller the fish, the hotter the grill should be. If the fish sticks or breaks when you attempt to turn it or to take it up, then odds are you didn't let the grill get hot enough to start with. Too, grease it well at the onset.

Either salt the inside and outside of the fish up to an hour before broiling, or sprinkle the inside with pepper and lemon juice just before it goes on the heat. Whole fish may be split or not, depending on your preferences and on the size. Even when the fish has a thick skin well cushioned with fat, basting will add to the flavor. Once the translucency of the flesh has clouded to opaqueness, the fish will be ready for serving.

PLANKED FISH. These days if you can't easily come by a clean, sweet hardwood plank several inches thick, you can use almost any handy slab, shake, or other piece of wood of suitable size by first sheathing the working side with aluminum foil. The wood should be slightly longer and wider than the split fish.

Nail or peg the opened and flattened fish to the plank with the skin side toward the back. Salt and pepper. Either spread it with butter or margarine or brush it with cooking oil. Lean near the fire, turning the plank now and then and occasionally basting. As soon as the fish is flaky, it is ready. The saltiness of melting butter touches up the taste. If you've enough to go around, serve each fish with its individual hot plate attached.

BAKING FISH IN CLAY. This really seals in the flavor, but you need the kind of fine sticky clay that makes good log cabin chinking. If it isn't already wet, work it with water until it reaches the consistency of a stiff dough. Then mold it about an inch thick completely over the whole fish. Bury in hot embers until you have what resembles a hard, hot block. Baking will take about 15 minutes per pound of fish. When you break open the shell, you'll find such externals as fins and scales embedded in it, leaving a steaming savory feast.

POACHED FISH. Use serving size portions. Place in a frypan. Barely cover with hot salted water, tomato juice, or milk. Add diced onions if you want. Cover and simmer for about 10 minutes or until the fish is flaky. Then remove the fish and thicken the remaining gravy by stirring in flour and margarine. Pour the hot sauce over the fish and serve.

When fish is so poached in salted water, an egg sauce is a particularly fitting accompaniment. Melt 2 tablespoons of margarine in a separate pan. Blend in 2 tablespoons flour. Gradually stir in 1 cup of milk and cook about 5 minutes or until the sauce is thick and smooth. Remove from the heat. Season with ½ teaspoon salt and a sprinkle of black pepper. A ¼ teaspoon of paprika and 1 teaspoon of dried parsley will add eye and taste appeal. Finish by stirring in 2 finely chopped, hard boiled eggs. This sauce can be richly made with dried milk and eggs.

Fish may also be cradled in cloth or cheesecloth, lowered into salted bubbling water, and simmered gently until done. This is an easy way to prepare for recipes demanding flaked cooked fish. It is also a satisfactory way to cook a large salmon, part of which is to be eaten cold.

FISH CAKES. Colonel Townsend Whelen taught me this way of making fish cakes. You'll need:

1	small onion, chopped fine
2	tablespoons shortening
1½	cups cooked fish
3	cups diced, boiled potatoes
½	teaspoon salt
¼	teaspoon black pepper
1	tablespoon dried egg
½	cup water

Fry the onion in a small amount of the shortening until soft. Then mix with fish, potatoes, and seasoning. Stir the egg in the water. Add this and the remainder of the shortening to the other ingredients. Form into small cakes ¾ inch thick and fry in a greased pan until brown.

Another way both the Colonel and I like fish cakes on occasion is in the proportions of:

1	cup cooked fish
2	cups mashed potatoes
2	eggs, fresh or reconstituted
3	tablespoons shortening
½	teaspoon salt
¼	teaspoon pepper

Mix the potatoes and fish. Then stir the other ingredients into the mixture. Form cakes as before and fry them slowly until you can't wait any longer.

FISH CHOWDER. You can prepare for this before leaving on your vacation by packing and sealing dehydrated equivalents of the following or similar ingredients, except for the bacon and fish, in a plastic bag. Or you can make a quart of it on the spot with:

1   cup diced potatoes
½   cup diced carrots
2   tablespoons diced bacon
1   tablespoon chopped onion
½   cup dry milk
1½   tablespoons flour
2   cups liquid (that from cooked vegetables plus water or fluid milk)
2   cups flaked cooked fish

Cook the potatoes and carrots until tender in just enough boiling water to cover. Drain and save liquid. Fry bacon until crisp, adding onion long enough to make it tender.

Add milk powder and flour to the liquid and beat until smooth. Cook over low heat, stirring constantly until slightly thickened. Then combine all ingredients and heat thoroughly.

FISH PIE. Don MacDougall's most popular dish when he cooked for a Canadian Government survey party in the neck of the wilderness where I was fishing the other summer was fish pie. This Don got going by fitting an uncooked pie crust into what he described as a "real deep" casserole. A layer of fresh boiled fish, shredded, came next, then ½ inch of boiled rice, another thickness of fish, and so on. Each layer was sprinkled with salt and nutmeg.

Don then made a white sauce by melting 2 tablespoons of butter in a saucepan, slowly blending 3 tablespoons of flour with this, and seasoning the whole to taste. Then, all the time stirring, he gradually added 2 cups of milk and brought the sauce to a simmer.

He finally took a fork, punched holes in the pie, and cascaded the white sauce into these. A sliced onion went on top, and the whole concoction disappeared into a moderate oven for an hour.

ROE. This is so relished in Alaska that a stratagem there at the time of the herring runs is to anchor hemlock limbs along the shore so that roe from the spawning fish will catch in the branches. This roe is drained, seasoned with salt and pepper, and sauteed in moderate heat until brown on both sides. Cooking time is about 12 minutes. Add lemon juice to butter that's been heated to a delicate brown and pour this over the hot roe.

You'll also find herring roe scrambled with eggs in the 49th State. For about ½ pound of roe, add 1 tablespoon vinegar and 1 teaspoon salt to 2 cups boiling water. Add the roe and simmer 15 minutes. Drain and remove membrane. Mash the roe. Combine with 6 eggs, 6 tablespoons thick milk, ½ teaspoon salt, and ⅛ teaspoon pepper. Scramble the mixture in 2 tablespoons margarine or other fat in a frypan over low heat. Garnish with parsley, water cress, or such and serve hot.

LING LIVER. This is what Vilhjalmur Stefansson, greatest of the recent explorers, has long considered the finest delicacy the North has to offer. I've eaten a lot of ling, too, caught within casting distance of our Hudson Hope, British Columbia, homesite on Canada's Peace River. It certainly would be difficult to contest Dr. Stefansson's contention. The way I like these delicately flavored livers best is lightly fried in butter or margarine and eaten at once as is.

If you catch a good mess of this freshwater codfish, which many scientists call living fossils, and want to serve up something special for company, get a couple of frypans going. In the first, fry the vitamin-rich livers very lightly as before. In the other, fry some diced onions in butter or margarine until they're soft but not brown. A volume of diced onions about half that of the livers is about right. When the onions are ready, put them in with the livers. Stir both together gently, not breaking the livers, and cook a minute or so longer. Serve over hot buttered toast.

SHELLFISH

If you'd like to enjoy a wonderfully lazy day in the sun, with the nearly certain promise of catching a delicious meal, shellfishing is hard to beat. Everyone is sure to get something—spiny lobsters, or scallops, or maybe abalone in their mother-of-pearl shells. And what's better eating? Matter of fact, some of the best fun of all can be gathering driftwood, putting on a big kettle of salt water, and doing your feasting right on the shore.

CRABS. It's perhaps the crabs that provide more good sport and fine dining than any other North American salt water delicacy. There are so many ways to catch these pugnacious individualists that no one should have much trouble in getting his share. Just a chunk of meat tied to a string will turn the trick. Crabs attracted to it will hold on so persistently that you can easily yank them, dripping, from the water. By moving quickly enough at low tide, you can also scoop crabs of all dimensions out of the shallows where they sometimes lurk by the hundreds in swaying sea grass. A night light will bring them, swimming like luminous ghosts, to within easy reach of a long-handled net.

Any rake, its sharp tines blunted by tape, will excite some of these crustaceans to combat if advanced slowly through grasses and seaweed. When they've clamped tight, just lift them out. Similarly blunted garden forks will also serve. Or you can just poke around with a stick, pinning the crab if necessary until you can flip it into the damp burlap bag or pail of brine you're carrying.

Crabs are plunged live into boiling salt water. After 20 minutes of seething, they're ready for breaking open and eating with melted butter. Or the cracked legs may be dipped into a mixture of egg and crumbs, then fried in butter until brown and delicious. How about when crabs are in the soft-shell stage? Leaving the delicate new shell undisturbed, just saute them in a little butter. Once you've finished devouring the first batch, odds are you'll be out looking for more.

CLAMS. Then there are the clams. Almost all our coastal waters are enriched with these, and at least half the fun is getting out to harvest them. Sandy beaches, salty mud flats, gravel-loaded reefs, bright headlands, and foggy bays all yield their savory treasures. These vary from tiny bean clams, which after storms can sometimes be picked up by the hundreds along Southern California beaches, to huge geoducks weighing a dozen pounds and more.

Some of these clams are dug with shovels, rakes, forks, hoes, and trowels. Others are felt by barefooted waders who

then casually reach down and transfer them to a convenient bag or basket. There are even clams, such as the
succulent rough piddock, that hollow out homes in rocks
and are hunted with such unlikely tools as sledge hammers
and chisels.

On many a beach, the technique is to stroll along and
tap the hard packed sand ahead, all the time watching for
tiny holes to appear. At this sign that a clam is on the
move somewhere beneath, the idea is to begin instantly
digging on the seaward side. Some experts scoop away only
the hard top surface, then grope for the fleeing clam with
their hands. With a lot of species, you have to move surprisingly fast.

If there's any way clams can be cooked more delectably
than they have been for centuries at New England clam
bakes, then a lot of us haven't discovered it yet. All you
have to do is dig a pit on the beach, line it with rocks,
and kindle a roaring fire within. When the burning driftwood has crumbled to hot coals, spread on fresh wet seaweed. The clams go in next. They are immediately covered
with more soggy live kelp. Then come such old standbys
as unhusked corn and potatoes in their jackets, and a final
topping of more wet seaweed. A thick layer of sand seals
in both the heat and the wonderfully fragrant steam.

After about an hour, if you can wait that long, the now
dry seaweed is raked out. The food is gingerly extracted.
And everyone begins making with hot melted butter. But
if your appetite precludes even these relatively simple preparations, just lay your live clams on a piece of sheet metal
under which driftwood is flaming in all its different colors.
When the shells have opened, cut out the clams, dip them
in butter, and wash them down with sips of their own shell-
cupped juices.

CLAM CHOWDER. Clam chowder is widely acclaimed.
A sound rule is to make it of equal volumes of shucked
clams, peeled and diced potatoes, and milk. Other ingredients can include a diced onion and several strips of
bacon or salt pork. Boil the potatoes 5 minutes. Fry the
bacon or salt pork until crisp and then brown the onion

with it. Put together in a dutch oven or large pot and cook just short of simmering until the potatoes are done. Let some melting butter or margarine spread over the top. Salt and pepper to taste.

STEAMED CLAMS. This one brings memories of some particularly congenial hours spent with good companions beside rousing fires. A good way to get ready for such sessions is by washing your clams well in several changes of water, then spreading them out in a big shallow pan. Barely cover them with cold water, with 1 cup of salt to every 3 gallons of water, and let them stand 3 or 4 hours to cleanse themselves. This process you can help along by sprinkling on a cup of corn meal. Then, before you use the clams, make sure each is still alive. Any with yawning shells that don't close when handled should be discarded.

Place the clams in a dutch oven or large kettle. Add ½ cup boiling water for every 4 quarts of clams. Put on a tight lid and allow to steam over the fire until the shells partially open. This usually takes about 15 minutes.

Set the pot in the middle of the table. Have dishes of melted butter ready. Ladle some of the steaming hot broth into individual cups. Then let everyone use his hands, opening the shells one by one, stripping off the membrane and the outside of the neck, swishing the clam a bit in the broth, then dipping it in the butter, and plopping it into the mouth. By being careful not to disturb the sediment in the bottom of the cups, you can intersperse the eating with frequent sips of the rich salty liquid.

CRAYFISH. These are found under rocks and logs and in the banks of most streams although, inasmuch as they scavenge mostly at night, they are not too often noticed except by gourmets like the raccoon. However, these fresh-water crawdads will cling to bait with the same avidity as crabs. Cook them whole in a small amount of boiling, salted water until the crayfish turns red. Then peel and eat as you would lobster or crab. Don't throw away the tasty stock that remains. Add some diced vegetables to it, season if necessary, and you'll have some memorable soup.

ABALONE. Abalone are prizes along the Pacific Coast.

Once you've pried these great mollusks from rocks at low tide, scoop them from their bright shells with the same large screwdrivers or tire irons, trim off the dark sections, slice into thin steaks, and pound until soft. Dip these steaks into beaten egg, then cracker crumbs, and fry about a minute on each side. Abalone's distinctively delicate flavor, many believe, is enhanced by lemon juice.

Abalone chowder, too, is unforgettable. You'll need:

      4   slices diced bacon
      6   slices pounded and diced abalone
      1   large diced potato
      1   finely chopped onion
      1   small clove garlic, crushed
    1½   cups hot water
      1   teaspoon Worcestershire
      3   cups hot milk
          salt and pepper to taste

Brown the bacon. Then drain all but 3 tablespoons of the drippings from the pan. Add the abalone, the raw potato and onion, and the garlic. Saute until well browned. Now add the water, cover the pan, and simmer until the potatoes are tender. Blend in the remaining ingredients. Ladle out piping hot.

OYSTERS. There are the savory bay scallops, the cockles, prawns, shrimp, the rock lobsters, and the picturesque and exciting conches. There are also the tasty mussels that in the United States and Canada are found inland as well as along the coast. And there are the oysters; some of them even attached to the roots of trees. No other waters anywhere in the world will give the family or individual more fun or finer eating.

It is the oysters that guarantee some of the best meals our open places can provide. Eat them live. Roast them like clams. Roll in eggs, milk, and seasoned crumbs, and then fry in hot fat about 2 minutes or until brown. Steam and serve in the shells with melted butter. Shuck, drain, sprinkle with seasoned and buttered bread crumbs, and broil on the half shell for 5 minutes. Simmer them into stew with salt and pepper, butter, and a quart of milk per pint of shellfish. Alternate them on a green wand with slices of bacon and cook over the coals of the campfire.

Or conjure up what's known as Angels on Horseback with:

  1   pint oysters
 12   slices bacon
 ½   teaspoon salt
 ⅛   teaspoon pepper
  2   teaspoons dried parsley

Drain the oysters. Lay each oyster on half a slice of bacon. Sprinkle with salt, pepper, and dried parsley. Loop the bacon around the oyster and fasten with a toothpick or whittled skewer. Arrange the oysters on a rack in a shallow pan and bake them in a hot oven or in the reflector baker before a leaping fire. Pick up by the toothpick or skewer and eat hot.

ET CETERA

FROG'S LEGS. "The one dish that has lingered longest in my memory," Colonel Townsend Whelen tells me, "was comprised of 6-inch brook trout with many frog's legs which two of us 12-year-old kids prepared alongside a brook in the north woods."

Frog's legs are not unlike chicken in texture and flavor. Both front and hind are edible. The smaller the frog, the tenderer and sweeter they are. Strip the skin off like a glove. Either grill over open coals or fry in butter or margarine over low heat for 5 to 10 minutes or until the meat comes away easily from the bones. For frying, they may first, if you want, be rolled in lightly salted and peppered flour or bread crumbs. If you prefer a crusty coating, dip them between rollings in egg diluted with an equal volume of cold water. You can often gather a little water cress nearby whose spiciness will help bring out the flavor.

TURTLES. My experience has been with snappers. Get it biting on a stick, steady it with a foot on the shell, and behead it with an ax. Cut off the claws. Then turn it over and cut the skin all the way around. Skin the hide down the legs to the feet which can then be easily disjointed. Now with the help of a sharp knife in the case of snappers, or with a saw or ax with varieties such as terrapins, cut through the substance connecting top and bottom shells and pry off the latter. The entrails can then be easily reached and discarded.

If the turtle is a small one in ratio to the appetites involved, simmer it in the shell until the meat has cooked free. But if you've more turtle than you can eat, settle for cutting out the four quarters. Brown the meat in margarine or other fat in a heavy frypan. Add several sliced onions and enough water to cover. Cover and simmer until the meat is tender. Fork this onto mounds of mashed potato, cover with gravy made by stirring enough flour with the pan juices to thicken them, and fall to.

EELS. I've caught and eaten eels while trout fishing in New England and the Maritime Provinces, and this elongated fish outdoes all normal expectations. I like them skinned, cut into 2-inch pieces, salted, and then browned on both sides in the frypan with several tablespoons of margarine or butter.

FISHERMAN'S REPRIEVE. "White man crazy," a friend of mine, Howard Cook the artist, says an Indian guide told him once. "Look at watch to see if hungry."

Here's a fish dish which boasts its own built-in alarm clock for arousing even the most sated appetites. Listen to its taste-tingling sizzlings, catch a whiff of its subtly imposing aromas, or on occasion even as much as a glance at its goldenly darkening deliciousness, and good intentions are rerouted in favor of better and more immediate ones.

As a matter of fact, this recipe is one I generally reserve until the tag end of a successful season when, although he may not admit it, even the most dedicated purist would just as soon sit down to something besides the ordinary run of poached fish, steamed fish, baked fish, broiled fish, and of course fried fish.

It's a particularly good creation for which to make your preparations before taking off on a fishing trip. Outdoorsmen readying for an angling holiday can mix the necessary

components at home except for water with which to reconstitute eggs and cream.

The following recipe is geared to enough fish to feed
a hungry foursome:

       4   eggs
       1   teaspoon allspice
       1   finely chopped garlic clove
       2   tablespoons thick cream
            salt
            pepper
            flour
      ⅛   pound margarine
       1   teaspoon chopped parsley
       1   lemon

If using fresh products, break the eggs into a dish. Add
the allspice, garlic, and cream. Then rub salt and pepper
in proportions of a teaspoon of salt to every ¼ teaspoon
of pepper into the fillets and soak them in the well beaten
mixture 5 minutes. Sprinkle with flour. Fry them in the
margarine until flaky.

Remove the fish and place on a platter or preferably on
individual preheated plates. Now add any of the unused
margarine to that remaining in the pan, stir in the chopped
parsley, and squeeze lemon juice over both. Pour over the
hot fillets.

For the streamside version of this fish dish, substitute
equivalent amounts of powdered whole eggs, parsley flakes,
dehydrated cream, and dried lemon juice. Seal in a plastic
bag with a hot iron or adhesive cellulose tape. When ready
to use, add enough water to make a thick batter and
proceed from there.

Chapter 7

BANNOCK, SOURDOUGH & OTHER BREADS

About the only cooking odors that even approach the aroma of bread baking outdoors are the sizzling smell of good grilled bacon, coffee bubbling in the heat of a campfire, and fat venison sputtering over hardwood coals.

This is just as well because, unless you can replenish it frequently, bakery bread soon becomes moldy, stale, and thoroughly unappetizing in the out-of-doors. Furthermore, its airy softness is unreasonably bulky and unsubstantial when it comes to packing. All these shortcomings are especially apparent when you consider that even the rankest greenhorn can break himself off a hot chunk of steaming bannock after a few minutes of practically foolproof effort.

Sourdough bread, too, is particularly designed to solve the problems of the ofttimes unskilled wilderness cook. Considerable folklore has sprung up around this pioneer staple which, early proving its ability to rise under just about any condition short of freezing, gave veteran northerners their name.

You hear tales of sourdough that has been kept going ever since gold rush days near the turn of the century. Many such accounts are completely true. The main difference between the folklore and the facts is one of cleanliness. There's actually no big need to worry about the admonition of old bushmen that if sourdough turns orange or yellow, it's still good; but that if it takes on a moldy greenish hue, it should be discarded and a new starter mixed.

When I first began log cabin living at Hudson Hope, British Columbia, I followed the practice of trapper neighbors and kept the sourdough starter in a surely handy lard pail. The difficulty was: the acids in sourdough corrode metals, discoloring and subtly changing the sponge. But more about that in a moment.

Another custom of the country I briefly adopted was that of keeping the sourdough working by dropping in leftover pancakes, crusts, and the like. This procedure, I discovered, adds nothing to the flavor while often worsening it considerably. Such haphazard additions, furthermore, are apt to keep you discarding spoiled starters and beginning new ones. More about that, too.

In other words, there are some good easy ways around the bread dilemma. Here are a few of these detours.

FRYING PAN BREAD. This is the famous bannock of the open places. The basic recipe for one hungry outdoorsman follows. If you want more, increase the ingredients proportionately.

1   cup flour
1   teaspoon baking powder
¼   teaspoon salt

Mix these dry, taking all the time you need to do this thoroughly. Have the hands floured and everything ready to go before you add liquid. If you are going to use the traditional frypan, make sure it is warm and greased.

Working quickly from now on, stir in enough cold water to make a firm dough. Shape this, with as little handling as possible, into a cake about an inch thick. If you like crust, leave a doughnutlike hole in the middle. Dust the loaf lightly with flour, so it will handle more easily.

Lay the bannock in the warm frypan. Hold it over the heat until a bottom crust forms, rotating the pan a little so the loaf will shift and not become stuck.

Once the dough has hardened enough to hold together, you can turn the bannock over. This, if you've practiced a bit and have the confidence to flip strongly enough, can be easily accomplished with a slight swing of the arm and snap of the wrist. Or you can use a spatula, supporting the loaf long enough to invert the frypan over it and then turning everything together.

With a campfire, however, it is often easier at this stage just to prop the frypan at a steep angle so that the bannock will get direct heat on top. When crust has formed all around, you may if you wish turn the bannock over and around a few times while it is baking to an appetizing brown.

When is the bannock done? After you've been cooking them awhile, you will be able to tap one and gauge this by the hollowness of the sound. Meanwhile, test by shoving in a straw or sliver. If any dough adheres, the loaf needs more heat. Cooking can be accomplished in about 15 minutes. If you have other duties around camp, twice that time a bit farther from the heat will allow the bannock to cook more evenly.

OTHER COOKING METHODS. Instead of slanting the pan in front of the fire to cook the top side only, you can often bake it throughout at this second stage. This may be accomplished by the use of an existing boulder or some such reflecting surface, perhaps several large stones laid up beside the campfire for the purpose. When the reflecting area is hot, lean the pan with its back to this and its face to the direct heat.

A reflector can also be made by thrusting several stakes in a line a foot behind the fire to support an expanse of aluminum foil. Or, with a small bannock, you can just bend a small sheet of foil in an arc over the frypan so that the heat rising about the pan will be reflected back down onto the top of the food.

You can also scoop a small pit in front of the campfire, rake a few red coals into it, and set the frypan on these so the bannock will be cooked both by the embers below and the blazing forelog of the fire above. For best results, this forelog should be a well burning one that's lying several inches off the ground at this point and blazing upwards with a generally vertical flame.

Suppose you're short on utensils and long on appetites? As soon as each loaf is crusty enough to hold its shape, slide it out of the pan and lean it on the ground near enough to the campfire to finish cooking. Immediately start another.

Bannock is also cooked with a minimum of attention in ovens of all kinds. This is a major reason for considering one of the folding wood stoves with ovens when traveling by car, boat, or horse. These stoves come in various models and sizes. The next handiest convenience, when you have the room for it, is a folding camp oven, preferably one with a heat indicator. Besides their uses with wood fires, these make baking with a manufactured-fuel stove—and, incidentally, with that charcoal grill when you get back home—a simplicity.

Bannock, in any event, never tastes better than when devoured piping hot around a campfire. It should then be broken apart, never cut. A cold bannock sliced in half, however, and made into a man-size sandwich with plenty of meat or other filler in between is the best lunch ever.

REFLECTOR BAKER. Light and compact varieties of the reflector baker, which our pioneer ancestors used for baking in front of open fireplaces, are still invaluable out-

REFLECTOR BAKER.

door equipment. The modern articles are made of brightly reflecting metals such as aluminum. They fold flat for easier carrying. Because they operate on the principle of reflecting heat to all parts of the cooking food, maintenance of their efficiency depends on their being kept reasonably clean and bright.

These portable ovens provide the simplest and most convenient means of baking and roasting with an open fire. They are also used in conjunction with ovenless stoves. Not only breads and biscuits, but fish and game as well, come out hot and appetizing. You merely stand the reflector before a blazing fire or hot stove. The temperature you regulate by moving the contraption toward or away from the heat. Food is placed in a pan on the center shelf of the reflector oven and occasionally turned end for end so the baking will be more uniform.

Here is a fine way to cook bannock in loaf form. For instance, you want some handy slices between which to sandwich cold venison for the next day's lunch. Use the basic bannock recipe, probably in at least double proportions, but shape the dough into a loaf. Dust lightly with flour. Lay in a warm, greased pan. Place this in the oven. Bake with occasional turnings of the pan until you get a good looking crust and the testing sliver comes out without any dough adhering.

BISCUITS. Start with the basic bannock recipe. Work 3 tablespoons of solid shortening per cup of flour into these dry ingredients. Mix thoroughly, perhaps by cutting through the flour and shortening again and again with two dull knives, until the mixture has the consistency of coarse meal.

REFLECTOR BAKER USED WITH FOLDING STOVE.

Then, working quickly, add enough water or milk to make a dough just soft enough to be easily handled. From ¼ to ⅓ cup of fluid per cup of flour will generally suffice. If the dough becomes too sticky, rapidly scatter on a little more flour. For best results, knead no more than half a minute.

Flatten the dough speedily into a sheet about ¾ inch thick. A cold bottle or can makes an effective rolling pin. Cut square biscuits with a sharp cold knife or press out round ones with perhaps the top of the baking powder tin. Dust each with flour.

Place on a lightly greased pan or sheet. Bake in a very hot oven or reflector baker until a rich brown, by which time the biscuits should have risen to about 2 inches high. These biscuits can also be cooked in a frypan like bannock, in which case you may have to turn each one several times to assure even cooking. If you don't care for crust, keep them close together. Or bake them in a dutch oven, as suggested later in this chapter.

Want something special? Dip each biscuit into melted shortening before baking.

BAKING POWDERS. When liquid is added to baking powder, gas is released. This is the same harmless carbon dioxide that gives such beverages as ginger ale their bubbliness. Its function in breadstuffs is to raise the dough. Without some such effervescence you'd end up with a chunk of hardtack; the way to make this, incidentally.

It follows that you want to prevent as much as possible of this gas from wastefully escaping. Aside from speed, you can conserve it several ways. Cold fluid, as might be expected, releases the carbon dioxide more slowly than hot. It is also better to do as much of the necessary mixing as possible with a cold spoon or peeled stick rather than with the warm hands.

Why not just put in more baking powder? The answer is that food tastes better and digests more easily with a minimum of this acid-alkali combination. Some outdoor cooks do tend to take out insurance by using more than the teaspoon of baking powder that's generally sufficient for each cup of flour. It's true that strengths of this leavening agent vary. Furthermore, all baking powder tends to become weaker with age, particularly if the container has not been kept tightly closed and in a dry and preferably cool place. It's sound practice to stir baking powder a bit before measuring, partly to break up any lumps but mainly to assure a more uniform mixture of ingredients. The outer layer is apt to lose some of its leavening power because of contact with air.

Directions on the particular can if the contents are fresh, experimentation if they are not, will provide a functional yardstick if you've any doubts. Double action baking powder, the so-called combination type which releases part of its gas when heated, packs more power than either the tartrate or the calcium phosphate varieties. The recipes in this book are geared to it.

The ideal, insofar as flavor and digestion are concerned, is to use the smallest amount of baking powder that will raise the breadstuff enough for your liking.

How to find out if the baking powder in your camping outfit is still active? Stir a teaspoonful into ½ cup of hot water. If the mixture doesn't bubble diligently, better use sourdough instead.

MIXING THE DOUGH. Easiest and most economical way is to carry a small sheet of thin plastic. Bark may also be used, but at best it's a nuisance. Wax paper or foil is an answer for motorized campers.

Prospectors, trappers, and other professional outdoorsmen still widely continue the pioneer practice of mixing bannock in the flour sacks themselves. Just make a small hollow in the flour. Drop the salt and baking powder into this. Then, stirring with the fingers of one hand, add the water gradually until the resulting dough has picked up all the flour it needs. Press and pat into shape. Cook.

BANNOCK CHANGES. Variations on the basic bannock recipe are innumerable. Inclusion of a tablespoon of sugar with every cup of flour will make for a more pronounced taste and a crisper crust. Fresh or powdered eggs, ½ to 1 egg for every cup of flour, will add thickness and richness.

Substitution of milk for water, or the addition of powdered milk, will improve both flavor and characteristic golden brownness.

Addition of a shortening, usually from 1 to 3 tablespoons per cup of flour, will increase tenderness. This is especially desirable in winter sports weather when even larger proportions of fat are sometimes necessary to keep the breadstuff from freezing hard on frosty trails. Solids like butter, margarine, bacon drippings, and lard are most effective when either creamed with the sugar or thoroughly mixed with the flour. Liquids such as cooking and salad oils, which make for a more crumbly but not so tender product, may be added mixed with water, milk, and any fresh eggs.

Such fruits as raisins, currants, and blueberries make bannock tastier, although their inclusion calls for the use of a bit more baking powder. Combine these fruits with the dry ingredients to avoid any overmixing. Spices, particularly nutmeg and cinnamon, are unusually zestful when their odors mingle with the keenness of pine trees and wood smoke.

MAPLE MUFFINS. You don't need maple trees for these. If you want, just make up some of the substitute maple syrup described elsewhere in this book. Then take:

2 eggs
⅓ cup milk
½ cup syrup
4 tablespoons liquid shortening
2 cups flour
2 teaspoons baking powder
¼ teaspoon salt

Add the eggs, either whole or dried, to the milk and beat together. Mix the syrup and shortening. Stir this into the eggs and milk.

Combine the flour, baking powder, and salt. Add the rest, mixing just enough to moisten the dry ingredients. Pour into a greased muffin pan and bake in a moderate oven or reflector baker. About ½ hour should do it. If these muffins are not devoured on the spot, loosen them in the pan, tip them so that air can get around them, and put them in a warm place.

SNOW FOR EGGS. In the North when we have lacked eggs for this and other breadstuffs, we have successfully used snow instead. Fresh dry snow is best for this purpose. It is rapidly stirred in just before the breadstuff is put over the heat. It must not be allowed to melt until the cooking is underway, for its function is entirely mechanical.

The air-loaded flakes of snow hold the ingredients apart. Cooked while these are so separated, such breadstuffs come out airy and light. Egg is able to accomplish the same end result, as you can appreciate by watching the way an egg readily beats into air-holding froth whose elasticity heightens its raising and spacing prowess. Two heaping tablespoons of fresh dry snow will take the place of every egg in the batter.

HOMEMADE DRY MIX

Fresh bannock is a simple thing to cook on the trail, even when the nearest utensil is a dozen miles away. Then the handiest method is to mix the dry ingredients before leaving the base of supplies. In fact, you can make up a number of such batches at home, sealing each in a small plastic bag. This mix has multiple short-notice uses.

The following basic mix, given here in one-man proportions, will stay fresh for six weeks or more in camp if kept sealed, dry, and reasonably cool.

    1   cup all-purpose flour
    1   teaspoon double action baking powder
    ¼   teaspoon salt
    3   tablespoons oleomargine

If this mix is being readied at home, sift the flour before measuring it. Then sift together the flour, baking powder, and salt. Cut in the margarine with two knives, with an electric mixer at low speed, or with a pastry blender, until the mixture resembles coarse meal. For increased food value, add 2 tablespoons of powdered skim milk for every cup of flour.

Place in plastic bags. Seal with a hot iron or with one of the plastic tapes. A large quantity can be made at once, of course, and divided into smaller portions. Before using, it is a good idea to stir the mixture lightly.

If compounding this mix in camp, do it with the ingredients at hand and in the simplest way possible. Any solid shortening may be utilized if the mix is to be used within a short time. Such mix may be carried in a glass jar or just folded in wax paper.

DRY MIX PRODUCTS

FOR HOT TRAIL BREAD. When the fire is going and everything else is ready, quickly add enough water to basic mix to make a firm dough. Shape into a long, thin roll, no more than an inch thick. Wind this ribbon on a preheated green hardwood stick, the diameter of a rake handle, so trimmed that several projecting stubs of branches will keep the dough in place. A particularly sweet wood for the job is birch. Hold the bannock in the heat, occasionally turning it, for a couple of minutes. Once a crust has been formed, the stick may be leaned between the fringes of the fire and some reflecting surface such as a log or rock for the 15 minutes or so required to form a tasty brown spiral. Or you can just shove a sharpened end of the stick into the ground beside the fire and turn this holder now and then while readying the remainder of the meal.

FOR FRYING PAN BREAD. When ready to go, add to mix about ⅓ cup of cold water for an easily handled dough. Cook like regular bannock.

FOR DROP BISCUITS. Mix with a little less than ½ cup cold water to make a soft dough. Drop by the spoonful atop a hot greased metal surface and bake in a very hot oven or reflector baker for 10 to 15 minutes.

FOR FRUIT COBBLERS. Proceed as with the above biscuits, but drop each daub of dough atop a frying section of apple, apricot, or other cooked dry fruit.

FOR MUFFINS. Add 1 tablespoon sugar, 1 well beaten whole or reconstituted egg, and ½ cup milk. Stir just enough to dampen all the dry ingredients. Fill greased muffin rings, improvised if necessary from aluminum foil, about ⅔ full. Bake in a hot oven about 20 minutes. Eat at once. For a dessert, cook with a teaspoon of marmalade or jam atop each muffin.

FOR SHORTCAKE. Add 1 tablespoon of sugar to make half a dozen medium-size shortcakes, which will assure a pleasant change of diet in berry season. Mix with ⅓ cup cold water to form an easily handled dough. Flatten this to ¼ inch and either cut squares with a knife or punch out ovals with something like a can top. Brush half of these with melted margarine. Cover each with one of the remaining pieces. Bake in reflector baker. Serve hot with fruit.

FOR CORN BREAD. Add a previously mixed 1 cup corn meal, 1 tablespoon sugar, 1 beaten egg, and 1 cup milk, stirring only until blended. Bake in hot oven or reflector baker about half an hour. Corn bread, like biscuits and baked potatoes, should be served as promptly as possible.

FOR FLAPJACKS. Add ½ cup milk, with which a whole or dried egg has been mixed, to the homemade dry mix. Stir only enough to moisten the flour. Cook like regular flapjacks.

FOR DUMPLINGS. Stir in ¼ cup of cold milk or water. Proceed as with regular dumplings. These can also be dropped by the tablespoonful atop a meat or vegetable casserole and baked in a hot oven approximately 20 minutes.

FOR COFFEE CAKE. Stir 3 tablespoons sugar into the mix. Combine a scant ¼ cup milk with 1 egg, fresh or dried, and stir well into the mix. Pour into shallow greased pan. Sprinkle something such as nutmeg, cinnamon, powdered instant coffee, and sugar over the top if you want. Bake in a hot oven or reflector baker about 25 minutes. Delicious!

SOURDOUGH

Sourdough was the first raising agent ever used in bread making. The primitive leaven contained wild yeasts as well as numerous kinds and types of bacteria, some of which produce gas and acids. If desirable organisms were to gain supremacy, the leaven was a success. If the fermentation was dominated by undesirable organisms, the product was inferior. Knowing all this, we can now control our sour-dough to a large extent.

You can still make a primitive sourdough starter by mix-ing a cup apiece of plain flour and water in a scalded jar, covering it loosely, and placing it in a warm place to sour. If the first results are not satisfactory, you may try again with a new mixture. Trouble is, you run into all sorts of different flavors and consistencies. If you will enlist the help of store yeast, however, you can almost always come up with a satisfactory starter of your own on the first try.

SOURDOUGH STARTER. The starter can be readied at home. Once you have it, you have commenced growing your own yeast. That's what you are actually using when you bake with sourdough. Here's the sure, simple way to begin:

> 2 cups flour
> 2 cups lukewarm water
> 1 yeast cake or package of dry yeast

Mix the flour, lukewarm water, and yeast thoroughly. Then set overnight away from drafts in a warm place. By the next morning, the mixture should be putting forth bubbles and a pleasant yeasty odor. This over-all process needn't stop for as long as you're going to be in the wilder-ness.

For best results, keep the starter in a well washed and scalded glass or pottery container. Never leave any metal in contact with it. Keep the starter as much as possible in a cool spot. As a matter of fact, if you want to store the starter or part of it for a period of months, just freeze it.

The sourdough starter can also be kept fresh and clean by drying. If you want to carry it easily and safely, work in enough flour to solidify the sponge into a dry wad. A good place to pack this is in the flour itself. Water and warmth will later reactivate the yeast plants for you.

Starters occasionally lose their vigor, particularly in cold weather. Old-timers then sometimes revive them with a table-spoon of unpasteurized cider vinegar. This puts new acetic acid bacteria on the job. A tablespoon or two of raw sour milk or cream, of unpasteurized buttermilk, or of cultured buttermilk or cultured sour cream will get the lactic acids functioning again.

Sourdough starters should never be stored in a warm place for very long. Heat encourages organisms hurtful to yeast to grow at an extremely rapid rate. These may soon gain sufficient control to produce putrefactive changes; the reason for some of the unpleasant smells one occasionally runs across in old starters. Another result is that the starter becomes progressively weaker in dough-fermenting ability.

The sometimes necessary solution? Begin a new starter. This is a practical reason for including some spare yeast in the camping outfit. Best to take is recently dated, packaged dry yeast. Stored where reasonably cool, this will keep several months or more.

A sourdough starter is best kept going by the addition of flour and water only. The starter, unless temporarily frozen or dried, should be so fed about once a week at least. If you are regularly cooking with the starter, this process will take care of itself.

SOURDOUGH BREAD. If commencing from the beginning, set your starting sponge as already directed. The commercial yeast is used only to get the starter going. From then on, the mixture will grow its own yeast. When doubling a recipe, by the way, you needn't double the starter.

Take your starter. Add enough flour and lukewarm water in equal volumes to make about 3 cups of sponge. Let this stand in a warm location overnight or from 6 to 8 hours, whereupon it should be bubbling and giving off an agreeable yeasty odor.

From here on, the general procedure remains the same. Take out, in this instance, 2 cups of sponge. Place the remainder aside. That's your next starter. No matter what the recipe, at this stage always keep out about a cup of the basic sourdough.

To these 2 cups of sponge add the following:

    4 cups flour
    2 tablespoons sugar
    1 teaspoon salt
    2 tablespoons shortening

Mix the flour, sugar, and salt. Make a depression in the center of these dry ingredients. Melt the shortening if it is not already liquid. Blend it and the sponge in the hollow. Then mix everything together. A soft dough should result. If necessary, add either flour or fluid. The latter may be water or milk. Knead for 3 or 4 minutes on any clean, floured surface.

"Keep attacking," I can still hear an old trapper cautioning, eyes blinking amiably behind thick-lensed spectacles. "Don't gentle it. That is where most cheechakos make their mistake. Too much pushing and pressing lets the gas escape that's needed to raise the stuff. Just bang the dough together in a hurry, cut off loaves to fit your greased pans, and put them in a warm place to raise."

The dough, once it has plumped out to double size, should be baked some 50 to 60 minutes in a moderately hot oven or reflector baker that, preferably, is hottest the first 15 minutes. Baking should redouble the size of the loaves. One tests "in the usual way," the old trapper added. He explained, probably because it seemed necessary, that the "usual way" is to wait until the loaves seem crisply brown, then to jab in a straw. If the bread is done, the straw will come out dry and at least as clean as it was when inserted.

Sourdough bread is substantial in comparison with the usual air-filled bakery loaf. It keeps moist for a satisfactorily long time. When the bread is made according to the preceding suggestions, the flavor is unusually excellent, being especially nutty when slices are toasted. If your crew likes real tasty crust, bake the bread in long slim loaves to capitalize on this outstanding characteristic.

BAKING IN THE GROUND. During the gold rush days at the turn of the century, when gravel punchers stampeded past my present Hudson Hope, British Columbia, homesite toward where dust lay yellower and more beckoning beneath the northern lights, prospectors used to bake sourdough bread in the shallow steel vessels used for panning gold. A few still do, for that matter.

A shallow hole was scooped in the ground, often in the heat-retaining sand of a stream bank. A fire was allowed to burn to coals in this cavity. Dough, in the meantime, was rising between two gold pans. Some of the ruddy embers were raked out of the hole. The pans were inserted and covered with the hot residue, plus maybe a few coals from the regular campfire. One hour's cooking in this makeshift oven was generally the minimum. The bread wouldn't ordinarily burn if allowed to remain longer. The crust would just thicken and become more golden, that's all.

You don't need gold pans to do this today. Other utensils, as for example two preferably large heavy frypans, will accomplish the same thing. If the metal is light, insulate it all around with a thin covering of ashes.

DUTCH OVEN. This highly effective oven of heavy cast iron, described in an earlier chapter, will bake biscuits and breads deliciously both below and above ground. Heat the contraption first, setting the lid on a good solid fire and easing the pot atop that. When the pot is hot, you should be all set to go.

Say you want to bake a mess of baking powder biscuits. Drop a blob of grease into the pot and work it around a bit. While it's melting, ready the biscuits. Put them in the pot

DUTCH OVEN.

and plant this solidly and evenly above a bed of coals and ashes. Clank on the lid. Heap additional coals onto that. The fact that the lid has been preheated to a higher temperature than the pot should balance the natural rising tendency of heat sufficiently to cook the tops and bottom of the biscuits uniformly.

Take a look after about 10 minutes. If the biscuits aren't already taking on a healthy tan, rake the accumulating cinders and ashes from the lid and substitute more live coals. Dutch ovens require a certain amount of cooking experience, but the biscuits should ordinarily be ready in a dozen or 15 minutes.

Bread, taking longer to bake, is better adapted to underground cooking. For this, start in the forenoon by digging a hole somewhat larger than the oven and filling it with a blazing hardwood fire. A basic precaution? Be sure this pit is in mineral soil, well away from roots and humus, so that the fire can not spread in any direction. When the blaze has burned down to coals, shovel out about half of them. Set in the preheated and greased dutch oven with a big round sourdough loaf bulging in it. Ease the oven around until it's setting evenly. Then rake the embers and ashes back in until the utensil, except for its upraised bail handle, is hidden.

You need a certain bit of experience here, too. If it seems that the coals are going to be too ardent, insulate the oven with an inch or so of ashes. In any event, seal in the heat with several inches of dirt. Then spend the afternoon getting enough trout or grouse to go with those crusty hot slices that will be awaiting you at suppertime.

BEATEN SOURDOUGH BREAD. This bread is especially popular with outdoorsmen cooking for themselves. One reason is that it's unnecessary to touch the dough with the hands, sometimes a particular boon as when you've been blazing a trail and your fingers are sticky with pine pitch.

Proceed as with regular sourdough bread. Instead of kneading the dough, however, beat it for two minutes. Then leave it standing in the mixing bowl until it has bubbled itself to lightness.

Add 1 teaspoon baking soda. Mix another minute. Then turn into a well greased container and let stand 10 minutes in a warm place. Bake in a moderately hot oven or reflector baker 50 to 60 minutes or until done.

SOURDOUGH FLIPPERS. A lot of fishermen, campers, and other frequenters of the farther places don't figure they've started the day right until they have stoked up with a stack of hot, tender, moist sourdough flapjacks. These flippers, as sourdoughs often call them, are so easy to prepare that there's no need for even the greenest tenderfoot to be dependent on store mixes. They're so tasty and wholesome, furthermore, that many a vacationist looks ardently for more when he's shut in again by city streets.

For a couple of breakfasters, add 2 cups flour and 2 cups lukewarm water to your sourdough starter. Set overnight away from drafts in a warm location. The next morning return the original amount of starter to its scalded glass or earthenware container. To the remaining batter add:

2 eggs, fresh or dried
½ teaspoon salt
1 tablespoon sugar
1 teaspoon soda
1 teaspoon warm water
2 tablespoons liquid shortening

Mix the eggs, salt, and sugar with a fork. Melt the baking soda in the teaspoon of warm water. Stir all these into the batter, along with either cooking or salad oil, or melted lard, margarine, etc.

For variations from time to time, if you ever want them, add a little whole wheat flour, corn meal, bran flakes, or such to batters after the starter has been saved out.

If the flapjack batter becomes a bit too thick to pour easily, thin it with just enough milk. Flour, on the other hand, will provide stiffening. But if the batter is on the thin side, the flippers will be more tender.

Once the preferably heavy frypan or griddle is hot, grease it sparingly with bacon rind. Do not let the metal reach smoking temperatures. Turn each flipper once only, when the hot cake starts showing small bubbles. The second side takes about half as long to cook. Serve steaming hot with margarine and sugar, with syrup, or with what you will.

SOURDOUGH WAFFLES. Mix a little thicker sponge than for flapjacks. Let stand overnight as usual. Save out the original amount of starter. To the remaining sourdough add:

> 1 teaspoon salt
> 2 tablespoons sugar
> ¼ cup liquid shortening
> 2 eggs
> 1 teaspoon baking soda

Stir the salt, sugar, and melted margarine or other shortening smoothly into the batter. If you have whole eggs, add the yolks; then fold in the beaten whites and the soda. If you are using dehydrated eggs, add them and the soda to the batter. Cook on a hot, greased waffle iron until brown.

SOURDOUGH MUFFINS. Set the sponge the evening before as for flapjacks. The next morning take out the original starter and handle as usual. To the remaining sourdough add:

> 1½ cups whole wheat flour
> ½ cup sugar
> 1 teaspoon salt
> ¼ cup skim milk powder
> 1½ teaspoons baking soda
> 1 cup raisins
> ½ cup liquid shortening
> 2 eggs

Mix flour, sugar, salt, powdered milk, and soda. Add either the raisins or perhaps blueberries or some similar wild fruit.

Make a cavity in the center of these blended ingredients. Mix the egg and the liquid shortening in this depression. Then stir only just enough to moisten everything.

Pour into greased muffin tins and bake in a hot oven or reflector baker for 20 minutes or until done. If the muffins become ready before the rest of the meal, loosen and tilt them in the pan, so that air can circulate around them, and lean them near the heat where they'll stay warm.

SOURDOUGH FRENCH BREAD. The nutty, toasty crustiness of this bread really goes well with the substantial fare on which hearty outdoor appetites thrive. To make 2 loaves you'll need:

1 cup water
½ cup milk
4 cups flour
2 teaspoons salt
2 tablespoons sugar
1½ tablespoons shortening
1½ cups sourdough starter

Bring water to a boil and mix with milk. Cool to luke-warm. Mix the flour with the salt and sugar in a large container. Make a bowl-like depression in the center.

Mix the lukewarm liquid with the sourdough starter in this well. Blend with the dry ingredients until you get a soft dough, but do not knead.

Cover and move to a warm place to rise until about double in bulk. This should take some 2 hours. Then turn out on a lightly floured mixing surface. This may be an easily carried sheet of plastic.

Roll half the dough into a large rectangle. Fold the 2 long sides toward the middle. Then roll together like a jelly roll. Do the same with the other half of the dough.

Sprinkle 2 tablespoons of corn meal lightly over the nearest thing you can come by in the way of a large greased baking sheet. Aluminum foil can be used. So can two large frypans. Place the loaves with their smoother sides uppermost. With a sharp knife make diagonal slits every couple of inches across the top of each loaf.

Now for the crust, take:

1 teaspoon cornstarch
1 teaspoon cold water
½ cup boiling water

Mix the cornstarch and cold water. Pour into the boiling water in a pan. Bring to a brief boil. Allow to cool. Then brush the loaves with it.

Now cover the loaves and place in a warm spot to double once more in bulk, which will usually take about another hour. Afterwards, brush the loaves a second time with the cornstarch mixture.

Commence baking in a hot oven or reflector baker for 15 minutes to set the crust. Then brush the loaves a third and final time with the cornstarch preparation. Reduce the heat to moderate and continue baking 30 minutes or until the bread is done and golden brown. Baking the bread longer, with less heat, will make for even thicker crust. The dutch oven really does a job with this bread.

CORN

CORN PONES. Mix two cups corn meal, 1 teaspoon salt, and 1 tablespoon shortening. Add enough milk, about 1 cup, to make a stiff dough. Shape into thin ovals. Bake in a hot oven or reflector baker a half hour or until rich brown.

ASH CAKES. Form the above dough into balls the size of eggs. Roll in flour, or wrap in foil or clean sweet leaves. Bury in hot ashes at the edge of the fire.

HUSH PUPPIES. Colonel Townsend Whelen makes these by mixing 2 cups yellow corn meal, ¾ cup flour, 2½ teaspoons baking powder, and 1 teaspoon salt with 1 cup water to make a medium thick dough. Drop big gobs into deep hot fat. Cook until a rich brown. Hush puppies are particularly good with fresh fish. In fact, the Colonel and a lot of us prefer cooking them in fat where fish and onions are also being fried.

GOLDEN CORN BREAD

        1 cup yellow corn meal
        1 cup flour
        ½ teaspoon salt
        2 teaspoons baking powder
        1 egg
        1 cup milk
        ¼ cup melted shortening or oil

Mix the corn meal, flour, salt, and baking powder as thoroughly as possible. Beat the egg and add the other liquids to it. Then combine everything, stirring just enough to moisten. Pour into a greased pan. Bake in a hot oven for half an hour.

FRYPAN CORN BREAD. Get this cooking a half hour before come-and-get-it time. For two hungry men you'll want:

> 1 cup corn meal
> 1 cup flour
> 2 tablespoons sugar
> 1 teaspoon salt
> 2 teaspoons baking powder
> 2 eggs
> 4 tablespoons liquid shortening
> 1 cup milk

Combine the dry ingredients. If using fresh eggs, beat them separately. Blend the eggs, shortening, and milk. Then quickly mix everything.

Pour the batter into a warm, well greased frypan. Cover and place immediately over low heat.

SPOON BREAD. This is the recipe that Colonel Whelen's daughter, Mrs. William G. Bowling, uses for spoon bread; good when eaten with butter or margarine along with the main dish instead of potato, and also when served with syrup to provide a special treat for dessert.

> 2 cups milk
> ½ cup corn meal
> 1 teaspoon salt
> 1 tablespoon melted butter
> ½ teaspoon baking powder
> 3 eggs

Scald the milk in a pan by heating it nearly to the boiling point. Stir in the corn meal bit by bit. Continue cooking for several minutes, stirring to avoid scorching. Then remove from the heat and add the salt, melted butter, baking powder, and the egg yolks beaten until light. Beat the egg whites stiff and fold them in.

Pour the batter into a buttered baking dish in which it will lie about 2 inches deep. Bake for 30 minutes or until the spoon bread is roofed with a thick brown crust.

CANOE BREAD. This went well on the most recent

deer hunting trip I took by canoe down the famous Half
Moon of the Southwest Miramichi River, shortly before the
New Brunswick freeze-up. Matter of fact, the hunting and
the eating were so good that the ice caught us. I had to
cache my canoe above Big Louie rapids and walk out to
the railroad, and I've never had a chance to go back
after it.

For enough hot bread for two of us, it took:

    4 tablespoons shortening
    1 teaspoon salt
    ¼ cup corn meal
    2 teaspoons baking powder
    1½ cups flour
    ½ cup water

The amount of flour was always approximate because we
were spending as many hours as possible in the bush and
shying away from any unnecessary culinary chores. We
dropped the shortening in one gob in the top of the rolled-
down flour sack. The salt, baking powder, and corn meal
went atop it. Then the cook for that particular meal worked
the ingredients into the lard, picking up whatever flour
clung to them. He next dented the flour with his fist, poured
in the ½ cup of water, and without any delay mixed a
soft wad of dough.

Flattened, this went into a warm, greased frypan for
cooking over birch coals. The salty, thick, brown crust
always tasted particularly good after a hard, dehydrating day
among the alders.

FLAPJACKS TO DUMPLINGS

FLAPJACKS FOR TWO. I ate these once with King
Gething who, having forgotten his skillet, used a long-
handled prospector's shovel instead. King first scoured the
shovel in sand, then doused it in the Peace River, and finally
swiped it lightly with a piece of bacon rind. The handle
proved an unexpected convenience.

    2 cups flour
    2 teaspoons baking powder
    ½ teaspoon salt

    2 tablespoons sugar
    2 eggs
    1½ cups milk
    2 tablespoons liquid shortening

Combine the dry ingredients, including the powdered milk if that's what you have in camp. Beat the eggs if they are whole, and combine with the shortening and the fluid. Otherwise, reconstitute the dried eggs and combine in the same way. When everything is ready to go, mix the whole business very briefly into a thin batter. Overmixing will make these tough. For this reason, slightly lumpy batter is preferable to one that's beaten until smooth. Cook the same as sourdough flippers.

DUMPLINGS. Nothing sets off a hearty outdoor stew like steaming hot dumplings. These are a cinch to make, and they have the additional advantages of meaning neither separate cooking nor extra washing. The following recipe should satisfy two ravenous campers. About a dozen minutes before mealtime take:

    2 cups flour
    2 teaspoons baking powder
    1 teaspoon salt
    2 tablespoons margarine
    1 cup milk

Mix the dry ingredients. Work in the margarine or other solid shortening. Make a bowl-like hollow in the center. Have everything ready to roll, for these dumplings should be cooked only 8 to 10 minutes, and then the meal should be served immediately. Have the broth simmering above enough meat and other solids so that the dumplings will not sink below the surface.

Now pour the milk into the well in the middle of the dry ingredients. Mix quickly and gently with a folding, rather than a stirring or whipping, motion.

Moisten a large spoon in the broth. Use it to place large spoonfuls, apart from one another, atop the stew. Cover tightly. After several minutes, you may if you want turn each dumpling carefully and speedily. Re-cover immediately and continue simmering until light and fluffy.

Then serve without delay. If any dumplings remain for second helpings, place them in a separate hot dish so they won't become soggy.

CORN MEAL DUMPLINGS. These are good for a change. To make the same amount as above, you'll need:

1½ cups corn meal
½ cup flour
2 teaspoons baking powder
1 teaspoon salt
3 eggs
¾ cup milk
2 tablespoons liquid shortening

Mix the dry ingredients. Beat the eggs, milk, and shortening together. Have the stew simmering and 15 minutes from being done. Or whenever you prefer with dumplings, which are actually drop biscuits cooked in boiling liquid, have broth seething in a wide stewpan.

Quickly blend the dumpling batter. As before, add it by the large, separate spoonful to the bubbling liquid. Cover tightly. Allow to simmer 15 minutes. Then remove the dumplings before they lose their featheriness.

CHAPTER 8

MAIN AND SIDE DISHES

BACON. "Bacon," a sourdough friend translated when asked what he meant by saying he'd gorged himself with vast quantities of *tiger*. "That's because it's striped. Sounds nobler when called tiger."

The main troubles that camp cooks experience with bacon arise from their submitting it too soon to too much heat. Not only is the bacon thus burned and toughened, but very often the frypan becomes a mass of leaping flames. Aside from resulting offenses to taste and digestion, this is wasteful if nothing worse. The nearly 3,000 calories per pound that fat side bacon contains lie largely in its grease, any excess of which should be saved, particularly in the bush.

We'll do better to start the bacon in a *cold* frypan and to fry it slowly over a very few coals raked to one side of the blaze. Move and turn the bacon from time to time. If you like it crisp, keep pouring off the grease. Don't waste any of this, though. It has numerous camp uses.

More satisfactory still is the practice of laying the strips well apart in a pan and baking them evenly to a golden brown in a moderately warm reflector baker.

Slabs of bacon have a tendency to mold. This mold can be harmlessly wiped off with a clean cloth moistened either in vinegar or in a solution of baking soda and water.

"BOILED" EGGS. Get enough water boiling in a pan to cover the eggs by an inch. Place the eggs in the pan with a spoon and let the temperature immediately drop to a simmer, keeping it that way until the eggs are done. With all egg dishes, moderate heat is necessary if you want to avoid toughness. Usual preferences here range between 2½ and 3½ minutes of cooking, depending on how stiff you like the whites. Remove and break open at once. Serve immediately, preferably in heated dishes.

HARD BOILED EGGS. Get things started the same way as above. Keep the eggs simmering, completely covered, for 8 to 10 minutes. Then remove from the heat and plunge into cold water. If the shells are cracked slightly before the eggs cool, peeling will be easier.

Campers sometimes get their hard boiled and raw eggs mixed. There's an easy way to tell the difference. If the egg will spin freely, it's cooked. The only condition that will cross you up is when the eggs are frozen.

POACHED EGGS. There's a gimmick to this one. Fill a frypan 2 inches deep with water, with roughly a teaspoon of salt for every 4 cups of water. Bring the water to the bubbling point. Then take a spoon and start the water revolving in one direction.

Now slide each egg gently into the water from a saucer. The movement of the liquid will keep the whites from spreading. Dip some of the water over the top. Three minutes of simmering suits most people. Or once the eggs are in, you may set the water off the heat for 5 minutes. Try these eggs sometime on a small mound of buttered rice, noodles, spaghetti, macaroni, or potatoes.

SCRAMBLED EGGS. The addition of milk has a tendency to toughen scrambled eggs. Instead, add 1 tablespoon of cold water for each egg. Mix the eggs and water well with salt and pepper to taste. Heat a tablespoon of fat in a frypan just hot enough to sizzle a drop of water. Pour in the egg mixture and reduce the heat. When the eggs have started to harden, begin stirring them constantly with a fork. Remove while they're still soft and creamy.

FRIED EGGS. Have about ½ inch of fat warm, not hot. Break in your eggs. Keeping the heat low so that the whites won't become tough and leathery, baste the yolks until they are well filmed. Salt, pepper, and serve on a hot plate.

Or get a tablespoon of fat just hot enough to sizzle a test drop of water. Break in the eggs. Take the frypan off the heat at once. Baste the eggs with hot fat 3 or 4 minutes.

OMELET. Break the eggs into a bowl or mixing dish. Add 1 teaspoon water for each egg. For a 3-egg omelet, season with ¼ teaspoon salt and just a dash of pepper.

Beat vigorously with a fork until yolks and whites are blended.

Melt 1 tablespoon butter (1 teaspoon for each egg) in a frypan until it just begins to brown. Pour in the eggs. Keep shaking and slanting the pan slightly while cooking so as to keep the omelet from sticking. As soon as the bottom of the omelet starts to harden, slip a thin spatula or knife well under the edges and lift the middle of the omelet so that uncooked egg can flow beneath it. This liquid egg, incidentally, will repair any resulting breaks and tears.

An omelet takes only about 5 minutes from shells to heated plates. It is done as soon as the eggs no longer run freely but the top still looks moist and creamy. Omelets will toughen if they are allowed to brown at all. Fold the omelet by tilting the pan sideways with one hand and then lifting the uppermost section about ⅓ over the middle. Now tilt, shake, and slide the folded omelet onto the hot plate. It's actually easier to make one such easily handled 3-egg omelet for each camper than to try to manipulate any more than, at most, a 6-egg omelet.

FRENCH TOAST. For half a dozen slices of hard bread, beat 3 eggs well. Add 1 cup of milk, 3 tablespoons sugar, and 1 teaspoon vanilla. Melt 3 tablespoons of margarine or other fat in a frypan. Dip each slice of bread in the egg mixture and brown lightly on both sides in the skillet. Sprinkle with cinnamon while hot and serve at once with sugar and margarine, tart jelly, or syrup.

TOMATOES, ONIONS, & EGGS. This nourishing and easily digestible dish, with the mild and provocatively elusive flavor, is unusually good when someone hauls into camp late, especially as its preparation is both simple and swift. Proportions, which are flexible, may be varied in ratio to appetite.

For two late arrivals, brown a couple of diced onions with a little grease in a frypan. When these have cooked to a dark blandness, add a small can of tomatoes. Let these begin to bubble. Then break in 6 eggs. Season with salt and pepper. Keep scrambling over low heat until fairly dry.

EGGS ON HORSEBACK. Rub your 2-pound, inch-thick

steak with salt, pepper, and a suggestion of mustard. Pan broil in a heavy frypan, searing quickly on both sides and then cooking more slowly until done to taste.

Meanwhile, melt 2 tablespoons of margarine or butter in another pan. Add 2 tablespoons chopped onion, a small can of mushroom sauce or ½ can of condensed mushroom soup if either is available, and 3 tablespoons of undiluted evaporated milk. When these are hot, fork in 6 eggs and, stirring, cook to the desired consistency. Or use powdered eggs and milk.

Trot the sizzling steak, cut in two, onto prewarmed plates. Saddle each half with the scrambled eggs. This recipe makes just enough breakfast for Colonel Whelen and me if no one else wanders into camp.

EGG IN A HOLE. Make a hole in the middle of a slice of bread or bannock. Toast one side of the slice with margarine or butter in a frypan. Turn over. Add more grease if the frypan seems dry. Then drop an egg into the hole and fry to suit, on one side only.

WHELEN SANDWICH. You'll need bacon, onion, eggs, cheese, seasoning, and patience enough to make seconds and maybe thirds. For each sandwich start 2 slices of bread toasting over the heat. Cut a slice of bacon into small bits. Fry these until they are crisp, pouring the excess grease into the camp shortening can. Fork the bacon together into a small rectangle and place a slice of onion atop it. Cook the onion until it begins to soften and tan.

Then break an egg over it. Puncture the yolk with the fork. Salt and pepper. Cover with a square of cheese. Cook slowly until the egg is done and the cheese has melted. Place each such serving between two slices of toast. If any watercress is handy, add several sprigs of that. With the average camp frypan you can usually have four such sandwiches going at once.

WELSH RABBIT. Melt 1 tablespoon margarine or butter in a pan. Add 1 tablespoon flour, ⅛ teaspoon pepper, and ¼ teaspoon salt. Mix thoroughly. Gradually stir in 2 cups of grated, shredded, or diced cheddar cheese, as aged and tangy as is available. Keep stirring over low heat until the cheese has melted. Heat ½ cup of milk and stir that in gradually and thoroughly. Add a slightly beaten fresh or reconstituted egg. Cook an additional 2 minutes. Serve at once on toast or hot crisp crackers.

APPLE CASSEROLE. Apples and cheese have always gone together, and this holds true when you combine them in a casserole. Special reflector baker and oven dishes such as the following help break the occasional monotony of cold rainy weather when your fire will be going anyway. You'll need:

    1 cup dried apples
    1½ cups water
    1½ cups soft bread crumbs
    1½ cups milk
    4 eggs
    1½ cups grated yellow cheese
    1 teaspoon salt
    ⅛ teaspoon black pepper
    ¼ teaspoon dried mustard
       paprika and dried parsley

Chop apples. Bring slowly to a boil in the water and simmer 5 minutes.

If the bread or bannock crumbs are not soft, soak them a few minutes in the milk. Beat the eggs well. Best cheese to use if you can is the old-fashioned yellow cracker-barrel variety, as sharp as you like. Mix the crumbs, milk, cheese, salt, pepper, and mustard. Add to the apples. Stir into the beaten eggs.

Pour into a shallow, well-greased baking dish. Bake in a moderately slow oven or reflector baker until the ingredients have become set and lightly browned on top. This should take about ½ hour. Sprinkle with paprika and dried parsley and call for everyone to heave to.

POOCH IN A POUCH. Let everyone impale a frankfurter, canned or fresh, on the peeled end of a sharpened green stick. Make some bannock dough (see chapter on breads). Roll out and cut into narrow, 5-inch-long ribbons. Or so mold a ball of dough between the palms. Spiral one of these strips around each of the "dogs." Press the dough firmly together at each end to hold it in place. Bake over the edge of a small campfire, turning slowly, for about 5 minutes or until done.

BAKED TOMATOES. Drain the juice from a large can of tomatoes. Use for beverage. Mix with the remaining solid portions: 1 cup cubed toast, 1 teaspoon salt, ½ cup sugar, and 2 tablespoons margarine. Spread this out in a greased pan or baking dish. Sprinkle with bread crumbs. Bake in a moderate oven or reflector baker 25 minutes.

NOODLES TO MACARONI

QUICK EGG NOODLES. Beat 2 eggs with ⅛ teaspoon salt until foamy. Blend with 4 tablespoons flour. Pour steadily in a thin stream into simmering broth, stirring all the time. Cook 2 minutes. Then serve immediately.

MACARONI, SPAGHETTI, NOODLES. A ¼ pound of any of these uncooked doubles in volume to about 2 cupfuls cooked and makes an average portion. Cook each such portion in 2 quarts of boiling water seasoned with 2 teaspoons salt.

Break the macaroni into small bits before cooking. Let the spaghetti and noodles gradually soften in contact with the boiling water and so adapt themselves to the pan. Stir occasionally to avoid sticking. Boil, uncovered, only until the macaroni or other paste is tender but still firm. Test by chewing. The time varies with different pastes but averages between 8 and 12 minutes. Drain immediately, as by holding the lid over the pan in such a way that just enough of an opening is left to allow the water to run off.

BAKED MACARONI AND CHEESE. Boil ½ pound macaroni in 4 quarts of water with 4 teaspoons of salt, according to the preceding directions. Cut ½ pound of cheese into cubes. Open a small can of tomatoes.

Alternate layers of cooked macaroni with cheese in a greased pan or baking dish, seasoning each layer with salt and pepper. Add 1 tablespoon of solid tomato to each layer. Then pour enough tomato over everything to come within ½ inch of the top. Roof with sliced onion if you want. Bake in a hot oven or reflector baker until well browned.

BEANS, ET AL

BEANS. The various dry beans and their cousins, the dry peas and lentils, are favorite old-time dehydrated foods. All provide hearty nourishment because of their carbohydrates which the body transforms into energy. They contain some B vitamins. Besides such minerals as iron and calcium, they furnish protein which the body needs for building and repairing its organs and tissues. They are, furthermore, both inexpensive and fairly easy to prepare.

Although split peas and lentils can be cooked without soaking, the ordinary beans may be soaked overnight. Preferably, however, they can be started by first bringing the water to a boil for 2 minutes. After they have then been soaked an hour, they will be ready to cook. The brief precooking, too, will guard against any souring if they are to be soaked in warm weather. Cooking should then be done in the same water, so as to preserve flavor and to conserve vitamins and minerals.

Here is the whole story:

Start with 1 cup of	Soak in water	Add 1 teaspoon salt; boil gently	Will yield at least
Black beans	3 cups	About 2 hours	2 cups
Blackeye beans	2½ cups	½ hour	2½ cups
Cranberry beans	3 cups	About 2 hours	2 cups
Great Northern beans	2½ cups	1 to 1½ hours	2½ cups
Kidney beans	3 cups	About 2 hours	2¾ cups
Lentils	2½ cups (No soaking needed)	½ hour	2½ cups
Lima beans, large	2½ cups	1 hour	2½ cups
Lima beans, small	2½ cups	About 45 minutes	2 cups
Navy (pea) beans	3 cups	About 2½ hours	2½ cups
Peas, split	Best made into soup as they break up easily during cooking		
Peas, whole	2½ cups	1 hour	2½ cups
Pinto beans	3 cups	About 2 hours	2½ cups

CAMP BAKED BEANS. "Take 3 cups of dried navy beans. Pick out any small pebbles you may find. Soak the beans overnight in cold water, and the next morning put to boil in a large kettle with a tablespoon of salt. Boil for about

2½ hours, adding boiling water as the fluid level goes down.

"Then drop in about a dozen 1-inch cubes of salt pork or bacon with the rind on it. Keep bubbling for about an hour and a half more or until the individual beans are soft, but not mushy. You have been keeping about 2 inches of water on top of the beans in the kettle. This water is now the finest of bean soup. Pour most of it into another container and serve while hot, but leave enough so that the beans are still quite damp.

"Then, usually the next day, place these beans about 2 inches deep in a pan, shift the cubes of pork or bacon to the top, sprinkle a little sugar over the entire surface, and bake in a reflector baker or oven for an hour or more, until they become a little brown on top." (Colonel Townsend Whelen)

BAKED BEANS. Soak a pound of small dry beans along with 6 thinly sliced onions overnight in enough cold water to cover. The next morning cook below the boiling point until the beans are done. Add water if necessary.

Cut ½ pound bacon or salt pork into 1-inch cubes. Mix 1 cup sugar, 2 tablespoons dry mustard, and 1 cup catsup. Now place alternate layers of this, the beans and onions, and the meat in a pot. Save enough bacon or pork with which to top everything generously. Bake in a moderate oven or reflector baker until crusty brown.

QUICK-COOKING BEANS. But if you are bean hungry and don't want to waste that much time in camp, you can heat up a meal of processed and cleaned quick-cooking beans in a few minutes. Directions are given on the packages.

Like the old German Erbswurst, pea and bean powders now available also make excellent and filling soups with a minimum of time and trouble. Stir such concentrates into hot water and bring everything to a simmer, making the soup as thick or thin as you like.

HOPPING JOHN. Start this, suggests my friend, H. S. Mathews, by bringing ½ cup washed blackeye beans to a boil for 2 minutes in 3 cups water. Then cover and allow to soak 1 hour. Add ¼ pound diced bacon or salt pork. Simmer, covered, 1 hour or until the beans are tender. Add

½ cup raw rice, plus a dried hot red pepper if you have one, and cook another 15 minutes or until the rice is tender. Add boiling water if more liquid is needed. Season to taste. This is really something when a campfire leaps at dry spruce logs, and the stars come out one by one.

PEA SOUP. Now and then there are few things more delicious when the bunch gets home, cold and agreeably tired from a long day's hunt, than a bowl of thick, hot pea soup. This sort of thaws everyone out and loosens the stomach kinks in preparation for more thorough enjoyment of that roast or steak.

Fast cooking split peas, both green and yellow, are now available that save the bother of overnight soaking and over-tedious cooking. Let a pound of these simmer until tender in 4 cups of meat stock, or in bouillon made by dissolving 4 chicken bouillon cubes in 4 cups of water. Then crush the peas with a spoon or fork and continue simmering, covered, along with salt and pepper to taste and a finely chopped onion.

The finishing touch, as far as I'm concerned, is furnished by those small chunks of bacon or salt pork scattered through the savory hotness. Put these in now. Here's the place, too, for that flavor-filled bacon rind you've been wondering what to do with. When everything is cooked, keep the soup hot and ready on the back of the fire.

LENTILS. Barely cover 1 cup of quickly cooking lentils with cold water, season with ½ teaspoon salt, and simmer until just tender.

Start 4 shredded or chopped strips of bacon in a cold frypan. When there is enough fat, add 4 diced onions. Stirring, cook until soft. Then add the lentils and mix thoroughly. Cook slowly for 20 minutes, covered unless there is an abundance of liquid. Season with paprika, parsley flakes, and if necessary with a little additional salt.

CORN MEAL

CORN MEAL MUSH. Mix 1 cup of corn meal with 1 cup of cold water. Get 3 cups of water, seasoned with 1 teaspoon salt, bubbling diligently. Pour in the corn meal mixture slowly and stir for 5 minutes or until the combination has thickened. Move to low heat for 30 minutes and occasionally stir. If it becomes necessary to thin this, use boiling water. A double boiler is a handy gadget when you're making corn meal mush or polenta. It's often easy to contrive one, as by arranging several pieces of silverware in the bottom of a pan of boiling water and setting the mush pot atop those.

If you prefer a thicker mush to begin with, use a total of 2 cups of water for every 1 cup of meal. Such mush may also be used with margarine as a vegetable, sliced cold for frying, or topped with molasses and milk for dessert.

POLENTA. Mix 1 cup yellow corn meal with 1 cup cold water and 1 teaspoon salt. Now get 3 cups of water simmering. Gradually stir in the corn meal mixture. Then, moving to the low heat, stir constantly about 5 minutes or until thickened.

Now pour a small layer into the bottom of a greased pan. Cover with liberal spoonfuls of canned tomatoes. Pour in more corn meal mush and top this time with slices of cheese. Do this until you have at least 4 layers. Finish off if you want with some sliced onions. Place in an oven or reflector baker and bake for 45 minutes or until the cheese has melted.

SCRAPPLE. "Take the head of a pig, wild boar, peccary, or any of the deer tribe. Remove eyes and tongue, then boil head in enough water to barely cover until the meat comes off the bones. Remove the meat from the stock, and let both cool, skimming most of the grease off the stock; strain the stock. Take 2 pounds of corn meal for every 3 pounds of meat. Bring the stock to a boil, slowly stir in the corn meal and cook to a medium-thick mush, adding a little hot water to thin it if there is not enough stock. Mix into each pound of meat ½ teaspoon salt, ¼ teaspoon black pepper, and a teaspoon of onion juice. Add the seasoned meat to the mush and cook in a double boiler for an hour. Then pour it into a greased pan and let it cool. To serve, cut this scrapple loaf into slices about ⅓ inch thick, like slices of bread, and fry until brown in a little bacon fat. Serve very hot. I had scrapple for breakfast twice a week for the first 21 years of my life. Fine grub." (Colonel Townsend Whelen)

RICE

The quickly cooking rices are a particular boon to outdoor cooks. Just follow the brief directions on the package.

Or if you want to boil some of the old fashioned variety, rub ½ cup of rice between the fingers in several changes of cold water, or in cold running water, until the water stays clear. Drain. Get 4 cups of water boiling briskly, put in 1 tablespoon salt, and then gradually add the rice. Lift the rice now and then with a spoon or fork to discourage sticking. Boil 20 minutes or until tender. Easy way to test is by biting or by rubbing a kernel between the fingers. There should be no hard spot in the center. Drain, saving the water for soup or mulligan. Rinse with hot water. Place the resulting 1½ cups or so of boiled rice near the fringes of the fire to dry.

CAMP RICE. Just what old trail cook Ted Boynton accomplished with rice would have been enough to assure his popularity with any pack horse outfit. Hewn down to indoor proportions for my wife's benefit, Ted's favorite recipe in that category went:

"Hack up 2 large onions and a fist-sized chunk of sow belly. That's salt pork, Vena, though bacon will do. Brown 'em a mite in a kettle. Add 2 cups of b'iling water and a cup of rice. B'il rice until soft. Don't do no stirring, for cripe's sake.

"Excuse me . . . Well, er, be heating half a big can of tomatoes, a teaspoon of salt, a tablespoon of sugar maybe, a teaspoon of celery seed if any's in camp, and a pinch of black pepper which with my hands is a quarter-teaspoon. Add these to the cooked rice. Sprinkle on grated cheese like . . . like aitch. Then you sure don't want no lost dudes wandering into camp for awhile."

OVEN RICE. Measure 2 cups boiling water into a pan

or baking dish. Add ½ teaspoon salt. Stir in 1 cup rice. Cover and bake in a moderate oven or reflector baker about 35 minutes or until tender.

FRIED RICE. The nutty flavor of this is so good with such repasts as steaks, chops, and fried grouse that sometimes you don't know in which direction to reach first for seconds. Stir and cook 2 cups boiled rice in 2 tablespoons fat in a frypan over low heat for about 5 minutes. Add 2 tablespoons chopped, preferably green onions and if you want a similar volume of cooked meat chopped and shredded into tiny bits. Cook this several minutes longer. Then break in 1 egg. Season with 2 teaspoons soy sauce or with salt to taste. Stir vigorously until the egg is set.

RICE WITH GAME. For rice with rabbit and other small game, melt 2 tablespoons margarine or butter in a pan. Add a chopped small onion, stirring until tender and tan. Gradually add 1 cup rice, shaking until the grains are coated with fat. Cook until lightly browned. Add 2 cups of the hot stock, cover, and simmer until the liquid is absorbed and the rice tender. Spread on the individual plates, add a slab of butter to each portion, and top with the meat.

GREEN RICE. Melt 2 tablespoons margarine or butter in a pan. Stir a chopped small onion in this until it is lightly browned. Add 2 cups cooked rice, 1 cup warm milk, and 1 tablespoon powdered parsley.

Beat 2 eggs with a fork. Mix with 1 teaspoon salt and 1 cup grated, shredded, or cubed cheese. Add these to the above. Mix thoroughly. Bake in a moderate oven or reflector baker for about 45 minutes or until firm.

Or try this version. Mix 2 cups of hot cooked rice with 2 tablespoons melted margarine and 1 tablespoon powdered parsley. If you can come by them, add small amounts of shredded watercress, young mustard, or dandelion leaves, etc. Season the savory result with salt to taste and serve.

PILAFF. Stir 1 cup raw rice in 3 tablespoons shortening in a frypan over low heat until the rice begins to tan. A small, chopped onion may also be included. Season with salt and pepper. Then pour on 2 cups broth or bouillon. Canned soup may be used instead, mushroom being a tasty choice. Cover the frypan and simmer over very low heat for about 30 minutes until the rice is tender and almost dry. If the rice is nearly dry, however, and is still hard in the center, add a bit more hot liquid and cook as long as necessary. Top with butter or margarine.

RISOTTO. Saute 2 small chopped onions in 3 tablespoons of shortening until soft. Add 1½ cups of the more solid parts of a can of tomatoes and stir and heat until bubbling. Add 3 cups of broth or bouillon, 1 teaspoon salt, and 1 cup raw rice. Cook covered over low heat for about 30 minutes or until the rice is tender and almost dry. Stir in ½ cup of shredded or grated cheese, sprinkle with paprika and powdered parsley, and serve hot.

WILD RICE. Wash this well in cold water. Stir ½ cup into 2 cups of boiling water, seasoned with ½ teaspoon salt. Cover and simmer without stirring for about 30 minutes or until the wild rice is tender.

Only drawback to this delicacy, unless you harvest it yourself for free, is the expense of the purple-black seed with its smoky sweetness, so excellent with game and poultry. However, there are a couple of other ways to approach the same distinctive flavor you'd come by after a hard day of harvesting this seed of tall freshwater grasses.

For one: mix 2 cups of regular hot boiled rice with ½ cup of hard bread or bannock crumbs that have been browned in 3 tablespoons of margarine or butter. Salt and pepper to taste.

For the other: if you happen to be in New Mexico or other pinon country when pine nuts are ready, gather a quantity of these. Then mix 1 cup of regular boiled brown rice with 1 tablespoon melted butter or margarine, salt and pepper to taste, and 2 tablespoons shelled pine nuts. I ate this first in the shadows of the tall Sangre de Cristo Mountains where a century before Kit Carson had likely sat down to some of the same.

A FASCINATING INTEREST

When the family is away on vacation together is an appropriate time for the cooks of the household to take as much of a rest as possible from culinary cares. One way to do this, while maintaining satisfactory relations with both appetites and digestions, is by scheduling a series of simple though hearty dishes.

Here are a few that not only fulfill these specifications but which have the added enhancement of combining tradition and color. They are special recipes of the North, so termed by the Hudson's Bay Company which, incorporated May 2, 1670, was already a century old before the United States was more than an absent-minded dent in one of Paul Revere's teapots.

"There is no mystery about cooking," this world's oldest trading corporation assures the future managers of its present fur trading posts, in cooking classes where the following dishes are among those shown to be quickly and easily prepared with materials normally available in out-of-the-way places. "You can become a good cook with a little practice, a dash of patience, and a pinch of common sense. Cooking can be a fascinating interest!"

ONE DISH MEAL. Variations on this theme are numerous, but here's a favorite at many H.B.C. trading posts.

    1   can kidney or lima beans
    1   can tomatoes
    1   can sausages
    1   small onion, chopped

Grease a baking pan. Combine the above in it. Season with salt, pepper, and 1 teaspoon sugar. Sprinkle with bread or bannock crumbs. Bake in a moderate oven 20 to 30 minutes.

CHEESE BALLS. Grate or chop preferably dry, stale cheese. Mix it with an equal volume of flour. Add salt and pepper to taste, ½ teaspoon mustard, and bind with a well beaten egg. Drop by the spoonful into hot fat and fry until a light brown. In the Far North they serve these over boiled macaroni, topped with tomato sauce hot from the fire.

STOVIES. Put 1 tablespoon of bacon drippings, margarine, or such in a frypan or baking dish. Peel 5 potatoes and slice them into the utensil. Salt and pepper to taste, cover tightly, and cook atop the heat or in an oven or reflector baker until tender, stirring occasionally. When the potatoes are nearly done, slice or dice one of the canned meats, add this to the potatoes, and finish cooking.

VEGETABLE CASSEROLE. You can get this started in a hurry by opening small cans of peas, corn, and tomatoes. You'll also need a cup of bread, bannock, or cracker crumbs, seasoned with 1 teaspoon salt and ⅛ teaspoon pepper. Arrange the vegetables in layers. Sprinkle each layer with the seasoned crumbs. Dot the top with margarine or crisscross it with strips of bacon. For a one-dish meal, cut any of the canned meats into small pieces and include layers of this. Bake 25 minutes in a moderate oven or reflector baker.

BADGER SQUAWS. Cut the contents of a small jar of dried beef into small pieces. Add to it ¼ cup of milk and 1 can of corn. Heat thoroughly. This goes well with crisp, fresh crackers.

IRISH SCALLOP. This is the Arctic Circle version. You'll need: 2 boiled potatoes, salt and pepper, and a can apiece of corned beef, mixed carrots and peas, and tomato soup. Grease a pan or baking dish. Spread the corned beef over the bottom. Cover with the carrots and peas, adding a little of the liquor and saving the rest for some other use. Slice the boiled potatoes over this. Salt and pepper to taste. Pour the can of tomato soup over everything. Bake in a moderate oven or reflector baker ½ hour.

TRAVELING WINTER TRAILS

On an outdoor trip anywhere, especially across ice and snow in weather so cold that the breath makes a continual fog, food is a consideration second only to water. The more drastic the conditions that may be encountered, the more essential it will be to plan the meals intelligently beforehand.

On short enough journeys, time and effort on the trail can be saved by cooking as much of the food as possible before heading into the whitened wilderness. You may find it worthwhile, too, to keep ahead of your appetite all the way by cooking the next day's meals at the previous night's camp. This is particularly true in regions where fuel is scarce, as high above the timber line or in the northern Land of Little Sticks.

Certain dried foods, augmented so as better to meet winter conditions, may as well be carried ready mixed. Flour, baking powder, margarine, salt, and sugar can be stowed in closed containers in proportions for individual bannocks. (See chapter on breads.) In extremely cold weather, use more than the accustomed amount of shortening in these bannocks to provide extra nourishment and to prevent the breadstuff from freezing hard. You'll appreciate a larger proportion of sugar, too.

Here are a few suggestions for rations for winter trails, tried personally above the frost-furred tree line in tall country or up under the aurora borealis in the Far North. They are recommended, too, by the Hudson's Bay Company for use by its own men in and about the red-roofed trading posts it still operates in the North.

ONE-DISH BEAN STEW. Bean stew makes a nourishing and palatable dish, particularly when the still white cold is so extreme that wood smoke, instead of coiling out of sight, spreads above the campfire like an enormous banner. The preparation of this one-dish meal is commenced back at the base by soaking dried beans overnight. Partially bake or boil these. Mix in any kind of fresh or canned meat cut into very small segments. Add canned tomatoes. Flavor with molasses, spices, and if you want with beef extract.

Cook until the beans and meat are well done. Then pour the mixture into a shallow pan and allow to freeze. When frozen, break into small pieces and carry in a cotton bag. To use, simply heat what you want in a pan along with a little water.

When carrying frozen foods under such conditions, be sure to keep them frozen hard until they are required for use. Do not take any more of an item than you immediately require into a heated place. Leave the remainder in the cold, out of the way of hungry animals both small and large.

CARRYING FOOD IN COLD WEATHER. Any bacon should be sliced before one sets off on such a trip. It may also be partly cooked beforehand. The slices, in either event, can be frozen separately and carried this way until needed. Potatoes freeze into something resembling marble, so if you want to pack along some of these, boil them until they are a bit on the hard side. Slice thinly and put out to freeze in individual pieces. Carry the frozen chips in a cotton food sack. They will go well heated in the fat from fried bacon.

MEAT BALLS. Meat balls will provide another one-dish repast. Mince up venison or any kind of meat. Add a little milk, some bread crumbs, potatoes or any other vegetables you want, and whatever spices you prefer. Grated cheese and tomato catsup add to the taste. Shape into flattened meat balls. Partially cook and then freeze them. They will be ready to eat on short notice on the trail or in camp. Merely thaw them out and heat them in a pan with some water. You can prepare fish balls in the same general manner, substituting fresh or canned fish for the meat.

CEREAL

Prepare according to the instructions on the package.

A favorite camp cereal of a lot of us is oatmeal. The quickly cooking variety saves time. Way I do is ready it the night before by adding ½ cup oatmeal and ½ teaspoon salt to 2 cups cold water. A ¼ cup of raisins, more or less, plump out overnight to add flavor. The next morning I hunch far enough out of the sleeping bag to get the fire going, put on the covered pan, and let the contents come to a boil before setting it to one side for a few minutes. Then I either pour in evaporated milk straight out of the can, or in colder weather add a liberal spoonful of margarine, and begin satisfying the inner man.

This is really luxury when deepening cold has condensed, close above the throbbing earth, a twinkling ceiling of ice crystals to which the smoke of your solitary campfire ascends in an unwavering pillar.

CHAPTER 9

THE VEGETABLE STORY

BAKED POTATOES. A good way to cook this native American vegetable is to bake the large ones in their skins in hot ashes, not glowing coals, until they become pretty well blackened on the outside. They're done when a thin, sharpened stick will run through their middles easily. Rake out, break in half, and serve at once with margarine and salt.

A more complicated way to go about this on occasion, in camps near civilization, is to cut well scrubbed potatoes lengthwise into 3 slabs. Lay thin slices of onion, salted and peppered, between these sections. Then reassemble each potato, wrap in a sheet of heavy foil or several thicknesses of lightweight foil, and bake in a nest of ashes among hot coals for about a half hour or until done, turning once during this period.

Potatoes may be scrubbed, rubbed with melted fat or salad oil, pricked with a fork, (or prepared as above and held together with skewers) and baked in a hot oven or reflector baker. This method is handiest when combined with some other cooking, as about an hour of baking is required.

BOILED POTATOES. Scrub enough potatoes, choosing those of equal size as far as possible so they'll cook uniformly. Cover with boiling water, seasoned with 1 teaspoon salt for every 3 potatoes. Simmer, covered, 20 to 30 minutes or until an inserted fork indicates they're tender. Drain, peel if you wish, season with salt and pepper, and cover to keep warm and to prevent sogginess.

Or, particularly if you're in a hurry, peel. Cut into uniform pieces. Drop into cold water for a short time to prevent darkening. Cook, covered, in a small amount of boiling salted water until done. Then handle as above.

MASHED POTATOES. If you're going to mash your

potatoes, peel and slice them rather thin. Boil in salted water until very well done. Drain and return to the heat until the remainder of the water has evaporated. Mash—a round bottle being a handy backwoods implement at this stage. Salt to taste. Sprinkle on a few flakes of pepper. Add 1 tablespoon melted margarine, and if you want ¼ cup hot milk for every 2 medium-size potatoes or their equivalent. Whip with a fork until fluffy. Top with a little paprika and powdered parsley, if you have any, and serve at once.

POTATO CAKES. An easy way to make potato cakes is to shape cold mashed potatoes as desired, then to cook them slowly in margarine or drippings, turning once, until they are tan and crusty.

POTATO ROULETTES. Add ¼ cup milk, 4 tablespoons grated or shredded cheese, and your idea of enough salt and pepper to 2 cups mashed potatoes. Beat until light. Drop by the spoonful into a greased pan. Bake in moderate oven or reflector baker.

FRIED POTATOES. "The most tasty way I know of to fry camp potatoes," opines my writing partner, Colonel Whelen, "is first to boil them peeled for 20 minutes, then to slice them into ¾ inch cubes. Have ¼ inch of lard or other cooking fat sizzling in the frypan. Put in several onions that have been chopped up fine. Before these have become much more than a light brown, add the cubed potatoes while the grease is still very hot.

"Now remove the frypan to a part of the fire where the fat will just simmer. Cover with a lid or tin plate. Let the contents bubble and cook in their own steam, occasionally giving them a turn with a spoon. Add salt and plenty of black pepper. Serve just before the potatoes begin to get hard on the outside."

FRYPAN POTATOES. Start 3 slices of bacon in a cold frypan and cook until crisp. Remove the bacon and pour all but a tablespoon of the drippings into the camp shortening can. Add a sliced and chopped onion, forking the bits around until they have started to brown. Break up the bacon and return it to the pan. Slice in 4 potatoes.

Flatten out the slices and cover them at once with a

minimum amount of water. Bring this to a simmer and keep the potatoes cooking until they've started to break to pieces and to thicken the liquid. Add hot water if any more is required. Salt, pepper, and eat as soon as the potatoes are ready.

HASHED BROWN POTATOES. Heat 4 tablespoons margarine, cooking oil, or other shortening in the frypan. Add enough potatoes, peeled and cut very fine. Salt and pepper. Then press down and cook over low heat until brown and crisp on the bottom. Loosen this crust with a knife. Then cover the frypan with a plate and invert it quickly, so that the potatoes will come out with the brown underside on top.

POTATO BALLS. Cut into very small pieces 2 large, peeled, raw potatoes and 1 small onion. Beat an egg with ½ teaspoon salt. Mix everything thoroughly and drop by the tablespoonful into hot, deep fat. Remove when brown, drain, and serve hot.

POTATO AND ONION PUFF. Cook equal quantities of potato and onion together. Mash. Add milk, margarine, and 1 or 2 well-beaten eggs. Beat until fluffy. Season with salt and pepper. Spoon into a greased pan. Top with grated or sliced cheese if you want. Bake until browned.

HASH. Colonel Whelen hustles together hash by chopping cooked meat with an equal volume of boiled potatoes. Salt and pepper to taste, and add one or all of the following: chopped onion, fresh or powdered celery, and parsley flakes. Moisten the mixture with soup stock, bouillon, thin milk, or water. Spread thickly on a greased pan. Set over slow heat 20 minutes until the bottom of the hash is well browned, or cook in a reflector baker with moderate heat.

BAKED HASH.

1	can corned beef
2	cups cold boiled rice
3	diced raw potatoes
1	can tomato soup
¼	cup bread crumbs
	salt and pepper
	margarine

Break up the corned beef with a fork. One of the other canned meats may be used instead, of course, in which case it may be easier to cube it. Place the meat, rice, and diced raw potatoes in alternate layers in a greased pan or baking dish. Season well. Empty a can of tomato soup over them. Sprinkle the top with ¼ cup of bread crumbs, dot with margarine, and bake in a moderate oven 20 minutes.

POTATOES H.B.C. Chop 5 or 6 cold boiled potatoes very fine and arrange them in a greased baking pan. You'll also need:

2	tablespoons margarine
1	tablespoon flour
1½	cups milk
¼	teaspoon pepper
1	teaspoon salt
1	egg
¼	cup grated cheese
¼	cup dry crumbs
1	tablespoon melted margarine

Make a cream sauce of the margarine, flour, milk, and seasonings. Add the egg and grated cheese. Pour this sauce over the potatoes, allowing it to run through the pieces. Cover with buttered crumbs, made by melting a tablespoon of margarine and mixing this gently with a fork into ¼ cup of dry bread, cracker, or bannock crumbs. Bake in a hot oven or reflector baker 15 minutes.

POTATO PANCAKES. Here is an old German way of making potato pancakes which are especially delicious outdoors, particularly when served with such wild fare as roast goose or venison pot roast. "They aren't the lightest food in the world," admits Duncan Hines who suggested them to me. "But like most German cookery they impart to the diner a feeling of solidity that is not quite heaviness. If I were to describe it in a word (and I am not by any means sure that I can) the word would be 'honest,' for it fills the hollow spaces and it is good and, after all, what more can we ask of food?"

1½	pounds raw potatoes, peeled
2½	tablespoons flour

1   teaspoon salt
2   eggs beaten
3   slices bacon, diced (optional)
    vegetable shortening

"Grate the potatoes and drain off the juice. Add the remaining ingredients to the potatoes and mix well. In a pan, heat enough shortening to make ¼ inch. The shortening should be sizzling hot. Drop the potato mixture from a spoon into the hot fat. Fry, turning once, until golden brown on both sides. Dry on absorbent paper and serve with applesauce."

POTATO SALAD. Here's my favorite year-around recipe for potato salad, unless you already have one of your own. For use as a main dish for 2 people, scrub and boil 6 medium potatoes, removing them from the salted water while they're still hard. Peel as sparingly as possible so as to preserve the utmost flavor and nourishment. Hard boil 6 eggs at the same time; then plunge them under cold water and peel them.

Slice some of the hot potato into an earthenware bowl, if one is at hand, or into whatever else is handy. Slice some egg atop it. Now pour on a liberal amount of preferably olive oil or of salad oil. Douse on about ¼ as much vinegar. Salt and pepper. Sprinkle on a very small amount of powdered garlic if you have any and if you don't object to it. Paprika and dried parsley will add eye and taste appeal. Repeat, keeping on doing this until you've used all the potatoes and eggs. Cover so that the flavor will permeate everything.

Preparing this salad half a day or more ahead of time will give the best results. Take off the lid once or twice and carefully, so as not to break up the eggs and potatoes, spoon the mixture around a bit to redistribute the oil and vinegar.

BOILED ONIONS. Peel the onions. These will cook more uniformly if all are about the same size. Large onions may be sliced before boiling. If you want, carry on these operations with the vegetables held under water.

Cover with salted boiling water. Cook, uncovered, some

20 to 35 minutes or until the onions are tender but not broken. The water, incidentally, will be excellent for soups and such. Drain, add your idea of enough butter or margarine, and season with salt and pepper.

ONION SOUP. A good time to make this is when you have plenty of broth on hand from game. Or you can use canned beef bouillon, bouillon cubes, etc.

Saute 2 large sliced onions very slowly in 2 tablespoons of margarine or butter. When they are just barely tender, but not brown, add 4 cups of broth or bouillon. Simmer slowly for 20 minutes. Season to taste with salt and pepper. Either serve as is or, if you've plenty of provisions and would like to start the meal off with something a little special, with the solids strained out to leave a clear soup.

ONION SOUP AU GRATIN. Saute 2 large, sliced onions very slowly in 2 tablespoons of margarine or butter. When they have become lightly browned, add 4 cups of broth, canned bouillon, or water in which 4 beef or chicken bouillon cubes have been dissolved. Salt to taste. Then simmer 15 minutes.

In the meantime, cut a substantial slice of preferably sourdough bread for everyone. Spread lightly with prepared mustard if you want. Cover with grated or sliced cheese and toast until crisp in the reflector baker or oven. If no reflector baker or oven is available, the bread can be toasted on anything from a campfire grate to a forked green stick, then turned, covered on the hot side with cheese, and very slowly toasted on the other side until crisp throughout. Put each slice in a bowl, breaking the toast into bits if necessary, and cover with the hot soup.

ONION SAUCE. An easy way to make this is to combine a package of dehydrated onion soup mix with 2½ cups of boiling water. Cover and simmer 10 minutes. In the meantime, stir 2 tablespoons flour into ½ cup cold water. Add this bit by bit to the simmering mix. Cook, stirring, until sufficiently thickened.

WHITE SAUCES. For the fat in these white sauces, a good idea is to use margarine, butter, and sometimes bacon drippings for extra flavor if the sauce is to be combined with mildly flavored foods. One of the bland cooking fats or oils will be entirely satisfactory if the sauce is to be used with more highly flavored foods.

	Thin	Medium	Thick
Milk:	1 cup	1 cup	1 cup
Flour:	1 tablespoon	2 tablespoons	3 to 4 tablespoons
Fat:	1 tablespoon	1 to 2 tablespoons	2 to 3 tablespoons

Melt the fat. Blend in the flour to make a smooth mixture. Slowly add the milk and cook over very low heat until thickened, stirring constantly. Add salt to taste, about ¼ teaspoon of salt per cup of milk usually being sufficient. Then cook 3 to 5 minutes longer, stirring occasionally.

ROAST CORN. You'll want sweet, young corn for this. Carefully strip the husks down to the end of the ear, leaving them attached. Pull off the silk. Soak the corn in cold salted water for ½ hour. Drain. Then brush the kernels with margarine or butter and sprinkle them with salt and a little pepper. Pull the husks back up around the corn and twist tightly together. Make a hollow of coals at the edge of the campfire, cover it with an inch of ashes, lay in the corn, cover with more ashes and then hot coals, and roast about ½ hour. Peel the husks back again and use as a handle.

If you're where there is green corn, probably aluminum foil is available, too. If you want, then, wrap and twist each ear tightly in foil before consigning it to the ash-insulated coals. This way you can poke the corn around occasionally to assure more even cooking, and even take a look, while it is roasting to taste.

VEGETABLES IN GENERAL

Few raw vegetables except for potatoes, onions, occasional corn and such, and the wild varieties detailed in a separate chapter are cooked in most vacation camps. The following general table, therefore, will save you time and trouble.

As you no doubt already know, heating fresh vegetables destroys a certain amount of their food value, so they should be cooked as quickly as possible and only until tender. Some of the valuable food elements also seep out into water, so vegetables should be boiled in the least possible amount of fluid, and this liquid should be used for soups, sauces, gravies, beverages, etc. Leafy vegetables, in fact, may profitably be lifted directly from the rinse into the pan and cooked without added water. Otherwise, start the vegetables in boiling water to reduce cooking time. The pan should ordinarily be covered.

If the vegetables are left in large pieces, fewer of the important nutrients will either oxidize or escape. Though washing is essential, vegetables should not be allowed to soak. A small brush is a help, for cooking in skins whenever possible will retain the maximum goodness. Potatoes, for example, are preferably scrubbed and boiled or baked with the skins intact. Matter of fact, a lot of us prefer eating skins and all except, of course, when the hide is badly charred from roasting in the campfire.

As for the practice of adding baking soda to vegetables, this is a prime destroyer of vitamins. The way many of us chronic wood loafers figure, if you're going to the trouble of fetching and preparing vegetables, you may as well get the maximum good out of them.

TIMETABLE FOR COOKING VEGETABLES

Vegetable	Boiling Minutes	Baking (Hot Oven) Minutes
Artichokes, French	20-30	
Jerusalem	15-25	
Asparagus (whole or butts)	10-25	
(tips)	5-15	
Beans, green wax (whole, pieces)	15-25	
Beans, lima	20-30	
Beets, young (small, whole)	30-45	40-60
mature (small, whole)	45-90	60-120
Beet greens	5-15	
Broccoli (stalks & buds)	8-25	
Brussels sprouts (whole)	8-20	
Cabbage, green (quarters)	5-15	
green (shredded)	3-10	
Cabbage, red (shredded)	8-12	
Carrots, young (whole)	10-25	35-45
young (sliced)	8-20	30-40
Carrots, mature (whole)	20-30	60
mature (sliced)	12-20	

Cauliflower (whole)	10-20	
(flowerets)	8-10	
Celery	10-20	
Chard, Swiss	10-25	
Corn, on cob	5-15	
Eggplant (sliced)	10-20	
Endive, curly	10-20	
Kale	10-25	
Kohlrabi (sliced, quarters)	20-40	
Leeks	12-35	
Okra (sliced)	10-30	
Onions, green (scallions)	8-15	
mature (quarters, whole)	20-35	50-60
Parsnips (quarters, whole)	10-30	30-45
Peas, green	5-20	
Potatoes, Irish (medium, whole)	20-40	45-60
Potatoes, Irish (quartered)	15-25	
Potatoes, sweet (whole)	20-35	30-45
sweet (quartered)	15-25	
Rutabagas (sliced, diced)	20-30	
Salsify (sliced, cubed)	15-20	
Spinach	5-10	
Squash, winter, Hubbard (pieces)	20-40	40-60
winter, Acorn (halves)	10-20	60
summer (sliced, halves)	10-20	30
Tomatoes	15-20	15-30
Turnips (whole, halves)	20-40	
(slices, cubes)	10-30	
Turnip greens	10-25	

Chapter 10

EATING FOR FREE

Think back to your really memorable camping, fishing, and hunting vacations. Isn't there a double-barreled combination that points up every one of them? It doesn't much matter if you were tenting in one of the national parks, stalking whitetails Down East, tracking grizzly in pelting Spring snows, or surf casting with the family for Pacific yellowtail. Wasn't a large part of the fun: (1) the grub, (2) and the kind of appetite that let you enjoy it!

Ever notice something else? Maybe you're one of the tribe who don't go much for liver most of the year. If so, how about breakfast the morning after you've been the first warrior in camp to bag a deer? Do you periodically listen to family complaints about fish bones during the workaday weeks? Then doesn't the conversation take a turn after the wife and kids have had a hand in filling that platter with bluegills?

Here's another thing you can mark down in your diary. The same deal will even work with spinach, when it's a wild spinach and you've gathered it yourself.

It will also work with numerous other wild vegetables and fruits. These grow everywhere. If you pack your rods and rifles far enough North, as a matter of fact, there is no nonedible vegetation whatsoever with the exception of one breed of mushrooms. Some of the lichens are bitter, it's true. But when this acidity is soaked out, such a variety as the familiar Iceland Moss is so nutritious that it's packaged and widely sold as food and tonic for convalescents.

The pick of the wild foods will upgrade your meals while you're fishing, hunting, or camping. That's not all. Back home they'll keep right on guaranteeing you some of the best eating there is—plus the continued incentive to get outdoors in the woods and fields, where the really healthy appetites are born.

PICK INSTEAD OF PACK. A lot of times you want to get a few miles deeper into remote country where the hunting and fishing are better. The outfit you're packing is just too heavy, however. So, reluctantly, you settle for less. This usually means you have to work harder for even the small ones. As for those record-busting trophies, they're just not around.

The next time, you figure, you're going to travel lighter and farther. With careful planning you find you can save weight and space on nearly every item in your outfit. When it comes to grub, though, you're still going to need a minimum of 2¼ pounds of reasonably waterfree provisions each day to keep enjoying yourself under full power.

Yet there's a way you can reasonably lop a pound a day off those basic food requirements and still have the rugged, tasty, healthy meals you need to make it a real vacation. This is a method once used by our frontiersmen and still employed today by sportsmen, explorers, and other experienced outdoorsmen who regularly journey into the most inaccessible regions of this continent. It's a technique you can adopt with every assurance of success from the start. I know, for I've used it with increasing satisfaction for the past two decades.

The grubstake I generally pack on extended hunts when space and weight are at a premium includes: flour, oatmeal, side bacon, oleomargarine, sugar, salt, rice, jam, tea, and either baking powder for bannock or baking soda for sourdough. For those days when game is going to keep me pretty well occupied, I add a few of the dehydrated vegetables and fruits.

What about the sacks of onions and spuds, that bag of oranges, the bunches of celery, odd cabbages and cauliflowers, lemons, carrots, parsnips, and the occasional head of lettuce I used to try to keep in a moistened cloth bag just a couple days longer? They stay where they are until I get back to where transportation is no longer a problem. So do those heavy cans of berries. Why bother with the bulk, heft, care, waste, and expense of such vegetables and fruits when you can pick them as you need them?

Besides meaning the difference between an easy pack and a troublesome one, adding from season to season the recognition of a couple more wild edibles can become an engrossing and practical hobby, as well as a thrifty and healthful way of introducing new delicacies to the table. You don't even have to lug your pots and pans into wilderness country to begin finding wild eatables. They grow everywhere.

There are actually thousands of wild eatables, far too many to cover in this chapter. If you are particularly interested in the subject, however, you'll find quite a few pictured and discussed in my Stackpole book devoted entirely to the problems suggested by the title, *Living Off the Country*. A very large number, along with detailed drawings, also appear in another of my books published by the Stackpole Company, *How To Go Live in the Woods on $10 a Week*.

You don't need to be any sort of an expert to begin taking immediate advantage of this free grub. There are so many edible wild fruits and vegetables, in fact, that their very number scares off a lot of people before they start. There's no good reason for this last. Recognizing a half dozen or so will do the trick. That's all of a choice many old woodsmen bother with, anyway.

As far as that goes, just about every camper, fisherman, and hunter reading this already knows at least a dozen wild eatables, although perhaps not as sources of nourishment. You're afraid you may be an exception? Then here's a tip. Don't wager any folding money against yourself until we've had a look at some of the more widespread of the free foods.

ROSE HIPS. For example, there is a familiar berry that, although you've maybe never sampled it, has the flavor of fresh apples. More important, its juice is from 6 to 24 times richer in Vitamin C than orange juice. Throughout much of the continent you can pick all you want the greater part of the year, even when temperatures fall a booming 60° below zero. As for recognizing this fruit, no one with a respect for brambles and a modicum of bush savvy is going to get the wrong thing by mistake. It is the rose hip, the ordinary seed pod of roses everywhere.

These rose hips have a delicate flavor that's delicious. They're free. They're strong medicine, to boot. Studies in Idaho found the scurvy-preventing vitamin in the raw pulp running from 4,000 to nearly 7,000 milligrams per pound. Daily human requirements, to give you a yardstick, are estimated to be 60 to 75 milligrams.

Three rose hips, the food experts say another way, have as much Vitamin C as an orange. We don't pay much attention to these gratuitous vitamins in the United States and Canada. But in England during World War II, some 5 mil-

ROSE HIPS.

lion pounds of rose hips were gathered from the roadsides and put up to take the place of then scarce citrus fruits. Dried and powdered, rose hips are sold in Scandinavian countries for use in soups, for mixing with milk or water, to make hot and cold drinks, for sprinkling over cereals, etc., all of which they do admirably.

You get the good from this cousin of the apple, one of the many members of the rose family, whether you eat it off the bushes, cut up in salad, baked in cake or bannock, or boiled into jam or jelly. Matter of fact, plain dried rose hips are well worth carrying in a pocket for lunching on like raisins. To prepare them for this latter use, just cut each in half. Remove the central core of seeds. Dry the remaining shell-like skin and pulp quickly, as in a cool oven or in a kettle suspended above the fringes of a small campfire.

What I like to do with rose hips, when I catch my wife Vena in a cooking mood, is turn them into syrup. Snip the bud ends from a freshly gathered batch. Then cover the fruit with water and boil rapidly until soft. Strain off the juice. Return the pulp to the kettle, add enough water to cover, and make a second extraction. For every 2 cups of juice you end up with, add 1 cup of sugar. Boil until thick. Pour into sterilized bottles. That's all. Poured over steaming sourdough hotcakes blue-black winter mornings when the Northern Lights are still ablaze, this syrup never lasts us long.

Here's an extra hint. Don't throw away the pulp. Press it through a sieve to remove seeds and skins. Add half as much sugar as pulp. Put in clove, cinnamon, and any other spices or flavoring agents to taste. Heat covered until the sugar is dissolved. Then uncover and cook slowly until thick, stirring to prevent sticking. Pack in sterilized jars and seal. Voila! Fruit butter!

BERRIES. It's difficult to hunt or fish across a corner of North America, from the very deserts to the glittering ice cakes of the Arctic Ocean, that doesn't regularly yield wholesome and often delectable wild fruit. Until you count them, you may be surprised at how many you can name.

There are the numerous common grapes and cherries and

plums, the uniquely flavored little wintergreens, and there
are the crab apples that thrive wild from the southern states

AMERICAN RED CURRANT. These spell jams, pies,
and jellies.

to the 49th State. There are the startlingly red but less familiar berries of the mountain ash that, crushed in water and sweetened, give a drink like lemonade. There are also the reddish-orange soapberries which, beaten with a little

AMERICAN RED RASPBERRY.

Even expert botanists have trouble trying to tell the numerous members of the raspberry family apart. Six are illustrated on this and following 3 pages. I don't bother, I just eat them.

sugar, foam into a salmon-colored froth that backwoodsmen still serve up as a pudding.

But there are the common blueberries, gooseberries, cranberries, and their ilk that every year fill out by the thousands of tons. And there are such other abounding members of the rose family as strawberries, blackberries, and raspberries—whose young stems and stalks are also tasty, and whose very leaves can be profitably steeped for tea.

THIMBLEBERRY.

TRAILING RASPBERRY.

CLOUDBERRY.

NAGOONBERRY.

SALMONBERRY.

PRICKLY PEAR. There's also the unlikely prickly pear. You don't know this one? Ever notice the little thorny knobs, ranging from the size of apricots to the size of large lemons, that bulge from the padlike joints of cactus? Those are the fellows. Actually, the spine-bristling skin of this fruit of the cactus is so unmistakable that any difficulties lie not in identifying but in picking. An easy way to go about this? With leather gloves and a knife.

STRAWBERRY.   Various forms of these are familiar everywhere.

BOG CRANBERRY.   Found in northern climes the world over, this member of the cranberry family is smaller than commercial varieties but is at least equally delicious.

Depending on the kind of cactus, the ripened colors of prickly pears vary from tawny green and purplish black to the choicest of them all—the big red fruits of the large *Opuntia Megacantha* of the continental Southwest. To eat any of these Indian figs, as they're also known, slice off the ends, slit the hide lengthways, and scoop out the pulp.

LOWBUSH CRANBERRY. Picked in the original 48 States and northward over the entire top of the globe, these cook up with sugar into delectable jams, jellies, and sauces.

BOG BLUEBERRY.

BARKS. Speaking of unlikely foods, there are forests of them. If in the back of your mind you figure that one day you may possibly be up against it for grub, perhaps because an accident to a companion keeps you in camp after your regular supplies are exhausted, it'll be reassuring to remember that the inner bark of the familiar birches is a historically important emergency food. You can eat it as is. The flavor, although sweetish, is also neutral enough to warrant its being added in chunks and strips to soups and mulligans. It retains its aromatic spiciness even when dried for easier packing.

As far as that goes, the lodgepole and other pines have an inner bark that is eatable both raw and cooked. A fishing crony of mine in the Yukon goes so far as to assert that this is at its finest when scraped from the south side of a young pine while the sap is rising. The poplar's sweetish sap layer, between the wood and the bitter outside bark, is also sustaining both raw and cooked.

You're not ordinarily going to bother doing it, but it may also be handy one day to know that dwindling flour stores have been augmented more than once with the dried and powdered inner barks of such trees as the poplar, birch, slippery elm, and the pines. I've eaten cakes made of straight lodgepole pine flour that was cooked, incidentally, with the white lard rendered from black bear fat. This breadstuff is dry and somewhat flat tasting. But it's an outdoor grub that will stand by you in a pinch. Realizing deep down that no matter what emergency overtakes you in the wilderness you're not likely to have to go hungry—well, I suppose that's one more reason why an individual gets to feel safe, secure, and never more relaxed than when out with rod, gun, or camping outfit in the primitive places.

GREENS. So you didn't think you knew at least a dozen wild eatables? If I were a wagering man, I'd be willing to lay odds that you've passed that dozen mark already. And we haven't even mentioned the wild lettuces, spinaches, and some of the other fine greens that are abundant nearly everywhere.

If you have ever sat down to a well prepared feed of wild vegetables, maybe you've noticed that they seem to taste better than domesticated varieties. I'll let you in on a trade secret. They are better.

Green leafy vegetables, to give just one example, deteriorate very quickly. Even when purchased as fresh as obtainable from the finest nearby market, they'll already have lost a sizeable proportion of vitamins. Some of the food values of greens diminish as much as one-third during the first hour after picking. But gather them fresh from nature's own garden and eat them while they're at their tastiest, and you'll enjoy the best they have to offer. It's a happy way to sharpen a satisfactory hunger, too.

LAMB'S-QUARTER. In a lot of hunting and fishing camps the acknowledged pick of the edible greens is lamb's-quarter. The tender tops of this wild spinach, which has none of the strong taste of market varieties, are delicious from early spring to frost-withering fall. The entire young plant is good from the ground up. Even from the older ones a quantity of tender leaves can usually be stripped. However, the pale green leaves with their mealy-appearing underneaths and the slim stalks are not the only taste-tempting compo-

LAMB'S-QUARTER.

nents of this green, also widely known as pigweed and goosefoot. Indians long used the ripe seeds for cereal and for grinding into meal. The tiny gleaming black discs, which develop from elongated dense clusters of small green flowers, are also handy for giving a pumpernickel complexion to camp breads.

Along with other of the more tender leafy greens, lamb's-quarter can be given a little more taste on occasion with the help of a vinegar sauce. Such a flavorful acid also tends to

DANDELION.

preserve the vitamins in such vegetables. Alkalies, on the other hand, such as the commonly but inadvisedly used baking soda, destroy an unnecessary proportion of these food values.

For 4 cups of loosely packed greens, make with: 1 small onion, 4 slices bacon, ¼ cup vinegar, ¼ teaspoon salt, and pepper to taste. Shred the greens if they are large. Dice the onion. Mix. Then chop up the bacon and fry it until the bits become brown and brittle. Put in the vinegar, salt, and pepper and bring to a simmer. You now have two choices.

SEASHORE PLANTAIN. This representative of the plantain family, which is distributed throughout the world, finds favor whether used raw in salads or cooked like spinach.

You may pour the sauce over the raw greens. Or you may add the greens to the sauce and cook over low heat until they are limp. In either event, serve immediately.

PLANTAIN. Plantain is almost as good as lamb's-quarter. Furthermore, plantain is as well known to most of us as are the similarly prepared and eaten dandelions, although not usually by name. It is the short stemless potherb whose broadly elliptic green leaves rise directly from the root about a straight central spike. This singular spike blossoms, although you've possibly never noticed it, with minute greenish flowers that later turn into seeds. At any rate, you see plantain all over the world; even growing through sidewalks in New York, San Francisco, and Boston.

Plantain leaves make excellent greens. Fact is, the greener they are, the richer they are in Vitamins A and C and in minerals. Way I like them is boiled. What holds for plantain, when it comes to this common if often murderous method of cookery, goes for the other wild greens as well. Unless it means standing over a riled trail cook with a cleaver, try to see that all these are cooked only until just tender and still slightly crisp. This takes a surprisingly brief time. Even with such a formidable green as young nettles, which like prickly pears are best gathered with leather gloves and a knife, once the salted water has reached the boiling point and the dark green nettles have been dropped in, they'll be tender almost immediately and ready for that crowning pat of butter or margarine as soon as they're cool enough to eat.

The simple gimmick with these wild vegetables is to start them in a minimum amount of boiling water and to cook them, covered, as rapidly and briefly as possible. Young plantain and such can actually be lifted directly from the rinse to the saucepan and cooked without added water. For two liberal servings of slightly older greens, ½ cup water and ½ teaspoon salt will do the job. When the greens become tougher, a full cup of water may be required. Any of the vitamin-and-mineral-swarming fluid remaining should be used, as in soups, gravies, sauces and the like, unless there's some reason against this such as unusual bitterness. Me, I drink it.

WILD GREEN SOUP. Speaking of soups, though, here's a cream of wild green soup that really starts the mouth tingling; especially when you come in dehydrated from a day of hunting or fishing and get that first whiff of it, all

NETTLES.

GOOSETONGUE. Here is another of the plantains. Used like the rest, it is also sometimes canned for winter use.

steaming and savory. To go with 2 cups of chopped or
scissored young mustard greens—or one of the other spicier
greens such as dandelions, watercress, young wild radish
tops, etc., if mustard isn't at hand—start slowly heating a
quart of milk, not allowing it to boil.

Meanwhile, melt 2 tablespoons of butter, margarine,
bacon drippings, or any other edible fat in a saucepan over
low heat. Gradually stir in 1½ teaspoons salt, ⅛ teaspoon
pepper, and 2 tablespoons flour. Add a finely minced small
onion. Then pour in the hot milk bit by bit. Cook gently for
5 minutes. Drop in the greens and, stirring occasionally,
continue to heat just below the boiling point until these are
just tender. Sprinkle with paprika if you have any. Serve
at once.

MUSTARD. Mustard, which flourishes wild over most
of the globe, is universally recognizable because of its brilliant yellow flowers that become almost solid gold across
many a field and hillside. This green, whether used in soup
or elsewhere, is most agreeable when it first appears. The
young stalks from which the leaves grow directly are not
hard to identify, particularly as older mustard is often
blooming in the same patch. These slightly peppery leaves
are enjoyable raw. So are the young flowers with their then
subtle pungency. The entire young plant goes well cooked
with fish and game.

Even when you come upon wild mustard after it's grown
old and tough, the easily gathered seeds are hard to equal
for garnishing salads, adding to pickles and such for that
extra seasoning, giving a final authority to barbecue sauces,
and lending a wisp of zip and zest to venison mulligans.
Mustard's very name comes from its seeds, being a corruption of *must-seeds* which harks back to ancient Roman-oc-
cupied Britain when these were processed by saturating
them in a solution of grape juice or *must* as it was sometimes called.

Incidentally, table mustard can be made in camp by
finely grinding wild mustard seeds, as between two stones,
and adding enough water to make a paste. After that it's

up to you. Commercially prepared condiments often contain such additional ingredients as vinegar, flour, salt, turmeric and other spices, and occasionally horseradish. This latter white-flowered member of the mustard family, with the pungent white roots, also grows wild.

FIREWEED. Fireweed, which in summer gives an unforgettable amethyst hue to vast fire-blackened stretches below some of my favorite sheep and goat ranges west of the Alaska Highway, is another wild vegetable difficult to mis-

FIREWEED. Young leaves, stems, and flowers are edible both raw and cooked. The young shoots, conspicuous because of red stems and bright green succulent leaves, are an asparagus substitute.

DWARF FIREWEED.   Young leaves and stalks, mixed with
a few buds for color and flavor, make fine salad and boiled
greens. They all toughen and become increasingly bitter
with age.

take. Thousands of square miles of burnt lands from the Aleutians and Greenland to Mexico soften to magenta annually, so showily do these tall perennials flame into spike-like clusters of flowers. Try cutting the young stems into sections and boiling them in a small amount of salted water until tender. This way they resemble asparagus. More mature stalks can be peeled and their sweetish interiors eaten raw. Young fireweed leaves cook up into satisfactory greens. But even if you can't get to these until fall, all is not lost. Steep them for tea.

HORSETAIL. Another wild green, notably simple to identify is the young horsetail. Nearly every fisherman and hunter has made his way through stands of this small green plant which prospers along corduroyed toteroads, about shaded brooks, and in other cool moist locations. Ever notice, when you've been relaxing on a log, how some of these give the impression of miniature pine forests? Others are reminiscent of whimsically dwarfed bamboos. The reason? The horsetail grows in two different forms.

The infertile horsetail has a single thin stem which resembles the trunk of a tiny pine all the more because of green shoots that branch out from it in a series of levels. The fertile horsetail thrusts upward in one bare stalk. This ascends in joints which a lot of us occasionally find ourselves pulling idly apart, section by popping section. The fertile horsetail is also known as the scouring rush; the gritty surfaces of the older plants make them handy articles to grab by the handful for scrubbing pans after an outdoor meal. As for eating, the outer tissues can be removed from the young shoots of both varieties and the somewhat sweetish interiors eaten raw.

OTHER WILD FOODS. In other words, there's no shortage of familiar wild vegetation that's good to eat. Plain ordinary clover, including both flowers and leaves, is a nutritious garnish for any salad. As for the sweet roots, try the Indian practice of dipping them in game drippings and then smoking them a bit over the smouldering outskirts of a campfire. Peeled young burdock stalks are another aspara-

gus substitute. So are the upper parts of peeled young cattail shoots. Or shake the golden pollen from mature cattails
and mix it half and half with the regular flour in pancake
batters.

CATTAIL.

SPRING BEAUTY. The tender young leaves of this close relative of Miner's Lettuce can be added raw to salads or briefly cooked in a small amount of salted water for serving as a green vegetable.

Stems and leaves of the well-known miner's lettuce—whose clinching feature is the way a pair of leaves grow together part way up each short stem and form a cup through whose middle the stalk continues—are estimable salad fodder when young and a better-than-average spinach substitute when older.

As for kinnikinic, after you've filled up on the sustaining if blandly dry red berries, you can make yourself a smoke with the leaves. Dried and pulverized, these have been a frontier tobacco substitute for centuries.

Laziness in doing unnecessary things can be a great virtue. What I mean, one hungry outfit has only so much time and

KINNIKINIC.

energy. Why lug along a load of fresh vegetables and fruits on your outing if you can gather them fresher as you need them? A lot of time you'll do better to take instead enough other essentials to let you penetrate farther back of beyond, to where the big ones are holed up. A couple of good mottoes for most any vacationist to pin to his rucksack are: travel lighter, go farther. Pick instead of pack.

DULSE. This seaweed that grows attached to rocks is often added to soups and stews. It's also eaten fresh, a favorite method of preparation being to singe it quickly as by briefly dropping it into a hot frypan. Dulse is often dried in the air and stored for later use.

GIANT KELP. You can make pickles from these long
hollow stalks.

HIGHBUSH CRANBERRY. These have a distinctive sweetish sour odor and flavor which require a cultivated taste. However, they can get to be one of your favorite wild fruits. Frozen in winter, the berries melt pleasantly against the tongue like sherbet.

SALAL.   Want a taste treat? Try cooking up a few of these
western wintergreen fruits in your applesauce. Indians dried
them for winter feasting.

SERVICEBERRY.   Also known as Juneberries, the numerous
members of this family are used like the blueberries they
resemble. Millions were once gathered to flavor pemmican.

WILD CUCUMBER. The tender young shoots are among my favorites in the spring because of the cucumberlike flavor they impart to salads. The oddly growing little berries are worth eating later.

BEACH ASPARAGUS. Also known as Glasswort, this is often boiled as a potherb. However, it finds its main flavor when pickled. Very young plants blend especially well into salads predominated by oil and vinegar.

SOURDOCK.   This member of the widespread dock family
has tender young leaves that, more delicious because of an
acid tang, make excellent salad greens as well as a fine
cooked vegetable.

BRAKE. This is perhaps the most widely distributed and abundant of the ferns. The young fiddleheads, when some six to eight inches tall and still covered with a rusty scruffy material which is peeled off, are boiled and eaten like asparagus. They are not fit to eat when older.

MOUNTAIN SORREL. The leaves of this member of the buckwheat family have a piquant acid taste that make them favorites for eating raw. The plant is also boiled as a green.

LABRADOR TEA. This evergreen's leaves, with their green tops and woolly underneaths, make an enjoyably aromatic tea when used in moderation. Another name is Hudson's Bay Tea. Two or three leaves are occasionally refreshing to chew raw.

WILD CELERY. The peeled young stems and leaf stalks, tasting and smelling like celery, are relished raw. The young leaves are excellent when cooked with fish.

COWSLIP. The leaves, along with the thick hollow stems, should be boiled before flowers appear. (The leaves are not edible raw.) The buds become a delicacy when pickled in vinegar. Even the roots are good, looking like sauerkraut when they're boiled.

WINTERCRESS. This member of the mustard family is valued both as a salad green and as a potherb. The bitterness, found pleasant by many, increases with age and can be lessened by cooking in several changes of water.

CHAPTER 11

TOPPING IT OFF

ICE CREAM. Ice cream is one of the quickest and easiest of all desserts to make outdoors, especially after a fresh snow. Best for the purpose are dry flakes. You can also use the granular interior of the perpetual snowbanks found in the higher mountains, although the result will be more a coarse sherbet.

Just empty a can of evaporated milk into a large pot or bowl. A similar amount of dry milk, reconstituted with water, will do as well. Add 2 tablespoons of sugar, ⅛ teaspoon of salt, and some flavoring. Vanilla or one of the other extracts will serve. So will cocoa, powdered coffee, and the like. Mocha? Balance 2 teaspoons of powdered instant coffee with 1 teaspoon chocolate; enough, incidentally, for a quart of ice cream. If the flavoring, as for instance chocolate syrup, is already sweet, just omit the sugar.

Then quickly stir in fresh snow to taste. More sweetening and flavoring may be added at the end if you want. For this reason it is safest to go light on these initially. Otherwise, you'll have to repair any mistake with more milk and snow —not that this isn't a good excuse.

Three varieties that come out especially well, if you happen to like them to begin with, are the universally favored vanilla, rich dark chocolate with overtones of peppermint extract, and banana ice cream made with that particular extract.

TREELESS MAPLE SYRUP. The sugar maple grows only in North America. Like all green trees, it mysteriously changes water and carbon dioxide into sugar. So exceptional is the sugar maple's capacity for storing the sweet that this talent is a double boon. In autumn it produces some of the loveliest hues of the American forest; in spring, the amber succulence of maple syrup.

The only trouble many wilderness cooks have is that these latter activities are largely confined to such Eastern regions as the St. Lawrence Valley, New Brunswick and Nova Scotia, and such New England States as New Hampshire and Vermont. But there's a slightly incredible way around. You'll need:

 6 medium potatoes
 2 cups water
 1 cup white sugar
 1 cup brown sugar

Peel the medium-sized potatoes. Boil uncovered with 2 cups water until but 1 cup of fluid remains. Remove the potatoes, for use any way you want. Stirring the liquid until the boiling point has again been reached, slowly add the sugar. Once this has entirely dissolved, set the pan off the heat to cool slowly.

"Ghastly concoction," the old mountain man who gave me the formula nodded agreeably when, the initial time around, I first sampled the elixir at this primary stage. "Like home brew, it has to be aged in a dark place. After a couple of days in a bottle it'll be noble."

See if that first spoonful you doubtfully try doesn't seem to justify your worst suspicions, too. But bottle the syrup and tuck it away for several days to age. Taste it again at the end of that time and see if you, also, aren't pleasantly amazed.

HARD SAUCE. For hard sauce, cream ½ cup butter or margarine and gradually add 1½ cups of preferably powdered sugar. Beat until creamy. Toward the end add ½ teaspoon vanilla or some other flavoring.

CRANBERRY SAUCE. You frequently come across wild cranberries in the fall. Although smaller than domestic varieties, they are quickly picked. For a sauce that's particularly good with game, bring 1½ cups of water and 1 cup of sugar to a boil. After 10 minutes, drop 2 cups of washed cranberries into the syrup and let it continue to boil until the berries pop.

DRIED APPLES. These vary considerably. It will pay to buy the best obtainable, although outdoors most any dried apples taste delicious. Before using them, you'll ordinarily be best satisfied if you trim away any remaining portions of the core. Bruises should be cut out, too.

Brands differ, but on the average it takes about 7 pounds of fresh apples to make 1 pound of dried. Pressed into a measure, 1 pound of dehydrated apples contains some 4 cups of raw fruit. These cook up to roughly double bulk.

Applesauce, which may not get a second glance in the city, is relished in the open as a side dish with meat, as part of the stuffing for birds, atop cereal, and in numerous forms as a dessert. When the mercury threatens to shrink out of sight, try mixing some applesauce with evaporated milk and setting it in the cold, covered against the intrusion of small wild folk. The result will be a super ice cream, crystalline enough to eat easily.

Applesauce is handily enough made by simmering 2 cups of dried apples plus ⅛ teaspoon of salt in 4 cups of water until tender. If you want to go to the bother, press the cooked apples through a colander or such while they're hot. Stir 4 tablespoons of sugar and 1 teaspoon of nutmeg or cinnamon into the finished product, unless your palate dictates otherwise. Lemon or lemon juice, fresh or dehydrated, is also generally favored when available. Want something different? Coriander gives a piquant flavor. So does plain, everyday vanilla.

BAKED DRIED APPLES. Put 2 cups dried apples in an equal volume of boiling water. Set immediately off the heat and allow to stand 1 hour. Grease a shallow baking dish. Place the apples and liquid into this. Sprinkle with ½ teaspoon nutmeg, ½ teaspoon cinnamon, and 1 cup sugar. Slice ½ cup of margarine over the top.

Bake in a moderately hot oven or reflector baker ½ hour. Serve hot with milk. Or if you're where you can do it, mix up a quick batch of vanilla ice cream with the help of preferably light snow, as described elsewhere in this chapter, and put a few spoonfuls of that atop the hot apples.

APPLE CRUMB PUDDING. This takes on an even more pleasant campfire flavor if for the ½ cup of fat needed you mix bacon drippings with margarine or butter. Grease a baking dish with part of this. Put in 2 cups applesauce. Rub together ¾ cup of preferably brown sugar and an equal volume of flour with the remaining fat until crumbly. Spread this over the apples and bake everything in a hot oven or reflector baker 15 minutes.

APPLE APPEALS. Make enough bannock biscuits to go around, according to the directions in the chapter on bread. Top each—after the bottom crust has formed and the bannock has been turned if it is being cooked atop the heat; at once if the bannock will not have to be turned—with slices of dried apple that have been brought to a simmer in just enough water to cover and then allowed to cool in their own juice. Over these spread thin yellow slices of tangy cheese. A dutch oven, reflector baker, or regular oven is best for preparing this dessert.

STEWED PRUNES. Cover the prunes with cold water, bring to a bubble, and keep barely simmering until the fruit is soft.

Or let the prunes plump up overnight in enough water to cover. Cook slowly in the same fluid until done to your taste. Then add sugar if you like. Some also like to include lemon. Sometime when you want a particularly delectable syrup, try soaking and cooking the prunes in strong black tea. You won't be able to detect the tea taste, by the way. A little cinnamon and lemon will improve even this singular flavor.

PRUNE BREAD. Soak a pound of prunes in cold water until they are juicy and plump. Then remove them, take out the pits, if any, and cut or chop the fruit into small bits. Cover with 1½ cups boiling water. You'll also need:

2½ cups sifted flour
1½ cups sugar
1 teaspoon cinnamon
1 teaspoon salt
2½ teaspoons baking soda
2 eggs
½ cup melted shortening

Sift or mix together the flour, sugar, cinnamon, salt, and baking soda. Add the prunes and water. Beat the eggs or stir together the equivalent amount of dried eggs and water. Mix these, then the shortening, into the other ingredients. Pour into a greased bread pan and bake in a moderately slow oven or reflector baker for 1 hour or until done. Remove from the pan and cool.

STEWED APRICOTS. Cover the dried apricots with cold water. Bring this to a dancing boil for 15 minutes or until the fruit is tender. Another way is to cover the apricots with hot water, set them away from the heat for 2 hours or so, and then simmer slowly in the same water until soft. During the final few minutes of cooking, add sugar to taste if you care for any additional sweetening. I don't.

DRIED APRICOT COBBLER. We used to get cobblers a lot back at century-and-a-half-old Kimball Union Academy in Meriden, New Hampshire. Essentially, as you know, these are deep-dish New England fruit pies, aptly flung together in a hurry and unerringly topped with a biscuit mixture. In the woods you can bake these practically by ear, using both wild and dried fruits. Here is a basic recipe featuring dried apricots:

> 2 cups dried apricots
> ½ cup sugar
> 1 cup water
> 3 tablespoons lemon juice
> 3 tablespoons margarine
> ½ teaspoon cinnamon
> 3 tablespoons sugar

Wash the apricots and cut into pieces. Cover with water and cook until tender. Add the sugar when almost done. Transfer the hot fruit to a baking dish or casserole and add lemon juice if available. Dot with margarine. Sprinkle with cinnamon and the remaining 3 tablespoons of sugar.

Spoon soft biscuit dough over the fruit. Cut vents to allow steam to escape. Bake in hot oven or reflector baker about 30 minutes or until crust is done. Serve hot with whipped evaporated milk, vanilla ice cream, etc.

For the crust:

> 1 cup sifted flour
> 1 tablespoon sugar

1 teaspoon baking powder
½ teaspoon salt
2 tablespoons shortening
½ cup milk

Mix the flour, sugar, baking powder, and salt. Cut in the shortening. Have everything ready to go. Then quickly stir in enough milk to make a soft dough. Spoon this dough immediately atop the fruit and get the whole thing into the preheated oven without delay.

DRIED FRUIT TURNOVERS. A blend of dried apricots and prunes is good for these turnovers, although numerous other such combinations are pleasing, whether devoured hot from the fire or eaten cold for lunch. Simmer a heaping cup apiece of apricots and pitted prunes with 1½ cups of water until the fruit begins to come apart. Then stir in 1 cup sugar, 1 tablespoon flour, ½ teaspoon nutmeg, and 5 tablespoons margarine.

Make the pastry by creaming ½ cup of butter or margarine, then mixing in 1 cup flour and 2 tablespoons water. Roll into a sheet. Cut out 8 ovals about the size of a saucer. Fill each with fruit, fold over, press the edges together, and prick the tops with a fork to make a vent for steam. Bake in a moderately slow oven or reflector baker until tan and crisp.

PEACH SHORTBREAD.

3 cups quick-cooking oats
½ cup sugar
¼ cup flour
¼ teaspoon salt
¾ cup margarine
1 teaspoon vanilla extract
stewed dried peaches

Mix the dry ingredients. Cut in the margarine. Finally, stir in the vanilla extract. Press across the bottom of a greased oven pan. Put in a preheated moderately warm reflector baker or oven and bake 1½ hours or until lightly browned. Cut or break into chunks. Drench with stewed dried peaches.

BERRIES AND DUMPLINGS. This is a cinch when you

camp in blueberry, raspberry, blackberry, strawberry, saskatoon, and other berry country. Just pick enough berries for dessert. Stew them over the campfire, sweetening them the way you like them. When you're ready to sit down to the main meal, drop on a white dome of dumplings. Cover the pot tightly.

When the dumplings are done, take out and top each with a spoonful of margarine. Spoon the hot berries over them. Pour on some milk if you want. And see what everyone's idea is about the dessert for the following meal.

STRAWBERRY SHORTCAKE. All you need for this tiptop treat is wild strawberries and hot bannock. To match about 2 quarts of berries, freshly picked and left standing drenched with a cup of sugar, here's one way to go about the latter:

> 2 cups sifted flour
> 2 tablespoons sugar
> 2 teaspoons baking powder
> 1 teaspoon salt
> 4 tablespoons shortening
> ½ cup cold milk (or more)

The first time I ever ate this one was on Ottertail Creek, in the middle of the Canadian Rockies, with trapper and riverman Billy Kruger doing the cooking. We'd run out of lard a week earlier. Instead, Billy used some oil he'd previously rendered from a couple of young grizzlies.

Billy Kruger commenced the rites by sifting all the dry ingredients together into a bowl. He worked in the shortening, then stirred in enough cold milk to make a soft dough.

This dough Billy kneaded very briefly on a floured board. Using a clean cold bottle, he rolled it out about ½ inch thick. Half of the dough he laid in a greased pan and dotted with chunks of canned butter. The other half he spread on top. If you prefer individual biscuits, just cut the dough into ovals with a floured can top or glass. Baking in a very hot oven or reflector baker takes 12 to 15 minutes.

Afterwards we carefully separated the steaming layers, ladled the sweetened berries between and above, and fell to it. Raspberries, blueberries, saskatoons, blackberries, and similar wild fruits are also good with this hot bannock.

WHIPPED CREAM. That particular summer evening we crowned the shortcake with whipped cream made from evaporated milk. There's a simple gimmick to this. Milk and utensils have to be icy cold. This we arranged easily enough by submerging bowl, beater, and can of milk in the mountain stream that sparkled past Billy Kruger's cabin on its way to mingle with the Peace River.

So chilled, most evaporated milk quickly whips to about triple volume. A couple of tablespoons of lemon juice can be used to increase the stiffness after the milk is partially whipped. Some bush cooks also use an envelope (1 table-spoon) of unflavored gelatin, dissolved in a minimum of water, for this purpose.

FRIED WILD STRAWBERRIES. Clean 4 cups of fresh strawberries except for their stems. Chill the berries as much as possible, perhaps by partly immersing their container in a brook or spring. Keep the berries dry.

For the batter, beat 1 egg with 1 cup of milk. Then add 1 tablespoon melted margarine, ⅛ teaspoon salt, ¼ cup sugar, and 1 teaspoon vanilla. Blend thoroughly. Mix 1½ cups flour with 3 teaspoons baking powder. Combine with the egg mixture and beat until smooth.

Hold each chilled berry by its stem and dip carefully into the batter. Then drop into hot deep fat and fry until well browned. This will take about a minute. Save what you don't eat on the spot to mete out with whipped cream for dessert.

OPEN STRAWBERRY PIE. To make a 9-inch pie shell, sift together 1 cup of sifted flour and ½ teaspoon salt. Cut in ½ cup of shortening. For the flakiest and tastiest pie crust, use rendered bear grease.

Handling the crust quickly and lightly, add only enough water, about 3 teaspoons, to make a dough that will hold together when rolled. Roll out and spread on a greased pie pan. Bake in a hot oven or reflector baker for 12 to 15 minutes or until done.

Simmer together 1 cup of crushed wild strawberries, ½

cup sugar, and 2 tablespoons of cornstarch until they've become thick and syrupy. Meanwhile, pack the cooked pie shell with the ripest and juiciest strawberries you have. Drench them with the hot strawberry syrup. Chill and serve.

This pie is delicious, too, when similarly prepared with raspberries, thimbleberries, blackberries, and such. Sweetening may be varied to taste.

APPLE PIE. Make enough pastry for a 2-crust pie. If you don't already have a favorite recipe for pastry, the one with the strawberry pie is a good one. Roll out thin and line a deep 9-inch pie pan or plate, heavily greased with margarine.

> cooked dried apples, chopped
> 1 cup sugar
> ½ teaspoon nutmeg
> 4 teaspoons flour
> 4 tablespoons corn syrup
> ¼ pound margarine

Dot the lower pie shell, once it is in the pan, with half the margarine, sliced thin. Mix the sugar, nutmeg, and flour. Sprinkle half of it over the bits of margarine. Heap the pie tin full of chopped cooked apples and pour the corn syrup among them. Sprinkle on the remaining sugar, nutmeg, and flour.

Fold on the top layer of pastry. Cut a pinetree of vents in the middle of the top crust to allow steam to escape. Slice the other half of the margarine over it. Bake in a preheated hot oven or reflector baker for 40 to 50 minutes or until the crust is done.

The uneven heat that a lot of outdoor cooking contraptions put out gives trouble sometimes by overcooking the rims of pies. One solution is to overturn the empty pie plate on a sheet of aluminum foil, maybe before you leave home. Draw a line ½ inch beyond the edge of the pan. Take away the pan and draw a second circle 1½ inches inside the first. Cut out this foil crust-protector with scissors. Laid over the fluted edges of the pie, it will shield the dough from overbrowning.

DRIED APRICOT PIE.

  3 cups cooked, unsweetened apricots, drained
  ½ cup apricot juice
  1 tablespoon cornstarch
  ½ cup sugar
  ⅛ teaspoon salt
  1 tablespoon margarine

Drain the cooked, unsweetened apricots. Combine ½ cup of the juice from the cooked fruit with the cornstarch, sugar, and salt. Cook and stir until thick and clear. Remove from stove and melt in the margarine.

Arrange the apricots in a pastry-lined 9-inch pie pan. Pour the juice mixture over them. Top with pastry strips. Bake in a hot oven or reflector baker for about 30 minutes or until the pastry is done. This is really a treat when big wet flakes begin tumbling thickly among the pines.

GOOSEBERRY PIE. Double-crust gooseberry pie was famous back in colonial days. Just blend 3 cups of fresh ripe gooseberries, 1 cup of brown sugar, and 2 tablespoons of flour. The crust story is the same. Bake in a hot oven or reflector baker for 15 minutes to seal the crust and deter any running over. Then lower the heat to moderate and bake for 35 to 40 minutes more or until the pastry is brown on top.

BLUEBERRY PIE. This pie isn't so solid with thickeners such as arrowroot, tapioca, or cornstarch that it will hold stolidly together while you punctuate your conversation with the occasional forkful. As a matter of fact, most campers who sit down to this particular dessert are glad to hold up on the repartee for awhile and to finish off with a spoon.

All you need besides the pastry is 4 cups of fresh blueberries, 1 cup sugar, and ¼ cup of melted margarine. As for the cooking, it takes place in a single operation.

Line a greased pie pan with pastry. Mix the berries, sugar, and margarine. Pour them into the uncooked shell. Top with the upper crust, being sure to cut vents. Bake in a preheated, moderately hot oven or reflector baker about 50 minutes or until the crust is golden tan.

BLUEBERRY SLUMP. Bring 4 cups blueberries, 1½

cups sugar, 4 tablespoons cornstarch, and 1 teaspoon nutmeg slowly to a boil in a heavy saucepan. While the mixture is simmering, make a batter of:

> 4 tablespoons sugar
> 3 tablespoons shortening
> ½ cup milk
> 1½ cups sifted flour
> 1½ teaspoons baking powder
> ¼ teaspoon salt

Cream the sugar and shortening. Add the milk and blend thoroughly. Mix the flour, baking powder, and salt. Stir rapidly into the other ingredients.

Then begin dropping the batter, spoonful by spoonful, over the bubbling berries. Cover and cook at the same speed for 10 minutes. Serve hot with cream, if you have it, or with vanilla ice cream if there's snow for quickly stirring together a bowlful.

RASPBERRY SLUMP. Here is a variation of Blueberry Slump adjusted to raspberries. This recipe can also be used for prunes, dried peaches, blackberries, etc. by gearing the sugar and spices by taste to the natural flavor of the fruit.

> 1 cup sugar
> 1 tablespoon cornstarch
> 1 cup boiling water
> 3 cups raspberries
> 1 tablespoon margarine
> ½ teaspoon cloves
> ½ teaspoon cinnamon

Mix the sugar and cornstarch in a pan. Slowly add the boiling water and, continually stirring, bring to a simmer for a minute. Add the raspberries to the syrup. While the mixture is bubbling, proceed as in the preceding Blueberry Slump recipe.

CITRUS FRUIT PEEL. Oranges, grapefruit, lemons, and other citrus fruits are so much trouble to come by in many parts of the wilderness that when you get any, you may as well utilize them to the fullest possible degree. Instead of throwing away the skins as you would in the city, why not make candied peel?

Peel can be kept until you accumulate enough to bother with by immersing it in salt water. This will also remove some of the bitter taste. The skins should then be well rinsed in fresh water, boiled until tender, cut into bite-size bits, and slowly simmered in a thick sugar syrup until transparent. Drain as in a coarse sieve. Cool on a plate. Then roll in either powdered or granulated sugar.

Or if the fruit is eaten quickly, just gather the dry peel. If you want to cut down on any later bitterness, which on the other hand many relish, remove some of the white underneath of the skin with a spoon. Cut the peel into strips, perhaps with scissors. Put the peel from a dozen oranges, for example, in a saucepan along with 1½ cups water and 3 cups sugar. Simmer slowly until clear. Then proceed as above.

For something a little different, candied peel may be dipped in melted chocolate. Adding one of the instant coffees to the chocolate in proportions of 2 to 1 will give you a mocha flavor. Lay on paper to cool and dry.

SOURDOUGH CAKE. Sourdough (see chapter on breads) is still on the job those blusterous, rainy days when the masculine cook's mind turns to such possibilities as camp cake. Here's the way with that old stand-by, chocolate:

1	cup thick sourdough starter
1	cup water
1½	cups flour
¼	cup dry skim milk

Mix. Allow to ferment for several hours near the warmth until light and bubbly. Then in a separate pan blend:

2	cups sugar
½	cup shortening
4	squares bitter chocolate
2	eggs
1	teaspoon vanilla
½	teaspoon salt
1½	teaspoons baking soda

Rub and stir the sugar and shortening together until fluffy. Melt the chocolate and add that.

If using whole eggs, separate the whites and yolks. Beat

the yolks. Add the vanilla, then the salt and soda. Mix thoroughly with the sugar, shortening, and chocolate. Or just mix reconstituted dehydrated eggs, vanilla, salt, and soda, and add these. In either case, blend this second combination with the sourdough. If the egg whites are separate, now beat them stiff and fold them into the batter.

Pour into a large greased pan. Bake in moderate heat for 25 to 30 minutes or until done.

Cool. Then, if you want, ice with your choice of frosting. For a clear brown caramel coating, for instance, just stir a cup of sugar in a heavy frypan over moderate heat. When the sugar melts, spread it over the cake with a hot table knife.

TOMATO SOUP CAKE. Cream 2 tablespoons of shortening with 1 cup sugar. Add 1 well beaten egg. Sift together 2 cups flour, 1 teaspoon cloves, ½ teaspoon mace, ½ teaspoon nutmeg, ½ teaspoon baking soda, and 3 teaspoons baking powder. Stir these into the above, along with 1 can of condensed tomato soup. Add 1 cup seeded raisins, lightly floured.

Pour the batter into a small greased pan. Bake in a moderate oven 1 hour or until done. And unless you're an old hand with this sort of thing, be ready to be rather pleasantly surprised.

INDIAN PUDDING. Before Columbus and his cohorts mistakenly reached this continent while en route somewhere else, the rest of the world had never heard of redskins, corn, nor of course of Indian Pudding. The latter has done well to retain its distinctive name so long, during which time a native American bird has been dubbed a turkey and another equally American vegetable has achieved fame, even here, as the Irish potato.

Indian Pudding is something we like, particularly about the time of the first autumn snowfall when you can manufacture a bowl full of vanilla ice cream in about 5 minutes flat. It's also something in the mountains in summer, up by the snow line, although then the secondary enrichment you have to settle for is a more pebbly sherbet.

Scald 4 cups of whole milk in a double boiler. Gradually

stir in 5 tablespoons of corn meal and cook 15 minutes, constantly stirring. Then add: 2 tablespoons of margarine, ½ teaspoon salt, ¼ teaspoon nutmeg, ½ teaspoon cinnamon, ½ teaspoon ginger, 2 well beaten or well mixed eggs, and 1 cup molasses. Turn into a greased baking dish, pour on 1 cup of cold milk, and bake in a slow oven or reflector baker 1½ hours.

H.B.C. PLUM PUDDING. If you're going to be hunting in the bush with a friend or two on Thanksgiving and want to have something a little special for that occasion, you may be interested in going prepared to make one of the aromatic Hudson's Bay Company puddings which—traditionally varying in accordance to what ingredients have been at hand—have crowned many a holiday feast in the silent places since the Company was founded May 2, 1670.

The following components can be mixed at home and sealed in a plastic container:

4	cups sifted flour
4	teaspoons baking powder
½	teaspoon cinnamon
½	teaspoon nutmeg
1	cup brown sugar
½	cup white sugar
¼	cup finely chopped glaceed fruit mix
2	cups seedless raisins
1	cup currants
4	tablespoons dehydrated whole egg
6	tablespoons dehydrated whole milk
¼	teaspoon powdered lemon juice

When the memorable day arrives, shake and stir all these ingredients together, along with 2 cups finely minced suet. This can be either beef suet brought for the occasion or animal suet obtained on the spot. Add 2 cups water to make a cake batter. You will have also packed along a heavy cotton bag, and this you will have just wrung out in hot water and sprinkled inside with flour. Pour the batter into this. Tie the top tightly, leaving plenty of room for expansion.

Place this immediately in a pot filled with sufficient boiling water to cover. Keep it boiling 3 hours, turning the bag upside down when the pudding starts to harden so that all the fruit will not settle to the bottom. As the cooking continues, shift the bag occasionally so it will not scorch against the sides of the receptacle. At the end, dip this cloth container briefly in cold water and carefully remove the fabric so as not to break or crumble the pudding.

Serve this plum pudding hot with some appropriate sauce. Butter and sugar, flavored with some spice such as nutmeg or an extract such as lemon powder, will suffice. So will the thick juice from boiled dehydrated fruit.

Every time I enjoy one of these in the bush, I think of Voltaire acidly describing the North two centuries ago as "A patch of snow inhabited by barbarians, bear, and beaver." He should have seen the top of this continent when it's in a holiday mood.

Chapter 12

POTPOURRI

BAKING TEMPERATURES. If space and weight are no problems, one thing to do while accumulating experience is to bring along a small oven thermometer unless such is already attached to your cooking contraption. One costs only a few cents, occupies very little room, and takes much of the initial guesswork out of baking with outdoor fires. The following table will then apply; all temperatures mentioned in this book being the commonly used Fahrenheit, whereby at sea level fresh water freezes at 32° and boils at 212°.

Slow oven	250° to 325°
Moderate oven	325° to 400°
Hot oven	400° to 450°
Very hot oven	450° to 550°

If you're starting out with no such thermometer, you will be able to get a fairly accurate idea of the temperature by using the following test. With experience, of course, you'll be able to make the same approximations by holding the bare hand in the heat. In the meantime, sprinkle some white flour in a pan and place this in the heated oven or baker. If you're short on flour, a piece of white tissue paper can be used instead.

Turns light tan in 5 minutes   Slow Oven
Turns medium golden tan in 5 minutes
                                                                Moderate Oven
Turns deep dark brown in 5 minutes   Hot Oven
Turns deep dark brown in 3 minutes
                                                                Very Hot Oven

FOOD AT HIGH ALTITUDES. When pioneers first pushed their way westward into Rocky Mountain country, they had trouble for a time in successfully boiling such staples as vegetables and meats, while favorite bannock and occasional family cake recipes turned out to be dismaying failures.

The difference in atmospheric pressures was, and still is, the cause of such difficulties. Just as the pressure of water is greatest at the bottom of the sea and lightest just below the surface, so it is in the ocean of atmosphere in which we live. The pressure of the air is greatest below and at sea level. It becomes comparatively less the higher we climb.

Water, being under less pressure the loftier the altitude, boils at lower and lower temperatures the higher we go. This means that foods boiled or simmered at higher altitudes require a correspondingly longer cooking time. There are so many variations in foods themselves that it is difficult to give any definite rules. In general, such cooking times must be increased from 4 to 11 percent per 1,000 feet above sea level. Until you've had experience with a particular food, a safe rule is to add roughly 10 percent per 1,000 feet. A few minutes before that time is reached, start testing or tasting.

MOUNTAIN CAKES. Cake recipes may be modified by using the following table. Results vary with different types of cake, however, so the following data can be no more than a general guide:

Baking powder
3,000 to 4,000 feet
         Use ⅞ teaspoon for every cup flour
4,000 to 6,000 feet
         Use ¾ teaspoon for every cup flour
6,000 feet and above
         Use ½ teaspoon for every cup flour

Sugar
For rich cakes which contain ½ cup or more of fat and over 1 cup of sugar per 2 cups of flour, decrease the sugar ½ tablespoon for every 1,000 feet rise in elevation above sea level. Lean cakes containing less fat and less sugar than above do not need this sugar correction.

Liquid
At high altitudes, cakes tend to be more dry. In-

creasing the liquid ½ to 1 tablespoon results in a more moist and less crumbly product.

MILE-HIGH BREADS. With bannock and similar bread-stuffs: up to 5,000 feet, use 1 teaspoon of double action baking powder for every cup of flour as suggested elsewhere in this book. At 7,500 feet, decrease this to ¾ teaspoon baking powder. At 10,000 feet, use only ½ teaspoon of baking powder. Other ingredients remain the same. Follow the recipe for the nearest altitude.

At high altitudes, sourdough and other yeast bread should be allowed to rise for a shorter time, only until about doubled in bulk. Either that, or less leavening should be used. The first technique assures better results.

Because flour dries out faster at high altitudes, it may be necessary to use more liquid to compensate for this loss and to give the dough the desirable consistency.

WATER. Water from springs and streams that flow from clean and uninhabited North American country is usually safe for drinking and cooking. In the wilderness lake regions of northern United States and Canada, the water from these bodies, unless there are many camps on the shores or along the courses running into them, is also generally pure. This does not always hold true, however. Even if it did, we are not always familiar enough with a region to know the condition of a watershed a short distance away.

When we have the slightest doubt about whether or not water is pure, it should be treated as though unsafe. This includes not only the water we drink. It also involves the water used for cooking and for washing.

Cooking and eating implements that have been washed in contaminated water can carry disease germs even though the cooking water is pure or is boiled in the process of cooking. In some localities, uncooked vegetables such as lettuce and radishes are unsafe. Water can often be cleared by letting it seep into a hole dug a few feet from a shore, but such filtration does not assure purity.

PURIFYING WATER. The easiest and most practical way to sterilize doubtful water is to boil it. At or near sea level, hard boiling for five minutes will do the job. For

every additional 1,000 feet altitude, a safe all-around precaution is to increase the boiling time one minute.

Or you can use halazone tablets which may be secured
at most sporting goods stores. A small two-ounce bottle
containing 100 tablets costs about 50 cents and takes up less
room than a 12-gauge shell. Because this process depends
on the release of chlorine gas, the tablets should be fresh
and the container kept tightly closed. Dissolve one tablet in
a quart of water and let it stand for ½ hour. If the water
is murky or particularly doubtful, both the time and the
number of tablets may well be doubled. Slosh a little of
this water over the lips of the container after the first few
minutes to sterilize these. Then cover the receptacle as
tightly as possible.

In Mexico and other semitropical and tropical regions,
chlorine-releasing compounds can not be depended upon.
Water there should either be boiled or, when this is not
convenient, treated with Iodine Water Purification Tablets.

ICE. Ice is no more pure than was the water from which
it was frozen. Although heat destroys bacteria and parasites,
cold very definitely does not.

COOLING WATER. In warm country, water may be
chilled without ice to a palatable temperature by the use of
water-cooling bags. These commonly hold up to several
gallons and are slightly porous so that a little fluid continues
to seep out and to wet the outside. This exterior moisture
evaporates in the air and so lowers the interior temperature.
The process may be quickened by hanging the bag in a
breeze. This water you can purify at the same time by
dropping in the necessary tablets.

SNOW. The only precaution that need be taken with
pure snow in the wilderness is to treat it like ice cream and
not put down too much at once while overheated or chilled.
Aside from that, clean snow can be safely eaten any time
you are thirsty in the bush.

Wilderness snows, after all, afford in flake form the
purest of distilled water obtainable from the atmosphere.
Snow's primary drawback is that a considerable amount is
required to obtain the desired quantity of water. You soon

WATER-COOLING BAG.

learn to break off sections of any available crust. Heavy granular snow from former storms, you find, is usually more convenient still.

This lower water content is quickly evident the first time you melt snow in the noon tea pail. Particular care has to be taken not to burn the utensil, particularly as snow also acts as a blotter. This is a reason why a few mouthfuls seem actually parching. The safest technique when you want to boil the kettle is to melt snow in small quantities until the bottom of the container is protected with several inches of water. You can then begin filling it with more and more snow until the required amount of liquid is obtained.

These shortcomings are more than compensated for by the fact that snowfall makes water readily available throughout the woods, mountains, plains, and deserts it whitens. All one has to do is scoop up clean handfuls while walking along. The body requires considerably more water in cold weather than most of us would ordinarily expect. For one thing, the kidneys then have to take over part of the process of elimination otherwise accomplished by the perspiration glands. For another thing, the comparative dryness of the air increases the amount of body water removed from respiratory passages. The immediate results if such water is not reasonably replaced? Listlessness and fatigue! Snow used in place of drinking water, far from being harmful or dangerous, is therefore an extremely healthful convenience.

DISH WASHING. Washing dishes is not really much of a chore if you have some system about it and if you always clean up immediately after a meal. With your cook kit, you'll find it helpful to include such items as detergent, two small tough cellulose sponges or dish cloths, a little dish mop for that hot campfire water, and scouring pads that combine steel wool or such with soap.

While you are eating, have your largest kettle over the fire heating dishwater. Or at the jumping-off spot, perhaps, buy a cheap tin dishpan if you've the room and ditch it when the trip is over. This will not take up much space if you select a model into which other items in your outfit can nest.

If you prefer, you may take along a small canvas wash basin. Such a 7-ounce affair that I've carried on go-light trips for years is 4 inches high and 12 inches in diameter. It squashes down flat to pack.

Every camper, as he finishes his meal, scrapes his prob-

CANVAS WASH BASIN.

ably nearly clean plate into the fire. When you are through with the frypans, pour off all grease and wipe them clean. Then fill them with water and put them on the fire to boil. Do the same with any kettle containing the sticky residue of mush.

Down at the creek or lake shore you will find clusters of grass or other vegetation such as scouring rushes, with mud or sand adhering to the roots. Pull up a clump and use it to scour the outside of pots and also both the interior and exterior of the frypans before you wash them. Pans in which cereals like rolled oats have been cooked are particularly bothersome. If you will put a little square of butter or oleomargarine in the water when you are preparing the cereal, it will make the pot ten times easier to clean.

If you have a pet aluminum pot whose exterior you want to keep bright, coat the outside with a film of soap before you place it on the fire. All trace of black will then quickly wash off. Eventually, most kettles get thoroughly darkened on the outside with soot which sticks most tenaciously and which can scarcely be removed by anything short of abrasives. But this soot does no harm whatever and even makes food in such a kettle cook faster and more evenly. If you scour with sand or with muddy vegetation, very little will rub off on other things when you pack. It is customary to have a canvas bag in which to stow the nest of pans and kettles. This helps to keep them from blackening other articles in the outfit. Individual fabric containers may also be convenient.

It has been the experience of a great many of the old sourdoughs in Alaska and the Northwest that when a utensil used for cooking meat is washed with soap, they get bad digestive disturbances akin to poisoning and that this ceases when such washing is stopped. One way to clean a steel frypan is to heat it very hot, then quickly plunge it into cold water. If this does not remove all the dirt, then scrub with sand and rinse in clear boiling water. Another way of loosening grease is to fill the pan with water into which some wood ashes have been dropped and allow the whole thing to come to a boil beside the blaze.

OUTDOOR COOKING TERMS

Bake   To cook by dry heat, as in a reflector baker or oven.

Baste   To moisten cooking food with melted fat, drippings, or other liquid.

Boil   To cook in water, or liquid mostly water, at boiling temperature (212° F. at sea level). Bubbles rise continually and break on the surface.

Braise   To brown in fat, then cook in covered pan, with or without added liquid, over fire, in reflector baker, dutch oven or other oven. Larger pieces of meat cooked by braising are called pot roasts.

Broil   To cook uncovered by direct heat over an open fire.

Deep-fry See french-fry.

French-fry To cook in a deep receptacle, in enough hot fat to cover or float food.

Fricassee	To braise individual serving pieces of meat, poultry, or game in a little liquid—water, broth, or sauce.
Fry	To cook in fat.
Grill	See broil.
Marinate	To let foods stand in a liquid (usually mixture of oil with vinegar or lemon juice) to add flavor or make more tender.
Pan-broil	To cook in very lightly greased or ungreased heavy pan on top of stove. Any fat is poured off as it accumulates so food does not fry.
Pan-fry	See saute.
Parboil	To boil until partly cooked.
Plank	To cook and serve on wooden slab or board.
Poach	To cook under the boiling point covered in hot liquid.
Pot-roast	See braise.
Render	To free fat from connective tissue by slowly heating until fat melts and can be poured off.
Roast	To bake in hot air, in reflector baker or turning over open fire, without water or cover.
Saute	To cook in a small amount of fat.
Scald	To heat to a temperature just below the boiling point.
Sear	To seal surface by exposing it to intense heat.
Simmer	To cook in liquid just below the boiling point. Bubbles form slowly and break below the surface.
Skewer	To pierce with pointed stick.
Steam	To cook food in steam over boiling water. Food is steamed in a covered container, on a rack or in a perforated pan above boiling water.
Steep	To extract flavor and other values by soaking in hot but not boiling water.
Stew	To boil or simmer in a small amount of liquid. Meats are stewed at simmering temperatures.
Toast	To brown, and occasionally blacken, by dry heat.

ONE INGREDIENT FOR ANOTHER

For these	**Substitute these**
1 whole egg, for thickening or baking	2 egg y o l k s. Or 1 tablespoon dried whole egg plus 2 tablespoons water. (Varies with product.)
1 whole egg in a batter	2 tablespoons of fresh dry snow, stirred in just before baking.
1 cup butter or margarine for shortening	⅞ cup of rendered bear or other animal fat, with ½ teaspoon salt. Or 1 cup hydrogenated fat (cooking fat sold under brand name) with ½ teaspoon salt.
1 square (ounce) chocolate	3½ tablespoons cocoa plus ½ tablespoon fat.
Nut meats	Similar amount of browned rolled oats. Peanut butter will do, too.
1 teaspoon double acting baking powder	1½ teaspoons phosphate baking powder. Or 2 teaspoons tartrate baking powder.
Baking soda in breadstuffs	Equal amount of the white of hardwood ashes.
Sweet milk and baking powder, for baking	Equal amount of sour milk plus ½ teaspoon soda per cup. (Each half teaspoon soda with 1 cup sour milk takes the place of 2 teaspoons baking powder and 1 cup sweet milk.)
1 cup sour milk, for baking	1 cup sweet milk mixed with one of the following: 1 tablespoon vinegar. Or 1 tablespoon lemon juice. Or 1¾ teaspoons cream of tartar.
1 cup whole milk	½ cup evaporated milk plus ½ cup water. Or 4 tablespoons dry whole milk plus 1 cup water. (Varies.) Or ⅓ cup nonfat dry milk plus 2½ teaspoons

	table fat and ¾ cup water. (Varies.) Or 1 cup skim milk plus 2 tablespoons melted table fat or salad oil.
1 cup skim milk	⅓ cup nonfat dry milk plus ¾ cup water. (Varies.)
1 tablespoon flour, for thickening	½ tablespoon cornstarch, potato starch, rice starch, or arrowroot starch. Or 1 tablespoon granulated tapioca.
1 cup cake flour, for baking	⅞ cup all-purpose flour.
1 cup all-purpose flour, for baking breads	Up to ½ cup bran, whole-wheat flour, or corn meal plus enough all-purpose flour to fill cup.
Commercial jelling agent for jelly making	1 level teaspoon Epsom Salts for each 5 pounds of fruit.

MEASURING FOODS

Part of cup	A compact nest of aluminum measuring spoons will enable accuracy and can also be used for eating. Measure dry ingredients before liquids.
Cup	Check at home the relationship of nesting drinking cups to standard measuring cup. If necessary, mark.
Molasses, syrups	These will bother less with clinging and sticking if you'll either first chill the measuring implement in cold water or lightly grease it.
Sugar	Pack brown sugar firmly into cup or spoon. Press or sift any lumps out of granulated sugar and measure like flour.

Solid fats

When fat comes in one-pound rectangular form, 1 cup or fraction can be cut from pound which measures about 2 cups. With quarter-pound rectangles, each of these equals ½ cup or 8 tablespoons.

You can measure a cupful, too, by packing firmly into cup and leveling off top with knife. Water method may be used for part of cup. To measure ½ cup fat, put ½ cup cold water in 1-cup measure. Add fat, pushing under water until water level stands at 1-cup mark. Pour out water and remove fat.

White flour

If you can, sift once onto a piece of plastic if that is most convenient. Lift lightly into cup. Don't pack. Don't shake or jar cup, or flour will settle down again. Level off top with knife.

Other flours

This also includes fine meals, fine crumbs, dried eggs, dry milks. Stir instead of sifting. Measure like flour.

Baking powder, etc.

Cornstarch, cream of tartar, and spices are included in this group. Stir to loosen. Fill spoon lightly to overflowing. Level with straight knife.

COMMON U. S. FOOD MEASURES

A dash, pinch, etc. . . . . less than ⅛ teaspoon
60 drops . . . . 1 teaspoon
3 teaspoons . . . . 1 tablespoon
2 tablespoons . . . . 1 fluid ounce
4 tablespoons . . . . ¼ cup

6 tablespoons .... ⅜ cup
8 tablespoons .... ½ cup
16 tablespoons .... 1 cup
1 cup .... 8 fluid ounces
2 cups .... 1 pint
1 gill .... ½ cup
4 gills .... 1 pint
1 pint .... 16 fluid ounces
2 pints .... 1 quart
1 quart .... 32 fluid ounces
4 quarts .... 1 gallon
1 pint milk or water .... 1 pound

CANADIAN LIQUID MEASURES

1 cup .... 8 fluid ounces
1 pint .... 20 fluid ounces
1 quart .... 40 fluid ounces
1 imperial quart .... 1¼ U. S. quarts
4 imperial quarts .... 1 imperial gallon
1 imperial gallon .... 5 U. S. quarts
One imperial quart, figured exactly, equals 1.2003 U. S.
quarts.

DRY MEASURES

2 pints .... 1 quart
8 quarts .... 1 peck
4 pecks .... 1 bushel
British dry quart equals 1.0320 U. S. dry quarts.
Legal weights of a bushel of corn, barley, potatoes, etc.
vary in different regions.

ORDINARY AVOIRDUPOIS WEIGHT

16 drams .... 1 ounce
16 ounces or 7000 grains .... 1 pound
14 pounds .... 1 stone
2000 pounds .... 1 short ton
2240 pounds .... 1 long ton

PROVISIONING TABLE

Calories	One-Pound Portion	Outfitting Data
2709	Almonds, shelled, dried	1 cup shelled—5⅓ oz.
1680	Apples, dried	1 lb. dried—8 lbs. fresh
1634	Apricots, dried	1 lb. dry—5½ lb. fresh
1047	Bacon, back	3 slices, 2½″ diam. x ¼″—3½ oz.
2855	Bacon, side	1 lb.—20 to 24 slices 2½ to 3 slices—2 oz.
1219	Banana, dried	3½ oz. dried—about 1 lb. fresh
1536	Barley, brown, whole	2 tbsp. dry—1 oz. yield ½ cup cooked
1525	Beans, dried, kidney	1 lb.—2⅔ cups 1 lb.—7 cups cooked
1512	Beans, Lima	1 lb.—2⅓ cups 1 lb.—6½ cups cooked
1535	Beans, Navy	1 lb.—2⅓ cups 1 lb.—6 cups cooked
977	Beef, corned, canned	3 slices 3″ x 2½″ x ¼″ —3½ oz.
922	Beef, dried or chipped	2 thin slices—1 oz.
1004	Bologna	1 slice—4½″ diam. x ⅛″—1 oz. 16 slices to 1 lb.
3248	Butter	1 lb.—2 cups
1587	Cabbage, dehydrated	1 lb. serves 50 1 serving ⅓ oz.
1641	Carrots, dehydrated	1 lb. serves 25 1 serving raw—4 oz. cooked
2619	Cashews	4 to 5 nuts—½ oz.
1804	Cheese, cheddar	1 lb. cheese grated— 4 cups
1676	Cheese, cheddar processed	

Calories	One-Pound Portion	Outfitting Data
433	Cheese, cottage	1 lb.—2 cups, serves 8 1 serving, ¼ cup—2 oz.
1684	Cheese, cream	2 tablespoons—1 oz.
1679	Cheese, Swiss	1 slice, 4½″ x 3½″ x ⅛″—1 oz.
905	Chicken, canned, boned	½ cup—3½ oz.
2273	Chocolate, bitter	1 lb. melted—2 cups
2282	Chocolate, milk, plain	
2413	Chocolate, milk, with almonds	
2403	Chocolate, bittersweet	
2136	Chocolate, sweetened, plain	
1329	Cocoa, dry	1 lb.—4 cups
	Coffee, roasted	1 lb.—5½ cups finely ground, makes 50 cups. Contains, in solid state, 1316 calories.
1649	Corn meal, yellow	3 cups weigh 1 lb.
4013	Corn oil	1 lb.—2 cups
1642	Cornstarch	1 lb.—3½ cups (stirred)
4013	Cotton seed oil	1 lb.—2 cups
1287	Dates, dried, pitted	1 lb. pitted and cut—2½ cups
655	Eggs, fresh, whole	1 doz. extra large—27 oz. up 1 doz. large—at least 24 oz. 1 doz. medium—21 to 24 oz.
2688	Egg, dried, whole	¾ cup powder & 1½ cups water—1 doz. fresh eggs
1530	Farina, dark	3 tbsp. dry—1 oz. yield ¾ cup cooked

Calories	One-Pound Portion	Outfitting Data
1677	Farina, light	1 lb.—approximately 2⅔ cups dry
357	Figs, fresh, raw	2 medium—4 oz.
514	Figs, canned in syrup	½ cup weighs 3½ oz.
1223	Figs, dried	3 cups (44 figs)—1 lb.
2838	Filberts, shelled	1 cup—4¾ oz.
1643	Flour, buckwheat, light	1 cup—4¼ oz.
1574	Flour, dark	1 cup—4¼ oz.
1659	Flour, rye, light	1 lb. rye flour—about 4½ cups 1 lb. sifted—5⅔ cups
1442	Flour, rye, dark	
1632	Flour, wheat	All-purpose flour—4 cups per lb. sifted Cake flour—4¾ cups per lb. sifted Pastry flour—4¾ cups per lb. sifted
1586	Flour, self-rising	4 cups per lb. sifted
1510	Flour, whole	Whole wheat flour stirred —3¾ cups per lb.
317	Fruit cocktail, canned	No. 2 can—1 lb.
1739	Gelatin, dessert powder	2½ cups per lb. 1 oz. pkg. makes 4 to 6 servings
1643	Hominy, grits	3 cups per lb. 3 tbsp. raw—⅔ cup cooked
1400	Honey	1 lb.—1⅓ cups
1262	Jam, assorted	3 level tbsp.—2 oz.
4091	Lard	2 cups per lb. 1 oz. measures 2 tbsp.
1530	Lentils, dry	2⅓ cups per lb. 2½ tbsp. dry—1 oz.— yields ½ cup cooked

Calories	One-Pound Portion	Outfitting Data
1928	Liverwurst	1 slice 3″ diameter ¼″ thick—1 oz.
1723	Macaroni	1 lb. 1″ pieces—4 cups 1 lb. cooked—12 cups—weighs 4 lbs.
624	Milk, evaporated	1 lb. tin & equal water—1½ pts. fresh milk
2231	Milk, powdered, whole	1 lb.—3½ cups 4 tbsp. level & 1 cup water—1 cup fresh milk
1642	Milk, powdered, skim	3.2 oz. makes 1 qt. ⅓ cup & ¾ cup water—1 cup fresh skim milk
1142	Molasses	1 cup weighs 11 oz.
107	Mushrooms, fresh, raw	4 large or 10 small—3½ oz.
1728	Noodles, containing egg	1″ pieces—6 cups to 1 lb. 1 lb. yields 11 cups cooked
1794	Oats, meal or rolled	1 lb.—5⅔ cups ⅓ cup makes 1 cup porridge
3266	Oleomargarine	1 tbsp.—½ oz.
4013	Olive oil	1 lb.—2 cups
308	Peaches, canned in syrup	2 halves & 3 tbsp. juice—4 oz.
1634	Peaches, dried	1 lb. dried—5½ lbs. fresh
2613	Peanut butter	1 lb.—2 cups
1219	Pears, dried	1 lb. dried—5½ lbs. fresh
193	Peas, fresh	2.2 lbs. whole—1 lb. shelled (3 cups)
1540	Peas, dried, green	2 tbsp. dry—1 oz. yields ½ cup cooked

Calories	One-Pound Portion	Outfitting Data
1562	Peas, split	2¼ cups—1 lb.
3159	Pecans, shelled	1 lb. in shell yields ⅓ lb. meats
3410	Pork, salt, fat, with rind	2 slices 4″ x 2″ x ⅜″— 3½ oz.
318	Potatoes, fresh	1 lb. as purchased—3 to 4 servings
1620	Potatoes, dehydrated	1 serving—1 oz. dry—4 oz. reconstituted
1034	Prunes, dried, with pits	Sizes—large 20 to 40 per lb., medium 40 to 60 per pound., small 60 to 100 per lb.
1725	Prunes, dried, pitted	1 lb. cooked with 2 qts. water gives 2½ qts.
1217	Raisins, dried	Seeded, 3¼ cups—1 lb. Seedless, whole, 2¾ cups —1 lb.
1648	Rice, brown	2 tbsp. dry—1 oz. yields ½ cup cooked
1629	Rice, white	1 lb.—2⅛ cups, 7 cups when cooked
1682	Rice, wild	1 lb.—3 cups 1 oz.—3 tbsp.—1 serving
1787	Salad dressing, French	2 tbsp.—1 oz.
3211	Salad dressing, mayonnaise	2 tbsp.—1 oz.
1531	Sardines in oil	15 sardines 3″ long— 5 oz.
784	Sardines in tomato sauce	
1817	Sausage, salami in casing	1 slice 4½″ diam., ⅛″ thick—1 oz.
1164	Sausage, weiners, raw	7 to 9 per lb.
4010	Shortening, vegetable, Crisco, Spry, etc.	1 lb.—2¼ cups

Calories	One-Pound Portion	Outfitting Data
1719	Spaghetti	1 lb. broken—4¾ cups
3437	Suet	1 lb. ground suet— 3½ cups
1676	Sugar, brown	2 cups (firmly packed) —1 lb.
1747	Sugar, granulated, white	1 lb.—2¼ cups
1747	Sugar, icing	1 lb.—3½ cups
1747	Sugar, loaf	Flat tablets, 100 to 1 lb.
1580	Sugar, maple	1 piece 1″ x 1¼″ x ½″ —½ oz.
1299	Syrups, corn	1⅓ cups per lb.
1123	Syrups, maple	1½ cups per lb.
1633	Tapioca, dry, pearl	2¾ cups raw—7½ cups cooked
	Tea	1 lb.—6 cups dry makes 200 to 300 cups
2969	Walnuts, shelled	1 lb. in shell—½ lb. meats
		1 lb. halves—4½ cups
1639	Wheat, germ	1 tbsp.—1/6 oz.
1544	Whole wheat, dry	⅓ cup dry—1 oz.— ¾ cup cooked

This chart may be used for scientifically planning a light and compact grubstake made up largely of high-energy rations.

The nutrient values, based on official researches of two governments with standard United States and Canadian foods, will vary somewhat in different localities. Dehydrated products will, naturally, differ to an even broader extent, depending not only on the original raw products but also on processing methods. Seasonal variations have not been noted, being minor in the aspects here considered.

WILDERNESS COOKERY

Outdoor trips have a way of sneaking up on an individual. Better start planning now for that next adventure back of beyond.

You're not going vacationing to spend your time cooking and eating. On the other hand, the right kind of meals will never taste better than when appetites are sharpened to a wonderful edge by healthful outdoor living.

EXTRA RECIPES

EXTRA RECIPES

NEXT TIME BRING:

INDEX

The
CHANGE
in the
WEATHER

People,

Weather,

and the

Science of

Climate

WILLIAM K. STEVENS

DELTA TRADE PAPERBACKS

A Delta Book
Published by
Dell Publishing
Random House, Inc.
1540 Broadway
New York, New York 10036

Copyright © 1999 by William K. Stevens

Dell books may be purchased for business or promotional use or for special sales. For information please write to: Special Markets Department, Random House, Inc., 1540 Broadway, New York, N.Y. 10036.

ISBN: 0-385-32007-8

Reprinted by arrangement with Delacorte Press.

Book design by Nicola Ferguson

Manufactured in the United States of America
Published simultaneously in Canada

March 2001

10 9 8 7 6 5 4 3 2 1

BVG

To Joan

Contents

Contents

Introduction

Chicago/July 1995
The most lethal weather disaster in the city's history arrived not with the terrifying roar of a tornado but quietly, deceptively, until America's third largest metroplis lay immobilized under a suffocating blanket of heat and humidity unprecedented in meteorological records.

For four days, from July 12 through July 16, a stagnant high-pressure system sat over northern Illinois like the lid on a pressure cooker, trapping the torrid, clammy air mass. No trace of clouds graced the sky by day; no wind mitigated the misery. On Thursday the thirteenth, the temperature rocketed to 106 degrees Fahrenheit at Midway Airport. Stepping outside was like stepping into a furnace. Roads buckled. Electrical transformers blew out.

But what made the heat wave unique in weather annals was that it remained both so hot and so humid at night. At 3:45 A.M. on the fourteenth, observers at Midway recorded a temperature of 93 degrees, with a dew point of 80 degrees—nearly as humid as a tropical rain forest and about as moist as it has ever gotten in the summer as far north as Chicago. By combining the temperature and humidity in a single measurement, meteorologists found that the "apparent temperature"—a measure of the actual discomfort and biological danger for people—did not dip below 89 for two nights in a row and rose as high as 125 (at 6:00 P.M. on July 13).

That combination had never been recorded before.

The miserable nights meant no respite from dangerously high heat stress for people without air conditioning, mostly poorer and older Chicagoans. Some had nailed their windows shut and were afraid to go out because of street crime. Emergency workers took thermometer readings of up to 120 degrees in some dwellings. The unremitting heat impaired the working of enzymes essential to respiration. In scores of cases, this led to rapid breathing, mental confusion, stupor, coma, and death. The victims were extra vulnerable, living as they did in a northern city where people are not acclimated to such extreme heat and humidity.

Victims jammed hospital emergency rooms. The body temperature of some had soared to 107 and 108 degrees. Most of those who were treated, typically by spraying them with cold water and administering fluids intravenously, survived. But on Friday night, Dr. Edmund R. Donoghue, the chief medical examiner of Cook County, got a call at home advising him to prepare to handle forty dead bodies at the morgue the next day. Ordinarily there might be fifteen or twenty on a Saturday morning. When he arrived, eighty-seven cases actually faced him and his staff. Trucks continued to deliver corpse after corpse. The morgue's refrigerator holds two hundred bodies and was quickly out of space. Refrigerator trucks were brought in to store the overflow. Extra doctors, autopsy technicians, investigators, and body-bearers arrived, and soon a steady stream of dead bodies shuttled from the trucks to the autopsy tables and back.

The morgue was a sink of private tragedy and personal horror. In an office there, nineteen-year-old Tanisha Baker wept over the death of her mother, forty-year-old Joella Tucker. "She had laid down complaining about the heat and never woke up," Montrell Stephenson, a family friend, told a reporter. Outside, technicians taking a breather found their gruesome task and the sight of so much death hard to endure. "Oh, man, I don't want to go back in there," said one medical worker.

"I've never seen anything like this in my life," Dr. Donoghue said at the time. "We're overwhelmed." In the end 583 people died from the regionwide heat wave, most of them in Chicago. In terms of deaths, Dr. Donoghue said later, it was the city's biggest mass disaster. The next biggest was the 1979 crash of a DC-10 on take-off from O'Hare International Airport in which 270 people were killed—fewer than half the number of victims in the 1995 heat wave.

More people died from the Chicago heat that week than ordinarily die in an entire year in the whole United States from floods, hurricanes, and tornadoes combined.

Recriminations followed. How could the disaster have happened when warnings of the developing heat wave had been issued days in advance? One answer was subsequently given by the National Oceanic and Atmospheric Administration. The severity of the heat wave, said the agency, was so rare that it was simply not recognized as a public health emergency. "Unfortunately, a heat wave connotes discomfort, not violence; inconvenience, not alarm," said Kathryn D. Sullivan, the leader of a national disaster survey team that investigated the event.

At least Chicago was spared a possible encore to the disaster. Had a storm system come through while the humidity was still high, there could have been unprecedented flooding. The region had dodged that bullet.

But not for long.

Chicago/July 1996
Almost a year to the day after the end of the 1995 heat wave, the skies opened up over northeastern Illinois as never before, and the region suffered its worst flood disaster in recorded weather history.

Once again the air was loaded with moisture, but this time there was no high-pressure cap over the region. While this made the temperatures cooler than in 1995, it also enabled thunderstorms to move freely through the area. And they did, in three phases. On the afternoon of July 17, it rained so heavily that visibility in some localities was down to zero. Chicagoans welcomed the rain, since the region had been in a drought. "There were cracks about three-quarters of an inch wide in the ground outside the office," Paul Merzlock, a meteorologist in the National Weather Service Chicago office, recalled later. "Twenty minutes after it ended, there wasn't even any standing water; the ground absorbed it rapidly and there was virtually no runoff."

So far, so good. Then the second phase began. In the afternoon one severe thunderstorm cell after another moved along an east–west front west of the city, drenching the same localities again and again and spinning off at least one tornado.

The third, most damaging and terrifying phase began in early evening and lasted well into the next morning. The tornado threat tailed off but the rain intensified, falling in solid sheets that at times deposited four inches an hour. With the rain came crashing thunder and unbelievable lightning, generated in monster thunderheads reaching as high as eleven miles into the sky. Generally speaking, the more precipitation there is in a thunderstorm, the more lightning as well. Late on July 17 and early on July 18, the lightning was almost continuous— "just like if you were in a disco with a strobe light going," Merzlock remembers. "You couldn't get out to read the rain in the gauge for fear of being struck," he said. Several houses were set afire, and in a half-mile-square piece of earth near Joliet, observers recorded more than 3,300 cloud-to-ground lightning strikes. Thirty-year veterans of the Weather Service had never known the like.

The *New York Times* described the deluge as "biblical." The heaviest rains fell in a broad swath stretching nearly seventy miles from near Rockford, northwest of Chicago, southeastward through Aurora, to Joliet and Chicago's southern suburbs. Five to ten inches of rain were common across the affected area, and the 16.91-inch rainfall recorded in twenty-four hours at Aurora established a new all-time record for Illinois. "That's pretty amazing," said Merzlock, "considering that a lot of hurricanes don't provide that much rainfall in any one place."

With the rains came the floods. As with thousands of other families, the water drove Kurt and Debbie Krueger and their four children from their home. All that long night, Mrs. Krueger said later, the family kept looking out to see how high the creek behind their house in suburban Orland Park had risen, "but we couldn't tell; it was too dark." The creek answered them in the morning when water came pouring in the back door. The roof collapsed, and the family huddled together, waiting for firefighters to rescue them in a boat; by this time the neighborhood streets were canals. A neighbor got to them in his boat first, about 6:00 A.M., and off they went: the six Kruegers, the neighbor, a German shepherd pup, two cockatiels, a parakeet, two sparrows that Mrs. Krueger was nursing back to health for an animal hospital, and armloads of keepsake photographs. "When you're in an emergency situation," she said, "you just do it—get the kids up and out and the animals up and out, and yourself last."

The living room was flooded to a depth of eighteen inches, and when the family returned, Mrs. Krueger said, "there were worms everywhere, in every room, crack, and wall." They lost almost everything. But they had flood insurance. Nine of every ten eligible Illinois families did not. After the flood, more than 70,000 applications for disaster aid were filed, and more than $100 million in outright grants was dispensed. Crop damage was in the tens of millions of dollars.

Afterward, experts calculated that such a widespread and intense rainfall normally would be likely to occur only once in a thousand years or more.

It was, said Merzlock, "off the chart."

Madrid/November–December 1995
In the year between Chicago's two unprecedented weather catastrophes, top scientists and governmental representatives from around the world gathered in Spain's capital to extract from a vast and often confusing body of knowledge a succinct judgment about what was happening to the earth's climate. Intellectual electricity crackled and political intrigue rumbled through the meeting hall a mile or so from the Prado, Madrid's famed art museum, where the delegates gathered in semicircular rows with each country's name on a placard in front of its delegation. The setting was like a science fiction movie in which the world unites to discuss an invasion by extraterrestrials.

But this discussion had to do with a global threat posed by earthlings themselves. As the scientists and politicians met, 1995 was already assured of being the warmest year for the world as a whole, since people began keeping weather records in the mid-nineteenth century. The average surface temperature of the globe had gone up by about 1 degree Fahrenheit over the preceding century, with greater increases the farther one moved away from the equator; by comparison, the world had warmed by only 5 to 9 degrees, depending on whose measurement one accepts, since the depths of the last Ice Age 18,000 to 20,000 years ago. The rate of warming, scientists calculated, was faster than any experienced in the previous 10,000 years. Mountain glaciers were retreating and the sea level was rising. Far-northern climes were becoming warmer and greener, and some wild creatures like butterflies were shifting their ranges northward. Two years earlier, the upper Mississippi River basin had suffered through its worst flood disaster in memory. And extreme weather like that of Chicago was becoming more common in the United States.

Were human activities responsible for all this?

That question was the most urgent one to be tackled at Madrid by the Intergovernmental Panel on Climate Change (IPCC), chartered by the United Nations to advise the world's governments. The prime suspect in climate change was carbon dioxide. Present in the atmosphere only in minute quantities, it nevertheless exerts a powerful warming effect on the planet by trapping heat in the atmosphere; without it, earth would probably be an ice ball. But the burning of fossil fuels such as coal, oil, and natural gas, which produces carbon dioxide, was boosting atmospheric concentrations of the powerful "greenhouse gas" well above preindustrial levels, with no end to the rise in sight. Environmentalists insisted that this was surely the root cause of the climatic changes. The fossil fuel industry and its lobbyists argued just as forcefully that the climate was not changing, and that even if it were, the changes stemmed from natural fluctuations in the climate system. Both sides found support from one segment or another of a wide spectrum of scientific views.

Always before, the IPCC had waffled on the crucial issue of whether the observed changes were being caused by human activity; natural variability, the panel said, could account for them just as easily. But now important new evidence had been brought to bear on the question of whether there was a human imprint on climate, and many delegates sensed that history was about to be made as the Madrid meeting convened.

The new evidence came from an examination of not just the trend in average global temperature but of the regional patterns of temperature change. Climatologists had come up with a new way to separate the global trend from the climate system's natural fluctuations. They knew that in addition to heat-trapping greenhouse gases, sulfate droplets and particles were also being poured into the atmosphere by industrial processes. These sulfate aerosols, as they are called, cool the atmosphere in their local regions by reflecting sunlight. By using computers to simulate the simultaneous impact of greenhouse gases and aerosols on the atmosphere, the scientists had discovered that the combination produced a peculiar and distinctive pattern of temperature change that was highly unlikely to result from natural changes in climate. When analysts compared this simulated pattern with actual observations over the previous thirty years, they found a reasonably good fit. The fit was far from perfect, but this was the first time scientists had been able to distinguish the human imprint on climate with any clarity at all.

This finding was presented and explained to the Madrid gathering by Benjamin D. Santer of the United States Lawrence Livermore National Laboratory, a cautious, no-nonsense young scientist whose courage and backbone, as will be seen, were to be sorely tested by industry attacks that came close to wrecking his life and work. Not, however, before he presented to the IPCC what turned out to be a winning case for human influence on climate. In the end, after laboring painfully over every word well into the night, the group issued a landmark finding in the annals of climatology: "The balance of evidence suggests a discernible human influence on global climate."

The sentence was a model of caution, a product both of customary scientific circumspection and political compromise. It did not say whether humans were responsible for a lot of the climate change or a little. But for the first time, the world's most authoritative climate group had officially tied human activity to observed climatic change.

The panel went on to predict that the average surface temperature of the earth would rise by about 2 to 6 degrees Fahrenheit by the year 2100, with a best estimate of about 3.5 degrees if greenhouse-gas emissions were not reduced. This would be about half as much as the planet has warmed since the coldest part of the last Ice Age. The warming would not stop at the end of the twenty-first century but would continue into the next century, the panel concluded. By 2100, it said, climate change would be causing widespread ecological, economic, and social dislocations, some benign but most adverse. Deserts would expand. Climate zones would shift. Rising seas would displace hundreds of millions of people. Some island nations could all but disappear. Agriculture in some parts of the Third World would be severely damaged, while northern wheat belts might expand. Some forests might vanish and some species of organisms might be extinguished because they could not adapt to the warming fast enough. Tropical disease outbreaks could increase. Water supplies would be enhanced in some regions but diminished in others.

Of all the effects, the scientists said, extremes of precipitation and temperature, of flood and drought, probably would be the most obvious and common way in which climate change makes itself known to people in their everyday lives, at least in the early years and decades.

If that turned out to be true, the Chicago catastrophes of 1995 and 1996 would be but a prologue.

BUT WHAT DID those catastrophes signify for the here-and-now? Did they signal any kind of an immediate trend?

The answer may lie behind reflections of the Great Smoky Mountains in the big mirrored windows of a generally nondescript modern building in downtown Asheville, North Carolina. There, in the National Climatic Data Center, part of the National Oceanic and Atmospheric Administration, records stretching back to the nation's earliest days provide perhaps the world's most complete set of data on weather and climate, collected over the centuries from a succession of observers across the country and around the globe. Some of the observations on file were made by Thomas Jefferson. Others come from the logs of clipper-ship captains. Taken together, the books and filing cabinets and computer tapes in Asheville comprise much of the raw material with which to determine whether something truly new is going on with the weather today.

Thomas R. Karl, a trim, bespectacled, darkly handsome climatologist with a pleasant button-down manner and a quietly judicious tone, is the data center's director. Growing up in Chicago, he never wanted to be anything but a weather man. Data and the analysis of data have been his main game, and this affinity for the demonstrable and the tangible—for hard proof—long made him skeptical about whether human action is changing the climate. But his views have evolved, and that evolution in some ways symbolizes and epitomizes the evolution of the greenhouse debate itself. Today, he believes, it is getting harder and harder to deny the human imprint on climate. For him, he says, "There was no eureka moment; it's a gradual accumulation of evidence. You come to a point where you would have to purposely try to look the other way not to see some of these things hitting you in the face."

Tom Karl has had a ringside seat at the scientific debate over climate change, and he has published a blizzard of scientific papers on the subject, but his signal contribution so far is perhaps the analyses he and others at the data center performed in the 1990s to determine whether America's weather has been getting more extreme—as the IPCC predicted it should.

They found that it had. Karl and company examined the American weather record since 1910 to determine whether there were any unusual trends in temperature and precipitation. The analysis revealed, in the words of one of their scientific papers, "a persistent increase of extreme events" since the mid-1970s.

Chicago's 1995 heat wave and 1996 deluge were part of that pattern.

What jumps out most arrestingly from the numbers are the precipitation statistics. The Karl crew found that not only had overall precipitation increased in the twentieth century but also that an increase in extreme precipitation events, heavy rain and snowstorms, accounted for most of the upward trend. The reason, say Karl and other climatologists, is that a warming atmosphere causes more water to evaporate and is capable of holding more water vapor to start with. So in a warmer world, the atmosphere holds more moisture. Moreover, the vapor accumulates more rapidly as the warming proceeds. Result: When a storm system develops in this more highly moisturized atmosphere, more precipitation is likely to fall.

Extra-high atmospheric moisture was a key factor in the Chicago catastrophes of 1995 and 1996. And extranormal precipitation was a factor in the upper Mississippi flood of 1993, the Pacific Northwest flood of late 1996, and the Ohio River, Red River, and Oder River floods of 1997. These were floods of a magnitude unknown in recent memory. And while no single weather event can be linked to a global warming trend, Tom Karl for one warns that as the global climate warms, damaging floods will in general become more frequent. Likewise, although no single rainstorm or snowstorm can be laid at global warming's door, cloudbursts and blizzards can be expected to become more severe. People laughed when it was suggested that a January 1996 blizzard that buried parts of the northeastern United States in a record snowfall might have been made worse by global warming. But in general, that is just what would be expected as atmospheric circulation whisks warm, moisture-laden air from the Gulf of Mexico or Caribbean to the North, where cold air turns the moisture to snow.

How closely can the more extreme weather be tied to the greenhouse effect? The scientists in Asheville analyzed their data from the United States to see whether there was any evidence of telltale climatic changes that the computer models say will result from greenhouse warming. These indicators include much-above-normal daily low temperatures; extreme or severe drought in the summer; above-normal wintertime precipitation; and a much-greater-than-normal proportion of precipitation from extreme one-day events. Karl and crew calculated that there was only a 5 to 10 percent chance that the rising incidence of extreme weather could be caused by anything other than the greenhouse effect.

That figure is somewhat shy of the statistical assurance that would convince many scientists, but it may be well above what might convince a prudent person that something different is going on.

Chicago/2070

Predicting what the climate will be like in any given locality seven decades hence, when the children of babies born today will be in early middle age, is a highly chancy business. But a reasonable scenario can be sketched out based on what mainstream climatologists expect would happen in temperate regions generally.

By 2070, if the world economy is still burning fossil fuels at the rate it did in the late twentieth century, the amount of carbon dioxide in the atmosphere could be nearly double what it is today—although such projections are highly uncertain. If that happens, says Tom Karl, the average summertime temperature in Chicago might be about 5 degrees warmer than it is now. In general, Chicago's climate would be more like that of Richmond or Louisville, reflecting a worldwide poleward shift of climatic zones.

This is not all to the bad. On average, spring would come earlier and fall later. There would be more frost-free days, lengthening the growing season. The higher levels of carbon dioxide would spur plant growth; not only would Chicago likely be greener, it would be green longer. The region's once-vast and magnificent prairies, with their tall grasses and spectacular wildflowers, now existing only in small, isolated remnants and lovingly cared for by conservationists, could expand their range by displacing abundant forests to the north.

But events like the 1995 heat wave and 1996 flood would probably become more common. An analysis by Karl and his associates has shown that a killer combination of temperature and humidity like that of 1995 would be perhaps five times more likely than now; the chance of this happening at some time in July, now 1 in 20, would rise to 1 in 4. It is likely that the apparent temperature (what used to be called the temperature-humidity index) would stay at that peak two days in a row, thereby repeating the 1995 disaster, once every four to ten summers. Remember, such a thing had never been recorded in modern weather records before 1995. Summers in general would be hotter, and heat waves that now last two or three days might last four or five.

Death rates would rise among those who did not have air conditioning, and electricity bills would rise for those who did.

Like many temperate regions, Chicago would be wetter, and most of the increase would be accounted for by extreme precipitation events like that of July 1996. Those events would also become more common, and in general they would drop more rain than today's heavy rainfalls. "Instead of seventeen inches in twenty-four hours, you might see twenty-three inches," says Karl, speaking of the all-time record set in Aurora. Between rainstorms, increased heating would evaporate more moisture from the ground, leaving cracked earth like that observed by Paul Merzlock just before the 1996 deluge hit and causing short-term droughts. In years when the vagaries of atmospheric circulation guide rainstorms away from the area, as sometimes happens, the resulting drought would be more severe.

Paradoxically, the winters could be worse as well, or at least snowier. "It could very well be that at the transitions of the seasons there will be less snow," says Karl, since it would be generally warmer and precipitation would be more likely to fall as rain. But in the middle of winter, it would still get cold enough to snow. "You are still going to have to deal with below-zero temperatures in 2070," says Karl. With more moisture in the air, more snow would fall; January and February might see record blizzards.

All of this is very iffy, and even if it all happens, the timing could be different. Moreover, many surprises may lie ahead. It is nevertheless apparent to many climatologists that Chicago and the world have entered a new climatic period. Already, says Tom Karl, the climatic record has been "tilted"—you can't use the trends of the last 150 years as a guide to what will happen in the future.

Neither we nor the earth's climate system has been in just this place before. We are moving into terra incognita.

WHAT IS GOING ON now is the latest chapter in a grand drama that began with the formation of the earth and its atmosphere starting about 4.6 billion years ago. Ever since life emerged about a billion years later, the workings of the atmosphere have in large measure set the conditions for its existence, and living things have in turn modified the atmosphere itself. Much later, climatic change became a driving force in human evolution, a key to why we are the way we are. And like other organisms, humans have been in thrall to weather and climate ever since. Now it appears that people may for the first time be reshaping the climate system on a global scale—with even further consequences for human life.

This book is an account of that grand drama. The story contains a number of broad themes that might provide valuable lessons as people try to understand the weather around them and come to grips with the climate changes now under way and those that might develop in the foreseeable future.

One theme, or lesson, is that extreme climatic change has occurred many times over the ages—throughout earth history, in fact. So the story begins with the cataclysmic birth of the earth and its climate system and goes on to trace the titanic swings of climate that have punctuated the past.

A second theme is that the fate of humanity has been inextricably bound up with climate. So we will explore the ways in which the earth's evolving climate shaped human evolution. Then we will look at the impact of climatic change on the unfolding of human civilization.

A third theme is that in the long sweep of history, people have begun to understand the workings of the climate system only recently, and their understanding is incomplete as they confront the consequences of their own impact on the system. The story therefore chronicles humans' often halting, fumbling, conflicted attempts to make sense of weather and climate, first through myth and superstition and later through the powerful intellectual tools of science. Understanding has come only through struggle, and each new insight about how climate and weather work has challenged conventional wisdom. One result is that scientists today have a fairly comprehensive though imperfect picture of how the system functions. We will explore that still-evolving model of the atmosphere. All of this bears importantly on the big climate questions of the day and on the debate swirling about them, to which the last half of the book is mostly devoted.

Are we indeed changing the climate? If so, how importantly? What are the likely consequences? What should be done about it? These are questions of the gravest import for human society, and the attempt to answer them has been the subject of a juicy and contentious scientific argument. Science proceeds not in a vacuum but is rather an expression of the lives, character, foibles, disputes, rivalries, and talents of its practitioners. Much of climate science, in particular, is carried out today in a political crucible. The argument over climate change is examined here largely through the eyes, work, insights, and intrigues of the scientists involved.

Although something of a consensus has emerged lately among mainstream scientists that the atmosphere is warming and that human activity is at least partly responsible, widespread perplexity and confusion continue to attend the question of climate change. One reason is that the weather itself has seemed so incomprehensible to so many people. Another is that various vested interests on both right and left have muddied the waters of understanding through what might charitably be called a selective reading of scientific evidence. Opposing claims and counterclaims, often exaggerated and distorted, have frequently characterized the debate.

As the world counted down to the third millennium, the extremes of the debate became more shrill. On one end of the spectrum, a what-me-worry? contingent preached a gospel of climate benignity. This point of view, often trumpeted by some political conservatives and representatives of the fossil fuel industry, held that whatever climate change comes will be benign. "Warm is good" was their mantra. At the other end, a London-based publication called *The Ecologist* asserted editorially that "if we wait any longer for conclusive evidence to corroborate what we know to be likely, it will be too late to avoid the very real possibility of catastrophic, runaway climate change that—in the century to come—could make much of our planet effectively uninhabitable."

One recent book raises the apocalyptic specter of a great storm of unimagined magnitude and duration, coming soon, followed by a new ice age that would kill billions of people and convert most of the United States to a frozen wasteland.

The supermarket tabloid press has fairly screamed out a similar message. Some samples from 1999:

Hottest summer in History Will Fulfill a Final Bible Prophecy: THE SECOND COMING YEAR 2000! Weird weather Will Herald the End of the World . . . Say Worried Bible Scholars. (From *Weekly World News* [London])

And:

THE GREAT FLOODS TO COME! Shocking Bible Warnings Confirmed by Global Weather Scientists. Worst in 100 Years. Raging Rivers pour into inland cities. Giant tidal waves smash all coasts. Deadly plagues unleashed. What you need to do to survive, PLUS more. (From *The Sun* [London])

So this book is also an attempt to provide a guide through the shoals of exaggeration and cant, using mainstream climate science as chart and compass. The course is foggy, but the best way to prepare for the voyage is to equip oneself with reliable information. It is hoped that this book will help fill that need.

It is hoped further that as the grand drama unfolds in these pages, readers will develop a renewed appreciation of how we today fit into nature's long history. For all its ups and downs, as will be seen, the earth's climate has been unusually tranquil during our lives and those of our immediate ancestors.

We in the twentieth century have been relatively lucky. The lesson of the past is that our luck could change at any time, with or without human intervention in the workings of climate.

[PART ONE]

[1]

Origins

FOR AT LEAST a million years and hundreds of thousands of gen-erations, the ape-people survived essentially unchanged.

The average ape-woman weighed about 65 pounds, and the ape-man about 100, and they stood three to four feet tall. Each had a brain about the size of an orange—roughly as big as that of the species they most resembled, the chimpanzees. Like the chimps, they spent much of their time in the treetops of the thick, lush African forest. The fruits they mostly lived on grew there, and the forest canopy offered safety from ground-dwelling saber-toothed cats and other killers for whom the ape-people were easy prey. Three million years in the future, the inheritors of the ape-people's genes would deduce that the ape-humans' daily routine, like the chimpanzees', was to move through the forest, picking fruit as they went, scavenging an occasional piece of carrion, and killing and eating an occasional small animal. After combing perhaps two or three miles of landscape in a day they would retire to the treetops, there to sleep in relative safety from the predators below.

In most other ways, there was a wide difference between the ape-people and the chimps. The former walked upright, on two legs, the first species of their evolutionary family to do so routinely. But not all the time. The result, as often happens in evolution, was a compromise: The ape-human could neither climb as well as an ape nor walk as well as a modern human. The ape-people, it would seem, lived a two-part existence—in the trees and on the ground. In a departure from the ape lifestyle, their walking ability enabled them to venture farther into open spaces within the forest to look for food; they were not tied so closely to what was available in the trees.

Their world was hardly an Eden. The ape-human probably could not run fast, and so would have been unable to escape from a big cat or hyena without a substantial head start. Constant vigilance was necessary while on the ground, and numerous ancient skulls crushed by carnivores testify that the ape-human was more prey than predator.

Nevertheless, the ape-people have to be judged an evolutionary success: Their kind persisted perhaps ten times as long as modern humans have so far existed.

A little less than 3 million years ago, that long and successful run was coming to an end. Great forces were about to transform not only the world of the ape-people but also the ape-people themselves. No mysterious black monolith, planted on the savanna by some extraterrestrial force to strike the spark of humanity, was responsible. Rather, great ice sheets were beginning to grow far to the north. The Inheritors, with bigger brains amplified by computers, would later deduce that the ice sheets were accompanied by a drop in the temperature of the North Atlantic Ocean of as much as 25 degrees Fahrenheit, causing cooler, drier air to blow from Europe over Africa. They would also discover that as the northern ice sheets grew higher, they diverted colder, drier air toward the homeland of the ape-people.

The effect of these far-reaching climatic changes was to make Africa drier. This in turn shrank the forest refuges of the ape-people and expanded the open grasslands. All of this forced a survival crisis on the ape-people and the other animals of their world. They would have to adapt or die.

Out of the crisis would emerge the genus *Homo*, our genus.

Behind that development lay more than four and a half billion years of an unimaginably complex and violent coevolution of the earth's climate system and the life it shaped, and by which it was reshaped in return.

THE EARTH AND ITS ATMOSPHERE were born of fire and fury, setting in motion vast processes that are still playing out today and that will continue, scientists believe, for eons to come.

As far as modern scientists can tell, a slowly rotating cloud of dust and gases like hydrogen and helium, perhaps 15 billion miles across, a nebula floating in interstellar space, began to contract. Gravity pulled the smaller dust particles toward larger ones and the cloud began to spin faster and faster, flattening into a disk. Gradually, as the particles compressed into a single mass, the nascent sun materialized. Ever more intense compression boosted the temperature of the mass to nearly 2 million degrees Fahrenheit, setting off nuclear fusion. In fusion, hydrogen atoms combine to form helium, and energy is released as sunshine.

As the sun formed, not all the material in the rotating disk was drawn into it; some continued to orbit the new star. From this rocky material, the planets formed. No earthlings were around to see this, of course, but astronomers have observed many such disks around young stars, and they are confident that our solar system formed in the same way.

In the currently favored scenario of the earth's birth and the formation of its atmosphere, everything happened quickly, relative to geological time. Myriad chunks of rock orbiting the sun coalesced into the building blocks of planets. These planetesimals, as scientists call them, then began to merge with each other, and soon a planet took shape. As it grew bigger, its gravity force increased, attracting more and more planetesimals. The shock of the colliding planetesimals created such heat—several thousand degrees—that all of the naturally occurring water, nitrogen, and carbon in the planetesimals and on the new earth was instantly vaporized.

When the proto-planet reached only three-tenths of its eventual diameter of almost 8,000 miles, it began to hold the vaporized chemicals in its gravitational field, and an atmosphere thus started to accumulate.

Scientists cannot be exactly sure about what the early atmosphere was like. "We don't have any direct data," says James F. Kasting of Pennsylvania State University, an expert on the early earth and ancient climates. "We're sort of relying on theoretical models we build up partly on computers and in our heads."

But according to the dominant view, a key constituent of the early atmosphere was the one that provokes such contention today: carbon. Reacting with sunlight, it took the form of carbon dioxide, a powerful heat-trapping greenhouse gas. Like other greenhouse gases, carbon dioxide lets visible radiation from the sun penetrate to the planet's surface, where it is absorbed and reemitted as infrared radiation. Then the greenhouse gas reabsorbs this heat-producing radiation and bounces part of it back to the surface, warming the planet. Water vapor is an even more potent greenhouse gas, and most of the early atmosphere consisted of water in the form of steam. This combination of factors, along with heat from the interior, might have made the earth some 2,000 degrees Fahrenheit warmer than it otherwise would have been.

The young earth is thus believed to have been a largely molten ball hidden behind a cloud of steam. For perhaps 100 million years, or maybe in as few as 10 million, it continued to absorb hits by planetesimals big and small. Some were probably the size of full-fledged planets. The single most violent and jarring event in the earth's history took place in this early period, it is widely believed by scientists, when a planet-size body struck the earth a glancing blow, chipping off massive chunks that reaccreted to form the moon.

The formation of the earth and its atmosphere were largely completed between about 4.6 billion and 4.5 billion years ago. If all the time between 4.6 billion years ago and today were compressed into a century, the main period of the earth's formation would have taken between one and a half and three years. For about the next fifteen years (some 700 million years in actual time), heavy bombardment by smaller planetesimals, asteroids, and comets continued. Eventually, as the raw materials of the accreting earth were used up, bombardment slowed and the new planet cooled enough to allow the steam in the atmosphere to condense and fall as rain, forming the first ocean. Asteroids and comets still crashed into the earth from time to time, and if they were big enough, as they often were, they would revaporize the ocean. Eventually it would condense again. This may have happened repeatedly.

OUT OF THE CHAOS, the earth's landmasses and precursors of the continents materialized. Plates of solid crust must have been floating atop a global layer of partly molten rock by about 4 billion years ago. By 3.5 billion years ago, parts of the crustal plates may have grown thick enough to rise out of the oceans, creating the first land.

A sort of equilibrium set in as the bombardments tailed off. Much of the water in the atmosphere condensed to form oceans for the last time, and this greatly reduced the greenhouse effect. But the greenhouse warming probably remained intense, thanks to carbon dioxide left over from the bombardment era.

Today the atmosphere holds only a minute trace of the gas, but along with other greenhouse gases including water vapor, the most important, it is more than enough to keep the planet from freezing. Without the natural greenhouse effect, the average surface temperature of today's earth would be about 63 degrees below zero Fahrenheit. With it, the temperature is nearly 60 degrees above zero. Twenty thousand times the amount of today's atmospheric carbon dioxide is locked up, as some form of carbon, in the earth's rocks; if even a tiny part of that had been circulating in the atmosphere during the earth's formative stages, it would have warmed the planet beyond human imagination. There could have been several thousand times as much carbon dioxide in the early atmosphere as now, producing a megagreenhouse atmosphere and trapping more than enough heat to offset what has come to be known as the Faint Young Sun effect. In the earth's formative years, the sun was 30 percent weaker than it is now, and it strengthened only slowly.

As it did, the earth's dense atmosphere thinned and carbon dioxide levels dropped, exerting a cooling effect that now acted to counterbalance the sun's increasing warmth. Scientists today see this as part of an elegant thermostatic feedback loop linking the atmosphere, the land,

and the oceans. It developed early in the earth's history and still operates today. Without it, scientists like Kasting believe, the earth could never have developed a habitable climate. It works this way: Rainfall removes heat-trapping carbon dioxide from the atmosphere and changes it to carbonic acid contained in rainwater. In a process called weathering, the carbonic acid in the rain reacts chemically with silicate rocks on the ground, releasing calcium and a form of carbon into the groundwater. These chemicals flow into streams, rivers, and ultimately the ocean, where tiny organisms use them to make protective shells of calcium carbonate. Eventually some of the shells settle to the bottom and become part of the ocean sediment.

The earth's crustal plates come into play at this point. The planet's mostly solid mantle, just under the crust, is in a constant, slow roiling motion, and this keeps the surface plates moving. When the plates move apart, commonly under the sea but also on land, molten rock from the mantle spurts upward through the gap to create volcanoes. But when plates converge, the edge of one plate slides under the edge of another—subduction, the process is called. The calcium carbonate ocean sediments that began as atmospheric carbon dioxide are subducted as part of the sliding plate. This exposes the carbon-bearing sediments to great pressure and high temperatures, reconverting the carbon in the sediments to carbon dioxide. It reenters the atmosphere through volcanic eruptions, thus completing a grand cycle.

This carbonate-silicate cycle, as it is called, takes more than 500,000 years to complete, and many scientists believe it acts as a thermostat in this fashion: If the earth's surface temperature increases, more water evaporates from oceans, rivers, and lakes, just as in a birdbath in the summer's heat. As a result, when the evaporated moisture eventually condenses high in the atmosphere, there is more rain. More rain means that more carbon dioxide is removed from the air. The heavier rain also erodes rocks faster, allowing the carbon from the atmosphere to be recycled through the earth system in greater quantities. With less carbon dioxide in the air, the earth cools. If it gets too cold, however, less water evaporates from the planet's surface; there is less rain to remove carbon dioxide from the atmosphere, and the gas builds up again and rewarms the earth. Scientists believe this ponderous thermostat is what keeps the earth's temperature within very broad bounds over the long term. It may have kept the global climate relatively stable as the Faint Young Sun gradually became brighter. In any event, the earth's climate when compared with that of other planets in the solar system is like Goldilocks's ideal porridge: not too hot, not too cold, but just right for life.

LIFE FIRST APPEARED near the end of the period of heavy bombardment, probably as early as 3.8 or 3.9 billion years ago and certainly by 3.5 billion. Given repeated vaporization of the global ocean, it may have materialized several times, through chemical reactions of one sort or another, only to be repeatedly erased. The first microscopic fossils of living things appear about fifteen years into our century-long, telescoped version of earth history. They were exceedingly simple forms: single cells shaped like little balls or rods or filaments made of linked cells. Those that lived in the deep sea were white; those on the surface were blue, green, or purple. None of these creatures used oxygen in its metabolism, and there was little or no oxygen in the atmosphere. Eventually these algal cells coalesced into larger mats that imparted splashes of color to a bleak, rocky world.

From its inception, it appears, life altered the earth's climate. Some bacteria consume carbon as they perform photosynthesis. (This is the chemical process in which bacteria and plants convert the energy of sunlight into sugars—a process that today ultimately nourishes the vast majority of complex life on earth.) By using up carbon dioxide during photosynthesis, the early bacteria helped reduce atmospheric concentrations of the heat-trapping gas, thereby promoting a more moderate climate. But they made up for this depletion, at least partly, by producing methane, another greenhouse gas. They also gave off oxygen as a by-product, a sort of environmental afterthought that would have enormous implications for the planet's future.

And that is essentially the way things stood for about the next 1.5 billion years, until about 2.2 billion years ago, roughly halfway through earth history. All the major elements of the climate system—the atmosphere, greenhouse gases, the oceans, the land, the movement of crustal plates, volcanism, the carbon cycle, living organisms, and of course the engine driving the entire system, the sun—were firmly in place and functioning.

BY ABOUT 2.2 BILLION YEARS AGO, the earth's climate had cooled substantially as the carbon cycle settled into its routine. Now it would plunge to one of the two coldest extremes in the planet's history.

So deep and pervasive was the chill that it froze much of the tropics. Glacial ice crept to within 11 degrees of the equator, roughly the latitude of the modern countries of Panama and Costa Rica. It is possible that ice covered the entire globe: Snowball Earth. It was Icebox Earth for certain, and life apparently survived by retreating to the ocean depths, possibly seeking refuge near undersea volcanoes or persisting in patches of ice-free water.

What could have caused the earth to go from the Hadean heat and violence of its infancy to glacial cold? The answer apparently lies in the interplay of greenhouse gases, the evolving sun, rising amounts of atmospheric oxygen produced by bacterial photosynthesis, and continent-building.

One possible scenario runs like this: By now there was enough oxygen in the air to create a planetary chain of chemical reactions that drastically reduced the amount of heat-trapping methane in the atmosphere. With this major greenhouse gas removed from the scene, temperatures plunged. But this time the thermostat did not stabilize the climate system. The reason may be that as more continental crust formed, it presented more rock surface to be weathered and thereby accelerated the rate at which carbon dioxide was being removed from the atmosphere; there was not enough of it left to keep the planet from freezing.

In time the first great glaciation ended. No one is sure just how and why, but it may have been that the interaction among the carbon cycle, the building of continents, and the sun's gradually increasing luminosity achieved some new equilibrium. However it happened, the planet embarked on a billion years or more of ice-free existence. Life-forms proliferated. Many more kinds and colors of photosynthezing algae appeared. A menagerie of protozoa evolved.

A second bout of glaciation—actually several separate bouts—plunged the earth into its deepest ice age ever between 750 million and 550 million years ago. One arresting theory says that each of the bouts of deep freeze was followed by a catastrophic warming and that the back-and-forth switches from extreme cold to extreme heat happened this way: During the cold phase, carbon dioxide emissions from terrestrial volcanoes built up gradually in the atmosphere, eventually reaching a threshold where trapped heat thawed the planet, possibly in as short a span as a few thousand years. The thawing had two further effects: With less ice and snow, less heat was reflected from the earth, warming it even more; and the warmer atmosphere evaporated more water from the ocean. The resulting increase in water vapor intensified the greenhouse effect, producing the superwarming.

WHEN THE SEESAW BETWEEN intense cold and intense heat ended at last, life exploded, expanded, and took on innumerable new forms. For the first time, there were multitudes of organisms big enough for a modern human to see, if one had been around at the time. On our compressed century-long scale of earth history it is now Year 87. Geologists mark this as the start of the Cambrian period, 540 million years ago, and from that point onward the earth's living things became ever more complex and various, spreading out of the ocean and onto the land. By 500 million years ago, most of the modern groupings of marine animals had appeared. By 400 million, the first small plants were growing on land. By 350 million, the first creepy-crawlies—scorpionlike arthropods—were scuttling across the ground, followed soon by the first insects and the first four-footed amphibians.

But severe climatic changes brought about by the interplay of plate movements, rock weathering, volcanism, the sun's growing strength, and fluctuating levels of atmospheric carbon dioxide continued to alter the environmental rules of the game from time to time, wiping out large chunks of the global biota and opening up opportunities for new life-forms to replace them.

The biggest of these biotic catastrophes and rebirths, around 250 million years ago (about Year 94 on the compressed century time scale), coincided with a merger of all the world's continental plates to form a single supercontinent, which scientists today call Pangaea. It extended over both poles, providing a lot of surface on which ice could accumulate. Glaciers probably formed there, and if so, they would have locked up so much of the earth's fixed and finite water supply that sea levels would have fallen drastically. The sea level did indeed fall, although some scientists suggest that the cause might have been changes in the earth's mantle that enlarged the ocean basins. In any case, it appears that as the receding ocean exposed the seafloor, many marine species died out.

Exposure of the ocean bottom also may have set in motion chemical reactions that removed oxygen from the atmosphere and added carbon dioxide to it; animals had less oxygen to breathe, and carbon dioxide would have rewarmed the earth. At about the same time, volcanic eruptions in Siberia, dwarfing any of our time, may have added to the climatic instability by injecting sun-reflecting aerosols into the atmosphere over the short term and adding still more carbon dioxide in the long term. As the carbon dioxide reheated the globe, sea levels rose again, wiping out organisms that had established themselves on exposed continental shelves.

Exactly how the interplay of all these factors worked to cause the extinction is unclear. But the drastic global changes involved, coming near the end of what geologists call the Permian period, wiped out about 90 percent of all species in the ocean, more than two-thirds of all reptile and amphibian families, and 30 percent of insect orders— the only time insects have ever undergone a mass extinction. Before the Permian extinction, most marine life consisted of stationary creatures that sat on the bottom of the sea, lying in wait for prey or filtering food from the water. Afterward, free-swimming fish and mobile animals like squids and snails dominated.

One complicating factor in the ancient climatic equation appears to be that the proliferation of life removed more and more carbon dioxide from the atmosphere. As more plants photosynthesized and then died, or were eaten by animals that then died, more organic material containing carbon was buried. This reduced the amount of atmospheric carbon dioxide from what it would have been otherwise. It also put vast quantities of carbon into deep storage. For tens of millions of years before the Permian catastrophe, great swamps with luxuriant stands of plants covered much of the Northern Hemisphere. When plants died during this fecund period, they were rapidly buried in water. This forestalled complete decay and short-circuited the return of carbon to the global cycle by cutting off oxygen to the bacteria that decompose plants. As the dead vegetation accumulated it turned to peat and then lignite, and then coal.

Today that coal is being globally recycled by humans who dig it up and burn it, reconverting the carbon back into atmospheric carbon dioxide. Likewise, as plants and animals were buried and compressed in sedimentary rocks in nonglaciated lands between about 350 million and 65 million years ago, their remains were converted to oil and natural gas.

In our era, burning of all these fossil fuels is steadily increasing the amount of heat-trapping carbon dioxide in the atmosphere. Life, through *Homo sapiens,* is exerting its impact on climate in a new way.

AS THE GREAT SAGA of climate and life draws closer to the present, it reveals itself to scientists in ever greater detail, through a variety of clues that are unavailable for earlier eons.

Experts can, for example, infer the climate of a given time and place—say, 100 million years ago in the Arctic—by looking at plant and animal fossils; an alligator, for instance, cannot live in a cold climate. Scientists can also drill into lake and ocean sediments and glacial ice, and by examining and dating successive layers they can read the ancient climatic record as revealed in the kinds of pollen found and in the chemical content of air bubbles and the shells of tiny animals.

And what they have read in this fashion about the fascinating period called the Cretaceous, from about 140 million to 65 million years ago (Years 97 to about 98.5 on our compressed century-scale of earth time), tells them that this was the warmest interval since the great Permian extinction—Hothouse Earth.

In the mid-Cretaceous, there were no large ice sheets. The climate of Hudson Bay, the Bering Sea, and the Yukon resembled that of twentieth-century Florida. (By this time, Pangaea had long since broken up and the continents were approaching their present shapes and positions.) Alligators and dinosaurs—this was their heyday—lived above the Arctic Circle, on the north slope of Alaska. Trees grew where there is now tundra. The fossils of early primates, which lived only in warm climes, have been found in Cretaceous rocks on Ellesmere Island, only 500 miles from the North Pole.

Palm trees grew on the land where Chicago would someday sit.

During this time, the average global temperature was some 10 to 20 degrees Fahrenheit higher than now. And since the earth was 5 to 9 degrees colder in the depths of the last Ice Age 20,000 years ago than it is now, 15 to 30 degrees might represent the possible range of natural variation in the average global temperature—given the present configuration and arrangement of the continents and present levels of solar radiation.

The Cretaceous came to an end suddenly, about 65 million years ago, with another mass extinction that, while not so severe as that of the Permian period, is much more familiar because it wiped out the dinosaurs. The most popular explanation is that a comet or asteroid crashed into the earth in the Yucatán, producing a cloud that blacked out the sun for months, shutting off photosynthesis and thereby starving the animals. Some scientists continue to cling to alternative explanations. In any case, sometime after the great extinction, about 50 million years ago, the earth embarked on a long, pronounced cooling trend. While there have been scores of spikes above the trend line (our present warm climate is one such spike) and valleys below it, the basic trend itself has continued to the present day.

By about 36 million years ago, there was once again ice at the poles and Antarctica was freezing. About 14 million years ago, in what geologists call the Miocene epoch, the drop in global temperature steepened. It is now late in Year 99 on our century-scale calendar of earth history, and the stage is set for the entrance of humans.

[2]

Children of the Atmosphere

O N THE VELDT of what is now Namibia, seas of tall, golden grasses studded by crook-branched, flat-crowned acacia trees stretch out to the east, toward the nearby Kalahari Desert. Dry riverbeds cut across this savanna landscape, and in the summer wet season, walls of water fed by torrential monsoon rains occasionally flood the gullies, just as they have since the first members of the human line appeared in Africa some 2.5 million years ago.

As a girl, Elisabeth Munchmeyer often rode off from her stepfather's sheep ranch on her own, striking out on horseback across the golden grass. The Kalahari bushmen, relying on knowledge of the environment gleaned by ancestors reaching back to the fateful appearance of the first members of our genus, taught young Elisabeth what plants were safe to eat. She learned firsthand about the dangers of leopards, lions, snakes, and scorpions. Zebras, giraffes, and great herds of wildebeest and springbuck populated her youth. Years later, long after marriage had changed her name to Elisabeth Vrba and she had become a tenured paleontologist at Yale University, she pined for her homeland's open spaces, its gorges and canyons. Connecticut's lush greenery closed her in, depriving her of a horizon.

But in her intellectual world, the horizons remained expansive. The savanna lived on there, the savanna of 6 million to 1 million years ago, when the forebears of *Homo sapiens* were evolving in the very part of the world she rode across as a girl. In exploring that ancient environment through the proxy agent of fossils, she came up with one of those fresh, elegant insights that instantly elevates a scientist above the crowd. This particular insight propelled climatic change to center stage as a likely stimulus of human evolution.

As is often the case in science, the events that led to her transformational insight happened by accident. If her naval officer father had not been killed in World War II, her mother would not have moved with two-year-old Elisabeth from Hamburg to what was then German West Africa. If Elisabeth hadn't later met and married George Vrba, a civil engineer, she never would have quit her doctoral studies in molecular biology at the University of Witwatersrand in Johannesburg to join her new husband in Pretoria. And if she hadn't moved to Pretoria, she would never have encountered C. K. (Bob) Brain of the Transvaal Museum, one of the prime centers of research on human origins, about whom she heard from a colleague at a dinner one evening. Determinedly searching for some field in which she could continue working toward a Ph.D., Vrba thought that Brain's work at the nearby Swartkrans cave, one of the mother lodes of early prehuman fossils, sounded wonderful, and it was arranged for them to meet.

"So I came to see him," Vrba recalls, "and he took me to a great big room, piled with big rocks. You could see there were fossils inside. He said, 'These are antelopes, and there are hundreds, and nobody wants to do them. They're just lying there. Do you want to do them?' "

"Do them" meant using acid in a painstaking process to remove rock material encasing the fossils. It looked like a terrible job. "I said, 'I don't know, I never thought of this,' " Vrba remembers. "I said, 'Look, I'll tell you what. Can I come for six months and browse around and see whether I can do it or not?' " With that, she plunged into the lonely and tedious task of cleaning ancient antelope skulls and liberating them from their imprisoning rock, at no pay, and for a time she wondered about the wisdom of her decision.

But gradually she realized that the fossils were revealing to her an exciting evolutionary pageant. She made them the subject of her Ph.D. dissertation, in which she described and classified hundreds and hundreds of ancient antelopes. Once the classification was complete, and she compared the fossils with the bones and teeth of modern antelopes, patterns came popping out. One of the most intriguing patterns was that the kinds of antelopes present in Africa varied, in waves, over time: Sometimes species that live in moister, wooded environments predominated; at other times those that live in drier, grassland surroundings were ascendant.

Vrba realized that if she could determine the mixture of types of antelopes in a given stratum of dated fossils, she could tell whether a wet or dry climate prevailed in a given slice of ancient time. Once she had performed this analysis, it became clear that the African climate had changed repeatedly over the long term. And the broad time period in which her many species of antelopes lived was the same one in which the ancestors of all modern people first appeared and then evolved into something approaching human form. Presumably, the proto-humans were subject to the same climatic changes as the antelopes. Could it be that the emergence of both antelopes and proto-humans was triggered by climatic change?

The idea that climate had an effect on the birth and death of species was an old one, going back to Charles Darwin. But few had paid much attention to it in later years. It is "a long and unexceptional, unquestioned tradition among geologists," says Vrba, that massive physical changes—usually climatic ones—coincide with massive turnover in the kinds of animals that lived on earth. What she did was take this concept a step further by wondering whether turnovers also might occur on more limited regional or even local scales and by extending the idea to human evolution.

Pursuing this line of thought, she discovered what appeared to be two distinct evolutionary pulses associated with proto-humans. In the first pulse many of the typical groups of African antelopes that live in a dry, grassy environment appeared on earth for the first time around the end of the Miocene period 5 million years ago—roughly the same period in which the first ape-people, called australopithecines by scientists, were believed to have split off from the ape line.

In the second and more pronounced pulse, a wave of extinctions of antelope species and emergences of new ones occurred between 3 million and 2.5 million years ago—close to the time when, according to fossil discoveries, the first members of the genus *Homo,* our genus, appeared.

Vrba concluded that the same forces that caused the periodic turnovers of antelope species also caused the evolutionary changes that produced proto-humans—hominids, they are called. The hominids, she postulated, simply rode along on waves of general evolutionary change. She called these waves turnover pulses, and her idea became known as the turnover-pulse hypothesis. The hypothesis has not yet been subjected to enough proof to elevate it to a theory, an idea generally regarded as an accurate enough version of reality to be relied on as a building block of science. But in the late 1990s it was the most compelling hypothesis in its field, setting the terms of a debate over how—not so much whether as how—climate critically shaped human evolution.

What caused the pulses of evolutionary change? The most likely explanation, Vrba said in papers published in 1974 and 1975 in the journal *Nature,* was that a cooling of the global climate had made subtropical Africa drier. This, in turn, was what caused the forests to shrink and the grasslands to expand, transforming the habitat in which both the antelopes and the early hominids emerged and subsequently evolved.

The paper was a bombshell among those who study human origins. At the time, the favored view of evolution held that it proceeded gradually, over millions of years, as species competed with each other and nature selected the winners. Now new ideas were afoot. Two American paleontologists, Stephen Jay Gould of Harvard University and Niles Eldredge of the American Museum of Natural History, had just dropped their own bombshell, postulating that individual species remain essentially unchanged for millions of years and then disappear suddenly, to be replaced just as suddenly by new species. This theory of "punctuated equilibrium," which ran counter to the popular idea of gradual evolutionary change, created a furor, but over time it was increasingly accepted.

Vrba took this idea two steps further. First, she said, the main driving force in the sudden extinction of one species and sudden birth of another, including the first hominid species, was environmental change, specifically climatic change; and second, it caused not just a single species here and there to disappear and be replaced by another, but rather whole panoplies of species at once. In some cases, rapid environmental change simply wipes out a given species. In others, some members of a species are luckily endowed with genetically determined characteristics that enable them to adapt to the change, outlasting those that do not have the characteristics; the result is a new species. In still other instances, environmental change geographically isolates different populations of the same species, which diverge from each other through random genetic mutation and become two new species.

But environmental change—which frequently means climatic change—is the key in all these instances.

THE PARTICULAR CLIMATIC CHANGE linked to the first appearance of hominids was the sharp speed-up about 14 million years ago of the post-Cretaceous cooling trend. So pervasive was the cooling that the Antarctic ice sheet became permanently fixed. Some scientists say that a drop in atmospheric concentrations of carbon dioxide may have triggered the cooling. Others say it might have been caused by changes in ocean currents caused by changes in landforms. Whatever its cause, the cooling was expressed in Africa primarily as an increase in aridity. A drier climate favors grasslands over forests, and fossilized vegetation from across sub-Saharan Africa shows that grasslands had indeed expanded and that forests had contracted, by the end of the Miocene period, between 6.5 million and 5.5 million years ago.

At about the same time, two of the earth's crustal plates whose edges abutted each other in eastern Africa were moving apart, deepening the Rift Valley that cuts north and south through Ethiopia, Kenya, and Tanzania. Land east of the rift rose higher than that to the west, and so became cooler and drier. New mountains also rose on either side of the Rift Valley, altering atmospheric circulation patterns so that the dryness of East Africa was accentuated, while the climate remained moist west of the valley. East Africa thus became a prime cradle of human evolution.

The apes living in East Africa before the big change probably would have experienced heavy monsoon rains in the summer. The rains created thousands of crocodile-filled lakes and saturated the lush subtropical forests with moisture. One pictures our remote ancestors, dripping wet, hunkering down in the branches of the forest canopy to endure the assault of drenching storm fronts racing in from the Atlantic.

No single ape would have lived long enough to notice the change, but gradually the rains came less frequently and dropped less water than before. This appears to have been a crucial environmental change leading to the human line. It allowed grasslands to expand and forced forests to shrink, cutting the African landscape into a patchwork mosaic of forest and savanna. As a result, says Vrba, formerly continuous populations of some forest-dwelling ape and monkey species probably were divided into isolated subpopulations living in forest fragments. "Think of a monkey species," Vrba says. "It used to be continuously distributed across the forest. Now it's sitting in ten little islands. It's still a forest animal. It's not living in the savanna. But because it's cut apart, it genetically diverges. I think that is how I visualize the beginnings of hominids: Some of the apes got cut apart in a forested island and diverged to become hominids." This exact kind of species divergence, she says, has been seen in some modern monkeys.

In time, the main thing that set the early hominids apart from early apes was that they walked on two legs. Without this facility, the newly evolved hominids would have been, in effect, just another species of tree-dwelling ape. How and why did they begin to walk upright? The answer remains shrouded in the mists of antiquity, but Vrba and others believe that the expansion of the grasslands may have prompted hominids to spend more time on the ground, either traveling to find food in the increasingly separated forest patches or foraging on the grassland itself.

The oldest hominid fossils clearly indicating that their owners walked upright are 4.2 million years old. These creatures, members of a species dubbed *Australopithecus anamensis,* were a little bigger than chimps and similar in some respects to both apes and modern humans. By 3.9 million years ago, the form of ape-human known to have persisted for at least the next million years had appeared. Called *Australopithecus afarensis* (a more southern version was designated *Australopithecus africanus*), this was the slender man-ape with the half-human, half-ape body architecture and the orange-size brain we met in the opening of Chapter 1.

Then, sometime before 2 million years ago, the ape-human disappears from the fossil record. About the same time, there appear the first members of the genus *Homo*—direct descendants of the ape-human and the founder of the human line to which *Homo sapiens* belongs. The first skulls indicating that early *Homo* had a bigger brain than the ape-people show up at about 2 million years ago. The brain was also shaped differently from that of the ape-people, with a larger frontal lobe that could accommodate more sophisticated information processing. *Homo* was flatter-faced, with smaller grinding molars, a weaker jaw, and larger front teeth than the ape-human. Standing perhaps 5 feet 8 inches tall, this new species had longer legs, with bones shaped more like ours, indicating that it had shifted permanently to life on the ground. And it used tools—primitive, unrefined stone flakes—as knives and pulverizers.

Other, heavier, bigger-boned species of hominids, called robust australopithecines, were also evolving from the ape-humans at this crucial juncture in human evolution. What happened, says Vrba, "was a splitting up of the lineages—all hell's breaking loose." Exactly how many kinds of hominids erupted from this evolutionary spasm is unknown, but paleontologists today tend to think that the human genealogy at this point was not at all like the straight-line progression of traditional textbooks but rather more like the multiple branches of a bush. The idea of this "radiation" of species, as evolutionary biologists call it, is made more persuasive by the fact that it happened simultaneously with Vrba's well-documented radiation of antelopes and with radiations of African bats, rodents, and shrews as well.

ONCE AGAIN global climatic change appears to have stimulated this dramatic and fateful evolutionary pulse. Between about 3 million and 2.6 million years ago, there was yet another relatively steep downward step in the more general, overall global cooling trend of the post-Cretaceous world, accompanied by a further drying of the African climate and expansion of its grasslands. The dry period coincided with the first appearance, since before the Cretaceous era, of large North American and European ice sheets—the most dramatic manifestion of the long-term post-Cretaceous global cooling. One theory says that the gradual closing of the Isthmus of Panama was responsible for this plunge into ice age conditions. According to this view, the closing of the isthmus redirected ocean currents so that they altered the transport of heat to the North Atlantic region, setting in motion the on-again-off-again glaciations that have lasted to this day. Another theory says that the cause was the continuing rise of the Himalaya Mountain chains, which realigned atmospheric circulation patterns and drew down atmospheric carbon dioxide by thrusting up more weathering surfaces.

Peter deMenocal of Columbia University's Lamont-Doherty Earth Observatory believes that throughout the age of the ape-humans, the climate regime of sub-Saharan Africa was independent of that farther north. But once the northern glaciation began, he says, the polar ice sheets promoted cooler and drier conditions in subtropical Africa. Based on computer simulations, he calculates that glaciation caused a drop of as much as 25 degrees Fahrenheit in the surface temperature of the North Atlantic Ocean and by 3.5 to 10 degrees over West Africa. The contrast between the cold Atlantic and the warmer African continent intensified trade winds, according to this analysis, blowing cooler and drier air from Europe over Africa. An independent analysis of pollen from sediments just off the western coast of Africa seems to support these findings.

The ape-people would have experienced all of this as diminished rainfall and, more important, as the onset of more sharply delineated wet and dry seasons. Now the monsoon rains from the west, off the Atlantic, were lighter. Subtropical Africa was now bone dry for much of the year. Consequently, the grasslands expanded even more at the expense of the forests.

These factors, Vrba and others believe, combined to create a crisis of survival for the ape-humans and many of their fellow creatures. First, the shrinking of the forest both deprived the australopithecines of security and reduced the supply of forest fruits and nuts on which they largely relied. Second, the onset of sharper seasons drastically cut food supplies everywhere in the neighborhood in the dry season. So the hominids were forced, according to this line of thinking, to search a wider area to get enough food. And that meant adapting to life on the ground full time.

An alternative view, held by Rick Potts, an expert on human evolution at the Smithsonian Institution, says that *Homo* emerged not as part of a general evolutionary pulse brought on by a single shift to a cooler, drier climate but rather as a response to continuous climatic change over time. It was the very fact of change, according to Potts, that provided the evolutionary impetus. While there was a general trend in the direction of cooling and drying, he says, the climate often shifted back and forth between relatively cool-dry states and warm-wet ones. This in turn caused forest and grassland habitats to coalesce and break apart again and again.

Either way, the changing environment would have put a premium on a rapidly developing human ability: thinking, and especially planning ahead. This in turn put an evolutionary premium on the development of more powerful information-processing equipment: a bigger brain. In this situation, says Vrba, natural selection favors two characteristics: brains and locomotion. "And then think of the bonus," she marvels. "You get upright in order to walk around, and what have you got? A beautiful pair of free hands to make tools, to carry babies, to carry things. I think the whole thing went together."

It was by no means certain that these pioneering proto-humans would survive, and if their bold full-time move into the dangerous grasslands had failed, we probably would not be here today. It may be that many populations made the shift to the ground but were wiped out en masse by predators, with only a few groups surviving. But the dice fell right for at least one population, and hominids for the first time were freed from the constraints on brain and body development that had kept the ape-people on an evolutionary treadmill for so long.

Bands of early *Homo* soon began foraging farther from their home bases and exploiting a wider variety of food, including meat. Although the ape-people probably had supplemented their diet with small mammals and carrion, meat would have had an increasing value to *Homo,* particularly when vegetation disappeared during the driest periods of the generally drier climate. It also provided a more concentrated source of nutrition for a *Homo* mother, enabling her better to bear the increased metabolic cost of nourishing a child while its bigger, calorie-hogging brain was growing most rapidly. At the same time, according to one hypothesis, a shift to meat-eating means an animal can devote less of its body's energy to breaking down the cellulose in plants, leaving more energy to be devoted to the brain.

While *Homo* was evolving in this more sophisticated direction, the other offshoot of the ape-people—the heavy-bodied robust australopithecines—adapted to the drier, more seasonal climate in a different manner. They limited themselves to one kind of habitat, the denser vegetation along rivers, where they concentrated on eating coarse, hard seeds and tubers that were difficult and time-consuming to harvest and afforded relatively meager nutrition. While *Homo* became a versatile, wide-ranging generalist, the robust australopithecines backed themselves into an evolutionary corner. While one species could be flexible in the face of adversity and so persevered, the other eventually passed from the stage after a million-year run.

NEITHER THE POST-CRETACEOUS global cooling trend nor the alternating wet-dry African climatic cycles ended with the emergence of *Homo;* both continued to exert an evolutionary force on the human line. The wet-dry cycles continued to oscillate within the overall drying trend, in phase with the waning and waxing of northern ice sheets, according to Peter deMenocal. The waxing and waning of the ice, in turn, took place according to a rhythm dictated by long-term cycles in the earth's position and movement relative to the sun. There are three of these cycles, overlapping. The conventional wisdom among experts is that taken together, they constitute the pacemaker of the ice ages.

The shortest cycle, which is repeated in periods of 19,000 and 23,000 years, is a wobble in the earth's rotation (comparable to the wobble of a spinning top as it slows down). The second movement is a variation in the tilt of earth's axis, which shifts by about 3 degrees over a 41,000-year cycle. In the third movement, earth's orbit stretches slightly from nearly circular to more elliptical and back again every 100,000 years or so. The combined effect of these cyclical movements is to slowly but constantly alter the angle and distance from which the sun's energy strikes the earth—especially the northern part of the Northern Hemisphere, where the great glaciers ebb and flow.

When the orbital movements allow less sunlight to fall on those latitudes, millennium after millennium, less snow melts in the summer. As it accumulates, it gets compressed into ice, and the glaciers grow. This astronomical theory of glaciation was advanced in the 1920s by Milutin Milankovitch, a Serbian mathematician, but confirmed only in the 1970s and 1980s, when analysis of chemical clues contained in the shells of tiny marine creatures called foraminifera, buried in ocean sediments, found that the comings and goings of the ice coincided with the orbital movements.

From the onset of the Northern Hemisphere glaciation about 2.8 million years ago until about a million years ago, it appears, the glaciers advanced and retreated according to the 41,000-year, 23,000-year, and 19,000-year Milankovitch cycles, with the 41,000-year cycle dominant. The warm-wet and cold-dry cycles in Africa followed suit, constantly altering the African environment. But even as the cycles continued their inevitable rhythm, according to deMenocal, the larger trend of global climate took two more pronounced temperature step-downs.

The first of these may have given the evolutionary push from which emerged the major link between early *Homo* and modern humans. The link species, tall and long-legged with the body of a powerful run-

ner, is today called *Homo erectus*. These creatures represented a prodigious leap in evolution. It was not simply that *Homo erectus* had
better tools, making two-surfaced, sharp-edged hand axes, to replace
the simple, unrefined stone flakes used by earlier *Homo* species. What
really set *Homo erectus* apart was that it was the first hominid to strike
out from Africa, colonize much of the world, and show itself able to
survive in a wide range of climatic and environmental conditions.
Within a very short time after its appearance, *Homo erectus* had
spread across Asia as far as what is now China and Indonesia—perhaps
to escape a long African drought that accompanied the cooling and
forced them out of their African homeland. Some speculate that the
cooling may also have opened the way for this expansion out of Africa
by locking up so much water in ice that shrinking seas exposed a wide
land bridge between Africa and Asia.

The second pronounced drop in temperature took place about
900,000 years ago, inaugurating a new climatic era in which the periodic swings above and below the downward trend line became higher
and deeper than ever, and the ice sheets grew more massive. This
marked the onset of a pattern of alternating glacial and interglacial
eras that is still in place and in which modern humans burst onto the
scene. The pattern is that of repeated ice ages lasting 100,000 years or
so, interspersed with brief warm periods, or interglacials, of 8,000 to
perhaps 40,000 years.

We live in the most recent of these interglacial periods, now about
10,000 years along.

The pattern of each 100,000-year glacial episode has been similar: a
gradual descent into widely fluctuating degrees of deep cold, punctuated by relatively brief warm periods that come on suddenly, followed by an abrupt bounce back to full interglacial warmth.

Paleoclimatologists remain puzzled as to how the climate system
has been responding so strongly to the 100,000-year Milankovitch cycle, to the weakest of the Milankovitch pacemakers. Many scientists
believe the 100,000-year cycle triggers complex and far-reaching
changes in the ocean-atmosphere system that do the actual work of
bringing on the ice ages. Others point to the possibility of powerful

feedbacks within the climate system that amplify the 100,000-year cycle.

Still another thought is that once the Milankovitch cycle starts to warm the northern latitudes, glaciers start to melt and push more freshwater into the sea. The influx of freshwater could dilute the salt that makes heat-carrying ocean currents sink, rise, and perform their function of transporting heat around the globe. This could cause the currents to weaken or stop, depriving northern climes of heat. And, of course, the carbon cycle must be involved in some way. Analysis of air bubbles trapped in Antarctic ice show that atmospheric carbon dioxide rises and falls in rough parallel with the ice age cycle. Recent studies of the bubbles have suggested that the warming that ends an ice age is touched off by the Milankovitch cycle but is then amplified by carbon dioxide released by the decay of plants whose growth and spread was stimulated by the initial warming. The warmth would be amplified still further when the melting of the ice sheets means less sunlight is reflected off the earth.

Whatever combination of stimuli and feedbacks drives the ice ages, it has periodically buried much of the Northern Hemisphere in ice up to two miles thick; the last time, the ice moved as far south as the Ohio Valley in the United States and to a line stretching from England to the Ukraine in Europe. The human family from *Homo erectus* onward has persevered through it all.

With *Homo erectus,* the family may have gone a long way toward liberating itself from the influence of climate and environment as an evolutionary force. Some experts in human origins believe that from then on, culture—the whole complex of tools, knowledge, communication, social relations, political organization, and economic strategies that flows from intelligence—began to overshadow the biological aspect of human evolution. The most striking early evidence of this, says Niles Eldredge, was the migration of *Homo erectus* out of Africa. "In other words," he has said, "instead of speciation or extinction marking this particular spasm of global cooling, we see the expansion of a tropical-adapted species (*H. erectus*) northwards" into cold, coniferous forests almost in the shadow of the ice sheets. There they probably would have experienced climate and weather much like that of Alberta or Saskatchewan today: extremely cold winters and hot summers.

With that, the human family had expanded its ecological niche beyond the tropics and subtropics of Africa to encompass the world.

THE LAST TIME that climate may have had a direct shaping role in human evolution was in connection with the emergence, dominance, and eventual demise of the Neanderthals and the appearance and subsequent ascendancy of modern humans, the species called *Homo sapiens sapiens*.

The entire history of the Neanderthals as a species, which succeeded *Homo erectus* and lasted from 300,000 to 30,000 years ago, took place mostly in glacial times, on what was then the northern fringe of humanity's turf. The bodies of the classic European Neanderthals reflected this. They were short and squat, sturdier than a modern human, with a relatively long trunk and short legs. Experts interpret this as an adaptation to cold; such a physique, squat and compact like that of Eskimos, conserves heat. The Neanderthals also had very large noses and nasal passages, the purpose of which may have been to warm and moisten the cold, dry ice age air. They had large babies, too, and size helps babies survive in cold climates.

During the Neanderthals' long tenure, they had seen all the extremes of ice age climate, from the long, deep periods of cold to the brief, warm interglacials. In the last interglacial period before today's, some 120,000 years ago, cold Arctic air for the most part remained near or north of Iceland, as it does now except for brief excursions southward in the winter. In those days, hippopotamuses lived in the River Thames. But in the longer periods of glacial chill, the polar air migrated far southward. Ice covered Britain, and the Thames was home not to hippos but to polar bears. The average annual temperature in Europe was 12 to 18 degrees Fahrenheit colder than today's, and wintertime temperatures routinely plunged to 50 below zero. Hurricane-force winds roared down the ice sheets in blasts that may have topped 100 miles an hour. Even far away from the ice itself, constant winds and subfreezing temperatures made outside survival precarious, just as it is in the Arctic and Antarctic now. Much of Europe was simply uninhabitable.

Between the extremes of full interglacials and full glacial chill were many degrees of warmth and cold, wetness and drought, as the ice age climate continually oscillated. Every 5,000 or 10,000 years, the cold would suddenly moderate, though not matching the warmth of a true interglacial. Within fifty years or less, the air would warm and moisten. Forests would invade what had been tundra, and forest animals like deer and wild boar would replace tundra creatures like reindeer, mammoth, and woolly rhinoceros. In these benign times, the growing and hunting seasons lengthened, prosperity reigned, and everyday life was comparatively easy.

A hot argument has raged over whether the Neanderthals were an evolutionary dead end or instead contributed to the gene pool of today's humans; recent evidence cuts both ways.

While there may have been some interbreeding, some experts believe that the Neanderthals basically were replaced by a more flexible, adaptable, and opportunistic species: us. And climate was probably a major factor in a long chain of events leading to the takeover.

No one is sure just what led to the emergence of modern humans. One theory has long held that several populations of them evolved independently from *Homo erectus* in various parts of the Old World. But another theory says that all people alive today are descended from a single ancestral population that evolved in sub-Saharan Africa sometime after 250,000 years ago, or from a nearby but non-African branch of this population, or both.

How the original ancestral population of *Homo sapiens sapiens* came to appear "is anyone's guess," says Christopher Stringer of the Natural History Museum in London, a chief proponent of the out-of-Africa theory. "It's one of the black holes in the data."

Some things seem clear, however, according to Stringer. By about 200,000 years ago, in his view, there lived in Africa at least 100,000 adult members of the population of hominids from which modern humans directly evolved. Subsequently, the Northern Hemisphere plunged again into deep glacial cold and Africa became drier. Both the Sahara and Kalahari Deserts expanded, forming two impenetrable arid bands across the continent. It may have been then that the first truly modern people evolved from one population of near moderns who were genetically isolated behind these climatic barriers in one corner of Africa.

If Stringer is right, the survival of the line leading immediately to us was a very near thing. DNA analysis suggests that at one point, the ancestral cohort of moderns may have shrunk to a core breeding population of only 10,000 highly vulnerable adults. This population apparently began to expand seriously only when the last interglacial period before today's warmed the planet, ended that period of African aridity, and shrank its deserts. Fossilized skeletons indicate that shortly afterward, between 120,000 and 80,000 years ago, the first truly modern humans appeared outside Africa, in the Middle East.

Bit by bit, according to the Stringer scenario, modern people trickled out of Africa and into the rest of the Old World. By 40,000 years ago they had arrived in Europe. By 30,000 years ago they were leaving widespread evidence of their cultural superiority. These newcomers, called Cro-Magnons in western Europe, lived in fixed settlements with complex social arrangements at least some of the time, and some of them decorated the walls of caves with elegant paintings of wild horses, mammoths, reindeer, bison, lions, and bears. As part of this flowering of culture, they even produced beads and pendants on a standardized model that one would expect from an assembly line.

Immediately after arriving in Europe, in Stringer's view, modern humans began competing with Neanderthals for resources, a competition that became sharper in the colder periods when life was harder. Ironically, the Neanderthals may not have been served well in this competition by the big bodies they had evolved as an adaptation to cold. Modern humans neutralized this advantage with better clothing, better fires, and better shelter; meanwhile, the Neanderthals were stuck with an oversize body that required more food to sustain.

The bigger advantages held by the moderns, in Stringer's view, were their superior organizational ability, social cohesiveness, and proclivity for wide-ranging exploration. By comparison, the Neanderthals were solitary, sedentary stay-at-homes. The Neanderthal species probably died out, Stringer and coauthor Robin McKie wrote in their 1996 book, *African Exodus,* "because its social groups were small . . . so that when times were hard, during harsh climatic changes when food was scarce, *Homo sapiens* were simply able to call on better organizational backup, and share ideas with a bigger group of individuals. We had the big battalions."

As the moderns' population grew, they had to stake out new hunting territory to support their increasing numbers, and they began to monopolize the hunting grounds. Neanderthals probably were pushed into marginal habitat, some of them possibly retreating to mountain valleys during warmer periods but finding little space when glacial cold snaps forced them back to lower elevations.

By 30,000 years ago, *Homo sapiens sapiens* was the last hominid species left on earth. By 20,000 years ago, it was on the march around the world. And in only a few more short millennia—5,000 to 10,000 years at most—it would inhabit the entire globe in such numbers as to seem invulnerable.

But it would never escape the pervasive and powerful impact of climate.

[3]

The Turbulent Holocene

When the last Ice Age began relaxing its grip on the earth some 18,000 years ago, the world's climate subsequently became more equable, pleasant, and serene, making it possible for civilization to flower. At least, that has long been the conventional wisdom. It is true that as the glaciers shrank, new areas opened up to human habitation, especially in what are now the midlatitude temperate regions. And by the standards of earth history, the present interglacial period, our interglacial, has indeed been calm and moderate. Think of the planet's fiery, violent birth. Think of Snowball Earth. Think of the Cretaceous Hothouse. Think of the more recent ice ages.

But by any reasonable scale of human reckoning, the millennia since the last glaciation have been anything but serene. On the contrary: The earth's climate over that period often has been harsher and more disruptive than anything experienced by anyone alive today. Present and future climatic changes should be considered in this light; the forces at play in the not-so-distant past could come into play again.

The climatic upheavals of the last 10,000 years have been at least as influential as climatic stability in shaping the course of human society.

Modern humans, in fact, were set irrevocably on the road to civilization not by the onset of a period of climatic tranquillity but rather by a major climatic disruption attending an erratic transition from glacial to interglacial conditions.

Agriculture was the key. It was farming that provided people with a resource base that enabled them to punch through the limits to population growth imposed by what can be gleaned from the wild; for the first time, one of the earth's species had been liberated from constraints imposed by the local ecosystem in which it lived. And it was the need to manage the expanded resources that brought about more elaborate social organization and thus more complex societies.

The transition from hunting and gathering to agriculture took place first in the Levant, in the Middle East. According to one scenario, advanced by Harvard archeologist Ofer Bar-Yosef, it happened as a result of long-term changes in rainfall following the last Ice Age.

The Ice Age expressed itself in the Middle East primarily as a prolonged dryness. Then, for 5,000 or 6,000 years, the world warmed inexorably if unevenly as the glaciers retreated. With the warming came a wetter Middle Eastern climate. During this mild and relatively moist period, a culture of hunter-gatherers called the Natufians (after an archeological site in the Judean hills called Wadi-al-Natuf) grew up and flourished in the Levant. This was a settled people—the first, in fact, known to settle in one place (albeit with temporary outlying hunting camps) as a permanent way of life, without eventually backsliding to the nomadic lifestyle characteristic of most of human prehistory.

These homebodies luxuriated in a pleasant Mediterranean climate whose highlight, for purposes of subsistence, was winter rain. The rains would come from the west, sometimes in the form of crashing thunderstorms, sometimes as steady downpours that lasted for two or three days and then yielded to two weeks or so of sunshine. As the temporary warming proceeded, the rains fell more heavily on the Natufians and their surroundings. Dry lakes and small ponds filled up again. The ground was probably quite muddy at times, but the compensation for this inconvenience was immense: Forests expanded, fruits and seeds grew in abundance, and game animals proliferated in the luxuriant vegetation.

The Natufians hunted gazelles, deer, birds, and reptiles, and gathered the abundant plants and fruits. They reaped wild grains like wheat and barley with flint sickles and ground them with stone mortars and pestles. The natural bounty gave the Natufians a stable, predictable, and reliable resource base. They could now support large permanent settlements characterized by semisubterranean houses, elaborate buildings and storage facilities. They probably had a sophisticated social structure, as evidenced by badges of rank made from seashells.

Then, about 12,000 years ago, the world plunged abruptly back into near-glacial conditions for several centuries. No one is exactly sure why. One favorite theory is that melting water from the vast Laurentide ice sheet in North America poured into the St. Lawrence River, which unloaded it into the North Atlantic. This sudden, massive influx of freshwater, it is believed, upset the salt balance of the great oceanic current that supplies heat to the North Atlantic region, weakening or even halting it. Another theory is that large-scale melting of icebergs could have had the same effect. A third possibility is that the freshwater came from the increased precipitation that would accompany a warming climate.

Scientists call this brief reglaciation the Younger Dryas event. The name comes from a roselike herb called dryas, which lives in Arctic and alpine climates; it is the first plant to reappear after a glacier retreats. The Younger Dryas disappeared as quickly as it came, with warm conditions reasserting themselves in no more than a human lifetime and perhaps less. Fossils of tree pollen and plant remains at the bottom of ponds in New Jersey and Connecticut, for instance, have told scientists that the average annual temperature of what is now the New York region bounced sharply upward by 5 to 7 degrees Fahrenheit in a period of no more than fifty years. Ice corings from Greenland show that most of the rewarming occurred in short 10-degree jumps taking place in less than a decade, and some studies have found that these sudden jumps extended beyond Greenland to the wider world.

There is perhaps a big lesson for the future in this, since such findings are part of a growing body of evidence that indicates that the climate system in the past has undergone big changes suddenly rather than gradually, with abrupt shifts from one state to another. The traditional view of climatic change held that the system responds to "forcings"* such as increasing carbon dioxide or stronger solar radiation in much the way a stereo set does: Turn the volume knob and the sound gradually gets louder. But now they suspect that the system often behaves more like an electrical switch: Increasing pressure has no effect until a certain threshold is reached, and then the switch clicks abruptly over. It may even be, some experts believe, that this nonlinear sort of behavior is the dominant mode of climatic change.

The abrupt changes associated with the Younger Dryas transformed the Natufians' stable world. At first, the people probably would have noticed simply that the rains didn't come as often or fall as hard. And because the abrupt climatic change probably took time to affect the vegetation, the cooling and drying probably had only a gradual impact on the bounty of the land. In time, as the impact became more obvious and more serious, the Natufians' campfire conversations might well have been dominated by the changing climate and how to cope with it. As their world reverted to relative dryness, old heads might have recalled the lush, moist world of their parents' time and wondered aloud what had gone wrong. They might have prayed to their gods for help, but to no avail; in the end, the long drought induced by the delayed last gasp of the last Ice Age severely reduced the supply of wild grains, fruits, and vegetables.

The Natufians could have tried to cope in a number of ways, says Bar-Yosef, but in the last analysis "the only solution was to start cultivating." He believes that the Natufians already had figured out how to sow and cultivate the seeds of wild plants but that they had never taken up this laborious chore on a large scale until the Younger Dryas forced them to. Since the Natufians were already reaping wild grains, it was just a short, easy step for them to start saving seeds, planting

---

* External sources of heating and cooling change the climate. These include greenhouse gases and solar radiation, which warm the atmosphere, and volcanic aerosols, which cool the atmosphere by reflecting solar radiation.

them in the next wet season, and growing enough food to last through the year. Agriculture was born, and by saving more and more seed and planting more ground, food supplies could be expanded far beyond what could be taken from the wild.

This combination of factors has not been found to exist any earlier, anywhere else in the world. Some experts argue that agriculture would have been invented sometime, someplace, without the push given by climatic change; population inevitably goes up dramatically as soon as settled communities become established, requiring a new food source. And, in fact, agriculture subsequently developed independently in other parts of the world. But if Bar-Yosef and others are right, climatic change in the Middle East did stimulate cultivation for the first time. From there, an almost straight path leads to the rise, in Mesopotamia, of the first cities and civilizations.

THE END OF THE Younger Dryas ushered in, for the world, the interval known as the Holocene period—the most recent of geological and climatic epochs, and the one in which we live.

For the Middle East, the cradle of Western civilization, the early Holocene meant the return of a warmer, wetter climate. Agriculture, now irrevocably established and essential for a bigger population, took off. Almost immediately the domestication of wheat, barley, peas, and beans spread northward from the Levant into Turkey and from there southward into Mesopotamia, advancing at about half a mile a year as the expanding population of farmers moved into new territory. By about 8,000 years ago small agricultural villages dotted the entire Fertile Crescent. One of them, today called Tell Leilan, persisted for some 5,000 years on the plains of northern Mesopotamia. And then suddenly, between 4,600 and 4,400 years ago, it blossomed into one of the first of the world's city-states. It was a planned, built-from-scratch city called Shekhna, and its population expanded sixfold within 200 years. As many as 20,000 people lived there, prospering in a land not so much of milk and honey as of thick stands of wheat and barley.

This was a plum ripe for picking. South of Shekhna, between the Tigris and Euphrates Rivers, the rulers of another Mesopotamian city-state, called Akkad, cast envious eyes northward. Unable to resist the temptation, they conquered Shekhna, annexed the surrounding agricultural region, and converted it into the breadbasket of the world's first empire—that of the Akkadians, a vast expanse (for its day) stretching 800 miles from the headwaters of the Euphrates in present-day Turkey southward to the Persian Gulf. For a century the Akkadians rode tall and lived high under the famous Sargon and successive rulers.

Then Akkad suddenly vanished. The traditional explanation of the ancients was that the overweening pride of Naram-Sim, Sargon's grandson and strongest successor, had angered the gods. To punish Naram-Sim, according to the legend, the gods sent barbarians from the northern highlands to attack and conquer the Akkadian towns. But the real reason, it appears today, was that Akkad fell victim to a severe change in climate—apparently the first to bring an ancient civilization to its knees, but not the last.

Yale archeologist Harvey Weiss and an American-French team of scientists analyzed ancient soils at the ruins of Akkadian cities and found that a drought set in, beginning about 4,200 years ago and lasting 300 years—300 years!—with catastrophic consequences. Akkad, it appears, literally dried up. Or at least its breadbasket, the source of its wealth and power, did. The great drought was part of a broader pattern of aridity that devastated the whole Middle East, dotting the region with abandoned towns and setting off mass migrations. It may, in fact, have been global. The drought was certainly one of the major climatic events of the last 10,000 years—and an important example of the Holocene climate's ability to bite the hand of man.

DROUGHTS OF A persistence and severity totally outside the experience of recent generations appear to have been something of a regular occurrence throughout much of the Holocene.

In our time, California droughts—for all their cost and misery— have not lasted longer than six or seven years. But the climatic record of the Holocene is studded with droughts stretching for decades and even centuries. Archeological and climatic evidence is beginning to sketch a picture of their impact on ancient civilizations in the Americas.

The rise and fall of a number of pre-Inca cultures, for example, were in sync with alternating periods of wet and dry climate lasting from two to four centuries, according to Lonnie Thompson, a paleo-climatologist at Ohio State University. Thompson and colleagues have reconstructed those ancient patterns of climatic boom and bust by analyzing a 1,500-year climate record contained in ice cores retrieved from the Quelccaya glacier in the Peruvian Andes. One of these was a thirty-two-year drought, beginning in A.D. 562, that forced a pyramid-building pre-Inca society called the Moche to pull back from the fertile floodplains on which it had spread out and concentrate into one of the Western Hemisphere's first urban cultures, a planned city of 10,000 to 15,000 people that modern people have named Pampa Grande. Eventually, it is believed, drought alternating with floods caused by the torrential rains caused by the climatic phenomenon called El Niño played a key role in the disintegration of Moche society.

A few centuries later and farther north, drought may also have applied the coup de grâce to another pre-Columbian urban society, the famed Maya of Central America. Archeologists have long argued about the cause of the Mayas' sudden collapse, citing such possibilities as overpopulation, war, overexploitation of natural resources, and climate change. In 1995 a team of scientists led by David A. Hodell of the University of Florida found clues in lake sediments in Yucatan that the years A.D. 800 to 1000 were the driest two centuries of the middle to late Holocene in that area—and that the long drought coincided with the Maya collapse. Other experts noted that even if the drought was regionwide, it was unclear whether climate change was the prime cause of the Maya collapse or whether it was simply the final straw.

Perhaps the most startling and best-documented case of cultural collapse caused by ancient American drought is that of Tiwanaku, a rich and powerful state that was South America's most advanced pre-Inca empire. Dominating an area about the size of California that extended from the Andean high plateau in the vicinity of Lake Titicaca to the Pacific coast in what is now Bolivia, Chile, and Peru, the empire lasted about seven centuries and reached its peak of power and wealth about 1,000 years ago.

The core of Tiwanaku's economy was an ingenious system of intensive agriculture. A Tiwanaku field consisted of acres of raised, crop-bearing earth platforms created by removing soil from the corridors between them. The dug-out corridors became canals, enabling crops to survive drought up to a point, and retaining heat from the sun that warmed the fields and limited danger from frost at the high Andean altitudes. For centuries this system dominated the agricultural economies of South and Central America, and the raised fields covered millions of acres. The system was abandoned before the arrival of Europeans in America, and the reason was long considered a mystery.

In Tiwanaku's case, at least, it would seem to be a mystery no longer. The Quelccaya ice cores clearly document an extended drought that afflicted the region starting between A.D. 950 and 1000 and continuing, with fluctuations, until 1410. The drought was of "horrendous proportions," says Alan L. Kolata, an archeologist at the University of Chicago who has extensively studied Tiwanaku and its fate. Slowly at first, the empire's agricultural underpinning began to succumb. Tiwanaku's rulers may have realized their peril only slowly, since just fields on the outskirts of the empire were affected at first. Kolata believes that Tiwanaku may have staved off disaster for a time by reconstructing the raised fields in areas nearer Lake Titicaca where the water table was higher.

In the end, he says, the empire's agricultural engineers could not cope with such a long and intense drought. The raised fields had been able to withstand earlier, lesser droughts, but between 1000 and 1100, they were abandoned. So were Tiwanaku's cities. Their residents scattered and began raising alpacas and llamas. The political state collapsed.

THE DROUGHT THAT DID IN TIWANAKU also affected western North America. In what is now California, centuries-long droughts may have been the rule rather than the exception for the last 3,500 years. By reading evidence locked in the trunks of trees long submerged in water, paleoclimatologist Scott Stine, at California State University at Hayward, in 1994 discovered droughts that lasted from 892 to 1112—roughly coinciding with the Tiwanaku drought in the Andes—and from 1209 to 1350. The trees analyzed by Stine grew in the beds of lakes, swamps, and rivers in and near the Sierra Nevada, including Mono Lake, during a period when drought dried up the water and exposed the lake beds. The trees drowned when the droughts ended and the water rose again. Through a combination of growth-ring analysis and radiocarbon dating, Stine calculated that the water level had dropped by as much as fifty feet during drought periods. From this he concluded that the droughts were not only far longer but also far more severe than either the California drought of 1928 to 1934, the worst in that state in this century, or the more recent dry spell of 1987 to 1992.

Between the two ancient droughts, Stine discovered, the water in Mono Lake rose higher than it has been at any time in the last 150 years, suggesting that the California climate was wetter during that comparatively brief interval in the twelfth century than it is now. He found that the last 150 years have been the third wettest period in the last three millennia. But wet periods are comparatively rare. "The vast majority of years during the past 3,500 years," Stine says, "have been much drier than what we've come to expect to be normal in California." Today's equable California climate, it seems, has been a somewhat infrequent luxury.

Severe drought also had a profound impact on the early history of Europeans in America. The fate of the Lost Colony of Roanoke Island, the first English settlement in North America, is one of the most enduring mysteries of American history. In 1998 an analysis of annual growth rings in bald cypress trees turned up a severe drought that might be the key to the mystery. The longest-lived trees in eastern North America, bald cypresses, commonly live 600 to 800 years and sometimes far longer. Some that are alive now were also alive in the late sixteenth and early seventeenth centuries in southeastern Virginia, the climatic zone of both the ill-starred Roanoke colony, founded in

1587 on a coastal island in what is now North Carolina, and the subsequently successful Jamestown settlement, established two decades later a few miles farther north.

An analysis led by David W. Stahle, a specialist in tree-ring studies at the University of Arkansas, found that both the Roanoke colonists and the Jamestown settlers walked right into the worst droughts of the last 800 years in that part of the country. Severe drought would have reduced the colonists' food supplies and probably eliminated any surplus held by the Indians with whom they traded. The Indians themselves may have been afflicted by famine, as was documented in an earlier drought, from 1562 to 1571, by a Spanish priest.

On August 22, 1587, the worst year of the Roanoke drought, the colony's leader sailed for England to obtain relief supplies. England was preparing to meet the Spanish Armada, and no ships could be spared, so it was three years before a relief expedition returned to Roanoke Island. No one was there. Precisely how the end came for the Roanoke colonists is still not clear. But the drought has now been nominated as the root cause of the colony's disappearance. It "might well have survived if not for the drought," says Warren Billings, a historian at the University of New Orleans who is an authority on the early settlements.

The analysis also showed that the worst seven-year drought in 700 years coincided with the foundation and early years of Jamestown, when thousands died of malnutrition and disease. The colony at one point nearly starved to death and came within a hair of being abandoned. Only last-minute relief from England enabled it to escape the Roanoke colony's fate and go on to become the first lasting English settlement in the New World.

More recently still, killer droughts surpassing the Dust Bowl of the 1930s often converted much of North America's midsection into vast stretches of windblown, Sahara-like sand dunes right up into the nineteenth century. The Dust Bowl was bad enough, as anyone who lived through the 1930s or has read John Steinbeck's *The Grapes of Wrath* knows. That drought, the worst of the last century and a half in America, stripped much of the southern Great Plains of their topsoil after farming had exposed the soil to wind erosion, triggering a mass migration of destitute farmers from the plains to California. In Steinbeck's account, the unforgiving wind "cried and whimpered over the fallen corn" while people huddled in their houses and did not go out without donning goggles and tying handkerchiefs over their faces.

Droughts as severe as the Dust Bowl have not been unusual on the Great Plains, according to a 1998 study by Connie Woodhouse and Jonathan T. Overpeck, two federal scientists. They concluded that "a 1930s-magnitude Dust Bowl drought has occurred once or twice a century over the past 300–400 years, and a decadal-length drought once every 500 years."

From time to time, even more severe droughts have converted some parts of the plains to Sahara-like conditions. Daniel Muhs, a geologist with the United States Geological Survey in Denver, has used both historical accounts and analysis of soil strata to reconstruct with colleagues these great droughts of the past. The reconstruction makes it clear that when textbooks and maps of the mid-nineteenth century referred to the continent's midsection as the Great American Desert, it was not some exaggeration in the minds of effete eastern mapmakers. It really *was* a desert.

As explained by Muhs, great stretches of the plains from Texas and New Mexico to Nebraska and South Dakota consist of classic sand dunes. One area, the Nebraska Sand Hills, is the biggest dune field in the Western Hemisphere. The only thing holding the dunes in check is a thin cover of prairie vegetation. When the atmosphere settles into a long-term pattern of no rain and high heat, as it sometimes does, the vegetation dies and the dunes are uncovered. The wind blows the constantly shifting sands great distances, expanding the dune field.

Oldtime explorers have provided obscure but startling accounts of what the country looked like when this happened. In 1810, for example, Zebulon Pike wrote this about parts of Kansas and Colorado: "These vast plains of the western hemisphere may become in time equally celebrated as the sandy deserts of Africa; for I saw in my route, and in various places, tracts of many leagues, where the wind had thrown up the sand, in all the fanciful forms of the ocean's rolling wave, and on which not a speck of vegetable matter existed."

The most recent of these desert-making droughts materialized as recently as the 1860s. Since then the dunes have been stable, although aerial photographs show that in the 1930s some were already "going active," as Muhs puts it, when the drought of the Dust Bowl era ended.

It takes little stretching to imagine what it would be like should the dunes appear again. Muhs says some highways and railroads probably would be buried. Cattle ranges would disappear, as would large tracts of wetlands where ducks and other waterfowl live and breed. Sand would rain on farmlands downwind, and some dunes might migrate onto adjacent farms and possibly into some towns.

"It would be pretty catastrophic, I think," Muhs says.

DROUGHT IS NOT THE ONLY way in which Holocene rainfall patterns have shown themselves to be a rough climatic customer. The last 10,000 years in North America have also seen frequent extremes of flooding, much of it surpassing anything recorded in modern times.

James C. Knox of the University of Wisconsin has examined the geological strata of floodplains in the upper Mississippi Valley for the last 7,000 years, searching for evidence of ancient floods. His main clue was the size of rocks found in various strata; the larger the rocks, the bigger the flood required to move them. Knox's analysis revealed that between 3,300 and 5,000 years ago, the upper Mississippi Valley experienced frequent floods of a size that in more recent times has occurred, on average, once every 500 years or more. The great upper Mississippi Valley flood of 1993, the worst in living memory, was in that class. Knox's sediment record revealed that even larger floods had occurred between about 1250 and 1450.

The timing of the big floods, Knox says, suggests that they are more likely to occur when the climate is changing. In one case, the increase in flooding coincided with a transition from a period of warm, dry midwestern climate to a cooler, wetter one. The second surge occurred during the transition from what in Europe is called the Medieval Warm Period to what is called the Little Ice Age. These two periods have long been taken, in conventional wisdom, to represent convenient extremes of Holocene climate and of its impact on human society.

The Medieval Warm Period came first. In the conventional view, it dominated Europe's climate from about A.D. 900 to about 1300. This was the period of the Viking expansion, the Norman conquest of England, and the beginnings of the first nation-states. In the period's warmest years, Eric the Red established the first Norse colony in Greenland. (Although the land was warm enough to allow settlement, it was far from green; Eric, who named it, was a promoter.) His son, Leif Ericson, sailed the northern route to North America through mostly iceless waters, putting himself into history books as the first European to reach the New World. And the Domesday book, the census of William the Conquerer's new kingdom following his famous victory at Hastings in 1066, lists thirty-eight vineyards in Britain.

Whether the Medieval Warm Period was global in extent is unclear; many experts are highly skeptical. California's megadroughts and the collapse of Tiwanaku did roughly coincide with this period of European balminess. But the most that can be said on the basis of available evidence, a number of scientists insist, is that notable warmth affected some parts of the globe from time to time roughly a millennium ago.

"The evidence for the Medieval Warm Period is flimsy in the extreme," says Philip D. Jones, who with colleagues at the highly regarded Climate Analysis Unit of the University of East Anglia in England has been looking at past climates as revealed by tree-ring analysis and other "proxy" evidence of temperature trends. Even in Europe, Jones says, the warm period may not have been all it is cracked up to be. For instance, he suggests, too much may have been made of the vineyards in Britain. "You could have vineyards now in England," he said, although they would not be economically viable except in parts of the South. Also, he says, "you don't know what sort of volumes of grapes they were growing or whether the wine was any good." Likewise, he says, it is likely that Greenland's climate during the Viking colonization was not all that salubrious. The Norse, after all, came from western Norway, a pretty cold place. Greenland, though it might have been able to support the colony for a time, might have looked good only by comparison with Scandinavia.

Medieval Warm Period or no, the European climate switched to a clearly colder regime in the last decades of the thirteenth century. The Greenlanders noticed it first, when sea ice, which had been absent from their trading routes, began to choke the shipping lanes. By the mid-fourteenth century, the climate was becoming increasingly cold and harsh, and Greenland itself increasingly uninhabitable. Farms were abandoned, trade with Denmark and Norway dwindled, and by 1500 the Norse had entirely disappeared from the island.

Thus developed the Little Ice Age, an on-again, off-again period of cold and climatic misery that afflicted much of the Northern Hemisphere from the thirteenth through the nineteenth centuries and affected the Southern Hemisphere as well: Mountain glaciers advanced in all parts of the world. In Europe, cold summers sometimes brought crop failures, and famine sometimes ruled Britain and the continent. Almost every European country lost entire harvests from time to time, and lack of food touched off waves of migration out of eastern Europe. Some who stayed were reduced to eating pine bark, dogs, and cats. Some sold their children into slavery or even ate them, too.

Glaciers thickened and coursed down mountainsides. In 1645, at Chamonix at the foot of Mont Blanc, people who had seen the ice flatten farms and villages appealed to the Bishop of Geneva for help in saving their town. At the margin of the ice, the bishop conducted an exorcism. The ice receded a bit but later surged again, and again the bishop was called. Similar scenes played out across Europe. Sometimes glaciers advanced down side valleys in the Alps, blocking the main valleys and in effect forming dams that penned up lakes behind them. Many times the ice dams gave way, letting loose floods that roared down the valleys. The Little Ice Age was also the time of Hans Brinker and the silver skates, when Holland's canals were frozen. North America felt the cold era's sting, as well. In the winter of 1779–80, New York harbor froze and people walked from Staten Island to Manhattan. The ordeal of George Washington's Continental Army at Valley Forge and Morristown was made immeasurably more miserable by unusual cold.

But recent studies reveal a complex Little Ice Age picture in which colder periods of varying length alternated with warmer ones at different times in different places. It might be better, Jones and others say, to forget about the idea of a Little Ice Age or a Medieval Warm Period and focus on specific decades or centuries in specific regions as being especially cold or warm, rather than putting a name to a broader but less precisely drawn era.

A big lesson for today's climate debate that emerges from all this, some scientists say, is that a big change in the average global temperature is not necessarily required to wreak climatic havoc. While the Little Ice Age brought severe misery to parts of Europe, for instance, the average global temperature was probably never more than a degree and a half cooler than today. This may mean that other parts of the globe were warmer than Europe and North America.

One way of putting this magnitude of global change into perspective is to remember that the average global temperature was only 5 to 9 degrees colder in the depths of the last full Ice Age than it is now. Another is to note that when Mount Pinatubo in the Philippines erupted in 1991, the sun-reflecting haze of sulfate droplets that it cast aloft cooled the globe temporarily by about 1 degree (up to 1.5 degrees in the Northern Hemisphere). That is a small cooling; nevertheless, in the summer of 1992 it was accompanied by record low temperatures in the northeastern quadrant of North America. Around the Great Lakes and in northern New England, July temperatures dipped into the 30s, and summer in some places was effectively canceled.

Similarly, only modest changes in global temperature accompanied the megafloods of 3,000 years ago in the upper Midwest. What makes the difference, Knox suggests, is that even a relatively small change in temperature may be able to shift the long-term average position of storm tracks and air masses. These are what determine where it rains and where it does not. Scott Stine says he believes that the centuries-long megadroughts of the last millennium in California could have been caused by a long-term change in atmospheric circulation and precipitation patterns triggered by a natural, modest global warming. In this case, the jet stream would have shifted away from California, leaving it chronically parched.

Knox suggests that periods of climatic disruption may be associated with the instability that comes with a period of rapid climatic change, like the one that may now be in progress. But "that's just wild speculation," he says. "I can't document it."

ALTHOUGH THE MEDIEVAL WARM PERIOD and the Little Ice Age are perhaps the two most commonly cited examples of long-term climatic variability in the Holocene, newer evidence suggests that there have been many such oscillations in the last 10,000 years and that several of the fluctuations have been much bigger.

A variety of evidence contained in corings from the Greenland ice cap, for instance, indicates that a plunge to much colder temperatures than those of the Little Ice Age took place about 8,000 years ago in the North Atlantic region. "This is a big event, clearly something that affected a huge chunk of the world, and it's a lot bigger than modern humans have ever experienced," says Richard Alley, a paleoclimatologist at Penn State. It indicates, he says, that the Holocene might yet spring a surprise or two—"and we won't like it."

Moreover, large, sharp climatic transitions have taken place regularly in more southerly latitudes. In a study of ocean sediments, Peter deMenocal found that sea-surface temperatures off subtropical North Africa have fluctuated abruptly every 1,500 years or so. In the cold phase of the oscillation, they fell by 5 to 15 degrees within 50 to 100 years and possibly less. The result was a severe curtailment of seasonal rains in subtropical Africa. Then the pattern reversed just as abruptly, producing heavy rains and creating widespread lakes in what is now the Sahara. "The transitions are sharp," says deMenocal. "Climate changes that we thought should take thousands of years to happen occur within a generation or two" at most. The changes certainly "would have rocked somebody's world," he said.

Separate analyses of ocean sediments by Gerard Bond at Lamont-Doherty have found that the 1,500-year fluctuations extended at least to the North Atlantic, regularly bringing centuries-long cold spells like the Little Ice Age to that region. Are we now in an intervening warm period between one of those dips? It is hard to tell. The 1,500-year cycles "are not perfectly periodic, so we don't really know where we are in detail—it's not that cut and dried," said Delia Oppo, a paleoocea-nographer at Woods Hole Oceanographic Institute.

On the broadest scales, too, the temperature profile of the Holo-cene has been uneven and erratic. The maximum Holocene warming in central North America, for instance, took place between 9,000 and 6,000 years ago. At the same time, according to proxy data, the Medi-terranean was cooler and wetter—and Richard Alley's big North At-lantic cold spell came during that interval, as well. In the last 6,000 years there has been a general global cooling, with many spikes and troughs above and below the general trend line at different times and places.

If nature were to take an unaltered course, it seems likely that the Holocene would continue its erratic behavior. That likelihood is bol-stered by emerging evidence of the climate's behavior during the last interglacial period before this one. That was the Eemian period, which began about 130,000 years ago. Evidence from ice cores, pollen records on lake bottoms, and deep-ocean sediments suggests that dur-ing the Eemian, the climate oscillated suddenly and often between great extremes on time scales as short as a decade. At least in its early stages, the Eemian may have been a little warmer than the Holocene has ever been.

But the Eemian also plunged often into severe cold. The worst of these cold episodes, according to analysis of pollen records, brought a return to full glacial conditions for northern and eastern Europe. In some places the temperature dipped as low as 50 degrees below zero, with an average in the coldest months of 4 below. The super-cold peri-ods did not appear everywhere; western and southern Europe seem to have been relatively warm and stable. Recent research has provided further evidence of erratic climatic behavior during the Eemian: When the Eemian period was about 12,000 years old, big Northern Hemisphere ice sheets began to build up again, presaging a new ice age. But the North Atlantic region as a whole stayed warm for another 10,000 years. In those last 10,000 years of Eemian warmth, the juxta-position of cold ice sheets and a warm ocean could have produced monster storms in North America. (Warm air next to cold air, as we will see, is a recipe for violent weather.)

So far, the Holocene has yet to experience anything as dramatic as what happened during the Eemian, and neither of those warm periods has matched the truly titanic temperature fluctuations of the ice ages. But it is also abundantly clear that even the Holocene climate has produced swings and extremes, some of them sharp and abrupt, "large enough to dwarf changes seen in the instrumentally based climate record of the last 150 years," in Jonathan Overpeck's words.

Daniel Muhs puts it another way: "We like to think of whatever climate we're in as normal, and our natural assumption is that it will keep on that way. That is a very tenuous assumption."

Will the past be prologue? Whatever humans are doing to the climate, says Overpeck, our biggest worry in the future may have to do with whether the Holocene will dish out new climatic extremes naturally.

Could human interference with the climate system trigger surprises even if nature doesn't serve them up? Or could it make them worse? Questions like these have infused weather and climate with an urgency unprecedented in modern life.

[PART TWO]

[4]

A World Full of Spirits

I N EVERY HUMAN'S MIND is a unique model of reality; not reality itself, but rather an approximation of the real world. The brain's relatively simple circuitry, for all the wonder it inspires as one of evolution's most notable products, cannot encompass the full complexity of nature. From earliest times, many human brains together produced a collective, evolving model of the world, held together and transmitted to future generations first by word of mouth and art, and then by writing and cameras and electronic devices. But even collectively, the human model falls short of the real thing and probably always will.

So it is with weather and climate, quintessential expressions of nature's complexity. Exactly how the earliest humans tried to make sense of the ever-present, inescapable rhythms of storm, heat, cold, flood, and drought that ruled their everyday lives as outdoor hunters and gatherers is lost in deep prehistory. So are the mental models they built. But here and there are small clues. Cave paintings in Europe, for instance, clearly reflect an awareness of the seasons by portraying bison in spring molt and wild horses in shaggy winter coats. Surely the people who made the paintings looked to the behavior and state of these and other animals as harbingers of seasonal change—one of countless weather signs that would in time coalesce into a rich and diverse body of traditional weather wisdom in use to this day. But how did the earliest members of our species account for the origins, significance, and workings of weather and climate? How did the long intellectual journey that led to our present-day understanding of weather and climate begin?

One way to get at the question is to ask how more recent hunters and gatherers like American Indians have traditionally tried to explain and make sense of the weather. Here the answer is clear: Weather and climate were seen as manifestations of a world dense with spirits and were believed to result from interactions among people, animals, and supernatural beings, which often took on and combined each other's characteristics.

In Iroquois tradition, for instance, a giant spirit named Ga-oh dwells in the Far North, where he holds the reins on four animal spirits, which personify the winds. When Ga-oh unleashes Bear, wintry blasts sweep the land. Panther leads the west winds. Moose brings east winds, clouds, and heavy rains. And when Fawn is unloosed, gentle zephyrs from the south blow across the land and spring arrives.

In his winter travels, North Wind often stops to rest and smoke his pipe at the lodge of an old man named Gau-wi-di-ne, who is winter incarnate. Gau-wi-di-ne, old man Winter, calls down the snow, freezes the waters, and sends the sun packing southward. By and by a pleasant, strapping young warrior glowing with warmth knocks on old man Winter's snow lodge. The old man orders the youth away, but the younger man stays to light his pipe. Winter, boasting of his strength, threatens the young man. But the warrior, not intimidated, merely smiles and points out that the old man's power is weakening and that Ga-oh is already calling Winter's friend, North Wind, back home. He warns Winter to depart, also, and quickly, before the sun arrives. "Who are you?" the old man asks. "I am Go-hay, Spring!" the younger man answers. He opens the lodge door, and as Fawn leads in the South Wind, a great bird enfolds old man Winter to its breast and bears him off northward.

The Ojibwa or Chippewa, a Great Lakes tribe, have an origins-of-weather myth that might well have been inspired by the transition from the Ice Age to the warmer Holocene. In that transition, melting ice made the Great Lakes expand, flooding many thousands of square miles. The myth tells of a cold so bitter and snow so deep that the Squirrel spirit leads the Ojibwa on a search for warmth. They eventually find leather bags containing cold, rain, snow, storms, and sunshine. Squirrel tears open one of the bags and warmth rushes out. It melts the snow, and the earth is flooded. In this version of the flood myth, the Duck spirit rescues the people by bringing up mud from the bottom to create new land.

Flood myths abounded among American Indians, and if this is any guide at all to the thinking of prehistoric hunter-gatherers and Neolithic farmers, such myths may have originated very early in the human experience, perhaps tens of thousands of years before they were later written down as ancient legends. The best known of those, of course, at least in the West, is Noah's biblical flood. A roughly contemporary Babylonian myth describes a great flood encountered by the heroic warrior Gilgamesh. Flood legends also bloomed in India, Southeast Asia, the Pacific islands, Australia, China, and parts of Europe. In most of them, a divine hand is responsible for the deluge. All of this is vivid testimony to the pervasive impact of flooding on people and their sensibilities through the ages.

Next to floods, thunder and lightning may have terrified and fascinated the ancients more than anything else. This is not surprising, since thunderstorms are among nature's most spectacular and frightening phenomena as well as the most common and familiar: Every day about 40,000 thunderstorms occur in the world. By one calculation, there are 1,800 in progress at any given moment. Today, in the United States, thunderstorms are second only to flash floods as a cause of weather-related deaths, which in turn kill more people than any other natural disaster.

We now know that thunderstorms develop from purely physical causes when the atmosphere becomes warm, moist, and unstable. A thundercloud forms when the warm, moist air rises into cooler air above, either because the ground is simply warmer than usual or because the interaction of two air masses, one warm and one cold, forces warm air to rise. The rising moisture condenses in the cooler air aloft, forming clouds. If the force of the rising air is strong enough, it will continue moving until it reaches the stratosphere and the top of the cloud flattens out into an anvil form. Ice crystals and hail collide within the cloud, and according to one theory the collision imparts opposite electrical charges to each, setting the stage for the formation of lightning. The lighter, positively charged ice crystals are borne upward by the rising air, while gravity drags the heavier, negatively charged hailstones downward. This separation of positive and negative charges creates the potential for lightning, which commonly occurs when the buildup of negative charges in the bottom of the thundercloud rushes toward the positively charged ground at some 270,000 miles an hour, creating a lightning bolt. The bolt heats the immediately surrounding air by 50,000 degrees Fahrenheit, more than quadruple the temperature of the sun. The air expands explosively, producing a high-pressure shock wave that causes thunder.

The ancients knew none of this, of course, and so they typically ascribed thunder and lightning to the gods. For many American Indian tribes (and possibly, by extension, for many prehistoric hunter-gatherer societies), thunder and lightning were the province of animal spirits. The most famous is the thunderbird, revered as one of the most powerful of spirits by many tribes across North America but especially on the plains, where thunderstorms are especially numerous. This huge, eaglelike spirit, widely depicted in Indian art, was often thought to produce thunder by beating its wings and to make lightning by winking its eyes. To the Brule band of Sioux, thunderclaps came from the voice of the thunderbird, Wakinyan, and the rolling thunder that follows the first clap was produced by the cries of his children. No one ever saw thunderbirds, since they were swathed in dark clouds, but they were among the most revered of deities on the plains. Some tribes considered thunder and the thunderbird synonymous, and the first arrival of both on the semiarid plains, in the spring, was a red-letter day.

To the ancient Babylonians, Hebrews, Hindus, Germans, Greeks, Romans, and Scandinavians, thunder and lightning were the weapons of the gods. Zeus, the chief god of the Greeks, was armed with both. By shaking his shield, he produced storms. Sometimes he would use the weapons to influence earthly events, as in the Trojan War. "Zeus the Cloudbringer thundered furiously from Mount Ida and sent his burning lightning against the Greeks," according to Homer's *Iliad*. Thor, the red-haired Norse god of thunder and storms, bringer of rain, was a fierce warrior who engaged in unending combat with a horde of giant demons. His favorite weapon was a hammer, which he hurled at his enemies and which always returned to him. Thunder and lightning were a by-product of each hammer stroke.

Around the world, storm gods came in a wide variety of incarnations limited only by human imagination. Virgil's *Aeneid* tells of two rival horned gods of wind who battled over the Trojan fleet, blowing from opposite directions and whipping up a big storm. The fleet is saved only when Poseidon, god of the sea, gets angry at the invasion of his domain by the wind gods and banishes them. An ancient Japanese demon called Fujin carried a bag from which he produced both gentle zephyrs and typhoons. Another Japanese spirit, Raijin, beat on drums to make thunder, as did an ancient Chinese god, Lei Chen Tzu, who was also the custodian of lightning and carried an ax with which to split trees. He would announce approaching thunderstorms by riding the clouds with Fei Lien, the dragon god from whose powerful lungs issued the wind. To Australian aborigines, the summer monsoon called forth an angry god named Lightning Man, whose arms and legs were lightning bolts that struck the ground as he moved through the clouds. In India, it was the Hindu god Indra who produced storms.

As is recorded in Genesis, the Israelites believed that God's first act of creation was to start a wind moving across the waters. In Celtic tradition, the wind is the province of fairies. The Seneca Indians believed hurricanes were the thrashings of a big bear. Whirlwinds were regarded as evil spirits by some Indians, but the ancient Isrealites considered at least one whirlwind benevolent: the pillar of cloud in which God appeared to guide Moses and his people to the Promised Land.

Almost everywhere in ancient meteorology, rainbows were seen as pathways to the gods. In Siberia, Japan, Australia, Polynesia, and the Americas, shamans used rainbows to climb to heaven. Often the rainbow and its accompanying calm signified that people were at peace with the gods again.

The widely varying impact of climate on people is reflected in the character of their weather gods. In ancient Egypt, for instance, the life-giving floods of the Nile were predictable and beneficent, as was the prevailing north wind that cooled the land enough to make life there feasible. Consequently, powerful gods like Ra (the sun god) and Osiris (controller of the Nile) were mostly benign. But in nearby Mesopotamia, the floods of the Tigris and Euphrates were unpredictable and harsh desert winds alternated with torrential rains. Mesopotamian gods like Enlil—so powerful that the wind he controlled was believed responsible for keeping the sky and earth separated—were therefore seen as harsh and punitive.

In the Old Testament, weather was under the control of Yahweh, the one and only God, who used it to discipline, reward, and further the fortunes of the Israelites. In Psalm 135, the psalmist praises God: "He causeth the vapors to ascend from the ends of the earth; he maketh lightnings for the rain; he bringeth the wind out of his treasuries." On Mount Sinai, God promises Moses: "If ye walk in my statutes, and keep my commandments, and do them, then I will give you rain in due season . . ." (Leviticus 26:3–4). Conversely, failure to follow God's ways invites meteorological and climatic punishment. In Deuteronomy 28:24, one of the prescribed curses for disobeying God is a drought: "The Lord shall make the rain of thy land powder and dust: from heaven shall it come down upon thee, until thou be destroyed." When the commandments are broken, God acts accordingly. The ultimate punishment, of course, was Noah's flood.

But when his chosen people deserved it, Yahweh also used weather to help them defeat their enemies. Responding to a plea from Samuel, God saves the Israelites by directing "a great thunder" at the attacking Philistines, throwing them into such a panic that Israel is able to vanquish them (I Samuel 7:10). And there is the famous intervention in which God sends the plagues on Egypt until Pharaoh releases the Israelites from bondage. One plague is thunder, hail, and fire (which some modern scholars interpret as lightning). Mortals often asked Yahweh for specific weather favors. To impress on his sinful people that they must change their ways, Samuel called on God to send thunder and rain against the wheat harvest, "and the Lord sent thunder and rain that day: and all the people greatly feared the Lord and Samuel" (I Samuel 12:18).

According to Matthew, God in the person of Jesus gave a direct demonstration of his meteorological powers. At sea, while Jesus is asleep, a storm arises and his disciples fear for their lives: "And his disciples came to him, and awoke him, saying, Lord, save us: we perish. And he said unto them, Why are ye fearful, O ye of little faith? Then he arose, and rebuked the winds and the sea; and there was a great calm. But the men marveled, saying, What manner of man is this, that even the winds and the sea obey him!" (Matthew 9:25–27).

EVEN AS PEOPLE RELIED on the divine and the supernatural to explain the ultimate causes of weather and climate, they were laying the foundations of a more practical meteorology based on observation of weather events and manifest in a profusion of weather proverbs.

In the Old Testament, Elijah predicts rain by sending his servant to look toward the sea—that is, westward, whence came storms—for weather clues. Six times the servant goes and sees nothing. On the seventh trip he spies "a little cloud out of the sea, like a man's hand" (I Kings 18:44). On the basis of this small sign, Elijah warns Ahab to be on his way to Jezreel before rain stops him. Sure enough, "it came to pass in the mean while, that the heaven was black with clouds and wind, and there was a great rain." Presumably, the successful prediction greatly enhanced Elijah's status as a prophet.

In the New Testament, Jesus chides the Jewish priests: "When it is evening, ye say, It will be fair weather: for the sky is red. And in the morning, It will be foul weather today: for the sky is red and lowring. O ye hypocrites, ye can discern the face of the sky; but can ye not discern the signs of the times?" (Matthew 16: 2–3).

This, of course, is an early reference to one of the best-known weather proverbs in the world:

> Red sky at night, sailor's delight.
> Red sky at morning, sailor take warning.

Present-day meteorologists say there is considerable truth to this proverb, which has spread around the globe in varying forms—one entry in a vast folklore of weather that has accumulated by word of mouth since preliterate times.

The red-sky proverb was one of some 200 signs intended to predict rain, wind, storm, and fair skies that made up *De Signis Tempestatum* (*On Weather Signs*), the first written compendium of rules for weather prediction. Compiled some 300 years before Christ by the Greek philospher Theophrastus of Eresos, the pupil and immediate successor of Aristotle, *On Weather Signs* laid the basis for all subsequent attempts to predict the weather empirically—that is, on the basis of observation and experience.

The red-sky proverb stakes its modern-day claim to validity on the fact that dry dust particles in the air, which signify low humidity and therefore fair weather, scatter light so as to create a red or pink sky. Conversely, a gray sky in the evening means the air is saturated with water droplets that probably will fall as precipitation the next day. But since the proverb is based on the west-to-east movement of weather systems only in the midlatitudes, it does not apply to other parts of the globe.

Many other weather proverbs and folk beliefs also have some truth to them, including this one:

> Ring around the moon or sun,
> Rain before the day is done.

When conditions are right, light passing through ice crystals in high, thin clouds can create a halo around the moon or sun. Two varieties of this kind of cloud, cirrus and cirrostratus, often materialize ahead of the thicker clouds and precipitation of an approaching warm front. Thus a halo sometimes might predict rain or snow.

There is also a good meteorological explanation for this proverb:

> When the dew is on the grass,
> Rain will never come to pass.
> When grass is dry at morning light,
> Look for rain before the night.

The formation of dew requires a clear, calm night typically associated with a high-pressure system, and high pressure generally means fair weather. On the other hand, the wind and clouds that accompany an approaching storm system prevent dew from condensing on the grass.

A variety of sayings purport to predict a coming storm by detecting a rise in humidity, including these:

> When stones sweat,
> Rain you'll get.

> I know ladies by the score
> Whose hair, like seaweed, scents the storm;
> Long, long before it starts to pour
> Their locks assume a baneful form.

High humidity, often a precursor of rain, does indeed cause condensation on rock. And "bad hair day" has become a common complaint in present-day America. When humidity rises, human hair absorbs moisture and becomes longer. For curly-haired people, the extra length means more curl. For people with straight hair, the added length makes the hair limp and bodyless. One kind of hygrometer, an instrument for measuring atmospheric humidity, is based on this principle: A pointer attached to a bundle of hair traces changes in humidity on a graph as the hair lengthens and shortens. (Blond hair is favored because it responds faster.)

Prehistoric people, living as close to nature as they did, undoubtedly took note of animal behavior as it relates to the weather, and weather lore consequently is rich in animal signs.

Geese fly high when barometric pressure is high and weather is fair, and low when pressure is low and bad weather is due. Ants travel in single file when humidity is high but scatter when it is low. (Humidity, it has been suggested, affects the trail of pheromones that ants leave as way markers.) Flowers open and close in response to humidity. ("The daisy shuts its eye before rain.")

The cricket, it has been said, is the poor man's thermometer, and scientists say that while not perfect, it is not bad. The rule of thumb is to take the number of cricket chirps one hears in fifteen seconds on a summer night, then add forty to get the temperature in Fahrenheit.

These and hundreds of other animal-to-weather links abound in folklore, but their utility varies widely, as does that of proverbs in general. Even when they are valid, proverbs do not allow for sudden changes in meteorological conditions. They do not enable one to look hundreds of miles to the west, where the weather to be expected four or five days hence is shaping up now. They might suggest that rain or snow is to be expected, but not really when, and not how much. Nor are they uniformly applicable to different parts of the world; some proverbs formulated in Europe, for instance, may not apply in America.

And some proverbs are flat-out, demonstrably false, as with the famous saying "Lightning never strikes the same place twice." Actually, the higher the structure, the more likely it is to be struck multiple times. The top of New York City's Empire State Building, for example, is struck an average of twenty-three times a year. Once it was struck eight times in twenty-four minutes.

Another weather fantasy is that the width of the brown band encircling the body of the woolly bear, the caterpillar of the tiger moth, can predict the severity of the coming winter. Observations simply do not bear this out.

Nor is it true that when squirrels gather a lot of acorns, a hard winter is coming. "We think it reflects the weather of the *past* spring and summer, which is the primary determining factor on the size of the acorn crop; squirrels will usually gather whatever is available," said Jim Wagner, a veteran forecaster and climate analyst for the United States National Weather Service.

Some seasonal proverbs make some sense. One holds that "if October and November are snowy and cold, then January and February are likely to be open and mild." There are numerous examples of this in the northeastern United States, said Wagner, and they may reflect a rearrangement of large-scale air masses that tends to take place between late November and late December. Another seasonal proverb predicts "The first snow comes six weeks after the last thunderstorm in September." Again, this does not hold exactly. But in the northeastern United States, says Wagner, the last thunderstorm of the season usually is in September, while the first snow (at least inland, away from the ocean's moderating influence) usually falls in late October or early November—about six weeks later.

But linking seasonal weather forecasts with particular events or particular days is highly suspect in most cases. Consider perhaps the most famous of these linkages in the United States, Groundhog Day.

By tradition, the groundhog, or woodchuck, emerges from hibernation on February 2, midway between the winter solstice and the spring equinox. If the rodent sees its shadow, according to the tradition, there will be six more weeks of winter; if not, an early spring is just around the corner. The tradition is believed to have originated with sixth-century Germans who, realizing that February 2 was the midpoint of winter, observed the behavior of hibernating bears as a clue to whether spring would be early or winter would continue. When a group of Germans later settled in Pennsylvania, they transferred the role of prognosticator from the bear to the groundhog.

(The Pennsylvania Dutch, as they are called, are also believed inadvertently responsible for the saying "It's raining cats and dogs." The original saying was "It's raining to keep in the cats and bring out the ducks." Apparently, the pronunciation of "ducks" somehow became "dogs.")

The "official" meteorological groundhog for about the last century has been Punxsutawney Phil, named for the small western Pennsylvania borough where he lives in a glassed-in hutch in the town library. (There have been many Phils, of course, since a groundhog lives only about four or five years.) Every February 2, the nation's eyes turn to Punxsutawney, where, amid parties and general hoopla, Phil is dragged out into the glare of daylight and the television spotlight.

So how has Phil done? Meteorologists at Pennsylvania State University have checked. In the first ninety-three tries since 1896, says

Lee M. Grenci, one of the Penn State crew, Phil saw his shadow eighty-five times. But if average temperatures for the ensuing month of February are taken as the measure of proof, then Phil's record is not a stellar one. In only thirty-five of the eighty-five years was the February temperature at State College, about sixty miles east of Punxsutawny, below normal. That amounts, says Grenci, to a forecasting skill of only about 41 percent—less than would be expected by chance. Furthermore, says Grenci, while temperature does play a role in determining when groundhogs awake from hibernation, there is utterly no scientific basis for any claim that the circumstances of the emergence can predict what weather lies ahead.

Even more famous as a homespun predictor than Phil, perhaps, is the *Old Farmer's Almanac.* Almanacs purporting to make long-range forecasts mainly on the basis of astrology appeared in Europe about 400 years ago. They easily made the jump across the Atlantic. Benjamin Franklin owed much of his early fame to his publication of *Poor Richard's Almanac,* which sold an average of 10,000 copies a year for a quarter of a century. Franklin's almanac was a bit tongue-in-cheek. Many of its forecasts were not what one would call confident, authoritative, or precise; Franklin often hedged. For instance: "Snow if not too warm about this time." And "March many weathers."

Poor Richard's Almanac was succeeded in 1792 by what is today the *Old Farmer's Almanac.* It attempts to predict not only seasonal weather up to more than a year in advance but also weather for specific periods of as short as a week or less. How has the almanac performed on long-range forecasts? Again, the Penn Staters have checked and, on public television, have issued report cards on the almanac's performance. The grades are based on a comparison of the almanac's prediction for the previous month for various regions of the country (whether it was supposed to be wet, dry, cold, warm, or whatever) and the weather that actually developed. The highest grade attained in the first two years of comparisons was a B-minus; most were Cs and Ds. "I think our response to that was 'Even blind squirrels find a nut once in a while,'" said Grenci. "They're bound to hit it sometimes by chance, or just by studying climatology" in search of patterns. For instance, the

January thaw, coming in the third week of January, is a fairly reliable but not infallible recurring phenomenon.

Some years ago a scientist at the University of Illinois examined the almanac's long-range forecasts and found them to be correct about as often as would be expected by random chance alone. But "it is very difficult for us to comment intelligently" on the almanac's forecasts, says Robert Livezey, chief scientist of the National Weather Service's prediction branch, "because we really don't know what goes into them. Their methodologies are vague. They're cast in terms where you can't set up a clear 'Yes, this is right,' or 'No, this is wrong.'"

The almanac's owners decline to divulge the precise basis on which the forecasts are made, except to say that it involves an analysis of such factors as weather cycles, solar cycles, ocean temperatures, and past years in which atmospheric conditions were similar to those expected in the year to be forecast. The exact formula, according to the almanac's Web page, "is kept safely tucked away in a black tin box at the Almanac offices in Dublin, New Hampshire."

The almanac itself says it has "traditionally" been 80 percent accurate, but its editors say that is obviously not true for every region of the country all the time.

Modern, computer-based long-range forecasting does not always ring up good results, either, thanks to a chaotic streak in the atmosphere's behavior. Government forecasters can do little more than try to forecast the probability that a given region of the country will experience above-normal, normal, or below-normal temperatures and precipitation for a month or a season. As of 1998, the best the National Weather Service had ever done in its long-range forecasts was to achieve an accuracy rate of 75 percent for the winter of 1997–98 in the United States. That season's strong El Niño event exerted a heavy influence on American weather, giving the forecasters something to hang their hats on. Usually, they say, the long-range seasonal forecasts have a success rate well below 50 percent.

Sometimes the almanac blows a forecast spectacularly. But sometimes, said Grenci, it also hits the nail spectacularly on the head—as when it predicted months in advance that Florida would be struck by a major hurricane during a certain week in August 1992. It was. Hurricane Andrew, the most destructive storm ever to hit the U.S. mainland, roared ashore as forecast. "It's kind of fun" when the almanac scores big, said Grenci. But should the almanac therefore be relied on? "We always tell people who believe in the almanac, 'For the next year, plan all your activities, especially the outdoor ones, based on the *Farmer's Almanac.* Don't look at any weather page or any other weather forecast.' I don't think anyone's taken us up on it. That's not a criticism. I look at the almanac, like the groundhog, as fun. I don't get upset about it. Hopefully no one, either the forecasters or the critics, takes it too seriously."

Why do some people swear by it? One reason may be that science can seem cold, and meteorologists—devotees of science who nevertheless do not have a perfect record—are frequent targets of public dissatisfaction. The words "farmer" and "almanac," on the other hand, coupled with the publication's venerable ties to early American history, tend to evoke warm, fuzzy, salt-of-the-earth feelings of trust and to suggest that Everyman is as good as the experts. "If it were the *Old Meteorologist's Almanac,*" said Grenci, "I don't think it would sell."

Given the limitations of proverbs and almanacs, what is the modern weather-watcher to make of them in general? Can they be trusted?

Even in the past, traditional weather wisdom has been beset by skeptics, as in this counterproverbial German parody:

> When the rooster crows on the dunghill,
> The weather will change or stay as it is.

One piece of advice, offered by George D. Freier, the author of a 1989 book called *Weather Proverbs,* is to treat proverbs as an adjunct to modern-day science-based forecasts and even then to look for several signs in combination rather than basing a judgment on just one.

WHILE GODS, SUPERSTITION, AND PROVERBS ruled the effort to understand weather and climate throughout most of human history, and still command allegiance today, the seeds of a more rational alternative were sown well before the Christian era. In this new kind of mental model-building, humans tried to explain the workings of the atmosphere—and its effects on everyday life—in terms of natural physical phenomena that operated independently of any divine influence.

So began the scientific tradition that drives modern meteorology and climatology.

The models of reality built by science are called theories, and scientists rely on observations of what is going on in nature to test and flesh them out. The rain gauge is most likely the first instrument devised for making weather observations. Rainfall measurements were made as early as the time of the Mauryan emperors in India, some 2,300 years ago, and in Palestine some 300 years later. Records carved in stone 4,400 years ago make it clear that the Egyptians had been measuring the annual height of the Nile floods for nearly 700 years even then. But until the seventeenth century A.D., people had no other means of accurately checking what their eyes and common sense told them about weather and climate. Nature is deceiving to the casual eye; intuition is often wrong, and one can easily go astray in the absence of precise observational data.

That did not stop ancient civilizations from spinning theories, some fanciful and some surprisingly on or close to the mark. In the earliest civilizations, people often looked to the heavens for answers. At about the same time that the Mauryans were measuring rainfall, Chinese astronomers used their observations to develop a calendar that divided the year into twenty-four segments and specified the type of weather to be expected in each. Even earlier, the Babylonians tried to connect weather and climate with the stars. The Egyptians followed suit, and the expression "dog days of summer" can be traced to one of their astronomical-meteorological models. They believed that the heat of what we today call the dog days was produced when Sirius, the dog star, appeared in the sky between about July 3 and August 11. Heat waves resulted, according to the Egyptians, from the combined energy radiated by Sirius and the sun—a patently false theory, since Sirius is so far away that the impact of its energy on the earth is all but nonexistent.

The distinction of being the first to make regular meteorological observations and to try to devise coherent theories of weather and climate belongs to the ancient Greeks. H. Howard Frisinger's 1977 book, *The History of Meteorology: To 1800,* laid out this early history in great detail, and the following brief summary of the Greek's and medieval scientists' contributions is largely distilled from it. As early as around 600 B.C., a Greek philosopher named Thales, who lived in Asia Minor and steeped himself in the astrometeorological works of the Babylonians, was writing about the solstice and equinox. Thales apparently knew about, but did not understand, the basic functioning of the earth's hydrological (or water) cycle, in which water evaporates and returns to the earth as precipitation. Two of Thales' disciples, Anaximenes and Anaximander, propounded a theory that thunder and lightning were produced by air impinging on clouds. And Anaximander, in a stunning insight for his day, was the first to define winds correctly as "a flowing of air."

A century later, the philosopher Anaxagoras of Athens employed his meteorological observations to try to explain summer hail, and in so doing became the first to deduce that it gets colder as one goes higher into the atmosphere. Other philosophers could not figure out why hail should fall in the summer, when it is warm. Anaxagoras theorized that water would freeze at high altitudes in the summer. He also knew that heat causes objects to rise; thus, on a hot summer day clouds would rise to greater heights, where moisture would freeze and fall as hail. Anaxagoras did not understand why this was so and got the explanation wrong, but his basic insight was true.

Around the same time, a Sicilian Greek named Empedocles postulated a basic view of the physical world that would endure for some 2,000 years. He maintained that the universe was made up of four basic elements: earth, water, fire, and air. Each was associated with one of four basic qualities: cold, moisture, heat, and dryness. Empedocles tried to explain differing climates and seasons in terms of a clash between fire and water. Summer came when fire dominated, winter when water did.

Aristotle, student of Plato and tutor of Alexander the Great, pulled together the weather knowledge of his age and attempted to mold from it the first comprehensive theory of meteorology. In a treatise called *Meteorologica* (from which the term "meteorology" is derived), he took Empedocles' four-element idea as the basis of his theory. He conceived of the atmosphere as consisting of three concentric spherical layers about the earth: first water, then air, and then fire.

The layers of earth, water, air, and fire were not rigidly demarcated, in Aristotle's view, but instead were constantly interchanging with each other. The sun was the primary agent of this mixture: Its heat acted on cold water to produce warm and wet vapors, which in turn produced clouds and rain. It also acted on the cold and dry earth to produce hot and dry vapors that provided the makings of wind and thunder.

Aristotle was right in his idea that the sun's heat evaporates moisture, but much of the rest of his theory is fanciful. One reason may be that he declined to rely on what meager weather observations were available. While predecessors like Anaxagoras used observations to try to build their theories, working from data to theory, Aristotle concocted his theory first and then tried to use observed phenomena to explain it. This led him into error, including denials of the correct ideas that wind is the result of moving air and that hail is produced high in the atmosphere.

The Greeks made many other errors largely because they did not possess the necessary instruments to gather meteorological data. Theories spun out of one's head thus overwhelmed observed evidence. Still, *Meteorologica* was a landmark in the intellectual struggle to understand the atmosphere. It became the Western world's reigning authority on weather for more than two millennia.

In succeeding centuries there were elaborations and annexes to the Aristotelian theory, and some countertheories were propounded in parts of Europe where classical learning had not reached. Early in the Christian era, the greek astronomer Claudius Ptolemy of Alexandria was the first to divide the world into climatic zones based on the amount of solar illumination they received; that is, northern zones were colder, southerly ones warmer.

In the eighth century A.D., England's Venerable Bede revived, independently of the Greeks, the pre-Aristotelian idea that wind is "air disturbed or in motion, as may be proved with a fan." But he incorrectly described thunder as a result of "the clashings of clouds driven by the winds which are conceived among them."

Five centuries later another Englishman, Roger Bacon, added a caveat to Ptolemy's theory of climatic zones by noting that they had to be altered to account for topographic features such as mountains, which could block the movement of cold air and thereby affect a given region's climate. And while he accepted Aristotle's basic model of the atmosphere, he insisted that experimentation and evidence were more important in science than devotion to the authority of the ancients.

This was a precursor of things to come, but Bacon's voice was a lonely one: Aristotle reigned supreme as medieval scholars turned for enlightenment not to nature but to the ancient texts. Meanwhile, the pseudoscience of astrological weather prediction flourished on a parallel course.

And that was where the enterprise of trying to understand the atmosphere remained stuck, its progress blocked by slavish devotion to the Aristotelian model, for another 400 years.

That model would be shattered by the First Meteorological Revolution.

[5]

The First Meteorological Revolution

B Y THE SEVENTEENTH CENTURY, the Aristotelian edifice was crumbling. Scientists no longer felt themselves bound to classical authority and began to rely on experimentation, observation, and evidence in place of imaginative speculation. Meteorology was swept up in this rush of reason, and many of the scientific figures of the age—René Descartes, Galileo Galilei, and others—helped liberate the study of the atmosphere.

Central to this intellectual insurgency was a new conception of nature and a new attitude toward knowledge, both set out with revolutionary impact by Descartes, the French thinker who fathered modern philosophy. All matter and motion in the universe, he said, can be measured, and the behavior of the physical world can be described entirely by a single set of mathematical laws. In exploring this world, he insisted, you must suspend belief in the evidence provided by your senses and rely instead on objective investigation. Frisinger recounts Descartes' basic principles: Never accept anything as true unless the investigation clearly tells you it is. Divide problems into small parts and attack them one by one, proceeding from the simple to the complex. Seek out relationships. Be as complete and thorough as you can. Never allow prejudice to cloud your judgment.

In *Les Meteores,* his treatise on meteorology, Descartes tried to show that the weather can be explained by the general physical principles that he believed determined the physical behavior of the universe—a far from obvious observation back then. His own attempts to explain the weather on this basis, however, were in some respects no more successful than Aristotle's. He did get some things right, or nearly so. For instance, he determined correctly that clouds are made up of water droplets and that when the droplets get large enough, they fall as rain, or as snow if the air is cold enough. But other conclusions were wide of the mark: for instance, his finding that thunder was caused by one cloud falling on another.

Descartes provided the governing philosophy and the general method that ever since have formed the basis of modern science, including the science of weather and climate. And his enthusiasm for the study of meteorology helped rekindle interest in the subject. But in the specifics of weather, he fell into error because he still did not have the means to follow his own advice to mistrust one's senses in favor of quantitative investigation; there was just no way to measure adequately what went on in the atmosphere. Without proper instruments, there would be little chance to move beyond abstract speculation, proverb, and folklore.

The seventeenth century remedied this deficiency, in a flowering of invention that produced the thermometer for measuring temperature, the barometer for measuring air pressure, and the first effective hygrometer for measuring humidity, the amount of invisible water vapor in the air. To this day this troika remains the Big Three of instruments for making observations of weather and climate at and near the earth's surface. The invention of the thermometer and barometer in particular, in the words of the twentieth-century British meteorologist Sir Napier Shaw, "marks the dawn of the real study of the physics of the atmosphere, the quantitative study by which alone we are enabled to form any true conception of its structure."

Ground zero for the development of these two essential instruments was the Italy of Galileo's era. Galileo himself, best known as the first person to use the telescope to discern the true relationships of the planets and stars (and for being persecuted by the Inquisition as a result), is credited with devising the first thermometer, almost casually, with his left hand, as something of a parlor trick.

Galileo's thermometer, which he produced sometime in the late 1500s or early 1600s while at the University of Padua, consisted of a glass tube with an egg-size glass ball at the end. Realizing that air expands when heated and contracts when cooled, Galileo warmed the glass bulb by putting it in his hand and dipped the other end of the upright tube in a vessel of water. When he removed his hand, the glass ball quickly cooled. As it did, the air inside the tube contracted and water from the vessel below rose in the tube to replace it. Galileo used this instrument to discern "degrees," as he called them, of heat and cold. In later life, he resurrected this laboratory curiosity with the idea of perfecting it for sale, but abandoned the project when he discovered there was no money in it.

Galileo's thermometer was wildly inaccurate, mainly because it responded to changes in air pressure as well as temperature. It fell to his patron in Florence, Grand Duke Ferdinand II of Tuscany, to solve the problem. Ferdinand filled a glass tube with wine, whose expansion under the influence of heat was independent of air pressure, and sealed the end of the tube. This hermetically sealed thermometer yielded readings unaffected by external air pressure.

As the seventeenth century progressed, countless kinds of thermometers were constructed and tested, with varying kinds of scales and fluids, including distilled alcohol. In 1714 the German physicist Gabriel Daniel Fahrenheit, working in Holland, fashioned the first mercury thermometer with a reliable scale. On the Fahrenheit scale, the freezing point of water happened to fall at 32 degrees and the boiling point at 212. In 1742 a Swedish astronomer named Anders Celsius proposed a new scale on which zero would represent the boiling point and 100 degrees the freezing point. A year later this centigrade, or Celsius, scale was reversed, with zero representing freezing and 100 signifying boiling. It quickly gained favor in scientific work, and by the end of the eighteenth century the thermometer had developed to the point where it could be relied on for accuracy.

Today, of course, the Celsius scale is used universally in atmospheric science and other areas of scientific study and in countries on the metric system, which is most nations in the world, while the Fahrenheit scale is in common everyday use in the United States. (To convert Celsius to Fahrenheit, multiply by 1.8 and add 32.)

The barometer, too, came out of the intellectual ferment of the Florentine court of Ferdinand II. Always on the lookout for ways to torpedo Aristotelian thought, the scientists there, possibly at Galileo's instigation, gleefully set up experiments designed to demonstrate the falsity of Aristotle's assertion that a vacuum could not exist anywhere. A student of Galileo's succeeded in creating one by putting water in a tube closed at one end but open at the other. Once filled, the tube was turned upside down and its end placed in a container of water. When water ran out of the tube into the container, a vacuum remained. In a variation on this experiment, a protégé of Galileo's named Evangelista Torricelli substituted mercury for water. He stopped up the open end of the tube with a finger, turned it upside down, placed the open end in a basin of mercury, and removed his finger. Some of the mercury ran out of the tube into the basin, merging with the mercury in it, but some stayed in the tube—and its level fluctuated.

How to explain the fluctuation? Torricelli wrote: "We discussed this force that held up the quicksilver [as mercury was then called] against its natural tendency to fall down. I assert that it is external, and that the force comes from outside. On the surface of the liquid in the basin presses a height of 50 miles of air; yet what a marvel it is that the quicksilver rises to the point at which it is in balance with the weight of the external air that is pushing it!"

Torricelli had stumbled on a way to measure the variations in air pressure that create much of the weather in a given locality. Other scientists discovered in short order that such variations in atmospheric pressure were related to the appearance and departure of storms: Pressure dropped rapidly before a storm and rose when the weather turned fair. Today we also know that differences in atmospheric pressure from one part of the atmosphere to another are responsible for the strength of winds: In a perpetual attempt to achieve an equilibrium, high-pressure air rushes toward low pressure, and this rush is the wind; the sharper the pressure difference, the stronger the wind.

(Although air seems weightless, the combined weight of its molecules pressing on a surface at sea level exerts an average force of about 14.7 pounds per square inch. This is enough to support a column of mercury 29.92 inches high in Torricelli's barometer—and that is the most common way in which barometric pressure is still described, even when more modern mechanical barometers based on a different principle are used. Scientists today often use other units of barometric pressure, such as millibars, because they are better suited to scientific work.)

Hygrometers to measure humidity had been constructed as early as the 1400s, and various refined new types appeared in the 1600s. Many of these, like the hair hygrometer, exploited the sensitivity of one sort of material or another to humidity, and these were employed extensively for the next two centuries. The Florentine school produced a hygrometer based on condensation caused by cooling, but it never really caught on. The standard modern method employs two side-by-side thermometers, one dry and one covered by a wet cloth. Air is made to flow over the two instruments. Depending on how much water vapor is in the air, the difference in temperature measured by the two thermometers will vary. By comparing the two measurements and factoring in atmospheric pressure, the value of the air's humidity is calculated.

With the appearance of all these instruments, plus improved rain gauges and the anemometer, which measures wind direction and force, scientists were equipped for the first time to set up extensive networks for measuring the properties of weather.

Like boys with new toys, the scientists of the seventeenth century enthusiastically began playing with their new meteorological instruments. Descartes himself took the first barometer readings in Stockholm, as part of a plan to test the instrument simultaneously there and in Paris. But the first observation network was established by—who else?—Grand Duke Ferdinand II, who was not all that great a Medici ruler but whose status as a pioneer in modern meteorology is unchallenged. Ferdinand sent thermometers, barometers, and hygrometers to picked observers in Florence and six other cities in northern Italy. Paris, Innsbruck, Warsaw, and Osnabruck were soon brought into the fold, creating the first international weather observing network. The observers took readings of temperature, pressure, humidity, wind direction, and cloud cover. They entered the readings on forms and sent them to Ferdinand's academy, the Accademia del Cimento, for analysis and comparison. Church pressure forced the academy to close after a decade of operation, but it had shown the way for those who were to establish extensive observational networks in the eighteenth and nineteenth centuries.

By the late 1700s, fifty-seven colleges, universities, and scientific academies had joined to form an observational network in North America, Russia, Europe, and Greenland. It, too, functioned for about a decade; then it disintegrated in the turmoil following the French Revolution and the death of its director. An eighteenth-century network was also established in Britain, and James Madison and Thomas Jefferson teamed up from 1776 through 1778 to make the first simultaneous weather observations in America. But it was not until the mid-nineteenth century that the telegraph enabled observations to be collected fast enough to be useful in making forecasts. France established the first telegraphic weather network in 1856 after an unexpected storm ravaged the French and English fleets off Balaklava during the Crimean War.

WITH THE ABILITY to collect masses of quantitative data, scientists from the late seventeenth century onward found themselves in a better position to understand the dynamics of the atmosphere, to discern average temperature and precipitation levels, to measure extreme departures from these averages, to track the natural variability of weather and look for predictable patterns. The way was now open for them to try to make more precise predictions of the daily weather while at the same time getting a handle on the longer rhythms and broader scales of weather that constitute climate.

As the data-driven observational revolution got under way, a parallel revolution in theory was beginning to yield new understanding of the atmosphere's physical workings. Ever since, these two lines of meteorological thought—the data-driven (or empirical) line and the physics-driven theoretical line—have alternately raced ahead of each other, intersected, and combined to broaden and deepen the understanding of weather and climate. Sometimes the empiricists would be in the ascendant, sometimes the theorists. But from the beginning the two lines from time to time would merge and stimulate each other, with a crush of data sometimes demanding a new physical explanation or a new theoretical insight demanding more data for proof.

In the seventeenth and eighteenth centuries, European scientists following the intellectual trail blazed by Descartes began to identify general physical principles that govern the functioning of the material world, including the atmosphere. Sir Isaac Newton elucidated the laws of gravitation and motion. The Irish physicist Robert Boyle established the relationship between the volume of a body of air and its pressure. The French physicist Jacques Charles pinned down the relationship between temperature and the expansion and contraction of air. An English chemist, John Dalton, teased out a law governing the behavior of gases under pressure, opening the way for calculating atmospheric water vapor. Working from Newton's system, scientists derived the law of conservation of mass, which says that matter can neither be created nor destroyed; it can only change its state. Later, in the nineteenth century, the same principle would be established for energy.

Just as important, the people who discovered these and other laws also reduced them to mathematical expressions, which meant that they could in theory be combined with data to analyze and calculate the behavior of the atmosphere.

Researchers began trying to apply the basic physical laws to weather as soon as they were discovered. And almost immediately the science of the atmosphere leaped forward. For the first time, humans began contemplating the atmosphere from a wider perspective. Always before, men and women had thought of weather as a here-and-now phenomenon; what was happening over the horizon was unknowable and therefore irrelevant. Now came the first hint of a major shift in viewpoint.

One of the earliest manifestations of this shift was a realization that the motion of the atmosphere is continuous and global. The first to describe its basic motive scheme was Britain's royal astronomer, Edmund Halley, whose life spanned the latter half of the seventeenth century and the first half of the eighteenth. Halley is best known today for the comet that bears his name, but he was a broad-gauged scientist well steeped in both the new physics of the atmosphere and the growing empirical tradition. Halley had been one of many scientists working on the most popular meteorological problem of his day, the relationship between barometric pressure and altitude. (The French physicist Blaise Pascal ultimately proved that atmospheric pressure decreases with height.) Halley's work on the question got him to wondering about the cause of winds. Drawing on his own meteorological observations and those of seafarers, and combining this information with his knowledge of the new physics, he postulated that the basic cause of the winds was the sun's heating of the equatorial regions.

Halley reasoned that since air rises when it is warmed and cooler air moves in to replace it (a process called convection), and since the equatorial regions are the hottest part of the world, warm equatorial air must rise and move toward the poles, while colder air from the north moves away from the poles to replace it. This movement of air, Halley said, creates the world's major wind patterns. He thus became the first to tie the general circulation of the atmosphere to the sun's heat—the first, in fact, to conceive of the general global circulation itself. To illustrate his point, he created the first global map of the trade winds, which blow from east to west near the equator. It showed, for the first time, a sharp line of division between the tumultuous wind system of the midlatitudes and the more regular patterns of the tropics.

But Halley could not explain why, if the major winds flow from the tropics to the poles and back, the trade winds blew from the east. This fell to another Englishman, George Hadley, who in 1745 nominated the earth's rotation as being responsible for altering the circulation.

❖   ❖   ❖

ANOTHER ASPECT OF general circulation is that storms are not stationary; they move, and in somewhat predictable ways. Until the mideighteenth century, it had been generally assumed that storms were born, played out, and died in a single place—they did not move across the earth's surface. It was Benjamin Franklin, better known for his "discovery" of electricity, who shattered this misconception. On October 21, 1743, Franklin later wrote, "a storm blew up" in Philadelphia and "continued violent all Night and all next Day" so that "neither Moon nor Stars could be seen." This was a big disappointment to him, because he had been looking forward to a lunar eclipse that the storm obscured. Not long afterward, he read in the Boston newspapers that the city's skies had been clear on the night of the eclipse but that a severe storm had struck that city a day later, sending flood tides sweeping over the docks, destroying boats, and submerging waterfront streets.

Franklin concluded that the same storm which had struck Philadelphia then moved northeastward to hit Boston. In succeeding months he collected reports from travelers and newspapers from Georgia to Nova Scotia, and satisfied himself that at least in this part of the world, storms tended to take a northeasterly path up the Atlantic Coast.

He had discovered the northeaster, a spectacular manifestation of atmospheric circulation that is a staple of winter and spring weather along the eastern seaboard of the United States. Franklin also noted the curious fact that although the general course of the storm was in one direction, its attendant winds came from many directions, blowing most characteristically from the northeast, off the ocean, to the west and southwest, over land. He suspected that this had something to do with the storm's internal behavior, but try as he might, he never solved the puzzle.

THE SOLUTION CAME some eighty years later, and with it an explosion of research and argument from which would emerge the first clear understanding of the characteristics of storm systems like hurricanes, northeasters, thunderstorm clusters, and tornadoes.

A key insight came in 1821, when a huge September hurricane churned up the East Coast and slammed into New England. A few weeks afterward William C. Redfield, a seafarer's son, onetime harnessmaker's apprentice, storekeeper, and self-taught scientist, took a walk through the area hit by the storm. As a youth he had hiked all the way to Ohio and back to see his family there, and a walk across Connecticut must have been like a stroll in the park to him. Because he was able to walk so far, he became the first person to discern the internal circulation pattern of a hurricane.

At Middletown, in south-central Connecticut, Redfield noticed that all of the trees blown down by the hurricane had fallen with their tops pointing toward the northwest. But when he got to northwestern Connecticut, seventy miles away, the tops of the downed trees pointed in the opposite direction, toward the southeast! From this, Redfield inferred that the hurricane had been a vast whirlwind, pinwheeling its way slowly across the state.

With this flash of understanding, Redfield discovered the action of the cyclone—the whirling vortex of wind and precipitation whose various forms include the hurricane (and the typhoon, its Pacific incarnation), Franklin's northeaster, the tornado, most blizzards, and the major form of garden-variety thunderstorm system.

For the next decade, while he served as head of a Hudson River barge line, Redfield researched the question, analyzing ships' logs and tracing wind patterns on maps. Finally he published his theory of North Atlantic storms. In them, he wrote, the winds blow not in a straight line, as had always been assumed, but rather in a spiral fashion, rotating about a central axis. The rotation is counterclockwise in the Northern Hemisphere and clockwise in the Southern. Once launched, he wrote, a North Atlantic hurricane moves northwestward at an average speed of about thirty miles an hour until, in the latitude band roughly from Florida to Virginia, it turns to the north and northeast and churns its way to eastern Canada.

Redfield's theory was confirmed by other investigators and won almost instant acceptance. But scientists can be a contentious lot, and the Redfield theory ignited what would become known as the American Storm Controversy. Redfield's chief antagonist in the argument,

James P. Espy, a onetime schoolteacher who had turned to meteorology, came at the problem from a different direction. He focused on the matter of convection—the rising of warm air in accord with physical principles long-since established in Espy's time. Convection, Espy insisted, was the driving force in storms. He argued as follows: As the earth's surface warms, the air becomes more highly charged with water vapor. As the warming air rises, it carries this vapor with it. The farther it rises, the lower the atmospheric pressure, and the air expands. As it expands, it grows colder. If it rises high enough, the cold condenses some of the water vapor, forming clouds. A storm is born.

This did not conflict with Redfield's conclusions, but Espy went a step further. There is no whirlwind, he said, no circulation about an axis, no vortex. Instead, he insisted, the winds of a storm are a product of the convection and they blow inward toward a storm's center from all directions. Espy spent the remainder of his days vainly trying to demonstrate this behavior.

A third disputant joined the fracas. He was an academic, a chemistry professor at the University of Pennsylvania named Robert Hare. Drawing on his laboratory work with electricity, Hare argued heatedly that storms were touched off by differences in electrical charges between the sky and the earth.

The three scientists argued to the end of their days about the behavior of cyclones. Eventually Hare's theory fell by the wayside. But those of Espy and Redfield, between them, contained major elements of what is today the conventional wisdom about cyclones.

IN THE MID-NINETEENTH CENTURY, national weather services popped up around the planet and data-gathering expanded enormously. In the back-and-forth interplay between theory and data-gathering, data were clearly ascendant. Meteorological number-crunching ruled the day. The age of statistics had dawned, and there began a remarkable romance between stats and weather, rivaled today only by similar romances between stats and sports and stats and economics. The rise of statistics led directly to a new branch of atmospheric inquiry: climatology. Climatology, in fact, came to be defined in statistical terms. Its stocks-in-trade were averages of temperature and rainfall, departures from normal, ranges of extreme weather, and variability of temperature and precipitation over various time scales. The wealth of data and the statistics extracted from the data also made it possible, for the first time, to look for patterns and cycles in the climate's behavior and to identify a welter of climatological "laws." For instance:

- The farther one gets from the moderating influence of the ocean, the wider the daily range in temperature.

- In midlatitudes, the wind blows harder, on average, in winter than in summer.

- Precipitation increases with altitude up to moderate heights, then lessens.

When meteorologists focused more closely on their tables, graphs, and especially maps, they discovered a number of other regularities in weather behavior. They found that in the Northern Hemisphere, air generally flows counterclockwise around the center of a region of low pressure; that the wind blows harder in the southern part of a low-pressure area; and that it tends to be colder in the western and northern parts. The coldest weather, they learned, usually is found in areas of high pressure, while most rain falls in areas of low pressure. By charting the courses of storms on their maps, they discovered that in the northern midlatitudes, weather systems tended to move generally from west to east.

From these data-derived discoveries was compiled a list of hundreds of rules to guide forecasters. Given the speed of the telegraph, it became possible to use the new rules to produce finer-scale pictures, in something approaching real time, of the movement of weather systems.

Equipped with this knowledge, meteorologists of a hundred years ago set to work each day to make their daily forecasts. Pulling together their telegraphed reports, they made maps that charted barometric pressure patterns, temperature, precipitation, humidity, winds, and cloud cover. Having done this, they applied their welter of rules to construct a mental picture of what the weather was likely to do the next day. Often they simply assumed that any storm system would continue its previous day's path. There was much seat-of-the-pants judgment in this exercise, and it involved at least as much art as science. And it required no theoretical understanding of atmospheric physics. It would rule weather forecasting for another half century.

But already, the first stirrings of the Second Meteorological Revolution were being felt.

[6]

The Second Meteorological Revolution

T HE REVOLUTIONARY STIRRINGS came from Norway; specifically Bergen, a seaport that commanded a clear view of the developing storms that constantly swirled across the Atlantic and the North Sea from Britain and Iceland. There, in a burst of creativity lasting less than a decade, a remarkable team of meteorologists led by a Norwegian physicist named Vilhelm Bjerknes revolutionized ideas about the behavior of the atmosphere in the midlatitudes of the Northern Hemisphere, where most people on earth live. These are the latitudes where extratropical cyclones breed, wreak havoc, and die; where cold air masses clash with warm ones, giving rise to the fronts and jet streams so familiar today. When the climate changes, the changes are largely expressed through these atmospheric machinations. But before the Bjerknes team began its research work early in this century, weather experts had only a hazy understanding of the dynamic forces at work.

Bjerknes, a lean, craggy-faced man with an ascetic mein, who wore rimless glasses and looked every inch the stereotypical scientist, had a dream: to combine observation with theoretical knowledge of the atmosphere's dynamics in such a way that future weather could be calculated mathematically and precisely. To succeed at this would be to propel the science of the atmosphere ahead by light-years. No one had ever made such a proposition before, but Bjerknes's faith in the physical laws convinced him that such a thing was possible. If so, it could make meteorology more science than art for the first time, consigning the map-based, empirical approach then in use to the trash can.

Bjerknes's father, C. A. Bjerknes, had pioneered the study of the movement of fluids, of which atmospheric circulation is an example. In the 1890s, while working at the Technical University of Stockholm, Vilhelm Bjerknes took a big step toward the goal of calculating the weather on the basis of physical principles. He derived the mathematical equations that describe how varying pressure, density, and other factors determine the movement and circulation of fluids. This circulation theorem, as it was and is called, opened the way for his groundbreaking research program and for much of modern meteorology.

Germany invited him to head a new geophysics institute at the University of Leipzig, and there, starting in 1913, he began his work. It started well, but after World War I broke out, the German authorities insisted that Bjerknes put theory aside and concentrate on practical military meteorology. Combined with food shortages and other restrictions, this impelled Bjerknes to leap at the chance when the Bergen Museum invited him to leave Germany and join another new geophysics institute being organized in his homeland.

The Leipzig years had not been a total loss. In 1917, as he was leaving Germany and going to Bergen, Bjerknes wrote to his longtime friend and confidant, the Swedish physicist Svante Arrhenius, as follows: "For the first time, we have made headway with meteorological prognosis based on dynamical principles. How much practical significance this might have, it is still too soon to say. But as theory, it looks promising."

One of his first tasks in Bergen, however, was to expand the country's skimpy observational network. The Norwegian researchers would get no help from Britain and Iceland, since their weather reports were now kept secret by the military. So Bjerknes recruited naval sentries along the Norwegian coast, farmers, fishermen, and lighthouse keepers as his observers. They made reports several times a day by telephone, and the reports were coordinated in Bergen to provide the best meteorological data base yet accumulated anywhere up to that time. Combining these data with Bjerknes's circulation theorem and other physical principles, the Bergen School, as the team of less than a dozen people was soon known, began creating its picture of how the atmosphere functions. As the picture started to take shape, Bjerknes at the end of 1917 confided to Arrhenius that "it feels satisfying when it turns out that atmospheric phenomena develop according to the laws of nature."

Jacob Bjerknes, Vilhelm's twenty-year-old son, made the first breakthrough. The characteristics and behavior of cyclonic storms was the meteorological problem of that era, and most meteorologists believed that precipitation surrounded the center of a cyclone uniformly. Jacob Bjerknes found that things were a lot more complicated. A midlatitude storm moving from west to east, he discovered, typically functions like this: As viewed from above the storm, air does indeed circulate around the center of a low-pressure area, but precipitation develops in only two quadrants of the swirling vortex. First, a tongue of warm air coming up from the south gets swept into the winds of the southeastern quadrant of the whirling cyclone, which are circling around its center in a counterclockwise direction. In that southeastern quadrant, the leading edge of the warm air collides with cold air that has been moving down from the north. In this collision, the warm air is forced to a higher altitude, where the moisture in it condenses and a broad band of rain is produced. That is part one of the storm's precipitation behavior.

In part two, the cyclone's pinwheeling winds sweep cold northern air around behind the storm, to the west and southwest, where its leading edge collides with the flank of the original tongue of warm air arriving from the south. The cold air burrows under the warm, again forcing it upward, where precipitation takes place. But this forcing happens faster and more abruptly, producing quick, violent thunderstorms with heavy rain.

Jacob Bjerknes named this second, more violent line of rain the squall line. The first line was called the steering line. All during the autumn of 1918, he refined and tested the new idea. In another letter to Arrhenius (who will figure in this narrative in another historic context, that of global warming), Vilhelm Bjerknes wrote that "steering-lines and squall-lines sweep past incessantly and provide him with the best material he could desire for his work."

Work by another member of the Bergen School named Tor Bergeron suggested that in some cases, the squall line catches up with and merges with the steering line. Follow-up studies showed that there are many variations on the basic theme and that cyclones have varying life histories. This went a long way toward staving off criticism of the new idea.

In perhaps the ultimate linkage between theory and real-world data-gathering, the Bergen School went back to scanning the skies for clouds, as people had done since the beginning, as Elijah had done to prove his skills as a prophet. In Bergen, as real storms rolled by, the Bjerkneses looked to the sequence of clouds for evidence of their new theory.

From the perspective of an observer standing to the southeast of an approaching storm fitting the Bjerknes description, high, wispy cirrus clouds herald the approach. These clouds thicken, cover more of the sky, and become progressively lower as part one of the storm (the steering line) nears. The clouds turn dark and heavy—nimbostratus—and a steady rain falls. Then the skies clear, signaling the end of part one. Part two's arrival is advertised by a line of billowing cumulus clouds, then the towering castles of cumulonimbus, the classic thunder cloud. The squall line sweeps by, with heavy rain, crashing thunder, and scary lightning. Finally, the storm continues on its way east or dissipates, and skies become clear again.

This more precise knowledge of storm behavior enabled Jacob Bjerknes to make substantially more accurate storm forecasts. But the Bergen School minimized this success, for much work remained. To do it, the group moved into a wonderful, big old frame house on the edge of Bergen's city park, where the Bjerknes family lived on the first floor and the Bergen School's working area occupied the second. There, with the senior Bjerknes often carrying wood for the fire, his team worked at long wooden tables. A young woman named Gunvor Faerstad took the telephoned observations and entered them on maps in a neat hand that forestalled what might have been crippling clutter and confusion.

From the patterns that materialized on the map, it gradually dawned on the group that what lay behind the development of storms was a broad clash between large masses of cold and warm air. The key to the cyclone, Vilhlem Bjerknes said, was not low pressure but rather the sudden discontinuity between warm and cold. Within the storm itself, this discontinuity is embodied by the intrusion of the tongue of warm air into the cold. But now the Bergen School had its sights trained on bigger theoretical game.

One breakthrough came when Halvor Solberg, another member of the team, realized that individual cyclones were connected, that somehow they fed off each other to create a line of storms following each other that Vilhelm Bjerknes likened to "pearls on a string." By determining at what stage in its life history any one of these storms had reached, it now became possible to predict how the next one on the string would behave.

The larger significance, however, lay in Solberg's realization that the "pearls" were strung out along a line of contrast between warm and cold air masses. And in a letter to a colleague, he pithily laid out a sweeping new idea that extended the emerging new theory of storms to global dimensions.

Solberg told of discovering a line of temperature discontinuity "which stretched right across the map from one side to the other. There is no doubt at all that this line continues all around the Pole. . . . To the North of the line we have 'cold Polar air,' to the South we have 'warm Equatorial air.' It is only along this line that rain falls, in most cases at least. It marks the front battle-line between two bodies of air and that is why it has such a contorted course, since now the warm and then the cold has dominance over the other."

Cold fronts. Warm fronts. Battle lines. Dominance. The images, drawn from World War I, constituted an entirely new way of understanding and expressing the broad circulation patterns that produce temperate-zone storms.

The Bergen group went on to explain why storms sometimes do not develop along lines of temperature contrast, as would be expected (there has to be enough moisture in the air), and why some storms are worse than others (the more moisture in the air and the greater the temperature contrast, the stronger the storm). Bergeron delineated four classifications of air masses that could be used in making forecasts: relatively dry continental masses, wetter maritime masses, frigid polar masses, and warm tropical masses. The regions of high pressure characteristically associated with these masses, the Bergen group found, were just as important in forecasting storms as the low pressure associated with the cyclone itself.

In 1926 the main members of the Bergen group began to disperse, with Vilhelm Bjerknes returning to the study of theoretical physics with which his career had begun. Jacob Bjerknes remained for some years, but when the Nazi occupation of Norway caught him on a trip to the United States in 1940, he stayed and became a meteorology professor at the University of California at Los Angeles. There he continued his research, expanding it, as will be seen, to encompass the phenomenon known as El Niño.

It fell to another member of the Bergen School, a Swedish researcher named Carl-Gustaf Rossby, to put the crowning touch on the theory of air masses, cold fronts, warm fronts, and cyclones. The line of discontinuity between cold and warm air masses that encircles the globe in temperate latitudes assumes a wavy form when viewed on a map, twisting sinuously like a moving snake. This wave is relatively close to the ground, and Rossby had been studying it for some time. His attention was also attracted by great, high-altitude winds that sweep along above the edge of the surface front. He found that if one looks down on the top of the globe, this high-altitude river of air describes four to six southward bulges plunging deeply into warmer southern air. North of the wavy bulges, the air is cold. These high-altitude planetary waves, or Rossby waves, as they became known, progress slowly around the globe, with their position setting the basic terms for weather everywhere in the northern temperate zone.

The upper-level stream of winds that defines the bulges and marks the boundary between warm and cold air was named the jet stream by

Rossby, and its path corresponds generally to that of the surface front. The strength of storms at the surface, Rossby had found by 1940 (he had by then moved to the United States), is directly related to the speed of the jet stream. If the jet stream is carrying air away from a region faster than it is flowing into a cyclone at the surface, the cyclone will be correspondingly stronger, with higher winds. When cyclones form in the midlatitudes, they do so under the leading, or eastern, edge of a southward bulge in the jet stream. In the trough of that bulge, where the jet stream's curvy path turns north, it imparts a counterclockwise spin to the air, and any storm below is further intensified.

Perhaps no one group of scientists has ever had such an impact on human understanding of weather, in such a brief time, as did the Bergen School. Some credit it with launching modern meteorology. Nevertheless, acceptance did not come easily. Scientists are by nature a skeptical lot, especially when challenged by a big new idea; it is not rare for them to defend the status quo doggedly. That being so, it was two decades before the Bergen School's ideas were fully embraced by the meteorological profession, despite their elegance and power. But in time they took over the field completely—truth ultimately wins out in science—and they still reign today, as a glance at any televised weather map quickly confirms.

BUT FOR ALL its accomplishments, the Bergen group fell short of Vilhelm Bjerknes's original goal of being able to calculate the weather numerically, based on the physical principles governing atmospheric dynamics. No one had yet taken a given set of global weather conditions, applied to them the mathematical equations describing atmospheric circulation, and made an accurate forecast for the next day.

The first to try to do so was a slightly eccentric Englishman named Lewis Fry Richardson. The son of a tanner in Newcastle, he studied a variety of sciences at Cambridge University and subsequently held a number of teaching and research positions in various fields. One of his big interests was mathematics, and in 1913 he picked meteorology as a field in which some of his mathematical ideas could be put to a good test.

Meteorology came to fascinate him. Among other things, he applied differential equations to the weather and studied atmospheric turbulence; once he tried to measure winds by shooting little pellets the size of peas into the air. But when World War I arrived, he had to pursue his new enthusiasm in unusual circumstances. As a Quaker, a committed pacifist, and a conscientious objector, he served as an ambulance driver attached to the French army from 1916 to 1919 (at one point attracting attention by trying to communicate with German prisoners in Esperanto). It was between ambulance trips to the battle front that he completed the world's first mathematical weather prediction. All his papers disappeared in the chaos of war, but they were later found under a pile of coal in Belgium and returned to him. He expanded them into a publication called *Weather Prediction by Numerical Process.*

The treatise described a practical method for reducing the atmosphere's physical processes to simple arithmetic that could, in theory, be carried out by an automaton. The heart of the prediction scheme consisted of seven equations expressing basic laws of physics as set out by Newton, Boyle, Charles, and the others. Taken together, these laws would determine the atmosphere's future behavior once certain initial conditions like temperature, pressure, atmospheric density, water content of the air, and cloud cover were specified. Actually fashioning these ingredients into a program of simple arithmetic took three or four years. Richardson tested the program while still at the front, carrying out all the calculations by hand over a period of six weeks. Even then, he was able to compute changes in the atmosphere over a short period of only six hours.

The test was a noble failure. If the atmosphere behaved as Richardson calculated, storm systems would move across the landscape at the speed of sound. Atmospheric pressure changes would be 145 times greater than those actually observed. The wildest of guesses, said Sir Napier Shaw, could not have been wider of the mark.

Near the end of his treatise, Richardson spun out a fantasy in which a computing machine comprised of human calculators churns out forecasts of the world's weather. The setting is a huge hall, arranged like a theater with the walls painted to form a map of the globe. People sit in galleries stretching around all four walls. Each person works on the weather in the part of the world where he sits, solving one equation or part of an equation on a slide rule or mechanical calculating machine. The work of each region is coordinated by a regional supervisor. In a pulpit atop a tall pillar in the hall sits the person in charge of the whole theater. He is like a conductor, but instead of flourishing a baton he shines a red light on any region that is going faster than everyone else and a blue light on laggards. Clerks in the pulpit collect the completed calculations and send them by pneumatic tube to a central analysis room.

Richardson estimated that even if the fastest mechanical desk calculators of the day were employed in this regimented human computing theater, it would take 64,000 people to predict the weather as fast as it happens. "Perhaps some day in the dim future," he wrote, "it will be possible to advance the computations faster than the weather advances, at a cost less than the saving to mankind due to the information gained.

"But that is a dream."

Was Richardson ahead of his time? Frederik Nebeker, in his 1995 book, *Calculating the Weather: Meteorology in the 20th Century*, believes not. Rather, he writes, Richardson's calculating scheme and trial calculations represented the state of the art of his time.

"Bjerknes pointed out a new road," he writes, "Richardson travelled a little way down it, and his example dissuaded anyone else from going in that direction until they had electronic computers to accompany them."

But others believe this undervalues Richardson's contribution. They argue that he laid out the basic equations for weather prediction, along with their numerical solution, in ways that are very similar to what computer modelers of the atmosphere do today. Richardson, they say, was indeed well ahead of his time.

BY THE 1940s, the demand for more accurate forecasts that could see further ahead was clear. World War II focused the problem. Weather had always had a potent impact on the fortunes of war. The storm that befell the allied fleet at Balaklava in the Crimean War was but one example.

In the summer of 1588, for instance, heavy storms and gales scattered and battered the Spanish Armada whose intention was to invade England, wreaking far more damage on the Spanish ships than did the English fleet. Queen Elizabeth I ordered a medal struck to commemorate the decisive role of the winds in the historic English victory.

At Waterloo in June 1815, heavy thunderstorms converted the battlefield into a quagmire, preventing Napoléon Bonaparte from moving his cannon; cannonballs would have stuck in the mud on impact instead of bouncing forward into enemy troops, as designed. Napoléon waited for the mud to dry, and the delay enabled enemy reinforcements to arrive in time to turn the battle against him.

In 1941, the Russian rainy season, called the rasputiza, made Russia's fields and roads so muddy that Adolf Hitler's advance on Moscow ground to a halt. German generals hoped that when autumn came, the ground would firm up again. It did, but the ensuing winter of 1941–42 came early and was the coldest since Russian temperature records were first kept in 1752. The mercury dropped to 30 degrees below zero Fahrenheit. The German troops did not have proper clothes. Much of their equipment stopped working. Snowstorms blocked trains, and the troops could not be resupplied. Hitler abandoned the drive for Moscow, and the Soviets soon launched their first counteroffensive.

General Dwight D. Eisenhower, commander of the Allied forces poised to invade German-occupied Europe from England in 1944, was determined not to make weather mistakes like those that did in the Spanish Armada, Napoléon, and Hitler. A storm would defeat the attempt to ferry soldiers across the English Channel in history's biggest amphibious invasion and to support them with naval gunfire if they did land as planned on the beaches of Normandy. Even in the absence of a storm, clouds could prevent the crucial parachuting of airborne troops behind the beaches.

As D-Day approached, Eisenhower and his staff met twice a day solely to hear the weather forecast and discuss its implications. The invasion was to be launched on June 5, and Eisenhower expected a forecast five days in advance. The chief staff meteorologist, Group Captain John M. Stagg of Britain's Royal Air Force, was unable to oblige. Given the forecasting methods of the day, which still involved considerable art, intuition, and subjective judgment, Stagg was able to generate forecasts only a day or two ahead. At that range, he turned out to be right: Stagg forecast bad weather for June 5, and Eisenhower's own description of that day's conditions bears out its accuracy: "Our little camp was shaking and shuddering under a wind of almost hurricane proportions and the accompanying rain seemed to be travelling in horizontal streaks."

Stagg then predicted an interval of relatively calm weather for June 6. Eisenhower decided to launch the invasion that day, and one factor in the decision may have been that he thought the Germans would not expect an attack in the weather that had been prevailing. Indeed, the Germans apparently did not forecast the break in the weather on June 6—testimony to the chanciness of that era's seat-of-the-pants forecasting. Stagg and his meteorologists reaped widespread acclaim for their accurate prediction. How much of it can be attributed to luck is unknown.

World War II technology provided a whole new foundation for the hardware of meteorology, notably the Allies' radar and the Germans' V-2 rocket, which, despite its initial use to rain death on British civilians, led directly to the launching of orbiting weather satellites. But the piece of wartime hardware that would have the most important impact on meteorology was the electronic computer.

Here was the means to make the dreams of Bjerknes and Richardson come true. And although few realized it at the time, it was also the means to revolutionize the study of the longer rhythms of climate—and to try to predict how humankind might change the climate in the future.

More than any others, two figures were responsible for harnessing the computer to the prediction of weather and the study of the atmosphere. One was John von Neumann, a Hungarian native who in 1930 moved to Princeton University, where, at the newly established Institute for Advanced Study, he gained a reputation as a world-class mathematician. The other was Jule Charney, a brilliant, effervescent theoretician who would become, by most accounts, the dominant figure of his generation in meteorology.

Von Neumann designed one of the first two electronic computers. Looking around for an application that would make the best use of his machine, von Neumann chose meteorology because, as a meteorologist named Philip Thompson later put it, he regarded the forecast problem as "the most complex, interactive, and highly nonlinear problem that had ever been conceived of—one that would challenge the capabilities of the fastest computing devices for many years."

Frederik Nebeker put it a bit differently: "What von Neumann most needed was a hitherto unsolved scientific problem that would yield to computational power and a problem of practical import to secure funding and impress the world. Meteorology served von Neumann well."

Von Neumann assembled a team, secured funding with the help and support of Carl-Gustaf Rossby, and launched what was called, simply, the Meteorology Project. (Rossby, by that time an American citizen, had become one of meteorology's leading lights and was a dynamic man of entrepreneurial spirit who liked to get things done.)

The project moved into an unprepossessing one-story brick building (in 1998 it was a child-care center) in a lovely pastoral setting at the Institute for Advanced Study in Princeton, across the street from the far more imposing main institute building with its dominating spire, where another scientist named Albert Einstein was in the end game of his career. The meteorology project moved slowly at first, but that changed when Charney arrived on board in 1948.

THE IMMEDIATE CHALLENGE was to translate atmospheric theory into a mathematical form that could be handled by a computer. Without that, nothing else was possible. Charney took on the task.

Jule Gregory Charney had been born in San Francisco on New Year's Day 1917, as Vilhelm Bjerknes was about to start the Bergen School and Lewis Fry Richardson was taking advantage of the time between ambulance runs to work out his scheme for calculating the weather. His parents were Yiddish-speaking Russian Jews who worked in the garment industry and displayed strong left-wing political sentiments. One of Jule's early playmates was Yehudi Menuhin, the child-prodigy violinist. Charney spent his youth in Los Angeles and New York, developing an intense interest in mathematics. Once, on the way home from a burlesque show with a friend, he stopped at a library to work out a problem he had thought of during the performance.

He was pursuing graduate studies in mathematics at the University of California at Los Angeles (UCLA) when Jacob Bjerknes arrived there in 1940 to organize a meteorology program. He was invited to join the new program, which carried a draft deferment, and accepted. Tall and dark, with an infectious smile and thick, curly hair, the youthful Charney was described by Morton G. Wurtele, a contemporary in the UCLA meteorology program, as "fun-loving, always ready for a joke, a laugh, a prank, verging on the lecherous, arguing politics at the drop of a slogan, eager to participate in, but without any special talent for, whatever athletic activity anyone proposed."

In those years Charney also developed a passionate interest in the dynamics of the atmosphere, Wurtele wrote in one of several essays in a 1990 commemorative book called *The Atmosphere—A Challenge: The Science of Jule Gregory Charney*. It was in this field—atmospheric dynamics—that Charney was to earn a reputation as perhaps the most creative atmospheric theoretician of his time.

In 1946, on his way to accept a fellowship in Norway, Charney stopped at the University of Chicago, intending to stay for only a few days but ending up staying for nine months. The reason was that Rossby was then at the university. The two men had what Charney later called "endless conversations," and Charney described the relationship as "the main formative experience of my life." Thus, seredipitously, is the scientific torch sometimes passed.

One of Charney's major achievements was to identify and describe a believable physical mechanism for the development and motion of large-scale atmospheric disturbances. The relationship between the high-altitude Rossby waves and the Bergen School's surface fronts was unclear at that time, and Charney produced a mathematically workable explanation of the way in which growing cyclones get energy from the upper-level wave. Other researchers, building on Charney's finding, revealed that the upper-level Rossby wave is critical in bringing together contrasting warm and cold air masses, thereby creating the surface front.

The key to Charney's success was his ability to simplify things, removing irrelevant factors and cutting through to both meteorological and mathematical essentials. It was this ability that opened the door to calculating the weather, and it led to another of Charney's major achievements: He simplified Lewis Fry Richardson's original equations of atmospheric motion, removing from them things—like sound and gravity waves—that have no significant impact on large-scale cyclones but that require considerable time to compute. Charney succeeded in boiling down everything to a single equation, and this brought the problem within the computational range of the first computers.

Charney had already done this when von Neumann invited him to become director of the Meteorological Project. At once, the project took off, and on Sunday, March 5, 1950, Charney, von Neumann, and company launched the first computerized simulation of the weather. The simulation, limited to a two-dimensional representation of what was happening at an altitude of 20,000 feet, continued twenty-four hours a day, with brief breaks, for thirty-three days, on the ENIAC computer (the first electronic one ever built) at a U.S. Army installation at Aberdeen, Maryland (Von Neumann's computer at Princeton was not yet ready). The results, Charney said at the time, showed that large-scale features of the weather could be forecast numerically and that there was now reason to believe a prophecy by Rossby that "we are standing at the threshold of a new era in applied meteorology."

By the spring of 1952, von Neumann's computer was up and running, and Charney and a formidable company that included Norman Phillips, Joseph Smagorinsky, Thompson, and George P. Cressman eagerly ran their first test. They chose to simulate the development of a storm that had already occurred: a huge and famous cyclone that engulfed much of the eastern United States on November 24 and 25,

1950. This Thanksgiving Day storm, firmly etched in the memories of many who went through it, lashed the mid-Atlantic coast with heavy rain and gales. Inland, it buried the countryside in some of the heaviest snows of the century. The author remembers, as a teenager in the Ohio Valley, waking to the falling flakes on Thanksgiving morning and later wading through the deepest snow in anyone's memory. The undrifted snow was waist high. It took a true disaster to close schools in those days, and the big blizzard shut them down for a week. The storm's impact was all the greater because the traditional forecasting methods of the time utterly failed to predict it.

Feeding the correct initial conditions into the Princeton computer, Charney got back a result that showed the storm developing. The position was not exactly right, and the simulated storm was not quite as intense as the real one had been. But it was a "stunning success by the standards of the day," Cressman wrote years later.

In late 1953 Charney used the computer to "hindcast" another storm that traditional forecasting had failed to predict. This one had dropped six inches of snow on Washington, D.C., on November 6, 1952. Cressman, who was there, remembered later that when the hindcast succeeded, Charney telephoned Harry Wexler, the director of research of the U.S. Weather Bureau, woke him from a sound sleep, and said, "Harry, it's snowing like hell in Washington on November 6, 1952."

As it became clear that numerical forecasts could outperform traditional ones, the skepticism that greets every major new scientific departure subsided and computerized predictions became routine. In 1954 the U.S. Weather Bureau, the navy, and the air force set up a joint forecasting unit, and on May 6, 1955, the unit began making daily forecasts by computer. That same year a group in Stockholm, directed by Rossby and a former student of his, Bert Bolin (of whom we will hear more later), also joined the club. By the mid-1960s, fourteen countries had joined.

The invention of the transistor and the resulting advent of solid-state electronics made computers ten times faster in one stroke. This in turn made it possible to resurrect Richardson's original seven equations of atmospheric behavior. In those heady days there seemed no limit to the accuracy of forecasts, and optimists foresaw the time when pinpoint predictions could be routinely made months or years in advance.

They reckoned without nature's perversity. The computer, it ironically turned out, revealed for everyone to see that it would never be possible to predict the behavior of the atmosphere with an exactitude matched by astronomers with their planets. A recognition had dawned, starting with the insights of quantum physics in the 1930s and 1940s, that many natural processes are not fully deterministic, as Newton would have it; they behave only in approximate ways. Prediction is only partly possible and must therefore be couched in terms of probabilities: What are the statistical chances that the atmosphere, for example, will behave in a certain way?

On top of that, a computerized weather prediction is highly sensitive to the initially specified atmospheric conditions. If the initial conditions specified for the computer depart even one iota from the actual condition of the real atmosphere (as is unavoidable), the computer's forecast will drift increasingly astray, until it bears no resemblance to what the weather actually will be in a few days or weeks. Because of this, the practical time limit for effective local forecasts by computer is today about a week, beyond which one could do about as well by guessing what the weather should be on the basis of past averages. Even within a week, an accuracy rate of about 70 percent is considered good—less in spring and fall, when the atmosphere is most chaotic. The forecast horizon could be extended if observations improved enough so that initial conditions could be specified more accurately, but even then the theoretical limit is thought to be about two weeks. Weather forecasting may always have an element of art and judgment to it.

There is another, in some ways more significant, benefit to computerized simulation of the atmosphere: More than ever before, it has directed the attention of atmospheric scientists to the entire global climate system. Edmund Halley's and George Hadley's elaboration of large-scale circulation patterns were two milestones on the way to a global perspective. The illumination of hemisphere-wide circulation patterns by the Bergen School and Rossby was another. In 1955 came still another.

That year Norman Phillips, a member of the Princeton team, used von Neumann's computer to reproduce, for the first time, the main motions of the whole atmosphere (or, in this case, the half of the atmosphere in the Northern Hemisphere). A subsequent refinement of the basic equations by Smagorinsky set the stage for modern weather and climate models. This consummation of the Second Meteorological Revolution would soon expand the horizons of those seeking to understand how the global climate system works, how it might be changing, and how it might behave in the future.

[7]

A Primer on Weather and Climate

ON SUNDAY, March 29, 1998, the eastern United States basked in record high temperatures for the season. The thermometer reached 82 degrees in New York and would hit 86 a day later. Buds began to pop out on trees prematurely. Repair services scrambled to field calls from householders wanting their air conditioners fixed. Nick Frattaroli, owner of a Dairy Queen franchise in Fairfield, Connecticut, ran out of ice cream. Spring fever gripped the region. It was all very strange, since only a week earlier New York had experienced its only substantial snowstorm of the 1997–98 winter.

Now the cold was in the Southwest, a region more noted for its blazing heat. Arizona was in a deep freeze. At Flagstaff, the thermometer plunged to a record low reading of one degree above zero on the morning of March 30.

It seemed as if the weather had gone crazy. But actually, even though the temperatures at both ends of the continent were extreme, this apparently bizarre turn of meteorological events offers a perfect illustration of one of the classic ways in which the circulation of the atmosphere dictates the weather on any given day, week, or month in the midlatitude temperate zones. The key idea here—as the Bergen School discovered—is that the midlatitudes are characterized by large-scale, discrete masses of air, some cold, some warm, some moist, and some dry. These masses move, and their position determines whether a particular day will be relatively warm or cold, wet or dry in a given place.

On March 29, 1998, for example, a vast mass of warm, moist, tropical air dominated the eastern United States, while an equally big mass of cold, moist maritime air from the Pacific dominated the West. The two masses met in midcontinent, where a powerful jet stream, racing from southwest to northeast along the edge of a southward-bulging Rossby wave, marked their boundary. Here, the clash of warm and cold air and the presence of lots of moisture set the stage for atmospheric violence in the form of thunderstorms. The unusually large temperature contrast between the two air masses portended especially strong storms with the potential to produce tornadoes.

This they did, in the late afternoon and early evening of March 29 in southern Minnesota. That morning the interplay between warm and cold air turned into a deadly minuet. It created a storm system in eastern Kansas that began moving northeastward with the jet stream, along the boundary of the two air masses, as storms are wont to do. By midmorning a cloud shield heralding the storm's approach blotted out what had been sunny skies over Minnesota. Thunderstorms with quarter-size hail drenched the Minneapolis–St. Paul area in midafternoon. Then, just before four o'clock, there appeared a monstrous example of what is called a supercell thunderstorm. This is a storm whose structure—two internal downdrafts separated from a tilted updraft that funnels moist air into the storm—enables it to persist for a long time, given enough moisture near the earth's surface to feed it. In this case there was more than enough moisture, thanks largely to the high humidity of the warm eastern air mass, whose wind pattern was sucking up water evaporated from the warm Gulf of Mexico and transporting it northward.

Inside a supercell, the interaction of winds of differing speeds produces a whirling motion, which becomes a vortex and then, frequently, a tornado. In Minnesota on that horrific March afternoon, meteorologists identified seven separate tornado tracks. The largest, a true monster, was a mile and a quarter wide at its base and cut a sixty-mile-long swath across parts of five Minnesota counties. In less than two hours, it nearly destroyed two towns, killed two people, injured thirty-eight others, denuded the landscape, toppled silos, and demolished hundreds of buildings.

The hamlet of Comfrey, population about 400, was virtually obliterated. In the larger town of St. Peter, most buildings were wrecked, including those of Gustavus Adolphus College, which lost its trademark, the spire of Christ Chapel. Every tree on campus was destroyed. There might have been real tragedy had not the students been on spring break. But there was horror enough. In St. Peter, six-year-old Dustin Schneider was riding in a van with his parents. The tornado picked up the van, blew it 150 yards into a farm field, and peeled back its top. Dustin disappeared. His body was found facedown in muddy water about sixty yards from the van. Rescuers thought they had a pulse once or twice, but Dustin died. The other casualty was eighty-five-year-old Louis Mosenden, who died the next day of injuries suffered when the twister destroyed his home in the town of Hanska.

The weather's torment did not cease after the tornado passed. It turned cold, rain fell and then sleet, delaying salvage efforts.

"How much more do we have to take?" one frustrated man in Comfrey shouted at the sky.

Heat in the East. Chill in the West. Atmospheric violence in the middle. Inevitable change in the weather. All are expressions of a global, seamless, constantly moving sea of air currents, temperature gradients, and moisture whose actions and reactions are largely chaotic and in some measure unpredictable; if the perpetually changing, minute-by-minute state of the atmosphere ever duplicates itself exactly, it does so rarely and then purely by chance.

The atmosphere is not without structure, however. In fact, a great deal of order underlies and sets bounds to the apparent randomness of atmospheric action. We have seen how some of the great minds of the past succeeded in identifying some aspects of this structure. Out of their work, and that of others, has emerged an imperfect, still-evolving picture—a communitywide mental model, as it were—of the climate system from which all weather flows.

The following primer on the natural workings of that system, as it is understood to operate in our geological era, provides basic tools both for making sense of the everyday weather in one's own backyard and for understanding the worldwide debate on climate change.

CLIMATE EVOLVES, and weather takes place, mostly in what is called the troposphere—the lower six to ten miles of the atmosphere. Compared with the earth itself, which has a radius of 3,958 miles, the troposphere is a thin planetary skin layer indeed. Yet about 80 percent of the atmosphere's total mass and almost all its water are concentrated there.

What happens in the troposphere begins with the sun, the ultimate driver of climate and of atmospheric circulation. The sun heats the planet, of course, but because the earth is a sphere the heating is uneven: Much more heat is delivered to the tropics than to the poles. The extra warmth causes tropical air to expand and rise. As it rises, it carries with it much moisture that the sun has caused to evaporate from the ocean's surface. The process is a form of what scientists call convection, which is vertical movement within the atmosphere. All the way around the equator, convection in the tropics forces warm, moist air aloft. As that air vacates the surface, the atmospheric pressure there drops, creating a permanent band of low air pressure girdling the globe at the equator.

The air cools sharply as it rises, and once it reaches the top of the troposphere, most of it spreads out toward the poles. The initial cooling, near the equator, causes the moisture in the air to condense, creating a permanent band of clouds and rain to accompany the globe-girdling band of low pressure. When the air that is moving toward the poles gets to about 30 degrees of latitude, in the subtropics, it sinks back toward the earth. In the Northern Hemisphere, this is about the latitude of Cairo, Egypt. When the air sinks, it adds to the air already at the surface, and high atmospheric pressure, generally accompanied by fair and dry weather, is the result. Most of the world's deserts are situated in these permanent areas of high pressure near 30 degrees of latitude.

Once the air has sunk back to earth, most of it returns to the equator. It does so because near the surface, it always moves from an area of high pressure to an area of low pressure in a perpetual, never-achieved attempt to reach an equilibrium, a single, constant global air pressure.

This movement of air in response to differences in air pressure, as we have seen, is known as wind. All the surface and near-surface winds on earth ultimately come back to the attempt to balance masses of air whose pressure has been made unequal by different amounts of heating in different places.

The movement of air from 30 degrees of latitude back toward the equator is called the trade winds. They complete a grand circuit of traveling air called a Hadley cell, after George Hadley.

But the story is not complete. Not all of the air that sinks to earth at 30 degrees returns to the equator. Some continues on its journey toward the poles. Moreover, winds obviously do not blow only north and south. Mostly, in fact, the main currents run east and west. The explanation lies in the earth's rotation, which distorts the flow of the winds. Consequently, the trade winds associated with the Hadley circulation blow as much from the east, in the Northern Hemisphere, as they do from the north. And when the air that heads on toward the pole reaches the midlatitudes, the winds blow largely from the west, and so are called westerlies. So, too, with the jet streams, the Rossby waves, whose sinuous, looping courses around the globe form the long-term boundary between the tropical air of the south (in the Northern Hemisphere) and the polar air of the north.

While the climate of the tropics and the polar regions is essentially stable—one is always warm and the other almost always cold—that of the midlatitudes gives true force to the old saying "If you don't like the weather, wait a minute." That is because the temperate zones are the earth's big battleground for competing air masses. It is here where the Bjerkneses' warm and cold fronts, and Charney's unstable interplay between those surface fronts and the high-level jet streams, play out their cyclonic dramas; where the temperature in a given locality can drop suddenly as a cold front moves through; and where great movements of air and temperature and moisture combine to create heat waves, cold waves, droughts, floods, and killer storms.

Here is also where the atmosphere's never-ending attempt to overcome the sun's unequal heating of the earth and establish equal air pressure around the globe produces its most complex and convoluted circulation patterns, compounding the large-scale movement of air masses from the equator to the poles. The earth's rotation is responsible for this, too. It creates vast eddies in the air, just like those in a river or stream, and it is these eddies that in large measure distribute and redistribute air, heat, and moisture.

One type of eddy is the cyclone of Ben Franklin, the Bjerkneses, and Charney: a rotating mass of low-pressure air spinning about a central vortex—counterclockwise in the Northern Hemisphere, clockwise in the Southern. Another type of eddy is the anticyclone, in which air circulates in the opposite direction from a cyclone—that is, clockwise in the Northern Hemisphere—around a center of high pressure. When a high-pressure system and a low-pressure system abut each other in a certain way, as often happens, their circulations merge to create extra-strong winds that blow in the same direction. Typically, these strong winds buffet a region just after a stormy low-pressure system has passed and the leading edge of a high-pressure system replaces it.

Low-pressure cyclones and high-pressure anticyclones tend to move from west to east across the North American continent in an almost steady parade, with the rain-bearing cyclones usually following the always-shifting curve of the jet stream—indeed, usually they are embedded in it. (Sometimes the path of the jet follows a more-or-less straight course across the continent. This is called a zonal flow. Sometimes it follows a curvy path, ascending sharply to the north, plunging sharply southward, and then turning northward again, forming a sort of S curve laid on its side. This is called a meridional flow.)

The dry, high-pressure anticyclones tend to precede and follow the passage of a storm front. Typically, the winds on the leading, or eastern, edge of a high-pressure air mass blow from the north and are cold or cool. In the center of the mass, it is calm and tranquil, and the temperature there is governed by that of the land below: It can be extremely cold in the center of a midlatitude high-pressure system in a snowy January and extremely hot there in a July drought. On the trailing edge of the system, winds blow from the south and are typically warm. As the system moves over a given point, that locality will progressively experience these several varieties of weather.

One of these big highs was in place roughly over Bermuda on our record-setting Sunday in March 1998, in such a position that the winds on its western side blew over the eastern United States from the southwest, transporting very warm air from the tropics to give the East its high temperatures. A few days later the system had moved away and temperatures in the East returned to normal—yet another illustration of the fact that in midlatitude weather, air-mass positioning is crucial.

Sometimes these high-pressure systems do not move and instead remain in place for days or even weeks. These "blocking highs," as they are called, can wreak great damage by allowing too much or too little precipitation to be delivered to a given locality, or an entire region, for too long.

One such instance of gridlock in the skies was largely responsible for the disastrous "500-year" flood of 1993 in the upper Mississippi River basin. What happened was that the large-scale movement of Rossby waves around the globe stalled; instead of progressing slowly eastward, the southward-bulging lobes of polar air that characterize the Rossby waves simply froze in place. As a result, three high-pressure systems, two in Canada and one in the eastern United States, also froze in position. This blocked the normal movement of air masses across the continent. Instead, a stationary line between cold and warm air remained in place over the Midwest for most of the summer, setting the stage for recurring thunderstorms there. To make matters worse, the locked-in circulation pattern continually delivered copious amounts of moisture from the Gulf of Mexico to the Midwest. Result: rain that seemed never to end. From June 1 to August 31, nearly forty inches fell on parts of Iowa, where the average for that period ranges from eleven to fourteen inches. Falling on ground that had already been saturated by spring rains associated with El Niño, this precipitation converted much of the region to a sprawling, many-fingered lake.

Five years earlier, in the summer of 1988, another blocking situation produced just the opposite effect in the Midwest. A huge high-pressure system sat in place over the middle of the country during all of June and early July, preventing moisture-bearing storms from bringing rain to much of the nation. It had been a dry spring to start with in many places. With little moisture for the sun to evaporate, most of its energy went into heating the ground, driving up the surface temperature. The air aloft was soon heated, as well, and this had the effect of strengthening the high-pressure system. Much of the upper Midwest got less than 40 percent of its June rainfall, and temperatures of 100 degrees Fahrenheit and higher were common. At the height of the drought and heat wave, virtually the entire eastern half of the country baked. This particular bout of heat and drought played a major, even historic, role in focusing public attention on the problem of global warming, as we will soon see. But its origins apparently were explained by the natural workings of the atmosphere and its role in recycling water through interactions with the oceans, freshwater bodies, the land, and the biosphere.

THE EARTH IS NOT called the water planet for nothing. About 70 percent of the earth's surface is covered by water. Its key role in weather and climate stems from a unique property: It is the only known substance that can exist in liquid form, gaseous form (invisible water vapor), and solid form (ice) within the relatively narrow temperature range found on the earth.

Like air, water moves, and again the sun is ultimately responsible for the movement. When the sun heats water on the earth's surface, some of it turns to vapor and rises into the atmosphere. This is called evaporation, and it happens everywhere there is surface water, given enough heat; but since the oceans have most of the water, most evaporation—85 percent—takes place there. The more heat, the more water evaporates. And the warmer the air temperature, the more water vapor the atmosphere can hold.

Once in the air, water vapor does many things. Not least important for our story, it is the single most powerful heat-trapping greenhouse gas at today's temperatures; without it, the earth would be frozen and devoid of life. Generally speaking, a warmer atmosphere—say, an atmosphere warmed slightly by emissions of other greenhouse gases like carbon dioxide—means more water vapor in the air, which in turn traps even more heat and warms the atmosphere further. This is called a positive feedback.

Water vapor is also, of course, the stuff of which precipitation is made. When the air's temperature allows it to hold no more vapor, the air is said to be saturated. The temperature at which saturation occurs is called the dew point. In the hot summer, if there is sufficient water about, the dew point will be higher, since there is more water vapor in the air—as anyone who has experienced a humid July in New York or Houston or Bombay knows. When the dew point is reached, the water vapor starts to condense; that is, turn back into a liquid. At ground level, the condensation forms dew, or, if the temperature is below freezing, frost. Water must have some surface on which to condense. In the air, this role is filled by tiny floating particles like sea salt, dust, and pollutants. The particles are called cloud-condensation nuclei, since the water that condenses on them forms clouds. At ground level, these clouds are called fog.

In the colder upper air of the mid- and high latitudes, the cloud droplets typically are in the form of ice crystals or are supercooled—although they are cold enough to freeze, they have not done so. In the warmer tropics, the droplets reach much higher altitudes before turning to ice. In both cases, smaller water droplets coalesce with bigger ones or with ice crystals. When the crystals or drops become heavy enough, they fall to the ground. The result, depending on the temperature at varying levels of the atmosphere, is rain, snow, sleet, or hail at ground level.

Some of this precipitation is intercepted and used by plants, animals, and microbes, which then give it up through respiration and, eventually, at death. Some is intercepted when it freezes and becomes ground-bound ice or snow. Some of this is released through melting, but in sufficiently cold regions most of it remains all the time. That which is not intercepted runs into lakes, rivers, streams, and underground rock layers, and from there it ultimately makes its way back to the ocean.

Thus is completed what scientists call the hydrological cycle, or just the water cycle. As Jon M. Nese and Lee M. Grenci say in their book, *A World of Weather: Fundamentals of Meteorology:* "Any given water molecule has likely been in an ocean, in a body of fresh water, in the atmosphere as an invisible gas, in a cloud, and in a raindrop or snowflake parachuting toward the earth's surface."

PEOPLE HAVE LONG LOOKED for regular cycles in weather and short-term climatic varibility, and it turns out that the climate system indeed pulses with multiple, overlapping cycles and oscillations. But thanks in large measure to the chaos factor, most are only approximately regular, and none is perfectly so, not even the best-known cycles: the daily cycle of heating and cooling caused by the earth's rotation and the seasonal cycle.

As everyone learns in school, these two cycles are the most familiar and reliable climate and weather-makers. The rise and fall of temperature as night and day follow each other are so familiar as not to require a second thought. The seasonal cycle, while equally familiar, is a little more complicated. It is occasioned by cyclical changes in the amount of sunlight falling on different parts of the earth, which is in turn a consequence of the earth's one-year orbital trip around the sun. If the planet were not tilted on its axis, there would be no seasonal change to speak of; in any given spot, the climate would be about the same year-round. But since the earth does tilt, first the Northern Hemisphere and then the Southern Hemisphere is pointed more directly toward the sun. First one hemisphere feels the sun's heat in greater force, and then the heat wanes as the other hemisphere warms to summertime temperatures.

On June 21 or June 22, the summer solstice in the Northern Hemisphere, the sun's rays fall most directly on the Tropic of Cancer, at 23.5 degrees north latitude. Three months later, on September 22 or 23, the autumnal equinox, the most direct heating is at the equator, and neither hemisphere gets more solar radiation than the other. On December 22 or 23, the winter solstice in the North, the sun's rays hit the Tropic of Capricorn at 23.5 degrees south latitude, most directly. And on March 20 or 21, the spring equinox, both hemispheres are again heated equally.

A long train of consequences ensues from these astronomical events, and together they add up to the single most important short-term influence on climate and weather.

First and most obviously to temperate-zone dwellers, the midlatitudes get generally warmer or colder depending on the season. Over the course of a single year, people in many midlatitude localities can experience temperatures above 100 degrees and well below zero. What is not so obvious—what baffles many people, in fact—is that the weather seems often to be out of phase with the "official," or astronomical, arrival of the seasons. Why are March and April so often so cold in the Northern Hemisphere? Why are September and even October so often so summerlike?

The answer is that there is a built-in delay in the climate system's response to changes in solar heating. The main cause of this lag is that the oceans, which cover 70 percent of the earth, warm more slowly than land: Water must absorb three times as much energy as land in order to warm by the same amount. On top of that, winds continually perturb the ocean, allowing colder water from the deep to mix with surface water. The ocean lag postpones the meteorological onset of a season by about a month beyond its astronomical onset. Thus, the warmest days of the year in the Northern Hemisphere midlatitudes occur, on average, in late July or early August, even though the astronomical peak of summer is in late June. Similarly, late January and early February are the coldest time of year on average, even though winter's astronomical peak is in late December.

Not only do the seasons have broad and major impact on temperature, they also drastically affect the general circulation of the atmosphere, and this influence is perhaps even more pervasive. In the tropics, for instance, temperature changes little year round, since the amount of incoming solar radiation in those latitudes is less affected by the earth's tilt. But in the Northern Hemisphere summer, the entire

complex of circulation, from the Hadley cells to the pole, shifts northward. This means that the globe-girdling band of low pressure, constant convection, and perpetual rainfall around the equator shifts
northward, taking precipitation with it. Result: The tropics do not have
four meteorological seasons based on temperature changes; instead
they have two seasons, wet and dry, based on movement of rainfall to
and away from the equator.

Other climatic features move away from the equator during the
hemispheric summer, as well. In midsummer, for instance, the jet
stream is far to the north (or in the Southern Hemisphere, to the
south) of its average annual position. Conversely, in the winter, it
moves farther south (in the Northern Hemisphere) than average, exposing more territory to cold polar air.

One of the most renowned varieties of climatic periodicity, as well
as one of the more famous aspects of seasonality, is the monsoon. Basically, the monsoon is an expression of a distortion in the general circulation caused by uneven heating of the ocean and the land (which
heats more and, as we have seen, faster). There are many such distortions around the world, not all of which cause monsoons, but all of
which disrupt and modify the idealized general circulation that begins
with the Hadley cells.

The most famous of monsoons is the one that every year affects India and the rest of South Asia. The term "monsoon" usually is equated
with heavy rainfall, which for the most part is accurate. For instance,
the June-to-August rainy season in Bombay, India, brings an average
of more than fifty-five inches of precipitation, while little more than
two inches falls during the rest of the year. Much of the heavy summertime rainfall—it falls in sheets that do justice to a hurricane—
comes because the earth-circling band of storms near the equator has
moved far enough north to affect Bombay. The rest comes from the
monsoon.

The essence of the summer monsoon is that the continents warm
more than nearby oceans. Continental heating is particularly severe in
India and the rest of subtropical South Asia, where the temperature in
Delhi tops 100 degrees in May and can rise to 110 or more during the
day while falling to only about 90 at night. This intense heating causes

air to rise, creating low atmospheric pressure at the surface. Into this gap flows moisture-rich air from the nearby Arabian Sea and Bay of Bengal. Combined with the rising air, the copious moisture forms clouds and rain. The air becomes superhumid and the temperature drops, but only a little. When the moisture-bearing winds from the ocean reach the Himalayas, they rise and cool. This boosts condensation of the extraordinary amount of water vapor in the air, producing the heaviest rains in the world.

As winter approaches, cold continental air reverses the pattern, producing a huge high-pressure system over Siberia that sends frigid air rushing southward. Although these cold winds are moderated by the time they pass over the Himalayas and reach India, they remain strong enough to carry to the ocean, spreading dry air across the subcontinent. This prevailing flow of dry air, the reverse in both direction and humidity of the summer's flow, also constitutes a monsoon, the dry winter one.

RARELY IS THE meteorological expression of seasonal change perfectly regular. One spring is not like the next, and some summer monsoons are wetter than others. A prime reason for this, apart from the chaos factor, is that a number of semiperiodic climatic changes interact with seasonal change to stir the meteorological pot.

Although many people have searched for regular, predictable climatic cycles on scales ranging from one or two years to decades, very few of the candidates have passed the statistical tests that would establish their permanency, and none is perfectly predictable. But a few variations that are more or less regular have been identified. They all involve oscillations between alternative, semistable climatic states that combine to make the atmosphere pulsate to perpetually interacting rhythms.

Two of the most important of these quasi-cycles are year-to-year and decade-to-decade oscillations in sea-surface temperatures in the North Atlantic and North Pacific oceans. These oceanic seesaws, about which much remains to be learned, largely determine whether the winter in Northern Europe, Asia, and parts of North America will be generally mild or severe over periods of twenty or thirty years. In each case, the surface temperature of the ocean seems to flip back and forth between two essentially stable states. Each state produces a different pattern of heating and atmospheric circulation over great reaches of the Northern Hemisphere.

In one phase of the Pacific Oscillation, the surface of the western three-fourths of the North Pacific area is cooler than normal, while the tropics are warmer. The tropical warmth extends northward along the North American coast to just west of the Gulf of Alaska. This creates a circulation pattern in which winters tend to be milder and drier in Alaska, Canada, and the Pacific Northwest; cooler in the Southeastern United States; and wetter in the Southwest. This pattern was entrenched for more than two decades beginning in the mid-1970s. It did not apply in every year, but it dominated the period as a whole. Before that, starting about 1945, the dominant pattern was reversed, and so were the atmospheric consequences. Temperature records contained in three rings show that these flips have come every twenty to thirty years for the last two hundred years. No one is exactly sure what causes the oscillation. Changes in subsurface ocean currents are one possibility. So is some sort of unexplained interaction between the tropical and midlatitude ocean.

More is known about the North Atlantic Oscillation, or NAO as it is called, although many questions remain there, too. As in the Pacific, sea-surface temperatures in the North Atlantic oscillate between two states, one warmer and one cooler. It so happens that starting in the 1970s, the NAO was in its cold-water phase. When that is the case, the westerly winds of the Northern Hemisphere become stronger, on average, as they blow across the Atlantic. Since the ocean is still warmer than the land, the stronger westerlies pick up more heat than normal and carry it across northern Europe and Asia, making for milder winters. Combined with the effects of the North Pacific Oscillation, this pattern made the Northern Hemisphere continents warmer than they might otherwise have been.

When the NAO is in its opposite phase, the westerlies shift southward and weaken; Northern Europe and Asia become colder and generally drier in the winter, while the Mediterranean and the Middle

East get more rain. This phase was dominant in the 1950s and 1960s, and this cooled off the northern continents. Coincidentally, the average global temperature—which had been rising steadily earlier in the century—leveled off in those decades. With the flip-flop in the NAO and Pacific Oscillation that came in the mid-1970s, the global temperature resumed its rise. (An alternative hypothesis says that the cooling-off of the northern continents in the 1950s and 1960s was caused by increasing emissions of industrial pollutants that reflected sunlight, which was then overtaken by greenhouse warming.)

There were signs that the NAO might be flipping back to its 1950s–1960s phase in the late 1990s, and based on past patterns, the Pacific Oscillation was due to flip, as well. But neither pattern was clearly established, and even if it were, it remained to be seen whether the rise in average global temperature would be interrupted again. If the flip occurred and the global temperature continued to rise, some scientists said, it would strengthen the case that the world is in the midst of an unusual overall warming.

No one is sure exactly what causes the NAO. One strong hypothesis focuses on the alternating parcels of warm and cold water—also of unknown origin—that lie deep in the ocean. According to this idea, these parcels are conveyed by great ocean currents (such as the Gulf Stream) around a gigantic eddy, called a gyre, that covers most of the North Atlantic; the approximately twenty years it takes each parcel to make the trip around the gyre accounts for the alternating nature of ocean temperatures.

While the twenty-year cycle appears dominant, shorter swings in the NAO of a year or two are superimposed on the decadal ones. And some scientists speculate that the decadal swings might be superimposed, in turn, on even longer ones. That is, some centuries might contain more twenty-year stretches of "warm" NAO conditions than others, or vice versa. Researchers at Lamont-Doherty, in fact, have uncovered evidence in deep-sea cores suggesting that century-scale swings in the NAO might have been responsible for the great Middle Eastern drought that brought down the Akkadian civilization more than 4,000 years ago.

The North Atlantic and North Pacific oscillations may be linked in some way by a third big Northern Hemisphere oscillation, this one in the Arctic. In the Arctic Oscillation, high-altitude winds that circle the North Pole near the Arctic Circle alternate between periods of relative strength and weakness, with consequences for weather and climate farther south. John Michael Wallace, an atmospheric scientist at the University of Washington, considers the Arctic and North Atlantic oscillations so closely interlinked that they are basically the same thing. The Arctic Oscillation also may be linked to the North Pacific Oscillation, but the connection is more difficult to discern because of the presence of another big actor in the Pacific: El Niño, to which we will turn soon.

ANOTHER SEMIPERIODIC OSCILLATION in the atmosphere is a reversal of direction of winds, from easterly to westerly and back again, high in the atmosphere above the equator. The period of this quasi-biennial oscillation as it is called, or QBO, is about twenty-eight months but has been more than three years and less than two. In statistical studies, researchers have linked the QBO to sunspot activity, the first time any such long-sought link between sunspots and the atmosphere's behavior has been demonstrated. But no physical explanation for the link has been offered, and many scientists remain skeptical. And since the QBO is so high in the atmosphere, existing only in the rarefield air above the troposphere, some scientists think its links to the weather are tenuous.

Nevertheless, it is one of several factors, along with the state of the North Atlantic sea-surface temperatures dictated by the NAO, that some experts take into account in attempting to predict in any given year the frequency of occurrence of the single most destructive weather system on earth: the tropical cyclone, commonly known as the hurricane and typhoon. And the frequency of hurricane occurrences itself may have a somewhat regular sort of rhythm to it—an often grim rhythm.

Hurricanes are supercyclones, their rains and winds intensified far beyond those of most middle-latitude cyclones (tornadoes excepted) by the superinfusions of heat and moisture they get from moving over the ocean for days at a time. In the Atlantic, they typically are born as tropical thunderstorms over the Sahel region of Africa, whose latitude happens to coincide with the permanent equatorial band of low pressure and rainstorms once it has shifted north for the summer. Starting in June, the Sahel spits out one little disturbance after another, which the trade winds carry out over the ocean. There, if conditions are right, they build into tropical storms and then into full-fledged hurricanes, defined as whirling storms whose peak sustained winds are measured at 74 miles per hour (mph) or better.

The warmer the sea surface, if other conditions permit, the more intense the hurricane. One measure of intensity is the atmospheric pressure inside the "eye" of the hurricane. The lower the pressure, the more air is rushing in to fill the deficit and the stronger the winds. Hurricanes are rated according to wind speed on what is called the Saffir-Simpson scale of intensity. Five categories are established. The most severe, those that cause by far the most damage, are in category 3, with peak winds of 111 to 130 mph; category 4, with winds of 131 to 155 mph; and category 5, with winds higher than 155 mph.

The classic path for hurricanes in the Atlantic region follows a generally westerly course from the coast of West Africa toward the Caribbean. Then, as other steering winds take them in tow, they typically turn northward and eventually dissipate over either dry land or the cold waters of the North Atlantic, depending on where prevailing air currents bring them.

William M. Gray of Colorado State University has put together an array of atmospheric indicators that has enabled him and a team of forecasters to try to predict how many severe hurricanes will develop in the Atlantic region in any given year. The state of the QBO is one element that Gray includes in the predictive mix (even though other experts believe it has little or no predictive power), as is the sea-surface temperature in the region where embryonic hurricanes hatched by the Sahel storm systems grow to maturity. Whether the Sahel is expected to experience a wet or dry year is another important factor. In wet Sahel years, more hurricane embryos form.

Gray has linked a long-running Sahelian drought that began in 1970 to suppressed hurricane formation and a quarter century of relatively light hurricane activity in the Atlantic that ended only in 1995. He now believes that the Atlantic is in for a similarly long run of relatively active hurricane years, thanks mainly to what he believes is a new phase in the North Atlantic Oscillation. If so, the probability that major hurricanes will strike the United States will be higher, and damage will be relatively more severe than in the past, when coastal development was a fraction of what it is today. But climate is chancy, and big disasters can happen even in an off-year for hurricane frequency. When Hurricane Andrew ravaged South Florida in 1992 to become the most costly natural disaster in American history, it did so in a "light" year of infrequent hurricanes.

Gray has been close to the mark in his predictions of seasonal hurricane frequency more often than not, but in 1997 the strongest oscillation of all blew him out of the water.

El Niño.

IN THE WINTER OF 1997–98, El Niño truly became a household word, at least in the United States, and nothing hammered home its image so emphatically as events at opposite ends of the country on Monday, February 23.

In the eastern tropical Pacific, sea-surface temperatures were at some of their highest levels ever measured—the chief defining characteristic of the climatic phenomenon known as El Niño. This abnormal heating produced more intense convection and heavier rains than normal and disturbed the atmosphere over great reaches of the ocean. One consequence was that the main North American jet stream split to form a second, southern branch over California and the southern United States. Thanks to the heating of the eastern Pacific, the subtropical branch carried prodigious amounts of moisture and extra energy, meaning that any locality in its path was at risk of severe weather. This set the stage for the disastrous events of February 23.

California and Florida, sun-and-fun meccas of the southern tier, drew the short straws. California had been pounded by El Niño rains all month, doubling the season's average rainfall and approaching or breaking records in many localities. But the storm of February 23 was the capper. It pushed the February rainfall accumulation in Los Angeles to a new record of almost 14 inches, surpassing a mark that had stood for 114 years. Santa Barbara recorded nearly 22 inches. For the season as a whole, one small Sonoma County town called Cazadero recorded more than 100 inches.

The final deluge on February 23 led to mudslides that carried houses away, severed roads and railroads, sent rivers over their banks, opened holes in highways, and fouled beaches by causing sewage to overflow. In Laguna Beach, in the middle of a pitch-black, windswept night, a wall of mud rumbled down hillsides, ousting people from their houses, pushing buildings off their foundations, and carrying cars away. "People were on top of their roofs, screaming for help," one resident, Denise Hibben, told the *Los Angeles Times*. Another, Elden Setterholm, said he "ended up doing the breaststroke in the mud."

Nine-month-old Tiffany Serabia was suddenly catapulted into the muck when the hillside behind her family's home gave way, smashed the house, and swept its occupants outside. A man spotted the infant and snagged her in time. She was "just a bundle of mud," he said.

Others were not so lucky. A twenty-five-year-old neighbor of Tiffany's died in the slide. In all, at least nine deaths were attributed to the storm. In San Luis Obispo County, the swollen Cuyama River, chewing away at a highway and undermining it, opened a sinkhole in the pavement. Into it fell a California Highway Patrol car, carrying its two occupants into the river and to their deaths. At Pomona College, two nineteen-year-old sophomores were killed when a eucalyptus tree blew over onto their car.

In the month of February alone, at least sixteen Californians died from El Niño–related storms, thirty-five counties were declared federal disaster areas, and property damage neared half a billion dollars.

Across the country in Florida, the same subtropical jet stream that brought the deluge to California created ideal conditions for the development of extra-strong thunderstorms and tornadoes, phenemona not usually seen in Florida at that time of year. On the night of February 22–23, three supercell thunderstorms formed, and tornadoes materialized within each. Cutting a southwest-to-northeast swath across central Florida, narrowly missing Disney World and the Kennedy

Space Center, they killed forty-two people, destroyed 800 homes, rendered another 700 unlivable, damaged 3,500 others, and turned thirty-four counties into disaster areas.

It was the most deadly batch of tornadoes ever to strike Florida, and in some respects the damage was as bad as that caused by Hurricane Andrew in 1992. Mobile homes took the worst hits. Trailer parks looked as if they had been bombed. One twister picked up Fred Padgett's trailer in Sanford and deposited it in the St. Johns River. Rescuers later found him clinging to an overturned houseboat, cut up, ribs broken, but alive. Tom Tipton of Kissimmee was among those who did not survive. He was asleep in his mobile home when a tornado blew it off its supports and smashed it into hundreds of pieces. An eighteen-month-old toddler was literally sucked from his father's arms, and died. Six-year-old Emma Smith, an English girl on vacation with her family, was saved from death when her cousin, eleven-year-old Claire Roberts, whisked her out of the bedroom of their rented villa just before the family's rented Dodge Caravan slammed down on Emma's bed.

Throughout the spring, the southeastern United States continued to suffer under the assault of spates of tornadoes that usually would strike farther north or west, in the swath of Texas, Oklahoma, and Kansas called Tornado Alley. El Niño's repositioning of the jet stream was given the dubious credit for this shift in the main area of tornado activity.

The 1997–98 edition of El Niño was one of the two most intense ever recorded, as gauged by the high sea-surface temperatures in the eastern Pacific, but its impact was not uniformly disastrous. While it brought the United States its seventh wettest winter in 103 years of record keeping (the wettest of all in the South), it also brought the second warmest. In the Northeast, what could have been record snows turned out to be copious rains instead. Heating and maintenance bills were lower, as was the incidence of heart attacks suffered while shoveling snow. American deserts literally bloomed in the unaccustomed rains; in the southwestern United States, normally arid landscapes offered up to delighted visitors a celebration of lush, radiant color. El Niño even reached onto the dinner table. The price of lettuce rose to almost $2 a head in New York supermarkets, thanks to shortages caused by El Niño's ravaging of the California lettuce fields. A sign in the window of the Fairway supermarket at Broadway and 74th Street advised customers:

> Due to (Don't Laugh) El Niño, All salad greens will be in short supply. Consequently, the price will be increased for the next few days. We should be back to normal soon. Thank you. Los Niños de Fairway.

And William Gray's prediction of a third heavy hurricane season in a row was blasted to smithereens. Lots of factors affect the growth and development of hurricanes once they form in the Atlantic, and one of the most important is El Niño. The changes in atmospheric circulation caused by El Niño strengthen westerly winds blowing across the region where hurricanes grow, and these winds tend to shear the tops of hurricanes apart before they can become truly dangerous. By suppressing hurricane development in this way, El Niño essentially aborted the 1997 hurricane season. For Florida, it was a grim trade-off: killer tornadoes, but no killer hurricane. (Gray, however, remained confident that the decades ahead would see heavy hurricane activity, at least in non–El Niño years.)

What caused all this was an on-again, off-again atmospheric phenomenon whose full sweep, impact, and functioning was scarcely understood or appreciated until the 1950s. El Niño has come and gone for millennia, at least. Its effects first emerge in recorded observations in the early eighteenth century. Since then a periodic warming of the waters has been apparent off the coast of Peru, where it drenches that country in abnormal rains and has caused widespread kills of fish on which the local economy depends. Since the warming waters tended to appear around Christmastime, the phenomenon was named El Niño (the boy), after the Christ Child. Until the mid-twentieth century, most scientists considered El Niño a local phenomenon of little or no global significance.

The foundation for understanding El Niño's broader reach was laid in the 1920s when Sir Gilbert Walker, the British director general of observatories in India, searched for an explanation as to why the monsoon rains sometimes failed to arrive. The monsoon had failed in 1899 (an El Niño year, although no one knew it at the time), shortly before Walker's arrival in India, casting the country into famine. Walker was never able to forecast the monsoon reliably, as he had hoped, but in three decades of observations and research he discovered an atmospheric oddity: Barometric pressure is usually high over the South Pacific and low over the Indian Ocean. The low is associated with the monsoon rains. But every few years this pattern reverses, with the result that South America is deluged with rain while India and Australia suffer from drought. Walker called this phenomenon the Southern Oscillation. His discovery was one of the earliest and strongest indications that the climate system is an interdependent global network in which meteorological events in one part of the world can touch off chain reactions that affect the weather in other parts.

But no one connected the Southern Oscillation with El Niño until Jacob Bjerknes—the same man who earlier had first explained how midlatitude storms form—got interested in the problem. Nineteen fifty-eight, the time of the concentrated earth studies known as the International Geophysical Year, was also the year of a major El Niño event. Intensified observations in the tropics provided Bjerknes with the data to propose the following explanation for how the system worked.

In the eastern tropical Pacific, the boundary between warm surface water and colder, deeper water is normally at a relatively shallow depth. This fosters high pressure, which sustains the east-to-west trade winds. The winds in turn push warm water westward, where it piles up against Australia and Indonesia, igniting the convection that provides rain for India and the southwest Pacific. But sometimes this elegant arrangement breaks down; the trade winds weaken, allowing warm surface water to move back eastward. The zone of most powerful convection comes with it, taking water vapor and rain away from the western Pacific and Indian Ocean and moving it east.

When the zone approaches the west coast of the Americas, it constitutes a major atmospheric disturbance; like a boulder dropped into a stream, it disrupts and reroutes currents, in this case, atmospheric currents like the jet streams. This creates the split that sends a subtropical jet across the southern United States and another one, farther north, scooting across the northern tier, where in some El Niño configurations like that of the 1997–98 season it tends to keep cold Arctic air walled off in Canada. Meanwhile, the increased convection and atmospheric water vapor in the eastern Pacific feeds moisture to the jet, setting the stage for heavy rains on the West Coast and increased tornado activity in the Southeast.

These seem to be the most frequent atmospheric consequences of a very strong El Niño event like the one in 1997–98. But not all events are the same. Weaker ones can have somewhat different impacts. For example, California has experienced drought rather than rain in a more moderate or weak El Niño. It must be remembered that El Niño, for all its power, is only one of a myriad of influences on the climate system; other factors can alter the pattern of its impact. In 1997–98, for instance, different general circulation patterns in the North Atlantic region and the eastern United States could have allowed cold Arctic air to drop well down into the United States—in which case the Northeast's wet winter heavy with moisture brought by the long-traveling subtropical jet could have been a spectacularly snowy one instead.

Sometimes, but less frequently, the oscillation goes to the other extreme, with sea-surface temperatures in the eastern tropical Pacific dropping well below normal. This mode has been dubbed La Niña, and it, too, has an impact on climate, though it has been studied less than has El Niño. Sometimes it merely intensifies weather trends that would have taken place anyway. But occasionally it has a major new impact. Some experts believe that shifts in circulation patterns caused by La Niña, for instance, played a major role in locking the 1988 North American drought into place for so long. And in the winter of 1998–99, it played a role in producing record snows in Buffalo and Chicago, record numbers of January tornadoes in the south-central part of the country, all-time low temperatures in Illinois and Maine, and double the normal amount of January rainfall, along with an extended spell of abnormal warmth, in New York.

Interest in the El Niño–La Niña cycle first heightened in the late

1970s, mainly because some scientists wondered whether the phenomenon might be linked to a series of especially severe North American winters in those years. Two scientists at the Massachusetts Institute of Technology, Mark A. Cane and Stephen E. Zebiak, tackled the problem by constructing a computer model that succeeded in reproducing the Pacific temperature oscillations characteristic of El Niño. In 1982–83 the strongest El Niño observed up till then (and still one of the twentieth century's two strongest) focused the public's attention on the phenomenon for the first time. No one had seen it coming, and Cane and Zebiak set out to determine whether their model could be used to predict El Niño's comings and goings in time to be useful.

First, they tried to "hindcast" the 1982–83 event, and succeeded handsomely. "It's probably the only thing I've ever done in science that worked the first time," Cane said later. The real proof would come if and when they succeeded in using the mathematical model to predict an El Niño event in advance. By 1986 the two scientists had moved to the Lamont-Doherty lab, and there they forecast a moderate El Niño for 1986–87. After some anxious months in which it seemed not to be materializing, it finally did. Still, skepticism abounded. It was largely dispelled when many experts predicted that El Niño would appear in 1990. Cane and Zebiak predicted that it would not, and they were right.

Since then the Cane-Zebiak model has been wrong, as they knew it would sometimes be, on at least two important occasions, the biggest being that it missed the 1997–98 event. But by then other modelers were on the case, most notably the Climate Prediction Center of the National Weather Service. Its models predicted in May 1997 that the coming winter would see one of the strongest El Niños ever experienced, maybe the strongest.

The Climate Prediction Center's forecast was impressively right. Before 1997 was out, El Niño had quieted the Atlantic hurricane season and produced killing drought in Indonesia, which fed forest fires whose smoke choked the cities of that region for weeks. Early in the growing season, breadbasket areas of India and Pakistan were dry, as would be expected, but this time El Niño let the monsoon proceed.

In the United States, much of the country passed a warm December and January thanks to El Niño, and in California, the much-feared storms on the whole had failed to appear. For months, in an orgy of hype and hyperbole, Americans had been blaming everything on El Niño—even the fortunes of some college football teams. Now people were wondering whether the experts were crying wolf. "If this El Niño gets much worse, I'm going to have to get stronger sun block," said Willy Parsons, a comedian.

Then came February, and vindication for the government forecasters, who successfuly predicted not only the arrival of El Niño but also the regional outlines of its impact on the United States.

By the end of the 1990s, it was apparent that El Niño had become a much more frequent visitor than was historically the case. Could this be related to a broader change in the global climate? And could a changing climate alter the other semiperiodic weather oscillations in the Arctic, North Atlantic, and North Pacific, with down-to-earth weather consequences for everyday life? As we will see, these hotly contested questions involve some of the most important ramifications of global climate change.

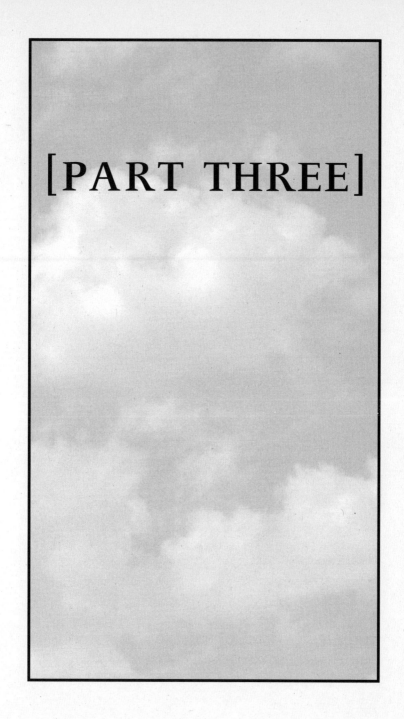

[PART THREE]

[8]

The Greenhouse Experiment

JUNE 23, 1988, dawned hot and oppressive in Washington, D.C. The temperature there would hit 101 degrees before the day was over. The rest of the East baked along with the capital. In central Pennsylvania, where men garbed in 1863 military uniforms were reenacting the battle of Gettysburg 125 years before, the weather was authentic—searing heat rose in shimmering waves off the bright green hills and swales, just as it had a century and a quarter earlier. Across the country, one of the most intense combinations of drought and heat since the Dust Bowl of the 1930s was almost a month old. The water level of the Mississippi River was at a record low. So much had evaporated that, in places, the great stream had slowed to a comparatively puny trickle. Barges could not get through. Some ran aground. At least half the wheat, barley, and oats grown in the northern Great Plains was lost. The U.S. Department of Agriculture declared a drought emergency in 40 percent of the nation's counties. In the West, the drought set the stage for a seasonlong siege of forest fires. Later in the summer, spectacular blazes whose extent and fury had not been seen in two centuries would sweep much of Yellowstone National Park. In all, 6 million acres would burn in the United States, the most in recorded history in one year.

With what seemed prophetic skill, U.S. Senator Timothy Wirth of Colorado had scheduled a hearing for June 23, at which scientists were to testify about a subject that had stirred enthusiastic concern in him and some other members of Congress: global warming.

By this time, scientists knew enough about the climate system and its impact on the natural world and human affairs to raise alarms about rising emissions of heat-trapping carbon dioxide and other greenhouse gases. Their understanding was far from complete. They were beginning to paint a picture of climate's influence on human evolution and early civilization, but a fuller appreciation of implications of the Holocene upheavals for present and future climate was still to emerge. Experts were only starting to focus on the ways in which a warmer atmosphere might alter everyday weather. They could not prove that emissions of greenhouse gases such as carbon dioxide, produced by the burning of fossil fuels like coal and oil, were in fact currently warming the atmosphere. But it did appear that the earth's surface had in fact warmed since the late nineteenth century. And many were convinced that if the world continued to burn fossil fuels as it was doing, it would be seriously risking a rise in the earth's temperature not seen in thousands, perhaps millions, of years. If this happened, scientists warned, the earth's climate would be disrupted and the global sea level would rise.

Environmentalists, seizing on what they saw as an overarching cause, cried catastrophe. Three years earlier scientists from twenty-nine countries had declared formally that the threat of climate change was clear enough so that world governments should consider policies to deal with it. This meant taking steps to control greenhouse gas emissions, which in turn meant finding some way to reduce the burning of fossil fuels—a prospect fraught with potentially grave economic implications, since the global economy essentially ran on fossil fuels. The heavy energy-using and energy-producing industries at the economy's core, sensing a threat to their well-being, weighed in on the issue, setting up a passionate debate that, as we will see, would blossom into a political and diplomatic problem of worldwide dimensions. The political argument also would spill over into the emerging scientific debate on global warming, as both environmentalists and industry lobbyists attempted to influence the scientific findings and to put their own spin on them once they emerged.

Despite all this, global warming had yet to excite much public interest as Wirth convened his 1988 hearing. Earlier congressional hearings had failed to make much of an impact. James E. Hansen, a forty-seven-year-old climatologist, and other scientists had testified at these hearings, most recently on a miserably rainy day the previous November. He had argued both before and after that appearance that people would pay attention to global warming only if the hearings were held in the summer, when it was hot.

Hansen had been one of the first investigators to harness computerized mathematical models to the study of the greenhouse effect. In 1981 some experts were focusing on the possibility that the globe was cooling off. But Hansen and his colleagues analyzed surface temperatures from 2,000 stations around the world and found that a century-long global warming trend had resumed after leveling off in the 1950s, 1960s, and early 1970s. The story made page-one news in the *New York Times,* but for the most part Hansen and his colleagues labored in relative obscurity in a small, out-of-the-way corner of the U.S. space empire, the NASA Goddard Institute for Space Studies, housed above a restaurant at 112th Street and Broadway in New York. The relative obscurity of Hansen's laboratory, combined with his naturally mild manner and even temperament, made him an unlikely candidate, at least on the surface, to shake up the world on an issue of such great magnitude as climate change.

Hansen's studies had convinced him, however, that greenhouse gas emissions were indeed warming the planet and changing its climate. And since no other reputable researchers were willing to say so flat out, in plain English stripped of the cautious qualifiers in which scientists tend to wrap their discourse, he determined to do so. He knew he was risking his reputation. On the morning of June 23, the day he was to deliver his testimony, according to Hansen's recollection, a senior official said in his presence at a meeting at NASA headquarters that "no respectable scientist would claim there is a causal relationship be-

tween the greenhouse effect and observed climate change." ("Greenhouse effect," in the context of those times, commonly was taken to
mean global warming caused by human activity.) Hansen, who had
been ignoring the meeting to write an oral summary of his upcoming
formal testimony, piped up: "I don't know if he's respectable or not,
but I know a scientist who's about to make that assertion." He caught a
few quizzical looks, but no one asked him to explain.

As the capital sweltered in waves of heat reflected from acres of
stone buildings and concrete parking lots and streets, Wirth told Hansen that he was shifting the order of testimony so that Hansen could
go first, in case the television cameras left early.

Hansen's statement was brief. He told the Senate Energy and Natural Resources Committee—and the world—that four of the warmest
years in 130 years of measuring the average global surface temperature had occurred in the 1980s. He noted that the first five months of
1988 had brought the highest global temperatures yet. He said it could
now be asserted with 99 percent confidence that the earth was warming and that it was a real change, not a temporary, chaotic fluctuation.
The cause of the warming, he testified, could be ascribed with "a high
degree of confidence" to the greenhouse effect: "It is already happening now." And finally, he said that the warming of the 1980s and predicted for the 1990s was large enough to affect the frequency of
extreme weather events—like heat waves and droughts.

Afterward, in what for him or any scientist was an extraordinarily
bold assertion, Hansen told Philip Shabecoff of the *Times:* "It's time to
stop waffling so much and say that the evidence is pretty strong that
the greenhouse effect is here and is affecting our climate now."

Hansen was careful not to attribute the 1988 drought directly to
global warming, since he knew—and said—that no single weather
event could be so attributed. Later he would make up a pair of dice,
one representing the climate of the United States from 1950 through
1980 and the other for the 1990s. The first die had two red sides, each
representing a hotter-than-average summer. The other had four red
sides. Global warming, he argued, was loading the dice, increasing the
odds that any given summer would be hotter than normal.

These finer distinctions and considerations of probability were lost in the immediate reaction to Hansen's testimony. Also lost in the sensational event in the Senate was the role of a conventional, natural blocking high-pressure system, possibly assisted by La Niña, in holding the summer's heat and dryness in place. No matter: Millions of people now believed that global warming was responsible for the drought and heat wave. Environmentalists were ecstatic, and Hansen became an instant hero to them. Many of his colleagues were less than thrilled and in fact criticized him harshly for, as they saw it, going too far—and, worse, doing it in a way guaranteed to gain maximum attention.

That it did. In one dramatic stroke, Hansen infused the question of climate change with palpable immediacy, propelling it out of the laboratory and into the public arena. Suddenly it was on the front burner of international politics. "I've never seen an environmental issue mature so quickly, shifting from science to the policy realm almost overnight," Michael Oppenheimer, an atmospheric scientist with the Environmental Defense Fund who had also testified on June 23, told the *Times*'s John Noble Wilford in August 1988.

For two centuries, people had been spewing heat-trapping waste industrial gases, mainly carbon dioxide, into the atmosphere. For a century and a half, a succession of scientists had been investigating what this might mean. For almost no time had anyone considered what, if anything, the world ought to do about it. Now all three streams of activity—industrial, scientific, and political—had converged as never before, and the outlines of a historic debate had suddenly popped into clear focus. We will return to that debate, and to Hansen and his work, once we have stepped back to examine the history of the global warming problem and of scientists' quest to understand it.

WE HAVE SEEN that between 350 million and 65 million years ago, great quantities of carbon were put into deep storage when plants and animals died and decayed and their remains were compressed into what eventually became coal and oil. This carbon was effectively removed from the global cycle in which it circulates through the earth, the oceans, the atmosphere, and living organisms.

The English, in the eighteenth century, became the first humans to begin putting the buried carbon back into circulation in a big way. Their instrument was the Industrial Revolution, beginning with the introduction and perfection of James Watt's steam engines. The engines were the catalyst for a number of ingredients that soon combined to transform England's economy and society, and eventually the world's.

Steam engines had two immediate effects. First, they rescued Britain's coal mines, many of which were about to be abandoned because no effective pump had been available to keep them clear of water. Steam engines gave them one, and coal mining was off to the races. Second, the engines made mechanical power independent of wind and water. Now factories could be built anywhere.

These two features might have found no immediate use had economic and social conditions in England not been ripe. The Industrial Revolution appeared there first because England had large amounts of free capital (other countries diverted much capital to the state), a sound monetary system compared with other nations, a mobile and adaptable labor supply, free markets, a social system that favored the starting of private businesses—and natural resources.

Of these, the greatest was coal. England in these decades was running out of wood to burn, and coal provided the perfect substitute for industrial purposes. Instead of burning wood to get charcoal for iron smelting, one could burn coal to get coke. England had lots of coal, and it was situated near seaports, making it easier to ship iron ore to where the coal was. The steam engine arrived on the scene just as the mining and metal industries were expanding and the need for coal was growing, and just as the techniques and machines necessary to produce the parts for Watt's machine had been invented. The steam engine, in time, was adapted to a wide array of manufacturing processes. All of these elements—new materials like iron and steel, new fuel, new machines, the factory system—eventually joined with transportation and communications innovations like the railroad, steamship, telegraph, telephone, and ultimately radio, automobiles, and airplanes to constitute what we know as the Industrial Revolution.

At the outset, the revolution was founded almost solely on coal, the fossil fuel with the highest carbon content and thus, pound for pound, the biggest producer of atmospheric carbon dioxide when burned. When the revolution crossed the Atlantic, it was fueled at first by wood burning (which also produces carbon dioxide), since North America was still thick with timber. As late as 1870, wood provided most of the fuel for American industry, but a mere fifteen years later coal was firmly in command.

The twentieth century ushered in the age of oil, and motor vehicles, of course, were the reason why. Until then demand for oil had been relatively minuscule. But when Henry Ford instituted mass production of automobiles, the petroleum industry took off worldwide. Oil joined coal as one of industrial society's two fuels of choice. Natural gas, favored especially for heating modern homes, completed the fossil fuel triumvirate that undergirds the modern global economy.

As the burning of these fuels increased, atmospheric carbon dioxide rose steadily, although it would be some time before scientists would know the rate of rise.

CONTRARY TO ASSERTIONS by some conservative politicians in the 1990s that global warming was a figment of the present-day liberal and environmentalist imagination, the issue has a long and distinguished scientific history.

The Industrial Revolution was just gaining headway when scientists began to investigate the atmospheric greenhouse effect. The effect was first pointed out in 1827 by the French mathematician and physicist Baron Jean Baptiste Joseph Fourier, who established a distinction between heat absorbed by the earth from the sun and heat reflected from the earth back into the atmosphere. The latter, he noted, passes less easily through the atmosphere, thereby raising its temperature.

Could humans modify the amount of heat retained in the atmosphere? Fourier thought so, but through what means? In a series of carefully controlled laboratory experiments in the 1850s and 1860s, an English scientist named John Tyndall isolated carbon dioxide and water vapor as the atmosphere's two most important heat absorbers, with water vapor the more powerful of the two. These constitute "true causes" of climate change, he said, with even small changes in carbon dioxide or water vapor being sufficient to alter temperature.

But how big a change would a given increase in carbon dioxide produce? As so often happened with big questions in atmospheric science, the attempt to provide an answer was made first in Scandinavia, where a talented Swedish chemist who would win the Nobel Prize (for other work) proposed in 1895 that long-term changes in the amount of carbon dioxide in the air could account for the comings and goings of ice ages. He was Svante Arrhenius, and he set out to take the investigation of the greenhouse effect a big step further by trying to pin down its magnitude. His idea was to construct a theoretical mathematical model and use it to calculate the changes in atmospheric carbon dioxide necessary to both boost the earth's temperature by about 14 degrees Fahrenheit and lower it by about 9 degrees. He figured, preliminarily, that this would require carbon dioxide to increase or decrease by about half.

Arrhenius, a rotund, 220-pound man who made friends easily and liked his parties, traveled in distinguished company. He was a close friend of Vilhelm Bjerknes. The two were members of a yeasty intellectual circle in Stockholm that considered science to be recreation as much as work. The goal of the group, called the Stockholm Physics Society, was to investigate the interworkings of the seas, atmosphere, solid earth, and cosmos. It was here that Bjerknes formulated the circulation theorem that underlies today's conception of weather and here that Arrhenius probed the greenhouse effect.

Arrhenius took as the basis for his calculations Fourier's concept of how the greenhouse effect actually works, which is really not like a greenhouse at all. The air inside a garden greenhouse is heated because it is enclosed and air currents cannot carry away the heat delivered by the sun's rays. The trapping of heat in the atmosphere works differently: Solar radiation is absorbed by the earth, and some of it, in infrared form, is then reradiated upward, where it is trapped and heats the atmosphere. Fourier's idea, still accepted today, was that this trapped heat is reradiated downward, warming the planet's surface and the air immediately above.

Arrhenius calculated the heating effect for various amounts of atmospheric carbon dioxide (like Fourier, he called it carbonic acid) at every 10 degrees of latitude from 70 degrees North to 60 degrees South during each of the four seasons. He made the calculation for 0.67, 1.5, 2, 2.5, and 3 times the observed atmospheric level of carbon dioxide. The calculations apparently took far longer than Arrhenius anticipated. He complained in letters how difficult it was to wrap up the "carbonic acid matter." He worked for a year to finish the problem, and at the end he produced a table, contained in a formal paper, setting out his results.

The ice ages, he wrote, could have been brought on by a reduction of atmospheric carbon dioxide to about half its value in the 1890s. By extrapolating from regional results, he figured that if the 1890s level of carbon dioxide were doubled, the average surface temperature of the globe would rise by 5 to 6 degrees Celsius, or 9 to 11 degrees Fahrenheit. This is roughly twice today's most widely accepted best estimate.

Arrhenius then went the extra mile by trying to calculate how long it would take for the amount of atmospheric carbon dioxide to double because of coal burning. This was apparently the first time anyone had linked the use of fossil fuels to climate change. He estimated that a doubling would take 3,000 years. Even then, he said with an optimism characteristic of his age, this would not be so bad—especially, one presumes, for Scandinavia. It would, he said in an 1896 lecture, "allow our descendants, even if they only be those of a distant future, to live under a warmer sky and in a less harsh environment than we were granted."

Other findings expanded on those of Arrhenius over the next few years. A key feedback mechanism that supposedly enhances greenhouse warming was pointed out by an American geologist named Thomas C. Chamberlin. The relatively small amount of warming produced by carbon dioxide, he said, was enough to increase atmospheric water vapor, a more powerful heat-trapper. This in turn would trap even more heat.

The first attempt to connect contemporary climatic change with the greenhouse effect came in 1938, when it was estimated by G. S. Callendar, a British meteorologist, that fossil fuel burning would increase the average global temperature by about 2 degrees Fahrenheit over the following century. After analyzing temperature data from 200 meteorological stations, he concluded that it had already risen by almost half a degree over the previous half century. Callendar saw no harm in this, predicting that carbon dioxide would spur plant growth, that agriculture would be enhanced "at the northern margin of cultivation," and that "the return of the deadly glaciers should be delayed indefinitely."

But most scientists in the early twentieth century put little stock in the greenhouse effect. They typically believed that an atmospheric trace gas found in such minute quantities as carbon dioxide probably had a negligible effect on climate. Consequently, little attention was paid to the greenhouse question well into the 1950s. The warming trend that Callendar had pointed out was tailing off, the globe was beginning to cool slightly, and even environmentalists were preoccupied with problems like nuclear fallout, local air pollution, and dirty water. Moreover, the general belief among scientists since Arrhenius (including him) was that the oceans would absorb most of the carbon dioxide being emitted and not release it to the atmosphere for a long time. The implication seemed to be that even if there was a problem, it was far off.

That idea began to change in the late 1950s, when it was discovered that the oceans were not taking up as much carbon dioxide as had been thought and that consequently more was remaining in the atmosphere. This finding was reported by two highly respected scientists, Roger Revelle and Hans E. Suess of the Scripps Institution of Oceanography. Because of the ocean's slowness in absorbing carbon dioxide, they wrote in the journal *Tellus,* it would stay in the air for centuries. The upshot, they wrote in a passage that has been quoted extensively ever since, was that "human beings are now carrying out a large-scale geophysical experiment of a kind that could not have happened in the past nor be reproduced in the future." Within only a few centuries, they wrote, "we are returning to the atmosphere and oceans the concentrated organic carbon stored in the sedimentary rocks over hundreds of millions of years. This experiment, if adequately documented, may yield a far-reaching insight into the processes determining weather and climate."

Indeed. And one of the most important pieces of documentation—in fact, one of the most important pieces of evidence ever to be produced on the climate question—was about to be supplied by one of Revelle's junior associates.

CHARLES DAVID KEELING, fresh out of Northwestern University with a Ph.D. in chemistry and with a job virtually assured in the booming postwar economy of 1953, had two career options. He could become an industrial chemist, working in a polymer laboratory on the East Coast, or he could be an environmental chemist on the West Coast. He chose the latter; it might allow him to get outdoors. He was hired as a postdoctoral researcher in a new geochemistry department being established by the California Institute of Technology in Pasadena. Caltech set him to work on extracting uranium from rocks, a task he found less than fulfilling. Looking around for something else, he got a chance to measure carbon dioxide gas in water and in the air above it. The object was simple, merely to find out whether the amount of carbon dioxide dissolved in lakes and rivers depended on the amount of the gas in the air. This pursuit, while it did allow him to get outdoors, presented a problem: There was no instrument on the market for measuring carbon dioxide in the small quantities required, namely parts per million. Following an old blueprint for such an instrument, called a manometer, Keeling built his own. It took about a year, but he wanted to make the instrument as accurate as possible. In the end, according to him, it was about ten times as accurate as it needed to be.

When the manometer was ready, he took out onto the roof of his laboratory building a hollow glass sphere from which he had pumped all the air. Holding his breath so as not to contaminate the sample with his own exhaled carbon dioxide, he opened a valve and let air flood into the sphere. Then he closed the valve and rushed back into the lab, separated the carbon dioxide from the air through a technique involving liquid nitrogen, put the carbon dioxide into the manometer, and compressed the gas under a column of mercury. This procedure produced a reading of 310 parts of carbon dioxide per million. He repeated the sampling and measurement over and over, even while his wife was giving birth to their first child, and soon they took the baby on a series of camping trips to Big Sur, Yosemite, and Olympic Park, where he made further measurements. Once a deer grabbed the notebook in which he was recording everything and ran off with it. Keeling gave chase and found the book, its cover chewed off but the data intact.

As the data accumulated, it described a peculiar pattern. Each day when the sun rose, the amount of carbon dioxide in the air began to drop, as would be expected when forest trees and other plants begin to perform photosynthesis and absorb the gas. Later in the day, as the sun went down, it increased again. The peculiar thing was that at its low point, in midafternoon, it always measured about 315 parts per million. No one had ever observed this, or at least reported it, before. Carrying his experiment to ever more remote places, like the 12,000-foot Inyo Mountains of eastern California, where gale-force winds continually mixed the air, Keeling continued to get the same reading: about 315 parts per million. Air samples from the equator also yielded the magic number of 315. These findings directly contradicted conventional thinking, which held that atmospheric carbon dioxide varies widely from place to place, depending on the amount of the gas being absorbed locally, by vegetation, or emitted locally, by burning. This concept was enshrined in the scientific literature of the day.

"I decided all the data in the literature was wrong," Keeling recalls. He was convinced that the level of carbon dioxide in the air was the same around the world, once atmospheric circulation had mixed the air thoroughly, as it constantly did.

Given his interest in the Great Carbon Dioxide Experiment, Roger Revelle was also naturally interested in knowing whether atmospheric concentrations of the gas were rising, and by how much. In 1957, the International Geophysical Year (IGY), he invited Keeling to come to Scripps. Keeling was also invited by Harry Wexler, director of the U.S. Weather Bureau (the same Wexler to whom Jule Charney, a few years before, had so gleefully reported the successful computer simulation of the 1952 Washington snowstorm), to come to Washington. Wexler was interested in making carbon dioxide measurements at a new observatory atop Mauna Loa, in Hawaii. Keeling chose Scripps, but also accepted Wexler's offer to use Mauna Loa, as well as some money from Wexler's IGY funds.

Revelle and Keeling, both strong-willed men, clashed over how to proceed. Keeling, convinced that carbon dioxide was the same everywhere once you got away from ground-level distortions, argued that he could detect any global trend by taking measurements at only a few stations continually, over a long period. Revelle insisted that the best way was to make lots of measurements in a one-time snapshot, then do it again some years in the future. Keeling caved in—but he also arranged for continuous readings to begin at Mauna Loa, whose elevation and isolation made it an ideal site.

The Mauna Loa measurements began in March 1958. By March 1959 Keeling had detected a trend in global atmospheric carbon dioxide. "As soon as we had two Marches at Mauna Loa," he says, "we could see it was going up." Plotted on a graph, the curve—now, long since, called the Keeling curve—reflects a seasonal rise and fall in carbon dioxide each year, as the change in seasons alters the carbon dioxide intake of the globe's vegetation. The pattern described is that of a regular sawtooth, reflecting a regular, seasonal rise and fall in the absorption of carbon dioxide by vegetation. But the regular seesawing pattern does not run in a straight line across the page. Instead, it marches steadily upward, describing an underlying year-to-year increase in atmospheric carbon dioxide. By the late 1990s, the global concentration had grown from Keeling's 315 parts per million in the late 1950s to more than 360 parts per million, an increase of about 15 percent.

The present-day concentration is the highest of the last 420,000 years, according to an analysis of atmospheric gases trapped in Antarctic ice that was published in mid-1999. It is 20 percent higher than in any previous interglacial period and double the typical concentrations during an ice age.

At first, as almost always happens with a major advance in understanding, Keeling's method and findings drew skeptical fire. "Looks like you've got a stuck instrument," some doubters said when confronted with the first, early evidence of globally uniform readings, according to Keeling. "It shook up a lot of people," he says. Given that new scientific assertions are often wrong, this skepticism is a healthy thing, an essential part of the testing and winnowing from which valid ideas emerge. The Keeling method and the Keeling curve passed the test; today they are generally accepted as solid. Even committed skeptics on the question of whether greenhouse emissions are changing the climate concede that atmospheric carbon dioxide is rising.

NOW THAT A RISE in atmospheric carbon dioxide had been established and quantified, the question of how much it would warm the earth invited, indeed demanded, renewed attention. Almost immediately, computerized mathematical models that were the lineal descendants of those first created by Charney and von Neumann became the primary tools for trying to answer it.

One of the first advances was a new version of Norman Phillips's first model of the atmosphere's general circulation, using Lewis Fry Richardson's original set of equations (which in the meantime had been altered so as to remove sound waves, since they are irrelevant to the climate problem). The improved model was devised by Joseph Smagorinsky, a member of the original Princeton group who in 1995 established the federal government's Geophysical Fluid Dynamics Laboratory (GFDL) in Washington, D.C., as the Princeton group's successor. None of these early models was global, not least because of limited computer capacity; instead, they all simulated the atmospheric workings of slices of the Northern Hemisphere. Until then computer models had been used mainly for short-term weather forecasting. But now, despite the models' limitations, Smagorinsky began using them to investigate the long-term dynamics of the climate system as well.

To this point, no one had yet been able to improve on Arrhenius's and Callendar's preliminary, first-cut estimates of carbon dioxide's effect on the temperature of the atmosphere. For instance, a German scientist, Fritz Möller, fell afoul of the water-vapor feedback problem.

When he tried to include it in his calculations of the greenhouse effect, he got wildly varying results. Sometimes the earth would warm, sometimes it would cool.

To work on the problem of incorporating the greenhouse effect in the general circulation models, Smagorinsky recruited a bright young Japanese physicist, fresh out of graduate school at Tokyo University, named Syukuro Manabe (universally called Suki). The son of a physician, Manabe had endured severe privation as a middle-school student in World War II. Smagorinsky was so impressed with Manabe's mental qualities that he invited him aboard on the strength of a single paper he had written and on Manabe's reputation as an acute identifier of problems to be investigated.

Manabe joined Smagorinsky's group in 1958, the year Keeling made his first carbon dioxide measurements at Mauna Loa, and in time he discovered the reason for the wild gyrations in Möller's recalculation of Arrhenius's and Callendar's greenhouse warming estimate. All of them, Manabe discovered, had overlooked a critical fact: When greenhouse warming heats the earth's surface, it alters convection, which affects the vertical transfer of heat through the atmosphere and thereby affects greenhouse warming, as well. Once Manabe and colleagues reformulated the climate model to reflect this, the calculation became stable. No more wild, inconsistent answers, no more crippling ambiguity.

Manabe and his colleagues in 1967 used their reformulated model to calculate the impact of a doubling of atmospheric carbon dioxide. It yielded an increase in average global surface temperature of about 4 degrees Fahrenheit—approaching the difference between an ice age and an interglacial. This was a landmark finding in its own right. But perhaps more important, Manabe, by accounting properly for convection, had established the basis for all future computer simulations of the greenhouse effect.

With the field of greenhouse modeling to themselves, Manabe and his GFDL colleagues unveiled a parade of landmark research. One of the most important of these milestones came in 1968, as GFDL was moving from Washington into a new, modern black-stone headquarters on the outskirts of Princeton. Manabe and a coresearcher, Richard Wetherald, devised the first three-dimensional computer model of the entire globe (the three dimensions being horizontal space, vertical space, and change over time). It was "fairly crude," says Wetherald, "but it had all the bells and whistles that we had in our models at that time." The model included, for instance, a number of important processes like the impact of ice and snow on the earth's temperature when they reflect sunlight back into space and, most important, the heat-amplifying effect of processes involving water vapor.

Manabe and Wetherald used this three-dimensional global model to estimate the impact on the earth's climate of a doubling of atmospheric carbon dioxide and came up with a rise in average global temperature of 5.4 degrees Fahrenheit. Just as important, the model said that the warming would produce an 8 percent increase in evaporation of water to the atmosphere, with an accompanying increase in precipitation globally.

When these results were published in 1975, they coincided with an update by Keeling of his carbon dioxide measurements, which showed beyond a doubt that atmospheric concentrations of the gas were steadily increasing. To Wetherald, the two papers coming together amounted to a watershed. "For the first time," he says, "people began to realize that this is a real environmental problem, not just an ivory-tower problem." The greenhouse question, he says, had left the realm of science fiction and entered the world of science.

For some people, maybe. But in the 1970s, global warming was barely on the public radar scope at all. In fact, scientists and the public were more interested in the prospects of a colder earth, not a warmer one. After rising to a modern-day peak in the 1940s, the average global temperature had cooled off and essentially remained stable in the 1950s, 1960s, and early 1970s. The Northern Hemisphere snow and ice pack had expanded. Reid Bryson, a respected climate expert at the University of Wisconsin, argued that man-made pollutants, including dust kicked up by overgrazing occasioned by the need to feed an expanding population, were reducing the amount of sunlight reaching the earth. A global cooling trend was in the offing, he held. A number of scientists agreed that cooling was more likely than warming, including Stephen S. Schneider, a rising young star in climatology who would later change his mind and become a highly visible and articulate advocate of the opposite view, namely that warming was more likely.

Was a new ice age on the way? Many asked the question in the 1970s, and in a 1974 book called *The Weather Machine*, the popular science writer Nigel Calder asserted that the possibility was real. He wrote that an ice age "could in principle start next summer, or at any rate during the next hundred years, with a ferocity that could not be mistaken for a 'mere' climatic fluctuation like the Little Ice Age." He argued that although the onset of a new ice age might be gradual, sudden plunges into glacial cold had taken place in the past and that this "favours a catastrophic view of the threat of ice."

Although many experts say that such arguments were never grounded in sound science, Calder's view nevertheless found resonance, especially in the United States, in the last half of the 1970s. The eastern part of the country suffered through extremely cold winters in the late 1970s. At one point, in January 1977, temperatures dropped to 25 degrees below zero as far south as Cincinnati and stayed in that general neighborhood for days. Cincinnatians, unwilling to venture out, suffered from cabin fever by the thousands. The author remembers the unbelievable chill of sharp winds off the Ohio River in 25-below temperatures. A year later heavy snows plagued the Northeast. To many, some icy new world did indeed seem a possibility.

Experts now attribute the bitter eastern U.S. winters of the late 1970s to, in Wetherald's phrase, "deep-diving Rossby waves that got frozen in place"—a classic case of atmospheric gridlock that in this instance allowed Arctic air to stay in position over part of the country for weeks.

As for Bryson's sun-blocking haze of pollution, it turned out to be not global but regional. Later, as we will see, this would complicate but in some ways help efforts to get a handle on the global warming question. In the meantime, the apparently lesser impact of pollution on planetary temperature convinced Schneider and others who had embraced the global cooling theory that they were wrong. (Contrarians on the global warming issue would take great delight in later years in pointing out Schneider's flip-flop. Schneider replies that his revised judgment was simply a natural outgrowth of the process of scientific inquiry. In this case, the inquiry's purpose was to sort out different external forcings on the climate system, an effort then in its early stages and one that continues today. The "ultimate test" of respectability in science, he says, is the ability to change one's mind when the evidence dictates it rather than hold blindly to a favorite or politically dictated hypothesis.)

As the 1980s began, new scientific players were making themselves heard, evidence was accumulating, and global warming (the term apparently had been coined by J. Murray Mitchell Jr., a government scientist, in the early 1960s) started to come of age as an issue. James Hansen was one of the first and most influential of these new players.

Hansen was born on a farm at Charter Oak, Iowa, in 1941, and he and a brother and five sisters were raised in nearby Denison. His father was a tenant farmer and his mother a waitress. Hansen made no special mark as a student but helped pay his way to the University of Iowa with money he made delivering newspapers. There he met and was inspired by James Van Allen, the physicist and astronomer who discovered the radiation belts around the earth that bear his name, and became a serious student. Hansen graduated with highest honors in physics and mathematics, earned a master's degree in astronomy, and in 1967 got his Ph.D. in physics with a dissertation on the climate of Venus. Immediately he was offered a research position at the Goddard Institute in New York. "I was so excited by the opportunity to study at a NASA laboratory that I drove all the way to New York without stopping to sleep," he told Karen Wright, who wrote a profile of him in the *New York Times Magazine* in 1991. After pursuing some research in the Netherlands, where he met his future wife, Anniek Dekkers, he was taken on as a researcher by Columbia University and soon, in 1972, was given a full-time job at Goddard.

In his early years at Goddard he was perfectly happy to explore the atmosphere of Venus, analyzing data on that planet's clouds sent back by the Pioneer spacecraft. Steve Schneider was at Goddard at the same time, working on the earth's climate. "Jim and I used to go out to lunch, to Tad's Steakhouse—we were eating high on the food chain; you could get a steak and a baked potato for five dollars in those days—and here was Jim, looking at me like [the earth's] climate was a hopeless problem." Hansen kept telling Schneider "what a crazy problem it was, but he was watching very carefully, and then he got sucked in even deeper than some of the rest of us. I kind of laugh about it."

What sucked Hansen in was work he undertook in 1975 in response to a request for help from Yuk Ling Yung, a postdoctoral researcher at Harvard University. By this time, man-made chemicals called chlorofluorocarbons, or CFCs, had been found to trap heat in the atmosphere just as carbon dioxide does, but even more effectively molecule for molecule. CFCs were widely used as refrigerants, as a component of aerosol sprays, and in fire extinguishers and plastic foam. (They also deplete the earth's protective ozone layer, which screens out ultraviolet rays that, if unblocked, could eventually wipe out most life on the planet. Ozone depletion and global warming are commonly confused as one and the same phenomenon, but the only commonality is that CFCs and a handful of related synthetic chemicals both deplete ozone and trap heat.)

Still other waste industrial gases were also suspected as being heat trappers, and Yung enlisted Hansen to help investigate them. In 1976 the two published a paper in the journal *Science* that tied an increase in these other gases, including methane and nitrous oxide, to the greenhouse effect. In effect, their findings helped to expand what people soon began calling the total "basket" of greenhouse gases. Carbon dioxide remained the most important, accounting for about 80 percent of the total basket's heat-trapping potential. As a result of this work, Hansen became so interested in the global warming phenomenon that he resigned from the Venus project in 1978 to devote full time to building a computer model of the earth's climate system.

"It's interesting to try and understand what's on another planet, but if our own planet is changing, that's even more interesting," he later told interviewer Bill McKibben.

So Hansen joined Suki Manabe as a pioneer in the relatively new and soon-to-expand brotherhood of climate modelers. Goddard's mainframe computer occupied an entire floor above Tom's Restaurant at 112th and Broadway, but for all its size it was a primitive machine compared with the smaller but much more powerful computers that would be available in only a few years. The three-dimensional general circulation model that Hansen and his colleagues programmed into it was based on an earlier model developed at UCLA and had somewhat different characteristics from Manabe's. One of the earliest calculations that Hansen performed was to estimate, as Manabe had, the global temperature change that would be caused by a doubling of carbon dioxide (or carbon dioxide equivalent if the full basket of greenhouse gases is considered).

Not surprisingly, Hansen got a different answer than did Manabe—a state of affairs that continues to this day in the world of computer modeling because of the limitations of models (more about this later) and imperfect knowledge of the climate system's workings. Even the same model often gives a different answer when run more than once. At this stage, in the late 1970s, Manabe's calculations were indicating an average global surface warming of anywhere from 2 to 3 degrees Celsius (3.6 to 5.4 degrees Fahrenheit) for doubled carbon dioxide. Hansen's calculation gave a higher result—3.9 degrees Celsius (7 degrees Fahrenheit), a potentially catastrophic number were it to be borne out in the real world.

The first of a long line of attempts by formal blue-ribbon panels of scientists to reach some kind of consensus on the greenhouse question came in the summer of 1979, when a group appointed by the National Research Council (a branch of the National Academy of Sciences that serves as the federal government's main scientific research arm) convened at Woods Hole, Massachusetts. It was, says Manabe, a panel of "geniuses," albeit none who was expert on global warming. It was headed by a figure guaranteed to command instant respect. He was none other than Jule Charney, then the Sloan Professor of Meteorology at MIT, who, not having previously been associated with the greenhouse question, had the additional virtue of detachment.

The panel's key finding set bounds to the emerging scientific debate that have proven surprisingly durable in the two decades since. Basing the finding on the Manabe and Hansen model results, the group concluded that a doubling of carbon dioxide would boost the average surface temperature of the earth by 1.5 to 4.5 degrees Celsius (2.7 to 8.1 degrees Fahrenheit), with a most likely figure of 3 degrees Celsius (5.4 degrees Fahrenheit). The panel judged that at then-current rates of emissions, the doubling would probably take place in the early decades of the twenty-first century. But it hedged this estimate by cautioning that the ocean's heat-absorbing capacity could delay the warming response to a doubling for several decades.

Manabe, for one, believes that the panelists simply took his number—"I've had all kinds of numbers, but it just happened to be 2 degrees [Celsius] at the time"—and Hansen's higher one of about 4 degrees as a likely range. Then, he believes, they added half a degree Celsius to each end of the range, as a margin of error, to get a likely range of 1.5 to 4.5 degrees Celsius. Finally, they apparently just split the difference to get a most likely figure of 3 degrees. In twenty years of scientific investigation since then, these numbers have remained the most widely accepted estimate of the climate system's basic sensitivity to forced change by greenhouse gases—everything else being equal, which, as will be seen, it is not.

In its bottom line, the panel said "it appears that the warming will occur" and that regional changes in climate that result "may well be significant," but it declined to say what those changes might be. Many scientists, Hansen among them, believed that while a global warming of 1.5 degrees might not be hard to adapt to, 4.5 degrees would dramatically change the earth's climate.

The Charney report, for all the weight of authority it carried among scientists, made less than an impressive public splash in a time when so many people, including some scientists, were worried about global cooling. Enter Hansen again. In 1981 came his study showing that although the globe had been warming until 1940 and had then cooled off for the next two and a half decades, it was warming again and by the late 1970s had risen, overall, 0.4 of a degree Celsius (about 0.7 Fahrenheit) over the preceding century. Hansen and his colleagues went further, predicting a global warming of "almost unprecedented magnitude" in the twenty-first century, possibly making the earth warmer than at any time since the era of the dinosaurs. It could, they said, even melt the West Antarctic ice sheet, which would raise the global sea level by fifteen to twenty feet, inundating many low-lying areas. They said that agriculture could be disrupted and that the melting of Arctic ice could open the fabled Northwest Passage across northern North America.

The major obstacle barring acceptance of the greenhouse theory, Hansen and his coauthors wrote in *Science,* "has been the absence of observed warming coincident with the historic carbon dioxide increase." Now, they said, that warming had been observed.

Response to the paper from scientists was mixed. Clearly, many believed, Hansen had gone beyond what had been pinned down solidly. Many subsequently lauded him for his courage but questioned his scientific judgment. Hansen's views got him into trouble with the government, which paid his salary, and not for the last time. The Department of Energy rescinded a promise to provide research funds to Goddard, forcing Hansen to lay off five people and reduce the scope of his research. The department also, according to Hansen, told an independent researcher that his funding would be canceled if he used the results from the Goddard climate model, which department officials described as an "outlier."

In 1983 the U.S. Environmental Protection Agency, with Hansen's help, issued a report detailing what it saw as the possible risks of global warming. That same year the National Academy of Sciences (NAS) undertook a far more detailed study than the Charney group had made and came up with a cautious bottom line. The NAS panel stuck with the Charney report's finding that a doubling of carbon dioxide would produce an average global warming of 1.5 to 4.5 degrees Celsius but said values "in the lower half of this range are more probable." The panel judged, however, that the evidence then at hand did not justify steps to shift the economy away from fossil fuels, and in any case, it said, some modification of climate appeared likely whatever steps were taken.

Meanwhile, paleoclimatologists were drilling through the ice of Greenland and Antarctica and coming up with striking new evidence of the link between carbon dioxide and climate. The ice corings showed that temperature and carbon dioxide rose and fell in tandem as glaciations came and went and came again over the previous

200,000 years. This did not prove that carbon dioxide caused changes in temperature. Indeed, the changes in carbon dioxide usually lagged slightly behind those in temperature, suggesting that warming causes more carbon dioxide to be released by the biosphere—a positive feedback of no small consequence, if true. But to Hansen, the significance of the ice corings lay elsewhere: They provided empirical evidence of the climate system's sensitivity to temperature change. That is, all the known forcings that caused the earth to warm up after the last Ice Age delivered energy equivalent to 7 watts per square meter. This produced a warming of about 5 degrees Celsius (9 degrees Fahrenheit), according to Hansen. If that is right, it implies that greenhouse warming, which delivers about 4.3 watts, would produce a warming of about 3 degrees Celsius (5.4 degrees Fahrenheit).

This evidence helped fortify Hansen's conviction that the greenhouse problem was real, serious, and of immediate concern. And so he broke with his colleagues and delivered his explosive testimony of June 1988. While many (especially environmentalists) praised Hansen for what they saw as a courageous act, he brought down a rain of criticism. The White House expressed displeasure, and Hansen became a semipariah in some climatological circles. Yes, it was true that he had gained more attention for the field and for the problem at the core of its work. But many thought his stance scientifically unsound, that he had gone beyond what the evidence allowed. The headline on a 1989 article in *Science* caught the essence of Hansen's position in those contentious days:

Hansen vs. the World on the Greenhouse Threat

The events of 1988 and 1989 might have taken a heavy emotional toll on Hansen. But there were other pressures in his life at the time, and they acted as distractions. His father died. His wife was diagnosed with cancer. Consequently, Hansen says, the controversy "went pretty quick." He remembers being "very calm" during the Hansen-against-the-world days: "There was a lot of pressure, but on the other hand it didn't really bother me."

After that Hansen tried to withdraw from controversy and concentrate on science but found it difficult for a while. He kept militating publicly for his agency, NASA, to launch a small satellite to measure key atmospheric properties vital to monitoring climate change. He offered to bet anyone that one of the first three years of the 1990s would turn out to be the warmest on record. He won on the first try, in 1990, and he continued to predict that the 1990s would be the warmest decade on record, with successive new annual records. In this, as will become clear, he was triumphantly right.

In time, Hansen would be elected to the National Academy of Sciences. But his most significant achievement was to galvanize the debate over climate and to crystallize the debate's critical questions: Is the earth really warming? Is the weather really getting to be more extreme, or does it just seem that way? Are observed changes in climate unusual when measured against the climate system's past behavior? Is the situation truly serious? If the answer to those questions is yes, what is the explanation? Is human activity responsible for the change?

We will now turn to those questions.

[9]

Is the World Warming?

T HE MEMORY has faded as extreme weather events have cascaded in the last two decades, but in the summer of 1980, the
worst sustained heat wave of the twentieth century in the United
States baked Texas and much of the rest of the country. This writer,
reporting in the *Times* from Houston on July 17 of that year, described
the summer as follows:

> Every morning it is the same. The air is pleasantly balmy as the first,
> faint light of day appears over the oaks and pines. But as soon as the
> sun peeks above the treeline, the heat is felt. By late afternoon it is
> 100 degrees or more, and fluffy white clouds, rainless clouds that
> don't show up on radar weatherscopes, drift across the sky atop tor-
> rents of air that blow from the Rio Grande to the Mississippi and be-
> yond, wreaking silent death and destruction.

Hundred-degree temperatures prevailed for day after day, and as
the summer progressed, the heat moved east and north from Texas. It

killed nearly 1,300 people, and the cost in agricultural losses, electricity use, buckled highways, and other damage amounted to almost $20 billion by the time the wave ended in September. But no one knew as it was unfolding that it was the century's most intense combination of heat and drought. It fell to Tom Karl, a thirty-year-old rookie analyst who had just reported for work at the National Climatic Data Center in Asheville, North Carolina, to help place it in historical perspective. As a result, he plunged almost immediately into the mainstream of climatic research—and into the maelstrom that was beginning to swirl about the question of global warming. Very soon he would become a key researcher and player in the emerging international discussion of climate change, and his evolving judgment on the issue—from skepticism that the atmosphere was warming and changing the earth's climate to firm acceptance—would reflect that of a substantial segment of the climatological community.

Thomas Richard Karl's fascination with weather and climate began early. When he was growing up in the Chicago suburb of Niles, just northeast of O'Hare International Airport, he and his father used to have forecasting contests, and young Tom developed a special fascination for keeping weather diaries and records, entering data point after data point and trying to discern patterns. It helped, he says, that his home happened to lie in a highly active and variable climatic zone— "Chicago is a great place; we had a lot of weather." He studied meteorology at Northern Illinois University and then at the University of Wisconsin, one of the two or three top meteorological institutions of the day in America, where he earned a master's degree. He chose Wisconsin largely because it was also a place with a lot of weather action; he ruled out California and the South as being "too boring, weatherwise." At Wisconsin, he came under the lash of hard-driving, authoritarian professors who had been Luftwaffe weather forecasters during World War II. "They pushed me so hard," he remembers. "I was really flat-out."

He did a stint as a television weather forecaster with a private weather service he helped establish in Madison but says he was "terrible at it," and the stint lasted only about six months. At something of a loss as to what to do, he tentatively took a position with the weather service's severe storms laboratory in Norman, Oklahoma, even moving his furniture there. The National Oceanic and Atmospheric Administration's Air Resources Laboratory at Research Triangle Park in North Carolina offered him a job at about the same time, and ultimately he opted for that. His task was to study the climatology involved in transporting air pollution and to help develop models for forecasting air-quality levels. It was, he says, "the best thing that ever happened to me," for two reasons: He was publishing papers and reaping the benefits of scientific conferences almost immediately, and the work made him appreciate "what you can do and can't do with data."

After a brief return to forecasting with the National Weather Service in Anchorage, Alaska ("Anchorage was okay by me, because there was a lot of weather"), he realized that he didn't want to do that for the rest of his life. His true love was working with data, and especially trying to extract climatic patterns from the historical record of weather observations. He began sending out applications. The Climatic Data Center responded, and in April 1980 he and his wife, Cindy, a math major and computer scientist he met in his undergraduate days, moved with their infant daughter (they later had a son as well) from Anchorage to Asheville.

The prospects for advancement, he was given to understand, were limited; if he was coming on board, therefore, he was doing it because he was interested in the science. As it turned out, eventually he would succeed on both levels, earning a reputation as one of the world's most talented, reliable, and productive analysts of climatic trends and, in 1998, becoming director of the Climatic Data Center, the world's premier repository of weather and climatic data.

From the beginning, Tom Karl and Asheville clicked. After the cold years of the late 1970s, and then with the torrid summer of 1980, interest in climatic trends was rising. What was going on with the weather? Was the climate changing or not? "I came into it just at the time when people were beginning to wonder, and the greenhouse question was starting to emerge," Karl says now. It was a clear case of the right man in the right place at the right time. The career of the climatologist who today might be called Mr. Data was truly launched, and it would evolve and mature along with the greenhouse issue itself.

In 1980, when Karl arrived in Asheville, people had not much looked at long-term climatic data in a truly rigorous and systematic way. The immediate task back then was to assess the historical significance of the heat wave. Was it unprecedented? Karl and his colleagues found that in one way, at least for the twentieth century, it was. Big droughts in the 1950s and especially the 1930s, the Dust Bowl era, were the champs. The 1980 drought, however, brought hotter temperatures than any other drought in the century.

But the 1980 heat wave had an impact on climatic science far beyond its immediate interest, and on Karl personally. It made him aware for the first time of the issue of global warming and climate change, and it was, he says, "the event that drove us to look at the records." The American weather records, it turned out, were a mess, a mass of raw data shot through with biases and distortions. This did not matter so much when an obviously extreme event like the 1980 drought popped up; it would stand out unambiguously. But when Karl and his colleagues tried to track national trends, it became obvious that the data records, in Karl's words, "weren't up to snuff." For openers, the millions of observations that constituted the record of atmospheric behavior were never intended for use in monitoring long-term climatic trends but rather for determining the daily weather and making short-term forecasts. That made it hard to adapt them for climatic research.

"I remember coming in here one day, scratching my head, and saying, 'This data's so bad, I don't see how we can believe anything,' " he said. Then, another time, it would look as if a trend really was there. "So one day, you'd say, 'This whole story's a crock, none of it's real.' And on other days, you'd say, 'It's amazing, how could all this fit together?' " as it sometimes seemed to do.

The first step, starting in 1980 and lasting for the next seven years, was to enter all the data on American weather into a computer data base. Without that, it was impossible to analyze long-term changes in climate. With it, researchers for the first time could extract climatic trends from the welter of information that until then had been locked away in archives. The United States was one of the first countries to do this.

WHILE KARL AND HIS colleagues were trying to make sense of the American climate record in the early 1980s, other climatologists were taking a broader look and trying to identify long-term global temperature trends. Among them were Phil Jones and Tom M. L. Wigley of the University of East Anglia in England. Jim Hansen's global temperature record had already suggested a warming trend over the preceding century, as we have seen. But much of the data on which all these researchers were operating basically came through the Climatic Data Center and then were redistributed. "We knew there were a tremendous number of problems" with the data, says Karl, and he was skeptical about whether a warming was going on largely because of this.

This kind of confusion and perplexity led to an intensive effort to clean up the data—that is, identify the sources of distortion, calculate the amount of error resulting from these biases, and correct the record accordingly. Big geographical gaps in data, especially in oceanic areas where the ships that measured the temperature seldom went, presented one source of error. So did the fact that observations became less trustworthy and abundant the farther one went back in time, especially in the nineteenth century. (Worldwide temperature records go back only to the mid-1800s.)

In England, Jones and Wigley teamed up with analysts at the British Meteorological Office in Bracknell (the Met Office, it is called), west of Heathrow Airport, in a daunting effort to bring some order out of the chaos of global climate data. It was tedious, labor-intensive work, but without it, efforts to identify global temperature trends would lack credibility.

One big source of distortion was that observers had used different observational methods at different times and places. For instance, in the nineteenth century and early twentieth century, ships measured sea-surface temperatures by lowering canvas buckets into the water.

Sailors, hauling the bucket up, would stick in a thermometer and stir it around until a steady reading was recorded, then enter the reading in a log book. The problem was that wind blowing on the porous bucket, combined with evaporation of water, would cool the water while the measurement was being taken. To complicate matters further, this distortion varied by location and time of year. And to add even more to the difficulty, wood, rubber, and metal buckets were also used, and in World War II, ships forsook these various uninsulated containers for an entirely new method: drawing the samples from ships' water intake tubes. That is the main method in use today, although measurements employing insulated plastic buckets agree well with intake measurements and are sometimes used. Two Met Office analysts, David Parker and Chris Folland, devised a complex way to correct the record for these biases, using mathematical equations that represent evaporation as a function of location and month of the year.

Surface temperatures on land present a different set of problems. For instance, a few decades ago a widespread relocation of observing stations from cities to rural airports took place. Heat-absorbing concrete, brick, and asphalt make cities significantly warmer than rural areas, and the switch to the countryside introduces a discontinuity in the records. On the other side of the coin, increasing urbanization in later years has steadily engulfed many observation stations, making them subject to distortion by what is called the urban "heat-island" effect.

Jones, Wigley, and their colleagues set out to collect, once and for all, every available land temperature record in the world, then combine them and scrub from the combined record as many distorting influences as possible. The task then became to cut the list down, correcting or eliminating readings from questionable weather stations. This required laborious checking of all the land stations. Sometimes the researchers were able to correct for the errors, but in many instances they were not and simply dropped these stations from the data set. In the end, Jones and Wigley eliminated 1,399 of the 3,276 stations they started with, leaving a data base of 1,548 stations in the Northern Hemisphere and 293 in the Southern. It was on this that the most ambitious effort so far to analyze the world's temperature trends would be founded.

To gauge how well they had eliminated the urban heat-island bias from the data, Jones and Wigley compared the data with a separate set of American data that Tom Karl and colleagues had extracted from their growing trove of "scrubbed" information. This data set included information mostly from rural areas, which would be free of the heat-island bias. The British data showed a slightly warmer temperature profile than did Karl's, but the difference was less than two-tenths of a degree Fahrenheit. Subsequent analysis of the heat-island problem by other researchers revealed a similar error for the globe as a whole of between one-tenth and two-tenths of a degree Fahrenheit over the twentieth century.

Having scrubbed the records as clean as possible, the Bracknell–East Anglia team was ready to produce its analysis of global average surface temperature. In short order, it would become the surface analysis most cited by the international community of climate experts. Tom Karl's group at Asheville would in time produce its own global data set and derive trends from it, but in the beginning the British and Hansen had the field to themselves.

In 1984 Parker and Folland published their results for ocean temperatures. Jones's group followed with land temperatures two years later. The two analyses showed similar, indeed, almost parallel, upward trends in global temperature. It is noteworthy that the ocean record by definition contained no urban heat-island bias, yet revealed essentially the same overall trend as the land record. By 1988 the researchers had combined the two data sets to create a single, global temperature record going back to 1856. In January 1989, with the global warming debate at a high pitch, they revealed their results in a Met Office press release. It made two main points: The six warmest years, globally, had all occurred in the 1980s, with the most recent year, 1988, the year when global warming leaped to the top of the international agenda, the warmest. And the average global temperature had risen by about 0.5 degree Celsius (about 1 degree Fahrenheit) since the beginning of the twentieth century. Both conclusions were instantly snapped up and became common currency in the debate. But in the press announcement, Parker offered a major caveat: "Whilst a warming of this amount is consistent with the 'greenhouse effect' caused by the rise in the levels of carbon dioxide and other man-made gases in the atmosphere, the earth's temperature fluctuates considerably due to natural causes, and no unambiguous connection can yet be made." Underlining the role of natural variability in the temperature rise, he pointed to the planet-warming effect of El Niño, which had peaked in 1987, as a factor in 1988's record warmth.

Indeed, despite the Herculean labors of the British group and other analysts of the climate record, many experts remained skeptical about whether the earth was warming. What began to change Karl's mind was one of the most remarkable—and contentious—enterprises in the history of climate science.

By 1988, researcher after researcher had weighed in on the question of climate change, and a number of study groups had tried to add up the findings. But science had moved on, and now the pressure of public events had created a need for a new assessment of the climate problem, one that could offer internationally sponsored, officially sanctioned, authoritative scientific guidance for policymakers and the public. The need flowed from a political imperative. With global warming so high on the agenda, pressure had intensified within the international community for a concerted attack on the issue. Not least, small island states in the Caribbean, the Pacific, and the Indian Ocean, fearful of being obliterated by rising seas resulting from a warmer climate, pressed for action. The United Nations General Assembly soon established a negotiating group, with representatives from virtually all nations, whose job was to fashion a convention, or treaty, to deal with the potential problem of climate change.

But previous scientific assessments of the problem, however good, were deemed insufficient as a guide to action. For one thing, most of the previous studies had not been carried out under international auspices, with international participation, and one country does not necessarily credit a report produced by another. A study by, say, the U.S. National Academy of Sciences might be helpful to that country— and, indeed, may make a contribution to a larger international assessment. But it is no substitute for a proper international study. "I don't ever hear German scientists talking about our Academy of Sciences report, and we don't talk about theirs," says Karl. "It's not that you ignore them, but it just doesn't have the impact, and it's not as comprehensive." Furthermore, while most of the assessments up to 1988 had come to the same basic conclusions on global warming, people in a bargaining setting tend to zero in on small differences in findings, not the larger similarities.

So, in November 1988, a nucleus of some thirty countries met in Geneva at the invitation of the World Meteorological Organization and the United Nations Environment Program to organize an international panel of climate scientists. Its job would be to comb the scientific literature and come up with a comprehensive assessment of climate change for use by the governments of the world. It was authorized to try to formulate realistic options for responding to climate change but not to propose solutions. While scientists were to control its operations and render its judgments, the panel's work would be reviewed, commented on, and lobbied about by affected interest groups, from environmentalists to fossil fuel producers. At several steps along the way, the emerging report would be reviewed not only by scientists but also by the governments involved, and they would have an active hand in summarizing, for policymakers, the detailed findings of the scientists. The process was designed, in effect, to produce not a wishy-washy ivory-tower conclusion but rather a concrete, decisive consensus on which practical action might be based.

The panel would soon come to be widely recognized (except by some scientific contrarians and some special interest groups who found its conclusions threatening) as the world's most authoritative voice on the science of climate change. Its organizers called it the Intergovernmental Panel on Climate Change, soon universally referred to by its initials, IPCC (by which it will be known throughout the rest of this book). Bert Bolin of Sweden, a greenhouse scientist of long standing and high repute, was chosen as the group's first chairman. Then sixty-three years old, Bolin would direct the IPCC for most of its first decade. Intellectually, he was a descendant of the Scandinavian school of atmospheric science, following in the footsteps of the Bjerkneses, Arrhenius, and Rossby. On his graduation from Uppsala

University in the mid-1940s, he joined Rossby, who had returned to Sweden after his years in the United States, to help create a European center for meteorology.

At first Bolin worked on computerized numerical weather forecasting, but Rossby asked him to shift gears and do research on atmospheric gases. This led to the carbon dioxide problem, and it became Bolin's central interest. When Rossby died suddenly, Bolin, then just over thirty years old, succeeded him as director of the meteorology center but continued his research. In 1960 he spent half a year working with David Keeling, and the two became good friends and collaborators. Over the years he took a leading role in a number of international climate research initiatives. So his background in computer modeling, his work on the greenhouse effect, and his international experience and contacts all made him a logical choice to head the IPCC.

In all, some 2,500 scientists would come to participate in the IPCC's work to some degree or other, with far fewer working on any given subtopic. At the outset, the British took over leadership of the panel's key working group on climate science. The driving force behind the British assumption of leadership apparently was none other than that country's prime minister of the 1980s, Margaret Thatcher, according to Geoff Jenkins, in 1998 the head of the Met Office's climate prediction program. Mrs. Thatcher, with a scientific background as a research chemist, had become a believer on the greenhouse question, and apparently her interest was more than passing. Once, after Met Office scientists briefed the prime minister on global warming, some people said it was the first they had ever seen Mrs. Thatcher not speak for half an hour, according to Jenkins.

Mrs. Thatcher freed up new funds for Britain's own climate research effort, which was expanded with the establishment of a new institute, the Hadley Center for Climate Prediction and Research, within the Met Office. So it was that in 1988, Mrs. Thatcher wanted her country to play a leading role in the IPCC. Her government's representative at the IPCC's organizational meeting at Geneva in November 1988 proposed that John Houghton, then head of the Met Office, be named chairman of the working group. He was, and Jenkins soon became coordinator of the working group's first report. The first IPCC scientific report, says Jenkins, "was a dream to do," mainly because the process "wasn't politicized at that time." No one knew what the political impact would be, and so the scientists could operate relatively unbothered by political pressures and more formal structures and procedures that appeared with future rounds of IPCC assessment. "We did things well," says Jenkins, "but we did them quite quickly."

The IPCC process was not without its critics. Contrarians charged that the leadership of the exercise was "self-selected." (Basically the leaders of the working group recruited the principal authors and other contributors to the study chapters around which the group's work was organized.) Contrarians also said that some contrary views were not given proper weight. Houghton and others denied this, saying that all relevant evidence that withstood the scrutiny of peer review was taken into account.

Tom Karl was chosen as one of three lead authors for the first report's chapter on observed changes in climate. (Chris Folland was the convening lead author, or chief author.) The experience was a watershed event for Karl, as had been the 1980 drought and, later, Hansen's congressional testimony. The first event had pushed him into looking at long-term climate trends. The second, he says, "really brought home very clearly that this wasn't an issue of how many angels can dance on the head of a pin; it wasn't just something we could sit back and discuss in papers. It really was an issue that was going to have a major impact." With the third event, the advent of the IPCC, Karl was led to see the bigger climate picture for the first time.

"Now, all of a sudden," he says, "you had scientists from around the world, in different disciplines, saying, 'Let's put what we have together in some coherent fashion and see what we know and what we don't know, what we can say and what we can't say.' " As a result, he believes, more actual knowledge was teased from the scientific literature than would otherwise have been the case: "Without the IPCC, I think there would be a lot more that we don't know. It's just hard to overemphasize the importance of getting . . . scientists around the world all looking at the issue with different perspectives and different disciplines."

A reasonably coherent picture of the broad subject of climate change did indeed emerge from the IPCC's work, leading to major reports in 1990 and 1995. We will turn to the IPCC findings from time to time as the rest of this narrative unfolds, beginning with the panel's assessment of what has happened to global temperatures.

DESPITE DIFFERENCES, by the end of the 1980s all the surface temperature records revealed a warming of the globe, on average, since the late nineteenth century. After subjecting all the temperature studies to close scrutiny, the IPCC, in its first report in 1990, synthesized them and pegged the average surface temperature increase at about 1 degree Fahrenheit—eight-tenths of a degree, actually, with a margin of error of plus or minus twenty-seven–hundredths of a degree. The estimate was slightly smaller than the actual year-to-year trend might suggest, since the IPCC expressed its findings in multidecadal averages that rise and fall over time. This tends to damp down especially high but temporary temperature spikes and especially low but temporary dips.

In its 1995 report, the panel reaffirmed its estimate of the surface temperature rise over the preceding century, but with an addition: Including later data, it now found that about half the warming since 1900 had taken place in the most recent forty years—contrary to a frequent assertion by skeptics that all or most of the century's warming took place before 1940. The report noted pointedly that the most recent forty years was the period in which surface data were most credible.

The 1995 report found further that readings taken by earth satellites and weather balloons showed a slight overall cooling of the troposphere after 1979. Greenhouse skeptics have often cited this as proof that there has been no recent warming. But the IPCC disagreed. After adjusting the post-1979 balloon and satellite records for the short-term effects of volcanic eruptions (which send up haze that cools the earth) and warming caused by El Niño, said the panel, these records also showed a slight warming, although not so large a one as the surface data. Satellite data do not extend back beyond 1979. But the data from weather balloons go back to the 1950s, and the panel noted that over that period, they show a tropospheric warming trend similar to that in the surface measurements.

The surface warming was not uniform. First, the IPCC noted, the warming of recent years was greatest over the Northern Hemisphere continents. Second, it noted that the range of temperature between night and day had grown smaller. This, Tom Karl and others had found, was because nights had warmed more than days. With this decrease in daily temperature range, the IPCC found, had come an increase in cloud cover. Karl and other researchers had also found that the warming was greater in winter than in summer. Very cold temperatures had become much less frequent, while hot nights in the summer were becoming more frequent. This matched what computer models said should happen in a world warmed by greenhouse gases. It also enabled the skeptics to attempt to argue that warming would be benign, and for a time Karl was a hero to the contrarians.

The IPCC in its 1995 report cited an especially edifying example of the impact that naturally occurring climatic events can have on temperature trends.

On June 16, 1991, the 4,800-foot Mount Pinatubo volcano in the Philippines erupted, after six centuries of dormancy, in eight mighty explosions that propelled a cloud of ash and steam almost twenty miles into the atmosphere. Against a surreal but coincidental backdrop of thunder, lightning, and rain, the eruption blackened the sky over Manila long before sunset and showered inch-thick rocks over hundreds of square miles. The eruptions lasted for days and combined with a tropical storm to create thick mudslides that buried homes in their path. The ash was so heavy that houses collapsed. Hundreds of thousands of people fled, and scores were killed.

The eruption's impact on climate was quieter and longer lasting, but no less dramatic. Pinatubo spewed great quantities of sulfur dioxide gas into the atmosphere, where the gas combined with water to form tiny supercooled droplets. The innumerable droplets created a global haze that reflected and scattered sunlight. The scattering produced spectacular sunsets as the haze spread around the globe in the months after the eruption. It also, according to the IPCC, reduced the amount of solar radiation hitting the earth by about 3 percent. As a result, the average global temperature dropped by about 1 degree Fahrenheit, entirely canceling out the global warming observed up to that time.

A number of scientists, notably Hansen, predicted at the time of the Pinatubo eruption that the temperature would bounce back up once the haze dissipated, in two or three years, and they were right. In 1994 it rebounded to the high levels of the 1980s, up till then the warmest decade on record.

The 1990s eclipsed the 1980s, although this fact was not apparent in time for the IPCC to reflect it fully in the 1995 report. The end of the decade, in fact, turned out to be the warmest of all.

As the 1990s began, Hansen had predicted that new average global temperature records would be set more than once in the decade. It happened first in 1990, then again, after the Pinatubo haze had dissipated, in 1995. As Phil Jones pointed out at the time, the first half of the 1990s were nearly half a degree warmer than the 1961 to 1990 average, which then served (and still does) as a standard benchmark against which temperature trends were commonly measured. The first half of the 1990s was warmer than any other half decade on record, including both halves of the 1980s, despite the two years of cooling provided by the Pinatubo eruption.

The planet cooled off a bit in 1996, and there was no obvious explanation, although short- or medium-term changes in ocean currents were named as one possible candidate. The cooling off was taken as an example of the impact of "unforced" natural variations—those caused by the climate system's internal churnings. David Parker and others pointed out at the time that a global warming trend would not be expected to be smooth and continuous. "One can get cooler years or even cooler decades owing to natural variation," he said. Phil Jones asserted at the time that there was still "an underlying upward trend" in global temperature. The decade's warming continued in 1997, as temperatures slightly exceeded the 1995 record. Responsibility for much of the increase was assigned to the 1997–98 edition of El Niño, one of the two strongest on record.

All during the 1990s, Tom Karl and his crew at the National Climatic Data Center had been building and refining a global temperature record of their own, and in January 1998 they began issuing monthly updates in global temperature trends. Their first reports were eye-popping: In the first six months of 1998, the average global temperature jumped by half a degree Fahrenheit from the same period a year earlier—a huge increase in terms of global averages, given that the world is now only 5 to 9 degrees warmer than in the last Ice Age. Again, El Niño was cited as part of the explanation. But Karl, newly named as director of the Climatic Data Center, called the jump "really rather spectacular" and said that El Niño was only part of the explanation; the underlying global warming trend was the rest.

As 1998 ended, the World Meteorological Organization, drawing together all the existing data sets, reported that the year was by far the warmest on record. It was the twentieth year in a row that the average surface temperature was above the 1961 to 1990 average. Seven of the ten warmest years on record had occurred in the 1990s, and the other three had occurred since 1983. Remarkably, new monthly high-temperature records were set in each of the eighteen consecutive months ending in October 1998. With El Niño having dissipated, it was universally expected that a slight cooling off would follow. (It did.) Many experts nevertheless expected the long-term warming trend to continue, and 1999 did indeed appear on track to become one of the warmest years on record, although not as warm as 1998.

Again, many differences between and within regions lay behind the long-term rise in average global temperature, with some places warming more than others and some actually cooling. While the global average was rising by about 1 degree Fahrenheit in the twentieth century, for instance, a 1996 analysis by Karl and his colleagues found that many parts of the United States—notably the entire northern tier of the country and the mid-Atlantic region—warmed by 2 to 5 degrees. Most of the Southeast, on the other hand, cooled by about the same amount.

As this is written, the IPCC is deliberating on its next assessment, due in 2001, and Karl's guess is that it will document a further increase, perhaps by as much as a quarter to half a degree, in the amount of average global warming observed in the twentieth century.

IF THE WARMING IS REAL, is it out of the ordinary?

The earth is apparently warmer now than at any time in the last 150 years, but is that unusual when measured against the sweep of climatic history? Certainly, it is piffling compared with the great swings of the remote past, with Icebox Earth, the Cretaceous hothouse, and even the alternating jumps between ice ages and interglacial periods. And when another ice age comes, what is going on today will pale by comparison.

That is not the most relevant question, however. What matters, from the standpoint of people alive now and in the foreseeable future, is how today's changing climate compares with the climate of the last 10,000 years, the Holocene, the period in which civilization developed.

As we have seen, the world has been buffeted during the Holocene by climatic changes far more severe and drastic than any experienced by anyone alive now, yet there is little or no evidence that the surface temperature of the world as a whole has varied more than a degree or two from what it is today. If a number of experts are right, there is already enough greenhouse warming locked into the system—but not yet realized because of the climate system's inertia in responding to greenhouse forcing—to raise the average surface temperature of the globe by perhaps another half degree in twenty years. If that happened, says Thomas J. Crowley, a paleoclimatologist at Texas A & M University, the global temperature would approach the highest level of the last 10,000 years (unless, of course, the warming were to be offset by a natural cooling). And if it reaches levels forecast by the IPCC for the end of the twenty-first century, says Crowley, "you have to go back millions of years to find global temperatures like that."

In one sense, the last 1,000 years is a particularly relevant period for comparison; the natural workings of the climate system are most similar to today's. Since the instrumental record goes back only a century and a half, analysts wishing to get a handle on temperature fluctuations before then must rely on proxy records like tree rings, ice cores, fossilized pollen in lake sediments, and the chemical traces contained in foraminifera on the ocean bottom. A number of efforts to reconstruct the temperature record of previous centuries have been made, and one of the most arresting surfaced in 1998. Michael E. Mann and Raymond S. Bradley of the University of Massachusetts, along with Malcolm K. Hughes of the University of Arizona, made one of the most comprehensive compilations of proxy evidence to date. Reaching back 600 years, to 1400, the analysts re-created the year-by-year temperature variations for that entire period in the Northern Hemisphere. (Remarkably, the proxy record closely matched the instrumental record for the twentieth century, for which both records are available.) The analysis revealed that the twentieth century was easily the warmest century of the six and that the warmest years of all were 1990, 1995, and 1997.

Taken together, the two records showed that the Northern Hemisphere's average surface temperature in the late 1990s was as much as 1.2 degrees Fahrenheit above the average for the benchmark period of 1902 through 1980 and a full 2 degrees warmer than the coldest years in the six-century record, in the early 1460s and early 1800s. Rarely before the twentieth century did the trend line rise above the 1902 to 1980 benchmark, and then only barely before dipping back down again. In the 1930s, it soars well above the line and stays there most of the time, with a sharp upward spike to new heights in the 1980s and 1990s. Those heights are reached nowhere else in the hemisphere-wide proxy record, not even during what would have been the Medieval Warm Period. In 1999 Mann, Bradley, and Hughes extended their proxy record back to the year A.D. 1000 and found that the twentieth century was the warmest century of the millennium, and 1998 the warmest year. The twentieth-century warming, it revealed, ended an overall Northern Hemisphere cooling trend that had lasted 900 years. But the researchers cautioned that large uncertainties in the data for the earlier centuries precluded any definitive conclusions about climate before about A.D. 1400.

Similar analyses have presented similar pictures, but all such studies must be interpreted carefully. Different conclusions can emerge depending on how one looks at the record. As the IPCC pointed out in its 1995 assessment, for instance, the years in which the instrumental record began represent one of the cooler periods of the millennium. Does this mean the twentieth-century warm-up was a natural recovery from the cooling of the Little Ice Age, as some contrarians have maintained? Mann and his coresearchers thought not. They concluded that until the twentieth century, a number of mostly natural factors combined to influence the climate, including changes in solar radiation and volcanic eruptions. But in the last few decades, they found, greenhouse gases had become the dominant influence—a conclusion that goes to the heart of the major climate debate of our time.

While the twentieth-century warming appears unusual in the context of the last millennium, it is "not clearly outside the range of climate variability for the last few thousand years," in the words of a 1999 report by the American Geophysical Union. (The union said there was nevertheless a "compelling basis for legitimate public concern" about climate change.)

Assuming the IPCC's predictions about future warming are right, it will take some more time for the warming to demonstrate how unusual it truly is—or is not.

In the meantime, there are abundant tangible signs of a warming world that go beyond a simple taking of the earth's temperature. Among them are a thawing and greening of the Great White North.

[10]

Signs and Consequences of a Warmer World

G LOBAL WARMING is becoming evident in many ways, but nowhere more clearly than in the earth's northern regions. That is where, so far, the warming is greatest, where its impact on the physical environment, flora, and fauna is most dramatic, and conceivably where economic dislocation caused by a changing climate might stir political awareness soonest.

As we have seen, land warms faster than the oceans, and most of the planet's land is concentrated in the Northern Hemisphere. In the northern reaches of those continents, one would expect the warming to be greatest of all, for two reasons. First, as a general warming melts the ice and snow that characterize those latitudes, less sunshine is reflected back into space, amplifying the warming further. As will become clear, this is just one part of a complex chain of rippling interactions and feedback loops that a change in temperature sets off, with consequences that reverberate from one end of the climate system and biosphere to the other. Once started, these chain reactions are wholly immune to control by humans and often impervious to full understanding, as well.

Second, in the sub-Arctic the atmosphere is more stable in winter and spring than it is in the temperature zones; much of the continental area lies north of the turbulence of the midlatitudes, with their jet streams and fronts and cyclones. In a more stable atmosphere, there is less mixing of air, and more heat is confined to the atmosphere's lower layers.

On top of all that, global warming may have touched off changes in large-scale atmospheric circulation patterns so that in winter, they distribute relatively warm air from the oceans onto the normally colder northern landmasses, a possibility we will explore later.

So it was that the IPCC in 1995 found that the warming was largest between latitudes 40 and 70 degrees north. Forty degrees is a line running roughly through Beijing, Denver, and Philadelphia. Seventy degrees is about the latitude of Barrow, Trondheim, and Murmansk. Within this band lies the sub-Arctic, including Alaska, Siberia, and much of Canada. There, the average annual temperature rise over the last thirty-five years has been three, four, even five times as great as in the world as a whole—up to 5 degrees Fahrenheit. Some parts of those regions, according to the NASA Goddard Institute for Space Studies, have warmed by 7 to 10 degrees. This is the world's primary bellwether region for climatic change. Because warming is exaggerated there, it becomes obvious there first, sending a strong signal that something different is going on.

People like Dwight Deely have noticed. Deely is a school administrator in Fairbanks, Alaska, for nine months of the year and the skipper of a sport-fishing charter boat for three, putting out from the southern Alaskan port of Valdez with parties of anglers seeking salmon and other game fish. One night in July 1998, Deely and a compatriot sat having dinner in the gloomy restaurant and bar best known as the place where, almost ten years earlier, the captain of the tanker *Exxon Valdez* downed his drinks before taking his ship out into Prince William Sound. There it turned left, as they say in Valdez, crunching onto Bligh Reef and disgorging into the sound the biggest oil spill in American history.

On that July night in 1998, with clouds wreathing the spectacular mountains that hem in Valdez and the midnight sun creating a perpetual twilight, Dwight Deely put his finger on a bigger, more pervasive, and potentially longer-lasting environmental change than the *Exxon Valdez* could ever have wrought. It seemed, he said, that Alaska wasn't as cold as it used to be. When he was a boy, he said, it didn't seem unusual for the temperature in Fairbanks to plunge below minus-40 degrees. These days, he said, it doesn't seem to happen that often. And then there are the glaciers. Take Black Rapids Glacier, which spills down the face of a mountain in the Alaska Range within easy view of travelers on the Richardson Highway, which runs the 360 miles from Fairbanks to Valdez. Black Rapids is a shadow of what it was, said Deely, and indeed, today it looks like a very thin necktie decorating the mountain's expansive front.

Often people's memories about weather and climate betray them; that is one reason why observations are made and records kept. But in this case, Deely was right on both counts. Many of Alaska's glaciers are receding, part of a general shrinkage around the world. And winters are indeed not as cold as they once were. "I remember my first New Year's Eve here," says Gunter Weller, a climate scientist at the University of Alaska in Fairbanks. That was thirty years ago, and when Weller poured a bottle of scotch into an ice tray, it froze. "These kinds of temperatures are not around as much," he said. An analysis of temperature trends by Weller and a colleague bears this out. In the last twenty years, the number of sub-40-degree days at Fairbanks has dropped markedly compared with the three decades before. Moreover, summers are warmer and longer. The permafrost is thawing, and clouds of insects that have been proliferated in a warmer climate are killing vast stretches of Alaska's evergreen forest. All this and more testify to substantial climatic change in Alaska, western Canada, and much of Siberia.

It is all part of a general northward shift of warmth and greenery.

THE BEHAVIOR OF SNOW in a warming climate is paradoxical. In really cold areas like the sub-Arctic and Arctic, it has often been, as they say, too cold to snow—not enough moisture can evaporate, nor can the cold air hold enough moisture, to sustain big snowstorms for very long. But with the warming of the sub-Arctic, snowfall has increased; the winter snows around Fairbanks are deeper than they used to be.

Farther south, however, in the northern tier of the Lower Forty-Eight and southern Canada, something different has happened, according to the IPCC: While snow can get quite deep when it does fall, wintertime precipitation now falls more often as rain rather than snow, and the average area covered by snow (of whatever depth) has shrunk. In fact, said the IPCC in 1995, less of the Northern Hemisphere as a whole is covered by snow, on average. In 1994 a study by Pavel Groisman of the State Hydrological Institute in St. Petersburg, Russia, along with Tom Karl and Richard Knight in Asheville (where Groisman would soon end up working) found that the average annual extent of snow cover in the hemisphere had decreased by about 10 percent in the previous two decades. More interestingly, perhaps, they also discovered an elegant feedback loop—part of the rippling, systemwide chain of nonlinear reactions that can be touched off by a change in temperature. In it, shrinkage of the snow area, caused by a warmer atmosphere, accentuates the warming further according to the following scenario: Besides cooling the planet by reflecting solar energy back into space, snow also prevents the escape of heat absorbed by the ground before the snow fell. This further helps to cool the air, counterbalancing the warming effect of any moderating winds that blow over the snow-covered ground. Thus, when snow covers the ground, the near-surface atmosphere has a hard time warming up when the sun shines. But remove the snow suddenly, as in springtime, and the temperature bounces right back up. Groisman, Karl, and Knight found that in the warmer atmosphere, with more snow melting in the spring than used to be the case, more trapped heat is released from the ground than before, and the earth also can absorb more solar energy. Result: Spring becomes even warmer, with April and May temperatures in the hemisphere generally higher than in earlier years.

As Karl said at the time, this may have been one reason why, recently, the first half of the year had tended to be warmer than the second half. It may also be one reason why, according to the IPCC, there is a clear trend toward fewer frosts in some areas; and why, according to David Easterling, a Tom Karl colleague, there are now slightly fewer days when the temperature of the Lower Forty-Eight falls below freezing.

This fits with another finding of recent studies: a trend toward an earlier spring. In 1996 David Keeling examined his records of carbon dioxide levels, looking for patterns in the seasonal rise and fall of the atmospheric gas (when plants shed and regain their leaves, respectively). Keeling's analysis of the timing of the seasonal drop of the gas in the Northern Hemisphere indicated that the springtime return of leaves was occurring about a week earlier than it had years prior.

A year later he joined in a study by Boston University biologist and climate researcher Ranga B. Myneni analyzing changes in solar radiation absorbed by plants as they perform photosynthesis. Using instruments aboard weather satellites from 1981 to 1991, the Myneni study focused on lands north of the 45th parallel, which runs roughly through Yellowstone National Park, Minneapolis, Ottawa, Boston, Bordeaux, Belgrade, and Vladivostok. The study affirmed Keeling's earlier finding. It also found that autumn arrived a bit later, making the growing season twelve days longer, on average, give or take four days.

The Northern Hemisphere is not only green longer, the Myneni study found, it is also greener, period—there was 10 percent more vegetation in the peak summer growing months of July and August in 1991 than a decade earlier. The enhanced greening also was evident in the temperate regions south of the 45th parallel but was substantially larger north of it. Part of the reason for the green-up is undoubtedly the fertilization effect that comes from higher amounts of atmospheric carbon dioxide, the fuel of photosynthesis. But the warming of the atmosphere also plays a part, Myneni believes. In particular, he said, the accentuated springtime warming identified by Groisman, Karl, and Knight could be stimulating plants to "green up" earlier.

The shift toward an earlier spring has also been confirmed by studies showing that plants are budding earlier in the year in Canada and that birds are laying their eggs earlier in Britain. And in a study reported in 1999, two German scientists, Annette Menzel and Peter Fabian, analyzed data on plant behavior at the International Phenological Gardens, a group of seventy-seven research sites spread across Europe that contain genetically identical clones of different species of trees and shrubs.

From 1959 to 1993 observers at the sites recorded the dates when buds first appeared, leaves unfolded, and the plants flowered; in the fall they recorded the dates when leaves turned color and fell from trees. Menzel and Fabian found that, on average, botanical spring arrived six days earlier in 1993 than in 1959 and that autumn was postponed by about five days. Noting that plants' response to seasonal changes are driven mostly by temperature, the researchers attributed the change to a general warming of the European climate.

ONE OF THE LONG-PREDICTED effects of global warming is that plant and animal species will shift their ranges northward and upward, to higher latitudes and altitudes, as they have done many times in the past in response to climatic change. But evidence of a present-day shift has been thin. An important breakthrough in research along these lines came in 1996, and it was the product of a remarkable research effort by a lone, determined scientist.

Camille Parmesan, now a biologist at the University of California at Santa Barbara but then at the University of Texas, set out in 1992 to find out whether the range of a western butterfly, the Edith's checkerspot, had shifted northward as would be predicted when the climate warms. She did it the old-fashioned way, by foot and, literally, by the seat of the pants. In 45,000 miles of driving and fourteen months of living out of a tent, she personally made on-the-spot surveys of more than 100 previously recorded populations of the Edith's checkerspot from Mexico to Canada and eastward to Colorado.

While a number of other studies have documented local shifts in animal populations, they have been considered inconclusive because they were too restricted to determine whether a species' entire range had shifted location. In some instances, the studies were not controlled to eliminate other causes of population shifts, such as air pollution or changes in land use.

After eliminating sites where such complications might distort results, Parmesan ended up with some 150 sites where Edith's checkerspots lived, scattered over the butterfly's full range. For 20 of the sites, observations and records of existing checkerspot populations were good enough so that she did not have to visit them. From 1992 through 1994 she drove to all the rest. At each site she looked for adult butterflies, caterpillars, eggs, and the host plants on which the eggs are laid and on which the caterpillars feed.

The hard work paid off when she analyzed the data. The numbers showed clearly that in the southern end of the butterfly's range, more populations had gone extinct over the century than in the northern range. In fact, populations in Mexico went extinct at four times the rate as those in Canada. The extinctions were "net" extinctions, that is, the number not counterbalanced by the starting of new butterfly colonies. Adding it all up, she found that the checkerspot's range had shifted northward by about 100 miles.

Parmesan also found that the butterflies had become more abundant at elevations above 8,000 feet, indicating that their range had moved upward. Checkerspots live up to 13,000 feet, above which there is not enough vegetation to support them. Below 8,000 feet, she determined later, the extinction rate increased.

Previous studies had shown that the checkerspots' population dynamics are sensitive to climate; gradual climatic change does not affect the butterfly directly, but instead interferes with its reproduction schedule by changing the growing period of the plants on which it depends.

There might be other explanations for the shift in range. For instance, predators and parasites might affect butterfly populations. But Parmesan says that the distribution of the predators and parasites has not increased or decreased with latitude. Although she tried to rule out all other possible causes of the range shift, she says, she "cannot say that climate warming has caused the shift; what I can say is that it is exactly what is predicted from global warming scenarios, that the butterfly's population dynamics are sensitive to climate and that other, smaller studies around the world have indicated evidence of north-ward shifts of species ranges."

Parmesan and twelve colleagues in Europe and America expanded the study method to encompass thirty-five European butterfly species and reported in 1999 that two-thirds had shifted northward by 22 to 150 miles over the twentieth century—a period when the warming trend over Europe was nearly 1.5 degrees Fahrenheit.

All in all, she says, "when you put it together, the picture that's coming out is that climate warming is affecting wild organisms."

THAT IS STARTLINGLY CLEAR in Alaska, if forest experts are right about what is going on there.

On the 360-mile drive down the Richardson Highway from Fair-banks in the interior to Valdez on the coast, the meaning of the phrase "purple mountain majesty" becomes as clear as it ever is. In the right light, tall, jagged peaks of the Alaska Range project a soft lilac hue. But as one approaches the spectacular Chugach Range on the southern leg of the trip, the color shifts subtly in the lower elevations. The land-scape still has a purplish look, but the purple has a gray cast to it. Whole mountainsides look dead, and in fact are; the white spruce that once adorned them have been killed en masse.

Once these purple-gray stretches of tree skeletons were a green and vital part of the spruce-larch-aspen tapestry that makes up the taiga, the great boreal forest that circles the globe's northern reaches. Today, in a stretch of 300 or 400 miles reaching westward from the Richard-son Highway, north of Valdez, past Anchorage, and down through the Kenai Peninsula, armies of spruce bark beetles are destroying the spruce canopy or have already done so. Often the trees are red instead of gray—freshly killed but not yet desiccated.

These are the most magnificent, most valuable trees in Alaska: tall, reaching 100 feet, most sought after by loggers, the cream of the crop economically and the signature tree of the taiga. The beetles are "basi-cally eliminating the canopy," Jerry Boughton, the Anchorage-based head of the U.S. Forest Service's regional forest health program, said in mid-1998. In the previous five years, he said, the beetles' assault on the spruce "just took off exponentially; it's an incredible phenomenon." Statistics are somewhat approximate, but they suggest that perhaps a third to a half of Alaska's white spruce have died in the last fifteen years.

Glenn P. Juday, a forest ecologist at the University of Alaska in Fairbanks, is one of several who believes the warming climate is fundamentally responsible for the decline of the taiga. This would make sense, since the boreal forest by definition flourishes in colder temperatures. But Juday has identified a number of specific factors that in his view have combined to put the forest under extreme stress.

One of them, strangely enough, is heavier snow. One day in mid-1998, Juday took a visitor to the Bonanza Creek Experimental Forest, a long-term ecological research reservation a few miles southwest of Fairbanks. At Bonanza Creek, not far from the Arctic Circle, white spruce trunks towered overhead, adorned by short, needled branches draped with delicate, wispy lichens. Juday pointed to the tops of two of the trees—they were missing, the crowns snapped off by the weight of snow. Normally, said Juday, snows in Alaska's interior have been light and fluffy. But with a warmer climate and more moisture in the air, they have become heavier. Two especially heavy snowfalls in the late 1980s and early 1990s broke off the tops of the trees. After that, the damaged trees became easy prey for insects.

That is not all. The warming climate, while bringing more snow to Alaska's interior in the winter, has also, perversely, made it drier in the summer. Warmth and lack of moisture, says Juday, have stunted the trees' growth. Not far away from Bonanza Creek, he pointed to a subtle but telling sign: The crowns of aspens looked thin and sparse, with small leaves. Crowns are where the most recent growth would have taken place. Finally, he said, the warming climate has stimulated outbreaks of tree-eating insects in general.

Most damaging of all has been the spruce-bark beetle outbreak. "It has moved into high gear in the last six or seven years," said Juday. "It's just rolling through the forest." Jerry Boughton takes a somewhat cautious view of the role of climate in the outbreak, noting that a number of factors have combined to cause it. For one thing, the forest is more susceptible to insect attack because it is older. "But certainly," he said, "the warming has created a better environment for the bark beetle to expand."

All in all, said Juday, the constellation of stresses promoted by the changing climate has put the taiga in real trouble: "We've got a sick forest here."

Whether the taiga will migrate northward, as forests have done in response to climate change in millennia past, remains to be seen. Some migration is expected, but there is not really all that much space between what is now the taiga's northern limit and the Arctic Ocean. Normally, forest types more tolerant of a warmer climate would move in behind the retreating taiga. But in Alaska's case, south of the state there is only ocean. Where would the trees come from? And if they don't come, what would Alaska's future look like? The answers to those questions are far from clear.

WHAT DOES SEEM CLEAR is the magnitude of the warming of the north. Three decades ago the temperature at Fairbanks would reach 80 degrees for a total of only about a week in the summer. Now it does so for three weeks. On average, summer days are about 11 percent warmer than they were thirty years ago. Over the same period, the extent of ice in the Bering Sea has contracted by about 5 percent. This has made hunting on ice more dangerous for native people and has increased coastal erosion, according to the proceedings of a 1997 workshop on the regional climate conducted by the University of Alaska under federal auspices.

On the Tanana River at the town of Nanana in the Alaskan interior, people since 1917 have been monitoring the exact moment when the ice breaks up in the spring. Four of the earliest breakups in that eighty-one-year span, as of 1998, came in the 1990s.

In the interior, the warming climate has brought both good news and bad news for Alaska's small agricultural industry (small because there is simply not that much suitable land). On one hand, the growing season is about 20 percent longer. But it doesn't rain as much, and crops are often parched. "It's changed dramatically since the eighties,"

Scott Miller, who grows barley, oats, and hay about two hours' drive south of Fairbanks, said as he prepared to drive a load of hay into town. As the thermometer approached 80 degrees, he explained that in the 1980s, there was rain almost all summer and even the danger of frost in July. "Now we're way on the other end of the spectrum," he said. "We're usually hurting for water, and there's more heat."

The heavier snows of winter and greater heat of summer have combined to cause Alaska's permafrost—perpetually frozen ground—to thaw. As it thaws, pockets of ice trapped in the soil melt, as well; where this happens, the land sometimes subsides and opens into big holes and depressions called thermokarsts. Over thousands of miles in Alaska's interior, patches of forest sink into thermokarsts and die as swamp water floods them. It is a frequent sight on the roadside: a stand of tamarack, gray, spidery, dead, rising from muskeg water.

Driving on roads affected by thermokarsting can be an adventure. Many stretches of highway are like ocean swells, lined by utility poles tilting at crazy angles because of thermokarsting. Trees also shift in the sinking ground, giving rise to the term "drunken forest." In some cases, thawing permafrost has forced the relocation of roads and runways, thrown houses off kilter, and caused buildings, roads, and bridges to be abandoned.

While some of the thawing can be attributed to construction, what is going on now is different; areas of undisturbed permafrost are melting. And many areas not yet thawed are on the brink of doing so, according to Vladimir Romanovsky of the University of Alaska, who studies the problem by analyzing boreholes drilled into the ground. Assuming the warming continues, many parts of Alaska will become free of permafrost altogether, and a new stability will set in. But damage could be considerable during the transition.

On the positive side, the warmer climate and longer summer clearly have allowed Alaska's booming tourist industry to expand, according to the 1997 study. But it has also had an occasional quirky effect on what the tourists do and see, and in one of them lies a clue to one of the most telling effects of climate change of all: the receding glaciers.

❖ ❖ ❖

ONCE, NOT SO LONG AGO, cruise ships would nose right up to the 200-foot-high face of Columbia Glacier, a three-mile-wide, thirty-four-mile-long river of ice that flows imperceptibly, majestically between sharp mountains and debouches into Prince William Sound some twenty-five miles west of Valdez. A forbiddingly desolate and hauntingly beautiful expanse of jagged gray ice whose massive weight and apparent permanence seem to say "I am forever," Columbia has long awed mere humans. Tourists aboard the cruise ships would marvel at the breathtaking, up-close sight of the glacier's front, the clear ice of its interior flashing aquamarine, reflecting back blue while absorbing all other colors of the spectrum. You still see travel brochures of scenes like that, but they are out of date, Dave Oberg, a professional pilot, said as he flew a visitor over the great glacier in a light pontoon craft in July 1998.

Today the glacier is not as permanent and unchangeable as its impressive mass suggests. It has receded eight miles since 1983. Before then Columbia's forward edge was anchored on a broad shoal formed by the great pile of rocky debris, or moraine, pushed out into the sound by the glacier as it advanced. When first studied in the late nineteenth century, Columbia advanced so rapidly that blocks of ice would fall on trees in its path. It stopped advancing in 1923, pulled back slightly, and then was stable for several decades. Each summer the glacier would retreat a little, then readvance in the winter, reattaching itself to the moraine. In 1983 it apparently failed to reattach. With nothing to anchor it, and with warm water underneath, it just kept on receding, at an average rate of about half a mile a year. Cruise ships can no longer get near the front wall, because the entire eight miles of water between the moraine and the ice front is choked by rapidly melting icebergs shed by the retreating glacier.

What triggered Columbia's retreat? "My belief is that it is climate," said Will Harrison, a glacier expert at the University of Alaska. One idea is that the warmer environment prevented the glacier from reattaching itself to the moraine. Once that happens, said Harrison, "you can't stop it; once the bullet's fired, that's it."

Every glacier behaves differently depending on the underlying geography, and tidewater glaciers like Columbia can be the trickiest of all, given the complicating factor of their direct interaction with salt water. But if anything, the state's landlocked mountain glaciers, taken together, send an even clearer message about climate. Recent mapping of a sample of nine Alaskan glaciers shows that most have gotten markedly thicker in their upper reaches, apparently because of heavier winter snows. But in their lower reaches, all the glaciers have thinned substantially because of more intense melting in the summer. In most cases, the melting at the base has exceeded the growth at higher altitudes, with the net result that the glaciers are shrinking. Harrison says the trend has been especially evident in the 1990s.

In July, with melting in full spate, waterfalls cascade down the mountainsides and into rivers made chalky by rocky dust ground to fine granules by the glaciers. The increased volume of meltwater flows quickly to the sea, contributing to a continuing rise in global sea level that, according to the IPCC, has amounted to four to ten inches over the last century. Alaska, in fact, may be the biggest contributor among glaciated areas to that rise, at least so far. There are more than a thousand glaciers in the state, making it the fourth largest ice province in the world, after Antarctica, Greenland, and the neighboring Queen Elizabeth Islands of the high Arctic. But it is still cold enough in the high Arctic so that much meltwater refreezes before it can flow to the ocean. The same is true in Antarctica; and although that frozen continent may pose a potential threat of long-term catastrophe if its huge ice sheets should melt, there is little or no evidence that melting there has contributed to the sea-level rise observed so far.

In Greenland, the picture is not completely clear; in 1995 the IPCC said there was not enough evidence to determine whether its ice sheet has changed over the last century. In 1999 NASA scientists reported, on the basis of airborne surveys with laser altimeters, that the Greenland ice sheet's southern half had shrunk substantially between 1993 and 1998. Each year, the surveys found, the sheet lost about two cubic miles of ice, enough to cover Maryland to a depth of one foot. While the results were surprising and significant, five years is not enough to discern a trend, and the studies continue.

But the picture is perfectly clear in sub-Arctic areas like Alaska and in high-altitude areas around the world: With some exceptions, there has been a general retreat of glaciers. The IPCC estimates that over the last century, the melted water from all these glaciers has contributed from three-quarters of an inch to two inches of the observed sea-level rise. Most of the rest has come from thermal expansion of the ocean; like most substances, water expands when it gets warmer. Whatever the glaciers' impact on the rise in sea level, which is expected to accelerate in the decades ahead, the more important immediate significance of their melting may be the strong evidence of a warming climate that it provides.

Rising global surface and atmospheric temperatures; corroborating evidence from bore holes; increased cloud cover; higher minimum temperatures; decreased snow cover; the thawing and greening of the north; shrinking glaciers; rising seas: As all the evidence began to fit into place, a clear picture displaced skepticism in many minds, including Tom Karl's. "It was just such an enormous amount of evidence to suggest that the climate had warmed that for me it became very convincing that our observations weren't fooling us," he says.

But some of the most important evidence of all, affecting as it does the everyday experience of everyday people, involves extreme weather like heavy rainstorms, blizzards, floods, heat waves, droughts, and record temperatures. Has a changing climate upped the ante, making these already extreme events even more extreme and more frequent?

[11]

Is the Weather
Becoming More Extreme?

T HE PEOPLE of Grand Forks, North Dakota, are weather-tough. Always have been, from the days when the place was an Indian trading post up to the present era of durum wheat growers whose harvests sustain the pasta market. Blizzards, subzero weather, spring floods from the Red River of the north, on whose banks the pleasant little town sits—they are used to it all. But in the winter and spring of 1996–97, Grand Forks found itself in a new ballgame altogether.

You could see it coming if you knew how to read the signs. From mid-November on, blizzard after blizzard battered the Red River valley. Normally, winter storm tracks tend to run somewhat south and east of the valley, tapping moist air flowing up from the Gulf of Mexico and carrying it to Iowa and eastward to Michigan. But in 1996–97, a slight shift in the position of the planetary Rossby waves moved the track somewhat farther north and west: rather than Iowa, the target was now Minnesota, where the Red River flows along the Minnesota–North Dakota state line. In the early fall, heavy rains saturated the valley, so that the water table was already high when winter set in. By

April seven blizzards had dropped a total of eighty-three inches of snow on Grand Forks, and even more on Fargo, seventy-five miles to the south. (The Red, which runs from south to north, flows into Grand Forks from Fargo.) The winter turned out to be very cold; not much snow melted.

"When we get snow, we don't lose it; it just sits there," said Allen Voelker, a meteorologist in the Grand Forks office of the National Weather Service.

As March turned into April, the equivalent of four to eight inches of water lay on the ground in the form of snow across the region. Then, on April 5, a combination blizzard and ice storm brought the valley to a standstill. The *Grand Forks Herald,* which names the big winter storms as the National Hurricane Center does for hurricanes, called the storm Blizzard Hannah. The electricity went out. People had no heat. And already the river was rising. Blizzard Hannah deposited an additional 2 to 4 inches of water. By now the season's total snowfall ranked as the deepest ever recorded for the region, which on average gets 35 to 40 inches a year. In Grand Forks it was measured at 98.6 inches, 9.5 inches more than the previous record. At Fargo, 117 inches of snow fell, 28 more than the previous record. In some places, nearly a foot of potential meltwater now lay in and on the ground.

But spring floods are something of a lottery. A deep snowpack does not necessarily guarantee a big flood, as Voelker has shown in a study of the subject. Much depends on the pattern of melting. A long succession of warm days but freezing nights is ideal for flood prevention: Snow melts readily during the day, but the refreezing at night slows down the melting and allows for a more gradual release of water. In 1993–94, when Fargo's previous record snowfall of 89.1 inches was established, that is what happened. Instead of a disastrous flood, the valley of the Red got a minor to moderate one.

When Blizzard Hannah hit, Grand Forks mayor Pat Owens said later, "I knew in my heart and mind that we were in for some hard weeks, but I did not know we were going to have the flood of the century." As all the world quickly found out, that is just what it turned out to be. After Blizzard Hannah, the weather warmed up to the 50s and stayed there. The worst-case scenario had materialized. "The runoff went really fast," says Voelker, and the Great Flood of 1997 was on.

Grand Forks had built protective dikes in the 1950s, based on its experience with floods up till then. Now the townspeople began digging snow away from the dikes and piling sandbags on top. If the flood got over, it would surely wipe out at least the Lincoln Drive neighborhood, a cozy enclave of neat houses lying not far from the river.

The battle was lost on April 17. At 1:20 A.M., Mayor Owens was advised as much. The workers were pulled off the dikes for their safety, and at 4:15 the mayor issued a mandatory evacuation order for the town. Mrs. Owens, a short, open, energetic woman who had been in office less than ten months, took to the radio and TV to plead with people to leave, soon earning the nickname the Little Spitfire for her energy and resilience in the crisis. "It was a scary feeling; all I could think of was the safety of the people," she said a year later in a conversation in her office in city hall, where water marks on the doors show that all desks on the first floor were submerged during the flood that was crashing in.

More than 50,000 people were driven from their homes. Many left with only the clothes on their backs and no idea of where they would go. Others were able to gather up what became known as the "three Ps"—pets, pills, and pillows. But there was very little time to act once the river overtopped the dikes. The flood literally chased people out. "The water was rushing so fast, it was unbelievable," the mayor remembers: It came through the sewers and spurted up through manholes and catch basins "like geysers." The drinking water and sewage systems were overwhelmed and useless. The flood crested at an unprecedented fifty-four feet, twenty-six feet above flood stage. As the crest moved across the Canadian border, the Red River was twenty-five miles wide. At one point, nearly 95 percent of Grand Forks was inundated. In East Grand Forks, Minnesota, right across the river, only eight houses escaped the water.

Thirty-six hours after Mayor Owens issued the evacuation order, four-foot-deep floodwaters shorted out an electrical system in a downtown building and started a fire, which quickly spread. Before they could even begin to fight the blaze, firefighters spent an hour evacuating forty apartment dwellers who had not left earlier. Most fire trucks could not get through the water-filled streets, and the few that succeeded could not fight the fire because there was no pressure in the hydrants. Firefighters had to contend with muddy, oily water polluted by chemicals. "They said that if you had a boat in there for any number of days, it would eat the finish right off," said the mayor. Firefighters had to hold on to their trucks to avoid being swept away by the toxic waters. One, Mitch Steien, told the *Herald* that even though he was six foot six and weighed 270 pounds, he needed all his strength to stand in the current while dodging floating chunks of ice and filing cabinets. Eventually the fire was extinguished with the help of airborne firefighters, but not before eleven businesses were destroyed.

When Mayor Owens saw the fire amid the flood, she said, "it was just like a fist hit me in the stomach." Photos of the scene became famous around the world in a year—and a decade—of weather extremes.

NINETEEN NINETY-SEVEN was the Year of the Flood, as record precipitation in the United States sent rivers and streams out of their banks in widely separated parts of the country, uprooted hundreds of thousands of people, killed at least ninety, and wreaked total damages estimated at well over $5 billion. In eastern Europe, along the German-Polish border, torrential summer rains created some of the worst flooding the region had ever experienced.

In the very first week of the year, northern California led the way. For weeks, heavy rains and snows fell on the Pacific Northwest, saturating a region that had already been soaked by record annual precipitation in 1996. Between Christmas and New Year's, more than 20 inches of rain fell in some places. In others, the precipitation came as snow. Squaw Valley got an unbelievable 102 inches in thirty-six hours. Then the temperature shot up, and unseasonable warmth produced what the Climatic Data Center called a "tremendous" snowmelt. Heavy rain in the Sierra Nevada contributed to the melting, and the resulting runoff devastated the Central Valley over the next few days.

Near Fresno on January 3, the San Joaquin River rushed by at a peak rate of 95,500 feet per second, nearly triple the previous record. On the other side of the Sierras, the Truckee River reached its highest levels ever and Lake Tahoe its highest since 1917. The Truckee flood put most of downtown Reno, Nevada, under water and closed the town's airport. Harrah's casino was shut for the first time in its sixty-year history. In all, half a million people were forced to evacuate in December and early January. Thirty-six people died, and damage was estimated at $2 billion.

It was the Ohio Valley's turn next. On March 1 severe weather with tornadoes and exceptionally heavy rainfall developed along a nearly stationary front stretching all the way from Texas to West Virginia. The tornadoes killed twenty-seven people, but the most remarkable feature of the vast weather system was its heavy precipitation. In parts of northern Kentucky, the rain averaged at least an inch an hour for twelve hours. Double-digit rainfall was widespread in the Ohio Valley and much of the surrounding region, and the rains fell on ground already loaded with water from earlier months (the northeastern United States, like the Northwest, also had record precipitation in 1996). Streams crested rapidly, and one of them, the Licking River, roared through Falmouth, Kentucky, pushing homes off their foundations and leaving behind more than a foot of mud. The Ohio River reached its highest level in thirty-three years, and the flood killed thirty-one people and caused $500 million in damage.

A month later Boston was hit by the April Fool's Day snowstorm of 1997. One to three feet of snow fell across a wide swath of the Northeast. Boston's twenty-five-inch blanket was the heaviest April snowfall on record there, and the third-heaviest for any month. No flood resulted, but the wet, heavy snow added to the pattern of unusually heavy precipitation experienced in much of the country. In many places the snowfall's water equivalent ranged from three inches to five inches.

For much of July, heavy rainstorms repeatedly struck parts of eastern Europe, pushing the Oder River, along the border of Germany and Poland, to its highest level in 300 years. In Germany, Poland, Hungary, Romania, the Czech Republic, and Slovakia, a million people were affected by the damage. Losses were estimated at $2 billion, and more than a hundred died.

Lesser floods associated with tropical storms afflicted the Gulf Coast and the Southwest, and as El Niño cranked up later in the year, much of the country's southern tier was soaked.

The journal called *Weatherwise* summed up the year this way: "The waters flowed so high this year in so many places that, when someone asks about the Great U.S. Flood of 1997, the proper response is, 'Which one?'"

THE POINT HERE is not that 1997 stood out but rather that in a strange way it had almost come to seem ordinary, an especially vivid example of a parade of extreme weather served up by the last decade of the twentieth century. Heavy weather has always characterized North America. According to the National Weather Service, the United States experiences more severe weather each year than any other country—more than 10,000 severe thunderstorms, more than 1,000 tornadoes, more flash floods and cyclones and heavy winter storms. Still, the 1990s struck many Americans as excessive. Heavy rainstorms and snowstorms in particular seemed to hit the country with uncommon frequency. In the lead-up to the Year of the Flood and in its aftermath, as well, they appeared in a sequence that sometimes, for all the havoc the storms caused, became almost numbingly familiar. Likewise, as many a casual observer of televised weather reports has noticed, it seems as if temperature records are being broken all the time. What follows is a detailed look at several recent instances of these precipitation and temperature extremes, leading inevitably into the question of whether they add up to a clear change from the recent past. First, temperature.

The temperature extremes of the last few years have involved both cold and heat, sometimes simultaneously. A particularly startling example was one we have already examined: record low temperatures in Arizona in late March 1998, while at the same time the Northeast experienced record highs—opposite extremes on the same day, producing killer tornadoes in the middle of the country. Anyone looking at the average temperature of the country that day would have found something resembling a wash; statistically, nationwide, things would have been about normal. But the extremes told a more dramatic and ultimately tragic story.

Likewise, in the winter of 1995–96, record low temperatures sometimes coexisted or alternated with unusual warmth. Several times that winter, the bulge of a Rossby wave and its associated jet stream dipped far to the south of its normal position, reaching deep into the Southeast and in effect expanding the perpetual pool of cold air that has the North Pole at its center. The cause of this expansion is not known, but it brought several new record low temperatures for individual states: 60 below zero at Tower, Minnesota; 47 below at Elkader, Iowa; 35 below at Elizabeth, Illinois; 25 below at Greene, Rhode Island. At the same time, a bulge of warm air surged up from the south into the plains states, and temperatures soared into the 70s as far north as Montana. While paralyzing cold gripped the eastern United States in January, southern California was basking in record warmth.

Even more arresting in another way are some recent examples of another kind of extreme: sustained high temperatures over a long period. In the early summer of 1998, for example, Melbourne, Florida, experienced more than twenty days with temperatures over 95 degrees. Florida's worst drought in fifty years contributed to the heat wave, whose probability of occurrence was put at one in a thousand by David Easterling of the Climatic Data Center. Later in that same summer, a drought and heat wave in Texas pushed temperatures to 100 degrees or above every day for a month, killing more than a hundred people. In July 1999, more than 250 people died in a month-long heat wave that spread from the northeast to much of the rest of the country. In New York that month, the temperature reached or exceeded 95 degrees on eleven separate days. Never had it been so hot so often since records were first kept in 1869.

One predicted consequence of a warming atmosphere is that heat waves will become more frequent. A 1998 study by federal scientists suggested that this has indeed happened in the United States since World War II. According to the study by Dian J. Gaffen and Rebecca J. Ross, research meteorologists with the National Oceanic and Atmospheric Administration, the frequency of extremely hot, humid days and of heat waves lasting several days increased substantially from 1949 to 1995. Most provocatively, the study found that the increase in the most stressful form of heat—the apparent temperature—was greater at night than in the daytime: Chicago 1995 was not an isolated incident, it seemed, but rather an especially lethal data point in an upward trend in killer heat waves.

For purposes of their study, Gaffen and Ross defined extreme heat as the highest 15 percent of temperature and humidity measurements, as recorded every three hours around the clock in July and August from 1961 through 1990. They said this threshold was closely correlated with levels above which, according to other studies, heat-stress mortality increases sharply. They analyzed records at 113 first-line government weather stations around the country, looking for information on both the true temperature and the apparent temperature, the measure of the combined impact of heat and humidity on the human body.

The apparent temperature, they found, was increasing faster than temperature alone, because humidity was increasing faster—as would be expected in a warming climate, with more water evaporating from the earth's surface. They found that over the forty-six-year study period, the annual frequency of days on which the thresholds of extremity were surpassed increased at all but 16 of the 113 stations. At some stations, the number of nights with extremely high apparent temperatures doubled, to about eighteen days a year from about nine days a year. Daytime increases were found not to be nearly as dramatic, as would be expected on the basis of model predictions.

The biggest trends were in some of the country's major population centers, especially from the Middle Atlantic states south to Florida, along the West Coast, and in the Southwest. Eight of the fifteen cities in which the trend was most pronounced were in the Southeast, including Miami, which topped the list nationally. Gaffen and Ross extended their study to look at three-day and four-day heat waves, and found that the number had increased by 88 percent. Two major caveats attached to the study. First, the urban heat-island effect may have skewed some of the temperature readings. But most of the trend could not be explained away that way, said Gaffen, because many of the stations were outside urban areas, and because the researchers looked for but did not find a correlation between population growth, a measure of urbanization, and temperature trends. Second, other experts said that the threshold of extremity adopted by Gaffen and Ross was not really selected on the basis of the relationship between health and extreme heat. Nevertheless, the study was the first of its scope to look for a trend in extremely hot days and nights. And it found one.

As ATTENTION-GETTING as temperature extremes can be, extremes of precipitation can be even more so, and some scientists believe precipitation actually may be more important in the context of a warming world and may tell us more about how the climate may be changing.

For the most part, the big snowstorms and rainstorms of the 1990s, along with their attendant flooding and damages, struck limited, even isolated, areas of the country. No one has personally lived through them all, and therefore no one has experienced the full range of extreme weather for the nation as a whole. That makes it difficult to discern a broader pattern and or appreciate the bigger picture; despite the drumfire of media coverage, what happens weatherwise in a distant part of the country seems remote from what happens close to home, and somewhat unreal.

Some recent events have nevertheless been big enough to get the attention of a huge slice of the country at a single stroke. One such monster storm afflicted almost the entire eastern United States in the second week of March 1993.

It began when a garden-variety cluster of thunderstorms developed over the Gulf of Mexico. A second, born in the Pacific, moved across Texas. A third dropped down across the middle of the country from the Arctic Circle. Any two, if combined, would have produced a significant storm. The jet stream that week was running generally southeastward from northwestern Canada, down through Minnesota to the Tennessee Valley, and finally up along the eastern seaboard. Frigid Arctic air lay on its northern and western sides, moist tropical air to its south and east. Over the Southeast, this jet picked up all three disturbances and merged them into one megastorm. The climate system had turned up "three cherries on the slot machine," Paul G. Knight, a Penn State meteorologist, told the *Times*.

So clear was the developing pattern that forecasters nailed it on the head: The jet would take this storm right up the East Coast, and it would be a monster, possibly the storm of the century. By some measures, it was. No winter storm ever recorded had been so intense—pressures at its center were as low as those in a hurricane, with winds to match—while at the same time affecting so wide an area. So big was the cyclone that the winds circulating about its center at one point lashed Boston and Atlanta simultaneously. No storm this strong had ever affected so many Americans at the same time. The Big One, as the Climatic Data Center subsequently dubbed it, inflicted every kind of stormy weather on one part of the East or another: blizzards, rain, sleet, thunderstorms, tornadoes, and those hurricane-force winds. For the first time, every major airport on the East Coast was closed at the same time by the same storm.

New York, which had been buried almost exactly 105 years earlier by the legendary Blizzard of 1888, got off relatively lightly this time; some of the precipitation turned to rain, and only a foot of snow fell on the city. But elsewhere—and this is what may have made the storm truly unusual in the context of climatic change—record snows fell. At the height of the storm, two to three inches of newly fallen snow an hour were common. Most places in the Appalachians got at least two feet. This single storm dumped fifty-six inches on Mount LeConte, Tennessee; fifty inches on Mount Mitchell, North Carolina, with fourteen-foot drifts; forty-three inches on Syracuse, New York, and the list goes on.

Four months later it was the Midwest's turn, and a number of climatic factors converged over many months to deluge the upper Mississippi River basin with record rains and produce the worst American flood in recent memory. The cooling of the atmosphere produced by the Pinatubo eruption may have inhibited evaporation in the previous summer, leaving more water in the soil than usual. Then, in the winter of 1992–93, a subtropical jet associated with El Niño sent abnormally heavy rains and snows into the region. Iowa had its deepest snowpack in fourteen years. Several spring storms saturated the already moist landscape. And as we have seen, a blocking high locked into place a weather pattern that continually shunted moisture from the Gulf to the upper Midwest, where it fell as rain after rain after rain.

For 400 miles along the Missouri River between Omaha and St. Louis and 500 miles along the Mississippi between Cairo, Illinois, and Minneapolis, the summer of 1993 was a waterlogged hell. Some stretches of the Mississippi remained above flood stage from March through most of August. Some areas that on average flood no more often than once a century were inundated. Des Moines, Iowa, was without drinking water for twelve days—the largest American city ever to be in that predicament for so long, at least in modern times. Destroyed bridges and flooded roads turned short commutes into 200-mile drives.

As the rivers spread out and reclaimed their natural floodplains, more than seventy-five small towns at bankside were totally flooded. Levees failed wholesale. Afterward, at least one small town, Valmeyer, Illinois, would simply give up and move to higher ground. Some 50 people died as a result of the floods, as did countless farm animals. More than 17 million acres of land were inundated in all, including 16,000 square miles of prime farmland. More than 85,000 people had to be evacuated, and 22,000 homes were damaged or destroyed. Total crop losses caused by flooding or supersaturated soil exceeded 35 million acres and $5 billion. Overall economic losses were estimated at more than $12 billion.

Perhaps the most significant thing about the Mississippi flood from the standpoint of possible climatic change is the heavy rain that contributed to it. Precipitation totals, according to a Climatic Data Center report, were "phenomenal." Iowa had its wettest summer on record, and neighboring states set records for parts of the summer. More to the point, the intensity of individual rain events was startling. Papillion, Nebraska, south of Omaha, reported an inch of rain in just six minutes during one thunderstorm. Several places in Nebraska and neighboring states experienced twelve inches in forty-eight hours. Seven inches in a little more than an hour sent a three-foot wall of water roaring through the town of Adrian, Minnesota, ripping big chunks of asphalt from the streets. One factor in the wet summer was the atmospheric gridlock that kept inflicting one storm after another on the region; another was the intensity of the storms themselves.

Over the next three years, it was unusually heavy snow that grabbed the headlines. In 1993–94, another instance of atmospheric gridlock created a quirky pattern that inflicted seventeen major snowstorms, almost one a week, on the New York metropolitan area.

The winter of 1995–96 was the snowiest of the twentieth century from Virginia to Massachusetts and the third winter of the most recent four with snow significantly heavier than normal in the East. Seasonal snowfall records were broken in Boston (the new record was 107.6 inches), New York (75.6 inches), Philadelphia (63.1 inches), Baltimore (62.5 inches), and Washington (46 inches). Seasonal records fell in parts of the Midwest and Ohio Valley, too, as Cleveland racked up 101.1 inches. At Marquette, Michigan, an astounding 250.8 inches of snow fell. Sault St. Marie was not far behind, with 222 inches. In both cases, the total was about double the seasonal average.

And on January 6, 1996, one of that cold winter's southward bulges of Arctic air plunged into the East and ran headlong into a mass of warm air. With the frigid air ensuring that the resulting storm's precipitation fell as snow, what became known as the Blizzard of '96 was under way. For three days it snowed across the northeastern quadrant of the country from Tennessee, Kentucky, and Ohio all the way to Maine. Record snowfalls blanketed the ground in many spots, especially from West Virginia and Virginia through New Jersey, where the blizzard was most intense. In Philadelphia, 27.6 inches fell in twenty-four hours; eventually the depth would reach 30.7 inches, smashing the previous record for total snowfall in a single storm by more than nine inches. A new state record of 35 inches was established in New Jersey. The old record had stood for ninety-seven years. At this author's home thirteen miles west of Manhattan, undrifted snow came up to the first-floor windowsill. A carefully placed yardstick said it was 30 inches deep. In Pocahontas County, West Virginia, it was a foot and a half deeper than that.

Just as suddenly as the cold and snow came, they yielded to unseasonable warmth and extreme rains. At Burlington, Vermont, the temperature hit 65 on January 19. Three inches of rain fell in twenty-four hours at Williamsport, Pennsylvania. The record snow cover melted rapidly, setting off floods in the Delaware, Susequehanna, upper Ohio, Potomac, and James River basins, with crests twenty feet above flood stage in some localities. The Potomac was swollen with so much water that it rivaled the flood caused by Hurricane Agnes in 1972, which killed 48 people and left 220,000 homeless. Combined, the 1996 blizzard and floods killed about a hundred people and cost an estimated $1 billion in damages.

WEATHER DISASTERS of epic proportions in some ways are not as important as smaller precipitation extremes that in the aggregate affect more of the country more frequently. These smaller, seemingly abnormal rainstorms appear to be happening with some regularity, but they make less of an impact in the national news. There is no dearth of examples.

On the October weekend in 1996 when the World Series was about to open at Yankee Stadium, a powerful northeaster struck metropolitan New York. Like many of its breed, the storm generated high winds and pushed flood tides ashore, inundating homes, toppling trees, and depriving tens of thousands of homes of power. None of this is unfamiliar to residents of the area, which is often under the gun of northeasters. What set the storm apart was its drenching rains. Nearly nine inches soaked parts of New Jersey, and new precipitation records for the date were set in several localities.

Ten months later, on the night of August 20 and 21, 1997, a string of thunderstorms slashed through southern New Jersey, dropping as much as 9 inches of rain in three hours. A total of 13.5 inches fell at Atlantic City International Airport, just shy of the state record of 14.8 inches for a single storm. "The first we knew about it was at 12:30 last night when the police called us to tell us that our cars were floating around in the street," Sue Ditmire, whose family owned a used-car lot, told the *Times* the next day. "When we got in here," she said, "the only things that were dry was what was in the top drawer of a four-drawer file cabinet and the two cars we had up on the lifts for repairs." Four bridges were taken out by floods and five feet of water covered some roads. Rainwater overflowed into reservoirs, forcing citizens to boil their drinking water. Total damage was estimated at $75 million.

But the point is illustrated most tellingly, perhaps, by a trio of rainstorms that occurred in the eastern United States between mid-June and mid-July 1998.

On June 13, 5.69 inches of rain fell on Boston, as recorded at Logan International Airport. This shattered the previous one-day record of 4.36 inches for a June rainfall, set in 1881. And it approached the all-time one-day record of 6.11 inches—set only a little more than two years earlier, on October 20, 1996. The June 1998 rain, which actually lasted over parts of three days and totaled nearly 10 inches in some places, caused widespread flooding, littered roads and rivers with raw sewage, and flooded basements. "I haven't seen rain like this before; it's amazing," Boston mayor Thomas M. Menino told the Boston *Globe*. "There are places that are flooding that never flooded before."

Two weeks later, it was Ohio's and West Virginia's turn. Over a weekend, eight inches of rain fell as a front stalled over the Ohio Valley and thunderstorms repeatedly pounded a triangular area straddling the Ohio River. In one sliver of turf in Ohio, a full foot of rain fell. "It was a real toad-choker of a storm," D. R. Smith, the emergency services director for Wood County, West Virginia, said of one of the downpours. In Parkersburg, the seat of Wood County, floods dislodged thirty-five mobile homes. Eighty people floated away in them and had to be rescued with boats and Jet Skis. Across the river in Ohio, 11 people were killed by floods or tornadoes and 9,000 people had to evacuate their homes. "This is the most devastation that this area has ever had, as far as I can remember," Captain Larry Simms of the Muskingum County Sheriff's Department told the *New York Times*.

Two weeks after that, nine inches of rain in four hours flooded Lawrence County in south-central Tennessee. Bridges, cars, and houses were washed away in Lawrenceburg, some seventy miles south of Nashville. "The water came up extremely fast, within minutes, and it is not common in that area, so there was not much warning," Randy Harris of the Tennessee Emergency Management Agency told the

Times. A handful of people were killed, and Lawrenceburg's 10,500 citizens were deprived of drinking water.

Six inches of rain. Eight inches. Nine. More than a foot. Is this kind of thing happening more often? Is the extraordinary becoming ordinary? Or does modern media coverage just make it seem that way?

IT IS A TRUISM among meteorologists that there is always abnormal weather somewhere and that behind every average lurk extremes like the droughts of the 1930s and 1950s. So do the nation's climatic records reveal any new pattern? Do hard data show an increase in the incidence of extreme weather events? Tom Karl and his colleagues in Asheville set out to find out.

They became interested for a number of reasons. By the early 1990s, the Asheville group was confident that it was doing what Karl described as "a fairly good job" of improving the global and national climatic data sets. But in analyzing those data sets, researchers had been focusing on averages of temperature and precipitation. Karl realized that with weather and climate, it is the extremes that are often most important. Extremes rather than averages are what cause damage. They are what people are concerned about and pay attention to. And already, even before the cavalcade of extreme weather events of the 1990s had unfolded, there was a perception that the weather was indeed getting more extreme.

So in 1993 Karl and company shifted their focus and started analyzing their digitized data collection to see whether there was any change in extreme weather patterns. In the first phase of this research, they identified all the instances of extreme heat, cold, drought, and wetness that had occurred at hundreds of locations across the country since the first decade of the twentieth century. "Extreme" was defined as the top and bottom 10 percent of the long-term climate record. The measurements were combined to produce a single index of weather extremity. The researchers found that since the late 1970s, the index had been about 1.5 percent higher than the average of the previous sixty-five years. This, they said, indicated "a persistent increase of extreme events." Similar surges of extreme weather were found to have occurred in the 1930s and the 1950s, but the one from the 1970s into the 1990s was longer-lasting.

The Karl group found no evidence of an increase in drought. But the analysis appeared to confirm what the deluges and blizzards we have just described may suggest to Americans who have lived through them: More precipitation is falling on the United States.

After about 1970, the analysis found, overall precipitation averaged about 5 percent more than in the previous seventy years. Such an increase "hints at a change in climate," the analysts wrote. In fact, they said, there was about a 90 percent chance that the increase represented a real, long-term climatic change. The increase was not uniform across the country, however. In some places, it was as much as 20 percent. The Northeast, the upper Midwest, and the south-central region with Texas as its anchor were affected most. In parts of the West and in northern New England, overall precipitation decreased.

Later phases of the analysis determined that precipitation across the Lower Forty-Eight as a whole had increased by 10 percent. This increase was most pronounced in spring and fall but was also apparent in summer. More rain was falling compared with snow than formerly, but the total amount of snow did not decrease because of the general increase in precipitation.

That general increase was ascribed to three main reasons. First, there were slightly more days when precipitation fell. Second, there were more heavy rainstorms and snowstorms than before—those delivering more than two inches of precipitation in twenty-four hours. Toad-chokers fall in this category. On average, the analysis found, the frequency of intense rainstorms and snowstorms had increased by about 10 percent. Intense storms were defined as those heavy enough to rank in the top 10 percent, in terms of the amount of precipitation delivered, at the start of the century. Third, heavy precipitation events were becoming heavier.

Thus, a clear picture was emerging: In general, Americans were having to carry umbrellas more often, since there were more days with precipitation than earlier. Moreover, those rains were more likely to be real soakers; a steady increase in precipitation was derived from extreme one-day downpours. Proportionately more precipitation was falling as toad-chokers, and these were becoming worse, making it more likely that more Americans would experience what Boston, the Ohio Valley, and Tennessee experienced during the early summer of 1998.

As a result of the increase in precipitation, the Asheville researchers found, more of the country was tending to be excessively wet—in contrast to the warm period of the 1930s, when severe droughts plagued the country. The researchers found that since about 1970, more than 30 percent of the Lower Forty-Eight had experienced a "severe moisture surplus" for at least one year. The study cited the Mississippi flood of 1993 as an "obvious example" of this. So, says Karl, were the floods of 1997. While many factors contributed to the floods, he says, excess precipitation worsened them. Atmospheric gridlock that kept certain regions in harm's way for weeks at a time may have been the major factor in some of the big floods. But that was not true of the Ohio River flood of 1997 and one-day floods like that of Chicago in 1996 and those of Boston, the Ohio Valley, and Tennessee in 1998: The rains that caused those floods simply dumped enormous amounts of water in a short period.

Trying to relate precipitation trends to floods and flood damage is an important but tricky business. More people die from floods, and floods cause more damage, than any other kind of natural disaster in the United States. Every year the bulk of federal disaster aid goes to flood victims. Worldwide, according to the Red Cross, more than 1.5 billion people were affected by floods in the quarter century before 1995. More than 300,000 of those were killed, and more than 80 million were made homeless. In the half decade from 1991 through 1995, flood-related damages totaled an estimated $200 billion globally, accounting for nearly 40 percent of all damage from natural disasters.

But does increased precipitation translate into increased flooding? The National Climatic Data Center says that despite the big floods of recent years, there is no evidence of general, widespread changes in flood frequency. This may be, say researchers at the center, because there have been too few studies of the question so far and because the problem is very complex. Many things can alter the destination, dispersal, and concentration of rainwater or snowmelt once it hits the ground, or even before; there are many slips between cup and lip. For instance, forest trees take up some precipitation on the way down, and forest soils impede runoff. Other examples of altering factors include the intervention of human influences like the sinking of land caused by the pumping of groundwater or the corseting of rivers and streams by dikes and artificial channels so as to make them run deeper, faster, and more destructively at flood time. So, while some scientists say that there appears to be some relationship between increased precipitation and flooding, they are only beginning to try to discover its nature and magnitude.

THE EXPERTS KNOW more about the crucial question of whether the observed increase in precipitation is related to the observed warming of the atmosphere.

Rain and snow condense from atmospheric water vapor, as we have seen, and a warmer atmosphere causes more water to evaporate from the oceans and bodies of freshwater. A warmer atmosphere is also capable of holding more water vapor than a cooler one. In fact, most of the warmer atmosphere's heat goes into converting liquid water to vapor than into warming the land. In general, this means there is more moisture available to developing storms, enabling them to produce more precipitation. There is a big element of chance in this, however, since water vapor, like the air currents that transport it, is ephemeral; patches of it move around, both horizontally over the ground and vertically in the atmosphere. A given parcel is also short-lived, lasting only about ten days. Things have to be just right for a parcel of vapor to intersect with a storm that can convert it to precipitation.

Most of the moisture available to any given storm—80 percent or so, according to calculations by Kevin E. Trenberth, a climatologist at the National Center for Atmospheric Research in Boulder, Colorado—comes from evaporation that has taken place more than 600 miles away from where the storm is. This is easily verifiable from earth satellites, which typically show entire rivers of vapor flowing from one region to another. In the United States, particularly in the winter half of the year, a lot of the moisture available for precipitation comes from the warm subtropics, typically the Gulf of Mexico or subtropical Atlantic. Trenberth says that this moisture travels as much as 600 miles a day, so that water vapor from the Gulf can fall as rain or snow in the Ohio Valley or Great Plains or Northeast Corridor only a day or so later.

Some people, especially greenhouse contrarians, scoffed at the counterintuitive suggestion, offered at the time of the northeastern Blizzard of '96, that enhanced moisture production stimulated by global warming might make blizzards worse. No single, specific storm can be said to have been made snowier in this way. Generally speaking, however, it is just what would be expected in a warming world. Global warming has not canceled winter and is not likely to do so in the foreseeable future: There still are those big pools of cold air in the Arctic, and they still will invade more southerly climes in the winter. As long as winter is around and a warming atmosphere produces more evaporation in the subtropics, so the reasoning goes, snowstorms still will develop and warming can be expected to make some of them worse.

Is there indeed more evaporation, and is the atmosphere consequently moister? As with temperature, discontinuities in methods of measurement complicate efforts to tell. After these technical difficulties are taken into consideration, according to the IPCC, evaporation in the tropical oceans is estimated to have increased over the last four decades. Studies also show that the amount of precipitable water in the atmosphere has increased. One, published in 1996 by Rebecca Ross and another U.S. government scientist, William P. Elliott, revealed increases in water vapor over the United States and part of the Caribbean of 3 to 7 percent per decade in recent decades. The figures applied to the layer of the troposphere reaching from the surface to about 18,000 feet. This layer, the lower 3.5 miles of the atmosphere, generally contains about 90 percent of all the atmosphere's moisture. The IPCC found in 1995 that increases tended to be greater at lower latitudes and that the regions where vapor was increasing were, in general, also those with rising temperatures. It also cited increases in precipitable moisture as great as 13 percent per decade over the tropical Pacific between 1973 and 1990.

AS OF 1999, Tom Karl's findings about increasing climatic extremes seemed to be widely accepted, although there was considerable discussion of what they signified. Many scientists said that since the data applied only to the United States, global conclusions should not be drawn. Others argued that the U.S. data were among the best and richest in the world, and thus should be taken as an indication of what may be happening more generally. Karl and his fellow researchers, for their part, said that while the trends had not yet persisted long enough to conclude that the climate had become systematically more extreme in the long term, that appeared to be the most likely conclusion.

One possibly portentous wrinkle, Karl believes, may be that a warmer climate and El Niño have linked up to play an important role in creating weather extremes. In recent decades, El Niño appeared more frequently than normal. Some experts believe global warming may be the reason why (a possibility to which we will return later). Be that as it may, Karl believes that the effects of El Niño—heavy rains, floods, and droughts—are being amplified by a warmer atmosphere. He suggests that "this is another example of the intensification of the hydrological cycle that we would expect with global warming."

Statements like that caused global-warming skeptics and contrarians to view Karl, formerly a hero to them, as something of a bête noir. To them, he was no longer the doubter; he had crossed the bridge and was now a believer. Publication of the mid-1990s work on weather extremes was the turning point. With that, Karl acknowledges, he "went from sort of the darling [in the eyes of contrarians] to 'This guy has completely gone over to the other side.' I was amazed by that."

For Karl, the evidence that global warming was altering the earth's climate had become impossible to deny by the late 1990s. "There comes a time," he said, "when you have to say 'I don't believe the earth is flat anymore.'"

Not least, Karl was convinced because the observational evidence was squaring in so many ways with what the most up-to-date computer models said should happen in a warming climate.

How accurate are those models? The question becomes crucial when scientists try to determine the cause of global warming and predict its future course. At this stage in the evolution of climate science, there may be no more important question.

[12]

Cloudy Crystal Balls

L EWIS FRY RICHARDSON undoubtedly would be astounded if he could see how his intellectual descendants in England, his country, have made real his dream of computing the atmosphere's behavior. The means are different from what he envisioned, of course— there is no gigantic computing theater, no slide-rule–wielding army of 64,000, no pneumatic-tube network for collecting weather calculations to produce a real-time global weather forecast. As things have turned out, there are robots instead of people, one of the world's most powerful supercomputers in place of slide rules and mechanical calculators, and electronic circuits instead of pneumatic tubes.

On the ground floor of the British Met Office's main building in Bracknell, in a wing named for Richardson, the two robots, gleaming silver and briskly efficient, shuttle snappily along two parallel tracks behind protective glass. They pause frequently, and their arms reach into one of five rotating, twenty-eight-faceted storage towers holding some 60,000 seventy-two-track tape cartridges capable of storing as much information as some 5,000 of the world's most advanced personal computers of the late 1990s. The robots pluck cartridge after cartridge from storage slots and, like a householder or office worker putting a disk into the A drive of a personal computer, insert them into receptacles from where the tapes' contents are conveyed electronically to a Cray T3E supercomputer a floor below. The computer itself is singularly unremarkable to look at: a box about eight feet high, dark gray with red trim.

But contained in the supercomputer was, as of mid-1998, one of the world's most advanced general circulation models for analyzing the climate system and predicting its behavior. On this particular day, the computer is running a number of jobs at once, as always. "It's flogging away all the time," says Dave Potter, the shift manager. A colleague interjects: "You can start the next model if you like, Dave, it's due up in about ten seconds." Just now the computer is forecasting that day's weather. At the same time it is simulating the impact on the climate system of all the human-induced climate forcings—greenhouse gases, cooling aerosols, and the like—since the 1860s. All the while, screens are keeping track of different simulations and the robots are scurrying to and fro.

"It's wonderful when it's working properly, but it's hell when something goes wrong," says Potter.

Computer models of the earth-ocean-atmosphere system have come a long way since the early days of von Neumann and Charney, Smagorinsky and Phillips and Manabe. As of the late 1990s, there were about twenty of them in the world. Imperfection is still their middle name, even when everything is working right in shops like Dave Potter's in England, in the United States, and Germany (and soon, in the most powerful simulation setup of all, in Japan). But they are getting better all the time, say scientists who have made it their specific job to evaluate them, and now are reliable enough to provide a useful if necessarily hedged reading of the impact of rising greenhouse gas emissions on climate, especially future climate. Contrarians forcefully disagree, asserting that the models reproduce reality poorly and therefore cannot be used to project future climate change.

One cannot begin to judge the merits of these competing claims—or know how far to trust mainstream scientists' projections of global climate change—without some knowledge of the models, their basic nature, their operation, their strengths and limitations, and their ability to simulate the natural workings of the atmosphere.

A MODEL, by definition, is just that—a model of reality. Like the models in people's heads, it is never going to match the real world exactly; the best that can be hoped for is an approximation. One reason is that there is such a large measure of chaos built into the climate system, making its behavior to some degree inherently unpredictable. Even if the atmosphere were perfectly predictable in theory, it is far too complex to be captured completely by any computer program now in existence or likely to be developed in the foreseeable future. But the human brain is even less capable of calculating the climate system's complex interrelationships in any detail, at any speed that would be useful; Richardson's theater full of people could never remotely have hoped to carry out in any useful time frame the vast number of calculations necessary to forecast, say, the impact of rising greenhouse gases on the global temperature a century hence.

Basically, a general circulation model is a computer program incorporating the fundamental equations expressing the atmosphere's behavior—the same equations, essentially, that Richardson laid out early in the twentieth century. The physical laws embodied in the equations govern the interlinked workings of the sun, the atmosphere, the oceans, the land, and all other elements of the climate system. Temperature, wind, pressure, clouds, snow, ice, water vapor, convection, turbulence, soil moisture, vegetation's effect on climate, ocean salinity, ocean heat, ocean currents, and other characteristics—plus their interaction—can all be simulated using these equations. One can enter into the computer any given set of initial conditions and set the model running. The model calculates the extent to which the basic physical laws create fluctuations in such things as temperature, precipitation, and wind over a specified time period. One then can introduce any kind of external forcing to see how the climate would change. This is what makes models useful, within limits, as tools for understanding how greenhouse gas emissions are likely to alter the global climate.

If the problem were a straightforward one of translating the warming potential of greenhouse gases to some numerical value, it would be a simple matter to calculate changes in the climate. One could almost do it on the back of an envelope. Mainstream scientists are confident that a doubling of atmospheric carbon dioxide, by itself and independently of other influences, would raise the average global temperature by about 2 degrees Fahrenheit. But as we know, there are many other influences on climate, and the system behaves in perverse and complex ways that can either strengthen or lessen the warming and also produce different effects in different parts of the world. Landmasses, snow and ice, the differential response of oceans and land to heating, the very shape of the globe in producing uneven heating and driving the general circulation—these and many other things complicate the task of prediction.

Everything is complicated further by various feedbacks, some of which enhance warming and some of which lessen it. One of these, for instance, is the role of ice and snow: Both cool the planet by reflecting solar energy. If the atmosphere warms, ice and snow melt, and their disappearance means that less of the sun's heat is reflected; the planet warms even more. This is called a positive feedback. One of the most critical feedbacks involves water vapor. When a warmer atmosphere causes more water to evaporate, the resulting vapor traps even more heat in the atmosphere than does carbon dioxide. This amplification is central to the greenhouse phenomenon; if it is less than most experts believe, the overall warming of the earth from greenhouse gases will be less than they think. There are also negative feedbacks, those that tend to counteract the warming. For example, warming increases low-level cloudiness, cooling the planet. For a model to be realistic, it must reflect with some accuracy the welter of interacting and often conflicting feedbacks.

SINCE THE ATMOSPHERE has so many properties, and limited computer capacities make it impossible to include every detail, the art of modeling is to try to include as many climatic factors in the model as possible while at the same time excluding those that are not absolutely essential; to simplify without oversimplifying. One of the most important simplifications involves the very structure of the model itself. Models cannot possibly compute climatic changes at every point in the atmosphere. So they make calculations at widely separated points, producing a more or less crude approximation of how the climate really behaves. Conceptually, the points form a three-dimensional grid typically rising ten to twelve miles above the earth's surface. A typical spacing between grid points today is about 150 miles horizontally and less than half a mile vertically. This "resolution," as scientists call it, is about twice as fine as a decade ago. But it still misses many processes, like cloud formation, for instance, that take place between grid points. So modelers estimate them from conditions such as temperature and humidity, within the grid space as a whole.

Simulating long-term climatic change presents difficulties that do not plague forecasters who use computers to predict the weather a few days ahead. In the latter case, computing power can be concentrated on a shorter period, making higher resolution possible. For long-term climate models especially, resolution is limited by the speed of the computer. And as computers have gotten faster and faster, resolution has improved. The Cray T3E at the Hadley Center makes possible a resolution at the global scale of thirty vertical levels and thirty-five to forty miles between points horizontally.

But the fastest computer imaginable cannot overcome another deficiency: incomplete knowledge about the workings of the atmosphere. This more than anything is what ultimately limits the models' realism. "How the natural world works—that's always going to be our problem," says W. Lawrence Gates, a climatologist at the Lawrence Livermore National Laboratory in California. He has long been a leader of international efforts to evaluate the models and has led that effort for the IPCC.

Perhaps the biggest gap in the science is lack of knowledge about the net effect of clouds on the earth's temperature. Low-level clouds reflect heat, while high-level cirrus clouds—the "anvils" at the top of a thunderstorm, for instance—trap it. Nor do atmospheric physicists fully understand how water vapor behaves in a warming atmosphere and the amount by which it amplifies the warming is therefore unclear. One foremost skeptic, Richard S. Lindzen of the Massachusetts Institute of Technology, has long insisted that the models misrepresent the physics of the water vapor feedback effect; it may, he says, lessen the warming rather than enhance it.

At this time, the models do not fully incorporate even well-established knowledge. Over the years, they have included more and more known features of the ocean-atmosphere system. One of the biggest advances of the 1990s, in fact, was the coupling of atmospheric models with reasonably realistic ocean models to produce a truly integrated simulation of the earth's climate system. The twenty full-dress models in existence as of 1998 were coupled ocean-atmosphere models. But coupling the ocean with the atmosphere came with a built-in headache: When simulating decades or centuries of climatic change, the coupled models tended to drift off into a clearly unrealistic never-never land. So the modelers fudged, readjusting the models to eliminate the artificial drift. By 1999 this problem seemed to be disappearing: Some models required no such adjustments, and an analysis by the Hadley Center found that the adjustments had no impact on the models' accuracy anyway.

The Hadley Center was also responsible for another big advance in the 1990s, one with major implications for the models' accuracy. For years the models appeared to be overestimating the amount of warming that had taken place over the last century. Many scientists suspected that this was because they did not include the cooling effect of sulfate aerosols emitted by industrial plants. Just like the volcanic haze from Mount Pinatubo, these aerosols reflect sunlight. But unlike Pinatubo, and unlike the greenhouse gases, their impact is not global but regional; they cool some parts of the world, mainly industrial regions and areas downwind, but dissipate long before they can affect the whole globe. The Hadley Center modeling group, led by John Mitchell, succeeded in the mid-1990s in including the aerosols in the models, with important results that we will explore shortly.

Given the imperfect and constantly questing nature of science, the modelers will never know whether they have included everything necessary to make the computer simulations real enough. "With any models, what you never know is what you haven't put in," says Jeremiah P.

Ostriker of Princeton University. He is an astrophysicist who uses computer models to study the universe. But, he says, there is a ready-made reality check: How well do the simulations made by general circulation models match up with the real world?

THE ANSWER IS, pretty well on the largest planetary scales but not at all well when one gets down to the regional scale and poorly to not at all on finer regional details.

One can see this graphically displayed in bright color, for instance, in the offices of Jim Hansen's Goddard Institute for Space Studies (GISS), six floors above Tom's Restaurant. The GISS model was one of the first to include a somewhat realistic ocean and to do "transient" simulations of the effects of doubled carbon dioxide. Until this model was developed, simulations had assumed a sudden, single jump to the doubled carbon dioxide state; it was much like taking before-and-after snapshots of the state of the climate. A transient run simulates the change as it would actually unfold, gradually over time, much like a movie. This produces different results, and they are considered more accurate.

On an autumn day in 1997, Makiko Sato, a physicist, sat at a monitor attached to the GISS computer. She punched keys to tap the model's output, and world maps appeared on the screen. On them global temperature patterns were displayed in colors ranging from yellow to orange to dark red for degrees of warmth and through shades of blue for degrees of cold. Maps on the right of the screen showed the pattern of global temperature changes that the computer, by hindcasting, had said should take place between 1979 and 1995. On the left, maps showed the changes that actually had taken place.

On the broadest, global scale, the computer got it about right: The hindcast had said the world as a whole should warm and that the Northern Hemisphere should warm the most, and in general that is how things looked on the map. But at the regional scale, the model got a lot of things wrong. It had "predicted" that eastern Canada would warm substantially, for instance, but instead it cooled quite a lot.

A single run of a single model is not enough from which to draw conclusions, but the fact is that many runs of many models show the same general pattern. And in terms of their general ability to mimic what goes in the real world, says Gates, the models have displayed a "progressive convergence toward what has happened in nature." For example, a transient run of the latest generation of descendants of Suki Manabe's models at the Geophysical Fluid Dynamics Laboratory recapitulates the upward curve of late twentieth-century average global temperature with remarkable fidelity. The short-term squiggles on the long-term trend line do not always match, but the overall trend line itself is reproduced quite faithfully.

It was in 1995 that Gates led the IPCC's effort to evaluate the models, an endeavor considered so important that the intergovernmental panel devoted one of the eleven chapters of its report to the subject. Among other things, Gates and his fellow evaluators looked at how well the models reproduce present and past climates.

First, the negatives. The Gates group found that the models poorly reproduce seasonal changes in snow, sea ice cover, and tropospheric temperatures. And while all the models portrayed seasonal changes in the exchange of heat between the oceans and the atmosphere, the changes were not always of the same magnitude as those observed. These changes are crucial to predicting regional patterns of warming and cooling.

One major failure pointed out by the IPCC has been the models' inability to reproduce the magnitude of the El Niño–La Niña oscillation. They do show the impact of El Niño on weather over the continents, but they consistently underestimate the warm sea-surface temperatures in the eastern tropical Pacific that define the phenomenon and dictate how powerful its influence will be.

On the positive side, the group found that, overall, the models successfully reproduce the changes in surface air temperature and broad-scale patterns of precipitation that occur with the change in seasons— including the comings and goings of monsoons, the seasonal shift of major rain belts and storm tracks, and the changing daily temperature cycle.

The 1991 eruption of Mount Pinatubo presented an important test of the models' fidelity to nature. Immediately after the eruption, Jim

Hansen asked his model to predict what the impact on average global temperature would be. The model responded that it would cool the globe by about 1 degree Fahrenheit and that the temperature would take two or three years to recover. That is what happened, although the model projection did not match the temperature fluctuations actually observed between the eruption and the full recovery. Other modelers achieved similar results, leading the IPCC to make this statement: "These results indicate that models can respond realistically to a sudden but short-lived radiative forcing that is comparable to that following an instantaneous doubling of [carbon dioxide], and raise our confidence in atmospheric models' ability to portray longer-term climate changes."

The fortuitous Pinatubo experiment suggests that the models get one of the most important attributes of the climate system about right: its sensitivity to heating and cooling from outside forcings. This sensitivity, obviously, is crucial to the debate over how much warming can be expected from growing emissions of greenhouse gases. The import of the Pinatubo experiment should not be exaggerated, however, because, as the IPCC pointed out, the simulations involved only short-term responses to external forcing of the climate system. They did not reflect the longer-term response of the deep ocean, which so affects long-term climatic changes.

After the IPCC issued its 1995 report, says Gates, models for the first time successfully simulated the size and frequency of the climate system's natural, internal fluctuations on several time scales. Doing so also is crucial to prediction efforts; if the models do not reflect natural variability with reasonable accuracy, their projections could be seriously off target. A number of models, Gates said, have reproduced natural fluctuations whose magnitude "looks realistic." But he cautioned that the unpredictability inherent in natural fluctuations—the chaos factor—means that predicting the timing of the fluctuations probably will never be possible.

The models have also successfully reproduced broad-scale climatic changes observed over the last century, including not only the average global surface temperature rise of about 1 degree (this was achieved only after the models included the cooling effect of aerosols) but also large-scale patterns of warming and cooling, both horizontally and vertically. This ability, as we will see in the next chapter, has been critical to efforts to determine whether human activity is responsible for the temperature changes.

Last, the models have attempted to reproduce the climate of the last Ice Age. The simulations have come up with an average global temperature about 7 degrees lower than today's. That is right in the middle of the actual range of 5 to 9 degrees estimated from proxy evidence.

The bottom line? Dick Lindzen, the skeptic, concedes that the models have some realism but scoffs at their predictive qualities. "I'm not saying the model output bears no resemblance at all to nature," he says. "In the gross figures, it looks plausibly similar." But that, he says, "does not give you forecast ability." He has gone so far as to liken the models to Ouija boards.

Gates disagrees, saying that "the ensemble of existing modern models is reliable" and "provides a firm basis for policy."

The key, many scientists say, is to interpret the models with care, recognizing their strengths and weaknesses, and with full appreciation of what they do and do not say to us. "Despite all the uncertainties, I think you can make useful estimates" of climatic change with the models, says Andrew P. Ingersoll, a planetary scientist at the California Institute of Technology who uses them to investigate the climates of other planets. "You just have to be aware of the uncertainties," he says. "It's just like any other scientific process."

The IPCC in 1995 judged coupled, ocean-atmosphere global circulation models to be "the most powerful tools available with which to assess future climate." But their results need to be read properly. One commonsense view says that while the exact numbers churned out by the models should be taken with many grains of salt, they nevertheless probably indicate the general direction in which the global climate is heading and give a rough idea of the magnitude of the change.

[13]

The Greenhouse Fingerprint

I S HUMAN ACTION responsible for global warming and its attendant changes in climate? The question presents a daunting puzzle that challenges the expertise and ingenuity of scientists to the maximum, but in the 1990s the pieces began falling into place. And as the effort to put them together intensified, politics intruded ever more boldly and insistently into the unfolding science of climate change. The effort to determine whether humans are putting their imprint on the global climate—and, if so, to what extent—became an ever more politicized struggle. Whatever the answer, the potential stakes could scarcely be higher, or more important in the long run to economic and political leaders around the world.

At the very center of this struggle was one of the first scientists to try to evaluate the accuracy of general circulation models: an American son of World War II–era German parents named Benjamin D. Santer. In the mid-1980s, as a Ph.D. student at the University of East Anglia, he helped pioneer the use of formal statistical methods to test the models. With that achievement under his belt and a degree testifying to it, he arrived in 1987 in Hamburg, Germany, at the age of thirty-two to take up employment at the Max Planck Institute for Meteorology. By then his life already read like something out of a novel. But he couldn't have imagined that he was about to embark on the most rewarding yet traumatic and painful chapter so far—and that in it, he would play a central role in trying to answer the most urgent climatological question of the day.

Santer's Jewish father, Dave (for Davis), escaped from Nazi-era Berlin and made his way to the United States at the age of sixteen. He never again saw his parents or younger brother, who died in concentration camps. He joined the U.S. Army, landed in the invasion of Normandy, and worked as an interpreter at the Nuremberg war crimes trials. Ben's Roman Catholic mother from Munich, named Lea, endured bombing raids, lost a child to pneumonia, was divorced from her soldier husband, met Dave Santer at a dance, and married him. They moved to Washington, where Dave went into business and Ben was born in 1955.

When Ben was ten and in school in Bethesda, Maryland, his father was transferred to Germany. Faced with the prospect of their three English-speaking children forced to sink or swim in a German school, Ben's parents opted instead to put them into a British army school. His British education availed him little when he applied for entrance to American colleges, so he decided to go to the University of East Anglia in Norwich, England. It was an ultimately fateful choice, since East Anglia has what is regarded as one of the world's premier climatic research departments. Santer had little physics or mathematics in his background but prospered at East Anglia nonetheless, graduating in 1976 with top honors in environmental science.

While there, he struck up an acquaintance with the man who would become his mentor, the physicist and front-rank climatologist Tom Wigley, then the director of the university's climatic research unit. But in the meantime, to Santer's dismay, American employers were no more interested in his British university credentials than American universities had been in his British high school education. He became something of an occupational vagrant over the next few years, working as a soccer teacher, a German teacher for Berlitz, and an assembler in a zipper factory. At that point, he says, he was "down and out in Seattle." He made two attempts to earn a doctoral degree at East Anglia, abandoning one because the subject (chemistry) ultimately failed to excite him and giving up the other when his father was mortally stricken with cancer.

After tracking down a somewhat annoyed German consul-general at lunch in Seattle, a desperate Ben Santer made a pitch for help in getting a job in Germany, where his parents were. Three months later he had one, with a German aerospace company. There, for the first time, he got seriously involved in climatology. His introduction to climate modeling came when he worked on a contract with the European Community, the purpose of which was to combine the predictions of global circulation models with models that attempt to predict the impact of climate change on such things as crop yields and water resources.

At last, things clicked. He was intrigued by climate modeling but also, more broadly, by "the idea that humans could have an impact on climate, and that this could have repercussions in all realms of human endeavor; it clearly had practical implications for many, many people and it was not just abstruse theoretical science, but something that could potentially impact normal people in their normal lives."

Searching for a way to get into the field permanently, Santer wrote to Wigley, and in 1983 he was back at East Anglia for a third try at a Ph.D.—this time in climate science. Under Wigley's tutelage ("Everything I learned about science I learned from Tom Wigley," Santer says), the new Ph.D. student went to work, for his thesis, on the problem of testing climate models to see how well they reproduced reality. This was basically a statistical comparison between computer simulations and real-world observations, building on Santer's long-held fascination with "how [statistics] could be used to solve problems."

In those days, few people had attempted to apply statistical rigor to the question of model validation; basically, they just made rough visual comparisons of model results and observations. Santer's thesis assessed the performance of several models in their attempts to reproduce a single variable, atmospheric pressure at sea level, only to discover that they did not perform well. (More recently, Santer performed the same analysis and found that the models were much improved.)

At the time, the Max Planck Institute in Hamburg was joining the front ranks of modeling labs by developing its own coupled ocean-atmosphere climate model. When Santer accepted an invitation to go to Hamburg for two years as a postdoctoral researcher, it was "sink or swim as a scientist," he recalls. "Up till then, I was like a bird being instructed in the theory of flight, a nestling. Now I was at the edge of the nest; it was either fly or it was a long drop to the ground."

For several months, though, Santer wasn't sure what he was supposed to be doing at Max Planck, until institute director Klaus Hasselmann took him under his wing and made a suggestion: Why didn't Santer work on the problem of detecting the signal of man-made climatic change amid the noise of natural variability? It was an area, not yet firmly in the spotlight, in which Hasselmann had done pioneering theoretical work a decade earlier.

With that, Santer plunged into the research that would at once make his name, threaten to ruin his reputation, and produce one of the most portentous and contentious findings in the history of climatology.

He enlisted in the search for the greenhouse fingerprint.

IF RISING GREENHOUSE GAS emissions are indeed warming the earth to the degree predicted by mainstream scientists, this should in time become obvious to everyone: There would be no other plausible explanation for so large a warming that so rapidly outstripped any other global climatic change of the last 10,000 years. But thus far, the warming is so small that scientists have found it extremely difficult to distinguish any possible human influence from the welter of natural climatic variations and fluctuations. It is as if the first, faint signal of a faraway radio station is just starting to emerge from static as one approaches the station. Yet in this case it is vital to detect the signal as soon as possible so that action to deal with greenhouse gas emissions can be taken if necessary.

But there are many ways in which the signal might be discerned, and here is where the puzzle comes in. As of the late 1980s, most efforts to pick out the greenhouse signal focused on the average global temperature. It turned out, however, that this variable, while familiar and convenient, responded to too many influences to allow experts to separate out any human influence from natural variability with much confidence. Largely as a result, the 1990 IPCC report declined to attribute any part of the previous century's observed warming to human activity; it could just as easily have had natural causes, the panel of scientists found. (On the other hand, the panel indicated that natural causes could be masking an even larger greenhouse warming than the surface temperature record reveals.)

So searchers for the greenhouse signal took another investigative tack. A warming world, they believed, would cause the climate system to respond in a number of characteristic ways that are unlikely to be produced naturally. How would they know what these ways might be? The general circulation models told them, and taken together, this ensemble of expected changes should produce a telltale pattern—the greenhouse fingerprint.

For instance, the models predicted that a warming world would produce more precipitation and that droughts and intense precipitation events should become more widespread and frequent. They also predicted that the rise in global temperature would be manifest not so much in the form of higher maximum temperatures as in higher minimum temperatures—that is, warmer nights and winters. In short, global warming would alter the pattern of weather extremes in distinctive ways.

In the early 1990s, Tom Karl and his crew in Asheville extended their study of weather extremes to include the question of whether the extremes they were documenting were a result of greenhouse warming. They concentrated on four indicators that could be matched up against model predictions: minimum temperatures much above normal; much above normal precipitation from October through April; extreme or severe drought from May through September; and a much greater than normal proportion of precipitation derived from extreme one-day precipitation events.

The results were averaged and combined to produce a "greenhouse climate response index." The researchers found that from 1976 on, the index was nearly 3 percent above the average for the previous years of the century; for the period from 1980 through 1994, it was 4 percent higher. Using statistical techniques, the investigators calculated that there was a 90 to 95 percent chance that these changes in extremes had been caused by greenhouse warming. But, Karl said at the time, that is not good enough; to be sure, he would rather have had closer to a 100 percent chance.

Karl and company also examined another variable that, according to the models, should be affected by greenhouse warming: short-term variations in temperature. The models suggested that a warming climate would damp down these variations; that is, temperature would vary less from one day to the next. This is what happens naturally in the summertime in temperate zones, and in the tropics the variations tend to wash out altogether; the temperature is relatively constant from one day and one month to the next. Greenhouse warming, the models said, should make the day-to-day swings in the temperate zones more summerlike, more tropical. Karl and his colleagues found that this had indeed happened. They examined temperature records from hundreds of places in the United States, the former Soviet Union, and China over the preceding thirty to eighty years and discovered that day-to-day variability had lessened.

Jim Hansen has adapted Karl's greenhouse climate response index to produce a "commonsense" climate index, based on practical indicators such as heating needs and frequency of intense precipitation. Its purpose is to provide a practical guide for the person in the street. According to the index, most trends are still too small to stand out above natural variability. The big exception is in Siberia and Alaska, where, as we have seen, warming has been dramatic. And it so happens that the models project this unusual Alaskan-Siberian warming to occur in a greenhouse world—another possible element of the greenhouse fingerprint.

As provocative as these indicators are, no firm cause-and-effect connection between them and any man-made global warming had been definitively pinned down by the mid-1990s. Moreover, the observed warming might be partly or largely caused by natural variations, such as changes in the strength of solar radiation. Some greenhouse contrarians have asserted over the years that this is the prime cause of whatever warming there has been. Their opponents retort that since the average global temperature has not varied much over the course of the last 10,000 years, variations in the intensity of solar heating could not be that great. The IPCC, for its part, said that changes in solar forcing over eleven-year sunspot cycles might equal "an appreciable fraction" of the heating caused by greenhouse gases. But these short-term changes come and go, said the panel, and their long-term impact therefore is probably small. By contrast, greenhouse emissions are sustained and cumulative over many decades. Over the last century, the panel said in 1995, solar forcing was "highly likely" to be considerably smaller than greenhouse gas forcing and was unlikely to be significantly larger in the twenty-first century. But the fact is that until 1978, when satellite-borne instruments came into play, there were no reliable measurements of solar irradiance, so the question remained open—a major thorn in the side of greenhouse fingerprint detectives.

IN THE LATE 1980s a small group of scientists began working on an entirely new approach to detecting the greenhouse fingerprint. The work focused first on putting together a suite of reliable greenhouse indicators, then rigorously, statistically, comparing observations of the climate's actual behavior with these indicators. Only by examining a variety of separate variables, these scientists reasoned, can a greenhouse detective be confident that the fingerprint actually has been found. "You want to look for it in a number of places so you don't get tricked by one," Tim P. Barnett of the Scripps Institution of Oceanography explained in 1991.

The indicators might include, for instance, global temperature patterns; the models said that the continents would warm more than the oceans, sub-Arctic latitudes would warm more than the Northern Hemisphere tropics, and the lower troposphere would become warmer while the stratosphere would become cooler. Other indicators identified by the computer models included vertical temperature patterns, increased water vapor, changes in seasonality, and the idiosyncratic temperature pattern produced by the combination of greenhouse warming and planet-cooling sulfate aerosols.

In 1987 Barnett and Michael E. Schlesinger, then of Oregon State University, published the results of the first attempt to demonstrate this fingerprint detection technique. They discovered that for most variables, not enough observational data existed to make a useful comparison between what the models predicted and what actually happened. There was enough, however, to enable them to examine three variables: tropospheric temperature, atmospheric pressure at sea level, and sea-surface temperature. The comparison of observations with computer predictions revealed a "marginally significant" carbon dioxide–induced tropospheric warming trend in the twentieth century but no such signal in any of the three variables over the preceding twenty-five to thirty-five years.

While the study's results were equivocal, the exercise was nevertheless an important step forward. As Barnett and Schlesinger pointed out at the time, it showed that some variables were more revealing of the greenhouse fingerprint than others.

Enter Ben Santer. Using the Max Planck Institute's state-of-the-art general circulation model, Santer and colleagues there tried to identify the most promising variables to include in a greenhouse fingerprint. Santer likens this approach to that of a doctor looking for the telltale diagnostic pattern of a specific illness to explain a general rise in body temperature. In the end, Santer concluded that geographical patterns of surface temperature and the vertical pattern of temperature variation from the bottom to the top of the atmosphere offered the best clues.

In 1992 Santer and a number of colleagues began putting all this together. That year he moved to the Lawrence Livermore National Laboratory just east of San Francisco, where he joined Lawrence Gates's climate research group. There he started working with a young climate expert named Karl E. Taylor, who, it turned out, had just collaborated with a third researcher, Joyce Penner of the University of Michigan, to produce an important piece of the detection puzzle. Taylor and Penner coupled a mathematical model of the behavior of atmospheric sulfur chemistry with a general circulation model to investigate the combined effect on global temperature of increasing carbon dioxide and sulfate aerosol emissions.

They found that the resulting pattern of global temperature, both "horizontally" at the earth's surface and "vertically" through the atmosphere, was quite different from that produced by carbon dioxide alone. In particular, there was a general cooling of the stratosphere and a general warming of the troposphere, with northern regions warming less and even cooling. This pattern is not one likely to be produced naturally. And, in fact, the pattern diverged sharply from the model simulation of the climate's natural behavior over the same period. Here was a possible indicator of human-induced climatic change that stood out from the noise in sharp, clear relief.

Santer and Wigley finally took the last step: comparing observations of the climate's actual behavior with what would be expected according to the Taylor-Penner study. Conferring at long distance, they devised a statistical method for making the patterns identified by Taylor and Penner stand out more sharply from the signal of average global temperature. Wigley soon moved to the United States, as well, setting up shop at the National Center for Atmospheric Research in Boulder. Together, mentor and former student undertook two landmark studies.

In one, they looked at the horizontal pattern of temperature change; in the other, the vertical. They found a good match between the actual global temperature pattern and the pattern predicted by the models. The correspondence was far from perfect (it appeared mostly at the hemispheric scale), but the statistical tests to which Santer and Wigley subjected the findings indicated that the match-up was unlikely to have resulted from chance. Moreover—and tellingly—the correlations became stronger over time, as would be expected as atmospheric concentrations of both carbon dioxide and aerosols increased.

The studies contained a substantial measure of uncertainty, stemming from the shortcomings of the models, the margin of error in temperature observations, and the lack of precise knowledge about the magnitude of external forcings on the climate system. They were nevertheless an eye-opener. "As far as I could see," says Wigley, the vertical pattern study in particular "was the nail in the coffin in implicating humankind as having some influence on the climate."

More than any other piece of evidence, the pattern studies would tip the balance when the IPCC gathered in 1995, as part of its second full assessment of the science of climate change, to take a new look at the question of whether humans were causing the change. The new findings would make that question the most important and contentious of the 1995 assessment round.

Santer was named the convening lead author of Chapter 8 of the emerging IPCC scientific report, the chapter dealing with detecting the signal of man-made climate change. The other three lead authors were Wigley, Barnett, and Ebby Anyamba, a Kenyan scientist then at the NASA Goddard Space Flight Center in Greenbelt, Maryland. Gates, Hansen, Hasselmann, Phil Jones, Tom Karl, and Taylor and Penner were all among the thirty-two other contributors to the chapter. This was the group that would largely refashion the IPCC's assessment of humans' relationship to climate change.

One must understand a little about how the group worked to appreciate the political furor that would soon engulf the IPCC over the fingerprint issue. The group's job was to comb the scientific literature and distill from it a basic statement of knowledge on the subject. The lead authors prepared a draft of the chapter, and the participants met regularly in workshops to shape and refine it. The evolving draft also was subjected to several rounds of review by still other experts, as well as by governments, and revised accordingly. Ultimately it would have to be examined and approved by the entire IPCC science working group, as would the 1995 report's other ten chapters.

In July 1995 the lead authors and contributors of Chapter 8 met at the Holiday Inn Sun Spree Resort in Asheville, North Carolina, for what in many ways was the key session in a series of meetings at which the science of climate change was intensely examined, thrashed, winnowed, and argued about. In this forum of his peers, Santer for the first time explained the results of the pattern studies to what Wigley called "a critical and appreciative audience." Round-faced, of medium height and weight, with short hair and a clear and fluent but controlled way with words, Santer is considered very good at explaining the arcana of science. As Wigley says, when Santer makes a presentation "he does it so clearly that everybody gets it."

"A lot of these meetings are boring; this was alive," said Michael Oppenheimer, an atmospheric scientist with the Environmental Defense Fund, who was a Chapter 8 contributor. "When Santer made his presentation the atmosphere was electric." The presentation, he said, was "mind-boggling to a lot of the scientists there," and it stirred great excitement.

By this time, many climate experts were fairly sure in their own minds that humans were causing the observed global warming, or part of it. The Santer-Wigley findings may have been the clincher for many. The Asheville group discussed the findings into the night in an attempt not only to be sure of what they meant but also how to translate them from mathematical formulas and graphical representations into everyday language for policymakers around the world. While politically essential, that can be an uncomfortable exercise for scientists: Formulas and graphs are precise. Their statistics, mathematical relationships, and curves express uncertainty and probability—a key attribute of climate science—with comfortable precision. Words, by contrast, are open to too many interpretations and shades of meaning.

When the conferees left Asheville, they were confident, as a group, of what the evidence said. The IPCC, it was clear, would break with its past and, one way or another, would convey the message that human activity did indeed appear to be modifying the earth's climate. How to say it was the problem, and that would be addressed in a November 1995 showdown in Madrid. There, in a plenary meeting of the IPCC science working group, politics and science would combine to produce a landmark scientific document.

THE WORLD DIDN'T WAIT for Madrid. Instead, the emerging findings exploded into the political realm. A post-Asheville draft of the entire IPCC science report found its way to the World Wide Web, from where it was readily plucked and made public. In September 1995 the world learned from the *New York Times* that in an "important shift of scientific judgment, experts advising the world's governments on climate change are saying for the first time that human activity is a likely cause of the warming of the global atmosphere." The page-one story cited a draft summary of the upcoming IPCC report, which said that the observed global warming of the last few years was "unlikely to be entirely due to natural causes and that a pattern of climatic response to human activities is identifiable in the climatological record." Wigley was quoted as saying, "I think the scientific justification for the statement is there, unequivocally."

The *Times* story cited the pattern studies as a major reason for the finding. It pointed out that the scientists still did not know how much of the warming might be attributable to human activity and how much to natural causes. It noted the imperfections of the computer models on which the finding was based. It quoted Richard Lindzen as saying that the models did not reflect the climate's natural variability very well and that there was therefore "no basis" for the claim that a human influence on climate had been detected. (We will meet Lindzen again.) And the story said prominently that while the draft summary of the IPCC report had been through at least one round of scientific review and that its wording could change, no substantial changes were anticipated in the full chapter on which the conclusion about humans' impact on the climate was based—Chapter 8.

The IPCC's change of stance was widely and prominently reported. Instantly perceived as a major landmark, it reenergized the climate debate, whose image on the public radar screen had weakened almost to the point of invisibility in the years since Jim Hansen's galvanizing congressional testimony in 1988 and the signing of a global climate treaty at the Rio de Janeiro Earth Summit in 1992. (The treaty and other political efforts to come to grips with the prospect of climate change will be among the subjects of Chapter 17.) So when the IPCC scientific working group met in Madrid for the final drafting of its new assessment, global warming was a hot issue once more: All the cross-cutting economic and environmental interests that had been stirred up in 1988 were quivering again.

When the IPCC science working group convened at its semicircular rows of tables in the meeting hall near Madrid's Prado art museum on November 27, 1995, it had two tasks. It is important to understand their nature, because it bears on what would soon emerge as a major threat to the IPCC's credibility. One task was to "accept" each of the eleven full chapters that made up the main body of the group's report and that were to stand as a full exposition of the state of scientific knowledge on climate change. Acceptance merely means that the IPCC certifies that the drafting and review process have been finished successfully. Debate over a chapter can take place within the working group, but the lead authors have the final word. The second task in Madrid was to "approve," line by line and word for word, a shorter Summary for Policymakers. Both the summary and the larger chapters were to be adjusted as necessary so that both conformed to the combined judgment of the working group as a whole and to each other.

While primarily a scientific group, the IPCC is also partly a political entity. The delegates at Madrid consisted not only of scientists but also of politically appointed representatives (many of them scientists as well) from ninety-six countries. The lead authors had final say over their chapters, a veto as it were. But in practice, both discussion of the chapters and the hammering-out of the summary were give-and-take exercises in which all groups took part. The delegates included interest groups like industry and environmental organizations, although their participation was limited because of time constraints.

On November 27 Santer presented the scientific findings contained in Chapter 8, as they had emerged from Asheville and been modified during the intervening months in accordance with myriad comments he had received from contributors and reviewers. Ensconced with Wigley and the working group's leaders on a raised platform with an overhead transparency projector and a screen, he laid out the essence of Chapter 8. Then he and Wigley submitted themselves to cross-examination from the floor. Opposition to the chapter immediately developed, especially from Saudi Arabia and other oil-producing nations that saw themselves as threatened by any attempt to reduce fossil fuel use. They made common cause with American industry lobbyists to try to weaken the conclusions emerging from Chapter 8. "They were trying to get us to say things we didn't want to say," says Wigley. "We never did, because it was wrong."

Acutely aware that detection of the greenhouse signal was a crucial and contentious issue, Sir John Houghton, the chairman of the meeting, directed an ad hoc drafting group to take it up and work out differences. Fifteen to twenty delegates from some half a dozen countries, including the United States, Britain, Australia, Canada, New Zealand, and the Netherlands, bent to that task. The oil-producing countries, which had been invited, unaccountably did not attend. When Santer later presented the breakout session's suggested revisions to the full working group, the Saudis again challenged it. Santer, quite hotly, some said, challenged them back. If the Saudis' objection had some basis in science, Santer wanted to know, then why hadn't they attended the breakout meeting?

In the end, the working group accepted the chapter—with the clear understanding, as explained several times during the meeting by Houghton, that the changes emerging from the discussion would be included in both the policymaker's summary and the final version of the underlying chapter. This is clearly revealed in the transcript of a tape recording of the Madrid deliberations.

When the working group turned to the question of how the bottom line of Chapter 8's findings ought to be worded in the Summary for Policymakers—the only part of the report most people would read—it remained perplexed about how to characterize the human influence on climate. Was it "detectable," or "identifiable," or "measurable," or "appreciable," or "significant"? "We went through about twenty-eight different words," recalls Oppenheimer. None satisfied everyone. At one point, remembers Bert Bolin, the IPCC chairman, he thought the key sentence went too far. In response, he came up with "discernible." Thus came about the official IPCC pronouncement that would transform the climate debate. It first set out the key caveats and uncertainties. Then it said: "Nevertheless, the balance of evidence suggests that there is a discernible human influence on global climate."

To Santer and others, this was too cautious a statement. In the debate, Santer said he thought "suggests" to be a lowest-common-denominator word. Furthermore, he said, just because the human impact cannot be quantified does not mean it is trivially small; indeed, he said, to be able to see any pattern correspondences at all between observations and computer models "requires that there is some signal that has risen above the regional-scale noise of natural climate variability, and we are seeing this." He said bluntly that using the two qualifiers, "balance of evidence" and "suggests," "is a compromise solution to deal with the concerns of the Saudi Arabian and Kuwait delegations" and of industry.

After the working group finished its deliberations, Santer, "exhausted and excited at the same time," flew to London and went directly to the Hadley Center in Bracknell. There, consulting long-distance with Wigley and Barnett, two of his coauthors, he revised Chapter 8 pursuant to the discussions in Madrid. The changes were many, but the bottom line of the chapter was basically unaltered. It was embodied, finally, in these three sentences: "Viewed as a whole, the results [of recent studies] indicate that the observed trend in global mean temperatures over the past 100 years is unlikely to be entirely natural in origin."

And: "Taken together, [the pattern studies] point towards a human influence on global climate."

And: "The body of statistical evidence in Chapter 8, when examined in the context of our physical understanding of the climate system, now points towards a discernible human influence on global climate."

But not everyone was happy with the crucial chapter as it finally emerged.

IN MAY 1996, in a crowded meeting room of the Rayburn Office Building on Capitol Hill in Washington, the fossil fuel industry and its allies struck back. Having only partly succeeded at Madrid in weakening the IPCC's conclusion about the human impact on climate, at best, they now set out to cast doubt on the credibility of the findings, providing a particularly hard-knuckled example of the intrusion of politics into science.

At the public meeting in the Rayburn Building sponsored by the U.S. Global Change Research Program, a federal government organization, Santer and Wigley explained the pattern studies and their results to a standing-room-only crowd. Several industry representatives were present, including William F. O'Keefe, the head of both the

American Petroleum Institute and the Global Climate Coalition, a lobbying group for the fossil fuel industry and its business allies; and Donald Pearlman, a Washington lawyer and longtime lobbyist on the climate issue for a group of U.S. power and coal companies. O'Keefe and Pearlman launched an attack on Santer, accusing him of secretly altering the IPCC report, suppressing dissent by other scientists, and eliminating references to scientific uncertainties. Santer and Wigley appeared "visibly shaken" by the attack, according to the author and journalist Ross Gelbspan, who was present.

That was only the beginning. Over the next few weeks Santer was the subject of numerous attacks by industry representatives and greenhouse contrarians. The Global Climate Coalition, for instance, charged him with rewriting Chapter 8 without proper authority, suggested that the integrity of the IPCC had been compromised or even destroyed, and accused Santer and the IPCC of "scientific cleansing." By design or not, this was a clear play on the term "ethnic cleansing," a policy of genocide carried out in the Balkan civil war of that time.

Frederick Seitz, a former president of the National Academy of Sciences (in the 1960s) and a well-known greenhouse contrarian, joined in the assault. He asserted that the final version of Chapter 8 was not the version approved in Madrid, that he had never seen "a more disturbing corruption of the peer-review process," and that Santer must "presumably" take the major responsibility. The effect of the changes, he said, was "to deceive policy makers and the public into believing that the scientific evidence shows human activities are causing global warming."

If the attackers thought Santer would be a soft touch, though, they were mistaken. This was a man who had dealt with adversity before, as witnessed by his down-and-out-in-Seattle days. Around that time, he had also gone through a life-and-death epiphany: To take his mind off his troubles, some friends had invited him on a mountain-climbing holiday in the French Alps. He fell into a crevasse and nearly died. He worked his way torturously toward "a little blue slit of sky" at the top of the crevasse to escape.

Santer struck back hard at his critics. The reference to "scientific cleansing" by the Global Climate Coalition, he said, was especially upsetting. Noting the deaths of his grandparents in concentration camps, he said it "raises all the wrong flags with me." He acknowledged that he had indeed made the changes in the October 9 draft of Chapter 8, but explained that he did so in response to the many scientists' comments made between October 9 and the late November Madrid meeting and at the meeting itself. In fact, he pointed out, the chapter was accepted on condition that it be revised in accordance with the wishes of the Madrid group. Far from papering over uncertainties, he said, the chapter treated them in great detail. (In fact, about 20 percent of the chapter's text was devoted to them.) He pointed out the obvious fact that the bottom-line conclusion had not changed; that it was phrased precisely the same way in both the pre-Madrid and post-Madrid versions.

He took Seitz to task in particular, pointing out that he had not been at Madrid and had not contacted him or any other IPCC scientists for their version of what had gone on there. Seitz, he pointed out, was not a climate scientist and had done no work in the field (his specialties were solid state and nuclear physics). Therefore, Santer said, Seitz was unqualified to judge whether the changes were scientifically justified. He accused Seitz of demonstrating "ignorance of both the topic and the IPCC process" and characterized Seitz's attack as "an apparent attempt to divert attention away from the scientific evidence of a human effect on global climate."

The attack on Santer and the IPCC ultimately backfired, as Santer's peers flocked to his defense. He was widely considered to be among the most careful and thoughtful of scientists and the straightest of straight arrows. It was "quite ironic that somebody like Ben should be accused of things like this, because I don't think you could find anyone less likely to do that sort of thing," said John Mitchell of the Hadley Center, who had been Santer's Ph.D. examiner a decade earlier.

Bert Bolin backed Santer fully and lashed back at the attackers: "I fully support the manner in which these lead authors consistently refused to bow to the very substantial pressure apparent in Madrid to modify the scientific conclusions for politically motivated or policy reasons." Houghton called the Global Climate Coalition's charges "rubbish" and accused Seitz of trafficking in disinformation. The American

Meteorological Society and the University Corporation for Atmospheric Research condemned what they called "a concerted and systematic effort" to undermine the scientific process, rather than "carrying out a legitimate scientific debate through the peer-reviewed literature."

All in all, said Mitchell at the time, the attack on Santer turned out to be "counterproductive from the standpoint of those trying to weaken the conclusions" of the IPCC.

The affair did expose a flaw in the 1995 IPCC exercise, one the critics exploited to the hilt in their attempt to indict the process. Despite assurances that any changes made in the report at Madrid would be introduced when the full IPCC met in Rome to accept the report two weeks later, the final version was not ready by then. Bolin said later that the "close scheduling" had made it impossible to complete the revisions in time. It was, Houghton said, a mistake that would not be repeated with future reports. In any event, the full IPCC accepted the science working group report and published the revised version.

To some, the Chapter 8 affair pointed up important differences between the way science normally works and the way it does, should, or must work in a political context. Steve Schneider and a historian of science, Paul N. Edwards, wrote about this in the Fall 1997 issue of *Ecofables/Ecoscience*, an occasional publication of Stanford University. "Formal procedures are relatively unimportant in scientific culture," they wrote. This, they said, is because scientists work in "very small social groups endowed with extremely strong and deeply entrenched (informal) norms." Further, they said, the pace of change in science means that "too much focus on formal rules would inhibit progress." But in a part-scientific, part-political setting like the IPCC, they maintained, this customary informality can have its dangers—as the flap over Chapter 8 illustrated. So while continuing revision of findings is a normal feature of scientific research, they concluded, doing things the way they were done in Madrid and immediately afterward is risky from a political point of view.

In the end, the IPCC conclusions about human influence on the climate system stood. In July 1996 high-level ministerial delegates from around the world, meeting in Geneva to take the first steps in negotiating reductions in greenhouse gas emissions, formally endorsed the findings. Tim Wirth, the chief American delegate, defended the report on behalf of the Clinton administration. The administration, he said, was "not swayed by and strongly objected to" the allegations about Chapter 8, and described the attackers as "naysayers and special interests bent on belittling, attacking, and obfuscating climate change science."

Still, the Chapter 8 affair did have an impact on the political argument over climate change. Within a few months eyes focused on Kyoto, Japan, where in December 1997 delegates from more than 150 countries were scheduled to conclude formal talks on reducing greenhouse gas emissions. The fossil fuel industry, while continuing to point up the uncertainty of the science, shifted its attack to the economic realm, predicting economic disaster if the world moved to place significant limits on emissions and therefore on fossil fuel burning. But as the pre-Kyoto debate heated up, opponents of binding limits on emissions more than once used the Chapter 8 issue to try to attack the credibility of climate science and argue that no binding action was justified.

AS THE QUEST FOR the greenhouse fingerprint charged ahead in the latter part of the 1990s, skeptics and contrarians continued to pose substantive scientific challenges. In late 1996, for instance, University of Virginia climatologist Patrick J. Michaels questioned the validity of one of the most vital underpinnings of the IPCC conclusion about humans' effect on climate—Santer and others' study showing how closely changes in vertical patterns of temperature in the atmosphere from 1963 to 1987 matched the models' predictions.

Michaels said that if the data are extended through 1995, the correspondence between the models and the observations disappears. When Santer obtained later data (which he said had not been available for the original study) and reran the analysis, he found that Michaels was partially right. Michaels's claim was accurate when the model simulation was of the before-and-after snapshot variety, the only kind of simulation available for the original analysis.

But when a more realistic "transient," or movie-style, simulation was used, a good correspondence between the models and the observations appeared once again. One physical explanation for this, Santer believes, is that patterns of warming and cooling evolve and change over time: Aerosol emissions have declined since the 1980s, for instance, allowing some previously cool areas of the Northern Hemisphere to warm. This generally corresponds with the movie-style model simulations. In fact, Santer says, the combination of the latest data and the latest, most realistic model simulations produces an even stronger correspondence between model predictions and observations—rather than a weak or nonexistent one, as Michaels claimed.

In response to critics and contrarians who suggested that uncertainties about humans' impact on climate were growing, Santer replied in 1997 that the general body of evidence that had emerged since Madrid actually "reinforces and fully warrants" the conclusions about human influence. Uncertainties, he wrote, are

> a fundamental part of any branch of science, not just climate science, not just climate change science. Although we will never have complete certainty about the exact size of the past, present and future human effect on climate, we do know—beyond any reasonable doubt—that the burning of fossil fuels has modified the chemical composition of the atmosphere.
>
> The question is not whether, but to what extent such changes in atmospheric composition have already influenced the climate of the past century and will continue to influence the climate of the twenty-first century.

Despite the continuing challenges, scientists at a number of laboratories were breaking new ground in the art and science of fingerprint detection. For the first time, they were trying to enrich the pattern studies by including in them the estimated impact of natural forcings like solar variability and volcanic eruptions. The impact of these natural factors varies over time, and if researchers could pin down these variations, they also could pin down their effect on temperature patterns over time. And if one could do that, it would be easier to identify the influence of natural factors and distinguish it from greenhouse forcing. For the same reason, researchers also were trying to quantify seasonal differences in the impact of greenhouse gases and sulfate aerosols on global temperature.

Through such strategies as these, the greenhouse detectives were hoping to produce a richer and more revealing model version of changing global temperature patterns—in effect, a quirkier, more idiosyncratic picture of the predicted combined effect of natural and man-made forcings on climate. "Richer" and "quirkier" mean that the effects of greenhouse gases and aerosols should be better defined: The physician would now have a more revealing set of symptoms to explain the general fever.

Early results of this combined spatial and temporal approach, said John Mitchell of the Hadley Center, indicated that for the half century between 1945 and 1995, "essentially you can't explain the current [temperature] record unless you take into consideration greenhouse gases and perhaps sulfates." Mitchell took part in a 1999 study led by a Hadley colleague, Simon F. B. Tett, in which modelers tried to isolate and quantify the major forcings that produced the last century's global warming. The researchers found that in the early part of the century, the warming could be explained by an increase in solar radiation or by a combination of stronger solar radiation and greenhouse gases. But after the 1970s, they found, when about half the century's warming took place, it was caused largely by greenhouse gases. The finding was tempered not least by the fact that solar irradiance was not directly measured until 1978. Nevertheless, Tom Wigley called it "another jigsaw puzzle piece."

Taking another tack, experts at the Max Planck Institute concentrated on refining statistical techniques for accentuating the signs of greenhouse warming so that they stand out from natural variability. One, Gabriele Hegerl, concluded from this sort of analysis that observed changes in temperature could not be explained by natural variability alone.

Santer and others expanded their detection studies to include hemispheric-scale variables like precipitation, changes in atmospheric circulation, the behavior of the North Atlantic Oscillation, and possible changes in the temperature difference between the poles and the equator. "What happens if you throw all these things in the pot?" said Santer. "That's the problem we've been looking into."

Still, the fingerprinting exercise continues to be plagued by uncertainty. Santer himself, once he was able to give full attention to his research again, attempted to document and quantify one important kind—uncertainty in observed temperature changes in the free atmosphere. He found that there was so much uncertainty that the use of any single data set in pattern detection studies should be avoided; several data sets should be used.

John Mitchell and David Karoly, an Australian scientist, both of whom did early work pattern studies and contributed to Santer's study on vertical temperature patterns, took over Santer's role as convening lead author of the fingerprint detection chapter for the 2001 IPCC assessment. Santer opted out, saying he wanted to pay more attention to his young son. He also had the future of the science itself in mind. "If I were to be involved in any way, shape, or form, certain people would use that as evidence of incorrectness," he said, also acknowledging his relief that he wouldn't be "nominated for lightning-rod-of-the-year award" when the report comes out in 2001.

As things turned out, he was nominated for an entirely different kind of award. In June 1998 it was announced that Santer had been named a MacArthur Fellow by the John D. and Catherine T. MacArthur Foundation. The award carried a no-strings-attached grant of $270,000—a prize known far and wide as the MacArthur "genius grant."

No genius is likely to identify the greenhouse fingerprint definitively anytime soon. Santer and virtually everyone else working on the problem believe that unambiguous detection of the greenhouse signal—especially the magnitude of the human impact—is some time away. There is "still a long way to go" before the jigsaw puzzle is completed, Wigley said in mid-1999, "but we're beginning to see the smile on the face of the Mona Lisa, I think—or perhaps it should be a frown."

When might the picture become clear? To some degree, Santer wrote in the fateful Chapter 8, the answer is in the eye of the beholder: Some scientists believe that uncertainties preclude any answer, while others claim that the signal of man-made greenhouse warming has already been detected.

Wherever the search for the greenhouse fingerprint leads, some skeptics undoubtedly will be permanently unconvinced. "Even if New York were under six feet of water," says Santer, "there would be people who would still say, 'Well, this is a natural event.'"

So we turn to the contrarians.

[14]

The Contrarians

ON JUNE 16, 1981, Jule Charney died at age sixty-four after a twenty-month-long battle with lung and pancreatic cancer. With him went a mind and personality that prompted the American Geophysical Union to cite him as the person who "guided the postwar evolution of modern meteorology more than any other living figure."

Two years later Richard S. Lindzen stepped into the big pair of shoes that Charney left as Alfred P. Sloan Professor of Meteorology at MIT. As with Ben Santer, Lindzen's father fled Hitler's Germany. He settled as a shoemaker in Webster, Massachusetts, where Richard was born in 1940. Later the family moved to the Bronx, where Lindzen Senior changed crafts and became a purse maker. "I think we were the first Jewish family in an Irish-Catholic neighborhood," Lindzen recalled later in a standard academic accent modified by a pronounced New Yorker's hard *g*, as in "Lon-GUY-land."

Like Charney, Lindzen was brilliant. He won Regents' and National Merit Scholarships at the front-rank Bronx High School of Science, graduating in 1956. The scholarships enabled him to go first to Rensselaer Polytechnic Institute and then Harvard University. Classical physics first attracted him, and then atmospheric physics. He achieved sufficient distinction as an investigator and theorist of atmospheric dynamics to be elected to the National Academy of Sciences at the relatively precocious age of thirty-seven. By then he had produced pioneering work involving regular changes in atmospheric pressure called tides and the quasi-biennial oscillation, the high-level equatorial winds that every few months change their direction 180 degrees. He was just forty-three and at the top of his intellectual game when he took over Charney's chair at MIT in 1983.

But while Charney in 1979 had lent his enormous prestige and credibility to the first effort to find a consensus on the greenhouse question, Lindzen channeled his brilliance and prestige in a different direction: He became perhaps the most formidable of would-be consensus busters. Charney's chairmanship of the 1979 consensus panel had resulted in the conclusion, still accepted by the scientific mainstream two decades later, that a doubling of carbon dioxide in the atmosphere would warm the earth by about 3 to 8 degrees Fahrenheit, with a best estimate of about 5 degrees.

That is simply bunk, Lindzen decided, and he has steadfastly maintained that the warming would be negligible. He based this forceful dissent on a conviction that atmospheric water vapor does not, in fact, amplify the warming effect of greenhouse gases as the modern greenhouse theory requires, and may even diminish it. Doubled carbon dioxide, he insisted, would consequently raise the average surface temperature of the earth by no more than about 1 degree Fahrenheit. Conventional wisdom held that the amplification does take place, and the 3- to 8-degree number was based on that. If Lindzen is right, then the theory on which the dominant view of global warming is based will come crashing down.

By the measure of professional reputation, Lindzen stood out among those who in the 1980s and 1990s made themselves vocal challengers of the dominant view—what might be called the establishmentarian or mainstream view—on climate change. So far in the part of this narrative dealing with global warming, the primary focus has been on that dominant view. It is forged from the results of myriad studies by active scientists doing original research, trying to tease out the secrets of the atmosphere, and is embodied in the products of successive attempts to fashion a consensus. The Charney report was the first such attempt; the IPCC was and is the most all-encompassing and influential one.

But true consensus, even though it does not require unanimity, is difficult to find in a field of knowledge so pervaded by uncertainty and so riddled by gaps in data as that of climate. Controversy, argument, and dissent are inevitable. So while the IPCC does succeed in achieving a consensus of sorts, its findings unavoidably amount to a compromise. Behind them lies a bigger range of opinion, with some IPCC scientists preferring to make bolder statements than actually emerge and some preferring more cautious ones. Moreover, many scientists with something to say about climate do not go public, do not participate in the IPCC and other attempts at forging consensus; they just do their work.

Not all opinions are equal, of course. Not all atmospheric scientists and meteorologists are experts on climate change. Even within the field of global warming research, an expert on one aspect of the problem might not be qualified to judge the merits of an argument on another aspect.

Moreover, opinions may tend to be affected by a person's professional perspective. For a long time, data-crunching climatologists were highly leery of computer modelers and their projections. Today that gulf has been bridged in some significant measure, as symbolized by Tom Karl's intellectual evolution. Likewise, scientists who have spent their lives studying natural climatic and meteorological phenomena may tend to look askance at suggestions that humans are having a significant impact on the atmosphere. Sometimes judgments may be skewed when an expert looks at the climate system not in the round, as a total, interdependent entity, but focuses only on one aspect, perhaps the aspect with which the expert is most familiar. There may also be something of a generational divide, with older scientists tending to be more resistant.

"A lot of my older colleagues are very skeptical on the global warming thing," William Gray of Colorado State University told the *Times* in 1996. Gray, best known for his yearly forecasts of Atlantic hurricane activity, is himself a skeptic on global warming; the climatic changes observed over the last few years are of natural origin, he says. There are many quiet skeptics, too, Lindzen and others insist. Many do not speak out, he says, because it doesn't pay. "Who needs to be in controversies?" he says, noting that the climate issue has drawn a lot of government funding: "Why spoil a good thing?"

Actually, the range of views among atmospheric scientists was and is more of a spectrum than a black-and-white division of opinion, with most scientists positioned somewhere in the middle. But at least since the late 1980s, a clear polarization of publicly expressed views has been evident. The debate, rightly or wrongly, has become cast as a dispute between "believers in global warming" and those who have come to be called the "contrarians."

Contrarians play a constructive role, many of their intellectual adversaries say, by raising legitimate criticisms that keep mainstream scientists honest and on their toes; that is the way science normally works. But other scientists bitterly charge, off the record, that some contrarians exploit and exacerbate uncertainties needlessly and even spread outright disinformation and misrepresentation. The upshot, according to this second view, is that contrarians more often obscure issues than clarify them, unnecessarily muddying an already muddy picture and sowing confusion rather than promoting enlightenment. Similar criticisms have been leveled at some environmentalists who inhabit the opposite extreme of the debate.

Not all contrarians make or subscribe to the same points, but insofar as there is a common contrarian position, it includes these main propositions:

- Available data do not solidly support the conclusion that the world is warming.

- If the global temperature is rising, the cause is solely or mostly natural.

- Any future warming caused by carbon dioxide emissions will be small, and the impact will be mostly beneficial.

- Computer models of the atmosphere are so flawed that their projections of future climatic change cannot be taken seriously.

- Climate science is still too uncertain to justify the costs involved in taking action strong enough to stabilize atmospheric concentrations of carbon dioxide.

Outside the scientific community, interest groups have deployed a full range of public relations weapons to amplify the two polarized positions on global warming. Environmental organizations have trumpeted the believers' position, while fossil fuel producers and big industrial users of fossil fuels, along with political conservatives, have promoted the contrarian view. In some cases, scientists espousing one view or the other also have been affiliated with the interest groups.

In the early 1990s industry groups, conservatives, and libertarians launched an assault on the idea that climate change was a serious and possibly catastrophic threat. Some used shrill words like "flash in the pan," "hysteria," and "scare talk" to characterize the idea of global warming. The Cato Institute, a free market, libertarian Washington think tank, in 1993 characterized the evidence that warming or harm from warming would occur in the foreseeable future as "ludicrously small." That same year the late Dixy Lee Ray, a former governor of Washington State and a former chairwoman of the Atomic Energy Commission, wrote a book in which she called carbon dioxide "an unlikely candidate for causing any significant worldwide temperature changes." This and other contrarian quotes were picked up and spread by right-wing radio talk-show hosts.

The conservative editorial pages of the *Wall Street Journal* and the *Washington Times* offered warm welcomes to contrarian essayists, who took full advantage of those forums. In mid-1993 Jeffrey Salmon, executive director of the contrarian George C. Marshall Institute in Washington, stated categorically in a magazine article that there was "no solid scientific evidence to support the theory that the earth is warming because of man-made greenhouse gases."

Many of these assaults were the work of nonscientists or scientists not trained or working in the field of climate or even in atmospheric science. Perhaps the most prominent of these was Frederick Seitz, the solid state and nuclear physicist and former president of the National Academy of Sciences who challenged the propriety of Ben Santer's revision of Chapter 8 of the 1995 IPCC report. But in 1998 Seitz's position took a sharp blow. The prestigious National Academy took the highly unusual step of disassociating itself from its former leader's views on global warming.

Seitz had circulated a petition among scientists calling for the American government to reject the 1997 Kyoto Protocol, the first international agreement to reduce greenhouse gas emissions. (We will consider the Kyoto agreement later.) The petition's backers said it was signed by 15,000 scientists, mostly physicists but also climatologists and meteorologists. What brought Seitz afoul of the academy was an attachment to the petition. It was what appeared to be the report of a scientific study concluding that carbon dioxide emissions pose no threat to the climate but instead amount to "a wonderful and unexpected gift from the Industrial Revolution."

The study, described by its authors as a review of research on global warming, concluded that "predictions of harmful climatic effects due to future increases in minor greenhouse gases [like carbon dioxide] are in error and do not conform to current experimental knowledge." On the contrary, said the report, more carbon dioxide would stimulate plant growth. The chief author of the study was Arthur B. Robinson, a physical chemist at what he described as "a very small, little research institute devoted mostly to the study of biochemistry," called the Oregon Institute of Science and Medicine, in Cave Junction, Oregon.

What got the National Academy's attention were the facts that Seitz, in his cover letter, had identified himself as a past academy president and that the Robinson study was printed in a format and typeface highly similar to the academy's journal, *Proceedings of the National Academy of Sciences*. In fact, the study had not been published anywhere. The academy's governing council thereupon formally disassociated itself from the petition and the study, saying in a statement that it "does not reflect the conclusion of expert reports of the Academy" and that it was never published in the academy's journal. The governing council also noted that the most recent academy report, in 1991, had concluded that "greenhouse warming poses a potential threat sufficient to merit prompt responses."

Seitz acknowledged that the academy was "not involved" and said he had urged the authors of the Robinson paper to "withdraw it" and submit it to a journal for publication. Robinson said the article was circulated before being published because the delay and copyright considerations would have prevented its being used in the petition drive. Eventually it was published in a medical journal.

The Seitz affair and the assaults of nonscientists aside, a number of contrarian scientists have been vigorous in pressing their arguments over the years. Arguably, the two most persistent and visible have been S. Fred Singer and Patrick J. Michaels.

SINGER, at the age of fourteen, fled Nazi-controlled Vienna aboard a children's transport train with other Jewish children and in time, after working as a teenaged optician in England, ended up at Ohio State University, where he received a degree in electrical engineering. After World War II service in a navy research laboratory in Washington, where he worked on antimine warfare and the design of an early computer, he was awarded a Ph.D. in physics from Princeton University. In the 1950s and 1960s he held several academic and government research posts in which he helped to pioneer the development of rocket and satellite technology. He worked with early instrumented V-2 rockets, is credited with devising the basic instrument for measuring atmospheric ozone, and became the first director of the National Weather Satellite Center in 1962. He founded the school of environmental and planetary sciences at the University of Miami in Coral Gables and was a deputy assistant secretary of the interior for water quality and research. He chaired a federal task force on environmental impacts of the supersonic transport. For some two decades he was a professor of environmental sciences at the University of Virginia.

Singer, too, was galvanized by Hansen's 1988 testimony on global warming—as an advocate for the opposing view. He became, in effect, a professional contrarian, leaving his position as chief scientist of the Department of Transportation in 1990 to found a think tank in Fairfax, Virginia, outside Washington, called the Science and Environmental Policy Project, specifically to write a book on the climate issue. Global warming was not his only target, though. He also debunked the idea that the earth faced a serious threat from depletion of the stratospheric ozone layer, which prevents ultraviolet solar radiation from wiping out terrestrial life. His campaign against the idea of ozone depletion struggled against an overwhelming consensus among scientists that the threat was indeed real, taking what was perhaps a fatal hit when the scientists who first identified the threat were awarded a 1995 Nobel Prize. The citation credited them with helping to deliver the earth from a potential environmental disaster.

But throughout the 1990s Singer maintained a drumfire of dissent on climate in the press, in books, correspondence, and monographs, on his think tank's Web site, and in countless speaking appearances. His role, he says, has been essentially that of an informed critic rather than an original researcher. He has made several basic points over the years, many of which have been contested by scientists on the other side of the question, and some of which are conceded.

One of the latter is that there is considerable uncertainty about the fate of human-induced carbon dioxide emissions once they enter the atmosphere. How long does carbon dioxide stay there? How long does it stay in the oceans? How rapidly does it recycle among the ocean, the atmosphere, and the biosphere? Uncertainty about the carbon cycle is indeed one of the major problems involved in predicting future greenhouse gas concentrations in the atmosphere and, thus, in predicting future warming.

Another Singer point generally recognized by climatologists is that the record of surface temperatures is imperfect. And he correctly points out that the computer models on which predictions of future climate are based produce varying results, that they do not model clouds very well, and that most require arbitrary adjustments.

All of which leads some scientists on the establishment side of the issue to say "so what else is new?" These points, along with many other uncertainties, are well recognized and taken into account by the IPCC assessment; that is why there are such large margins of error in both observations of past climate and predictions of future climate. "The part I've resented most about the contrarian attack is the pretense that they're the guys with the caveats," says Steve Schneider. "Almost all the uncertainties and caveats they raise are in the papers we write, and we get beaten [up] with our own caveats, with few exceptions."

Singer, many other contrarians, and even the IPCC agree that increasing carbon dioxide stimulates plant growth, resulting in a greener world. While Singer and others argue that this and longer growing seasons may already be benefiting agriculture, scientists in the mainstream say things are more complicated than that. They point out that plant growth is limited by available nutrients like nitrogen and phosphorus, not to mention water (although carbon dioxide stimulation also makes plants use water more efficiently). Faster growth may simply make plants less nutritious: They may get bigger by storing up more carbon, but the nutrient content may be diluted. In that case, an insect or a cow or a person must eat more vegetation to get the same amount of nourishment. Some developing countries may not be able to afford the increased fertilizer loads necessary to support faster growth without sacrificing nutrition. Moreover, because some kinds of plants benefit from carbon dioxide enrichment more than others, competitive relationships among them may be altered; certain weeds could gain an advantage over various crops, for instance, and some wild plants could prosper at the expense of others. Finally, some scientists believe that eventually a saturation point is reached, at which forest trees and perennial plants gain no more benefit from more carbon dioxide.

Like other contrarians, Singer maintains that the world has not warmed significantly in the last century and is not likely to do so in the future. While he calls the 1995 IPCC report a "superb compilation" of present-day knowledge about climate, he dismisses its key phrase—

that "the balance of evidence suggests that there is a discernible human influence on global climate"—as a feeble formulation that can "mean anything you want it to mean." In a 1996 letter to the *Wall Street Journal,* he wrote: "In the absence of any evidence for a current warming trend, this artful phrase is being used to frighten politicians into believing that a climate catastrophe is about to happen."

Even if the atmosphere does warm substantially, Singer maintains, that need not have detrimental effects on society. He argues that past civilizations not only survived but thrived in climates warmer than today's; colder climates, he says, are worse for civilization. But this cannot be established, says Phil Jones of the University of East Anglia, who with colleagues has studied past climates through proxy evidence. "We know that civilizations have been affected by major catastrophes—droughts and floods, and there may have been cold periods as well," he said. But "I don't know whether there is any correlation between advances in civilization and good climate or poor climate, because we don't have the local records to tell you that."

As for colder climates being worse, it is true that there was great famine and misery in Europe in parts of what is called the Little Ice Age. But Jones points out that the seventeenth century, a particularly cold period in Europe, coincided with some of the world's biggest advances in science—including the Europeans' discovery of the basic physical laws of the universe and the development of instruments to study the operation of those laws in the atmosphere itself. Then there was the century-long plunge back into ice age cold of the Younger Dryas, which, according to prevailing thought, established the climatic conditions in the Middle East that led to the birth of agriculture and thus to the rise of civilization.

In any case, say those in the mainstream of climate science, there is no record that the earth as a whole has warmed as much or as rapidly in the 10,000 years since the last Ice Age as it is predicted to warm in the next century. If the average global temperature does rise by the IPCC's best estimate of 3.5 degrees Fahrenheit over the next century, they say, it would be unprecedented in the Holocene.

❈ ❈ ❈

THERE WILL BE WARMING, says Pat Michaels. The question, he says, is how much, where, and when? Michaels's answer is not much, in the coldest parts of the world, at night and in the winter. He asks: Can that be all bad?

Ebullient, upbeat, and optimistic, Patrick J. Michaels, a professor of meteorology at the University of Virginia, sees his main role as that of synthesizing other people's research "in ways other people aren't willing to do; that is one job of an academic." It is especially appropriate, he says, for a state climatologist (which he is, in Virginia), whose job is the communication of scientific information. He reminds some of his scientist adversaries in the climate establishment, however, of a good defense lawyer—selectively mining the scientific literature for material to bolster his point of view, molding it into a case, and then presenting it. His outgoing personality, quick, retentive mind, and nimble tongue enable him to present it effectively and, for many of his hearers, convincingly. That, says Tom Karl, "totally goes against the grain of science." Michaels sees it differently. Rather than building a lawyer's case, he says, he is pursuing a scientist's hypothesis. The hypothesis, essentially, is that global warming will be small and on balance beneficial.

Along with Singer and some other contrarians, Michaels was a congressional witness much favored by the conservative Republicans who controlled Congress after 1994—just as Hansen and Manabe had been favored by "believer" senators like Tim Wirth and Al Gore. The Cato Institute, where he was a fellow, published some of his writings. But Michaels's most regular vehicle, month in and month out, was a biweekly newsletter called *World Climate Report*. It was partly supported by the Greening Earth Society, an advocacy group that pushes a coal industry point of view. Michaels used the newsletter largely to respond to current developments in climate research and the climate debate. There was seldom, if ever, any doubt about which way the spin would go: Michaels typically would attempt to minimize or explain away developments that bolstered the believers' case and trumpet those favorable to his. "God bless balance," Michaels said when asked about this characterization.

"Pat's probably done a lot for the field," says Tom Karl, "in the sense that he's made people be not so sloppy. You have to make sure your case is airtight because you know Pat's going to assail it; if there's any chance he can, he will."

Some scientists, however, accuse him of misrepresenting their work. Hansen, for instance, complained in 1998 that Michaels had misrepresented his decade-earlier global warming forecast as an "astounding failure." The 1988 prediction included several scenarios, Hansen says, based on different projections of how much greenhouse gas would be emitted in the 1990s and different assumptions about whether there would be volcanic eruptions to cool the climate. Michaels, says Hansen, picked the "warmest" scenario as a test of the prediction's accuracy over the 1990s. The observed warming was much lower. But it matched the Hansen scenario that actually played out in the real world over the decade, including both lower greenhouse gas emissions and the Mount Pinatubo cooling. Michaels had simply ignored the lower scenarios and compared, in effect, apples and oranges, Hansen said.

Michaels, the son of a mushroom farmer, was born in 1950 into the same northern Illinois culture as Tom Karl, and at about the same time. Like Karl, he kept a big set of weather records when he was a boy. He traces the roots of his dissent on the greenhouse question to his first graduate-student encounter with the energy balance equation, a mathematical expression of the relationship among the sun's energy output, earth's reflective properties, the greenhouse effect, and the earth's temperature. It was obvious that the greenhouse effect and the reflective properties could change, and Michaels felt sure that "the political process was going to discover this and abuse it." He describes the University of Chicago faculty at the time he studied there as "incredibly active on the left," and says that he developed the perspective "that scientists would abuse science for political purposes. I learned that lesson well. When I saw this equation, I said, 'This is the next one.' And that's what drives me."

While conceding (before Congress) that the surface observations show a global warming of about 1 degree Fahrenheit over the last century, Michaels has long pointed out that they also show most of the warming to be at night and in the winter. By 1998 he was also drawing on a study by a contrarian colleague, Robert Balling of Arizona State University, to say that 95 percent of the observed warming has been in the coldest, driest landmasses of the Northern Hemisphere. He asks whether warming can be anything but beneficial if it comes at night, in the winter, and in the coldest parts of the world.

Hansen says the 95 percent figure is "not anywhere near" accurate, noting that most areas of the world—not just the north—have warmed. Moreover, he maintains, the days and summers are warmer, too, just not as much warmer as the nights and winters. And in any case, he and others have said, warmer nights and winters are not necessarily benign: Warmer summer nights could mean more lethal summer heat waves, for instance, while warmer winters might have detrimental effects on plant life in the temperate zones, since some plants need winter's chill to germinate properly in the spring.

The issue on which Michaels disagrees most crucially with the establishment, perhaps, is that of how much future warming there will be. In 1998 he was asserting that it was likely to be about 1.5 degrees Fahrenheit or at the most about 2 degrees—hardly, he says, a catastrophic change. He notes correctly that projections of global warming for the next century shrank during the 1990s: Between 1990 and 1992, the IPCC reduced its best estimate of average global warming by the end of the twenty-first century from nearly 6 degrees Fahrenheit to about 4.5 degrees. The reduction resulted from the use of different emissions scenarios and a different model of the carbon cycle. In 1995 the estimate was reduced again, to about 3.5 degrees. This reduction resulted mainly from the inclusion of the cooling effects of aerosols in simulations of future climate. Testifying before Congress in 1998, Michaels said that the figure should be reduced to 1 degree Celsius (not quite 2 degrees Fahrenheit).

Actually, given the uncertain nature of future trends in greenhouse gas emissions, that is not outside the establishmentarians' ballpark ranges. The least-case warming predicted by the IPCC in 1995, which assumes a low emissions scenario and low sensitivity of the climate system to greenhouse gas forcing, amounts to just what Michaels was predicting in 1999—the same prediction he and other contrarians had been making for years.

If that turns out to be right, Michaels says, "we can all declare victory and go on to something else."

But the IPCC also has a worst-case scenario. Assuming higher greenhouse gas emissions and the high end of the climate system's supposed range of sensitivity to greenhouse gases, the panel in 1995 predicted a rise in the average global temperature of about 6 degrees Fahrenheit over the next century. That would be comparable to the difference between the last Ice Age and now.

The most critical factor in this range of possibilities may be that of the climate system's sensitivity to change. If Richard Lindzen is right on that, then there is not much to worry about.

DICK LINDZEN—chunky, black bearded, and bespectacled, looking very much like a stereotype of the academic theorist he is—had always considered himself a friend of the environment. But in the spring of 1989, he was invited to speak at a meeting of environmental groups at Tufts University. He stated his doubts about global warming. Then, he remembers, "one person after another got up, saying scientists can have their doubts but we don't have any. I developed this awful feeling that here was an issue that was running away, developing a reality that transcended the science." He was dismayed, he said, that "a community I had paid a lot of attention to [had] co-opted the science in a very serious way." So he set out to "make it more widely known that this was an open question."

He concentrated a fair amount of his fire on the general circulation models, which, in his view, were unnecessary to a climate researcher and, more to the point, so flawed as to offer no reliable basis for prediction. He also was one of the first contrarians to make a big point of the uncertain level of future greenhouse gas emissions. But his main point had to do with a central feature of the greenhouse theory: the water-vapor feedback. We have seen that greenhouse gases by themselves produce only a limited amount of warming. But this warming causes more water to evaporate into the air. And since water is also a greenhouse gas, and is so abundant and pervasive, it amplifies the warming—a positive feedback. Lindzen maintains that this feedback mechanism does not operate as advertised, and in fact may even act in the opposite direction by drying out much of the upper troposphere—a negative feedback. While the mainstream position holds that a doubling of atmospheric carbon dioxide, without the amplifying effect of water vapor, would raise the average global surface temperature by about 2 degrees Fahrenheit, Lindzen insists that it would probably be no more than about 1 degree.

The IPCC in its 1995 report acknowledged that the existence and strength of the water-vapor positive feedback was still to be established, despite its apparent effect on warming. (The report described the amplifying effect in the lower troposphere report as the "least controversial" of uncertainties involving water vapor.) Lindzen, for his part, said that "to be fair, the answer at this stage is that we don't know" how water vapor operates in the upper troposphere. As of 1998, Lindzen was studying data gathered by NASA satellites to check his hypothesis. "It looks promising," he said, "and there have been several other people who claim to find a negative feedback. At this point we're going slow, seeing what the accuracy of the data is, and so on."

Even though the issue is unresolved, Lindzen has been unwavering in his stout assertion that global warming will amount to little. In a field of research so obviously pervaded by uncertainty, Lindzen takes hits from colleagues for being so certain. Like the IPCC, most mainstream scientists specify a range of probability when asked how much they think the planet will be warmed by greenhouse gases. Lindzen does not; he says it will be 1 degree Fahrenheit or less, and that's it. This makes him suspect in some eyes. Steve Schneider considers Lindzen a "sharp" and "enjoyable" adversary in debate. "My fight with Dick," he said, "is that with a straight face he can tell people he knows the answer to a tenth of a degree, and I'm afraid I'd have to characterize that as arrogant nonsense. I allow a 5 or 10 percent chance he's right. He allows no chance that anybody else could be right. I don't know what line from God he has."

Not surprisingly, Lindzen sees it differently, explaining simply that he used what data he had to try to estimate the climate's sensitivity to a doubling of atmospheric carbon dioxide and that the figure came out to 1 degree or less. "I don't think we've made the case yet" that serious climate change is in progress, he says. But once, when asked if he could turn out to be wrong in the end, he left the door open a crack.

"I think it's unlikely," he said, "but it can happen."

Within the IPCC, at least, the opposite view prevails. For the first time, Lindzen will serve as a lead author of an IPCC chapter, in the 2001 report. It is the chapter dealing with atmospheric processes, like the behavior and impact of water vapor. It will be interesting to see how things turn out.

Assuming that the IPCC view of the issue does not change substantially and is generally right about global warming, how might the warming affect the world in the decades and centuries ahead? It is both the biggest and chanciest climate question of all.

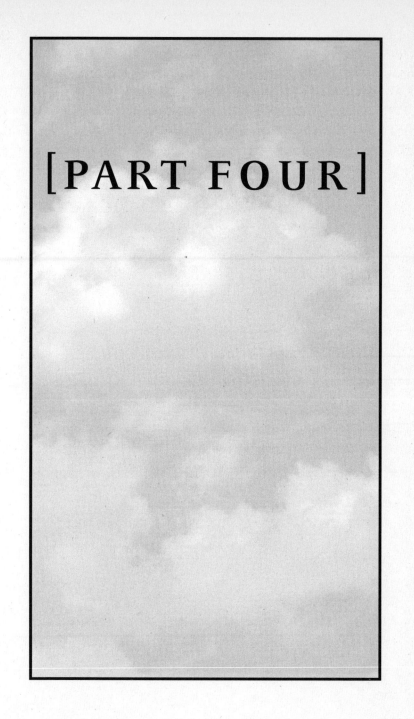

[PART FOUR]

[15]

Rising Seas

IN THE MORNINGS, as through most of the day and night, Paradise
Island hums. By 7:30 A.M., as the sun is already beating down with
tropical force, squads of buses and jitneys pull up to stops near luxury
hotels that flank the island's broad beaches. As the tourists are just finishing their early morning walks in the hypnotically rhythmic surf, the
clear turquoise water giving way to the almost purplish blue of the
deeper ocean offshore, streams of brightly uniformed service workers
pour into the hotels. One way or another, three-quarters of the Bahamas' permanent workforce owes its employment to the dollars spent
by the tourists, who outnumber them six to one.

Paradise Island is a narrow strip of land running east and west, separated from New Providence Island by the bustling harbor of Nassau,
the capital of the Bahamas. Water is everywhere, and some legends
have it that the Bahamas were the site of the mythical lost civilization
of Atlantis. So it was that at the end of the twentieth century, an age of
unusual enthusiasm for capital gain, entrepreneurs tapped into the
myth by creating, on Paradise Island, one of the world's gaudiest pleasure palaces: a megaresort costing nearly a billion dollars, an ornate
beachfront hotel-entertainment complex with 2,300 guest rooms,

thirty-eight restaurants, bars, and lounges, and the biggest gambling casino in the Caribbean region. The soaring orange-pink towers, arches, domes, and spires that were the signature of this tropical Xanadu became Nassau's dominant landmark. It was called, naturally enough, Atlantis, and it tried to live up to the name, or at least the illusion.

Every effort was made to make visitors feel as if they really were in the mythical lost undersea city. People walked through tunnels separated by glass from real underwater vistas populated by sharks, rays, groupers, lobsters, jellyfish, snappers, bonefish, porgies, angelfish, and tarpon—some 40,000 specimens in all, representing some 150 species of marine life. Real sharks, lionfish, lobsters, and piranhas patrolled the silent streets of a re-created "Atlantis," complete with supposed "Atlantean" hieroglyphics, diving paraphernalia, and scientific instruments.

In some ways the illusion was not so far-fetched. Sea level has varied widely over the millennia, and the fortunes of the Bahamas with it. And if mainstream projections of global warming are right, the Bahamas stand directly in harm's way as a result of rising seas not in some far-distant future well over the horizon, but in the foreseeable future of the next few decades. The IPCC, in fact, has picked out the Bahamas as one of the places most at risk from a changing climate.

In the depths of the last Ice Age, when the great glaciers locked up so much water, global sea level was about 400 feet lower than today and what is now the Bahamas was one massive island. But in some past interglacials, the seas in that locality may have been more than sixty feet higher than now. Eighty percent of the Bahamas is today only five feet or less above mean sea level, so it requires no great feat of imagination to determine what the consequences would be if the sea level should reach the peaks of the past. There would be no tourist industry, no crowds of hotel and restaurant workers stepping briskly toward their jobs every morning. On what used to be Paradise Island, most of the once-thriving tropical Xanadu would be a real underwater ruin, not just a manufactured illusion of one.

Could global warming boost the oceans to levels like that again?

In theory, yes. There is no clearer consequence and signal of global warming than rising seas. While uncertainties of magnitude and timing abound, the relationship is well accepted: A warmer atmosphere causes seawater to expand and glacial ice to melt. The warming of the last century, according to the IPCC, has been accompanied by a rise in global sea level of four to ten inches. In some places like the eastern United States, where coastal land is subsiding, the rise has been considerably more; in others, less. If the IPCC is right in predicting that the average global temperature will increase by some 3.5 degrees Fahrenheit over the next century unless greenhouse gas emissions are reduced, the oceans could rise by twice as much in the twenty-first century as they have in the twentieth, or even more. And that would not be the end of it; the rise would persist into the twenty-second century. "Sea-level rise is the dipstick of climate change," says Stephen P. Leatherman, director of the Laboratory for Coastal Research at the International Hurricane Center at Florida International University in Miami. A warming climate and rising seas, he says, are "pretty much hardwired" together.

If the earth warms as projected, thirty-five or forty highly vulnerable small island states—the Bahamas are a prime example—might find much of their territory threatened in the decades ahead. While many other coastal areas around the globe would also be in jeopardy, extinction would surely be the fate of many small island states should the long-term, worst-case scenario come true: collapse of the West Antarctic ice sheet and melting of the Greenland ice cap. The future of many of the warmest parts of the earth depends crucially on what happens to the coldest parts. Even without melting, the vast flotilla of icebergs shed by the retreat of Alaska's magnificent Columbia Glacier and other tidewater glaciers contributes immediately to the oceans' rise, as does water from melting mountain glaciers all over the world. Both are already expected to cause major difficulties and dislocations in the twenty-first century. But a global disaster of truly major proportions would ensue if Greenland or Antarctica were to shed all its ice. In either event, according to scientists' estimates, global sea level would rise by thirteen to twenty feet; if both took place simultaneously, the rise would be about double that, or even more.

No one is predicting that this doomsday case will materialize in the foreseeable future. Some estimates say that given the IPCC scenario for climate change, the West Antarctic ice sheet might not fully melt for perhaps 500 to 700 years. But some scientists say that human-induced global warming could cast the die much sooner, perhaps in the next century, making a collapse of the Antarctic sheet inevitable at some point. Moreover, the rise would not occur all at once; rather, it would develop gradually, perhaps in step stages, over time, and cata-strophic levels in some parts of the world could be reached sooner than five or seven centuries hence.

For the very long term, the question of how global warming might affect the Greenland and Antarctic ice sheets is both the biggest and the least understood question facing scientists as they grapple with the matter of rising seas. Much of the ice in polar regions, particularly in the Northern Hemisphere, is already floating on the ocean; if it were to melt, it would not cause the sea to rise. But the Greenland ice cap and most of Antarctica's ice are grounded; they would add to the oceans' volume if they were to melt or break off in blocks, a process known as calving. Sometimes this happens quietly, unobtrusively; a chunk of ice simply detaches itself from an oceanfront glacier and floats free. Other times great icebergs, potential ship-sinkers, crack off from the blue ice of the glacier front and plunge into the sea with a spectacular crash and a shower of spray.

In Greenland, water is routinely added to the ocean through both calving and runoff of water from melted ice, in about equal measure. But ice also reaccumulates when it snows on Greenland and the snow compacts. Scientists do not yet know whether the discharge of ice and water from Greenland into the sea presently exceeds the reaccumula-tion, or vice versa. Although laser altimeter surveys found that the Greenland ice sheet's southern half had shrunk markedly between 1993 and 1998, five years do not a trend make, and studies continue. If the IPCC's forecast is right, however, melting and calving will con-tinue to outweigh accumulation as the atmosphere warms further.

The situation in Antarctica is entirely different. It is the coldest place on earth; in 1983 the wintertime temperature was measured at minus 139 degrees Fahrenheit. Subfreezing temperatures chill most of the White Continent year round. Tourists who increasingly venture there enter a strikingly beautiful realm. Malcolm W. Browne, a *Times* reporter who is a veteran of five Antarctic trips, described it this way in a 1999 report: "The sights are stunning: towering blue, white and green icebergs and giant penguin rookeries near Palmer Station on the Antarctic Peninsula; vistas of the snow-covered Transantarctic Mountains across the sound at McMurdo; dancing solar halos around the sun at the South Pole." It is also a dangerous place, made so by the cold. Antarctica is a perpetual refrigerator; Browne noted the presence at an abandoned camp of early twentieth-century explorers of "the 89-year-old body of a husky dog that looks as if it just died." In such an environment, Browne pointed out, constant vigilance is the price of survival, even with modern gear.

The super-cold means that melting of ice from atmospheric warming is not much of a factor; the transfer of water from the Antarctic ice cap to the ocean comes from calving. In recent years attention has focused on Antarctica from time to time as big chunks of ice, some as large as small American states, have broken off extensions of the continent's ice sheets that reach out into the Southern Ocean as floating ice shelves. But again, these have no effect on sea level, since they are already floating.

What really concerns scientists is the West Antarctic ice sheet. Alone among the world's biggest ice sheets, it lies largely below sea level even though it rests on a rocky archipelago. A much bigger grounded ice sheet in East Antarctica is entirely above sea level. Although all or most of the planet's ice melted during the super-high temperatures of the Cretaceous, scientists do not believe that the amount of global warming predicted for the foreseeable future would be enough to dissolve the East Antarctic sheet.

But the West Antarctic sheet is vulnerable to warming ocean waters that lap at its margins. The margins consist of big floating ice shelves the size of Spain. They are fed by large, moving rivers of ice that flow from the interior of the West Antarctic sheet. Scientists believe that if the shelves melted or broke away in the warming water, it would allow the ice rivers to flow faster, but not that fast: It would be more like taking the cap off a bottle of stubborn ketchup than a bottle of water. Over time, however, the flow could deplete the West Antarctic's reservoir of ice, which would flow into the ocean. The IPCC predicts that, at least initially, global warming will increase precipitation over Antarctica, increasing ice accumulation and actually countering part of the global sea-level rise. But in time, some scientists believe, the outflow from West Antarctica would overwhelm the increased accumulation and cause the average global sea level to rise by thirteen to twenty feet.

That would be enough to submerge all of Florida's coastal cities, the Keys, and all of South Florida. Large chunks of New York City would also be under water, including much of East and West Sides and Lower Manhattan as well as the city's three airports. So would virtually all of Paradise Island (although part of the ruined towers of the Atlantis resort, if still in existence, probably would still rise out of the water). While no one can say just how much coastal territory would be lost all told, "it would be catastrophic," according to Vivien Gornitz, an expert on the subject in Jim Hansen's laboratory.

For a long time, no one was able to point with confidence to any instance in which this had happened in the past, in any sort of climate that compares with today's or that is predicted in the decades and centuries just ahead. Then, in 1998, investigators at Uppsala University in Sweden and the California Institute of Technology, led by Reed P. Scherer, reported evidence that the West Antarctic ice sheet, or part of it, did indeed collapse at least once during a previous interglacial period, most likely a warm interval some 400,000 years ago. The researchers analyzed sediments recovered from the area beneath the Antarctic ice and found the remains of microscopic marine creatures called diatoms, along with a chemical tracer called beryllium-10. Together, they said, the tracers provided evidence that at one time, marine conditions prevailed deep within the West Antarctic interior. While some experts were not convinced that this was the explanation for the placement of the diatoms, others said it strengthened the possibility that the West Antartic ice sheet could collapse at some future date; having done so once, it could do so again.

Recent studies from opposite ends of North America suggest that the sea level during that long-ago period was as much as sixty to seventy feet higher than it is now. In one study, Julie Brigham-Grette of the University of Massachusetts analyzed patterns of rocky debris left on ancient beaches, an indicator of sea-level height, in northwestern Alaska. "It's like a bathtub ring around the coastline," she explained, and it can be analyzed from aerial photographs. She concluded that at one juncture in the past, probably the interglacial period 400,000 years ago, the sea level was about sixty feet higher than today. In the Bahamas, researchers led by Paul J. Hearty, a regionally based expert on shoreline geology, found a similar sea level for that period by analyzing marine sediments.

THAT IS THE DIM PAST, and it may or may not be prologue to the dim future. What about the first few decades of the twenty-first century, the period on which the IPCC has focused its assessments of sea-level rise? That calculation depends directly, of course, on how much the world warms in the next hundred years, which in turn is affected by the rise in atmospheric carbon dioxide.

Over the years, people have predicted that carbon dioxide levels could double as early as the first few years of the twenty-first century and as late as the beginning of the twenty-second century, assuming that the world continues to burn fossil fuels at the present rate; as of 1999, the later twenty-first century was widely considered the most likely time of doubling. According to the establishmentarian consensus, this would raise the earth's average surface temperature from 1.5 to 4.5 degrees Celsius (about 3 to 8 degrees Fahrenheit), with a best estimate that has fluctuated between about about 2.5 and 3 degrees Celsius (about 4.5 to 5 degrees Fahrenheit). Any such projections are highly uncertain. On top of that, it is impossible to predict how much carbon dioxide will have been spewed into the atmosphere half a century hence, or even to know what kind of energy system and what kind of economy the world will have in fifty or one hundred years. (How could anyone have predicted today's technologies and economic profile with any certainty or precision a hundred years ago?)

In the face of this difficulty, the IPCC in 1995 used a middle-range scenario for its projections. It also took into consideration the expected cooling effect of sulfate aerosols emitted by industry. That is how the panel came up with its 1995 projection of future warming. As we saw early in this narrative, it called for a 2- to 6-degree Fahrenheit increase in the average global surface temperature by 2100, with a best estimate of 3.5 degrees, if no further action were taken to limit emissions of greenhouse gases. The warming would not stop in 2100, the panel said; only 50 to 70 percent of it would be realized by then.

So it is with sea-level rise, which follows warming as surely as night follows day. By the end of the twenty-first century, the panel said, the projected increase in temperature would induce a rise in global sea level of about six to thirty-seven inches, with a best estimate of about twenty inches. It said that the sea level would continue to rise for several centuries beyond 2100 as a result of human-induced global warming, even if atmospheric concentrations of greenhouse gases were stabilized by then.

These estimates, said the IPCC in 1995, represent "plausible scenarios of what could occur, not necessarily of what will occur." But if the best-estimates scenario were to play out, according to the panel, it would put at risk tens of millions of people in low-lying areas and on oceanic islands, mainly in the Pacific and Indian Oceans and the Caribbean region. The report highlighted the Bahamas, the Maldives, the Marshalls, Egypt, and Bangladesh as examples of countries whose territory and people would be in the greatest danger. Many people would have to flee, in effect becoming environmental refugees. The panel estimated that 46 million people currently experienced flooding as a result of storm surges each year. That number would increase to between 92 million and 118 million by 2100. A three-foot rise, in the high end of the range predicted by the IPCC, would seriously threaten the coastal zone on which Tokyo, Nagoya, and Osaka sit in Japan as well as the Atlantic and Gulf coasts and many of China's coastal cities.

Some stretches of American coastline would see rises higher than others, since the sinking and rising of coastal areas in response to geologic events complicates the picture. For instance, the average one-foot sea-level rise over the last century along the United States' mid-Atlantic coast has exceeded the global average, because the land level from northern New Jersey south through the Chesapeake Bay region is still recovering from its assault by the Laurentide ice sheet during the last Ice Age. The sheet depressed the earth's crust, causing it to "flow" forward ahead of the sheet's edge and creating a big bulge of rock ahead of the glacier. That bulge is still subsiding, and this adds to the relative rise in sea level—meaning that for that part of the coast, the projected rise in the twenty-first century would be above the global average. Similarly, the net rise in sea level would surpass the global average in places like Louisiana and Texas, where coastal land is sinking as petroleum and water are pumped out of the ground.

Computer models incorporating the IPCC projections indicate that sea level in the New York metropolitan area would rise by 3.5 to 10 inches by the 2030s, 7 to 17 inches by the 2050s, and 1 to 3 feet by the 2090s. When storm surges are superimposed on this, severe flooding would occur. A taste of this future, should it materialize, was delivered to the region in December 1992, when a powerful northeaster struck with nearly hurricane-force winds. The water rose 8.5 feet above average sea level at the Battery, the tip of Manhattan. The flooding forced many seaside communities in New Jersey and Long Island to evacuate and nearly shut down the metropolitan transportation system. Water poured into the subways, interrupting power and stopping trains. At one point, a commuter train was stalled seventy-five yards from the Hoboken terminal for an hour and a half as floodwaters cascaded down a stairway and onto the tracks. LaGuardia Airport was closed by the storm. Disaster officials said later that if the water had been only 2 feet higher, many people could have drowned in the subways. Out on Long Island, the storm breached barrier islands, destroyed more than 150 shorefront homes, and damaged hundreds of others.

Storms and flooding of that magnitude have been occurring, on the average, once every forty years in the New York area. According to the worst-case scenarios for sea-level rise, it could occur annually a century from now. Moreover, some of the storms would be even worse, with storm surges easily exceeding ten feet. If that were to happen, the surge would batter the foundations of the World Trade Center. The East River would invade Bellevue Medical Center, FDR Drive, and much of East Harlem. Entire neighborhoods on Staten Island would be submerged. In New Jersey, Newark Airport would be threatened and the Meadowlands would become a lake. Jones Beach, Fire Island, and Westhampton Beach would be fragmented into small islands. Since nearly every subway and train tunnel has openings below the ten-foot line, they could be flooded out.

But even without the subsiding land that exacerbates the problem on the East Coast, the prospect for the Bahamas is grimmer: The island nation's very survival may be at risk.

ONE SUNNY AFTERNOON in Nassau in December 1998, Philip S. Weech and Ulric Trotz sat under the shaded overhang of an outdoor restaurant called the Poop Deck and regarded the pink towers of the Atlantis resort across a harbor crowded with small boats. The harbor is the hub of a calypso island state with a long and yeasty history of traffic by all kinds of people, from pirates like Blackbeard to aristocrats like the Duke and Duchess of Windsor. Weech, a Bahamian native, is the senior hydrologist of the Bahamas government and chairman of the National Climate Change Committee in the prime minister's office. Trotz, from Guyana, is the Barbados-based director of Caribbean planning for adaptation to global climate change.

Basically, Weech said, the entire Bahamas consists of coastline, and much of the land is so close to sea level that serious flooding is already a recurrent threat. If the sea level rises and precipitation increases and storms become more intense, as predicted by the IPCC, much of Nassau and New Providence Island would be periodically and in some cases permanently inundated. At high tide just that very bright and stormless morning, Weech said, water came up through the storm drains and created puddles in densely packed neighborhoods where working Bahamians live in bright pastel houses. Some of the puddles had not yet receded by midafternoon. About two years earlier, the combination of a full-moon tide and a torrential downpour put much of the area under water.

What might a rise of twenty inches in sea level mean? First, said Trotz, "it means more volume of water coming farther inland" when storms come. Salt water might invade drinking water systems. Sewer systems might flood. Mangrove swamps that are the dominant coastal ecosystem of the islands could drown. Storm surges from hurricanes and northeasters would surely be higher by much more than twenty inches: Waves increase even more and take longer to recede. The beaches of Paradise Island would be largely or entirely eaten away, removing one of the island's biggest tourist attractions.

The beach that runs along the north side of Paradise Island, in front of the Atlantis and the Sheraton Grand Hotel, is today especially beautiful even by Bahamian standards. But as is also the case with most beaches in the eastern United States, it is less than 100 feet wide at high tide—more like 75 feet for much of its length. According to Steve Leatherman, who has done a study of the matter, a one-foot rise in sea level creates wave action that erodes away 150 to 200 feet of the kind of gradually sloping beach typical of the U.S. East Coast and Caribbean.

"People normally think that if you raise the sea level, all you do is flood the beach and that it's not that much of a problem," said Leatherman. "But permanent inundation is less than 10 percent of the problem." The other 90 percent is physical removal of sand by increased wave action. If all of this is so, and the sea rises steadily at the middle-range rate predicted by the IPCC, beaches on Paradise Island and the U.S. East Coast could erode completely away within two or three decades. Ordinarily, new beach would be created farther inland. But on Paradise Island and much of the East Coast, seaside development has closed off this possibility; the Atlantis, for example, is in the way. If the Atlantis or any successor resort is still around later in the next century, sea level may have risen enough for storm surges to push water into not only the hotels but most other structures on New Providence, as well. That is not so far-fetched, given that waves generated by the gigantic Halloween northeaster of 1991 broke well over the thirty-five-foot-high Nassau lighthouse.

A rising sea also would lessen the protection given to Nassau's fine harbor, which is buffered from the ocean by Paradise Island itself. This would be especially true in the event of a hurricane. Some computer models predict that global warming, by pumping more energy and moisture into the climate system, will make hurricanes more intense. If that happens, said Weech, a direct hurricane hit on the Bahamas, coupled with a higher ocean, could bring true catastrophe. "If a strong Category Five storm walks up the Bahamas," he said, "you could have a situation in which every island is devastated."

Not every threat posed by rising seas would come directly from the ocean itself. The Bahama Islands themselves consist of porous limestone—"Swiss cheese," Weech calls it. This karst, as it is known, is the classic matrix for underground aquifers, and in the Bahamas it holds freshwater. A rising sea, Weech says, would push salt water into the karst, raise the water table, and flood the land from within. Against this, no dike could protect.

While it might be possible to build on stilts and install floating piers, few good options seem to present themselves in the event that all these events should materialize—an eventuality, Weech and others pointed out, which is surrounded by uncertainties that frustrate intelligent planning. It might be necessary, he said, to prohibit development at the lowest elevations. But he acknowledged that if the worst case develops, the only recourse in some locations might be to "leave it where it is and live elsewhere." There are, he said, "no retreat options."

Studies in the Marshall Islands of the Pacific, which are in a situation comparable to that of the Bahamas, have found that either through erosion or flooding, 80 percent of the capital island's land would be lost if the sea level rises by three feet, the high IPCC estimate. "That means parliament, the ministry of foreign affairs, the college, the post office, the airport, at least one of the banks and major businesses" would go, said Espen Ronneberg, the Marshalls' United Nations delegate and a prominent player in international talks on climate change. "It would be a fairly large-scale disaster."

For the Bahamas, said Weech, "we are projecting a similar scenario." But, he said, "we're going to find some way of coping. We're never not going to call this home." The question, he said, is whether the world can get a handle on climate change before the islands' $600-million economy is destroyed. But his worst fear, he said, "is that I will not be able to leave my children a Bahamas like the one I've enjoyed all my life."

[16]

The Future Impact of Climate Change

No one at this point can possibly foresee how the complex relationship between uncertain climatic changes and the constantly changing nature of modern societies will play out. But it seems clear that if the world warms as much as mainstream science predicts, it will affect more aspects of life than one might think—human health, for instance, as we will see. In North America, at least, society might be able to cope rather easily with any single effect of climate change; with many effects at once, it is a different story. Nor will everyone and every place be affected the same. Inevitably, there will be positive and negative impacts, winners and losers. Whether the negatives and positives will cancel each other out is impossible to tell. Some experts believe one should not even try to calculate a balance; that while the exercise might have a sort of abstract logic, it is in the end a heartless sort of trading off. If northerners get to spend less on heating and snow plowing, and fewer people die from heart attacks while shoveling snow, or fewer suffer from hypothermia, does that make it all right when people somewhere else are drowned by flash floods or driven from their homes, or lose their homes, or die from nighttime heat stress?

A lot depends, of course, on how much the atmosphere actually warms. A warming in the low end of the range predicted by the IPCC would obviously bring milder and more easily handled climatic changes than one at the high end. That, too, is an imponderable; one can only spin out alternative scenarios. The uncertainties and difficulties of prediction are serious enough on a global scale, but they are even more frustrating when scientists move down from global phenomena to try to forecast future climatic changes at the regional and local level—how, for instance, the weather experienced by people every day, in a given place, might be altered. It is not just that computer models do not do regional details well, although that is a big part of the problem. The difficulty is compounded by the fact that climatic change does not operate in a vacuum; it interacts with a number of other stresses. Natural environments, not to mention human economies, themselves act in largely unfathomable ways, frustrating attempts to predict how climatic changes would alter the existing equation. On top of that, there is the possibility that climate change might not be gradual; that the system will surprise everyone by leaping abruptly and unpredictably to a new state. As we have seen, large, abrupt changes in climate have not been uncommon in the past.

The experts are not totally clueless, however, in trying to foresee long-term effects of global warming on weather in general. And they believe they also can identify, in a general, nonquantitative fashion, some ways in which particular regions, places, natural ecosystems, and human activities might be affected by climatic change.

One prediction is that the trend toward heavier precipitation and higher temperatures, including more heat waves with higher humidity, will continue. In fact, says the IPCC, small changes in the average global temperature can produce relatively big changes in the frequency of weather extremes—as is suggested, but not proven, by the Tom Karl studies. The bottom line is that global warming will probably mean more extremely hot days (and especially hot nights) and more heavy rainstorms and snowstorms, but fewer days and nights when it is extremely cold. (Commonsense intuition, in this case, appears to be right.) Some modeling studies have found that although the frequency of heavy rains will increase, the number of dry days also may increase, and dry spells might get longer: Warming would rev up the hydrological cycle, kicking both wet and dry extremes up to a new level. Twice in the summer of 1999, the New York region got a taste of what this can be like: On August 11, in the middle of one of the worst droughts in memory, up to five inches of rain flooded parts of Long Island. Sixteen days later, comparable downpours dropped as much as six inches across the area in a single morning, paralyzing mass transportation during the rush hour.

In short, the trends now in evidence would continue and become more apparent to the casual observer if the atmosphere warms as projected. "The climate reality is that if you look out your window, part of what you see in terms of the weather is produced by ourselves," says Tom Karl. "If you look out the window fifty years from now, we're going to be responsible for more of it."

Some models show that the largest changes in precipitation would be in the tropics. Storms like a highly unusual twenty-five-inch, three-day rainfall that saturated Nassau in June 1997 might become more common if that is true. If so, the Bahamas and other small island nations might be in for a double soaking from rising seas and heavier rain. In 1998 monsoon floods lasting two months, three times longer than any others on record, inundated two-thirds of Bangladesh. Whether this was related to global warming or not, it may provide a taste of what lies ahead if the forecasters are right.

ONE OF THE MOST intriguing questions about global warming's future impact is its possible effect on the large-scale circulation patterns that determine where it rains and does not, where it is colder, and where it is warmer. The El Niño–La Niña cycle is one case in point. As the century-long global warming trend resumed in the mid-1970s, the frequency of El Niño appearances increased, as well. For much of the 1990s, the warmest decade in the instrumental record, El Niño appeared more frequently than not and sometimes seemed to be almost continuous. Was this a coincidence, or were the two trends related?

Kevin Trenberth of the National Center for Atmospheric Research postulates that global warming may indeed be the cause of El Niño's more frequent visits. His hypothesis is that it could work this way: El Niño appears when warm water builds up in the tropics and then is depleted as some of the extra heat is transferred directly to the atmosphere over the Pacific (affecting rainfall patterns in many parts of the world, including California and the southern United States) and some is transported by ocean currents to higher latitudes. The effect is to raise the temperature of the globe as a whole, beyond whatever greenhouse warming might be taking place. As Trenberth points out, it has been suggested that the time interval between El Niño visitations is determined by how long it takes to recharge the system by reaccumulating heat in the ocean. One reason El Niño conditions have become more common, he says, may be that global warming has caused the warm pool in the Pacific to expand its area, thereby enabling the system to recharge faster or take longer to dispense its heat to the atmosphere, or both. It may be, he says, that this relationship developed not gradually but all at once, in a sudden change in the mid-1970s. Until then, he suggests, the modest global warming might have been accommodated by the normal workings of the climate system; but once a certain threshold was reached, it forced the system into a new mode of behavior. Not only might global warming make El Niño more frequent, Trenberth says, it might increase its magnitude as well, thereby intensifying its wide-ranging impact on the weather.

Until lately, researchers have had little success in projecting the impact of global warming on other aspects of atmospheric circulation, such as the relative position of warm and cold air masses and the strength and position of Rossby waves, jet streams, and surface fronts. But in 1999, studies suggested for the first time that the warming may be changing the frequency of existing Northern Hemisphere circulation patterns. In winter and spring, it was found, the climate system now favors a circulation regime that distributes relatively more warmth and precipitation to Eurasia, the North Atlantic region, and northwestern North America, while generally cooling the southeastern United States and drying out southern Europe and the Middle East. This is exactly the pattern that has been in place, on average, since the mid-1970s, the period of most rapid warming, and some researchers believe it could remain dominant over the next several decades.

The circulation patterns in question are those associated with the North Atlantic and North Pacific Oscillations and the Arctic Oscillation that may be the link between the two. In these oscillations, the climate of the Northern Hemisphere shifts back and forth between two preferred circulation patterns, or regimes. What actually changes is the predominant position and strength of the westerly winds that transport heat and warmth from the oceans onto the colder winter continental landscapes.

Researchers led by Tim Palmer, a climatologist at the European Center for Medium-Range Weather Forecasts in England, examined atmospheric circulation data for the last fifty years to see whether there had been any change in the relative frequency of different regimes. They found that there had: The phase that favors relatively warmer winters on the Northern Hemisphere continents had become more frequent. This, Palmer believes, is the main mechanism accounting for the unusually pronounced warming of Alaska, Siberia, and western Canada that we described in Chapter 10. He postulates that a warming atmosphere forced the change in frequency of regimes, although his study did not establish that.

Drew Shindell, a researcher at the Goddard Institute in New York, took the matter a step further. In a computer modeling study, he found that the Northern Hemisphere winter warming can be explained by the action of upper-atmosphere winds characteristic of the Arctic Oscillation, which in turn is the apparent link between the circulation regimes of the North Atlantic and North Pacific. In the Arctic Oscillation, the strength of high-altitude winds that circle the North Pole near the Arctic Circle shift back and forth between stronger and weaker states. Shindell says that at the altitude in question, from roughly six to twelve miles, global warming has the effect of strengthening the vortex of winds. In turn, the westerly winds off the Atlantic are strengthened, making northern Eurasia and western North America warmer and wetter. He offers no firm prediction of what future Northern Hemisphere winters will be like but suggests nevertheless that the current trend will continue for thirty or forty more years. If so, northern regions of Europe and Asia and, to a lesser extent, North America can continue to expect warmer winters, with more rain and, when it comes, heavier snow.

The larger conclusion suggested by Trenberth's hypothesis about El Niño, and by the work of Palmer and Shindell on Northern Hemisphere circulation, is that global warming, both now and in the future, may largely express itself as changes in the frequency of existing circulation regimes.

Beyond that, there is much to be learned about how climate change will affect everyday weather. For instance, the 1995 IPCC consensus found that it is simply impossible to say whether global warming will make hurricanes stronger, although some models have shown that it will. Scientists are equally at a loss to predict whether future warming will have any effect on how often hurricanes materialize, and where.

Some models indicate that the temperature contrast between the tropics and higher latitudes would be reduced in a warmer world, thereby robbing storm fronts of some of their energy. At the same time, there would be more water vapor in a warmer atmosphere, releasing more latent heat into the atmosphere when the vapor condenses as precipitation. The effect of this would be to pour more energy into storms, making them stronger and windier. The IPCC found it impossible to assess the net effect of these competing influences.

Some scientists suggest that the big eddies of air that define weather systems would become smaller. Others postulate that storms could become more intense, but fewer and farther between. But, said the IPCC, there was "little agreement between models on the changes in storminess that might occur in a warmer world."

THE LEAVES START turning color in August in northern Maine, New Hampshire, and Vermont, and by mid-September the hills and valleys of northern New England are already ablaze with the russets, oranges, reds, and yellows of maple and birch, becomingly set off in many places by stands of evergreen pine, spruce, cedar, and fir. By mid-October the peak of brilliance has come, and tourists by the carload flock the narrow roads to bask in one of the most famous displays of natural beauty in North America and to train their binoculars on the spectacular and accommodating moose. By then the foliage show has begun to move south, where it peaks in the New York and Philadelphia region in late October. As one goes south, the subtler, duller hues of oaks and hickories gradually displace the more brilliant maples, and soon, except in higher elevations, the show flickers out.

Does global warming mean that New England will exchange its bright autumn maples for less gaudy oaks and that its moose, which abhor warmth, will migrate north? What about its skiers' snows, mainstay of the tourist economy in winter? Or its trout, which need cold water?

Those who have considered New England's position do, in fact, believe that the magnitude of global warming predicted by the IPCC poses a potential, substantial threat to the region as people now know and appreciate it. Some decades from now, its brilliant foliage may have migrated farther north, with the southern boundary of the maple-and-conifer zone shifting into Canada, and oaks and hickories moving in from the south. Habitat for trout might be drastically reduced. Snow might be deeper when it comes, but the skiing season might be shorter, with snow coming later in the fall and turning to slush on the slopes earlier in the spring. The region would retain its characteristic accents and architecture, but climatically and ecologically, it might be more like New Jersey and Pennsylvania. At risk may be New England's very "sense of place," says Steven P. Hamburg, a forest ecologist at the University of Rhode Island. And since its sense of place is central to the region's important tourist trade, there might be serious economic repercussions as well.

As is already evident from the experience in Alaska, the impact of warming on forests around the world may be dramatic. According to the IPCC, the amount of warming expected over the next century would cause climatic zones in the Northern Hemisphere to shift northward by about 100 to 350 miles and upward in altitude by about 500 to 1,800 feet. This would cause a corresponding shift in the character of forest ecosystems. Some models suggest that a doubling of atmospheric carbon dioxide would expand the range of mixed, largely deciduous temperate-zone forests well into parts of Canada now covered by the evergreen boreal forest (the taiga), with the taiga taking over and almost eliminating the tundra farther north. Overall in North America, total forested land would increase. But in some places, particularly in midcontinent, grasslands and savannas would expand substantially.

The species composition of forests would change; the IPCC estimates that on a global average, one-third of the world's forests would be so affected, and that in some places entire forest types would disappear. Some high-altitude plant species—the edelweiss of the Alps is an example—might go extinct if it got too warm; there would be no place to which they could migrate.

Many scientists have feared that because the projected warming would be rapid, some natural ecosystems, including forests, might not be able to migrate fast enough and could die out. But recent studies have found that in the past, the rate of migration has been relatively rapid, too. For instance, Dorothy Peteet at Lamont-Doherty has found that the average annual temperature of the New York region jumped by 5 to 7 degrees Fahrenheit in only about fifty years as the earth was recovering from the last gasp of the last Ice Age, the Younger Dryas. In that brief period, cold-adapted tree species like birch, fir, and spruce all but disappeared from the region, while those adapted to warmer conditions, like oak and white pine, just as quickly replaced them. If the climate were now to warm further and quickly, said Peteet, "I would think the trees would do exactly what they did in the old days."

There is a big difference between then and now, however. People have so transformed the landscape that the old ecological rules may not apply as they once did. Agriculture and development have chopped natural ecosystems into disconnected fragments, which might well block the migration not only of trees but also, and especially, of the supporting cast of smaller plants, fungi, insects, and microbes, not to mention the birds, fish, reptiles, and mammals, that constitute a healthy ecosystem. Worse, some experts say, hardy weeds that thrive in disturbed ground could race northward ahead of other species as the climate warms and take over the landscape, accelerating a trend toward a simplification of natural ecosystems that is already under way. The result could be a serious degradation of biological variety and a weakening of the web of life.

Conservationists worry that nature preserves, Noah's Arks for many kinds of ecosystems, might be rendered useless and that the natural assemblages of species they are protecting may vanish, because they are locked into place and cannot move as the climate changes. On the other hand, a serious movement to restore natural landscapes has taken hold in the United States, and people might lend nature a hand by transplanting trees, flowers, and grasses to places where they could thrive better in a warming climate. And some kinds of ecosystems that are now in mortal danger, like midwestern prairies and savannas, could actually expand to more robust levels in a warmer world.

Increased carbon dioxide could foster faster growth and increased biomass of trees, shrubs, flowers, and grasses. But some experts say, as we have seen, that this might also reduce plants' nutritional value by increasing the proportion of carbon in plant tissues at the expense of nutrients. The deficiency could cascade through terrestrial ecosystems, affecting the well-being of countless plant-eating species.

Warming, said the IPCC, would foster more forest fires and pest outbreaks, such as the insect ravages already observed in Alaska's taiga. On the positive side, while forests would help counteract warming by absorbing some of the heat-trapping carbon dioxide from the atmosphere, some researchers say that this benefit could be relatively temporary, as ecosystems eventually become carbon-saturated. Moreover, large amounts of carbon could be released into the atmosphere, said the IPCC, as trees die during the transition from one type of forest to another. This would in some measure offset forests' increased uptake of atmospheric carbon dioxide. The short-term terrestrial carbon reservoir, including both vegetation and soils, is an extremely complex, constantly changing entity, the focus of an IPCC study scheduled for completion in 2000.

As THE GOOD-NEWS, bad-news aspect of global warming's impact on natural ecosystems suggests, climate change is almost bound to produce both winners and losers, gain and pain. A warmer New England's changing character, for instance, might result in economic disruptions but might also reduce the expense of heating, snow plowing, and road salting. While the midcontinent American corn belt might be hit hard by generally drier weather, the wheat-growing areas of northern North America and Russia probably would expand. Air-conditioning costs might soar in the summer across much of the country, but northern channels and ports might be ice-free longer, and permanent ice-free channels might open up in the Arctic Ocean, providing a new trade route between Europe and Asia.

American bass fishermen would be happy, because the range of that warm-water fish would expand; but those who love cold-water brown trout would have far less opportunity to pursue them, as streams warm up, eliminating habitat throughout much of the trout's range.

Globally, according to the IPCC, agricultural production could be maintained in the face of the projected warming. But the panel noted that while this assessment takes into account the beneficial effects of increased fertilization by increased atmospheric carbon dioxide, it does not account for possible increases in populations of crop-destroying pests or for the effects of extreme weather. Agriculture in some regions would be better off than in others. In North America, the shift to a new climate would require a fair measure of adaptation— replacing field crops with citrus fruits in the Southeast, for example. The farmers probably would be able to do it, but at a price. "There's no doubt we in the U.S. can adapt, but we shouldn't think those adaptations are cost-free," says Cynthia Rosenzweig, a research agronomist who works in Jim Hansen's shop and was an IPCC coauthor.

In many parts of the developing world, though, outright agricultural disaster could be lying in wait. Farmers in many of the world's poorer countries lack the expertise and resources to help them adjust. Moreover, the economies of many poor countries, especially in sub-Saharan Africa, are based on subsistence agriculture; any increase in the length or severity of droughts could push the many people already living on the brink of disaster over the edge—and their farm-dependent economies with them. The richer countries have spent billions of dollars on dams, reservoirs, pipelines, aqueducts, and irrigation systems to help them surmount dry spells. But in much of the developing world, this kind of infrastructure scarcely exists or is only now being built. "People in most developing countries really live with the climate; if the rains fail, their crops fail," says Peter H. Gleick, an expert on the subject, who is the director of the Pacific Institute for Studies in Development, an environmental research group in Oakland, California.

In the end, changes in the hydrological cycle may prove the most disruptive consequence of climate change. If rains do indeed become heavier but fewer and farther between, as predicted, both floods and droughts would afflict developing countries disproportionately more than richer ones. On the other end of the hydrologic spectrum, some regions that are now drought-prone could become even more so with global warming. Especially vulnerable are places like the American Southwest, the Middle East, and northern Africa. In the latter two regions, says Gleick, there might not be enough water both to meet everyday needs and to produce enough food as populations grow—even in the absence of climate change. Countries in those regions might have to import all or most of their food, becoming permanently dependent on the rest of the world. The atmosphere has always made some parts of the world water-rich and some water-poor. Global warming could widen these differences—or, if it should create changes in large-scale atmospheric circulation patterns, it could redistribute water resources. Indeed, in the remote past, warmer climates have sometimes brought wetter times to previously dry areas.

A CHANGING CLIMATE could have many wide-ranging and not especially obvious effects on human health. Take, for instance, the impact of heavier precipitation and flooding. If heavier rains do produce more and bigger floods, potentially fatal waterborne diseases caused by a wide array of viruses, bacteria, and parasites, like hepatitis and *E. coli* infections, could become a serious problem in the United States. Researchers are already discovering that the problem may be bigger than has been imagined. Many of the diseases are diarrheal in nature and therefore not seen as a public health threat even though they sometimes are; they do not "cause people to fall over or bleed out of the eyes or mouth," says Dennis Juranek, the associate director of the division of parasitic diseases of the federal Centers for Disease Control and Prevention. Consequently, the cause frequently goes unnoticed. "It has to be something big like Milwaukee" to attract attention, he said. The reference was to an outbreak of the *Cryptosporidium* parasite that infected 400,000 people and killed 50 to 100 in that city in 1993. Even so, he said, "we came within a hair's width" of failing to find that the oubreak was waterborne.

The fear is that heavier rainstorms and floods may increasingly overwhelm sewer systems, as was the case in Milwaukee. This tends to happen quickly, said Juranek, in the first hour or two after a storm, before people can react. By then the damage is done. As of 1998, scientists were taking the first steps in trying to pin down cause and effect, and were finding a statistically significant association between heavy rainstorms and waterborne disease. Researchers at the University of South Florida, the University of Maryland, and the National Climatic Data Center plotted more than 300 outbreaks of waterborne disease over the previous fifty years against the distribution of heavy rains. Although the study was not complete as of mid-1998, "We can demonstrate increased probability of waterborne outbreaks when there are extreme events," said Joan Rose, a microbiologist at the South Florida University.

A more obvious and more direct impact of a warmer climate on health is that of heat itself. One expert who has looked into the matter extensively is Laurence S. Kalkstein of the University of Delaware. In the 1980s he found that different cities in the United States have different thresholds at which hot weather begins to kill people. Residents of Dallas, Phoenix, and Jacksonville, for instance, are accustomed to higher temperatures than those of New York and Chicago. Kalkstein calculated the threshold at which mortality rises sharply to be 92 degrees in New York, 96 in St. Louis, and 81 in Los Angeles. Even though people in the southern tier are more used to high heat, they also have thresholds above which deaths increase; the thresholds are simply higher. Kalkstein found the threshold in Dallas, for instance, to be 103 degrees. The year 1998 offered two instances in which normally hot regions suffered from killer heat waves. In Dallas and much of the rest of Texas, more than 100 people died as a result of temperatures that exceeded 100 degrees for weeks on end. In India, the most intense heat wave in fifty years boosted temperatures above 120 degrees in some places, killing nearly 1,300 people. And a year later, there was that suffocating heat wave that brought the hottest July on record in New York and killed more than 250 people across the United States.

Not just any stretch of extremely hot weather will send the death rate soaring, Kalkstein found. It requires a special sort of extremely hot, humid, oppressive air mass that combines high moisture from the tropics with dry, torrid air borne on winds from southwestern deserts. These features distinguish the killer air masses from other types of hot weather systems. The killer systems are born in one part of the United States or another as large high-pressure domes and retain their coherence as they move slowly from region to region. Wherever they go, they bring clear skies and, most important, high nighttime heat and humidity that prevent vulnerable people, especially the young and old, from recovering from daytime heat stress. It is this lack of respite, as we have seen in the case of the 1995 Chicago heat wave, that is so lethal. Another factor in heat-related mortality, Kalkstein found, is the suddenness with which the temperature jumps above the fatal threshold. Without a sudden jump, he discovered, there is no jump in deaths.

What this suggests is that people can acclimate to hot weather when it is steady, as people who live in hot southern climates do. Will northerners so acclimate if global warming brings hotter summers? In one sense, probably yes. "If New York's climate becomes more like Jacksonville's and all the days stay about the same in the summer," said Kalkstein, "I think New Yorkers will acclimatize." The question, he said, is whether hotter short-term heat waves will be superimposed on top of a warmer summer season. In that case, he said, "we are going to get more deaths."

Another question is whether killer heat waves will become more frequent. Kalkstein found that lethal air masses do not visit any given city all that often. In St. Louis, where the phenomenon has been most extensively studied, this kind of air mass dominated summer weather only 7 percent of the time. In some years it appeared not at all. But if Tom Karl's calculations are right, the odds in favor of heat waves like the 1995 disaster in Chicago will rise as the climate warms. And Dian Gaffen's 1998 study showing an increase over the last half century in American heat waves, and especially in lethal combinations of extreme nighttime heat and humidity, suggests that such a trend already may be under way.

But won't a warmer climate also reduce cold-related deaths? The IPCC said that in the case of Europe, the net effect of a warmer climate on total deaths was unclear. In the case of America, Kalkstein believes, the increase in heat-related deaths is likely to outweigh the reduction in those related to cold. The main reason, he says, is that many cold-season deaths result from complications of diseases like the flu, which are transmitted in close indoor quarters. Global warming is not going to repeal winter, and people are going to continue to huddle indoors during cold months.

For years, a vocal group of scientists has been insisting that global warming will indirectly provoke an upsurge in diseases like malaria, cholera, and dengue fever. In theory, it seems a reasonable thing to suspect. Warmer climates do stimulate growth in populations of disease-carrying insects like mosquitoes. But things are not quite that simple, and for a long time scientists were unable to come up with much hard evidence to support these suppositions. The IPCC in 1995 said that some observed changes in disease patterns, as well as a heat wave in India that year, might plausibly have been early signals of the impact of global warming on health. But the panel said it was "not possible to attribute particular, isolated events to a change in climate or weather pattern."

Then, in 1997 and 1998, nature presented scientists with a research gift. El Niño, coming on top of a general global warming trend, boosted the earth's average temperature to levels previously unseen in the instrumental record. At the same time, El Niño brought heavy rains, droughts, and other extreme weather to many parts of the world. Here was a natural experiment that in some measure might provide a glimpse of the kinds of climatic changes that could lie ahead. So scientists zeroed in on the health effects that might be associated with El

Niño and discovered that while the evidence was circumstantial, consisting of correlations and coincidences, a fair amount of it did exist.

The World Health Organization (WHO), for instance, found that there had been "quantitative leaps" in the incidence of malaria around the world, coincident with extreme weather events associated with El Niño. Surveys by the WHO found that tens of thousands of people in Somalia and Kenya contracted another mosquito-borne disease, Rift Valley fever, after the heaviest rains in nearly forty years fell on the region. Some 200 people died, and the rains were attributed to El Niño. The incidence of cholera rose markedly in Latin America, and there, too, the jump was associated with El Niño rains and floods. In the southern Rockies, a warm, wet winter linked to El Niño produced a profusion of vegetative cover for deer mice, which transmit the deadly hantavirus to humans. The number of mice grew, and the deaths of at least three people were attributed to the disease. A killing drought in Southeast Asia, also linked to El Niño, allowed widespread forest fires to develop and produced air pollution that subjected thousands of urban dwellers to respiratory illnesses.

East Africa especially illustrated the risk to health posed by climate, argued Paul R. Epstein of the Harvard University medical school, who has long held the view that global warming will have a serious effect on health. In East Africa, he pointed out, simultaneous outbreaks of cholera, malaria, and Rift Valley fever followed El Niño's heavy rains and flooding.

But many experts urge caution. One problem "is that we may see some correlations" between climate and disease outbreaks, "but we don't know whether it's cause and effect," said Duane Gubler, director of the division of vector-borne infectious diseases at the Centers for Disease Control and Prevention. Another problem is that the spread of disease is a highly complex, often unpredictable matter that can frustrate attempts to track it even in the absence of any climatic influence.

In many ways, climatic factors do alter background conditions associated with the incidence of disease. Temperature, humidity, rainfall, and other weather factors do indeed influence the transmission of some diseases. In some cases, warmer temperatures prompt disease viruses to multiply. Heavy rain creates more places for mosquitoes to breed. Drought forces people to store water in open containers, with the same result. There is more to the story, however. Predictions that insect-borne diseases will spread from the tropics to temperate zones like the United States, for instance, overlook several facts. First, malaria, dengue fever, and yellow fever were once common in the United States. But public health practices like pest control, along with better housing and living conditions, have pretty much foreclosed large-scale epidemics. Many people predicted that a recent resurgence of dengue fever in the Caribbean and Central America might spread to the United States. But the advance of the disease appeared as of 1998 to have halted at the Rio Grande; while thousands of cases developed in Mexico, there were only a handful across the border in Texas.

Many experts on all sides of the question, including both Epstein and Gubler, agree that to the extent that climate change causes an increase in disease, the developing countries—again—are most vulnerable, since many have inadequate and in some cases almost nonexistent public health systems.

OF ALL THE POSSIBLE consequences of the expected global warming, none is so unsettling to scientists studying the subject as the possibility of unpleasant surprises. Greenhouse contrarians sometimes assert that the warming of the last century represents a natural recovery from the Little Ice Age. But what if, having come out of the Little Ice Age, for example, the world has entered one of Gerard Bond's 1,500-year cycles of natural global warmth? What would be the effect of further greenhouse warming on top of that?

Moreover, we have seen that the climate system is in many respects nonlinear; that it often changes not gradually and smoothly but abruptly, in fits and starts, responding to outside forcings (such as increasing greenhouse gases) less like the gradual turn of a volume knob than like the sudden flip of a light switch. In the case of greenhouse gas forcing of the climate system, the problem is that no one knows how far in the future some threshold might lie or when some climate trigger might be tripped. It is "like walking the plank blindfolded," says Thomas Crowley of Texas A & M. In nonlinear systems like that of climate, the possibility of surprise is enhanced. "When rapidly forced," the IPCC said in 1995, "nonlinear systems are especially subject to unexpected behavior."

If people knew what kinds of surprises lie ahead, they wouldn't be surprises. But one example of abrupt change frequently cited is the behavior of the North Atlantic oceanic currents that are the chief driver of the global conveyor belt that transports heat around the world. Wally Broecker of Lamont-Doherty has been the chief proponent of the idea that the on-again, off-again behavior of the ocean conveyor was responsible for sharp, rapid climatic changes in the past. Broecker once calculated that the currents, bigger and more forceful than a hundred Amazon rivers, deliver 30 percent as much heat to the North Atlantic region as comes from the sun. If the world warms as much as the IPCC projects, he says, it could set in motion a train of events that would weaken or halt the conveyor. Some computer modeling studies have supported this hypothesis.

How might this happen? In one possible mechanism, also supported by modeling studies, extra moisture evaporating from the oceans in a warmer atmosphere would be transported northward, where it would fall as rain and snow. This would deliver more freshwater to the North Atlantic, diluting the salt content of the conveyor where it sinks. Large volumes of surface water and heat are drawn from the tropics to replace the salty water that has sunk, thus setting the conveyor in motion. Less salt in the North Atlantic means less dense water. Less dense water fails to sink to the bottom. Since this sinking is what gives the conveyor belt its momentum—what causes it to move—less salt could weaken it or even make it stop.

One consequence of this could be to shut off the heat supply to Europe and to some extent to eastern North America. Some models suggest that the conveyor might be cut off late in the twenty-first century as a result of global warming. Broecker believes that would make Europe somewhat cooler than now while at the same time partly offsetting global warming in the rest of the world. "It's kind of ironic, but it's possible that the greenhouse warming we are likely to be producing now may lead to a warming period followed by a dramatic cold period," says Kendrick Taylor, a paleoclimatologist at the Desert Research Institute of Nevada at Reno, who has studied abrupt climate change.

It was just this sort of dramatic shift to sudden cold that characterized the Younger Dryas and touched off the chain of climatic events that led to the invention of agriculture. Broecker believes that since it probably would take a relatively large global warming to shut down the oceanic heat conveyor, the world would not get as cold as it did during the Younger Dryas. Still, the world would not necessarily be off the hook. Broecker believes, on the basis of the climate system's behavior in similar situations in the past, that it would not readjust itself smoothly to the weakening or stopping of the conveyor. It would do so, rather, in sharp, unpredictable "flickers" of change in global temperature before the system settled into a new state. He points out that in the past, as we have seen, these flickers have produced drastic temperature changes within periods as short as five years. If that happened in the next few decades, he says, it might mean disaster for world agriculture at a time when the world's population is peaking.

That is not all. If the past is any guide, the large, rapid changes in climate associated with the flickers would probably be propagated globally, by a process that is not yet understood. The abrupt climatic changes would be more widely distributed around the world and would have a bigger effect on weather than El Niño, Broecker believes. For an idea of what this might mean, think back to the havoc El Niño caused in the southern tier of the United States in 1998, with unprecedented tornadoes in Florida and floods in California. The details undoubtedly would be different in a world where the climate is shifting, flickeringly, from one state to another, but meteorological upheaval of some sort probably would result. No one can begin to say what the details of this upheaval might be: They would be a true surprise. "You could imagine a lot of things," says Broecker. "We are going into the unknown, and we probably never will be able to predict with any reliability what's going to happen."

The point is not that any of this will come about, though it might. It is that today's climate "is delicately poised with respect to the ocean circulation," in the words of Scott Lehman, a paleoclimatologist at the

University of Colorado, and that there may be a risk that human activity could destabilize the system in ways that would severely test people's ability to adapt.

"The climate system is very volatile," says Broecker. "It can do some weird things." It is, he says, "an angry beast, and we are poking it with sticks."

[17]

The Political Response

B Y THE END of the twentieth century, some 4 million years after the first known ape-people emerged from the crucible of climatic change in Africa, the bigger-brained inheritors of their genes had swelled in numbers to nearly 6 billion living individuals, loosely organized into a worldwide political and economic network of independent nation-states. The scientific and political leaders of these states had become well aware that they might now be accidentally altering the very climate system that had played a central role in the birth of their species and that serious disruptions of both human life and the natural world might result.

So it was that in the first two weeks of December 1997, in the ancient Japanese capital of Kyoto, representatives of more than 150 countries gathered for one of the most complex and difficult diplomatic negotiations ever undertaken. The objective of the delegates was to agree, for the first time, on specific, legally binding targets and timetables for reducing greenhouse gas emissions—the crux of the climate issue from a political and economic standpoint. Rarely, if ever,

had humans tried to exercise deliberate, collective foresight on an issue whose dimensions were potentially so vast yet so hazily discerned.
Kyoto in a sense was the culminating moment of an international initiative that had begun more than a decade earlier, an initiative remarkable in that it was launched not by any single country or bloc of
countries but by political and scientific organizations representing humanity at large.

The stakes were high indeed, and the ongoing political effort to deal
with the prospect of climatic change thus had proven to be one of the
most daunting of diplomatic tasks. For the simple fact was that in the
late twentieth century, the world economy ran on fossil fuels. Reducing their use would surely reverberate from one far-flung corner of
that economy to another. Just as climatic change would create both
winners and losers, so cutting greenhouse gases could make economic
winners of some countries and interest groups within countries, and
losers of others. All went to Kyoto having made their individual assessments of advantage and disadvantage. Blocs formed and re-formed.
Lobbyists abounded on all sides of the question. The atmosphere was
charged with tension and expectation. It was high politics on a global
stage, and not since Jim Hansen's testimony in 1988 pushed the climate question onto the front burner had the climate question attracted such a bright spotlight.

Insofar as people in general understood and paid attention to the
question, their attitudes appeared to bode well for greenhouse believers and ill for contrarians. Or so most public opinion polls at the time
suggested. A *Times* poll on the eve of the Kyoto talks found that only
16 percent of Americans said they believed global warming was caused
by natural climate fluctuations and only 13 percent said they thought it
would have no serious effect. Twenty-three percent said they believed
global warming was already having a serious impact, while another 43
percent said they thought its effects would be not be felt for some
time. But six of every seven people within that 43 percent said steps
were needed right away to counter global warming.

Sixty-five percent of those polled believed the United States should
take steps to cut its own emissions "regardless of what other countries
do." Only 15 percent said the United States should delay acting until

an international agreement could be put in place. The poll suggested further that most Americans thought that reducing greenhouse emissions would bring economic benefits rather than economic harm and that, in general, they strongly favored environmental protection despite its costs.

Findings like these were tempered by a subsequent study by opinion experts at Pennsylvania State University. It concluded that while "there can be little doubt that awareness of, and general concern for, global warming is almost universal," there was widespread misunderstanding of the climate question. Many people confused it with the problem of ozone depletion or viewed it, misleadingly, in terms of conventional air pollution. The study pointed out that while people can relate to weather extremes and variations in temperature and rainfall, global climate change is "far removed from direct experience." The clear implication was that most people do not see the possible connection between global warming and weather extremes. The Penn Staters found further that people tended not to see a connection between global warming and the heating and cooling of their own homes (which burn fossil fuel energy). Moreover, the researchers discovered, people generally would not accept a significant alteration of their lifestyle to attack global warming and that "in the complexities and uncertainties of daily life, global warming is far down on the list of things requiring attention." And compared with some other nations, like Canada, the European countries, and South America, the study concluded that concern in the United States was "modest to low."

The same could be said for many of America's political leaders as the international effort to take concerted action on the question of climate change was beginning in the mid-1980s. Some American politicians, including then-Senator Al Gore of Tennessee, leaped on the issue and called for national and international action to head off global warming. But the administration of President Ronald Reagan was distinctly cool to the idea, saying it was much too soon even to consider an international agreement limiting greenhouse gas emissions. The stance of the United States was and is critical, since it produces about a fifth of the world's carbon dioxide emissions and is by far the biggest emitter on the planet. Because of that, and because of its political and economic dominance, the United States is the world's 900-pound go-rilla on this issue as on so many others. In the eyes of much of the rest of the world, however, America has more often been seen, rightly or wrongly, not as a leader but as a foot-dragger and an obstacle to action.

With interest in global warming at its peak in the summer of 1988, George Bush made a campaign pledge that would come back to haunt him after he won the presidency. "Those who think we are powerless to do anything about the greenhouse effect," he said, "forget about the 'White House effect'; as President, I intend to do something about it." But less than a year into the Bush presidency, his advisors were sharply divided on the issue, and the president was under fire from en-vironmentalists and others who accused him of failing to live up to his election-year pledge. International and domestic pressures did finally force the Bush administration to add its voice to the many calls that were being made in 1989 for a multinational convention, or treaty, on climate change. Events moved quickly, and in late December 1989 the U.N. General Assembly set up a negotiating body to draft a climate convention and have it ready for signing at a world conference on the environment, the Earth Summit, scheduled for Rio de Janeiro in the summer of 1992.

As the countdown to Rio began, two factions warred within the Bush administration. One, led by John H. Sununu, the White House chief of staff and a political conservative, took a go-slow approach. Among other things, Sununu was worried about the economic conse-quences of reducing fossil fuel burning and about rushing into an agreement before all the facts were known. He also said he thought the drive to limit carbon dioxide emissions was the latest horse being ridden by advocates of "no-growth" development and economic poli-cies—anathema to a pro-growth conservative like Sununu.

The other faction, led by William K. Reilly, administrator of the En-vironmental Protection Agency, favored stronger and more forthright action. Reilly especially approved of "no-regrets" options—efforts to cut greenhouse gas emissions that would make sense in their own right even if global warming fears turned out to be unwarranted. Promoting greater efficiency in the use of energy would be one such option, for instance. In the run-up to the Rio Earth Summit, Reilly seemed to gain Bush's ear, and in that period the administration announced several dozen no-regrets actions that it was taking to promote emissions reductions. They were relatively modest energy-saving measures that would have little or no disruptive impact on people's everyday lives but that in the aggregate, it was hoped, would significantly reduce greenhouse emissions while saving money for consumers and businessess. The measures included, for instance, steps to strengthen efficiency standards for appliances; incentives for electric utilities to improve efficiency rather than build coal-fired power plants; increasing federal purchases of alternative-fuel vehicles such as those powered by natural gas; capturing methane, a powerful greenhouse gas, from landfills; planting more trees, which offset some emissions by absorbing atmospheric carbon dioxide; and establishing voluntary public-private programs to install more efficient lighting—Green Lights, the program was called.

In 1993 the newly elected Clinton-Gore administration formally adopted as official U.S. policy a goal that had until then been voluntary for the United States and other industrialized countries: reducing greenhouse gas emissions to 1990 levels by the year 2000. The administration also put forth its own action plan to achieve the goal. The plan relied mostly on a wide array of voluntary actions by business, industry, and homeowners to cut energy use. The Clinton White House, as had the Bush administration before it, said it believed stronger action, like a tax on the burning of carbon, or again raising fuel-economy standards for motor vehicles, was unnecessary.

Instead, the Clinton-Gore plan outlined some fifty measures that, taken together, provided a long and varied menu of ways to reduce energy use and, thereby, emissions. The plan also included the expenditure of nearly $800 million in federal funds, between 1994 and 2000, to stimulate some $60 billion in private investment in more energy-efficient technologies and practices. The plan looked remarkably like that adopted by the Bush administration under Reilly, but the Clinton-Gore plan (Gore was the administration's point man on global warming) expanded it and infused it with more money.

A good example of the plan's approach was the Green Lights program, which the Clinton administration continued and touted as an example of its cooperative public-private approach to emissions reduction. In that approach, government was to act as a catalyst for change and provide reliable technical expertise to private concerns. In Green Lights, the federal Environmental Protection Agency approached private companies to enlist them in an ingenious scheme to both save money and reduce emissions. An example was the American Express Company, which installed new energy-efficient lighting that saved it up to 40 percent on electricity bills at its fifty-one-story headquarters in Lower Manhattan. This simple expedient enabled American Express to cut annual carbon emissions by about 3,300 tons in New York and five other cities. By late 1995, 1,100 companies had been signed up for Green Lights. That was not all. In another type of leveraging exercised under the Clinton plan, Consolidated Edison, the utility company, provided a one-time rebate to American Express as an incentive for installing the more efficient lighting. By doing this for many customers, Con Ed hoped to reduce demand sufficiently to avoid having to build a new power plant; it would not only reduce carbon dioxide emissions, it would also save itself a big investment outlay.

Other measures on the Clinton menu, many of them patterned after the Green Lights approach, included setting higher efficiency standards for home appliances and awarding "Energy Star" labels as stamps of approval for energy-efficient office equipment and computers. Few of these measures intruded much on Americans' everyday lives and, indeed, would in the long run save them money. The administration calculated that together, its menu of no-regrets measures would cut total greenhouse gas emissions by the equivalent of nearly 440 million tons of carbon dioxide by 2000—while saving nearly $286 billion in energy costs between 1994 and 2010. The reductions, the administration figured, would be enough to bring emissions roughly back in line with the 1990 figure of about 5 billion tons. If that did not happen, said the Clinton team, stronger measures would be instituted.

It did not work. Substantial emissions reductions did take place. But energy demand created by an unexpected economic boom, coupled with soaring greenhouse gas emissions from the transportation sector, combined to ensure that total emissions continued to go up. One big reason was the surging popularity of gasoline-wasting sport utility vehicles, vans, pickup trucks, and minivans, which represented over half of the domestic passenger-car market by 1998. These light trucks were subjected to lower federal fuel-efficiency standards than the passenger cars they replaced, officially averaging only about 21 miles per gallon of gas, compared with passenger cars' fleet average of 28. In some cases, they were subject to no standards at all. In 1995, according to a calculation by the *Times*, the emissions from less than half a day's production of Ford Explorers, one of the most popular sport utility vehicles, more than canceled out all of American Express's emissions savings from Green Lights.

Motor vehicles accounted for one-third of all the carbon dioxide emitted in the United States—a big country that more than any other industrialized nation depends on cars and trucks to knit it together—and emissions from this source were growing faster than those from any other. But a combination of opposition by the auto industry and Congress, newly controlled by Republicans in 1995 after decades of Democratic dominance, frustrated any meaningful effort to control automotive emissions in the short term. Right-wing Republicans in Congress considered any action to combat global warming anathema. The leader of one key congressional committee, Dana Rohrabacher of California, scornfully characterized as "liberal claptrap" any concern about climate change.

"Nobody is under any illusions about how tough this is going to be," Gore said in 1995 of the attempt to reduce emissions over the long term. "It's at the outer boundary of what is possible in our world, but it is possible." As the evidence of climate change "inexorably accumulates," he said, "the degree of difficulty in getting support for effective responses will decline."

Clinton and Gore invested a lot of hope for the longer term in a collaboration between the administration and the auto industry to develop a family car that would travel perhaps 60 miles on a gallon of gasoline. While the effort was said by both parties to be on track as of 1998, the prototype was not due until early in the next century. Then it would still have to pass the test of the marketplace.

In the meantime, as America took two steps backward for every step forward in trying to reduce emissions, it became obvious that it would come nowhere near meeting its formal commitment to reduce emissions to 1990 levels by 2000. In fact, by the administration's own calculation as of late 1997, American emissions in 2000 would be 13 percent higher than in 1990.

CONSERVATIVE POLITICIANS and think tanks, along with lobbying groups for the fossil fuel industry and industries that use energy intensively, such as steel, automobiles, and utilities, argued that doing substantially more than America was already doing could send its economy into a tailspin. The question of how greater emissions reductions would affect the economy, however, is even more iffy than the debate over climate change itself. "There's a lot more uncertainty about the economics than about the climate," Dale W. Jorgenson, an economist at Harvard University who specializes in environmental questions, said during the run-up to Kyoto. The view of the fossil fuel industry represents one extreme of the debate. At the other extreme, environmentalists and industry advocates of alternatives to fossil fuel energy say the economy as a whole would become more robust in the long run because it would use energy more efficiently.

What is the truth?

Experts generally agree that emissions reductions would come at some cost to the economy, with the impact depending on the size and speed of the cuts. Energy costs probably would rise after mandatory caps on emissions took effect, and some industry sectors—coal, in particular—could be hit hard if they did not adapt quickly enough. Many experts also say, however, that the costs could be reduced substantially. One way is to reduce emissions by imposing a tax on fuels in proportion to their carbon content. The proceeds of the tax would be used to reduce other federal taxes, therefore offsetting the new bite on taxpayers and putting money back into the economy. A number of economists in the late 1990s saw this as the best way to proceed. But in the America of that time, a carbon tax would never have flown politically. So administration officials and supporting economists looked toward other cost-cutting strategies.

Foremost among these was the concept of what was called emissions trading. Widely favored among economists, it called for the government to set an overall cap on emissions. Individual companies would be issued permits allowing them to emit carbon dioxide and other greenhouse gases up to the limits of the cap. Companies could meet their targets in one of two ways. One way would be to reduce emissions outright, through technological means. Another would be for a company to purchase a permit to emit more than its allotment from another company that has reduced its emissions more than required. The money to be made from the sale of permits would act as an incentive for companies to be superefficient. The price of the emissions permit is set in the open market, like that of any commodity. This concept has in fact been tested in practice in the United States, where companies trade in permits to emit sulfur dioxide, an industrial pollutant. Advocates of the approach say it reduced sulfur dioxide by greater amounts than expected, and at lower cost, and that overall, it was much less costly than if the government had simply mandated reductions by way of traditional "command-and-control" regulations.

Another way to reduce costs, argued some economists, was to allow some flexibility in the timing of emissions reductions—that is, allow industries to wait until normal investment cycles play out before replacing old factory and transportation equipment with new equipment that is more energy efficient or that does not use fossil fuels. The IPCC in 1995 said there would be at least two replacement cycles over the next century and that each would offer the opportunity to adopt not only more energy-efficient technologies and practices but also non–fossil fuels like solar and wind power, electric and hydrogen-powered vehicles, fuels made from wood or grain, and, if safety concerns could be met, nuclear power. Even in the absence of exotic new power sources, many experts said, costs could be cut if government acted aggressively to stimulate the adoption of more mundane and conventional fuel-efficient technologies. Many such technologies exist, ranging from small things like devices that automatically shut off power to appliances when they are not in use, to big things like automobiles that deliver 60 or 70 miles to a gallon of gasoline, to more efficient ways of burning coal.

In 1997 a study by five of the U.S. government's national laboratories found that by vigorously promoting such technologies, carbon dioxide emissions could be reduced to 1990 levels by 2010 while saving enough energy to at least offset the cost of adopting the technologies. A number of other studies had come to similar conclusions, and some even found that the resulting efficiencies would boost economic growth nationally by 1 to 2 percent a year over the long run.

"Bottom-up" studies like the five-lab study, which try to add up the expected impact on the economy from the introduction of new technologies, probably overstate the potential energy savings, according to a 1997 assessment by Robert Repetto and Duncan Austin of the World Resources Institute, an independent research group in Washington. On the other hand, they also found that some "top-down" studies using computer models—which analyze the economy's overall performance and are favored by opponents of mandatory action to reduce emissions—tend to overstate the costs of reducing emissions. Typically, the top-down studies showed that reducing emissions to 1990 levels by 2010 would cut economic growth by 1 or 2 percent. Some predicted much greater losses.

Repetto and Austin found that estimates of the impact of reductions varied so widely because there was such a wide array of assumptions about economic uncertainties. For instance, the estimate turns out more optimistically if one assumes that the economy responds easily to changes in government policy, that non-carbon fuels are available and readily adopted, and that damages from air pollution and climate change are averted as a result. Opposite assumptions give a more pessimistic answer.

Studies that predict serious harm to the economy from a carbon tax or an emissions trading scheme are unrealistic, Repetto and Austin concluded, since they stem from worst-case assumptions.

Still harder than calculating the cost of reducing emissions is putting a dollar value on the benefits of avoiding damage from climate change—and on the benefits of global warming's positive aspects. Many experts say it is impossible. Harder still is trying to calculate really long-term costs and benefits out to like, say, 300 years. In these rarefied realms of analysis, uncertainties make economic calculation essentially meaningless. For instance, there is no way to know how much economic growth will take place in future decades or to predict the technological and energy profile of the world a century or two hence.

Even for the shorter term, the next two or three decades, many experts throw up their hands over the difficulty of gauging the economics of climate change. "If anybody tells you that he or she has the definitive answer as to the costs and benefits of particular climate change policies, I would suggest that you raise your collective eyebrows," Janet L. Yellen, the head of President Clinton's Council of Economic Advisers, told Congress in July 1997.

As the Clinton administration tried to decide what to settle for in Kyoto, the debate within the White House was all about economics. Clinton by then had become a believer on the greenhouse question itself, saying he found the mainstream science "pretty compelling." By Clinton's account, it was Gore who made him a believer. At first, the president told a White House conference in 1997, he was only "convinced that he [Gore] was convinced" on the question. But in time, the president said, he became convinced, as well. Clinton's conversion set up a tug-of-war within the administration, with Gore and his allies urging strong action both domestically and in Kyoto, while Clinton's economic advisors insisted on going more slowly.

As the Kyoto meeting approached, Clinton pledged that the United States would take stronger action to reduce emissions on its own, regardless of the outcome in Japan. The White House announced that it would ask Congress to spend $6 billion over the next decade to stimulate the development and spread of climate-friendly technologies and fuels and to provide incentives for industries and individuals to adopt them. After about a decade of experience with that, according to the plan, firm caps would be set on U.S. greenhouse gas emissions and an emissions-trading scheme would go into effect to achieve the reductions at least cost. The actual reduction targets would be whatever ones were agreed to in Kyoto, and the United States hoped that its decade-long timetable for achieving the cuts would be accepted there.

What would this mean for U.S. consumers? For about a decade, little or no action would be required of them. The incentives would be designed to encourage them to adopt more energy-efficient appliances, heating-cooling systems, and motor vehicles, and to encourage producers to make them available. Any rise in energy costs as a result of the new policy would await the imposition of the emissions caps around 2010. It would remain to be seen how much these costs could be reduced by emissions trading and how much they could be offset further by the decade's hoped-for gains in energy efficiency.

THE FIRST STEPS toward Kyoto were taken in 1985, when the United Nations Environment Program and the World Meteorological Organization, another U.N. agency, joined with The International Council of Scientific Unions to organize a twenty-nine-nation scientific conference in Villach, Austria. The conferees reached a quick consensus that research on climate change was not enough; now attention should turn toward economic and social policies to deal with it. Three years later, at the height of attention to global warming, government officials, scientists, and environmentalists from forty-eight countries met in Toronto and called for international action to achieve a 20 percent reduction in the use of fossil fuels by the year 2005 and, ultimately, a reduction of 50 percent.

The model for an international agreement, in many eyes, was an accord forged at Montreal in 1987 by forty countries, including the United States, placing specific limits on the production of synthetic chemicals that were said to be destroying the earth's protective ozone layer. Industry acceded to the agreement willingly, as Du Pont, the biggest producer, unilaterally stopped making the chemicals before the protocol required it.

But it was clear to everyone at the time that achieving a similar agreement on climate change would be far more difficult. While it was one thing to regulate a few chemicals made by a handful of companies, and for which there were relatively easy substitutes, it was quite another to reduce the use of fuels on which the entire world depended for heat, transportation, electrical power, and the general functioning of the economy. Nevertheless, the effort to negotiate a climate convention was launched.

In five formal negotiating sessions between February 1991 and May

1992, the European Community (later the fifteen-nation European Union) led the charge for the adoption of specific targets and time-tables for cutting greenhouse gas emissions. It was supported by the small island states and Japan. As the talks ripened, the Europeans pressed for the world's rich, developed, industrialized countries to commit themselves—on a legally binding basis—to stabilizing emissions at 1990 levels by 2000. The Bush administration opposed any targets and timetables, even while arguing that actions it was already taking would enable it to meet the Europeans' proposed standard. It favored a voluntary target.

A second major point of contention was the role of the world's poorer countries, many of which were just beginning to industrialize and emit increasing quantities of greenhouse gases. Organized as a formal caucus called the Group of 77, or G-77 (although it had more than 130 members), the developing countries were adamant from the start: Since the rich countries had gotten rich by burning fossil fuels and were therefore responsible for most of whatever global warming was in the cards so far, they should take the lead in controlling greenhouse emissions.

In making this demand, the G-77 occupied the moral high ground, arguing that the rich countries' emissions were a result of wasteful overconsumption, while for the poorer nations, it was a question of economic survival: Cheap fossil fuels were, at least for now, the only way they could generate the economic growth to provide their people with the bare essentials of life. Furthermore, the G-77 argued, if the rich countries expected the poor ones to adopt new greenhouse-friendly energy technologies, the rich countries must pay for them. These were powerful appeals, not only on grounds of basic fairness but also because the world's two most populous nations, China and India, with more than a quarter of the earth's people between them, put their weight solidly behind the position.

The G-77 was not monolithic, however. The small island states, for instance, were becoming the real hawks on global warming by pressing their case for strong, quick action to reduce emissions. At the other end of the spectrum, the oil-producing countries, led in this debate by Saudi Arabia and Kuwait, felt threatened by any attempt to reduce the use of petroleum and often dug in their heels or used delaying tactics. Early on, lobbyists for the fossil fuel industry linked up with the oil countries as allies.

So the lines were drawn. These basic blocs, and their basic stances on whether to go fast or to act with caution, would remain in place and control the international political debate on climate for most of the next decade.

In May 1992, in a final two-week negotiating round at U.N. headquarters in New York leading to the Rio summit, this interplay of political forces produced a treaty whose "ultimate objective" was to stabilize greenhouse gas concentrations in the atmosphere "at a level that would prevent dangerous anthropogenic [human-caused] interference with the climate system." All countries signing the convention would be legally obligated to take steps to rein in their emissions and would have to report periodically on their progress to the other signatories—in effect, submitting to peer pressure as a way of enforcing compliance.

The convention expressly embodied the idea that developed countries must take the lead. The Bush administration got its way, however, by insisting successfully on only a voluntary target for industrialized countries of stabilizing emissions at 1990 levels by 2000. In 1993, as we have seen, Bill Clinton made that a formal, binding target for the United States. While poorer countries acceded to the same general obligation to control emissions as the rich ones, they would be subject to no specific goals for the time being. The rich nations also agreed to provide new financial aid to developing countries to enable them to adopt greenhouse-friendly energy technologies.

While the compromise agreement fully satisfied no one, it did set in motion an international process for grappling with the question of climate change. By 1999, 176 countries including the United States had ratified the convention. But it did not take that long to demonstrate that if the nations of the world really were serious about reducing greenhouse emissions, the action taken so far was not going to get the job done.

❖   ❖   ❖

WE HAVE SEEN THAT the United States was a long way from meeting the Clinton administration's emissions reduction goal as it headed into the last half of the 1990s. As a group, the other industrialized countries were not doing much better. As of 1995 the Netherlands and Switzerland said they expected their emissions in 2000 to be lower than in 1990. But Britain and Germany were the only big Western countries able to say the same, and in each case there were special one-time circumstances: Britain had decided for reasons other than climate to phase out its coal industry and switch to natural gas, and after the 1990 reunification of East and West Germany, the East's bankrupt factories and power plants were demolished. With them went some of the highest emission rates in the world. The former Soviet Union's emissions also plunged when its economy plummeted after it broke up. But most of the industrialized world was having about as much trouble as the Americans in meeting the goals of the 1992 convention. And across Europe, an intensifying love affair with the automobile was making further gains problematical.

In the developing countries, fossil fuel use continued to surge. As of 1995, it appeared that China's reliance on its huge coal reserves would make it the single largest emitter of carbon dioxide by the third or fourth decade of the twenty-first century. As the rest of the developing world also industrialized, it was widely expected that the poorer countries would be outstripping the richer ones as emitters of greenhouse gases by the middle of that century.

Against this harsh prospect, the IPCC had warned in the fall of 1994 that even if worldwide emissions of carbon dioxide were capped at current levels, atmospheric concentrations would continue to increase for at least two centuries. Even if emissions were stablized at 1990 levels by 2000, it said in a special report, overall concentrations would still approach a doubling of the preindustrial level by 2100. The reason was that too much of the gas was already being spewed into the air to be reabsorbed quickly by the oceans and biosphere.

Clearly, the newly constituted conference of the parties to the Climate Convention concluded, further action was necessary. At their first meeting, in Berlin in April 1995, the parties set in motion a process to negotiate further cuts in the early twenty-first century by the rich countries, with a deadline of the end of 1997 for completing the talks.

The IPCC's second assessment report later in 1995 infused the debate with new vigor. There was, most important, the landmark finding of a "discernible human influence" on climate. Two other parts of the report concluded that it was better to take action sooner rather than later. It was true, the IPCC said, that putting off action might allow future technological advances to lower the cost of emissions reduction. But the panel also concluded that delaying too long would push too much of the burden onto future generations and mean that deeper emissions cuts would have to be made in the end. On top of that, a delay in action could increase the damage from climate change and boost the cost of adapting to it.

No great technological breakthroughs or big changes in lifestyle would be required to achieve substantial reductions in emissions, the panel found. It said that existing technology could achieve energy savings of about 25 percent in homes, businesses, and industrial plants over the next three decades and that the resulting reductions in greenhouse gas emissions could be even bigger. Energy use by motor vehicles could be cut by about a third over the same period by using more efficient drive trains, lightweight materials, and designs less resistant to air, the panel said.

All that was needed, the IPCC said, was for strong governmental policies to promote aggressive exploitation of existing energy-saving technologies.

THE HOME STRETCH to Kyoto began in the summer of 1997 as negotiators met in Bonn, Germany, the new home of the Climate Convention secretariat, to narrow the issues and thrash out many technical details. The crux of the negotiators' task, both in Bonn and Kyoto, was to determine the magnitude and timing of cuts in greenhouse gas emissions. One could not simply pick numbers out of the air, because every possible choice would have different economic and climatic consequences. Yet the uncertainties of economics and climate posed a quandary: If global warming turns out to be at the low end of the range projected by the IPCC and cuts in greenhouse emissions are too steep, requiring premature replacement of energy equipment, it will be too costly to the global economy. But if the warming is on the high end and the cuts are too small and too late, climatic damage will be more serious and it will still be too costly.

Even more frustrating, the effects of any level of cuts would not be apparent for many years, and it would be hard if not impossible to tell before then whether the right thing was done and, therefore, whether further action was needed. And if the cuts did succeed in reducing global warming, no one would ever know for sure how serious the warming would have been in their absence. Again, there would be no way to judge whether the level of cuts was appropriate.

"That is what's so difficult about this cockamamie problem," said Michael Schlesinger of the University of Illinois, who had long studied the issue.

Nevertheless, a raft of proposals surfaced. The two that realistically set the terms of the debate were those of the European Union and the Clinton administration. The Europeans called for cuts in the emissions of the greenhouse gases carbon dioxide, methane, and nitrous oxide of 7.5 percent by 2005 and 15 percent by 2010. The United States called for the rich countries to stabilize their emissions of those three gases, plus three others,* at 1990 levels by about 2010—in line with its domestic plan. The White House maintained that its proposal would reduce America's total greenhouse emissions by 30 percent from what they would otherwise be in 2010.

Reaching an agreement on emissions targets and timetables for rich countries was going to be difficult enough. But the issue most likely to torpedo the chances of a successful outcome in Kyoto was the perennial one of the developing countries' role. The U.S. Senate elevated the question to the status of potential deal-breaker. Under the U.S.

* The other three gases, which have a small impact on climate compared with carbon dioxide, are hydrofluorocarbons, perfluorocarbons, and sulfur hexachloride, all of which are produced by a variety of industrial processes for a variety of uses.

Constitution, the Senate would have to approve any Kyoto agreement by a two-thirds vote. If it did not, U.S. participation in the agreement would be barred. That would effectively sink the agreement, both technically (since the United States was the world's biggest emitter) and politically (since the ratification formula for putting the agreement into effect necessarily required U.S. approval).

But in late July 1997, the Senate adopted a nonbinding joint resolution saying that no agreement would be acceptable unless it both included developing countries and did no economic damage to the United States. Supporters of the resolution argued that failure to require any specific emissions-control action by developing countries would give them a competitive economic advantage over the United States. The resolution, sponsored by Democratic Senator Robert C. Byrd of West Virginia, a Senate heavyweight, and Republican Senator Chuck Hagel of Nebraska, a relative newcomer, passed by a vote of 95 to 0. One factor in securing the overwhelming vote might have been Senator Byrd's express endorsement of the mainstream scientific view on global warming. The Senate's insistence on commitments by developing countries ran directly counter to the Climate Convention's requirement that rich countries go first, even though the Senate five years earlier had ratified that requirement and it still remained in effect. To override that approval, the Senate would have to formally revoke ratification of the convention, an unlikely step.

At Kyoto, the developing countries held firm and refused even to discuss taking on specific commitments. To bolster their case, they could now point to a study by the World Resources Institute (WRI), which showed that many key developing countries had cut or eliminated energy subsidies and so were emitting less carbon dioxide than they otherwise would have. The changes were made for economic rather than environmental reasons, but the effect on emissions was the same. "It appears that developing countries are already doing a great deal to limit emissions—a fact largely overlooked in the current debate," said the WRI report.

Despite the impasse over the developing countries' role, the Kyoto delegates forged ahead. Little happened until higher-level ministers arrived for the last three days of the talks, and at the end it was sealed only at the highest levels of key governments, especially that of the United States. Bill Clinton and Al Gore broke the logjam. Gore had a strong personal incentive to see the Kyoto talks succeed. As the front-runner for the Democratic presidential nomination for the 2000 election, he would not look good if the Kyoto talks failed. He flew into Kyoto on Monday, December 8, as the talks entered their crucial last three days, and immediately told the American delegation, in his words, "to show increased negotiating flexibility." He also held out an olive branch to the developing countries: "We understand," he said, "that your first priority is to lift your citizens from the poverty so many endure and build strong economies. . . ."

For three grueling days and nights, and continuing well past a midnight completion deadline on December 10, the key parties slowly hammered out an agreement. Sleeping bodies were everywhere: draped over couches, propped against walls, sitting up at tables in the Kyoto International Convention Center. In those wee hours, China, India, and a handful of other developing countries threatened to torpedo the nearly complete accord over two issues: emissions trading and a proposal by a group of industrialized countries, including the United States, to allow developing countries to adopt binding emissions limitations voluntarily. China and India feared that trading would make it too easy for rich countries to avoid cutting their domestic emissions by, in effect, buying their way out. The United States was adamant that trading was necessary for it to contain the cost of emissions reduction and said it would sign no agreement that did not contain the mechanism.

In the end, as sunrise approached and the question was debated openly by the full group of 150 countries, Chairman Raul Estrada Oyuela of Argentina pulled key players aside, near the podium, and fashioned a compromise: Trading would be allowed, but only as a supplement to domestic emissions reductions, and negotiations on the specific rules of trading would be postponed. And there would be no provision on voluntary reductions by developing countries.

So it was done. The Kyoto Protocol, as it was now known, called for the rich countries collectively to cut all six greenhouse gases by an annual average of about 5 percent below 1990 levels for the period 2008 through 2012. Some were to cut more than that, some less, and the emissions of a few were allowed to grow because of special circumstances. Among the industrialized big three, the United States was to reduce emissions by 7 percent below 1990 levels; the fifteen-nation European Union, by 8 percent; and Japan, by 6 percent. The agreement also provided for emissions trading, both within and between nations.

And, in a step designed to speed emissions reductions in developing countries, the protocol established an international fund through which rich countries could gain emissions-reduction credit by investing in specific emissions-saving projects—more efficient power plants, for instance—in developing countries. If such arrangements became widespread, proponents of the fund hoped, it might help developing countries leapfrog the wasteful, heavy-carbon era of economic development and go directly to more greenhouse-friendly sources of energy.

The protocol permitted the Clinton administration to put in place its domestic plan that postponed U.S. emissions caps for a decade while providing financial incentives for consumers and businesses to adopt more energy-efficient technologies in the meantime. This would mean a relatively painless decade for consumers and even make it possible to save money through energy conservation. But environmentalists and others were concerned that a sudden imposition of emissions caps around 2010 might deliver an economic shock. They also worried that the protocol would allow the United States to avoid this shock—but also to avoid significant emissions cuts—by purchasing emission rights from other countries. Russia, for example, would have many to sell because economic weakness had pushed its emissions well below its cap.

Still, environmentalists hailed the Kyoto Protocol as a historic landmark, while the fossil fuel industry predicted economic disaster. But everyone knew that even though it was designed only as a first step, the prospects that it would ever go into effect were chancy.

[18]

Horizons

I MAGINE CHICAGO in 2100, given two different versions of the climatic future. In one version, the world has continued its reliance on fossil fuels for another century, and the climate has changed essentially as the IPCC now predicts. Chicagoans are putting their snow blowers away and hauling out their lawn mowers a month or so earlier than now. Winter is not as cold as it once was, especially early and late in the season. But it still comes, bringing midwinter snowfalls heavier than the oldest old-timers remember. Fed by a wetter atmosphere, the snowstorms bring the city to its knees for days at a time. Summers are 5 to 10 degrees hotter and more humid, as well. Every four years or so, on average, the citizens endure a killer heat wave like that of 1995. People with air-conditioning flee indoors, and their electricity bills soar. Those without are still trapped in ovenlike houses and apartments, and many die. Much more often than now, people are forced from their homes as heavy cloudbursts turn parts of the city into canals. Water supplies are contaminated, and even though many people boil their water, gastrointestinal disease spreads. At other times, the region bakes in droughts of unprecedented length and severity. The lush, flowered tapestry of tallgrass prairie that once was the region's ecological glory has expanded, but periodic drought turns the prairie brown, along with the rich farms of the Chicago hinterland.

In the other version, the world has greatly reduced or given up its dependence on fossil fuels. High-mileage automobiles powered by fuel cells or batteries or hydrogen crowd the Loop and the lakeshore. Natural gas, with its lower carbon content, has replaced coal and oil as a more climate-friendly fuel of choice for power generation—or may already have been supplanted itself by some non-carbon energy source like fusion power. To the degree that fossil fuels are still burned, energy-efficient industrial plants and appliances have long since cut fuel use. The net effect of all this is that atmospheric concentrations of carbon dioxide have been stabilized.

But Chicago's climate has changed anyway. While the changes are not as severe as in the first scenario, they are in the same direction and they still require the city and its people to adjust and adapt. The reason is that even if all greenhouse gas emissions stopped today, there would still be warming to come: The decades-long lag between emission of the gases and their effect on the atmosphere has not yet been fully played out. Moreover, it seems unlikely at best that atmospheric concentrations of greenhouse gases are going to stop building up anytime soon.

The two scenarios are, of course, highly speculative, given what we know about the difficulty, even the impossibility, of predicting changes in both climate and future emissions levels, and the actual details are bound to be different. But many experts believe that whatever combination of climatic changes may lie in store, change there is bound be. The global economy cannot turn on a dime. In an image that gained much currency in the late 1990s, turning the economy and its energy system to a new course is like turning a supertanker; it goes slowly.

Indeed, perhaps the main lesson to be drawn from the first decade of humankind's attempt to gain some measure of control over greenhouse gas emissions is how difficult that task is. The human economic and political system (if it can be called that), with its innumerable cross-cutting and competing interests, may be as complex as the climate system itself, if not more so, and as subject to inertia. Enormous effort, and no small measure of ingenuity, intelligence, and diplomatic skill went into fashioning first the framework Climate Convention and then the Kyoto Protocol. The world's first attempt to achieve emissions cuts through voluntary means, in 1992, nevertheless clearly failed. And as of 1999 there was serious doubt that the Kyoto Protocol would go into effect in time to achieve the targets and timetables it specified, if at all.

The protocol may have had some impact in the first year after its adoption. Industry, for instance, may have gotten a message that the world was serious about global warming and that the issue was not going to go away. A number of American industries that had adamantly opposed any mandatory action in Kyoto were singing a different tune afterward; while they still didn't like the protocol, they were taking a proactive stance in trying to do the most they could to reduce emissions. The protocol itself, however, was languishing in the Senate, which had not given up its insistence that developing countries take on specific emissions reduction commitments. While the Clinton White House signed the protocol in November 1998, it had yet to submit it to the Republican-controlled Senate for approval as of mid-1999. Meanwhile, hard-liners in the G-77, particularly China and India, continued their refusal to take on new commitments. Talks at the international level on the rules for putting the protocol into effect, such as those governing emissions trading, were dragging on.

Even if the protocol were to enter into effect immediately, the cuts it mandated would fall far short of stabilizing atmospheric concentrations of greenhouse gases—as had been clear for a long time. The Kyoto cuts would only slow down the rate of increase in overall atmospheric concentrations of greenhouse gases. Further cuts would be required if concentrations were to be stabilized.

Consequently, many experts were coming to believe that political and economic inertia would make it impossible to avoid a doubling or near doubling of preindustrial greenhouse gas concentrations some time in the latter part of the twenty-first century. Tom Wigley calculated in mid-1999, based on a new series of IPCC emissions scenarios generated for the panel's 2001 climate assessment, that carbon dioxide concentrations in 2100 would range between 558 and 825 parts per million. A doubling of preindustrial concentrations would place the level at 560 parts per million. Phil Jones, Wigley's longtime former colleague at East Anglia, believes that number will be substantially surpassed. "I think we're going to be somewhere near 700 or 750 parts per million by the end of the [twenty-first] century," he said. The implications of these estimates are sobering indeed. Assuming that the IPCC's new emissions scenarios are reasonably accurate, it would mean that a substantial measure of climate change is unavoidable. As the American Geophysical Union said in an official policy statement in 1999, there is "no known geologic precedent" for the conversion of carbon from underground into atmospheric carbon dioxide, in the amounts now being burned as fossil fuels, without changing the climate.

Wigley calculated on the basis of the new IPCC scenarios that the average global surface temperature would rise by 2 to 7 degrees Fahrenheit by 2100, with a best estimate of about 3.5 to 5 degrees, and that the rate of future warming would be noticeably higher in the United States. His global projection is slightly more than that of the IPCC in 1995. The reason is that sulfate aerosol emissions are expected to decline over the next century, lessening their cooling effect. Jones pegs the global rise a bit higher, at about 5 to 7 degrees Fahrenheit—by far the warmest climate in several million years, and about the same magnitude as the difference between the temperature now and that in the depths of the last Ice Age.

If a doubling or more of carbon dioxide concentrations is indeed unavoidable, many experts were saying in the late 1990s, more attention should be paid to adapting to the resulting changes in climate. In the late 1980s, there was a fair amount of talk and analysis on the adaptation front. But as the international negotiating process gathered steam, reducing emissions and preventing climate change eclipsed adaptation in the global warming debate. Attention returned to adaptation as the new century approached, although in most cases hard planning was yet to be done.

One reason was the uncertain impact of future climatic change. How can one plan to deal with a contingency whose details and dimensions are so unclear? "How can we make decisions now when we don't have the ability to predict exactly what will happen?" says Philip

Weech, the Bahamas hydrologist. The main thing he and his Caribbean friends have been able to do so far is to improve their monitoring of sea level. In many respects, people do not deal well even now with familiar weather-related disasters like floods and droughts. What will happen if both become more extreme, as mainstream science predicts? Of special concern are the developing nations. As we have seen, in many ways they are the most vulnerable to climate change. Countries like Bangladesh, Egypt, and China do not have the resources to protect their coastlines, even if they knew exactly what to plan for.

It seems unlikely that the best adaptation strategies will enable humanity to entirely cushion all the projected shocks, even if the climatic changes stemming from global warming turn out to be gradual and linear. As we have seen, however, there might be some nasty surprises. What if the changes turn out to be nonlinear, with the climate system jumping suddenly to a new state, as has happened in the past? How might global warming exacerbate the once-or-twice-a-century droughts of Dust Bowl magnitude that may come again through natural causes? What if global warming shuts off Wally Broecker's ocean conveyor belt and causes flurries of abrupt climatic changes that reverberate through the entire global climate system? What if Chicago, for instance, has to cope with drastic flickers in climate every decade or so? What other possible surprises might lie in wait? If anything has come clear in this word journey through the long history of people and climate, it is that humans are a resilient and adaptable species in the face of the elements. Adapt they will, one way or another. The issue is what the cost will be in pain and pleasure, and on the other side of the ledger, what benefits and opportunities climate change may bring.

If a doubling of atmospheric carbon dioxide is indeed inevitable, the story does not necessarily end there. There is no guarantee that the rise will stop once a doubling has been reached; that is only an arbitrary reference point, picked by scientists as a standard benchmark for analysis. The amount of carbon dioxide spewed into the atmosphere by human activity could conceivably reach three or four times the preindustrial figure, or more. That would surely bring true catastrophe for humans and much of the natural world.

In theory, according to modeling studies by James Kasting at Penn State, there is enough carbon buried underground in the form of fossil fuels—some 5 trillion tons—to raise peak concentrations of carbon dioxide to 1,100 or 1,200 parts per million if the whole reservoir were burned. This is roughly four times the preindustrial concentration. If different assumptions about the ability of the ocean and biosphere to absorb carbon dioxide are used, the eventual concentration could be twice that again, or eight times the preindustrial level. At present rates of fossil fuel burning, Kasting calculated, it would take 800 years to burn up the entire reservoir. This would raise the temperature of the earth to that of the mid-Cretaceous hothouse. Furthermore, enough carbon dioxide would persist in the atmosphere so that it would take a million years or so for concentrations to get back down to about where they are today. The reason, says Kasting, is that the ocean's ability to absorb carbon dioxide diminishes exponentially as more is absorbed. If all the fossil fuels were burned, the absorption ability would be overwhelmed. It is limited to begin with by the amount of carbonate and borate ions (electrically charged atoms) in the ocean waters, and there are only enough in the surface waters to take up about a third of the total fossil fuel inventory. Additional absorptive chemicals lie on the ocean's bottom, but it takes hundreds of thousands of years for carbon from the surface to reach them.

That being so, Kasting calculates, burning the whole fossil fuel inventory would cancel the parade of periodic ice ages for about the next million years. Some greenhouse contrarians say that would be all to the good. But the price would be steep: All the world's ice probably would melt, raising sea level to such heights that most of today's coastlines and coastal cities, where half of humanity presently lives, would be under water. The tropics probably would become uninhabitable—just as northern climes will become uninhabitable if the ice ages proceed naturally.

Until recently, experts generally thought that our interglacial period, the Holocene, was nearing its end and that the long, irregular descent into a new ice age could begin at any time, certainly within the next 1,000 to 2,000 years. Now that view has changed, and many scientists believe that the Holocene could last for another 10,000 to 20,000 years. The estimate is based on recent studies of ocean foraminifera, which show that the last warm period before the Holocene, the Eemian, lasted about 20,000 years and that an earlier warm period, about 400,000 years ago, was some 30,000 years long, maybe longer. This latter interglacial is now coming to be viewed as the better predictor for the length of the Holocene. The reason is that the combination of variations in the earth's wobble, tilt, and orbit is quite similar now to what it was then. As we have seen, those variations are thought to be the pacemaker of the ice ages. If the Holocene does last another 10,000 or 20,000 years, it means that if all the fossil fuels were burned, the peak of the human-induced global warming would come well before the next Ice Age; the earth would be in a sort of super-interglacial for several millennia.

Eventually, the present ice age rhythm will be superseded no matter what. The plates of the earth's crust and their landmasses continue to move toward or away from each other, and over tens and hundreds of millions of years they will evolve into new continental configurations. The earth's climatic regime will surely undergo drastic modifications as a result. That, too, will someday be moot: In the very long term, about a billion years from now according to astronomers' calculations, the sun will expand and turn the earth into a cinder. For humans, of course, such horizons are so far away as to be meaningless. But they do suggest how changeable the planet is, and how, despite our technological prowess, we are all at the mercy of the physical system called earth.

For our geological era, the first one in which fossil fuel burning by humans might substantially change the earth's climate, Kasting's estimates may mark the theoretical outer limits of the greenhouse effect. But it seems unlikely that humanity would burn up the entire fossil fuel reservoir. It is, as Wally Broecker has put it, "hard to believe we'd ever be that stupid." Might people someday manipulate the earth's climate on a large scale—by deliberately regulating the amount of atmospheric carbon dioxide, for instance—so as to frustrate the ice ages while avoiding a catastrophic warming? "Much as I dislike it," says Broecker, "you can see that the temptation is going to be very high" to manipulate the climate, "and the capability to do it will become very high, and so whether we'll resist, I don't know."

A number of last-ditch measures have been proposed should climatic catastrophe be clearly imminent or actually materializing. They involve counterbalancing climatic change through what is called "geoengineering." One such measure is the addition of iron to the oceans, which would spur the growth of the tiny marine plants called phytoplankton, which in turn would remove carbon dioxide from the air and help the planet cool off. At least one preliminary experiment has been carried out. Scientists added 990 pounds of iron to a twenty-eight-square-mile patch of the Pacific near the Galápagos, and the proliferation of plankton turned the sea from blue to green. But at best, even proponents of this approach say, its potential is modest; while it might help, it would not solve the problem.

Other possible geoengineering measures include reducing incoming solar radiation by, for example, purposely injecting reflective aerosols into the atmosphere or using large orbiting mirrors to reflect sunlight away from the planet. There are almost as many uncertainties surrounding these options as surround unintentional climate change, however, and the side effects are unknown. Geoengineering also would be expensive, and the IPCC noted in 1995 that the same money could be used to develop renewable energy sources. The panel also noted that geoengineering would have to remain in place for decades to centuries. Undertaking such measures only to halt them prematurely could deliver what the IPCC called a "climatic shock" of sudden greenhouse warming. So if geoengineering were to be employed, said the panel, it could become "a new, formidable, and quite possibly very costly societal responsibility." Geoengineering, it would appear, is a solution of last resort.

While such far-out calculations go on, the world may already be on the path toward a permanent decarbonization of energy production, quite apart from political efforts to control fossil fuel burning under the Climate Convention. "The decarbonization of the energy system is the single most important fact to emerge from the last twenty years of analysis" of the system, says Jesse H. Ausubel, an expert on energy and climate at Rockefeller University in New York. That is, he explains, energy production has been steadily moving from "heavy" high-carbon fuels to "lighter" ones with less carbon. Coal, the heaviest and most carbon-rich aside from wood and hay (which are almost pure carbon), was king for a long time. But over the twentieth century, it has given way increasingly to oil, which emits less carbon when burned, and then to methane, or natural gas, which emits less still. The coal industry is already essentially dead in Germany, Britain, and a number of other countries, Ausubel says, leaving the United States and China as the two biggest coal-burners on earth. Yet even in China, he says, coal production has been dropping lately. One reason is that to build an economy on coal requires building either a big railroad network to transport it or building power plants right at the mine mouth. Both are hugely expensive propositions.

In the decades just ahead, Ausubel believes, natural gas will prove the way to go. "We're entering the methane age," he says. "Gas is beautiful. Gas is plentiful. Gas is easy to transport. It has roughly half the carbon of coal. Over the next forty to fifty years, methane will be the leading and dominant fuel. After that we will be in a non-carbon economy." Nuclear power will play a role if the problem of waste disposal can be solved, he believes. Since the Chernobyl disaster in 1986, he calculates, 400 reactors in the world have run for the equivalent of about 5,000 years without a single accident. Hydroelectric power will play its part, he says, as will solar energy. But for the long haul, Ausubel nominates hydrogen as the fuel of choice. Environmentally clean, it emits no heat-trapping gases.

"Rapid evolution" along the current trajectory can take the world a long way toward a non-carbon economy, Ausubel says. Other strategies might ease the situation in the meantime. The planting of more trees, for instance, means that more carbon dioxide would be removed from the atmosphere—an activity for which countries would be able to earn credit for emissions reduction under the Kyoto Protocol. It is also technically possible to remove carbon dioxide from smokestack gases or, alternatively, to separate it out before burning, so that hydrogen is produced as fuel. But the cost of this alternative is high. The strategy is not easily applied to the transporation sector. And the separated carbon dioxide must be disposed of by storing it in exhausted oil and gas wells, in porous rock formations, or in the deep ocean. The ocean is the biggest repository, but no one knows what effect the influx of carbon would have on marine life, and the carbon stored there eventually would find its way through the carbon cycle and back into the atmosphere. Future generations would then have to deal with merely postponed consequences. Still, many experts believe that in the decades ahead, the capture and storage of carbon dioxide could play a role. But there is no panacea.

Ausubel and his colleagues at Rockefeller believe that over the next century, greenhouse gas concentrations will rise to about 500 parts per million despite continuing decarbonization, approaching a doubling of the preindustrial level and about 40 percent higher than now. While it seems all but certain that greenhouse concentrations will continue to increase substantially, where they eventually will wind up is anyone's guess. A decade after Jim Hansen energized the greenhouse debate by testifying to Congress that the human-induced greenhouse effect was real and was already being felt, he was pointing to the considerable uncertainty attached to estimates of future forcings of the climate system, both man-made and natural.

"The forcings that drive long-term climate change are not known with an accuracy sufficient to define future climate change," he and several colleagues wrote in late 1998. That uncertainty especially infuses estimates of future forcing by greenhouse gases, which depend in turn on inherently unknowable answers to questions about future emissions. Will future economic growth be fast, slow, or in between? Will new energy-efficient and non-carbon technologies be applied sooner or later? Will the capture and sequestration of carbon become cost effective? Will the decarbonization trend continue on its present trajectory, or falter, or accelerate? These are true imponderables. As a result, the IPCC for its 2001 assessment was giving up trying to provide a single "best estimate" or "business as usual" or "central case" for future emissions. Recognizing that emissions are unpredictable, the panel was instead outlining four different "story lines," based on different combinations of assumptions. (It was these preliminary scenarios on which Tom Wigley based his revised estimates of twenty-first century global warming.)

In the meantime, in our fleeting moment of geological time, something surely has been going on with the weather. Whether it adds up to a relatively lasting change in climate remains to be seen. So does the degree to which humans are responsible. We are still in uncharted waters, and it will continue to be difficult, at least for a while, to distinguish whatever influence humans are having on climate from the system's natural fluctuations. Some uncertainties are likely never to be fully resolved, but some things should become clearer.

Will the earth's temperature really warm up over the next few decades to levels not seen in millions of years? Will the seas rise, climatic zones shift, new agricultural bonanzas open up, new deserts develop? Will killer heat waves like Chicago's in 1995 become more frequent? Will toad-choker storms like that of Chicago in 1996 become more common, making floods worse and exposing more people to waterborne diseases? Are we in for worse droughts? Will the agricultural economies of Africa be devastated? Will El Niño visit the world more often, with greater ferocity? Will global patterns of atmospheric circulation change, dictating new rainfall and temperature patterns? How will greenhouse warming, to whatever degree it develops, interact with natural climatic changes? And how will that affect everyday life?

The experiment is running, and time will tell.

Postscript to the Paperback Edition

AS THE WORLD moved into the millennial transition year of 2000, signs of a warming earth continued to mount.

In perhaps the most striking revelation, an analysis by Tom Karl and his colleagues in Asheville disclosed that over the last quarter of the twentieth century, the average global surface temperature rose at a rate equal to about 3.5 degrees Fahrenheit per century. That was precisely the rate projected by the IPCC in 1995 for the twenty-first century as a whole. Now it seemed that the future was arriving ahead of schedule.

While no one knew for sure whether the rapid warming since the mid-1970s would continue, it was consistent with the rate predicted by computer models if greenhouse gas emissions are not reduced. For their part, Karl and his colleagues concluded that a string of record global temperatures at the century's end, in 1997 and 1998, and a near record in 1999, most likely represented the start of a new, more rapid planetary warming phase. There was only a small chance, they calculated, that this was not so.

In North America, Europe, and Asia—the big Northern Hemisphere land masses—1999 turned out to be the second warmest year on record, behind 1998. This came as a surprise, since 1999 was a year in which La Niña, El Niño's opposite number, dominated the world's climate, and La Niña exerts an overall cooling effect. Near-record temperatures in the face of La Niña had never been seen before; the warming trend, it appeared, had simply overwhelmed La Niña's coolness.

It seemed ever clearer that on local and regional scales, the warming was proceeding as model predictions said it should, at least in broad hemispheric outline. At the end of 1999, for instance, the *Times* compiled and published a hundred-year record of temperatures in New York's Central Park. The record revealed a century-long warming trend of 2.3 degrees—about twice as large as the global trend, as models had predicted for temperate regions generally.

The 1990s especially stood out. New York's warmest years of the century were 1990, 1991, and 1998. In 1991 and 1993 the city set records for the most days with temperatures over 90, thirty-nine in all. In 1990 the temperature fell below freezing on only three days, also a record. The most snow ever to fall on Central Park in one season, 75.6 inches, fell in 1995–96. Heavy winter precipitation, as we have seen, is consistent with a warmer atmosphere.

At the very end of the century, the United States set the third of three consecutive records for winter warmth. With an average temperature of 38.4 degrees Fahrenheit, the period of December 1999 through February 2000 was the warmest winter season of the previous 105 years in the Lower 48. In the eastern part of the country that year, winter effectively lasted about six weeks, from mid-January to the end of February. "Winter has shortened on both ends," said Mike Changery, one of Tom Karl's colleagues.

In another sign of warming that emerged near the turn of the new century, studies found that the extent of sea ice in the Northern Hemisphere had decreased by about 7 percent over the previous four to five decades, and that the perennial ice cover of the Arctic had shrunk by about 14 percent over the previous two decades. Further, an analysis of data collected by nuclear submarines found that the floating ice cover of the Arctic had become about 40 percent thinner than it was two to four decades earlier.

Again, this was in line with what the models predicted for far northern latitudes. And the melting of arctic ice raised anew the red flag about whether influxes of fresh meltwater into the North Atlantic might upset the oceanic conveyor belt that transports heat from the tropics to western Europe and eastern North America. Scientists feared that if this happened, a sudden shift in climate might at some point transform weather and disrupt life throughout the Northern Hemisphere in ways impossible to predict.

As evidence of a surface warming mounted, contrarians generally conceded that it was a fact, especially after a special panel of the National Research Council declared that the warming was "undoubtedly real." The panel said further that although satellite measurements showed little or no warming of the upper atmosphere over the preceding two decades, balloon measurements over a longer period of forty years revealed similar warming trends at the surface and in the upper air. Greenhouse believers seized on this to assert that one of the contrarians' key arguments had now evaporated.

But the dissenters argued that since computer models did not predict the apparent twenty-year disparity between surface and upper air temperatures, this offered a telling indication that the models are unreliable. They continued to assert that even though the planet might be warming, the cause was wholly or mostly natural, and that any warming over the coming century would be small.

Despite the cascading evidence of a warming, the jury remained out on the question of the human role in producing it. Experts in the scientific mainstream, citing recent studies, maintained that the rapid warming of the previous quarter century could not be explained without the greenhouse effect. Skeptics countered that the warming of the late twentieth century was caused by recurring natural changes in the circulation of heat-bearing ocean waters, especially in the Pacific. A group of eleven experts headed by Tim Barnett, one of the earliest seekers after the greenhouse fingerprint, concluded that the "most probable cause" of the warming was a combination of natural and man-made factors. But the elusive greenhouse signal, they said, was still obscured by the noise of natural climate variability. That state of affairs, they wrote in the *Bulletin of the American Meteorological Society*, was "not satisfactory."

As for those changes in Pacific circulation, researchers reported in early 2000 that for two years in a row, sea-surface temperatures in the Pacific had reverted to a pattern associated with more frequent La Niña events, which in turn means a generally cooler Northern Hemisphere, sharper swings between deep cold and abnormal warmth in the North American winter, and increased risk of drought in parts of the United States. Some experts said this regime might rule the next two or three decades, reversing an opposing regime that had dominated the late twentieth century and contributed to the Northern Hemisphere warming. It was this possibility that led some contrarians to argue that the warming since the mid-70s was mostly natural and that it might now disappear. But other scientists believed that the greenhouse effect would override these natural machinations and continue to warm the planet, as suggested by the unusual warming in 1999, a year in which the cool side of the Pacific oscillation dominated.

Meanwhile, yet other experts confirmed that the world's oceans had soaked up much of the warming of the previous forty years, delaying its full effect on climate. Scientists had long believed this to be so. This meant that some of whatever warming had been caused by the greenhouse effect so far—perhaps half, some researchers said—was still to be realized, and inevitably would materialize even if all fossil-fuel burning stopped immediately.

There remained absolutely no prospect of any such halt either right away or in the near future.

Acknowledgments

The writing of this book has been a highly satisfying project, made so by the subject itself but also by people who have helped and cooperated.

Without Flip Brophy, my agent, and Tom Spain, the book's editor, the project would never have gotten off the ground. Flip took an active part in its genesis and was responsible for taking it to Tom, who instantly seized on the concept and worked thoughtfully in helping to refine it. His care and good judgment in looking for and finding ways to improve the resulting manuscript were exceptional, and his many suggestions were right on target.

The generous support of the editors of the *New York Times* has been indispensable. I am grateful to them, most especially Cory Dean, the science news editor, for encouraging the project and allowing me to take the chunks of time necessary to complete the book. Her predecessor, Nicholas Wade, offered cooperation and encouragement in the early stages of the project, as did Jim Gorman. Mitchel Levitas, William E. Schmidt, and Dennis Stern were all supportive. Several colleagues in the paper's stellar science department provided information, aid, and insight, including William J. Broad, Malcolm W. Browne, Nicholas Wade, and John Noble Wilford.

On a broader level, the project would never have come about without the *Times*. The book is rooted in ten years' experience in reporting and writing about the science and politics of climate and weather for the newspaper. Any insights that may be reflected in the finished work are a direct outgrowth of those years of following the subject close-up. For that decade's worth of irreplaceable and fulfilling opportunity, I am eternally thankful to the *Times*.

I owe a debt of gratitude to the many sources who have spoken with me in connection with the book. Others were interviewed in connection with stories that appeared in the *Times*, and some of these were reinterviewed for the book. In this way the project has drawn on the expertise of dozens of scien-

Acknowledgments

tists—the producers and custodians of knowledge about weather and climate in our time. As a group, they have been uncommonly able and willing to talk, and many are quoted in the text. The book is theirs as well as mine (although, of course, they are not responsible for any errors of fact or interpretation).

Some were of special assistance. These include Richard Alley, Eric Barron, Bert Bolin, Wally Broecker, Peter deMenocal, Niles Eldredge, Fred Gadomski, Lee Grenci, Jim Hansen, Sir John Houghton, Geoff Jenkins, Tom Karl, Jim Kasting, Paul Knight, Dick Lindzen, Gordon Lupton, Mike Mac-Cracken, Jerry Mahlman, Syukuro Manabe, Pat Michaels, Todd Miner, John Mitchell, Richard Moss, Tom Mulhern, Michael Oppenheimer, Espen Ronneberg, Tom Ross, Ben Santer, Steve Schneider, Fred Singer, Joseph Smagorinsky, Kevin Trenberth, Elisabeth Vrba, Bob Watson, Philip Weech, and Tom Wigley. Some chapters of the manuscript were reviewed for scientific accuracy by Barron, deMenocal, Eldredge, Gadomski, Grenci, Kasting, Mahlman, and Vrba. Catherine Benjamin, Candace Crandall, Sylvia DeCotiis, Paul Edwards, Linda Livingston, and Anne Murrill were all helpful in moving the project along. Please forgive any omissions from this listing. They are entirely inadvertent.

As always, it has been my extreme good luck to enjoy the unwavering devotion, support, and encouragement of my wife, Joan Stevens.

—*William K. Stevens*
June 1999

Sources

The following people were interviewed expressly for this book. Some others quoted in the text appeared first in *New York Times* stories by the author and are not listed below. The stories in which they originally appeared are listed in the bibliography. Some among this latter group were reinterviewed for the book.

Richard Alley, Pennsylvania State University
Jesse Ausubel, Rockefeller University
Eric J. Barron, Pennsylvania State University
Ofer Bar-Yosef, Harvard University
Bert Bolin, chairman of Intergovernmental Panel on Climate Change, 1988–1997
Keith Briffa, University of East Anglia
Julie Brigham-Grette, University of Massachusetts
Wallace S. Broecker, Lamont-Doherty Earth Observatory
Mark A. Cane, Lamont-Doherty Earth Observatory
Dan Cayan, Scripps Institution of Oceanography
John R. Christy, University of Alabama at Huntsville
Candace Crandall, Science and Environmental Policy Project
Thomas J. Crowley, Texas A & M University
Michael Zammit Cutajar, executive secretary, United Nations Framework Convention on Climate Change
Dwight Deely, Fairbanks and Valdez, Alaska; school administrator and fishing guide
Anthony Del Genio, NASA Goddard Institute for Space Studies
Peter deMenocal, Lamont-Doherty Earth Observatory
Edmund R. Donoghue, medical examiner, City of Chicago

Sources

Craig Edwards, U.S. Weather Service, Chanhassen, Minnesota

Niles Eldredge, American Museum of Natural History

Richard G. Fairbanks, Lamont-Doherty Earth Observatory

Fred Gadomski, Pennsylvania State University

Lee Grenci, Pennsylvania State University

Paul Gross, United Kingdom Meteorological Office

James E. Hansen, NASA Goddard Institute for Space Studies

Paul Hoffman, Harvard University

Heinrich D. Holland, Harvard University

Sir John Houghton, chairman, Working Group I, Intergovernmental Panel on Climate Change

Geoff Jenkins, Hadley Center for Climate Prediction and Research

Philip D. Jones, University of East Anglia

Thomas R. Karl, director, NOAA National Climatic Data Center

James F. Kasting, Pennsylvania State University

Charles David Keeling, Scripps Institution of Oceanography

Paul Knight, Pennsylvania State University

Andrew Knoll, Harvard University

James C. Knox, University of Wisconsin

Debbie Krueger, homemaker, Orland Park, Illinois

Upmanu Lall, Utah State University

Stephen P. Leatherman, International Hurricane Center, Florida International University

Richard S. Lindzen, Massachusetts Institute of Technology

Harry F. Lins, United States Geological Survey

Robert Livezey, Climate Prediction Center, National Weather Service

Gordon Lupton, Hadley Center for Climate Prediction and Research

Michael MacCracken, United States Global Change Research Program

Jerry D. Mahlman, NOAA Geophysical Fluid Dynamics Laboratory

Syukuro Manabe, retired, NOAA Geophysical Fluid Dynamics Laboratory, Princeton University

Paul Merzlock, U.S. National Weather Service, Chicago, Illinois

Alden Meyer, Union of Concerned Scientists

Patrick J. Michaels, University of Virginia

Todd Miner, Pennsylvania State University

John F. B. Mitchell, Hadley Center for Climate Prediction and Research

Tom Mulhern, communications officer, City of Grand Forks, North Dakota

Michael Oppenheimer, Environmental Defense Fund

Patricia Owens, mayor of Grand Forks, North Dakota

David Parker, Hadley Center for Climate Prediction and Research

Peter Patterson, United Kingdom Meteorological Office

Roger A. Pielke, Jr., National Center for Atmospheric Research
Dave Potter, United Kingdom Meteorological Office
Richard Potts, National Museum of Natural History, Smithsonian Institution
Espen Ronneberg, Marshall Islands delegate to the United Nations
Tom Ross, NOAA National Climatic Data Center
Benjamin D. Santer, Lawrence Livermore National Laboratory
Michael E. Schlesinger, University of Illinois
Stephen S. Schneider, Stanford University
Phil Schumacher, U.S. National Weather Service, Grand Forks, North
  Dakota
Izumi Shimada, Southern Illinois University
Drew Shindell, NASA Goddard Institute for Space Studies
S. Fred Singer, Science and Environmental Policy Project
Joseph Smagorinsky, retired, NOAA Geophysical Fluid Dynamics
  Laboratory
Tony Socci, U.S. Global Change Research Program
Steven M. Stanley, Johns Hopkins University
Christopher Stringer, Natural History Museum, London
Simon F. B. Tett, Hadley Center for Climatic Prediction and Research
Kevin E. Trenberth, National Center for Atmospheric Research
Allen Voelker, U.S. National Weather Service, Grand Forks, North Dakota
Elisabeth S. Vrba, Yale University
Jim Wagner, Climate Prediction Center, National Weather Service
Robert T. Watson, chairman, Intergovernmental Panel on Climate Change,
  1997–
Philip S. Weech, government of the Bahamas
Harvey Weiss, Yale University
Gunter Weller, University of Alaska
Richard T. Wetherald, NOAA Geophysical Fluid Dynamics Laboratory,
  Princeton University
Tom M. L. Wigley, National Center for Atmospheric Research

Selected Bibliography

Chapter One

Barron, Eric J., Peter J. Fawcett, William H. Peterson, David Pollard, and Starley L. Thompson. "A 'Simulation' of Mid-Cretaceous Climate." *Paleoceanography*, Vol. 10, No. 5, Oct. 1995, pp. 953–962.

Crowley, Thomas J. "Remembrance of Things Past: Greenhouse Lessons from the Geologic Record." *Consequences*, Vol. 2, No. 1, 1996, pp. 2–12.

deMenocal, Peter B., and Jan Bloemendal. "Plio-Pleistocene Climatic Variability in Subtropical Africa and the Paleoenvironment of Hominid Evolution: A Combined Data-Model Approach." In Elisabeth S. Vrba, George H. Denton, Timothy C. Partridge, and Lloyd H. Burckle, eds., *Paleoclimate and Evolution, with Emphasis on Human Origins*. New Haven, CT: Yale University Press, 1995, pp. 262–288.

Erwin, Douglas H. "The Permo-Triassic Extinction." *Nature*, Vol. 367, Jan. 20, 1994, pp. 231–236.

———. "The Mother of Mass Extinctions." *Scientific American*, July 1996, pp. 70–78.

Evans, D. A., N. J. Buekes, and J. L. Kirschvink. "Low-Latitude Glaciation in the Palaeoproterozoic Era." *Nature*, Vol. 386, March 20, 1997, pp. 262–266.

Holland, Heinrich D. "Chemistry and Evolution of the Proterozoic Ocean." In J. William Schopf and Cornelius Klein, eds., *The Proterozoic Biosphere: A Multidisciplinary Study*. New York: Cambridge University Press, 1992, pp. 169–171.

Holland, Heinrich D., and James F. Kasting. "The Environment of the

Archean Earth." In Schopf and Klein, eds., *The Proterozoic Biosphere,* pp. 21–23.

Jones, Steve, Robert Martin, and David Pilbeam, eds. *The Cambridge Encyclopedia of Human Evolution.* New York: Cambridge University Press, 1992.

Kasting, James F. "Proterozoic Climates: The Effect of Changing Atmospheric Carbon Dioxide Concentrations." In Schopf and Klein, eds., *The Proterozoic Biosphere,* pp. 165–167.

Kasting, James F., and Thomas P. Ackerman. "Climatic Consequences of Very High Carbon Dioxide Levels in the Earth's Early Atmosphere." *Science,* Vol. 234, Dec. 12, 1986, pp. 1383–1385.

Kasting, James F., and Sherwood Chang. "Formation of Earth and the Origin of Life." In Schopf and Klein, eds., *The Proterozoic Biosphere,* pp. 9–11.

Kasting, James F., Heinrich D. Holland, and Lee R. Kump. "Atmospheric Evolution: The Rise of Oxygen." In Schopf and Klein, eds., *The Proterozoic Biosphere,* pp. 159–162.

Kirschvink, Joseph L. "Late Proterozoic Low-Latitude Global Glaciation: The Snowball Earth." In Schopf and Klein, eds., *The Proterozoic Biosphere,* pp. 51–52.

Lowe, Donald R. "Major Events in the Geological Development of the Precambrian Earth." In Schopf and Klein, eds., *The Proterozoic Biosphere,* pp. 67–74.

Lowe, Donald R., and W. Gary Ernst. "The Archean Geologic Record." In Schopf and Klein, eds., *The Proterozoic Biosphere,* pp. 13–18.

Press, Frank, and Raymond Siever. *Understanding Earth.* New York: W. H. Freeman and Co., 1994.

Schopf, J. William. "Paleobiology of the Archean." In Schopf and Klein, eds., *The Proterozoic Biosphere,* pp. 25–39.

Schopf, J. William, and Cornelius Klein, eds. *The Proterozoic Biosphere: A Multidisciplinary Study.* Cambridge University Press, New York, 1992.

Stanley, Steven M. *Children of the Ice Age: How a Global Catastrophe Allowed Humans to Evolve.* New York: Harmony Books, 1996.

Stevens, William K. "Evolving Theory Views Earth as a Living Organism." *New York Times,* Aug. 29, 1989.

Wade, Nicholas. "Evidence Backs Theory Linking Origins of Life to Volcanoes." *New York Times,* April 11, 1997.

Chapter Two

Crowley, Thomas J. "Remembrance of Things Past: Greenhouse Lessons from the Geologic Record." *Consequences,* Vol. 2, No. 1, 1996, pp. 2–12.

deMenocal, Peter B. "Plio-Pleistocene African Climate." *Science,* Vol. 270, Oct. 6, 1995, pp. 53–59.

deMenocal, Peter B., and Jan Bloemendal. "Plio-Pleistocene Climatic Variability in Subtropical Africa and the Paleoenvironment of Hominid Evolution: A Combined Data-Model Approach." In Elisabeth S. Vrba, George H. Denton, Timothy C. Partridge, and Lloyd H. Burckle, eds., *Paleoclimate and Evolution, with Emphasis on Human Origins.* New Haven, CT: Yale University Press, 1995, pp. 262–288.

Dupont, Lydie M., and Suzanne A. G. Leroy. "Steps Toward Dry Climatic Conditions in Northwestern Africa during the Upper Pliocene." In Vrba et al., eds., *Paleoclimate and Evolution, with Emphasis on Human Origins,* pp. 289–298.

Dutton, Jan F., and Eric J. Barron. "Miocene to Present Vegetation Changes: A Possible Piece of the Cenozoic Cooling Puzzle." *Geology,* Vol. 25, No. 1, Jan. 1997, pp. 39–41.

Eldredge, Niles. "Cretaceous Meteor Showers, the Human Ecological 'Niche' and the Sixth Extinction." Abstract of paper presented at conference on extinctions, American Museum of Natural History, April 1997.

Hill, Andrew. "Faunal and Environmental Change in the Neogene of East Africa: Evidence from the Tugen Hills Sequence, Baringo District, Kenya." In Vrba et al., eds., *Paleoclimate and Evolution, with Emphasis on Human Origins,* pp. 178–193.

Jones, Steve, Robert Martin, and David Pilbeam. *The Cambridge Encyclopedia of Human Evolution.* New York: Cambridge University Press, 1992.

Potts, Richard. "Evolution and Climate Variability." *Science,* Vol. 273, Aug. 16, 1996, pp. 922–923.

———. "Environments and Resource Change: An Outrageously Long-Term View." Paper prepared for Resources for the Future, Washington, DC, Dec. 4, 1996.

———. *Humanity's Descent: The Consequences of Ecological Instability.* New York: William Morrow & Company, 1996.

Ruemer, Jelle W. F. "The Effect of Paleoclimate on the Evolution of the Soricidae (Mammalia, Insectivora)." In Vrba et al., eds., *Paleoclimate and Evolution, with Emphasis on Human Origins,* pp. 135–147.

Shell, Ellen Ruppel. "Waves of Creation; Elisabeth Vrba Believes Climatic Changes Caused Evolutionary Pulses." *Discover,* May 1993, pp. 54–61.

Stanley, Steven, M. *Children of the Ice Age: How a Global Catastrophe Allowed Humans to Evolve*. New York: Harmony House, 1996.

Stevens, William K. "In the Ebb and Flow of Ancient Glaciers, Clues to Next Ice Age." *New York Times,* Jan. 16, 1990.

———. "Global Climate Changes Seen as Force in Human Evolution." *New York Times,* Oct. 16, 1990.

———. "Neanderthals: Dead End or Ancestor?" *New York Times,* Feb. 4, 1992.

———. "Dust in Sea Mud May Link Human Evolution to Climate." *New York Times,* Dec. 14, 1993.

Stringer, Christopher B. "The Evolution and Distribution of Later Pleistocene Human Populations." In Vrba et al., eds., *Paleoclimate and Evolution, with Emphasis on Human Origins,* pp. 524–531.

Stringer, Christopher B., and Robin McKie. *African Exodus*. New York: Henry Holt and Co., 1996.

Vrba, Elisabeth. "Ecological and Adaptive Changes Associated with Early Hominid Evolution." In *Ancestors: The Hard Evidence*. New York: Alan R. Liss Inc., 1985, pp. 63–71.

———. "The Environmental Context of the Evolution of Early Hominids and Their Culture." In R. Bonnichsen and M. H. Sorg, eds., *Bone Modification*. Orono, ME: Center for the Study of the First Americans, 1989, pp. 27–42.

———. "On the Connections between Paleoclimate and Evolution." In Vrba et al., eds., *Paleoclimate and Evolution, with Emphasis on Human Origins,* pp. 24–45.

———. "The Fossil Record of African Antelopes (Mammalia, Bovidae) in Relation to Human Evolution and Paleoclimate." In Vrba et al., eds., *Paleoclimate and Evolution, with Emphasis on Human Origins,* pp. 385–424.

Wade, Nicholas. "Neanderthal DNA Sheds New Light on Human Origins." *New York Times,* July 11, 1997.

Wilford, John Noble. "New Fossils Reveal the First of Man's Walking Ancestors." *New York Times,* Aug. 17, 1995.

———. "The Transforming Leap, From 4 Legs to 2." *New York Times,* Sept. 5, 1995.

Chapter Three

Bar-Yosef, Ofer. "The Impact of Late Pleistocene–Early Holocene Climatic Changes on Humans in Southwest Asia." In Lawrence Guy Straus, Berit

Selected Bibliography

Valentin Eriksen, Jon M. Erlandson, and David R. Yesner, eds., *Humans at the End of the Ice Age: The Archaeology of the Pleistocene-Holocene Transition.* New York: Plenum Press, 1996, pp. 61–78.

Bar-Yosef, Ofer, and Richard H. Meadow. "The Origins of Agriculture in the Near East." In T. Douglas Price and Anne Birgette Gebauer, eds., *Last Hunters, First Farmers: New Perspectives on the Prehistoric Transition to Agriculture.* Santa Fe: School of American Research Press, 1995, pp. 39–94.

Calder, Nigel. *The Weather Machine.* New York: Viking Press, 1974.

Crowley, Thomas J. "Remembrance of Things Past: Greenhouse Lessons from the Geologic Records." *Consequences,* Vol. 2, No. 1, 1996, pp. 2–12.

Cutler, Alan. "The Little Ice Age: When Global Cooling Gripped the World." *Washington Post,* Aug. 13, 1997.

Donnan, Christopher B. "Masterworks of Art Reveal a Remarkable Pre-Inca World." *National Geographic,* June 1990, pp. 16–33.

Gibbons, Ann. "How the Akkadian Empire Was Hung Out to Dry." *Science,* Vol. 261, Aug. 20, 1993, p. 985.

Hodell, David A., Jason H. Curtis, and Mark Brenner. "Possible Role of Climate in the Collapse of Classic Maya Civilization." *Nature,* Vol. 375, June 1, 1995, pp. 391–394.

Knox, James C. "Large Increases in Flood Magnitude in Response to Modest Changes in Climate." *Nature,* Vol. 361, Feb. 4, 1993, pp. 430–432.

Lamb, H. H. *Climatic History and the Future.* Princeton, NJ: Princeton University Press, 1977.

Levenson, Thomas. *Ice Time: Climate, Science, and Life on Earth.* New York: Harper & Row, 1989.

Muhs, D. R., and P. B. Maat. "The Potential Response of Eolian Sands to Greenhouse Warming and Precipitation Reduction on the Great Plains of the U.S.A." *Journal of Arid Environments,* Vol. 25, 1993, pp. 351–361.

Ortloff, Charles R., and Alan L. Kolata. "Climate and Collapse: Agro-Ecological Perspectives on the Decline of the Tiwanaku State." *Journal of Archaeological Science,* Vol. 20, 1993, pp. 195–221.

Overpeck, Jonathan T. "Warm Climate Surprises." *Science,* Vol. 271, March 29, 1996, pp. 1820–1821.

Sabloff, Jeremy A. "Drought and Decline." *Nature,* Vol. 375, June 1, 1995, p. 357.

"Science Watch; Return of the Ice Age." *New York Times,* Sept. 3, 1991.

Sherratt, Andrew. "Climatic Cycles and Behavioural Revolutions: The Emergence of Modern Humans and the Beginning of Farming." *Antiquity,* Vol. 71, No. 272, June 1997, pp. 217–287.

Shimada, Izumi, Crystal Barker Schaaf, Lonnie G. Thompson, and Ellen Mosley-Thompson. "Cultural Impacts of Severe Droughts in the Prehistoric Andes: Application of a 1,500-Year Ice Core Precipitation Record." *World Archeology*, Vol. 22, No. 3, 1991, pp. 247–270.

Stevens, William K. "Scientists Revive a Lost Secret of Farming." *New York Times*, Nov. 22, 1988.

———. "In the Ebb and Flow of Ancient Glaciers, Clues to Next Ice Age." *New York Times*, Jan. 16, 1990.

———. "Climate Roller Coaster in Swedish Tree Rings." *New York Times*, Aug. 7, 1990.

———. "Dry Climate May Have Forced Invention of Agriculture." *New York Times*, April 2, 1991.

———. "In New Data on Climate Changes, Decades, Not Centuries, Count." *New York Times*, Dec. 7, 1993.

———. "Severe Ancient Droughts: A Warning to California." *New York Times*, July 19, 1994.

———. "Data Give Tangled Picture of World Climate Between Glaciers." *New York Times*, Nov. 1, 1994.

———. "Great Plains or Great Desert? The Sea of Dunes Lies in Wait." *New York Times*, May 28, 1996.

———. "From Under the Sea, Signs of Climate Jolts." *New York Times*, Nov. 18, 1997.

———. "If Climate Changes, It May Change Quickly." *New York Times*, Jan. 27, 1998.

Thompson, Lonnie G., Mary E. Davis, and Ellen Mosley-Thompson. "Glacial Records of Global Climate: A 1500-Year Tropical Ice Core Record of Climate." *Human Ecology*, Vol. 22, No. 1, 1994, pp. 83–95.

Weiss, H., M.-A. Courty, W. Wetterstrom, F. Guichard, L. Senior, R. Meadow, and A. Curnow. "The Genesis and Collapse of Third Millennium North Mesopotamian Civilization." *Science*, Vol. 261, Aug. 20, 1993, pp. 995–1004.

Wilford, John Noble. "Collapse of Earliest Known Empire Is Linked to Long, Harsh Drought." *New York Times*, Aug. 24, 1993.

Chapter Four

Burroughs, William J., Bob Crowder, Ted Robertson, Eleanor Vallier-Talbot, and Richard Whitaker. *The Nature Company Guides: Weather*. New York: Time-Life Books, 1996.

Cerveny, Randy. "Power of the Gods; Ancient Cultures Were Grounded on a Fear of Lightning," *Weatherwise*, Vol. 47, No. 2, April/May 1994, pp. 20–23.

Erdoes, Richard, and Alfonso Ortiz, eds. *American Indian Myths and Legends*. New York: Pantheon Books, 1984.

Freier, George D. *Weather Proverbs*. Tucson, AZ: Fisher Books, 1989, 1992.

Frisinger, H. Howard. *The History of Meteorology: To 1800*. New York: American Meteorological Society/Science History Publications, 1977.

Laskin, David. *Braving the Elements: The Stormy History of American Weather*. New York: Doubleday, 1996.

Lee, Albert. *Weather Wisdom: Facts and Folklore of Weather Forecasting*. New York: Congdon & Weed Inc., 1976.

Nese, Jon M., and Lee M. Grenci. *A World of Weather: Fundamentals of Meteorology*. Dubuque, IA: Kendall/Hunt, 1996, 1998.

Schneider, Stephen H., ed.-in-chief. *Encyclopedia of Climate and Weather*. New York: Oxford University Press, 1996.

Turner, Frederick, ed. *The Portable North American Indian Reader*. New York: Penguin Books, 1977.

Chapter Five

Burroughs, William J., Bob Crowder, Ted Robertson, Eleanor Vallier-Talbot, and Richard Whitaker. *The Nature Company Guides: Weather*. New York: Time-Life Books, 1996.

Fleming, James Roger. *Meteorology in America, 1800–1870*. Baltimore: The Johns Hopkins University Press, 1990.

Frisinger, H. Howard. *The History of Meteorology: To 1800*. New York: American Meteorological Society/Science History Publications, 1977.

Laskin, David. *Braving the Elements: The Stormy History of American Weather*. New York: Doubleday, 1996.

Nebeker, Frederik. *Calculating the Weather: Meteorology in the 20th Century*. San Diego: Academic Press, 1995.

Reston Jr., James. *Galileo, A Life*. New York: HarperCollins, 1994.

Whipple, A. B. C. *Storm*, Planet Earth series. New York: Time-Life Books, 1982.

Chapter Six

Cressman, George P. "The Origin and Rise of Numerical Weather Prediction." In James Rodger Fleming, ed., *Historical Essays on Meteorology 1919–1995*. Boston: American Meteorological Society, 1996.

Jewell, Ralph. "The Bergen School of Meteorology; the Cradle of Modern Weather Forecasting." *Bulletin of the American Meteorological Society*, Vol. 62, No. 6, June 1981, pp. 824–830.

Laskin, David. *Braving the Elements: The Stormy History of American Weather*. New York: Doubleday, 1996.

Nebeker, Frederik. *Calculating the Weather: Meteorology in the 20th Century*. San Diego: Academic Press, 1995.

Nese, John M., and Lee M. Grenci. *A World of Weather: Fundamentals of Meteorology*. Dubuque, IA: Kendall/Hunt, 1996, 1998.

Phillips, Norman A. "Charney's Influence on Meteorology." In Richard S. Lindzen, Edward N. Lorenz, and George W. Platzman, eds., *The Atmosphere—A Challenge: The Science of Jule Gregory Charney*. Boston: American Meteorological Society, 1990, pp. 121–131.

Thompson, Philip D. "Charney and the Revival of Numerical Weather Prediction." In Lindzen et al., *The Atmosphere—A Challenge*, pp. 93–119.

Whipple, A. B. C. *Storm*, Planet Earth series. New York: Time-Life Books, 1982.

Wurtele, Morton G. "Charney Remembered." In Lindzen et al., *The Atmosphere—A Challenge*.

Chapter Seven

Albach/Hogan, Susan. "Comfrey Reels and Grieves as Damage Extent Becomes Clear." *Minneapolis Star Tribune*, April 1, 1998.

Burroughs, W. J. *Weather Cycles: Real or Imaginary?* New York: Cambridge University Press, 1992.

Burroughs, William J., Bob Crowder, Ted Robertson, Eleanor Vallier-Talbot, and Richard Whitaker. *The Nature Company Guides: Weather*. New York: Time-Life Books, 1996.

Cane, Mark A. *ENSO and Its Prediction*. Monograph. Palisades, NY: Lamont-Doherty Earth Observatory of Columbia University, 1997.

Chen, David W. "Unprepared for Seasonal Warmth." *New York Times*, April 1, 1998.

Doyle, Pat. "Desperate Effort to Save 6-Year-Old Victim Fails." *Minneapolis Star Tribune*, March 31, 1998.

Malnic, Eric. "Muddy Flood of Evidence Says El Nino Is Real." *Los Angeles Times*, Feb. 25, 1998.

Malnic, Eric, and Daryl Kelley. "Powerful Storm Socks Rain-Soaked Southland." *Los Angeles Times*, Feb. 24, 1998.

Meryhew, Richard, and Anthony Lonetree. "Toppled Spire Takes Wind Out of Gustavus Adolphus." *Minneapolis Star Tribune,* March 31, 1998.

National Oceanic and Atmospheric Administration. "California Flooding and Florida Tornadoes." Feb. 1998.

National Weather Service. "The Central Florida Tornado Outbreak of Feb. 22 and 23, 1998." March 25, 1998, Melbourne, FL.

Navarro, Mireya. "At Least 38 Die as Tornadoes Rip Central Florida." *New York Times,* Feb. 24, 1998.

Nese, John M., and Lee M. Grenci. *A World of Weather: Fundamentals of Meteorology.* Dubuque, IA: Kendall/Hunt, 1996, 1998.

Nordheimer, Jon. "Lives and Homes Destroyed in a Night of Deafening Fury." *New York Times,* Feb. 24, 1998.

Schneider, Stephen H., ed.-in-chief. *Encyclopedia of Climate and Weather.* New York: Oxford University Press, 1996.

Simon, Stephanie, Kate Folmar, and David Reyes. "Storm Kills Six, Inflicts Severe Damage in State." *Los Angeles Times,* Feb. 15, 1998.

Sinker, Howard, Pat Doly, Conrad deFiebre, and Allie Shah. "Extent of Storm Damage Starts Being Assessed." *Minneapolis Star Tribune,* April 1, 1998.

Sternberg, Bob von, Richard Meryhew, and Pat Doyle. "Along a 60-Mile Swath, an Unbelievable Trail of Destruction." *Minneapolis Star Tribune,* March 31, 1998.

Stevens, William K. "Scientist at Work: Mark A. Cane." *New York Times,* Dec. 31, 1996.

Weather Chart. *New York Times,* April 5, 1998, p. 39.

Zebiak, Stephen E. "Ill Winds." *The Sciences,* March/April 1989, pp. 26–31.

Chapter Eight

Arrhenius, Svante. "On the Influence of Carbonic Acid in the Air upon the Temperature of the Ground." *The London, Edinburgh, and Dublin Philosophical Magazine and Journal of Science,* April 1896, pp. 237–277.

Calder, Nigel. *The Weather Machine.* New York: Viking Press, 1974.

Callendar, G. S. "The Artificial Production of Carbon Dioxide and Its Influence on Temperature." *Quarterly Journal of the Royal Meteorological Society,* Vol. 64, 1938, pp. 223–240.

Crawford, Elisabeth. *Arrhenius, from Ionic Theory to the Greenhouse Effect.* Canton, MA: Science History Publications/USA, Watson Publishing International, 1996.

————. "Arrhenius' 1896 Model of the Greenhouse Effect in Context."

Selected Bibliography

Ambio, A Journal of the Human Environment, Vol. 26, No. 1, Feb. 1997, pp. 6–11.

Fleming, James R. "T.C. Chamberlin and H_2O Climate Feedbacks: A Voice from the Past." *EOS*, Vol. 73, No. 47, Nov. 24, 1992.

Hansen, James E. "The Greenhouse, the White House, and Our House." Paper presented to the International Platform Association, Washington, DC, Aug. 3, 1989.

———. "Global Warming: A Personal Perspective." Paper presented at the University of California at Irvine, April 18, 1997.

Howard, Janet. "Ahead of the Curve; CO_2 Sleuth Spends Career Tracking Buildup of Greenhouse Gas." *Explorations* (Scripps Institution), Vol. 3, No. 1, Summer 1996, pp. 18–25.

"James E. Hansen." *Current Biography*, May 1996.

Jones, M. D. H., and A. Henderson-Sellers. "History of the Greenhouse Effect." *Progress in Physical Geography*, Edward Arnold, Vol. 14, 1990, pp. 1–18.

Kellogg, William W. "Mankind's Impact on Climate: The Evolution of an Awareness." *Climatic Change*, Vol. 10, 1987, pp. 113–136.

Kerr, Richard A. "Hansen vs. the World on the Greenhouse Threat." *Nature*, June 2, 1989, pp. 1041–1043.

Manabe, Syukuro. "Early Development in the Study of Greenhouse Warming: The Emergence of Climate Models." *Ambio*, Vol. 26, No. 1, Feb. 1997, pp. 47–51.

National Research Council. *Carbon Dioxide and Climate: A Scientific Assessment*. Washington, DC: The National Academy of Sciences, 1979.

———. *Changing Climate: Report of the Carbon Dioxide Assessment Committee*. Washington, DC: The National Academy of Sciences, 1983.

Oppenheimer, Michael, and Robert H. Boyle. *Dead Heat: The Race Against the Greenhouse Effect*. New York: Basic Books, 1990.

Petit, John-Robert, et al. "Climate and Atmospheric History of the Past 420,000 Years from the Vostok Ice Core, Antarctica." *Nature*, Vol. 399, June 3, 1999, pp. 429–436.

Shabecoff, Philip. "Global Warming Has Begun, Expert Tells Senate." *New York Times*, June 24, 1988.

Weiner, Jonathan. *The Next Hundred Years: Shaping the Fate of Our Living Earth*. New York: Bantam Books, 1990.

Wilford, John Noble. "His Bold Statement Transforms the Debate on Greenhouse Effect." *New York Times*, Aug. 23, 1988.

Selected Bibliography

Chapter Nine

Associated Press. "U.S. Death Toll in Summer Heat Wave Put at 1,265." *New York Times,* Oct. 16, 1980.

Houghton, J. T., G. J. Jenkins, and J. J. Ephrams, Intergovernmental Panel on Climate Change. *Climate Change: The IPCC Scientific Assessment.* New York: Cambridge University Press, 1990.

Houghton, J. T., L. G. Meira Filho, B. A. Callander, N. Harris, A. Kattenberg, and K. Maskell, Intergovernmental Panel on Climate Change. *Climate Change 1995: The Science of Climate Change.* New York: Cambridge University Press, 1996.

Jones, Philip D., and Tom M. L. Wigley. "Global Warming Trends," *Scientific American,* Aug. 1990, pp. 84–91.

Stevens, William K. "Severe Drought Is Feared as Heat Withers 6 States." *New York Times,* July 17, 1980.

———. "In New Data on Climate Changes, Decades, Not Centuries, Count." *New York Times,* Dec. 7, 1993.

———. "A Global Warming Resumed in 1994, Climate Data Show." *New York Times,* Jan. 27, 1995.

———. " '95 Is Hottest Year on Record as the Global Trend Resumes." *New York Times,* Jan. 4, 1996.

———. "Experts on Climate Change Pondering: How Urgent Is It?" *New York Times,* Sept. 9, 1997.

———. "Ever-so-Slight Rise in Temperatures Led to a Record High in 1997." *New York Times,* Jan. 9, 1998.

———. "New Evidence Finds This Is Warmest Century in 600 Years." *New York Times,* April 28, 1998.

———. "Global Temperature at a High for First 5 Months of 1998." *New York Times,* June 8, 1998.

———. "Song of the Millennium: Cool Prelude and a Fiery Coda." *New York Times,* March 9, 1999.

Chapter Ten

Houghton, J. T., G. J. Jenkins, and J. J. Ephrams, International Panel on Climate Change. *Climate Change: The IPCC Scientific Assessment.* New York: Cambridge University Press, 1990.

Parmesan, Camille, et al. "Poleward Shifts in Geographical Ranges of Butterfly Species Associated with Regional Warming." *Nature,* Vol. 399, June 10, 1999, pp. 579–583.

Selected Bibliography

Stevens, William K. "Deeper Look at Cold, Snowy Winter Reveals Balmier Future." *New York Times,* Feb. 8, 1994.

———. "Western Butterfly Shifting North as Climate Warms." *New York Times,* Sept. 3, 1996.

———. "Greener Green Belt Bears Witness to Warming Trend." *New York Times,* April 22, 1997.

———. "Dead Trees and Shriveling Glaciers as Alaska Melts." *New York Times,* Aug. 18, 1998.

———. "March May Soon Be Coming in Like a Lamb." *New York Times,* March 2, 1999.

———. "Surveys Uncover Substantial Melting of Greenland Ice Sheet." *New York Times,* March 5, 1999.

Chapter Eleven

Belluck, Pam. "21 Dead or Missing as Storms Rage in East and the Midwest." *New York Times,* June 30, 1998.

Cayan, Dan, Kelly Redmond, and Larry Riddle. "El Nino/La Nina and Extreme Daily Precipitation and Streamflow Values." Scripps Institution of Oceanography 1999, www.wrcc.dir.edu/enso/percentile.html.

Daley, Beth, and Patrick J. Calnan. "Waterlogged—and Bracing for More." *Boston Globe,* June 15, 1998.

Grand Forks Herald and Knight-Ridder Newspapers. "Come Hell and High Water." *Grand Forks Herald* (Grand Forks, ND), 1997, pp. 22–25.

"Heavy Rain Causes Flood in Tennessee; at Least 2 Are Dead," *New York Times,* July 15, 1998.

Robert Henson, "Up to Our Necks; in 1997, the Floods Just Wouldn't Stop." *Weatherwise,* March/April 1998.

Karl, Thomas R., and Richard W. Knight. "Secular Trends of Precipitation Amount, Frequency and Intensity in the United States." *Bulletin of the American Meteorological Society,* Vol. 79, No. 2, Feb. 1998, pp. 231–241.

Karl, Thomas R., Richard W. Knight, David R. Easterling, and Robert G. Quayle. "Trends in U.S. Climate During the 20th Century." *Consequences,* Vol. 1, No. 1, Spring 1995, pp. 2–12.

———. "Indices of Climate Change for the United States." *Bulletin of the American Meteorological Society,* Vol. 77, No. 2, Feb. 1996, pp. 279–292.

Karl, Thomas R., Neville Nicholls, and Jonathan Gregory. "The Coming Climate." *Scientific American,* May 1997, pp. 55–59.

Kocin, Paul J., William E. Gartner, and Daniel J. Graf. "Snow! A Record Season." *Weatherwise,* February/March 1997, pp. 28–35.

Lins, Harry F., and James R. Slack. "Streamflow Trends in the United States." *Geophysical Research Letters,* Vol. 26, Jan. 15, 1999, pp. 227–230.

Lott, Neal. "The Big One! A Review of the March 12–14, 1993, 'Storm of the Century.'" National Climatic Data Center, Asheville, NC, Technical Report 93-01, May 14, 1993.

———. "The Summer of 1993: Flooding in the Midwest and Drought in the Southeast." National Climatic Data Center, Asheville, NC, Technical Report 93-04, Sept. 16, 1993.

Lott, Neal, Doug Ross, and Matthew Sittel. "The Winter of '96–'97; West Coast Flooding." National Climatic Data Center, Asheville, NC, Technical Report 97-01, January 1997.

McFadden, Robert D. "Storm Floods Many Areas and Kills 4." *New York Times,* Oct. 21, 1996.

National Climatic Data Center. "The Winter of '95–'96; A Season of Extremes." Asheville, NC, Technical Report 96-02, May 1996.

———. "March 1997 Tornadoes and Flooding." Asheville, NC, Technical Report, April 1997.

———. "Northeast Spring Snowstorm." Asheville, NC, Technical Report, May 1997.

———. "Central and Eastern European Flooding." Asheville, NC, Summary Report, August 1997.

Pielke Jr., Roger A., Mary W. Downton, Linda O. Mearns, and Naressa Cofield. "Relationships of Precipitation and Damaging Floods in the United States, 1932–1996." Paper presented to the American Meteorological Society, Dallas, TX, January 1999.

Ross, Rebecca J., and William P. Elliott. "Tropospheric Water Vapor Climatology and Trends over North America." *Journal of Climate,* Vol. 9, No. 12, Dec. 1996.

Smothers, Ronald. "Fast-Moving Storms Flood Slice of New Jersey." *New York Times,* Aug. 22, 1997, pp. 3561–3574.

Stevens, William K. "3 Disturbances Became a Big Storm." *New York Times,* March 14, 1993.

———. "'Monster' Is Just Wind on Coast." *New York Times,* March 15, 1993.

———. "East Still Hot, Midwest Still Wet and Here's Why." *New York Times,* July 9, 1993.

———. "Violent Weather Battering Globe in Last 2 Years Baffles Experts." *New York Times,* May 24, 1994.

———. "More Extremes Found in Weather, Pointing to Greenhouse Gas Effect." *New York Times,* May 23, 1995.

———. "Deep Jet-Stream Shifts Made the Blizzard Possible." *New York Times,* Jan. 8, 1996.

———. "Fewer Northeasters Pound U.S., but Punch Is More Powerful." *New York Times,* Oct. 29, 1996.

———. "Global Climate Stayed Warm in 1996, with Wet, Cold Regional Surprises." *New York Times,* Jan. 14, 1997.

———. "Wet Winter, Then Drought Are Linked to Florida Fires." *New York Times,* July 4, 1998.

Trenberth, Kevin E. "Conceptual Framework for Changes of Extremes of the Hydrological Cycle with Climate Change." *Climatic Change,* Vol. 42, 1999, pp. 327–339.

Voelker, Allen. "Anatomy of a Red River Spring Flood." National Weather Service, Grand Forks, ND, 1997.

Chapter Twelve

Barron, Eric J. "Climate Models: How Reliable Are Their Predictions?" *Consequences,* Autumn 1995, pp. 16–27.

Houghton, J. T., G. J. Jenkins, and J. J. Ephrams, International Panel on Climate Change. *Climate Change: The IPCC Scientific Assessment.* New York: Cambridge University Press, 1990.

Stevens, William K. "Computers Model World's Climate, But How Well?" *New York Times,* Nov. 4, 1997.

Trenberth, Kevin E. "The Use and Abuse of Climate Models." *Nature,* Vol. 386, March 1997, pp. 131–133.

Chapter Thirteen

Avery, Susan K., Paul D. Try, Richard A. Anthes, and Richard E. Hallgren. "Open Letter to Ben Santer." *Bulletin of the American Meteorological Society,* Vol. 77, No. 9, Sept. 1996, pp. 1961–1966.

Barnett, Tim P., and Michael E. Schlesinger. "Detecting Changes in Global Climate Induced by Greenhouse Gases." *Journal of Geophysical Research,* Vol. 92, Dec. 20, 1987, pp. 14772–14780.

Edwards, Paul N., and Stephen H. Schneider. "The 1995 IPCC Report: Broad Consensus or 'Scientific Cleansing'?" *Ecofables/Ecoscience* (Center for Conservation Biology, Stanford University), No. 1, Fall 1997, pp. 3–9.

Gelbspan, Ross. *The Heat Is On.* New York: Addison-Wesley, 1997.

Houghton, J. T., G. J. Jenkins, and J. J. Ephrams, International Panel on Climate Change. *Climate Change: The IPCC Scientific Assessment.* New York: Cambridge University Press, 1990.

Kerr, Richard A. "Greenhouse Forecasting Still Cloudy." *Science,* Vol. 276, May 16, 1997, pp. 1040–1042.

Kiehl, J. T., and B. P. Briegleb. "The Relative Roles of Sulfate Aerosols and Greenhouse Gases in Climate Forcing." *Science,* Vol. 160, April 16, 1993, pp. 311–314.

Masood, Eshan. "Lobbyists 'Belittle Climate Change Science.' " *Nature,* Vol. 382, July 25, 1996, p. 287.

———. "United States Backs Climate Panel Findings." *Nature,* Vol. 382, July 25, 1996, p. 287.

Michaels, Patrick J., and Paul C. Knappenberger. "Human Effect on Global Climate?" *Nature,* Vol. 384, Dec. 12, 1996, pp. 522–523.

Mitchell, J. F. B., T. C. Johns, J. M. Gregory, and S. F. B. Tett. "Climate Responses to Increasing Levels of Greenhouse Gases and Sulfate Aerosols." *Nature,* Vol. 376, Aug. 10, 1995, pp. 501–504.

Santer, Banjamin D. "No Deception in Global Warming Report" [Letter to the Editor], *Wall Street Journal,* June 25, 1996.

Santer, Benjamin D., Karl E. Taylor, Tom M. L. Wigley, Joyce E. Penner, Philip D. Jones, and Ulrich Cubasch. "Towards the Detection and Attribution of an Anthropogenic Effect on Climate." *Climate Dynamics,* Vol. 12, 1995, pp. 79–100.

Santer, Benjamin D., K. E. Taylor, T. M. L. Wigley, T. C. Johns, P. D. Jones, D. J. Karoly, J. F. B. Mitchell, A. H. Oort, J. E. Penner, V. Ramaswamy, M. D. Schwarzkopf, R. J. Stouffer, and S. Tett. "A Search for Human Influences on the Thermal Structure of the Atmosphere." *Nature,* Vol. 382, July 4, 1996, pp. 39–46.

Seitz, Frederick. "A Major Deception on Global Warming." *Wall Street Journal,* June 12, 1996, op-ed page.

Stevens, William K. "More Extremes Found in Weather, Pointing to Greenhouse Gas Effect." *New York Times,* May 23, 1995.

———. "Global Warming Experts Call Human Role Likely." *New York Times,* Sept. 10, 1995.

———. "In Rain and Temperature Data, New Signs of Global Warming." *New York Times,* Sept. 26, 1995.

———. "U.N. Climate Report Was Improperly Altered, Overplaying Human Role, Critics Say." *New York Times,* June 17, 1996.

———. "At Hot Center of Debate on Global Warming," *New York Times,* Aug. 6, 1996.

Chapter Fourteen

Crowley, Thomas J. Letter to the Editor. *New York Times,* Nov. 27, 1997.

Dlugokencky, D. J., K. A. Masarie, P. M. Lang, and P. P. Tans. "Continuing Decline in the Growth Rate of the Atmospheric Methane Burden." *Nature,* Vol. 393, June 4, 1998, pp. 447–450.

"Dr. Jule G. Charney Is Dead at 64; Worldwide Leader in Meteorology." *New York Times,* June 18, 1981.

Hansen, James, Makiko Sato, Jae Glascoe, and Reto Ruedy. "A Common-Sense Climate Index: Is Climate Changing Noticeably?" *Proceedings of the National Academy of Sciences,* Vol. 95, April 1998, pp. 4113–4120.

Hansen, James E., Makiko Sato, Andrew Lacis, Reto Ruedy, Ina Tegen, and Elaine Matthews. "Climate Forcings in the Industrial Era." *Proceedings of the National Academy of Sciences,* Vol. 95, Oct. 1998, pp. 12753–12758.

Houghton, J. T., G. J. Jenkins, and J. J. Ephrams, International Panel on Climate Change. *Climate Change: The IPCC Scientific Assessment.* New York: Cambridge University Press, 1990.

Michaels, Patrick J. "Kyoto Protocol: A Useless Appendange to an Irrelevant Treaty." Testimony before the Committee on Small Business, U.S. House of Representatives, Washington, DC, July 29, 1998.

Myhre, Gunnar, Eleanor J. Highwood, Keith P. Shine, and Frode Stordal. "New Estimates of Radiative Forcing Due to Well-Mixed Greenhouse Gases." *Geophysical Research Letters,* Vol. 25, No. 14, July 15, 1998, pp. 2715–2718.

Singer, S. Fred. Letter to the Editor. *New York Times,* Sept. 19, 1995.

———. *Hot Talk, Cold Science: Global Warming's Unfinished Debate.* Oakland, CA: The Independent Institute, 1997.

———. Testimony before the Committee on Small Business, U.S. House of Representatives, July 27, 1998.

———. Various biographical and substantive entries on web site of Science and Environmental Policy Project, 1998, www.sepp.org.

Stevens, William K. "Carbon Dioxide Rise May Alter Plant Life, Researchers Say." *New York Times,* Sept. 18, 1990.

———. "Scientists Confront Renewed Backlash on Global Warming." *New York Times,* Sept. 14, 1993.

———. "In New Data on Climate Changes, Decades, Not Centuries, Count." *New York Times,* Dec. 7, 1993.

———. "A Skeptic Asks, Is It Getting Hotter, or Is It Just the Computer Model?" *New York Times,* June 18, 1996.

———. "Experts on Climate Change Pondering: How Urgent Is It?" *New York Times,* Sept. 9, 1997.

Chapter Fifteen

Bloomfield, Janine. *Hot Nights in the City: Global Warming Sea-Level Rise and the New York Metropolitan Region.* New York: Environmental Defense Fund, 1999.

Browne, Malcom W. "Antarctica: As Gorgeous and Deadly Today as Ever." *New York Times,* April 9, 1999.

Houghton, J. T., G. J. Jenkins, and J. J. Ephrams, International Panel on Climate Change. *Climate Change: The IPCC Scientific Assessment.* New York: Cambridge University Press, 1990.

Schneider, David. "The Rising Seas." *Scientific American,* March 1997, pp. 112–117.

Schneider, Stephen H., ed.-in-chief. *Encyclopedia of Climate and Weather.* New York: Oxford University Press, 1996.

Stevens, William K. "Scientists Say Earth's Warming Could Set Off Wide Disruptions." *New York Times,* Sept. 18, 1995.

———. "Cushioning the Shock of Global Warming." *New York Times,* Nov. 30, 1997.

———. "Catastrophic Melting of Ice Sheet Is Possible, Studies Hint." *New York Times,* July 7, 1998.

United States Geological Survey. "Marine Isotope Stage 11; Stage 11: Back to the Future?" 1999; chht-ntsrv.er.usgs.gov/stage_11/stage11.htm.

Watson, Robert T., Marufu C. Zinyowera, and Richard H. Moss. *Climate Change 1995; Impacts, Adaptations and Mitigation of Climate Change: Scientific-Technical Analyses.* Report of Working Group II of Intergovernmental Panel on Climate Change. New York: Cambridge University Press, 1996.

———. *The Regional Impacts of Climate Change: An Assessment of Vulnerability.* Special report of Working Group II of Intergovernmental Panel on Climate Change. New York: Cambridge University Press, 1998.

Chapter Sixteen

Corti, S., F. Molteni, and T. N. Palmer. "Signature of Recent Climate Change in Frequencies of Natural Atmospheric Circulation Regimes." *Nature,* Vol. 398, April 29, 1999, pp. 799–802.

Dugger, Celia W. "2-Month Flood Breeds Havoc and Spreads Disease in Bangladesh." *New York Times,* Oct. 9, 1998.

Houghton, J. T., G. J. Jenkins, and J. J. Ephrams, International Panel on Climate Change. *Climate Change: The IPCC Scientific Assessment*. New York: Cambridge University Press, 1990.

Shabecoff, Philip. "Ferocious Storms and Drought Seen." *New York Times*, Dec. 7, 1988.

Shindell, Drew T., Ron L. Miller, Gavin A. Schmidt, and Lionel Pandolfo. "Simulation of Recent Northern Winter Climate Trends by Greenhouse Gas Forcing." *Nature*, Vol. 399, June 3, 1999, pp. 452–455.

Stevens, William K. "Heat Is More Lethal When It Is Unusual, Researchers Find." *New York Times*, July 31, 1990.

————. "Carbon Dioxide Rise May Alter Plant Life, Researchers Say." *New York Times*, Sept. 18, 1990.

————. "Global Warming Threatens to Undo Decades of Conservation Efforts." *New York Times*, Feb. 25, 1992.

————. "If Climate Changes, Who Is Vulnerable? Panels Offer Some Local Projections." *New York Times*, Sept. 30, 1997.

————. "From Under the Sea, Signs of Climate Jolts." *New York Times*, Nov. 18, 1997.

————. "If Climate Changes, It May Change Quickly." *New York Times*, Jan. 27, 1998.

————. "As the Climate Shifts, Trees Can Take Flight." *New York Times*, March 10, 1998.

————. "Scientist at Work: Wallace S. Broecker; Iconoclastic Guru of the Climate Debate." *New York Times*, March 17, 1998.

————. "Warmer, Wetter, Sicker: Linking Climate to Health." *New York Times*, Aug. 10, 1998.

————. "Water: Pushing the Limits of an Irreplaceable Resouce." *New York Times*, Dec. 8, 1998.

Watson, Robert T., Marufu C. Zinyowera, and Richard H. Moss. *Climate Change 1995; Impacts, Adaptations and Mitigation of Climate Change: Scientific-Technical Analyses*. Report of Working Group II of Intergovernmental Panel on Climate Change. New York: Cambridge University Press, 1996.

————. *The Regional Impacts of Climate Change: An Assessment of Vulnerability*. Special report of Working Group II of Intergovernmental Panel on Climate Change. New York: Cambridge University Press, 1998.

Chapter Seventeen

"Action Is Urged to Avert Global Climate Shift." *New York Times,* Dec. 11, 1985.

Andrews, Edmund L. "For Europe, Greenhouse-Gas Issue Is How Much to Cut." *New York Times,* Dec. 4, 1997.

Bord, Richard J., Ann Fisher, and Robert E. O'Connor. "Public Perceptions of Global Warming: United States and International Perspectives." *Climate Research,* Vol. 11, No. 1, Dec. 17, 1998, pp 75–84.

Cushman Jr., John H. "In Shift, U.S. Will Seek Binding World Pact to Combat Global Warming." *New York Times,* July 17, 1996.

———. "Senate Urges U.S. to Pursue New Strategy on Emissions." *New York Times,* July 26, 1997.

———. "President Plans Energy Savings in a Moderate Step on Warming." *New York Times,* Oct. 23, 1997.

———. "Public Backs Tough Steps for a Treaty on Warming." *New York Times,* Nov. 28, 1997.

Deutsch, Claudia H. "Still Defiant, but Subtler, Industry Awaits E.P.A. Rules." *New York Times,* May 27, 1997.

Kinzer, Stephen. "Nations Pledge to Set Limits by 1997 on Warming Gases." *New York Times,* April 8, 1995.

Lewis, Paul. "Thatcher Urges Pact on Climate." *New York Times,* Nov. 9, 1989.

———. "U.N. Takes Step Toward Global Climate Pact." *New York Times,* Jan. 3, 1990.

Shabecoff, Philip. "Scientists Warn of Earlier Rise in Sea Levels." *New York Times,* Nov. 3, 1985.

———. "Norway and Canada Call for Pact to Protect Atmosphere." *New York Times,* June 28, 1988.

———. "Parley Urges Quick Action to Protect Atmosphere." *New York Times,* July 1, 1988.

———. "U.S., in a Shift, Seeks Treaty on Global Warming." *New York Times,* May 12, 1989.

———. "E.P.A. Chief Says Bush Will Not Rush into a Treaty on Global Warming." *New York Times,* May 13, 1989.

Stevens, William K. "At Meeting on Global Warming, U.S. Stands Alone." *New York Times,* Sept. 10, 1991.

———. "White House Vows Action to Cut U.S. Global Warming Gases." *New York Times,* Feb. 28, 1992.

————. "Accord on Limits on Gas Emissions Is Said to Be Near." *New York Times,* May 8, 1992.

————. "143 Lands Adopt Treaty to Cut Emission of Gases." *New York Times,* May 10, 1992.

————. "Emissions Must Be Cut To Avert Shift in Climate, Panel Says." *New York Times,* Sept. 20, 1994.

————. "Price of Global Warming? Debate Weighs Dollars and Cents." *New York Times,* Oct. 10, 1995.

————. "U.N. Warns Against Delay in Cutting Carbon Dioxide Emissions." *New York Times,* Oct. 25, 1995.

————. "Trying to Stem Emissions, U.S. Sees Its Goal Fading." *New York Times,* Nov. 28, 1995.

————. "Industries Revisit Global Warming." *New York Times,* Aug. 4, 1997.

————. "U.S. and Japan Key to Outcome in Climate Talks." *New York Times,* Aug. 12, 1997.

————. "Doubts on Cost Are Bedeviling Climate Policy." *New York Times,* Oct. 6, 1997.

————. "Battle Stage Is Set." *New York Times,* Oct. 23, 1997.

————. "Cushioning the Shock of Global Warming." *New York Times,* Nov. 30, 1977.

————. "Greenhouse Gas Issue: Haggling Over Fairness." *New York Times,* Nov. 30, 1997.

————. "Gore, in Japan, Signals That U.S. May Make Some Compromises on Climate." *New York Times,* Dec. 8, 1997.

————. "The Climate Accord: The Outlook; Despite Pact, Gases Will Keep Rising." *New York Times,* Dec. 12, 1997.

Tyler, Patrick E. "China's Inevitable Dilemma: Coal Equals Growth." *New York Times,* Nov. 29, 1995.

"Where Sununu Stands." *New York Times,* Sept. 10, 1991.

"The White House and the Greenhouse" [Editorial]. *New York Times,* May 9, 1989.

Whitney, Craig R. "Scientists Urge Rapid Action on Global Warming." *New York Times,* May 26, 1990.

Chapter Eighteen

Ausubel, Jesse H. "Energy and Environment: The Light Path." *Energy Systems and Policy,* Vol. 15, 1991, pp. 181–188.

Broad, William J. "Debating Use of Iron as Curb of Climate." *New York Times,* Nov. 12, 1996.

Hansen, James E., Makiko Sato, Andrew Lacis, Reto Ruedy, Ina Tegen, and Elaine Matthews. "Climate Forcings in the Industrial Era." *Proceedings of the National Academy of Sciences,* Vol. 95, Oct. 1998, pp. 12753–12758.

Kasting, James F. "The Carbon Cycle, Climate, and the Long-Term Effects of Fossil Fuel Burning." *Consequences,* Vol. 4, No. 1, 1998. pp. 14–27.

Parson, E. A., and D. W. Keith. "Fossil Fuels Without CO2 Emissions." *Science,* Vol. 282, Nov. 6, 1998, pp. 1053–1054.

Socolow, Robert, ed. "Fuels Decarbonization and Carbon Sequestration: Report of a Workshop." Center for Energy and Environmental Studies, Princeton University, Sept. 1997.

Stevens, William K. "Experts on Climate Change Pondering: How Urgent Is It?" *New York Times,* Sept. 9, 1997.

———. "Experts Doubt Rise of Greenhouse Gas Will Be Curtailed." *New York Times,* Nov. 3, 1997.

———. "In Ancient Ice Ages, Clues to Climate." *New York Times,* Feb. 16, 1999.

Watson, Robert T., Marufu C. Zinyowera, and Richard H. Moss. *Climate Change 1995; Impacts, Adaptations and Mitigation of Climate Change: Scientific-Technical Analyses.* Report of Working Group II of Intergovernmental Panel on Climate Change. New York: Cambridge University Press, 1996.

Wigley, Tom M. L. "The Science of Climate Change: Global and U.S. Perspectives." The Pew Center for Global Climate Change, 1999.

Index